The Samuel Gompers Papers

Presented to
   Cumberland County College
By
   The International Brotherhood
   of Electrical Workers
Local 592   Vineland, New Jersey

THE
Samuel Gompers
PAPERS

VOLUME
3
Unrest and Depression
1891–94

Editors
Stuart B. Kaufman
Peter J. Albert

Associate Editors
Grace Palladino
Ileen A. DeVault
Elizabeth A. Fones-Wolf
Dorothee Schneider

UNIVERSITY OF ILLINOIS PRESS
Urbana and Chicago

90-499

© 1989 by the Board of Trustees of the University of Illinois
Manufactured in the United States of America
C 5 4 3 2 1

This book is printed on acid-free paper.

Library of Congress Cataloging-in-Publication Data
(Revised for vol. 3)

The Samuel Gompers papers.

Includes bibliographies and indexes.
Contents: v. 1. The making of a union leader, 1850-86—v. 2. The early years of the American Federation of Labor, 1887-90—v. 3. Unrest and Depression, 1891-94.
1. Trade-unions—United States—History—Sources. 2. Labor and laboring classes—United States—History—Sources. 3. Gompers, Samuel, 1850-1924—Archives. I. Gompers, Samuel, 1850-1924. II. Kaufman, Stuart Bruce.
HD6508.S218   1986   331.88′32′0924   84-2469
ISBN 0-252-01546-0 (vol. 3)
ISBN 0-252-01138-4 (set)

8

To
Herbert Gutman

CONTENTS

INTRODUCTION

"The Trade Unions," Samuel Gompers wrote in 1894, "are the reflect[ion]s in organized, crystallized form of the best thought, activity and hopes of the wage-workers." Claiming that they represented "the aggregate expression of [the] discontent of labor with existing economic, social and political misrule," he argued that the trade unions would not only protect the workers' present interests but could also expand and adapt to a changing industrial world. Many of his critics, however, dismissed pure and simple trade unionism as a strategy too limited to confront the challenges of late nineteenth-century America and too craft-oriented to meet the needs of factory operatives and the unskilled, immigrant, and female workers who constituted a growing sector of the workforce. Consequently, some activists championed a "new" socialist trade unionism that promised to unite labor's "economic and political forces" into a single movement, while others endorsed the program of multi-class political action favored by the People's (Populist) party. Gompers' debate with his critics on this issue raised questions of critical importance to the working class, reopening and revitalizing discussion of the structure and function of the labor movement, the role of politics and the state, and ultimately the tactics and the strategies that could best be employed by workers in this period of national unrest and economic depression.[1]

From Gompers' point of view, the ethnic, regional, and ideological diversity of the workforce, the uneven development of industry, and the varying degrees of labor organization nationwide required a movement that focused on trade issues — hours, wages, working conditions, and the like — that would provide workers with the common ground necessary for collective activity. He argued, moreover, that a system of benefits sustained by high dues would attract workers to the trade unions, create bonds of mutual self-interest, and insure the growth and permanence of those organizations. His opponents disagreed, pointing out that high dues barred low-paid workers, especially women, from joining unions, and that benefit systems often induced conserv-

atism among union members. Aware of these criticisms, Gompers
nonetheless believed that the history of organized labor confirmed
his position, and he pointed to the AFL's steady growth after 1886,
in contrast to the KOL's precipitous decline. If the labor movement,
in the years between 1891 and 1894, boasted a number of organizations whose structures and programs differed significantly from
those endorsed by the AFL—the KOL, the American Railway Union,
and the SLP, for example—no competitor demonstrated the organizational stability achieved by the Federation. With its affiliates' membership edging above the quarter of a million mark by 1894, it was
well on its way to becoming the leading, but by no means the only,
labor organization on the American scene.

As a corollary to his economic priorities and his concern for the
Federation's stability, Gompers maintained that partisan political debate would factionalize the AFL, and he cautioned affiliates against
committing the organization to a particular political party, even one
as sympathetic to labor issues as the Populists. From his point of view
and his reading of history, partisan political action had diverted, not
advanced, the labor movement, and he repeatedly pointed to the
collapse of the National Labor Union after it nominated David Davis
for president of the United States in 1872. Although his position was
not without its critics, Gompers insisted that "in the struggle for
improved conditions and emancipation for the toilers, what is wanted
is the organization of the wage-workers, not on 'party' lines, but on
the lines of their class interests. . . . Political liberty with[out] economic
independence is illusory and deceptive," he argued, for "only in so
far as we gain economic independence can our political liberty become
tangible and important. This may sound like political heresy," he
concluded, "but it is economic truth."[2]

If Gompers resisted efforts to move the Federation into "the political
arena by the nomination of candidates for national and State offices,"
he did not disdain politics or assume that trade unionism pure and
simple negated political efforts. Although evidence of government
intervention on the side of business confirmed his view that labor
could not rely on the state to protect its interests, he utilized the
apparatus of government—and his personal political contacts—to
influence government appointments, encourage the enforcement of
labor measures already on the books, and support legislation in labor's
behalf. "The politics of the American Federation of Labor is to secure
labor measures through any political party using every one of them
for the purposes of labor," he wrote, "but warning them to keep their
hands off when they propose to use us."[3] He actively pursued legislation in national as well as state capitals on such subjects as the eight-

hour day for government workers, woman and child labor, factory inspection, immigration, the importation of alien contract labor, the limitation of injunctions, the use of the automatic railroad car coupler and power brakes, and nationalization of the communication and transportation systems. He also endorsed such progressive measures of the period as woman suffrage and the popular election of U.S. senators. Finally, the AFL under Gompers sponsored test cases in the courts to require enforcement of such legislation as the Pennsylvania semimonthly payment law and the Indiana eight-hour law and supported suits contesting injunctions against strikes.

Gompers' documentary legacy from these years indicates that much of his energy focused on the mundane day-to-day business of organization building: establishing new national and local unions, attempting to persuade already existing bodies to affiliate, resolving jurisdictional disputes, and providing financial assistance to affiliates. He created an effective network of organizers, maintained a voluminous correspondence, and spoke and traveled extensively. Moreover, in 1894 he began editing the AFL's official journal, the *American Federationist,* the first issue of which appeared in March. This publication, for which Gompers had campaigned since the demise of the *Union Advocate* in 1887, offered a forum for trade unionists to debate Federation policy and allowed Gompers another opportunity to promulgate his ideas.

In his correspondence, speeches, and published writings, Gompers relentlessly encouraged the "thorough organization" of the entire working class, including blacks, women, and unskilled workers—but vehemently excluding the Chinese—promoting an ideal of labor solidarity rooted in the practical circumstances of economic self-interest. "You must bear in mind the fact that employers of labor care very little whether the workers in a certain industry are men or women," he warned one correspondent. "What they are after, particularly is to get their work done cheap and unless you make friends of your women co-workers you will make enemies of them; and both antagonistic to each other you will be playing into the hands of your employers."[4] Gompers took a similar stance in regard to black workers: "I am strongly of the opinion that it is essential for us to do all we possibly can in order to eliminate the consideration of a color line in the labor organizations of the country," he wrote. "If we fail to organize and recognize the colored wage-workers we cannot blame them very well if they accept our challenge of enmity and do all they can to frustrate our purposes. If we fail to make friends of them, the employing class won't be so shortsighted, and play them against us. Thus if common humanity will not prompt us to have their co-

operation, an enlightened self-interest should." Gompers had no objection, however, to racially separate organizations where existing
prejudices and predilictions seemed to require them. "It is useless to
be simply trying to ram our heads through stone walls," he advised
one correspondent; "recognizing the conditions which exist is the best
way we can secure the organization of all in a way which must ultimately bring about a unity of feeling and action among all toilers."[5]
In general, however, Gompers discouraged wage earners from organizing along ethnic, religious, or racial lines, and he held fast to
his conviction that economic interests would best unite the varied and
diverse elements of the working class.

At a time when most trade union activity remained independent
of the national Federation, Gompers attempted to promote unity in
the face of political, organizational, and regional factionalism in labor's
ranks. He faced conflicts among brewers, miners, painters, and shoemakers, jurisdictional disputes in the building trades, and disagreements within central labor bodies, as well as growing regional tensions
within the AFL. One conflict, involving West Coast brewers, grew so
intense by 1891 that he feared it would split the national labor movement, claiming that this fight threatened to split it "into two distinct
lines, one of the Pacific Coast, and the other of the remaining portions
of the country."[6] Such regional competition, which was echoed in
attempts to relocate the AFL's headquarters and which may well have
contributed to Gompers' defeat at the 1894 convention, led him to
stress labor's common interests over all other concerns.

Economic conditions in the early 1890s made these years still more
perilous for the labor movement. The financial panic in the spring
of 1893 triggered one of the worst depressions of the nineteenth
century. The hardship and unrest brought on by the economic collapse—as well as by such long-term economic developments in the
American economy as the enormous expansion and corporate consolidation in American manufacturing and the vast increase in American farm production in a fluctuating world market—precipitated a
succession of crises for farmers' and workers' organizations. Moreover,
capital's aggressive defense of managerial prerogative and its increased
reliance on the armed forces of the state, the injunction, and private
police to break strikes threatened to reverse whatever gains organized
labor had achieved. The strikes in Homestead, Coeur d'Alene, Tennessee, Buffalo, and New Orleans in 1892 and the Pullman strike in
1894 convinced Gompers that the American labor movement now
operated in quite a new context. The defeat of these strikes and the
growing influence of populist and socialist organizations placed severe
tests on his commitment to a strategy of political non-partisanship and

opened the way for a rigorous reappraisal of the AFL's position at the 1894 Denver convention.

This volume follows Gompers and the AFL through a challenging and significant period, years of depression and unrest. Looking back over his term of office, after his defeat for reelection in 1894, Samuel Gompers affirmed once again his belief that "the trade union movement is the natural class organization of the wage-workers in which they must seek present improvement as well as future disenthrallment." Reviewing his years of service to labor he maintained that "for office in the movement I care and cared nothing. To me the movement was greater than any man or set of men. . . . I have not been re-elected, and can fairly say that I have no regrets to express. I feel the consciousness of having performed my duty to the very best of my ability and with a single purpose, to benefit my fellow wage-workers. There is nothing that I have done in the cause that I would seek to undo," he concluded, "or words that I have expressed that I would unsay, except to do and say them with greater force and emphasis."[7]

Although the prospect of testing Gompers' social and industrial vision against historical evidence is a tantalizing one, it remains outside our jurisdiction as editors. Neither do we presume to evaluate the course he pursued. Instead we strive to present Gompers in the context of his times through documents drawn from a wide variety of sources—official and unofficial, published and unpublished—and we seek to illustrate the experiences and perceptions that contributed to his evolution as a labor leader. At the same time, however, we are well aware that Gompers and the AFL represented only one strain of a dynamic and increasingly complex movement. Thus we continue to include documents not authored by Gompers when they demonstrate contemporary criticisms that shed light on alternative labor bodies and philosophies or impart information pertinent to Gompers' assessment of an issue. On the whole, we have retained our non-intrusive editorial policy, utilizing footnotes to provide brief identifications, glossary entries for more detailed information, and occasional editorial essays. These essays are not intended as chapter divisions or to imply an organization of the book by subject, but are included to supply background information on significant or confusing issues or to provide an overview of complex developments that evolved over a lengthy period of time. Annotations of non-glossary items that appeared in previous volumes are not repeated here; however, the index will direct the reader to the volume and page where such pertinent information appears.

The documents for this volume, as was the case with *The Early Years of the AFL,* are drawn primarily from the Gompers letterbooks (now at the Library of Congress) and the records from the AFL's archives (now held by the George Meany Memorial Archives at the AFL-CIO and the State Historical Society of Wisconsin). This volume of the Gompers papers also includes documents from the *American Federationist* and from such important record groups as the AFL Executive Council Minutes and Vote Books and the National and International Union Correspondence. Supplementing this is other material, drawn from such sources as the labor press and mass circulation newspapers of the time, public documents, and other collections of private papers.

With three modifications in our rendering of typed or printed documents, the editorial style used in this volume remains essentially that outlined in our first volume, *The Making of a Union Leader.* To distinguish between our editorial insertions, which are signified by brackets, and parenthetical material enclosed in brackets in a typed or printed source, we now substitute parentheses when brackets are used in the original. Second, we have slightly expanded our policy of silently correcting typographical and spelling errors, as described in volume 1, and now no longer use brackets when inserting punctuation marks necessary to make the text sensible or letters obliterated from the original text if most of the word is legible. Finally, we omit routine secretarial notations in correspondence such as "enclosures" or "dictated by S.G."

ACKNOWLEDGMENTS

This volume of the Samuel Gompers Papers is dedicated to the late Herbert Gutman, who, at the time of his death, was Distinguished Professor of History at the City University of New York and a member of our project's board of editorial advisors. Through his scholarship and personal influence, Professor Gutman, more than anyone, broadened the concerns of American labor historians and heightened our understanding of the community and cultural settings in which workers' institutions were shaped. Thanks especially to Gutman, we have increasingly come to see the history of workers as rich, complex, and varied.

We are gratified by the labor movement's interest in its own history, exemplified by the AFL-CIO's recent dedication of its new facility for the George Meany Memorial Archives. Throughout the history of this project, the AFL-CIO has helped us in a variety of ways, providing access to records, permission to publish, and financial assistance. President Lane Kirkland, Secretary-Treasurer Thomas R. Donahue, assistants to the secretary-treasurer Wesley Reedy and James J. Kennedy, Jr., and the members of the Executive Council have gone out of their way to establish a partnership of support with other agencies interested in our progress.

Two federal agencies have provided the core of our annual funding as well as professional encouragement and support. They are the National Historical Publications and Records Commission (NHPRC) and the National Endowment for the Humanities (NEH). We would specifically like to thank Frank G. Burke, Richard A. Jacobs, Roger A. Bruns, Sara Dunlap Jackson, and Mary A. Guinta of the NHPRC, and Richard Ekman, Margot Backas, Jack Meyers, Kathy Fuller, and Dennis Romano of the NEH. Outright grants from these agencies have provided the backbone of our funding, and matching grants from the NEH have enabled us to attract support from the labor movement. Each year the AFL-CIO has made a generous grant to the project, and numerous unions have followed suit. We are pleased to acknowledge contributions from the Joseph Anthony Beirne Memorial Foundation of the Communications Workers of America and the following unions: the Associated Actors and Artistes of America, the Bakery, Confectionery and Tobacco Workers' International Union, the International Brotherhood of Boilermakers, Iron Ship Builders, Blacksmiths, Forgers, and Helpers, the International Union of Bricklayers and Allied Craftsmen, the United Brotherhood of Carpenters and Joiners of America, the International Brotherhood of Electrical Workers, the International Union of Electronic, Electrical, Salaried, Machine, and Furniture Workers, the Association of Flight Attendants, the United Food and Commercial Workers' International Union, the American Flint Glass Workers' Union, the United Garment Workers of America, the Glass, Pottery, Plastics, and Allied Workers' International Union, the American Federation of Government Employees, the Laborers' International Union of North America, the National Association of Letter Carriers, the International Longshoremen's Association, the International Association of Machinists and Aerospace Workers, the Mechanics' Educational Society, the Newspaper Guild, the International Union of Operating Engineers, the International Brotherhood of Painters and Allied Trades of the United States and Canada, the United Paperworkers' International Union, the United Association of Journeymen and Apprentices of the Plumbing and Pipe Fitting Industry of the United States and Canada, the American Postal Workers' Union, the Brotherhood of Railway Carmen of the United States and Canada, the Retail, Wholesale, and Department Store Union, the Service Employees' International Union, the American Federation of State, County, and Municipal Employees, the United Steelworkers of America, the International Brotherhood of Teamsters, Chauffeurs, Warehousemen, and Helpers of America, the International Alliance of Theatrical Stage Employes and Moving Picture Machine Operators of the United States and Canada, and the Amalgamated Transit Union. In addition, we continue to draw on the records of many labor unions that have granted us access to their files and permission to copy and publish pertinent material.

The University of Maryland at College Park has housed the project since we began our work, providing released time, office space and equipment, and student assistance. The History Department at the University, under the chairmanships of Emory G. Evans and Richard Price, has provided the project with encouragement, advice, and financial support. In addition, we would like to thank University of Maryland President John S. Toll, Chancellor John B. Slaughter and Vice-Chancellor William Kirwan of the College Park campus, Shirley Strum Kenny, former provost of the Division of Arts and Humanities, and Richard D. Brecht and James H. Lesher, acting deans of the College of Arts and Humanities.

We have been able to draw upon the collections and staffs of area libraries and research institutions that have been of invaluable assistance. These include the Library of Congress, which has provided our researchers with an office, the National Archives, the George Meany Memorial Archives, the Catholic University of America, and the Library of the U.S. Department of Labor. In addition, the staff of the McKeldin Library, where our project's offices are located, and especially Judith Cmero of the Inter-Library Loan Office, have been extremely helpful. Beyond these institutions located in our immediate proximity, we have continued to draw on the holdings of numerous other archives, notably the Tamiment Collection of the Bobst Library at New York University and the State Historical Society of Wisconsin. We are most appreciative of the resources of these institutions. Without them, it is difficult to see how we could have pursued our work in its current scope.

In addition to the individuals listed on the title page, a number of others have played key roles in producing this volume. Our research assistants, Mary Ann Coyle, Michael Honey, Katherine Morin, and Edwin Gabler, worked with us on researching, proofreading, and other day-to-day aspects of this labor-intensive effort. We consider ourselves fortunate to have had four colleagues of such exceptional intelligence, integrity, and commitment. Until her retirement Celia Ramos Gray undertook the grueling work of transcribing documents and typing all the accompanying editorial materials and notes; since then Vicky

Comer has carried this burden. Both have performed with competency and cheerfulness, for which we are grateful. Dolores Janiewski, project associate editor until moving to a teaching position at the University of Idaho, contributed to the selection and annotation of this volume prior to her departure, and Patrick McGrath continued to provide the project with exemplary translations of German-language documents. University of Maryland graduate students Frederick Augustyn, Marla J. Hughes, Gu Ning, Lizette LeSavage, Harold Eugene Mahan, Diane Miller, Elizabeth Robertson, and Kevin Swanson, and undergraduate student Tonya Little spent months in annotation work, proofreading, and other tasks requiring accuracy, discipline, and a dedication to the overall objectives of the project. In addition, we would like to thank professional colleagues for timely assistance on specific problems connected with this volume: Peter Argersinger for sharing his expertise on the populists, Richard Oestreicher for advice on the Detroit labor movement, and Barney Grogan for information from the records of the Hotel and Restaurant Employees' Union.

As they have done for our first two volumes, members of our board of editorial advisors rendered us invaluable assistance when they reviewed our third volume in manuscript form. David Brody, Melvyn Dubofsky, Philip Foner, Louis Harlan, David Montgomery, Maurice Neufeld, and Irwin Yellowitz were able to take time from their own busy schedules for this task. Their critical comments and suggestions provided our staff both with ideas for specific improvements and, in a more general sense, with an invaluable outside perspective. This volume is simply that much better for their help.

Notes

1. *American Federationist* 1 (Mar. 1894): 10-11; "The New York City Central Labor Federation to the Workingmen of New York," Nov. 14, 1891, below.

2. "An Article by Samuel Gompers in the *North American Review*," July 1892, below.

3. Ibid.; "To Eva McDonald Valesh," Feb. 9, 1892, below.

4. "To Bernard Dugan," Dec. 2, 1891, below.

5. "To Harry Ives," Nov. 10, 1892, below; "To David Watkins," July 17, 1893, below.

6. "To John O'Brien," July 29, 1891, below.

7. "An Editorial by Samuel Gompers in the *American Federationist*," Dec. 31, 1894, below.

SYMBOLS AND ABBREVIATIONS

ACS	Autograph postcard, signed
AFL	The American Federation of Labor
ALp	Autograph letter, letterpress copy
ALpS	Autograph letter, letterpress copy, signed
ALS	Autograph letter, signed
CMIU	The Cigar Makers' International Union
DCU	The Catholic University of America, Washington, D.C.
DLC	The Library of Congress
FOTLU	The Federation of Organized Trades and Labor Unions of the United States and Canada
Ia-HA	State Historical Society of Iowa, Des Moines
ICHi	Chicago Historical Society
ICU	University of Chicago
IU-HS	Illinois Historical Survey, University of Illinois at Urbana-Champaign
KOL	The Knights of Labor
MiU	University of Michigan, Ann Arbor
PDSr	Printed document, signature representation
PLSr	Printed letter, signature representation
SG	Samuel Gompers
SLP	The Socialist Labor party
T and ALpS	Typed and autograph letter, letterpress copy, signed
T and ALS	Typed and autograph letter, signed
TDp	Typed document, letterpress copy
TLcSr	Typed letter, copy, signature representation
TLp	Typed letter, letterpress copy
TLpS	Typed letter, letterpress copy, signed
TLpSr	Typed letter, letterpress copy, signature representation
TLS	Typed letter, signed
TLSr	Typed letter, signature representation
TWpS	Typed wire (telegram), letterpress copy, signed
TWpSr	Typed wire (telegram), letterpress copy, signature representation
WHi	The State Historical Society of Wisconsin, Madison

AFL, *Proceedings,* 1886	AFL, *Proceedings of the First Annual Convention of the American Federation of Labor* (1886?; reprint ed., Bloomington, Ill., 1905)
AFL, *Proceedings,* 1889	AFL, *Report of Proceedings of the Ninth Annual Convention of the American Federation of Labor, Held at Boston, Mass., December 10, 11, 12, 13, 14, 1889* (1889?; reprint ed., Bloomington, Ill., 1905)
AFL, *Proceedings,* 1890	AFL, *Report of Proceedings of the Tenth Annual Convention of the American Federation of Labor, Held at Detroit, Michigan, December 8, 10, 11, 12, and 13, 1890* (1890?; reprint ed., Bloomington, Ill., 1905)
AFL, *Proceedings,* 1891	AFL, *Report of Proceedings of the Eleventh Annual Convention of the American Federation of Labor, Held at Birmingham, Ala., December 14, 15, 16, 17, 18, and 19, 1891* (1891?; reprint ed., Bloomington, Ill., 1905)
AFL, *Proceedings,* 1892	AFL, *Report of Proceedings of the Twelfth Annual Convention of the American Federation of Labor, Held at Philadelphia, Pa., December 12, 13, 14, 15, 16, and 17, 1892* (1892?; reprint ed., Bloomington, Ill., 1905)
AFL, *Proceedings,* 1893	AFL, *Report of Proceedings of the Thirteenth Annual Convention of the American Federation of Labor, Held at Chicago, Ill., December 11th to 19th, Inclusive, 1893* (1893?; reprint ed., Bloomington, Ill., 1905)
AFL, *Proceedings,* 1894	AFL, *Report of Proceedings of the Fourteenth Annual Convention of the American Federation of Labor, Held at Denver, Colorado, December 10, 11, 12, 13, 14, 15, 16, 17, and 18, 1894* (1894?; reprint ed., Bloomington, Ill., 1905)

AFL, *Proceedings,* 1895	AFL, *Report of Proceedings of the Fifteenth Annual Convention of the American Federation of Labor, Held at New York, N.Y., December 9th to 17th, Inclusive, 1895* (1895?; reprint ed., Bloomington, Ill., 1905)
AFL Records	Peter J. Albert and Harold L. Miller, eds., *American Federation of Labor Records: The Samuel Gompers Era,* microfilm (Sanford, N.C., 1979)
The Early Years of the AFL	Stuart B. Kaufman et al., eds., *The Samuel Gompers Papers,* vol. 2, *The Early Years of the American Federation of Labor, 1887-90* (Urbana, Ill., 1987)
The Making of a Union Leader	Stuart B. Kaufman et al., eds., *The Samuel Gompers Papers,* vol. 1, *The Making of a Union Leader, 1850-86* (Urbana, Ill., 1986)
SG Letterbooks	The Letterbooks of the Presidents of the American Federation of Labor, 1883-1925, Library of Congress

CHRONOLOGY

1891	Feb. 9-Apr. 20	SG's trip to West Coast
	Mar.-May	Strike in Connellsville coke region
	Apr. 28	United Mine Workers of America calls off its eight-hour campaign
	May 11-12	National Union Conference in Cincinnati organizes People's party
	Aug. 16-22	Second International meets in Brussels
	Dec. 14-19	AFL convention, Birmingham, Ala.
1892	Apr.-July	Strike at Coeur d'Alene, Idaho
	July-Nov.	Strike at Homestead, Pa.
	July 4	James B. Weaver nominated for president of the United States by the People's party at its Omaha, Neb., convention
	July 6	Pinkertons arrive in Homestead
	July 11	Coeur d'Alene strikers blow up facility at Frisco mine and expel strikebreakers; state troops called in
	July 12	State troops arrive in Homestead
	July 14	Federal troops arrive in Coeur d'Alene
	Aug.	Switchmen's strike in Buffalo, N.Y., to demand enforcement of state's ten-hour law
		Miners' uprising in Tennessee against use of convict labor
	Nov. 8-11	New Orleans general strike
	Dec. 12-17	AFL convention, Philadelphia
1893	Jan.-Apr.	United Garment Workers strike in New York City
	May 1-Oct. 30	World's Columbian Exposition in Chicago
	May 5	Stock market collapse precipitates financial panic and major depression
	June 20	American Railway Union founded
	June 26	Governor John P. Altgeld pardons surviving Haymarket defendants

	Aug. 20	New York City trade unionists meet to formulate plan to cope with economic depression and unemployment
	Aug. 22	SG and trade union delegation meet with New York City Mayor Gilroy to press for municipal public works program to relieve unemployment
	Aug. 28	SG addresses International Labor Congress at the World's Columbian Exposition in Chicago
	Nov. 7	SG defeated in campaign for election to New York state constitutional convention
	Dec. 11-19	AFL convention, Chicago
1894	Mar.	First issue of the *American Federationist* published
	Mar. 25-May 1	March of Coxey's army to Washington, D.C.
	May 11-Aug.	Strike of Pullman workers
	June 11-12	Unity conference of AFL, KOL, populists, railroad brotherhoods, and various trade unions meets in St. Louis
	June 26-Aug. 2	American Railway Union boycott of Pullman cars
	July 2	Injunction issued against American Railway Union leaders
	July 3-5	Illinois State Federation of Labor conference of labor and reform organizations meets in Springfield
	July 4	Federal troops arrive in Chicago
	July 12-13	AFL Executive Council and union representatives meet at Briggs House, Chicago, and resolve not to endorse general strike in support of the American Railway Union's Pullman boycott
	Nov. 13-14	Congress on Industrial Conciliation and Arbitration meets in Chicago; SG speaks on Nov. 14
	Dec. 10-18	AFL convention in Denver
	Dec. 17	John McBride elected president of the AFL

Documents

Gompers and the Populist Movement

Farmers, no less than industrial workers, faced severe economic distress throughout the last two decades of the nineteenth century. Falling prices, tight credit, and crop failures sparked an agrarian protest and impelled farmers to organize to protect their interests. Beginning in the 1880s, farmers' alliances emerged in the South, North, and West as farmers worked to raise prices, regulate monopolies, and restore a flexible money supply. These organizations, which later formed the basis of the People's party, also sought to bring industrial workers into a coalition to promote populist political reform.

Although a number of these alliances attempted to enlist the AFL in their effort, Samuel Gompers advised delegates to the 1889 convention to remain aloof. The farmer-employers who comprised the bulk of these organizations had suffered from "many wrongs," he admitted. Nevertheless, "our purpose should be to organize and ally ourselves with the farm laborers whose condition is so wretched and whose living so precarious."[1] Even as the populist movement gained momentum in the 1890s, Gompers held fast to this position and sought, rather, to encourage fledgling, if short-lived, farm laborer organizations.

Farmers proved more successful in attracting the leaders of the KOL to their cause. Terence Powderly, A. W. Wright, and Ralph Beaumont, for example, attended the St. Louis meeting of farmers' alliances in December 1889 and helped draft a platform demanding reform in landholding and in the transportation and financial systems. The following December KOL leaders, at a meeting in Ocala, Fla., sponsored by the National Farmers' Alliance and Industrial Union of America (NFAIU), agreed to coordinate congressional lobbying efforts. Despite this apparent harmony, however, attempts to organize a populist political party split the Knights. While Beaumont, for example, took part in the movement to create a new party, Powderly feared that this political initiative might absorb and "kill" the declining KOL.[2] When James Sovereign, a strong party supporter, replaced Powderly as grand master workman in 1893, he reaffirmed the ties between the Knights and the populists.

With the formal organization of the People's party in Cincinnati in

May 1891, the populist movement became a national political force. After nominating General James B. Weaver of Iowa for president at a convention held in Omaha, Neb., in July 1892, the party garnered more than a million popular votes and twenty-one electoral votes in the election that year. Over the next four years it worked to build on this success and promoted a united front with labor, socialist, and reform elements in some sections of the country and an alliance with traditional politicians and parties in others. In a number of localities, trade unionists supported the party and ran for office on its ticket. Miners, machinists, printers, and shoe workers, especially in the West and Midwest, played important roles in this populist-labor alliance.

Growing trade unionist support for populist reform, spurred by the depression that began in 1893, induced the AFL's 1893 convention to instruct the Executive Council to "effect and perfect an alliance" with the farmers' organizations.[3] When representatives of the AFL, the KOL, the NFAIU, the railroad brotherhoods, and other organizations met in St. Louis in June 1894, however, the question of party politics again divided them. The AFL delegation, led by Samuel Gompers,[4] rejected a KOL proposal to support the People's party candidates, claiming that partisanship even on behalf of a third party would "imperil the economic integrity" of the AFL's affiliates. Since these affiliates were themselves in the process of considering the adoption of the Federation's own political program, the AFL delegates could not "assume to speak for the vast body of our membership, or pledge them to the support of any particular platform of principles."[5]

One month later, following an industrial conference in Springfield, Ill., which formed a labor-populist alliance in that state, Chicago reformer Henry Demarest Lloyd implored Gompers to help organize a meeting to establish a reform coalition that would support the People's party candidates calling for the collective ownership of the means of production. "This crisis is greater than that of 1776 and 1861," Lloyd argued, and he urged Gompers to "write your name by the side of our greatest patriots." Gompers refused, however, and reiterated his position in an October editorial. "To go to the ballot box as workers is one thing," he wrote in the *American Federationist*, "to attempt to swamp the trade unions and subordinate them to party organization is another."[6] Although a number of central labor unions, state federations of labor, and national unions pledged support for the populists, Gompers' position on the question remained unchanged; the AFL's involvement in partisan politics, he believed, threatened the very survival of the trade union movement.

Notes

1. AFL *Proceedings,* 1889, pp. 13-14.
2. Terence Vincent Powderly to Ralph Beaumont, Apr. 13, 1890, Terence V. Powderly Papers, DCU.
3. AFL *Proceedings,* 1893, p. 38.
4. P. J. McGuire and Frank Foster were also delegates.
5. *American Federationist* 1 (Jan. 1895): 267.
6. Lloyd to SG, July 30, 1894, reel 59, Files of the Office of the President, *AFL Records; American Federationist* 1 (Oct. 1894): 172.

To Charles Power[1]

Jan. 7th [189]1

Mr. C. A. Power,
Terre Haute, Ind.
Dear Sir:—

Your favor of the 30th. inst. asking for me to co-operate and to invite the Trade Unions, in the movement to hold a National Conference at Cincinnati,[2] Feb. 23rd. 1891 for independent political action in other words to create a third Party, came duly to hand.

In reply permit me to say that the proposed conference was well known to the delegates of the recent convention of the American Federation of Labor held at Detroit, Mich.[3] and that no action was taken upon the matter by them, hence since our organization is based upon the sovereignty of the members, rather than the autocracy of the Executive, I am in a measure bound by their non-action upon the subject matter.

If you will forward me a few of the calls for the conference, I will submit them to our Executive Council and obtain their advice upon it.

You express surprise that Mr. Powderly[4] was a party to the St. Louis agreement, then suppressed the call for the conference, and is now antagonizing the result of that agreement.[5]

You must pardon me if I cannot enter into a discussion of Mr. Powderly's consistency; that is a matter between himself, his constituents, and his conscience.

Very Respectfully Yours.　Saml Gompers.
President. American Federation of Labor.

TLpS, reel 4, vol. 5, p. 325, SG Letterbooks, DLC.

1. Charles A. Power, a Terre Haute, Ind., dealer in farm implements and a solicitor, was an organizer of the National Union Conference held in Cincinnati, May 11-12, 1891, that established the People's party. The Indiana delegation elected him to serve on the party's national committee.

2. At the farmers' alliance meeting in Ocala, Fla., in December 1890 supporters of a movement to launch a new political party formed a National Citizens' Alliance (NCA) to build third party support in the cities and issued a call for a national union conference to meet in Cincinnati on Feb. 23, 1891.

3. The AFL held its 1890 convention in Detroit, Dec. 8-13.

4. Terence Vincent POWDERLY, a machinist, was grand master workman (1879-83) and general master workman (1883-93) of the KOL.

5. Powderly was determined that independent political action, endorsed by the KOL as recently as its November 1890 General Assembly, should be non-partisan in character. After the NCA called a conference in Cincinnati for February 1891, he attempted to call his own conference. The organizers of the Cincinnati conference

deferred to his efforts by delaying their meeting until May, but a poor response to Powderly's call forced him to abandon his plans by February.

To Friedrich Engels

Jan. 9th. 1891

Mr. Fred. Engels,
#122 Regents Park Road. London (N.W.) Eng.
Dear Sir:—

I make so free as to write to you upon a question which I know you take a deep interest in, and from the further fact of having been a life-long devoted friend, thinker and writer to and for the labor movement.

You have no doubt received reports of the proceedings of the convention of the American Federation of Labor held at Detroit, Mich. Dec. 8th.-13th. 1890, but from what I know and see printed in some papers I am led to the belief that little if anything but a garbled, untrue yes, maliciously false report has reached you. Having respect for you and confidence in your judgment I desire as briefly as possible to recount the facts as they exist.

The American Federation of Labor is as its title implies a federation of Trade Unions, the constitution providing for "the encouragement and formation of local Trade and Labor Unions, and the closer federation of such societies through the organization of Central Trade and Labor Unions in every city, and the further combination of such bodies into State, territorial or Provincial organizations, to secure legislation in the interests of the working masses.

["]The establishment of National and International Trade Unions, based upon a strict recognition of the autonomy of each trade, and the promotion and advancement of such bodies.

["]An American Federation of all National and International Trade Unions, to aid and assist each other; and, furthermore, to secure National Legislation in the interest of the working people, and influence public opinion, by peaceful and legal methods, in favor of Organized Labor.

["]To aid and encourage the labor press of America."

By constitutional provisions we have endeavored to also make of the Federation more of a concerted effort on the part of the members of the various other trade Unions when the members of any particular one shall be in any conflict with their employers; in other words, to endeavor [to] carry on in practice the idea, "one for all, and all for one."

I speak thus fully of the constitutional provisions and the purposes of the American Federation of Labor in order that you may have a full and clear understanding of the formation of our organization, which unquestionably must have a bearing in forming a judgment upon the question at issue.

It is also necessary to add that the American Federation of Labor issues through its President what is termed certificates of affiliation or charters, these documents certifying to the fact of the fellowship of the National or International Trade Unions, or Central Labor Unions, or Trades Councils.

We have a very large number of Central Labor Unions of a local character throughout this country, in fact in almost every industrial centre. In the city of New York such an organization existed under the title of the Central Labor Union, but owing to a local quarrel a division took place, and the local Trade Unions formed what was termed the Central Labor Federation of N.Y. They applied for a charter to this office and I cheerfully granted it to them believing that they were honest, and well intentioned towards the labor movement. Together with others I urged on a reconciliation between the divided factions, which was accomplished, the Central Labor Federation having resolved to adjourn and surrender its charter to this office. I have a letter from its Secretary[1] stating that fact.

This union did not bring about harmony, and without going over the entire grounds as to the causes and how it was brought about let me say that most of the organizations formerly constituting the Central Labor Federation again organized a Central Labor Federation. They wanted the old charter returned which of course could not be complied with. They appealed from my decision, and I was sustained in that position.

They then applied for a new charter. It is now necessary to call your attention to the fact that pending the correspondence between the Secretary of the Central Labor Federation and myself, the American Section of the Socialist Labor Party of New York sent delegates and was represented in the Central Labor Federation. The Secretary of the Central Labor Federation in forwarding the application for a charter accompanied it, as is the custom, with a list of the organizations represented therein. Among the organizations represented was the American Section of the Socialist Labor Party. I called attention to the fact that the American Federation of Labor was a federation of Trade Unions and expressed the opinion that the Socialist Labor

Party or a section of it, as a party, could not properly be represented in a Trade Union Central Organization.

Of course this did not suit the views of the leaders of the Socialist Labor Party and they commenced to abuse me both officially and personally. Desiring to avoid conflict as much as possible, I referred the entire subject matter to the convention of the American Federation of Labor which was then but a few months off. At the convention every opportunity was given their representatives and those who held their views, as well as all others, to express themselves fully and freely upon the subject. One whole day and a half was consumed in its consideration and finally the decision not to grant a charter to the Central Labor Federation, so long as they have the Socialist Labor Party, as a party, represented therein, was adopted by a vote 1,574 to 496.[2]

I am free to say that in the discussion of the subject I took decided grounds that the Trade Unions were the natural organizations of the wage-workers, under present economic and social conditions to secure present amelioration and final emancipation of the wage-workers; that as a federation of Trade Unions the condition necessary to representation in a convention of Trade Unions is good standing membership in a Trade Union. This is the kernel of the whole dispute, and upon which I am willing to abide.

There has never yet arisen a question in our councils whether a man was a socialist or not, whether he was an anarchist or not, in fact the greatest freedom and latitude of thought have been not only permitted, but encouraged. Some of our best men and staunchest in holding as I do are well-known and avowed socialists.

I refer you to the documents I mail to your address with this as an evidence of the intelligent and progressive character of our movement. I regret that the proceedings of the Detroit convention are not yet printed, but shall forward you a copy as soon as they are received from the printer.

Our movement is anxiously endeavoring to keep in touch with the wage-workers, to help organize them, to make them self-reliant, to coalesce them into one grand whole struggling against the unjust conditions that exist, and to supplant them with such that the noblest aspirations of mankind has conceived or can conceive.

Pardon me if I intrude a little personal matter in this communication. They have accused me of being unfair and partial while presiding. I beg to assure you that if my experience of twenty-five years in the labor movement presiding in the majority of its most important gatherings would not teach me that an unfair presiding officer in a labor organization always accomplishes the very reverse of the tendencies of his unfair rulings, I certainly would be a dunce. So characteristic of impartiality is my reputation while presiding, that during a joint debate between Seguis Schevitch and Henry George,[3] I was the only one that both could agree upon, regardless of the well known fact that my views coincided with those of Schevitch as opposed to George.

I ask your pardon for intruding this lengthy letter upon you, yes in fact this subject, but I do so because as I have said I have respect for your judgment, and as a student of your writings and those of Marx and others in the same line I would not have your judgment formed upon the base of erroneous information.

If it is not asking too much, and you can find the time, I kindly request you to favor me in the interest of our great cause, with an expression of opinion upon the above at your earliest convenience and oblige,[4]

Yours Very Respectfully   Saml Gompers.
President. American Federation of Labor.

N.B. I enclose herein a copy of the report of the committee which was appointed at the Detroit convention, and which was finally adopted by the vote above referred to.[5]

S. G.

TLpS, reel 4, vol. 5, pp. 334-36, SG Letterbooks, DLC.

1. Ernest BOHM was secretary of the New York City Central Labor Federation (CLF) from 1889 to 1899.

2. See "Gompers and the Struggle between the Central Labor Union and the Central Labor Federation in New York City" and "A Series of Accounts of the 1890 Convention of the AFL in Detroit," Dec. 8-9, 1890, in *The Early Years of the AFL*, pp. 191-92 and 386-408.

3. SG presided over the debate, entitled "The Single Land Tax as a Basis of the Political Labor Movement," which took place on Oct. 22, 1887, in New York City. The parties were Sergius E. SHEVITCH, a member of the editorial board of the *New Yorker Volkszeitung* and an important figure in the SLP in New York City, and Henry GEORGE, a Philadelphia-born journalist, labor reformer, anti-monopolist, and unsuccessful candidate for mayor of New York City in 1886.

4. While Engels did not answer SG's letter, he gave his view of the matter on Jan. 29, 1891, in a letter to Hermann Schlüter: "Nor do I understand the [SLP's] quarrel with Gompers. His Federation is, as far as I know, an association of trade unions and nothing but trade unions. Hence they have the *formal right* to reject anyone coming as the representative of a labor organization that is *not* a trade union, or to reject delegates of an association to which such organizations are admitted. I cannot judge from here, of course, whether it was *propagandistically* advisable to expose oneself to such a rejection. But it was beyond question that it had to come, and I, for one, cannot blame Gompers for it.

"But when I think of next year's international congress in Brussels, I should have thought it would have been well to keep on good terms with Gompers, who has more workers behind him, at any rate, than the S.L.P., and to ensure as big a delegation from America as possible there, including *his* people. They would see many things there that would disconcert them in their narrow-minded trade-union standpoint—and besides, where do you want to find a recruiting ground if not in the trade unions?" (Karl Marx and Frederick Engels, *Letters to Americans, 1848-1895: A Selection,* ed. Alexander Trachtenberg [1953; reprint ed., New York, 1969], p. 233).

5. See "Special Committee's Report," Dec. 9, 1890, in "A Series of Accounts of the 1890 Convention of the AFL in Detroit," in *The Early Years of the AFL,* pp. 390-91.

An Excerpt from a News Account of a Meeting of the New York City Central Labor Federation

[January 10, 1891]

WEEKLY MEETING OF THE CENTRAL LABOR FEDERATION.

. . .

SAMUEL GOMPERS' LETTER.

The special order at 4 o'clock was "Action on the communication received last week from President Samuel Gompers" and published in full in these columns.[1]

After reading again the said communication, delegate Bohm moved that the delegates of the American Section, Socialist Labor party, be retained in the C.L.F. . . .

THE SOCIALISTS RETAINED.

The motion to retain the S.L.P. section, with the addition relative to the reply, was then put to a vote and adopted almost unanimously by the largest assemblage of delegates that has yet come together, only three votes being cast in the negative. Applause followed this result.

The reply sent to President Samuel Gompers by Secretary Ernest Bohm reads as follows:

REPLY OF THE C.L.F. TO GOMPERS.

Mr. Samuel Gompers, Pres. Am. Fed. of Labor.
Dear Sir and Brother:—

Your letter of the 27th ult. was duly considered at a regular meeting of the Central Labor Federation, held last Sunday.

In reply this body has instructed me to say that it does not agree with you in any of the statements therein made, except as to the mere fact that the Detroit Convention, upon those statements and others of the same character, denied a seat to our representative.

In the first place it is not correct to state, as you do, that *you* referred the C.L.F. matter to the Detroit Convention. This would imply that you had the power to prevent us from submitting our case to the said Convention, but kindly waived it. It would also imply that you made a temperate exercise, in an issue where you had already taken sides, of the power and influence which naturally attach to the functions of President of the A.F. of L.

The fact is, however, that the C.L.F. *appealed from your decision* to the said Convention, and from the moment its representative[2] appeared before the Committee on Credentials to the time when a vote was taken, all the influence and power you could command as President of the A.F. of L. was exerted against his admission:

1 — By speeches in which passionate appeals to vulgar prejudices took the place of sensible argument;

2 — By statements calculated to mislead the delegates;

3 — By your appointment, on the Special Committee referred to in your letter, of men notoriously opposed to our admission[3] and so evidently selected by you to report as you wanted, that, contrary to all parliamentary precedent, you failed to appoint on that committee the author of the resolution by virtue of which it was created,[4] for no other apparent reason than that he was an able and earnest supporter of our claim.

So far, indeed, were you carried away by your intense desire, not that justice be done to the C.L.F. if you had done it an injustice, but that your unjust decision be sustained at all hazards by the Convention, that you attempted, by personal and unjustifiable attacks, to descredit *bona fide* delegates of *bona fide* organizations represented in this body. And while intimating that the credentials of Ernest Bohm as delegate of the National Brewers' Union,[5] and August Waldinger[6] as delegate of the N.Y. United Machinists,[7] would not bear the closest scrutiny, not only you were putting forward as your mouthpiece the representative of a sham organization styling itself a Federal Union,[8] but you were appointing on the aforesaid special committee a certain Frank K. Foster,[9] boss printer, employer of labor, claiming to represent the Tackmakers' National Union,[10] but whose real business in the councils of wage-workers has been for years, notoriously, that of an agent of the Democratic party. This Foster was the Secretary of *your*

"Special Committee," and its report, which we shall presently consider, was his work.

The two first paragraphs of this report, as quoted in your letter, are for the most part made up of meaningless phrases, such as the professional politician has long been accustomed to use in his public treatment of the labor question. In so far as they contain anything that is at all tangible or comprehensible they are contradictory or untrue, and plainly intended to keep the wage-workers divided by hypocritical appeals to the right of individual opinion, even when such opinion is the product, not of reason, but of race prejudice, individual selfishness and "temperament."

The third paragraph states a flagrant untruth in language calculated to deceive. By the cunning addition of the word "partisan" to the word "politics," it falsely asserts that the A.F. of L. is committed against political action of any sort; whereas, in fact, the A.F. of L., at its Columbus Convention held in December 1886,[11] placed itself on record, by resolution, as unreservedly favoring and recommending independent labor movements of the working class.[12] Again it says: "We cannot logically admit the S.L.P. to representation and shut the door in the face of other political organizations formed to achieve social progress." Everybody knows that there is no such political organization in existence outside of the Socialist Labor party. But it is by deprecating "partisan politics" that partisan politicians succeed in excluding the S.L.P. from the councils of Organized Labor, while throwing wide open the doors of its central bodies and conventions to the old plutocratic parties under the borrowed name of "Tackmakers" and the fictitious one of "Federal Unions."

Finally, the conclusions and recommendations of the report ignore all the testimony and arguments presented on the side of the C.L.F. at the meeting held by the special committee.

We therefore believe that the Detroit Convention had no opportunity of fairly deciding our case. For the injustice done us, we blame you, and you alone. We believe that most of the delegates who were instructed to vote against us would now, in the light that has been cast upon the subject, be instructed to vote otherwise; and we appeal from the Detroit Convention to the various organizations represented therein, with the conviction that they will so instruct their delegates to the Birmingham Convention next year[13] as to admit the delegate that we shall send then and there.

And so long as the S.L.P. remains a pure labor party, having in view the abolition of wage slavery and the substitution of the cooperative commonwealth under a self-government of free workers, for the competitive system under a despotic government of plutocrats; so long as that party sends us as delegates honest representatives of the aspirations of labor, we shall prefer their company and co-operation to that of the Fosters and like agents of the boodle parties.

Fraternally yours, Ernest Bohm.

Cor. Sec'y.

. . .

Workmen's Advocate (New York), Jan. 10, 1891.

1. The letter, dated Dec. 27, 1890, and published in the *Workmen's Advocate* on Jan. 3, 1891, recapitulated the report of the special committee of the AFL convention that investigated the charter application of the New York City Central Labor Federation (CLF).

2. Lucien Delabarre SANIAL was a prominent leader of the SLP and editor of its organs the *Workmen's Advocate* (1889-91) and the *People* (1891).

3. The committee consisted of William J. Cannon, Frank K. Foster, John B. Lennon, Frank L. Rist, and William J. Shields.

4. Thomas John MORGAN was a Chicago machinist and brass finisher and a leader in the SLP.

5. The National Union of the United BREWERY Workmen of the United States.

6. August Waldinger, a New York City machinist, was financial secretary of the New York City CLF from 1891 to 1894 and an SLP nominee for various minor New York City offices in 1892 and 1894.

7. New York City machinists organized in the James Watt Assembly of the KOL beginning in 1881 and in other KOL local assemblies, all under the jurisdiction of District Assembly (DA) 49, by the middle of the decade. After an unsuccessful attempt to join together as machinery constructors' DA 198, machinists primarily from the James Watt and Harlem assemblies formed United Machinists' Union 1 in 1886. It affiliated with the AFL as Federal Labor Union (FLU) 4013 in 1890 and by 1891 had over 600 members organized in five sections.

8. Probably George Edwin McNEILL, who represented FLU 3873.

9. Frank Keyes FOSTER, a Boston printer, was active in the International Typographical Union, the KOL, and the FOTLU, and edited the *Labor Leader* in Boston from 1887 until 1897.

10. Tackmakers' Protective Union 4007 was affiliated with the AFL from 1889 until about 1893; Foster represented the union at the 1890 convention.

11. The convention met in Columbus, Ohio, Dec. 8-12, 1886.

12. "Resolved that the Convention urge a most generous support to the independent political movement of the workingmen" (AFL, *Proceedings*, 1886, p. 16).

13. The AFL held its 1891 convention in Birmingham, Ala., Dec. 14-19.

To the Wage Workers of the United States[1]

[January 11, 1891]

GOMPERS FIRES A SHOT OF HEAVIEST CALIBRE.

. . .

["]To-day the socialist party in this city is in the control of an element dangerous to true progress and a menace to the men it professes to serve, and I propose, as far as lies within my power, to protect them from the machinations of a clique whose presence in any movement bodes disaster to it. They dare not combat the Federation openly, hence they want to make the fight on me for my defence of its principles and policy. Their personal attacks on me are maliciously false. The situation demands that I should be personal and discuss the personnel of the leaders of this party.

["]It is a notorious fact that most of the leaders of the socialistic political party have proven themselves tricksters and wire pullers of the lowest order—dishonest in all their professions and false to the cause of labor. Let me cite a few instances. Philip Van Patton,[2] their earliest national secretary, was proven to be an embezzler of the pennies contributed by the members. Then there was Vincent Woy-tesek,[3] another of the evangelists of that political party, who was the socialistic bosses' candidate for Assembly. They forced the real labor candidate to withdraw from the field in his interests. To-day Mr. Woytesek is an active heeler for Tammany Hall.

["]Again, there was William Bartholomew,[4] their candidate for Congress. He also proved false to organized labor and became an active Republican heeler. The socialistic party has not forgotten that its other shining light, John Jahelka, ran for Congress at the dictation of the socialistic politicians for the purpose of drawing away sufficient votes to insure the defeat of a man who was pledged to the abolition of the tenement house cigar factories. His candidacy resulted in the election of Edward Einstein, a tenement house manufacturer.["][5]

NON-UNIONISTS FOR CANDIDATES.

["]Of Samuel Phillips, candidate for Assembly in the Seventeenth district,[6] I need hardly speak. He is best known as a non-union cigar manufacturer, from whom the cigar makers' union[7] twice withdrew their union label because he refused to pay union wages.

["]It is more in sorrow than in anger that I refer to these men, and I do so only to show organized labor the character of the element which seeks to control the industrial movement. The Latter Day Saints, Sanial and Vogt,[8] who are attitudinizing as leaders of the socialistic political party, are not much better. How Mr. Sanial edged his way into his role is a mystery; of his antecedents but little is known. My brief investigation of his record showed me that he has been known only as a scribbling advocate of every party that ever existed. He has been on both sides of every question, and several years ago he was the paid editorial advocate of the New England factory lords. Protection was then his professional hobby. He is now strutting about as the political boss of the socialists, and his ambition is to become known as the labor leader of New York. At a recent meeting of the Central Labor Federation he bullied delegates into reconsidering their honest decision and to resolve upon a policy detrimental to their interests and at variance with their expressed sentiments.

["]As for Hugo Vogt, the lawyer who joined Mr. Sanial in his cry against me, I have nothing to say, except that he is noted as a standing candidate for all nominations.["]

No Friends of Theirs.

["]Messrs. Sanial and company have seen fit to refer often to Thomas Morgan, their Chicago confrere, who fought for them at Detroit. They profess great admiration for him. They must be aware that he totally disagrees with them and is opposed to their tactics.

["]In the plainest language he declared that they had no right to force their political machine into the trades union movement or to provoke the quarrels which have marked their efforts. The best and wisest socialists outside of New York take this view of the matter.

["]The misleading and destructive element to which I refer never tires of chanting praises of John Burns,[9] George Tillott[10] and Thomas Mann[11] of England. These men are socialists, but first of all they are trades unionists, and never have they attempted to appear in a trades union congress or trades union council as representatives of the so-cialistic political party. On the contrary they have invariably attended such gatherings as delegates of trades unions.

["]The socialistic politicians as a party have always professed great friendship for trade unions, but that was only pretence. They are friendly only to those unions which they can control for their own dishonest schemes. But of unions noted for large membership, discipline and substantial treasuries, which conduct their affairs regardless of the wishes of the socialistic political party, they have ever been relentless enemies.

["]There are few men in the labor movement who have not an ideal of better social and economic conditions. Some might call this socialism. If it is, it is not the narrow party socialism, but of that broad and progressive character that towers over party or junto.

["]The German organ[12] of the clique of which I have been speaking suppressed the report of the Detroit Convention, thereby preventing the German speaking members of the Central Labor Federation from reading the clear and concise statement of the committee to which was referred the question in dispute.["]

NOT A POLITICIAN.

["]I have been accused of an itching for politics. Of the number of appointive positions offered me I will say nothing. A year ago a nomination for Senator (equivalent to an election) was tendered me. I felt that I had neither the right to accept nor to decline it without consulting the organized workmen of New York. As I did not seek the proffered honor I did not hesitate to decline it when I learned the sentiments of my colleagues.[13] Before the recent election I was positively offered the nomination for Congress, which I declined without hesitation. In view of these facts and the fact that I have ever held aloof from politics the accusation is absurd.

["]The socialistic bosses threaten my downfall. I doubt their ability to encompass anybody's downfall. But even should they succeed it would make little difference to me and none to the cause of labor for the man who holds the position which I occupy cannot take any other stand on the question of politics in trade unions except the one I have taken. It is the only logical stand that trade unions can take.["]

UNDEFILED BY POLITICS.

["]I have no word of censure for a man because of his views on political, social or economic questions, but I contend that trade unions are the natural form of organization for wage earners under existing economic conditions, and I propose (so far as I may be able) to keep them undefiled and free from alliance with any political party—no matter what name it may bear or how lofty its pretensions may be. Factions who wish to dally with hobbies and fine spun theories or desire to attitudinize as statesmen have no place in the ranks of trade unionism. Trade unionists are practical men: they must deal with the hard, stern, cold facts of everyday life—questions of hours and wages, which have the first and most pressing claim upon their attention.

["]A man may be a socialist or any other ist of his choosing, but we hold and shall insist upon his good standing in a trade union as a condition essential to his right to speak or act in a council of trades unionists.["]

New York Herald, Jan. 11, 1891.

1. The *New York Herald* described the following as "generous extracts" from SG's letter.

2. Simon Philip VAN PATTEN, who went by the name Philip Van Patten in the 1870s and 1880s, had served as national secretary of the Workingmen's Party of the United States (1876-77) and of the SLP (1877-83). In the 1890s he was operating an architectural firm in Hot Springs, Ark.

3. Vincent William Woytisek served as president of CMIU 144 during late 1881 and as secretary of local 1 of the Cigarmakers' Progressive Union until about 1885. He ran on the SLP ticket for the New York Assembly in 1882, and in 1884 was elected treasurer of the New York City Central Labor Union. During the late 1880s and 1890s he operated a saloon and sold real estate. About 1898 he became a lawyer.

4. Robert H. Bartholomee, a piano maker, was the SLP candidate for assemblyman for New York's tenth district in 1878.

5. In 1878 the SLP nominated John Jahelka for Congress in New York's seventh district. Cigar manufacturer Edwin Einstein, who ran on both the Republican and "anti-Tammany" tickets, defeated Jahelka and Tammany candidate Anthony Eickoff. Einstein served from 1879 to 1881.

6. Phillips was the SLP candidate for assemblyman in New York's seventeenth district in 1890.

7. The CIGAR Makers' International Union of America.

8. Hugo VOGT, a notary public, was a leader of the SLP in New York City.

9. John Elliott BURNS, a machinist, was a leader of the 1889 London dockers' strike and was a Member of Parliament from 1892 to 1918.

10. Benjamin TILLETT was general secretary (1889-1922) of the Dock, Wharf, Riverside, and General Labourers' Union of Great Britain and Ireland (DWRGLU).

11. Thomas MANN was president (1889-92) of the DWRGLU.

12. The *New Yorker Volkszeitung.*

13. See "A Translation of a News Account of a Nominating Convention for the New York Seventh Senatorial District," Oct. 26, 1889, "To the Committee of Notification of the Republican Party of the New York Seventh Senatorial District," Oct. 28, 1889, and "An Excerpt from a News Account of a Meeting of the New York City Central Labor Federation," Nov. 2, 1889, in *The Early Years of the AFL,* pp. 244-47, 249-51.

To John Ketcham[1]

Jan. 13th. [189]1

To the Hon. J. H. Ketchum,
#1329 K. St. N.W. Washington, D.C.
Dear Sir:—

Being aware that you are the Chairman of the Committee on Post Offices of the House of Representatives and have reported favorably upon the Bill to extend the beneficent effects of the Eight Hour Law to the Post Office Clerks,[2] I beg leave to say that I am aware of the crowded condition of legislation at present.

I have reason to believe that Mr. Speaker Reed,[3] and Mr. Mc-Kinley[4] are favorably disposed towards the Bill and would be willing to present a rule, as members of the Committee on Rules of the House, setting a date for the consideration of the Bill in question.

The constituents of Mr. Cannon,[5] of the same Committee, will also request him to favor a proposition of that character in the Committee on Rules, and I would suggest that you would also urge him on in that direction.

Of course it is superfluous at this time to say how unjust it is for this great Government to place it in the power of any one man to allow Post Office Clerks to work as many as eighteen (18) hours in a day and seven days in the week as is the case in our Post Office, and that the recent action of some people in the Post Office department to off-set the progress of the Bill in question by a increase in salaries, finds no actual responsive chord from the Post Office Clerks.

I earnestly hope that you may be successful in the passage of the Bill, and to say that if I can be of any further service in helping it on I am at your command.

Very Respectfully Yours   Saml Gompers.
President American Federation of Labor.

TLpS, reel 4, vol. 5, p. 340, SG Letterbooks, DLC.

1. John Henry Ketcham (1832-1906), a New York farmer, was a Republican congressman (1865-73, 1877-93, 1897-1906).

2. In July 1890 Ketcham introduced a bill to limit the hours of work of post office clerks and employees (H.R. 6449, 51st Cong., 1st sess., 1890); it did not become law.

3. Thomas Brackett Reed (1839-1902), a Maine lawyer, was a Republican congressman (1877-99) and Speaker of the House of Representatives (1889-91, 1895-99).

4. William McKinley, Jr. (1843-1901), was a Republican congressman from Ohio (1877-84, 1885-91); he subsequently served as the state's governor (1892-96) and as president of the United States (1897-1901).

5. Joseph Gurney Cannon (1836-1926), an Illinois lawyer, was a Republican congressman (1873-91, 1893-1913, 1915-23) and Speaker of the House of Representatives (1903-11).

From Henry Skeffington[1]

Office of General Secretary,
Boot and Shoe Workers International Union,[2]
Boston, Mass., Jan, 14, 1891

Dear Sir & Brother:

No doubt you were informed by the members of the Rochester Shoe Council who were in your city recently looking for financial aid, of the rejection of the proposition made by you conjointly with Bro. Sieverman,[3] Sec'y of the Rochester Shoe Council and myself, by the Boot & Shoe Manufacturers Association of Rochester.[4]

The history of the difficulty at Rochester can be summed up in a very few words. The P. Cox Shoe Co. of that city, desiring to forestall the introduction of a bill of wages in their Fairport, N.Y. factory, discharged several of the officers of our union at that place. They refused to consider the bill of wages or to re-instate our members. Several serious difficulties were pending in their Rochester factory, and after six consultations with the firm, our Gen'l Exec. Board decided to strike the Fairport factory. This was on the 31st of May last. The Rochester Shoe Council, finding that the work was being done in the Rochester factory, concluded to strike that factory also a few days after.

The annual convention of our International Union took place the 2nd of June,[5] and the action of the Rochester Shoe Council and members of our Gen'l Exec. Board in the P. Cox affair was unanimously endorsed. Since that time we have maintained the strike conjointly with the Rochester Shoe Council, and until recently have not missed a payment of those who came out on strike at our bidding. The International Union have levied assessments amounting to $1.40 per member on the entire organization for the support of Rochester. The Shoe Manufacturers Association of Rochester on the 11th of June last resolved to furnish financial assistance to the P. Cox Co., and also to furnish money proportionately to the number of their employes, to what is known as the Scab Fund. This Fund was used for the purpose of securing men and women in different sections of the country to go to Rochester and work in P. Cox & Co.'s shoe factories. A large proportion of the assessment paid by our members was used to buy off these scabs. A boycott was levied on the goods which worked very successfully. The Supreme Court of the state of New York has been invoked by Mr. Cox,[6] and an injunction served upon nearly all of our leading members in Rochester restraining them from paying any more money to the strikers. Injunctions were also served upon our members restraining them from paying any part of their wages to the strike fund. 30 of our members were sued by Mr. Cox for $50,000 damages. All of this failed to deter our membership from carrying on the fight against that firm. In Nov. last the Manufacturers Association notified the Rochester Shoe Council to the effect that unless the strike in the factories of the P. Cox Shoe Co. was declared off on Dec. 1st they, the Manufacturers Association, would lock out their employes. 21 firms thus engaged themselves to throw 2200 people on our hands. At the recent convention of the American Federation of Labor the representative[7] of the Central Labor Union of Rochester[8] made application for financial assistance, which was voted. I restrained him from placing a resolution before the convention asking for an assessment to be levied on the American Federation of Labor.

Word comes to me today that the Big organizations of Pittsburg, viz. the Amalgamated Association of Iron & Steel Workers,[9] the Flint Glass Workers,[10] and others are in favor of levying an assessment upon the American Federation of Labor. The Flint Glass Workers propose to loan us $5000 provided the Exec. Council of the American Federation of Labor endorses our application for the same. I presume this amount would be paid back from the fund massed, provided the assessment were levied in favor of the Rochester shoemakers by the Exec. Council.

This International Union has exhausted every resource to beg, borrow or steal money in aid of our members at Rochester. We are not securing sufficient money to buy bread for those people. My latest information is that the manufacturers have armed their scabs, and the ex-President of one of our unions, John E. Coyle, was shot down by a scab on last Saturday night, receiving four bullets and now lies between life and death.[11] I believe that the Manufacturers Association are becoming desperate. Recently they advertised in all the leading newspapers throughout the country for help to go to Rochester, and my opinion is that they made a miserable failure of it.

The shoe trade generally has not been so dull for five years. This has been caused by the advance in leather which began last August and continues at the present time. The manufacturers endeavored to advance the price of their shoes to meet the advance in the price of leather, but were met with a firm refusal on the part of the jobbers and retail dealers throughout the country. This has had the effect of so demoralizing our trade that ¾ of the shoemakers of this country are not earning an average of $4 per week, and have not done so since the 1st of Dec.

Our International Union has now reached the most critical period in its existence. For 20 years it has been the custom of the manufacturers here in the East, viz. Maine, N.H. and Mass., where ⅔ of all the Boots and Shoes in the United States are manufactured, to cut down wages an average of 10% in the appearance of the first snow storm. For the two years of its existence this International Union has fought this system. During the winter of 1889-90 we had 84 strikes against reductions, and won every one of them. This left our organization poor but undaunted in spirit. During the present winter we have not had a single reduction in wages throughout our entire jurisdiction. This is a great boon to us, but we are in danger of losing it as the manufacturers throughout the East, as I have reason to know, are watching Rochester very closely, and any disaster at that point would precipitate a general reduction. At the present moment our prospects are bright, for today comes a letter, a copy of which I send you, from Chicago, and in this connection, we are now negotiating for the formation of four new unions in that section. In consideration of the above facts I now, on behalf of the Boot & Shoe Workers International Union, and with the approval of our Gen'l Exec. Board, make application to the Exec. Council of the American Federation of Labor for an assessment to be levied upon the affiliated associations,[12] and I most urgently request you, as President, to call a meeting of the Exec. Council at Phila. on Monday, Jan. 19th.

The undersigned will be present at the meeting if notified by you that the same will be held.

Will you please notify me by wire at your earliest possible convenience if such a meeting is called.

Fraternally yours   For the Gen'l Exec. Board,
H. J. Skeffington
Gen'l Sec'y

TLS, Boot and Shoe Workers' International Union Records, reel 139, *AFL Records.*

1. Henry J. SKEFFINGTON was secretary-treasurer of the Boot and Shoe Workers' International Union (BSWIU) in 1889, and general secretary and general treasurer from 1890 to 1894.

2. The BOOT and Shoe Workers' International Union.

3. Frank A. Sieverman was a member of BSWIU 25 of Rochester, N.Y.

4. See *The Early Years of the AFL*, pp. 427-28, n. 1.

5. The BSWIU held its second annual convention June 2-6, 1890, in Rochester, N.Y.

6. Patrick Cox of Rochester, president of P. Cox Shoe Manufacturing Co., operated two factories in Fairport, N.Y., and one in Rochester, N.Y.

7. Joseph Bauer (1845-1938), a Rochester, N.Y., shoemaker, was a member of BSWIU 22 and was active in the Rochester Trades Assembly. He was elected to the New York assembly as a Republican in 1888 for one term.

8. The Rochester Trades Assembly was founded in 1888.

9. The National Amalgamated Association of IRON and Steel Workers of the United States.

10. The American FLINT Glass Workers' Union of North America.

11. On Jan. 10, 1891, John E. Coyle of BSWIU 82 of Rochester, N.Y., was involved in a fight with John Brennan, a working shoemaker, in a local saloon. Brennan shot Coyle twice in the chest, but Coyle survived.

12. The AFL did not levy an assessment in this instance.

From D. L. Alexander[1]

Office of General Secretary
The Axe and Edge-Tool Makers' National Union of America.[2]
Reedsville, Pa., Jany 17—1891

Dear Sir and Bro.

Enclosed find Post Office Money Order for Thirteen Dollars and Fifty Cents ($13.50) credit me for the same as follows—

Per Capita Tax 400 Members. December 1890.	$ 1.00
" " " " " Jany. 1891.	1.00
1st Assesment for Miners[3] @ 2c per Member "	8.00
1 200 Page Ledger	1.75
1 " " Day-Book	1.75
	$13.50

Please send Ledger and Day-Book to A. G. McClennan East Douglas Mass. *At once.*

I earnestly hope the Miners may be victorious in their Eight hour Movement, but in my opinion the surest safest and shortest way to obtain a universal Eight hour day thereby doing the greatest good to the largest number—is for the Labor Organizations to unite in a political movement to elect representatives to the Legislatures of the different States who will make and enforce laws such as Eight hour day—[,] Anti-Monopoly.[,] Contract Labor[,] Against Corporations Employing Pinkertons Detectives Etc. You will find outside of the large Cities a strong sentiment growing amongst the workingmen favoring such a movement and many are only waiting for an opportunity to Join in with Alliance[4]—K of Ls political combine. Unless the other Labor Organizations inaugerate or endorse some such a movement they are very likely to find their ranks greatly depleted in the next two years.

Will you be please be kind enough to send me a few sample copies of Labor Papers or tell me where I can obtain copies of the best Journals.

Hoping to hear from you soon. I am.

Yours fraternally   D. L. Alexander

G.S. Axe & Edge Tool Makers National Union of America.

P.S. Hurry books to East Douglas. Mass.

Send me latest password of A.F of L.

ALS, Axe and Edge Tool Makers' National Union Records, reel 138, *AFL Records.*

1. D. L. ALEXANDER was a founder and first general secretary (1890-91) of the Axe and Edge Tool Makers' National Union of America.

2. The AXE and Edge Tool Makers' National Union of America.

3. The AFL Executive Council designated the United MINE Workers of America to carry on the eight-hour campaign after the completion of the carpenters' drive.

4. The major organizations of farmers' alliances involved in the populist political movement were the National Farmers' Alliance and Industrial Union of America (NFAIU) and the Colored Farmers' National Alliance and Cooperative Union (CFNA). The state farmers' alliances of Texas and Louisiana merged in 1887 to form the National Farmers' Alliance and Co-operative Union of America. Known as the "Southern Alliance" because it developed state alliances throughout the South, it joined with the Arkansas-based Agricultural Wheel in September 1889 to become the Farmers' and Laborers' Union of America, and in December 1889 absorbed the Kansas and South Dakota farmers' alliances and became the NFAIU. By 1890 it had over a million members, with lecturers operating from coast to coast and in Canada, supported by a National Reform Press Association that united 1,000 newspapers from all sections of the country.

Racial restrictions of the southern alliances led to the establishment of a separate black organization, the CFNA, in 1888. It was an outgrowth of a Texas organization established in 1886. By 1890 it claimed to have a membership comparable to the NFAIU spread over sixteen states.

A third organization, the National Farmers' Alliance or "Northwestern Alliance," originated in Chicago in 1880 and developed a presence across the Midwest. Lacking an effective organizational structure or strong leadership, it had only about 10,000 members after the South Dakota Alliance withdrew to join the NFAIU in 1889. It played a peripheral role in the populist movement.

To Frances Dickinson[1]

Jan. 31st. [189]1

Dr. Frances Dickinson
Chairman Petition Commmittee N.A. Woman Suffrage Association.[2]
#70 State St. Chicago, Ill.
Dear Madam: —

With this I express to your address the petitions in favor of the Women Suffrage amendment now pending before Congress.[3]

The petitions represent a membership of 229252. In the course of a week or so I shall forward you others and continue sending them as they come in.

Sincerely hoping that the amendment may be submitted to the various legislatures and finally become a law of the land I am,

Truly Yours   Saml Gompers
President. American Federation of Labor.

N.B. You will find that nearly all the Petitions have the seal of the organizations affixed which of course gives them much more potency and effect.

S. G.

TLpS, reel 4, vol. 5, p. 405, SG Letterbooks, DLC.

1. Frances Dickinson, an ophthalmalogic surgeon and medical writer, was a lifelong advocate of woman suffrage.

2. In 1890 the National Woman Suffrage Association and the American Woman Suffrage Association merged to form the National American Woman Suffrage Association.

3. The woman suffrage amendment pending before Congress was originally introduced in 1878. Congress approved it in 1919, and it was ratified as the Nineteenth Amendment to the Constitution in 1920.

To Charles Saxton[1]

Jan. 31st. [189]1

Senator Chas. T. Saxton,
Senate Chamber, Albany, N.Y.
Dear Sir: —

Enclosed please find a crudely drawn amendment to the laws of the state of N.Y. in which it is sought to limit the judges of the courts of our state in issuing injunctions upon working people engaged in disputes with their employers.

By the same mail I forward to you copies of injunctions served upon working people engaged in struggles, both in Rochester and in Binghamton.[2] From a perusal of them you will see the flimsy pretexts used in order to defeat the working people in their efforts to aid each other in the contribution of money, or persuade their fellow-workers not to take work from employers with whom they are in dispute.

It is called bribery (in these injunctions) to pay working people a certain sum so that they may be enabled to buy the necessaries of life, in order to persuade them not to take work pending a trade dispute.

I kindly ask you to give this matter, as well as the other forwarded you yesterday your earnest consideration, and urge you to secure the enactment of either this law or one that will achieve the object in view.[3]

I also forward a copy of a bill which may cover the proposed law to prohibit or regulate the arming of private forces (commonly known as Pinkerton thugs) during labor troubles.[4]

All these measures to which I call your attention have received the approval of the convention of the State Branch of the American Federation of Labor.

I kindly ask you to preserve the injunctions I forwarded, but which you can use in your argument should you desire to.

Earnestly hoping that you will give these matters your early and favorable consideration I am,

Very Respectfully Yours   Saml Gompers.
President. American Federation of Labor.

TLpS, reel 4, vol. 5, p. 404, SG Letterbooks, DLC.

1. Charles T. Saxton was a Republican member of the New York senate from 1890 to 1894.

2. Between 2,000 and 3,000 cigarmakers in Binghamton, N.Y., struck for higher wages in June 1890. Less than 10 percent of the strikers were members of the CMIU, although CMIU 16 and 218 assumed leadership of the strike, which ended unsuccessfully in October. In 1891 the New York supreme court dismissed an application by the Binghamton Cigar Manufacturers' Association for a permanent injunction enjoining the union from picketing or paying traveling or strike benefits.

3. Possibly a reference to the bill in the state assembly to amend section 608 of the code of civil procedure, relating to injunction orders. It passed the assembly but did not become law.

4. In 1892 the New York legislature prohibited local authorities from importing men for special police duty (Laws of 1892, chap. 272).

From August Delabar[1]

Office of the International Secretary
Journeymen Bakers' & Confectioners' International Union of America[2]
New York, Feb 2 1891

Dear Sir & Bro

I unterstand you will go to the Pacific Coast,[3] can you let me know about the time you get to San Francisco Cal, also will you speack for us at a mass meeting of our people they are in a most misrable condition ther and just picking up a litle a litle push would ait [aid] greatly. the federation[4] out ther does nothing for us probebly you could also push our labol their the reason i write those [this?] is Frisco stants alone as far as we are consirnet [concerned] no other city ixept New Orleans has the same misrable Conditions 7 days work long hours mirable [miserable] bording & lodging sort of a truck system. please note our Statistic in Journal this week and the 3 [2?] next Take notice of SF Cal also the diverence betw 24 germ and 51 engl Union[5] a splentid material for you out their. our people have best time for a meeting on Sunday if you let me know wat Sunday you will be their and if you will speack for us i will at once make all other arangements be consitering this remember our men have no time to antent [attend] any of your other meeting wer you may speack They work every night hence my request, to speack to the bakers Separate hoping for a early and favoble reply I remain yours

Fraternally   Aug Delabar
Int Sey

ALS, Journeymen Bakers' and Confectioners' International Union Records, reel 138, *AFL Records.*

1. August DELABAR was secretary of the Journeymen Bakers' National Union (after 1890 the Journeymen Bakers' and Confectioners' International Union) from 1888 to 1892.

2. Journeymen BAKERS' and Confectioners' International Union of America.

3. Between Feb. 9 and Apr. 20, 1891, SG visited over twenty-five cities to promote the miners' eight-hour campaign, strengthen local labor movements, and resolve the Pacific Coast brewers' dispute. This was the first trip that took him to the Pacific Coast. On Sunday, Mar. 15, he spoke to a gathering of bakers at Metropolitan Hall in San Francisco.

4. The Representative Council of the Federated Trades and Labor Organizations of the PACIFIC Coast.

5. German-speaking bakers organized local 24; local 51 was for English-speaking workers.

To David Hill[1]

Feb. 7th. [1891]

Hon. David B. Hill,
Governor of the State of N.Y.
Albany, N.Y.
Dear Sir:—

A rumor reaches me that there is to be a change in the personnel of some of the offices in the State Government.

From my recent utterances published in the Press you no doubt have seen that such a course is most desirable and in the interest of the people. I desire to say however, that from my large circle of acquaintances, an extensive correspondence, and personal visitations, I have yet to learn of any complaint among the organized or unorganized working people, with the personnel or official conduct of the Chief and chief clerk of the Bureau of Labor Statistics, Mr. Chas. F. Peck, and Mr. Ed. J. Kean.[2]

Both the work and reports of the Bureau have reflected credit upon their department, and have been received by all classes of the community with manifestations of respect and confidence, hence should the rumor above referred to prove true, I trust you will give the matter herein referred to your earnest consideration, and believe me to be,

Yours Very Respectfully   Saml Gompers.
President. American Federation of Labor.

TLpS, reel 4, vol. 5, p. 420, SG Letterbooks, DLC.

1. David Bennett HILL was Democratic governor of New York from 1885 until 1892.
2. Edward J. KEAN, a New York City printer, was chief clerk of the New York Bureau of Labor Statistics between 1885 and 1891.

To Martin McMahon[1]

Feb. 9th. [1891]

General T. Mc-Mahon,
Senate Chamber, Albany, N.Y.
Dear Sir:—

I beg leave to call your attention to the fact that our organization is fully committed to all measures tending towards a reduction in the hours of labor of the working people of our country, and being aware of the fact that a Bill has been placed in your hands by Miss Ida M. Van Etten[2] of this city for the limitation of the hours of labor for Women and Children in the factories and mercantile establishments of this state, I beg to assure you that the Bill in question has my full endorsement and hopes that it may be enacted into law.

The same Bill has been introduced by the Hon. Senator Saxton in the Senate, and I earnestly hope that through your and his efforts we may have the satisfaction of relieving so large a number of over-worked and worthy people.

I understand that another Bill has been introduced seeking to limit the hours of labor of women and children in mercantile establishments. I am of opinion that considerable opposition will be manifested against it by reason of its unfair discrimination between the factory and mercantile employes, hence when such opposition can be avoided and the Bill have a larger scope I think that course should be pursued.[3]

Very Respectfully Yours   Saml Gompers
President. American Federation of Labor.

TLpS, reel 4, vol. 5, p. 424, SG Letterbooks, DLC.

1. Martin Thomas McMahon, a New York City lawyer and at one time a major general in the Union army, served as a Democratic member of the New York assembly in 1890 and of the New York senate from 1891 to 1895.

2. Ida M. VAN ETTEN helped organize the New York Working Women's Society in 1888 and for several years was a leading figure in organizing women workers in New York.

3. On Jan. 19, 1891, McMahon introduced two amendments to the 1886 factory regulation act, concerning the employment of women and children. One applied to factories and the other to mercantile establishments. The legislature failed to take action on either in 1891. In 1892, however, the legislature limited the employment in factories of minors under eighteen and women under twenty-one to sixty hours a week or ten a day, prohibited the employment of children under fourteen or of children unable to read or write English under the age of sixteen, and provided for the appointment of inspectors to enforce these regulations (Laws of 1892, chap. 673). In 1894 and again in 1895 the legislature failed to pass a bill further regulating the employment of women and children. In 1896, after an investigation into the working conditions of women and children, a compromise bill was passed that limited their employment in mercantile establishments to sixty hours a week and ten in any day except Saturday, except during the holiday period between Dec. 15 and Jan. 1. The new statute also prohibited the employment of those under fourteen except during school vacations and provided for work breaks and sanitary facilities. Enforcement was placed under local boards of health rather than the state factory inspector, and the law was generally not enforced (Laws of 1896, chap. 384).

To the Executive Council of the AFL

Feb. 10th. [1891]

To the Executive Council of the A.F. of L.

Fellow-Workmen: —

For years the Trade Unions of the far West and the Pacific Coast have been complaining that they are entirely neglected in the consideration of the Trade Unionists of the East and North.

I have been urged time and again in the interest of our movement to endeavor to allay this feeling and to arouse a fraternal and more close alliance between the wage-workers of the Coast and the rest of the country. Plans have been matured for such a trip and I finally consented making such statements to the recent convention at Detroit which were received with approval.

By the action of the convention suspending the Federated Trades Council of San Francisco for having within that Council a Brewers Union which refused to pay an assessment of their National body,[1] and the Brewers Nat. Union granting a charter in opposition to the existing but suspended local union, there has been such a war of factions that it seems that the whole people of the Pacific Coast and far West is aroused to an awful degree which may spread and disrupt the Trade Union movement, hence in view of the foregoing I have concluded to undertake the trip and try to settle these important questions, and I have strong hopes that I shall be successful.

Enclosed please find list of addresses and dates of the tour. Earnestly hoping that this course will meet with your approval, and trusting that our movement may be entirely successful I am,

Fraternally Yours   Saml Gompers
President. American Federation of Labor

N.B. The costs of the trip are to be covered by the organizations in the places I visit.

S. G.

TLpS, reel 4, vol. 5, p. 426, SG Letterbooks, DLC.

1. In January 1890 the National Union of the United Brewery Workmen of the United States (NUUBW) suspended local 16 of San Francisco because the local refused to pay a per capita assessment in protest against the establishment of the national union's weekly journal. Local 16 had branches in several West Coast cities. Its general secretary, Alfred Fuhrman, then organized the rival United Brewery Workmen's Union of the Pacific Coast and chartered West Coast locals. The NUUBW organized a new local 16 in San Francisco. In December 1890 the AFL convention suspended

the Representative Council of the Federated Trades and Labor Organizations of the Pacific Coast for seating delegates of Fuhrman's group. The rival brewery workers' organizations settled their differences at the 1891 AFL convention, and the Pacific Coast body united with the NUUBW at the latter's 1892 convention.

To P. J. McGuire[1]

Logansport Feb 11th [189]1

P. J. McGuire Esq.
1st Vice Prest. A.F. of L.
Dear Friend

Your favor of the 6th was forwarded here and I certainly regret that I was unable to see you before [my] departure and shall not be permitted [to] see you when you get to N.Y. on the 2[0th?].

By this time you, of course, know that I am out on that *long* trip. Everywhere I am meeting with the greatest success. Our movement has at last taken a firm hold on the hearts and minds of the wage workers and has their confidence as well as the respect of the people at large. The meetings I address are filled to overflowing. The press gives full and fair reports. The Lower Ohio House unanimously tendered their chamber to "Prest. Gompers of the A.F. of L." Here tonight it is expected that 2,000 people will be in attendance. I am making the best of [. . .]. At the Miners Convention[2] every evidence [of loyalty] was given to the A.F. of L. John McBride[3] came [out f]lat footed in his speech of what the U.M.W. owed [as a?] moral obligation to the Trade Unions of the country [&] to the A.F. of L. not to encumber their demand for eight hours with other demands. It was well received too in the face of a recommendation of Pres. Rae to demand "weighing of coal before screening."[4] Of course this demand is perfectly just but in view of the eight hour demand, probably, impracticable.

If there is a movement to place Kirchner on his feet again.[5] You can put me down for fifty dollars. Providing it will put him on his feet. I assure you that I haven't a dollar in the world but I am will[ing] to deprive myself of many things to help him and save our movement from a blot.

I wish you would read N.Y. Herald special letters of the tour.[6] My letter to the Ex. Council upon the subject of the trip[7] is I hope, satisfactory to you.

[Can] you find time to write me to any of the [addres]ses I sent you with last letter? I should [like] to [hear] from you *en route.* The trip is no easy job [as you?] know.

Best wishes to you and yours. I am

              Yours truly

ALp, reel 4, vol. 5, pp. 435-36, SG Letterbooks, DLC.

1. Peter James McGUIRE was secretary of the Brotherhood of Carpenters and Joiners of America (after 1888 the United Brotherhood of Carpenters and Joiners of America) from 1881 to 1901. He served as secretary of the AFL from 1886 to 1889, second vice-president from 1889 to 1890, and first vice-president from 1890 to 1900.

2. The United Mine Workers of America (UMWA) met Feb. 10-17, 1891, in Columbus, Ohio. SG attended the opening of the convention and addressed the delegates.

3. John McBRIDE was president of the Ohio Miners' Amalgamated Association from 1882 to 1889, the National Federation of Miners and Mine Laborers in 1885, the National Progressive Union of Miners and Mine Laborers in 1889, and the UMWA from 1892 to 1895. He was elected president of the AFL over SG in 1894 and was narrowly defeated for that office the next year.

4. John B. RAE was president of the UMWA from 1890 to 1892. At the convention Rae highlighted his opposition to company stores and the screening of coal. By screening coal prior to weighing it, mine operators paid miners only for the larger coal they mined. The convention adopted a resolution requesting state legislatures to forbid screening, but postponed action on the issue pending a joint conference between miners and operators in Pittsburgh, Apr. 7-9, 1891. At that conference Rae emphasized that the eight-hour issue was paramount to all others.

5. John S. KIRCHNER had been secretary of CMIU 100 of Philadelphia (1881, 1884-90), CMIU fourth vice-president (1885-87), and an organizer for Pennsylvania. SG's concern apparently related to Kirchner's drinking. See, for instance, SG to P. J. McGuire, Nov. 4, 1892, reel 6, vol. 8, p. 69, SG Letterbooks, DLC.

6. SG reported on his trip in a series of dispatches that appeared in the *New York Herald* between Feb. 10 and Mar. 7, 1891.

7. See "To the Executive Council of the AFL," Feb. 10, 1891, above.

To William Thorne[1] and Eleanor Marx Aveling[2]

            Evansville, Ind. Feb. 19th. 1891.

Mr. W. Thorne General Secretary and
Mrs. Elivanor Marx Aveling,
For the National Union of Gas Workers and General Laborers of
 Great Brittain and Ireland.
#144 Barking Road E. London, England.
Dear Comrades: —

Your favor of the First inst. calling attention to the action of designing and interested employers, who by various schemes endeavor

ie laborers from one country and to import or export
l from such countries to reduce wages, lengthen hours of
) introduce obnoxious conditions of labor, and your proposition ror the establishment of an International Secretary in each
country for the purpose of counteracting such influence[3] came duly
to hand.

In reply, permit me to say that the proposition entirely meets with
my views. There are two matters, however, which I desire to call your
attention to which may prevent its immediate culmination. One is
that I am just at this time engaged in an agitation and organizing
tour through the entire country from Maine to California in the
interest of the movement of the coal miners, selected by the American
Federation of Labor to make the demand for the enforcement of the
eight hour work day May first 1891, and which will prevent me from
laying the matter before the Executive Council of the A.F. of L. in
a tangible form before my return about the end of April. The second
consideration to which I respectfully call your attention is that it
appears to me such an understanding as you propose, and which all
sincere advocates of our cause must favor, should be approved and
inaugurated not only by one even if by your grand and wonderful
organization, but also with practically all of the Trade Unions of
Great Brittain and Ireland, Continental Europe, Australia, and the
American Federation of Labor for the American Continent.

However since most schemes that result in gigantic proportions
have humble beginnings it may do to start as you propose. I ask you
to bear the above in mind and to respond to it at your earliest
convenience. In the meantime endeavoring to secure the co-operation
referred to.

Permit me to add that I am in hearty accord with the hopes you
express that this movement as well as the aspirations of labor may
tend to the closer international Alliance to crystalize and attain the
fondest hopes for laborers; their amelioration and final emancipation.

Any letter you may kindly send will be forwarded to me to any
place I may be, at the time. With fraternal greetings

I am Sincerely   Saml Gompers
President. American Federation of Labor.

TLpS, reel 4, vol. 5, pp. 455-56, SG Letterbooks, DLC.

1. William James THORNE, a laborer and gas stoker, was a founder and general
secretary (1889-1934) of the National Union of Gas Workers and General Labourers
of Great Britain and Ireland (NUGWGL; after 1924, the National Union of General
and Municipal Workers).

2. Eleanor Marx AVELING served on the executive board of the NUGWGL from
1890 to 1895.

3. In December 1890 Thorne and Aveling prepared a circular letter on behalf of the NUGWGL. It called on labor organizations to establish international labor secretaries in each country to communicate information on labor difficulties to discourage the importation of strikebreakers.

An Article in the *Rocky Mountain News*

[February 28, 1891]

UNIONISM IS UPHELD.

Coliseum hall was crowded with people last night to hear and see the great leader of the trades unions and the champion of the eight hour movement, Samuel Gompers. Every seat was filled and the closest attention was paid to his words. On the platform were Lieutenant-Governor William Story,[1] Hon. Wolfe Londoner,[2] W. H. Milburn,[3] Hon. A. B. McKinley,[4] Hon. O'Mahoney,[5] W. H. Montgomery,[6] Adam Mensche,[7] Lester Bodine,[8] J. S. Appel,[9] Messrs. Plummer and Beale,[10] Mrs. Scott-Saxton,[11] and others.

The speaker has a fine presence and an excellent voice, and his hearers were so enthusiastic that they interrupted him frequently to applaud. The McCartney jury,[12] in charge of several deputy sheriffs, occupied a prominent place in the gallery and were among the most interested listeners.

President Montgomery of the trades and labor assembly, in a few appropriate remarks, presented Lieutenant Governor Story, the first speaker who was to welcome the visitor.

THE OFFICIAL RECEPTION.

Lieutenant Governor Story said: "On behalf of the people and on behalf of the trades union, it gives me pleasure to welcome you here as our distinguished guest.

"It is but a truism to say that happiness can not exist so long as the relations of capital and labor are not harmonious, but it is a truism that we have yet to consider. Accumulations of wealth should feel that their wealth is held in trust for the benefit of those who are less fortunate, and those who are employed should feel that there are reciprocal duties which they should recognize.

"We may say that you and your co-laborers have at least partially solved the great problem of labor. When it is universally recognized that no man should work more than eight hours a day, it will be the better for all mankind. (Applause.) It is because we know that this is your life work that we welcome you here tonight and bid you god speed on your mission."

Mayor Londoner was next introduced. He said: "Ladies and gentlemen, or men and women, if you please. The pleasant duty devolves upon me of welcoming—I was about to say, the Hon. Samuel Gompers, but when I met him at the city hall the other day and heard the boys all calling him Sam, I felt on familiar terms with him and so I say, Sam, you are welcome here to-night. (Applause.) This gentleman, who sits so calmly on this platform, wields more power than the president of these United States. (Applause.) His hobby, as it is called, is the eight-hour work day. I remember in my youth that a workman's life was a little better than a slave's. It is just such men as Sam Gompers that are creating a better state of things for the workingmen. In my own business I find that where I give my employes nickels in the shortening of hours they give me back dollars in their work. On behalf of every man, woman and child we outstretch our hand to this man and welcome him into our midst. I want to say to you Brother Sam that you have come to the garden spot of trades unions, where they flourish like a bay horse. (Laughter.) You are welcome to our city. (Applause.)["]

President Montgomery then introduced Mr. Gompers as the president of an organization of 750,000 working men and women.

RECEIVED WITH APPLAUSE.

When Mr. Gompers stood up he was greeted with a perfect thunder of applause. He said:

["]Mr. Chairman, Governor, Mayor, Ladies and Gentlemen—

["]I am unaccustomed to respond to addresses of welcome, more especially when tendered on behalf of a state or municipality. My responses are usually to those of the working people and I hope that you may take that as an offset to any of my shortcomings. The thing that the working people are most interested in is that we must have progress with order, for progress without order is disastrous. Hence that alone would prompt me to pursue the ordinary course. The reminiscences the mayor gave of his early boyhood days reminds me of an incident I met with the other day. An employe of one of the railroads entering Michigan, who worked from 6 o'clock A.M. to 11 o'clock P.M., fell heir to an estate and resigned. There was another young man who worked from 7 A.M. until 7 P.M., and he was approached by the superintendent of this railroad and asked to take the vacant place where he had to work from 6 A.M. until 11 P.M. But he refused, saying that he was afraid he might be ashamed of himself if he should meet himself coming to work in the morning when he was on his way home in the evening. (Laughter.)["]

Sympathy in Distress.

["]There is no question but that there are many honest people whose sympathies are with the laborers, but too many who sympathize with the working people in trouble will not see and extend their sympathies through and to organization. That much abused organization known as trades unions is the natural outgrowth of the economic conditions. It is just as natural for them to exist and continue in their work as it is for the rose to bloom and grow in the sun. It is perfectly natural for the people to organize, for we find it in all classes and orders of the human family and in the lower forms of life. Where there is greatest concentration there the best results are obtained. We see the beasts of the field going in herds, the birds of the air in flocks, to protect themselves. We find the railroad trusts, the bankers' associations, the stock exchanges, and you may run the gamut clear through and you will find the wealth organized. You find organizations among the professions. The doctors are organized, and woe to him who attempts to practice without conforming to a standard, and he is sure to be called a quack. And so with the lawyers. They have their associations. It is nothing more than a trades union of lawyers. (Applause.) A certain number of years at school is necessary. Let a lawyer be ever so eloquent and get up in court, and he would be asked by the judge — the walking delegate of the lawyers' union — (Laughter), if he was a regularly admitted lawyer. If he attempted to practice without following these conditions, he would be barred out and called a shyster. Can you blame us when we, from boyhood, aye, from infancy, follow the example of these men who have had so much the advantage of us in education, and organize? If it is necessary to those men who own great wealth, how much greater is the need for you, who own nothing, to organize? There are some people who make peculiar statements with regard to labor organization. They say that we are breeding a discontent into the minds of the wage workers with their lot, which, as some say with injustice to God, that He has ordained they should occupy.

["]You can judge of the condition of men by what they want. Ask the man who is walking on the street without shelter what he wants more, and if he doesn't say a drink more, he'll probably say he wants a square meal more. Ask the man who earns $1 a day what he wants, and he wants 25 cents more. Ask the man who has $800,000, and he will say $200,000 more, and then he'll be a millionaire, and ask the man who has $100,000,000 what he wants more, and he will say oh, I want millions more. He wants the earth. (Applause.) The wage workers of this world have begun to study the economical conditions of the world. They are going to be larger sharers in the products of their labor, and if I read the signs of the times aright, I think they are going to succeed. In this world of ours there are certain self-evident truths. Water runs down hill. Of course, human ingenuity may compel it to run up hill, but as a general thing water runs down hill. The sun does shine, and so with the labor movement. It is based on the justice of a people, and the objections that can be launched against it. The labor movement will live. Would you have us enjoy that contentment which the oppressor of the people always declared contentment? Would you have us to enjoy a peace like that which reigned at Warsaw. No. We do breed discontent. I don't want to be awakened from my sleep by fire bells, but I would rather be awakened than roasted alive. You show me a country where the people are contented and I will show you a nation of serfs. Discontent is an indication of progress. Discontent shows that the people are aware that there are those who would rob them and teaches that it will be dangerous for them to continue it. The only peace is the fruit of discontent. The organizations of labor stand as the harbinger of peace, of social progress.

["]Such discontent we preach and instill and praise to all the powers on high. The seed is taking root and you see it everywhere and it is honored by the presence of the governor, the mayor and other distinguished men to hear a cigar maker talk labor. (Applause.)["]

STRIKES NOT INCREASING.

["]The charge that is made against us is that we are continually increasing the number [of strikes]. To this charge I plead not guilty. To this I plead that not only is it not true, but the very reverse is true. Look to any of the various branches of industry and when they are not organized you will find the greatest number of strikes and when they are well organized the strikes are few. It is not a fact that working people are compelled to strike when their rights are invaded. We don't denounce strikes. I have heard that there was an organization which declared that they would never strike under any provocation.

["]If a conflict should arise which required a strike we won't back out. We have not enlisted for a month or a year; we have enlisted for the war. (Applause.) We say to the working people of all classes, organize, organize; and when you do, don't say that you do want to strike or that you won't strike, but prepare yourselves for a strike.

(Applause.) If you are prepared you won't have to strike. A judicious employer will think twice before he provokes his employes to strike when he knows they are prepared and ready for a strike. The man or woman who does not respect himself or herself will not receive the respect of others; and the wageworkers who are not organized show, so far as their condition is concerned, that they don't respect themselves.["]

LABOR WITHOUT BRAINS.

["]I will tell you a story. I don't want you to take offense. There was a union of butchers. They put labels on the meat. [']This piece of meat was dressed by a union man.['] A woman wanted a nice sheep's head for her husband's dinner. The butcher cut off a piece of lamb, and she noticed a label which said: 'This sheep was dressed by union men.' She refused to take it, saying that she wanted a non-union sheep's head. He took his cleaver, scooped out the brains and, handing it to her, said: 'Here, madame is a non-union sheep's head.' (Laughter and applause.) Now, I don't wish anyone to be offended. This is only a non-union sheep's head. (Laughter.) There are some who say that they don't want to belong to a union. They want to be independent. My friends, we want more dependence—mutual protection. What the traitor is to his country the scab is to his trade. He deserves the contempt he is [held in]. He has made himself a social scourge—a traitor. He is a parasite upon the result of the honest endeavor of the working people. There seems to me no money that is so iniquitous or that is more dishonorable to us as a nation than that insatiable greed which drags the children into the mills and factories and grinds their young bones into dollars.

["]To me it seems that the child of the nineteenth century should be something more than a machine. I know the horrors of child labor, and I have never lost an opportunity to appeal to my fellow men, to spare for God's sake, our children. (Applause.) Tho' some may say that it does not exist in our beautiful Colorado. It may exist. Wherever the industries become more concentrated it brings with it the horrors of child labor. Since there is still little interest at stake in your state see while there is still time, that a law is passed preventing the employment of children under 14 years of age. (Applause.) I know there are some who say that they must make cheap goods, but to sheol with cheap goods if the lives of children must be sacrificed. (Applause.)["]

SUPPLY AND DEMAND.

["]They say that all things are controlled by the law of supply and demand, and those who try to interfere with its workings will get hurt. They wish to reduce our wages, but we say we can't do with it. 'But you must.' This law of supply and demand is the answer that we get.

["]See how the capitalists work it. The coal merchants meet together and say, now unless something is done the law of supply and demand will bring down the price of coal. So one gentleman says, I move that the price of coal during the months of September, October, November and December shall be so much, and it is done. Now, how is it done? How do they get around the law of supply and demand? They shut down for a time and limit production. We are organized and we intend to limit the supply of labor by shortening the hours. (Applause.) You cannot improve the condition of the foundation of a building without improving the building and so you cannot improve the condition of the working classes without improving the condition of all classes of society.

["]The business man says that business is dull and gives as a reason that there is no money. He didn't mean that there was no money, but that the people didn't have enough money. The man says, 'Now, boys, I'll have to reduce your wages. If you're not fools, you'll take it.' The people haven't enough money to buy goods, so they solve it in this way. Reduce the wages so the people can buy more money. There is no more successful or prosperous community as when the people are well situated. Therefore, we say that the way out of this industrial darkest Africa is to give the people more wages, give them more time to cultivate higher tastes and morals.

["]I urge upon the men who hold the destinies of the people in their hands, consider these things. Don't antagonize us as you have in the past, or you will turn us so thoroughly against you that the words of the Bible will read to us, 'Whithersoever thou goest I will not go; whither thou lodgest I will not lodge. Thy people are not my people. Thy God is not our God.' I plead to you as well as to our workingmen. You find in our demands the crystallized wants of the workingmen. In dealing with us as a united order you are dealing with the crystallized laboring men.

["]But if you antagonize us and break up the organization, you will have to deal with disorganized wolves and wild animals, their hopes and aspirations blasted. So I ask you, friends, meet us as men. Don't ask us to crouch on our knees before you, for we have learned to stand up and look you squarely in the eye.["]

EQUAL SUFFRAGE.

["]Among the things we advocate is that the women should have equal suffrage with men. Within four weeks 229,000 trade unionists signed a petition for an amendment to the United States permitting women to vote. We not only work for equality of suffrage, but work and fight to obtain equal wages for her.

["]Last year we concentrated our efforts on the carpenters and joiners, and now we have selected the coal miners to make the demand on next May 1 that eight hours shall constitute a day's work and not a minute longer. (Applause.) I am travelling now over the country preparing the people for the struggle and I hope in the coming conference of the coal miners with the coal mine owners[13] that I can get them to concede the eight hour day without a struggle or bad blood. But if they refuse we will show them the strength of organized labor. May you all come to look upon the trades union question in its proper light and not antagonize it any more.["]

A COLORADO SOUVENIR.

When the speaker resumed his seat the audience raised a shout of applause that was deafening. President Montgomery got up and waved for silence. Stepping to the front he asked them to remain to the end of the programme. When quiet was once more restored he held up a little velvet case, and opening it, displayed a beautiful gold and silver medal, attached by silver chains to a gold bar engraved with the name "Samuel Gompers." The medal was the size of a silver dollar, of solid gold. Across the face of it, in raised silver letters, was the motto, "Eight Hours." "Presented by the Denver Trades and Labor Assembly, February 27, 1891."

Mr. Armstrong[14] then handed the medal to a little boy, and leading him forward, the proud recipient of the beautiful token of friendship and respect took it from the hands of the little fellow and seemed the more embarrassed of the two.

Mr. Montgomery then said: "If you will allow me I will place it over the heart of as true a man as ever lived. This gold and silver was mined by miners who worked eight hours, engraved by engravers who worked eight hours and received by the greatest champion of the eight hour workday."

Mr. Gompers stood without saying anything for a few minutes, and then said: "Well, you've got me this time. I'll say, friends, I'm deeply grateful for this mark of your appreciation, this gift of organized labor, my idol. There are some men who consecrate their lives to a cause, but I don't know of any duty that a man can consecrate his life to that is better than that of trying to make the way of his fellow men a little easier.

["]Some men devote their best efforts to religion, some to politics, but I have, after long consideration, consecrated my life to helping my fellow men to place at least one step forward in the progress. I accept this gift and I hope I may wear it many years with credit and honor and that you may never regret having given it to me, and that my numerous descendants may remember when they see it that Sam Gompers was a man who tried to help the people. My motto has always been to level classes, but to level up, not level down. (Applause.)["]

Rocky Mountain News (Denver), Feb. 28, 1891.

1. William Story, a Republican, was lieutenant governor of Colorado from 1891 to 1893.

2. Wolfe Londoner, a merchant, served as Republican mayor of Denver from 1889 to 1891.

3. William H. Milburn, a Denver printer and foreman, was president of International Typographical Union (ITU) 49 from 1889 to 1890.

4. Alexander B. McKinley was a lawyer and Democratic state senator representing Colorado's sixth district.

5. Probably Thomas F. O'Mahoney of Leadville, a member of the Colorado general assembly.

6. William H. Montgomery, a Denver printer, was a leader of ITU 49 and president of the Denver Trades and Labor Assembly (TLA).

7. Adam MENCHE was a Denver cigarmaker and AFL organizer.

8. Lester Bodine served as deputy commissioner of the Colorado Bureau of Labor Statistics from 1891 to 1892.

9. Jacob S. Appel was a Denver clothier and merchant.

10. Possibly Edmund V. Beales, manager of a Denver tailor shop, who entertained SG at his home on the evening of Feb. 27, 1891.

11. Mrs. Scott Saxton was an elocutionist and president of the Denver School of Expression.

12. George McCartney, a bookkeeper, was on trial for murder at the time of SG's speech. On Mar. 6, 1891, the jury found him guilty of involuntary manslaughter.

13. The sixth annual joint conference of Ohio and western Pennsylvania mine operators and miners took place in Pittsburgh, Apr. 7-9, 1891. It disbanded after an impasse developed over the miners' demand for an eight-hour day. SG was in the Midwest at the time and did not attend the conference.

14. Probably Hamilton Armstrong, a bookbinder who was elected president of the Denver TLA in July 1891.

An Excerpt from an Interview in
the *San Francisco Examiner*

[March 7, 1891]

LABOR'S LEADER IS HERE.

. . .

A PEN PICTURE.

The head of the American Federation of Labor does not look anything like the modern labor agitator as pictured in the minds of those who are more familiar with men of millions than they are with the millions who labor for their sustenance. As he stood on the lower deck of the Piedmont last night, he looked more like a well-to-do man of business than one who has spent the greater portion of his life at the hardest kind of labor—cigarmaking. He was dressed in a suit of dark clothes, dark heavy overcoat and high silk hat. A pair of well-fitting kid gloves completed his attire.

He is short of stature, being but a few inches over five feet in height. His complexion is dark and a pair of deep, black eyes light up a most pleasant face. He smiles almost constantly as he talks. His face is full and well rounded, and just a suggestion of a double chin adds an unmistakable tinge of good nature to his appearance. He is a little over forty-one years of age, or, to be exact, forty-one years, one month and eleven days, and though he has worked at his trade for over thirty years, he does not look to be more than thirty-five at most. A heavy black mustache, which bears evidence of careful cultivation, adorns his face.

"So you want to know the object of my visit? Well, the principal one, I may say, is to secure, as far as possible, moral and financial support for the eight-hour movement in behalf of the coal miners of this country directly and all organized labor. You know that last year the Federation inaugurated the eight-hour movement, taking the carpenters of the country as the trade through which the initiatory movement was made. That is now a part of the history of labor in this country. On the first day of May next a similar movement will be inaugurated among the coal miners. One of the objects of my tour has been to meet and confer with the owners of coal mines with a view of securing an eight-hour schedule throughout the country; to organize new branches of the Federation; to secure moral and financial support; to scatter broadcast the objects of the Federation; to put the claims of the wage-worker before the people in as fair and intelligent a manner as I can."

"And have you been successful in your mission so far?"

How He Has Been Received.

"That I cannot say as yet. But I can say that so far my tour has been a most pleasant one. I left Boston nearly six weeks ago and have been traveling almost constantly ever since. I have visited every city of prominence in the country, and everywhere I have met with the most courteous treatment. The mass meetings which I have addressed have been composed of large and intelligent audiences, and I believe so far good results will follow my efforts. In many places I have been welcomed by the officials of the cities and States through which I passed. At Salt Lake Governor Thomas[1] officially welcomed me to the Territory. It was the same in Colorado. The Governor[2] and other officials of that State welcomed me in their official capacities, and I was invited to address the Legislature then in session. While in Denver the Mayor of that city paid me every possible attention."

"What is the general condition of labor throughout the Eastern cities you have visited?"

"Labor prospects are brightening everywhere. There has been some stagnation, but a reaction seems to be setting in and it seems to me that the prospects of organized labor are brighter and better now than at the same time last year."

"What effort is the Federation making toward the enactment of legislation in the interests of the laboring classes?"

"Just now we are confining ourselves to State legislation. We want to have laws passed for the better protection to the life and limb of the workingman. We want a law on the statute book of every State that will put an end to that great evil, child-labor. There are many other pieces of legislation we would like to see enacted for the betterment of the condition of the laboring classes, and we are working to secure such from the various States. When we accomplish this purpose our next step will [be] in the direction of national legislation. But of that it is yet too soon to speak."

Straightening Out Kinks.

"What action, if any, will you take in regard to the differences existing out here between the United Brewery Workmen of the Pacific Coast and the National Brewery Workmen of the United States?"

"Ah, that is a little private affair that I hardly think would interest the public just now," replied the head of the federation pleasantly. "I would like to tell you, but it would not be proper. You see, there are numerous little kinks and twists constantly arising within our ranks that require straightening out. To do this is, of course, a part of my mission, but it is hardly just what the public care to read about. The public, I take it, are more interested in the eight-hour movement, and it is in the success of that movement, as I said before, that I am most deeply interested."

"Tell me something about yourself," said the reporter, as the Piedmont was nearing the slip.

"About myself? Why, there is hardly anything to be said about me. I am simply a workingman, doing the best I can in my way for the hundreds of thousands who have honored me for years with the Presidency of the greatest labor federation in this country. For thirty years I have been a cigarmaker, and have been a union man from the first. See, here is my card," and President Gompers proudly drew from his pocket a card which showed that he was a member in good standing of the Cigarmakers' International Union.

The card was No. 1. There are over 34,000 members of the union.

THE WELCOME HERE.

"I have been one of the officers of the union for many years, and this is my sixth year as President of the American Federation of Labor. What more can I say about myself?"

. . .

San Francisco Examiner, Mar. 7, 1891.

1. Arthur L. Thomas was the Republican governor of the Utah Territory from 1889 until 1893.
2. John Long Routt, a Republican, was the last territorial governor and first state governor of Colorado (1875-79); he served again from 1891 to 1892.

An Article by Samuel Gompers in the *San Francisco Examiner*

[March 8, 1891]

THE HOURS OF LABOR.

From the time that Aristotle declared that "that is the most perfect system of society which provides for the happiness of *all* its members" down to our present era, when we are living under a constitution based upon the theory "that all men are born free and equal," a struggle has been waged between the wealth-producers and the wealth-absorbers to obtain a larger share of the result of human exertions, commonly known under the name Labor. At one time the greatest aim in life and the loftiest aspirations were to develop the militant side of the human character; now we find, through the ever-increasing spirit of commercialism, the demand for greater industrial progress and development. And yet, while the new order of progress is still battling with the last vestiges of feudal and medieval conditions, the new order contains elements within itself struggling with each other for ascendency—for still greater progress—for the full realization of the declaration of that grand and earliest of philosophers, Aristotle.

There can be no question in the minds of observers that the greatest efforts and deepest thoughts of the human family are to conquer that most important of all things—Time.

How can we encompass the continent? How can we reach another part of the world quickly? How can we produce such and such an article swifter? are all in themselves questions that seek to conquer the fleeing moments of time.

On the other hand the wage-workers, who, being the producers of the wealth of the world, are considering for themselves the question which, while pressing upon the minds of others with so much persistency, is one that reaches nearest their life and being than all other considerations combined—Time.

Meet corporate power or the employing class under any circumstances and you will find the tendency on their part to secure the longest number of hours of toil from the workers. That hundreds of thousands of the people of the country are walking the streets in idleness, that those who are employed too many hours a day wearing away their lives and driving them to a premature old age and death, forms no part of their economic creed. They want all the time they can squeeze out of the human as well as the steam machine.

Argue with them that such a policy is short-sighted, that it is false political economy, and that it has a tendency to prevent the full development of the mental as well as the physical part of the human family, and puts a quietus upon industrial and commercial progress, and you will be met with a shrug of the shoulders, implying, "After me, the flood," or "Each for himself, and the d---- take the hindmost." He forgets, however, that if his inferred or uttered sentiments are fully carried out, his Satanic Majesty will be continually taking the hindmost, until he in the front rank will be reached, for he will then be the hindmost.

On the part of the wage-workers we also urge the consideration of the question of time, for to us there is no question of greater moment. How can we maintain the political rights achieved for the human family? How can we secure a larger share of the product of our labor? How can we prevent the pressing concentration of mind and muscle, brought about by machinery, from wearing our lives out prematurely? must be answered to the satisfaction of the constantly growing investigating character of the labor movement, and those who sympathize with the honest and noble aspirations of the membership of the American Federation of Labor.

We offer as a means to the solution of this problem the question of *a reduction in the hours of labor.* In other words the saving of time.

It must not for a moment be imagined that a reduction of the hours of labor would at all have the tendency to diminish either the productivity of the laborer or the aggregate production of the people, for it is demonstrable that wherever the hours of labor have been reduced it has been followed by an increased production per capita and as a whole.

Nor will the movement to reduce the hours of labor tend either to divert the trade or commerce of any country to that of any other, for, as a matter of fact, we see the evidence plainly that those industries where the hours of labor are lowest more thoroughly developed and successfully competing with the same industries in countries where the hours of labor are longer, yes, longest.

View the movement to reduce the hours of labor from any standpoint, and you will find it based upon science and economy, political and social necessity or expediency, and is in the line of progress and humanity.

A reduction in the hours of labor gives employment to the idle and increases the desires, wants and necessities of the whole people. Giving a greater and better market. A nobler manhood, a more beautiful womanhood and a happier childhood. Less poverty, idleness or drudgery. A greater and a nobler people to carry on the struggle for better and more humane conditions.

San Francisco Examiner, Mar. 8, 1891.

An Excerpt from an Article in
the *San Francisco Examiner*

[March 9, 1891]

A TRIP TO CHINATOWN.

President Gompers was last night given an introduction to the lights and shadows of Chinatown. Accompanied by President Fuhrman,[1] Secretary Kretlow,[2] C. J. Boyle,[3] Charles Grambarth,[4] V. A. H. Hoffmeyer,[5] L. J. Gannon[6] and Jacob Gassner[7] of the Federated Trades, President Tully Boyce[8] of the Miners and Mine Laborers' Protective Union of Vancouver, and Charles Bergman,[9] under the guidance of Sergeant Price[10] of the Chinatown squad, he was led through a labyrinth of dark, crowded, foul-smelling passages above and below ground, until several of the party were almost overcome with faintness and were glad to seek the comparative fresh air of the Chinatown streets. Sights that the President of the American Federation never saw before were opened up to his wondering gaze. Filth and a system of crowding men and women in cubby-like holes to live, eat and sleep to an extent that none but Chinese could endure were exposed for his benefit. From the elegantly fitted up quarters of the Bun Sun Low restaurant to the dark underground hole where the meals for a colony are cooked over a little fire in a discarded old oil-can the party was led by Sergeant Price, who explained the lives and methods of the Chinese to President Gompers. The opium dens and the manner of smoking opium attracted his attention to some extent, but most of all he seemed to be impressed by the dirt and the absolute absence of ventilation in rooms not more than ten feet long and about the same wide in which as many as fifty to sixty Chinamen were found at one time. After visiting all the usual points of interest, and climbing up and down rickety, dirty stairways leading to and from underground holes, the party visited the Jackson-street Theatre, where President Gompers was given a chance to observe the progress of a Chinese play. The leader of the American Federation is a man of thought more than words, and when he expressed his opinion of Chinatown by the few words "disgustingly horrible," he conveyed a great deal to the others in the party.

To-day he will be taken through Chinatown to visit and observe the workings of the Chinese cigar, boot and shoe and other factories.

Yesterday afternoon President Gompers was taken in a barouche and driven through the Park to the Cliff House and Ocean Beach. He expressed himself as greatly pleased with what he saw.

. . .

San Francisco Examiner, Mar. 9, 1891.

1. Alfred FUHRMAN was president of the Representative Council of the Federated Trades and Labor Organizations of the Pacific Coast (RCFT) in 1890, and of the Council of Federated Trades of the Pacific Coast (1891-92), and general secretary of the United Brewery Workmen's Union of the Pacific Coast (1890-92).

2. Henry Kretlow, a cigarmaker and president of CMIU 228 of San Francisco in 1890, served as recording secretary of the RCFT in 1891.

3. Christopher J. Boyle, a cigarmaker, served as financial and corresponding secretary of CMIU 228 from the late 1880s until 1892.

4. Charles Grambarth, a cigarmaker, preceded Alfred Fuhrman as president of the RCFT.

5. Volmer A. Henry Hoffmeyer was a musician and member of the Musicians' Mutual Protective Association of San Francisco. In the late 1880s he became a leading figure in the California Anti-Chinese Non-Partisan Association, the state assembly of the KOL, and the RCFT.

6. Lawrence J. Gannon was a tanner.

7. Jacob Gassner was a San Francisco cigarmaker.

8. Tully Boyce, a miner from Vancouver Island, B.C., was president of the Miners' and Mine Labourers' Protective Association of Vancouver Island and of the Provincial Federated Labour Congress. He was in San Francisco during SG's visit seeking support for his union's strike in the Wellington, B.C., collieries. (See "An Excerpt from a News Account of an Address in Seattle," Mar. 23, 1891, n. 18, below.)

9. Charles F. BURGMAN was a tailor and a socialist. He worked with Burnette G. Haskell in founding the Pacific Coast Division of the International Workingmen's Association in 1882, and between 1883 and 1885 served as business manager of Haskell's paper, *Truth.*

10. William Price was a sergeant with the San Francisco police department.

Excerpts from an Interview in the *Tacoma Daily News*

Portland, March 18 [1891]

PRES. GOMPERS TALKS

A *News* correspondent, obedient to telegraphic instructions, has interviewed President Samuel Gompers of the American Federation of labor. Mr. Gompers is a man of less than medium height, heavy set figure with a massive head set squarely upon a pair of broad shoulders. He is a man of pleasant address, of modest personal appearance and somewhat averse to talking to newspaper men. To your correspondent he said:

"This is my first visit to the Pacific coast and I am pleased to see the very excellent condition of organized labor, but much pained by the very apparent helplessness of the unorganized branches. I have not studied the existing conditions closely enough to give a very decided opinion yet; however, I like the climate. The opportunities, it seems to me, are better here for the young than in the older communities of the East."

"What about the eight hour question?"

"There is no question but that the near future is bright for the eight hour movement if the organized wage workers will concentrate their efforts for its achievement. I am fully aware that the establishment of the eight hour working day will not be the end of the efforts of the working people for economic and social reform; yet the great good a substantial reduction in the hours of labor will bring to the toilers of our country, the hundreds of thousands it will save from poverty will clear the path and prepare the working people to see the wrongs and injustices practiced upon them in ingenious and subtle ways. I understand that in the Puget Sound region many trades have already secured this concession, and I am prepared to receive many substantial, practical and demonstrated reasons why the eight-hour working day, is best not only for the employed but for the employer. I look forward to my visit there with a great deal of pleasure."

"How has the Federation grown?"

"The past year has witnessed our expansion in the recognition on the part of the wage workers of America that the trade union form of organization is the best to protect and advance their interests. The National Trades Unions have established 913 local branches throughout the country while 247 charters for local unions were issued from the office of the American Federation of Labor to such wage workers as have no National union in their trade or calling, the membership of all organizations represented in the Federation has increased with one exception from 5 to 35 per cent."

"Has the federation been successful?"

"There has been an increase in wages of from 7 to 25 per cent. in all lines except the silk workers, who, on account of dullness of trade, have suffered a lessening of earnings. The increase in wages and improved conditions has been shared proportionately. Statistics show that since organization there have been 563 authorized strikes of which number 389 were successful, 76 were lost, and 98 compromised. These were generally for a reduction of hours, increase of wages and maintenance of the rights of workers. It will be seen that our organizations are continually succeeding in making their members larger sharers in the product of their toil and doing work for them which no other organization on earth thinks it worth their while to deal with."

"Will there be an International Labor Congress?"

"Immediately after the United States Congress decided to hold the World's Fair at Chicago I issued an invitation to the organized wage workers of the world to be represented at an International Labor Congress at Chicago in 1893 and urged that no other be held that year. The response has for various reasons not been what I desired and hoped, yet I am convinced that if we are desirous of holding a successful International Labor Congress in 1893 we can do so, but we must be energetic and send our representatives to the one to be previously held in Europe."

. . .

"What in your opinion is the greatest evil labor has to combat with today?"

"Child-labor—by all means—child-labor. Of all the ills that mankind suffers from the unjust and cruel tendencies of modern methods of wealth-producing, this one seems to me to rise to the most horrible proportions. Our centers of industry, with their mills, factories and workshops, are teeming with young and innocent children, bending their weary forms with long hours of daily drudgery, with pinched and emaciated frames, dwarfed both physically and mentally, driving them to premature decay and death. The innocent smile of youthful happiness is soon transformed into wrinkles and other evidences of decay.

"The hope of the perpetuity of free institutions is endangered when the rising generation is robbed of the opportunity to enjoy the healthful recreation of the playgrounds or the mental improvements of the school house. The children of the workers have none to raise a voice in their defense other than organized wage workers, and they should and will take steps to protect them from the contemptible avarice of unscrupulous corporations and employers."

. . .

Tacoma Daily News, Mar. 18, 1891.

Excerpts from a News Account
of an Address in Seattle

[March 23, 1891]

FOR EIGHT HOURS.

. . .

MR. GOMPERS' ADDRESS.

At night the Cordray theater was crowded to the very doors with people who had come to hear the address of Samuel Gompers, president of the American Federation of Labor. Every seat and every inch of standing room was occupied, and there was a fair sprinkling of women in the audience. There must have been over 1,500 persons present.

Mr. Gompers proved himself far above the average of the orators who usually advocate the cause of labor. He has a strong voice, clear enunciation, an easy flow of strong Anglo-Saxon language, without any of those errors which mar the oratory of self-made men, and does not indulge in any flights of flowery eloquence or high-flown metaphor which appear ridiculous in cold type. He is evidently a man of training as an orator and a man of education—a fact which is the more to his credit, as he is self-educated. He has eloquence of the best kind— simple language, forcibly expressed with deep earnestness. His speech was characterized by the light of humor and sarcasm, and the fire of declaration in just the right proportion to keep his audience interested to the end and to make them regret the ending. This describes the manner and style of his speech. The matter will speak for itself. He was warmly applauded at all his telling points, and his denunciation of Governor Laughton's[1] vetoes brought down the house.

Abe Spring[2] announced that W. F. Cushing,[3] the intended chairman, had not returned from the convention at Oakesdale. He therefore called on F. J. Ware,[4] president of the Building Trades Council,[5] to preside. Mr. Ware then instructed James L. Barry,[6] secretary of the Western Central Labor Union,[7] to read the names of the presidents of the several unions and the other vice presidents of the meeting. Mr. Barry first called Mayor White,[8] the board of aldermen and house of delegates, and after a few minutes' delay the mayor, Aldermen Snyder,[9] Miller[10] and Korn,[11] Delegates Muldoon,[12] Barton[13] and Hart[14] came up and were warmly received. The other vice presidents were the presidents of the various unions and delegates to the Western

Central Labor Union and Building Trades Council. Mr. Ware then introduced Mr. Gompers, who was loudly cheered.

Mr. Gompers said:

. . .

["]I want to refer to some things which happened lately in your state, and to the gentleman who now occupies the position of governor in this state. I refer to Acting-Governor Laughton. (A hiss.) Save that till a little later—or don't forget it in the fall. The governor has mistaken his position. He does not argue as the governor of a proud state, but as the paid attorney of a corporation would. He has vetoed the anti-Pinkerton bill,[15] or the bill restoring the original rights of the people, and providing that the sheriff, mayor, governor or president is alone endowed with the duty of protecting life and property. But the corporation steps in without regard to any higher authority, but above the law, has a standing army of mercenaries, of paid hirelings without any law to regulate their conduct. The bill declares this body illegal, in fact provides that the sheriff or mayor is good enough for the people. But the governor says that it interferes with the right of a man to protect his wife and children, our right to gather around our cabins and protect our lives. Does any man mean to say that the governor was serious when he wrote that? If he was he was either a paid agent of that corporation—you know which corporation I mean— or he is an ass. At least, if he was not paid he ought to have been, and the corporations are by no means stingy in such matters. This standing army is composed of Pinkerton thugs, and the governor says they must not be interfered with.

["]The governor has within the last two weeks developed a faculty of either writing veto messages or having them written for him. He has vetoed the time-check bill,[16] and says the people can hold their time checks for years and then present them and draw 10 per cent. interest. The people who get time checks, as I am acquainted with them, do not carry time checks around with them for years and years. They want the money as soon as possible. The governor says that then the corporations would not issue them. That is what we want. We want coin. I do not think the governor would care to be paid in time checks.

["]I am not a politician, and do not care whether this man is a Republican or a Democrat. I denounce him because he vetoed the bill on which the people of this state were more a unit than any other. If you do not resist this wrong you deserve that he should do something worse to you.["]

Mr. Gompers then argued in favor of popular election of United

States senators, saying the positions should not be bartered out by the corporations without consultation with the people. He referred to a law recently passed by the California legislature to make boycotting illegal and defended the right to boycott.[17] He urged a boycott on the products of Chinese labor, saying: "Don't you think the Caucasian race is worth preserving?" declaring the Chinese and Caucasian races not congenial and that he would sooner endure the horrors of Dante's "Inferno" than live in Chinatown. He then urged a boycott on coal from the Wellington collieries[18] and on thread from Clark's thread mills.[19] He then began a powerful argument for the eight-hour movement, saying:

["]I call on you and call on the wage-workers of the United States to rise up in a mass and demand the enforcement of the eight-hour working day. We hear men say that their hours must be increased in order that they may get along. As a matter of fact, in the countries where the hours of labor are long the industries are not developed as they are in the countries where the hours of labor are short. The rich men of the countries where the hours of labor are long are paupers compared with the rich men of the countries where the hours of labor are less. The merchants send the products of the short hour countries into the long hour countries. When times are dull and people have not money to buy things with, the employer of labor says: 'Boys, times are dull; I contemplate closing up, but want to give you employment, and will keep running if you will accept a 10 per cent. reduction. Don't be fools, boys, and kick. Or you can work an hour longer to make it up. Mind you, the markets are glutted, the shelves are bearing down with the stock, the people have not money to buy things, so you must accept a reduction so that you can buy more; so also you must work an hour longer to make it up.['] It is only necessary to state the remedy to show how ridiculous it is. I say there is no market as prosperous as the home market, and no way to prevent a glut in the market better than to give the workmen more wages, and there is no means better than to give employment to the hundreds of thousands of men and women who are walking the streets hunting employment. We say that to reduce the hours means higher wages and better conditions for the employer also. Show me a country where the hours are long and I will show you where wages are low. Show me a country where the hours are short and I will show you where the wages are high. In any factory, those who enter first and leave last are those who receive the lowest wages and those who enter last and leave first receive the highest wages, because those who work eight hours cannot afford to work as cheap as those who work thirteen or fourteen hours; their time is more valuable. The men who work twelve, thirteen or fourteen hours very seldom have a dinner hour, while those who work eight hours surely have a dinner hour. The long-hour men go home, throw themselves on a miserable apology for a bed and dream of work. They eat to work, sleep to work and dream to work, instead of working to live. The man who goes home early has time to see his children, to eat his supper, to read the newspaper. That reading the newspaper creates a desire to be alone for half an hour, and that starts a desire for an extra room, just a little extra room. That extra room is a milestone in the record of social progress. It means a carpet on the floor, a chair, an easy chair, a picture on the wall, a piano or an organ. What does the man who works three or four hours longer want with an extra room? The gas is generally turned low so that he can sleep in order that he can work.

["]You will find that people get wages just enough to buy the things they consent to live on. It is so in this country. In China they get wages just enough to buy rice. It is so with the four-legged gentleman. Let the American people decide next week or next year to wear blue jeans and eat red herrings and crackers and you'll find that they would get just enough to buy blue jeans, red herrings and crackers. So the reverse is true; let the people demand an extra room with all that goes with it, and they will get wages enough to buy it. Time is the most valuable thing on earth; time to think, time to act, time to extend our fraternal relations, time to become better men, time to become better women, time to become better and more independent citizens.["]

Mr. Gompers then vehemently denounced those who reply to the demand for shorter hours that the workingmen want more time to get drunk, saying that if five out of 100 men go from a factory and get drunk the employer will say that all his men are drunk. When he gets drunk this moralist and hypocrite does it in private, is taken home in a cab, and goes on Sunday morning to church to pray sanctimoniously for his drunken workmen.

He then said the American Federation of Labor had concluded to abandon glittering generalities and concentrate its efforts on this reform. He told the great results of the carpenters' eight-hour strike last year, resulting in the establishment of the law for 55,000 carpenters, besides hundreds of thousands of others, without the shedding of one drop of blood. The federation had now decided to concentrate its efforts on the coal miners in the year 1891. They will meet their employers in convention in about a month and try to arrange to have the eight-hour day enforced, and he had hopes that the mine owners would concede their demands. He had been from end to end of the country, appealing to all whose hearts revolt against injustice. He appealed to the hearts of the people, and believed that before May 1 the mine owners would see that the people were on one side and they on the other in the battle of justice and right. He concluded with an eloquent appeal to his audience to join in striving for the recognition of the brotherhood of man.

Mr. Gompers sat down amid tumultuous applause. Votes of thanks to him, and to Mr. Cordray[20] for the use of the theater, closed the proceedings.

Seattle Post-Intelligencer, Mar. 23, 1891.

1. Charles E. Laughton, a Republican, served as lieutenant governor of Washington from 1889 to 1893. He was acting governor in 1891 during the illness of Governor Elisha P. Ferry.

2. Abraham Spring, a hod carrier and plasterer, was a member of the Western Central Labor Union (WCLU) in Seattle.

3. Walter F. Cushing, a compositor, was secretary-treasurer of International Typographical Union 202 of Seattle and president of the WCLU. He was the WCLU's delegate to the convention of the State Federation of Industrial Organizations, held Mar. 19 to 23, 1891, at Oakesdale, Wash. The meeting was the first between representatives of the Washington Farmers' Alliance and state labor organizations.

4. Fred J. Ware, a member of the Seattle Stone Cutters' Union, was general president of the District Building Trades Council of Washington and British Columbia (DBTC).

5. The DBTC was established in February 1891.

6. James L. Barrie, a member of Iron Molders' Union of North America 371 of Seattle, was secretary of the WCLU.

7. The WCLU was organized in 1888 by Seattle KOL assemblies and trade unions. Friction between these groups led to the expulsion of the Knights in 1891.

8. Harry White, a real estate broker, was Republican mayor of Seattle from 1890 to 1892.

9. William A. Snyder, president and manager of the Safe Investment Co., was a Republican member of the Seattle board of aldermen.

10. Amasa S. Miller, a Republican, was a Seattle alderman and a member of the board of directors of the Commercial National Bank.

11. Moses Korn, a Republican on the board of aldermen, ran a hardware and stove business in Seattle.

12. Frank M. Muldoon, a real estate salesman and notary, represented the second ward as a Republican in the Seattle House of Delegates.

13. Alexander Barton, a saloon keeper, was a Republican member of the Seattle House of Delegates from the fourth ward.

14. Charles Hart, a carpenter, was a Republican representative from the first ward in the Seattle House of Delegates.

15. On Mar. 14, 1891, Laughton vetoed an act that prohibited the maintenance or employment of a body of armed men by private persons or corporations in the state of Washington (senate bill 19). On Jan. 27, 1893, the legislature passed the bill over the veto.

16. Laughton vetoed house bill 128 on Mar. 9, 1891; it required that time checks issued in payment for labor be immediately negotiable and redeemable without dis-

count, and that they bear interest from date of issue. An effort to override the veto failed in the senate in January 1893.

17. Probably senate bill 233, "An Act to Declare . . . Combinations in Restraint of Trade and Production Unlawful." It was introduced in the California senate in January 1891 but not passed.

18. Members of the Miners' and Mine Labourers' Protective Association of Vancouver Island, B.C., working at A. Dunsmuir and Sons, struck in June 1890, demanding an eight-hour day, union recognition, and an end to compulsory trading at the company store. With support from a boycott of Wellington coal in San Francisco, union leaders continued the strike until November 1891 before accepting defeat.

19. Members of the National Cotton Mule Spinners' Association working at Clark's O.N.T. Cotton Thread Co.'s Newark, N.J., mills struck on Dec. 8, 1890. The dispute involved poor treatment by the mills' superintendent and overseers. With 800 men on strike, the firm instituted a lockout on Dec. 10 that idled the remaining workers, including between 1,200 and 1,500 unorganized women. By mid-January 1891 it had succeeded in reopening one of its three local mills, using spinners allegedly imported from Canada. The AFL placed a boycott on Clark's on Feb. 4. On Apr. 18 the union and the mill owners reached an agreement to call off the strike. Clark's agreed to rehire 40 strikers immediately and to take on others at its discretion. The mill superintendent indicated his intention to deal with the returning strikers in a conciliatory manner.

20. John F. Cordray owned Cordray's Theater in Seattle.

To Chris Evans[1]

Duluth April 1st [189]1

Chris Evans Esq
Sec'y. A.F. of L.
Dear Sir & Friend: —

This morning as about to begin the examination of the papers, your letters, applications &tc mailed to Seattle and forwarded to St. Paul, your telegram of yesterday announcing that the Ex. Council would hold a meeting at Pittsburgh Pa. at the request of the officers of the Miners to consider the trouble in the Coke Regions of that State.[2] I am free to confess that your dispatch startled me. It was the intimation that for the first time in the history of the Federation the president was not only not in attendence at a Council meeting but was not consulted in reference to holding one: — not even invited or requested to be present. There is no question but that I could be communicated with by wire for my whereabouts were known to all the members of the E.C. who had lists of the dates and the addresses of the places I went to. That an action of this kind is a slight to an Executive Officer is beyond doubt. I can bear the taunts, insults and bitter opposition of our enemies but the tacit action which declares louder than words that my presence is not necessary at, or my views consulted in reference to the holding of a meeting of the Ex. Council of the AF of L while holding the office of president, is humiliating in the extreme. I am free to say that if the president of the A.F. of L. is of such little consequence, if the position is but the fifth wheel to the wagon, more ornamental than useful I don't want to occupy it; and shall willingly lay it down. Yes place it in the hands of the E.C. to fill the position with one who is inclined to play the part of a figurehead. Had I been notified that a meeting of the E.C. was necessary and in view of the importance of the subject I would have cancelled every other engagement and come right on to the seat of trouble.

All through this trip, which has been conducted [. . .] at my command, and which was an awful burden of work, I have made the Coal Miners movement my central point of appeals. So far have my efforts been crowned with success that the Coal Miners are the observed of all the observing organized workers of the country and also the enlightened and sympathizing public. Yet in view of this when an important [meeting] of the E.C. is to be held to consider the Miners troubles I am ignored. To fill a position so unnecessary is not requisite and quite uncongenial to my taste and temperament. While in the labor movement I have always tried to be, and during further connection I shall try to be of some use.

Of course there has been some delay in the granting of charters during this trip, but not any that could be avoided. Ordinarily I should have no objection to the issuance by you of anything upon which there is not a [specific constitutional provision?] of the wording, but in the granting of charters the president is the one specified by that instrument to be responsible for the issuance of charters and you know how careful I have had to be in that matter to avoid pitfalls almost specially arranged.

In the matter of the Washington D.C. application defer and enquire from them which organizations are represented therein.

You will find several marginal notes on the returned letters (enclosed) which kindly attend to as per requests. The letters marked "preserve for my return" I want to answer them personally.

The kind wishes of yourself and office associates are highly appreciated and reciprocated. Believe me always

Yours sincerely   Saml. Gompers.

N.B. Please copy this letter in book. If the ink won't copy then have typewritten copy made and copied in book, you can sign my name.

ALpS, reel 4, vol. 5, pp. 700-703, SG Letterbooks, DLC.

1. Christopher EVANS, AFL secretary from 1889 to 1894, was secretary of the National Federation of Miners and Mine Laborers from 1885 to 1888.

2. On Mar. 2, 1891, mine operators in the Connellsville coke region of western Pennsylvania posted a new three-year wage scale reducing wages and establishing a nine-hour day. The miners, under the leadership of United Mine Workers of America District 4, whose members were also affiliated with KOL National Trade Assembly 135, then struck for maintenance of the old wage scale and the eight-hour day. The strike affected over 14,000 miners and eighty-one companies. It culminated in a riot on Apr. 2 at the H. C. Frick Coke Co., in Morewood, Pa., that resulted in the death of eleven miners. On May 23 the miners gave up the strike after intervention by militia and Pinkerton detectives and the importation of Italian laborers.

From Chris Evans

April 1st. [1891]

Friend Gompers: —

Your telegram to hand.

In reply I beg to say to you that had I thought that the meeting of the Executive Council would warrant the cancelling of your engagements I should have wired you to be there, but in conversation with Bro. Lennon[1] we concluded that it would be a matter of impossibility to have you there owing to the dates you had already made. In addition to that you will observe that there was only three days to get a vote from the members of the Council and meet in Pittsburgh. I wired to Bro. McGuire at Phila, was informed that he was not at home and [was] advised to wire him at Indianapolis, which I did, but failed to get any response.

On our way to Pittsburgh, Bro. Lennon and I called at Phila and also failed to meet with him there, so we concluded to come on to Pittsburgh and meet the Miners' officials.

The proposition enclosed[2] will I think be sufficient to convince you that it was better you did not cancel your engagements for the meeting referred to. I would also add that Mr. Rae informed me that they had notified the general Executive Board of the K of L to meet with us there, but they failed to respond to the call.

Hoping this explanation will be satisfactory and that you will wire your reply as soon as you receive this I am,

Fraternally yours   Chris Evans

TLpS, reel 4, vol. 5, p. 673, SG Letterbooks, DLC.

1. John Brown LENNON was general secretary of the Journeymen Tailors' National Union of the United States (after 1889 the Journeymen Tailors' Union of America)

and editor of the *Tailor* from 1887 to 1910. He was treasurer of the AFL from 1890 to 1917.

2. The miners' leaders requested the AFL's endorsement of a circular in support of the strike in the Connellsville coke region (see "A Circular Issued by the Executive Council of the AFL," June 1, 1891, below).

An Interview in the *Pittsburgh Press*

[April 13, 1891]

EIGHT-HOUR DAY.

Samuel Gompers, president of the American Federation of Labor, arrived in this city this morning, having completed his tour of the principal cities of the west and south in the interest of the eight hour movement in particular, and in general the organization of which he is the able head. The short and compact figure, swarthy complexion, long black hair, heavy and drooping black mustache, and the dark eyes of the president of the Federation are familiar to many of the members of Pittsburg labor organizations having been seen here on several occasions. President Gompers comes to Pittsburg for the purpose of delivering a public lecture to-morrow evening in Lafayette hall, as has been announced. He speaks here, as he has done elsewhere during his tour, under the auspices of the local national and international unions affiliated with the American Federation of Labor.

When he arrived he was met by William Martin,[1] ex-vice president of the national organization, and at once escorted to Mr. Martin's office. He seemed to be very much fatigued, and while according the newspaper representatives a cordial greeting, said that he did not feel in a condition to discuss any subject at length.

"After my lengthy tour and continuous speech-making," said President Gompers, "I have commenced to feel a reaction. The task which I will have completed after I make my address in Pittsburg to-morrow evening has not been an easy one. I arrived here from Toledo, where I delivered an address to a large assemblage yesterday. I have been all through the west, including San Francisco and all other places on the Pacific coast. I have been gone 10 weeks, and during that time delivered 56 addresses. The one in Pittsburg will make 57.

"It is putting it mild to say that I have been gratified with the interest displayed everywhere I have been in the subject of organized labor. Many of the largest meetings addressed were attended by many professional and business men. The reason that this was particularly gratifying to me was that I had the opportunity of disabusing their minds of many false impressions, and especially in reference to the eight hour movement."

Asked as to the progress of the movement and the prospect of success President Gompers replied: "There is no doubt that the eight-hour day will be the working day of the workingman in all trades and throughout the length and breadth of the country. Great progress has been made. The miners who were selected by the federation to inaugurate the movement, will be successful. There are about 240,000 miners in the country, about 170,000 of which are in what are termed the competitive districts, including Pennsylvania, Ohio, West Virginia, Indiana and Illinois. Nearly all of the latter number are union mine workers.

"May 1, the time fixed for the beginning of the eight-hour day, has not yet arrived, but already it has been conceded to many trades. The only national movement is that of the miners, but the local movements are successful. The eight-hour day has been granted to the carpenters of Chicago and to all the building trades of Denver, San Francisco, Salt Lake City, Tacoma, Seattle, Spokane, St. Paul, Minneapolis and many other places, both west and east."

President Gompers was asked to enumerate a few reasons for the belief that the miners would be successful, but he said he would prefer to leave argument on that point for his address to-morrow night. President Gompers was reminded of the argument that there was no national organization of coal operators, and that independent action and probable concession of the demands in some districts would work in the miners' favor, but he contented himself by replying in a very forcible way:

"The operators eventually will be compelled to allow the eight-hour day."

President Gompers' coat parted a little and displayed two very elegant medals, presented to him during his recent trip, one at San Francisco and the other at Denver.

"I always try to keep them concealed by keeping my coat buttoned," he said. "On a dining car, going between Tacoma and Seattle, a gentleman, I presume a drummer, who sat at the opposite side of the table, caught sight of them.

" 'You are well decorated,' he observed. 'Presume you won them in championship contests?'

"Not caring to make myself known, I replied, after a moment's reflection: 'Yes, yes; I won them in an eight-hour-day go-as-you-please.' As I had been engaged in an eight-hour-day movement and was going as I pleased, I regarded the answer as strictly truthful."

The lecture at Lafayette hall to-morrow will be free and open to all. The subject to be discussed is, "Labor organization and the eight-hour question."

Pittsburgh Press, Apr. 13, 1891.

1. William MARTIN was secretary of the National Amalgamated Association of Iron and Steel Workers from 1878 to 1890 and a vice-president of the AFL from 1886 to 1890. In 1891 he accepted a position as head of the Bureau of Labor of Carnegie Brothers and Co. (subsequently the Carnegie Steel Co.) and retained that position until 1893.

From John Elliott[1]

General Office
Brotherhood of Painters and Decorators of America.[2]
Baltimore, Md., April 27th 1891.

Dear Sir & Bro,

A proposition is made to me to have an injunction laid against the board of walking delegates in N.Y.[3] to restrain them from forcing our people out of employment,[4] would you kindly advise me in relation thereto. I am willing to go to any lengths to protect our members and if this could be effectually done would at once proceed in the matter. I had wrongly relied on the friendliness of the carpenters to stand by us in N.Y. but that hope is dispelled. The K. of L. seem to rule the roost and we have no show to sustain our union unless something of this kind can be done. I hope to have your views on the subject in time to reply to those who are advising this course.

I am not sure that such a move could be legally made and the idea of it is distasteful, as it might react to my disadvantage. Hoping to have your counsel as soon as possible.

I am fraty yours in Bd,   J. T. Elliott.

TLSr, Brotherhood of Painters and Decorators of America Records, reel 141, *AFL Records.*

1. John T. ELLIOTT helped organize the Brotherhood of Painters and Decorators of America (BPDA) in 1887 and served as its secretary until 1900.
2. The Brotherhood of PAINTERS and Decorators of America.
3. The New York City Board of Walking Delegates (BWD) began in 1884 as a social group of business agents from four construction unions. The delegates enforced union work rules and prevented the employment of nonunion men; they had the power to call strikes. In 1894 a jurisdictional dispute between the United Brotherhood of Carpenters and Joiners (UBCJA) and the American branch of the Amalgamated Society of Carpenters and Joiners resulted in the formation of two competing or-

ganizations, the BWD and the Building Trades Council. The two boards merged in 1902 to form the United Board of Building Trades.

4. In August 1890 the BPDA organized New York City paperhangers' local 182, which affiliated with the New York City Central Labor Federation (CLF). KOL paperhangers were organized in paperhangers' District Assembly (DA) 210; they claimed that local 182 was composed of delinquent members of their assembly. DA 210 was affiliated with the CLF's rival, the Central Labor Union (CLU), and the district assembly's master workman, James Archibald, served as the CLU's recording secretary. BPDA 182 protested that the BWD, of which Archibald was a member, supported the Knights and discriminated against BPDA members despite the fact that some of the walking delegates belonged to organizations affiliated with the AFL, the UBCJA in particular. In the late summer or early fall of 1891, the BPDA withdrew from the AFL, protesting its inadequate support; it reaffiliated in January 1892, however, with the situation in New York still unresolved.

To Richard Coles[1]

April 28th. [189]1.

Mr. R. T. Coles,
Garrison School, Kansas City, Mo.
Dear Sir:—

In reply to your favor of the 26th. inst. permit me to say that the sentiment of organized labor of the country is decidedly in favor of maintaining and encouraging the recognition of the equality between the colored and white laborers, so much so, that at the last convention of the American Federation of Labor a question arose as to the existence of a national union of machinists which is particularly located in the South and which prohibits colored machinists from becoming members.[2]

The Federation resolved to call for a convention of all machinists unions for the purpose of forming a national union which shall recognize no color line.[3] There are very many other instances of the same character to which your attention might be called, but I have not the time to search for verification just now.

The colored mechanics are admissible into very nearly all the trade unions of the country. In some localities where the race prejudice predominates the white and colored mechanics of the same trade or calling are organized in separate local unions, but attached to the same national organizations with the same rights, duties and privileges. In many of the industrial centres of the South the hod carriers and day laborers are very well organized. There are not many skilled mechanics among the colored workmen of the South.

As to the question whether skilled mechanics are in the increase among the colored men, it can only be answered relatively since as a matter of fact the opposition of the employing and corporate classes to all forms of apprenticeship system, desired by the unions of labor, together with the division and subdivision of labor, the degree of skill in all mechanism is on the decline.

Trusting that the information here given will be of some benefit to you in the preparation of the paper you refer to I am,

Very Respectfully Yours   Saml Gompers.
President. American Federation of Labor

TLpS, reel 4, vol. 5, p. 815, SG Letterbooks, DLC.

1. Richard T. Coles was principal of the Garrison School in Kansas City, Mo., an institution that provided manual training for blacks.
2. The National Association of MACHINISTS.
3. The International MACHINISTS' Union of America.

To John Elliott

April 28th. [189]1.

Mr. John T. Elliott,
Sec. B. Painters and Decorators of America.
1314 N. Fulton Ave, Baltimore, Md.

Dear Sir and Brother: —

Replying to your favor of the 27th. inst. asking my advice as to the advisability of laying an injunction against the Board of Walking Delegates of the city of New York to restrain them from forcing members of your Union out of employment in New York.

I would say that to my mind notwithstanding the great injustice that is being done your members it would be the most unwise course to pursue. Let your or any other union inaugurate such a proceeding and it would be resorted to by every non-unionist or unfair workman to defeat the ends of labor and the odium will forever attach itself to the name of the Brotherhood of Painters and Decorators for having started it and the enemies of the Brotherhood would take it up, spread it all over the country, and the members of your Unions could not successfully defend themselves against the charge.

I recognize and appreciate the injustice that has been and is being done the members of Union 182, and I cannot begin to enumerate the work I have done to endeavor [to] persuade the various Unions in the building trades of New York to stand by your Union, but there is a combination in New York which will listen to no reason and in which many of our good unions are innocent participants, and as a matter of interest to them either cannot or dare not for the present sever the tie that binds them to this combination. I have no hesitation in believing that the time will come, and that not at too great a distance, when the natural trend of the trade union movement will either establish a local union of the Brotherhood in this city or that the local union will attach itself to the Brotherhood, but as in all other cases of a similar character attempts to force it prematurely will not have the desired result. I think you can afford to bide your time and without exhibitions of anger which can only prolong or postpone the desired result.

By-the-way there was a time when you dared address me as friend apart from the formal "dear sir and brother," and I have yet to learn that I have done aught to you, any one else, or the cause of labor to merit your censure and unkind attacks which have been so widely published.

Of course I esteem the friendship of all men, and certainly did yours, but I do not think you will expect me to prove false to my convictions, yes I think you would even think worse of me were I to do so even to maintain the friendship of one whom I familiarly styled "Jack Elliott, My Friend."

Fraternally Yours   Saml Gompers.
President.

TLpS, reel 4, vol. 5, p. 814, SG Letterbooks, DLC.

To P. J. McGuire

May 2nd. 1891.

Mr. P. J. Mc-Guire,
124. N. 9th. St. Phila, Pa
In view extraordinary decision Miners[1] and necessity to consider situation, meeting Executive Council will be held, office of the Federation, Tuesday May 5th. ten o'clock in the morning.

Saml Gompers

TWpS, reel 4, vol. 5, p. 827, SG Letterbooks, DLC.

1. On Apr. 28, 1891, the United Mine Workers of America, weakened by the prolonged Connellsville strike and by internal dissension, cancelled its plans to undertake a general campaign for eight hours in the coal industry on May 1.

From August Delabar

Office of the International Secretary
Journeymen Bakers' & Confectioners' International Union of America,
New York, May 18 1891

Private and Confitentialy
Dear Sir & Bro
Alow me to asc you the folowing private confitential question since a few weeks i am again delegade to the Central Labor Federation have ben out since after the Detroit Convention my intention is to bring up the Organization to a good basis wich can be done, wat i wont to know is this, is their any other objections then the SLP. Section NY. to get a Charter from the A.F. of. L if their is and no chance to get one then i will not be a delegade however on the other hand i will and shall try to have the charter at once, it is usless to say more on the matter at present please answer at once but keep this privatly as i will your answer this is done by me in the enterest of our unnions in this city leving asite all party enterest or other essues, however i wont it kept among Us at present till i have eather gaint my point or give it up i am in favor of making the CLF the body of all Nat & Int Unions of the city unter a charter of the A.F. of. L. i dont thing their is room for another body and the CLU is N.Y. also run by DA 49 wich is gaining foot hold egain in the city even among the bakers unless Natl & Int local unions of this city will do somthing 49 will bring them to their sencis

Yours truly   Delabar

ALS, Journeymen Bakers' and Confectioners' International Union Records, reel 138, *AFL Records.*

To August Delabar

May 19th. [189]1.

Mr. Aug. Delabar,
Sec. Bakers and Confectioners Int. Union
150 Nassau St. City.
Dear Sir and Brother: —
  Your favor of the 18th. inst. came duly to hand and contents noted.[1]
  In reply permit me to say that I am more than pleased to learn from you that I have been even in the smallest degree instrumental in gaining the increased membership for your Union of the Pacific

Coast, and to say that if anything lies in my power at any time to aid your organization in any place my services are always at its command.

You ask me whether, if the Socialistic Labor Party were to withdraw from the Central Labor Federation, I would issue a charter from the American Federation of Labor to the C.L.F.

Permit me to say in reply that thus far I know of no reason why a charter should not be issued to them. You remember that in my speech at Detroit I stated in substance that in my opinion the S.L.P. could do a great deal for the Trade Union movement in the city of New York by withdrawing, for then quite a number of unions which were ready to join the C.L.F. but could not do so so long as the S.L.P. was represented therein. I am satisfied that that situation still prevails today, and if at any time this subject should come under discussion you can say that to my mind there is no question of either a victory on one side and humiliation on the other. In this great labor movement of ours sincere men should be above personal glorification, and I certainly hope that in some degree I can count myself among that number.

So far as the $2.00 are concerned you have my privilege to do with them just as you please.[2]

That as years go on we may witness the progress and triumph of labor's holy cause, and learn to know and appreciate each other better; struggling together for its achievement is the wish of,

Yours Fraternally   Saml Gompers.
President. American Federation of Labor.

TLpS, reel 4, vol. 5, p. 857, SG Letterbooks, DLC.

1. There are two letters to SG from Delabar dated May 18. One is printed above; both are to be found in the Journeymen Bakers' and Confectioners' International Union Records, reel 138, *AFL Records.*

2. Due to an error, Delabar was not able to receive a small refund owed him for the purchase of tickets on the Erie Railroad. When SG received a $2.00 refund for a similar purchase, he sent the money on to Delabar, who suggested donating it to the striking Connellsville, Pa., miners.

An Article in the *People*

[May 24, 1891]

IN THE COKE REGION.

Reports having appeared in the New York papers and probably also in all the capitalistic sheets throughout the country, that the strike of the coke workers was over and that a stampede had taken place among the men anxious for employment, *The People* telegraphed to its Scottdale correspondent for a true statement of the condition of affairs, and in reply received last night the following telegram:

Scottdale, Pa.; May 23 — Up to the present time 839 families have been evicted, and they are sheltered in canvas tents. Even under these circumstances they remain firm and steadfast. The district convention of Tuesday affirmed the unanimous wish of the rank and file by declaring for a continuation of the strike. An appeal has been issued for aid for the 3,000 families in destitute circumstances and to fight the unjust criminal proceedings instituted against the labor leaders who still carry on the fight for right and justice. Yesterday Capt. Loar[1] and his ten deputies were acquitted of the charge of murder for the killing of seven strikers at Morewood. Some of the old men have returned to work, but not in numbers sufficient to affect the general situation, and with the proper assistance the greedy barons can yet be compelled to recognize our honest claims.

The hopes for assistance on May first from the Federation of Labor were blasted and considerable disappointment, to say the least, was expressed among the men here concerning the failure of Mr. Gompers to sustain them. He had no money to give, he said, and he could secure none yet for two months.

Yet the prospects of success are reasonably bright and if the workingmen of the country come promptly to our aid, organized labor will have gained the greatest victory of the nineteenth century.

MR. GOMPERS SPEAKS.

Upon the request of a representative of *The People* for a statement in relation to his visit to the coke-region, Mr. Gompers said that he had been instructed by the Executive Board of the A.F. of L. to effect a compromise between the coke-workers and the companies, if the strikers were willing. On May 13 he went to Scottdale and conferred with [Messrs.?] Parker[2] and Wise,[3] the leaders of the strike, about his mission. These two gentlemen decided to call a meeting of the Executive and let him know what to do the next morning while he would be in Pittsburg. May 14 he received the instruction from that board to confer with Mr. Frick[4] about a settlement. He saw Mr. Frick, but that gentleman declining to even discuss the strike he was obliged to leave for New York that same afternoon.

Mr. Gompers declared that he did not, as some newspapers had published, discuss with the men whether they should remain with or leave the K. of L. The report that he had tried to induce them to leave the K. of L. was without foundation in fact.

People (New York), May 24, 1891.

1. James A. Loar, a Mt. Pleasant, Pa., dentist, was captain of Company E of the Tenth Regiment of the Pennsylvania National Guard. He and other members of the company served as deputy sheriffs in Morewood, Pa., during the Connellsville region coke strike. A grand jury indicted him and all but one of his deputies for the murder of eleven strikers.

2. C. M. Parker was secretary-treasurer of United Mine Workers of America (UMWA) District 4.

3. Peter Wise was master workman of UMWA District 4.

4. Henry Clay Frick, president of the H. C. Frick Coke Co., served as chairman of the board of Carnegie Brothers and Co. from 1889 to 1892 and Carnegie Steel Co. from 1892 to 1899.

To Jacob Hilkene[1]

May 25th. [189]1

Mr. Jacob Kilkene,
Sec. Architectural Iron Workers Union 5043 A.F. of L.
255 Cobourn St. Indianapolis, Ind.
Dear Sir and Brother:—

Your favor of the 20th. inst. came duly to hand and contents noted.

In reply permit me to say that while I agree with you in the view you express generally and in local trade unions, yet as a matter of fact when national or international unions are organized they frequently include and admit to membership those of various branches of the trade and, some kindred to them, in other words those who may be able to materially aid them both in times of peace or difficulty with their employers. For instance the Amalgamated Association of Iron and Steel Workers have probably twenty or more different branches of the iron and steel trade under their jurisdiction. The Int. Typographical Union[2] not only admits compositors, but pressmen, book binders and so forth. The Cigarmakers Int. Union admits not only cigarmakers, but packers, strippers and so forth, and so I might quote a number of others.

If the convention of the Architectural Iron Workers[3] recently held in Indianapolis, Ind.[4] decided upon admitting to their organization those kindred trades, there can be no objection provided they do not infringe upon the domain of other trade union organizations.

Hoping that this explanation will be satisfactory, and wishing both yourself and the organization success, I am,

Fraternally Yours   Saml Gompers.
President. American Federation of Labor.

TLpS, reel 4, vol. 5, p. 877, SG Letterbooks, DLC.

1. Jacob Hilkene was an Indianapolis iron worker and architect.
2. The International TYPOGRAPHICAL Union.
3. The International Union of the ARCHITECTURAL Iron Workers' Industry of North America.
4. The convention was held on May 21, 1891.

From P. J. McGuire

Office of General Secretary
United Brotherhood of Carpenters & Joiners of America.[1]
Philadelphia, Pa. May 28, 1891

Dear Sir and Bro:

I note what you say in regard to the letter I forwarded you from Mr. McBride,[2] Hot Springs, Ark. I think your course is quite right in reprimanding the Federal Labor Union for rushing into print so readily, and also all parties who have been so eager to give their differences newspaper notoriety. In the case of the application of the United Mine Workers for financial aid to sustain the Iowa Miners in their fight for eight hours,[3] I most positively vote "no," for the reason that there has been evident negligence on the part of the Secretary[4] of the United Mine Workers of America in not informing your office until now that they had made an exception of the Iowa Miners in their letter deferring or declaring off their movement for eight hours on May first. The action of the United Mine Workers of America in publishing through the newspapers the fact that they had deferred or declared off their movement for eight hours on May first, has placed the American Federation of Labor in a very uncertain light, which will require considerable explanation, and the sooner you can issue the circular you have in view on this subject,[5] the better it will be for the reputation of the Federation. In the published statement deferring this movement of the Miners, no mention of the Iowa Miners as an exception was ever made by the officials of the United Mine Workers of America. The "Journal of the Knights of Labor" last week has taken a position in this matter,[6] which is extremely offensive, not only to you, but to all Trade Union men; and the sooner the statement of our connection with the United Mine Workers is known to the public, the better it will be. The Newark Carpenters have declared their strike off without consulting this office, and immediately after they got all the moneys they asked for.[7] It is more than likely that I shall insist on a thorough investigation of that course, and I shall have something done in connection with such a loose method of closing a strike.

Yours, P. J McGuire

Note the Penn miners in W. Penna. have cut loose from United Mine Workers.[8] So has N.D.A. 135.[9] See yesterdays and today's Phila. Papers.

I will be in N.Y. tomorrow with my family. Will arrive at Liberty St depot 4 P.M. Friday. Meet me there and we will go down with family to Staten Island.

T and ALS, United Brotherhood of Carpenters and Joiners of America Records, reel 139, *AFL Records*.

1. The United Brotherhood of CARPENTERS and Joiners of America (UBCJA).

2. C. F. McBride was southern states district organizer for the UBCJA. The local press carried accounts of McBride's dispute with J. E. A. Hall, AFL general organizer for Hot Springs, Ark., regarding jurisdiction over organizing. On May 25, 1891, SG cautioned P. E. Dumas, secretary of Federal Labor Union 5327 in Hot Springs, against "airing the grievances of individuals in the labor movement" (reel 4, vol. 5, p. 878, SG Letterbooks, DLC).

3. The Iowa miners struck on May 1, 1891, for a new scale of wages and the eight-hour day. Most miners returned to work before the end of July on the employers' terms. The AFL agreed to loan the United Mine Workers of America (UMWA) $2,000 for this struggle. The 1891 AFL convention converted the loan to a donation.

4. Patrick McBRYDE represented KOL National Trade Assembly 135 at the founding convention of the National Progressive Union of Miners and Mine Laborers in 1888, and served as the new organization's secretary-treasurer (1888-90). He was secretary-treasurer of the UMWA from 1891 to 1896.

5. See "A Circular Issued by the Executive Council of the AFL," June 1, 1891, below.

6. In an article entitled "A Fool Leader," the May 14, 1891, issue of the *Journal of the Knights of Labor* accused SG of seeking personal notoriety and fame in urging miners to strike for eight hours and promising them financial support that the AFL could not deliver. It characterized the AFL's leaders as "cold-blooded, base-hearted scoundrels, unworthy of any trust or confidence by workingmen."

7. Under the leadership of the Newark District Council of the UBCJA, the carpenters of Newark and vicinity struck on May 4, 1891, for the eight-hour day. Initially five New Jersey unions were involved: locals 119 and 172 (Newark), 232 (Millburn), 477 (Orange), and 533 (Montclair). Local 22 of the United Order of American Carpenters and Joiners joined the strike May 8, and unorganized carpenters also participated in the strike. The UBCJA contributed $4,500 from its reserve fund for the strike, which ended unsuccessfully on May 25.

8. In March 1890 the Pittsburgh area railroad and river miners established District 5 of the UMWA. On June 9, 1891, after the UMWA had decided to forestall plans to strike for the eight-hour day, representatives of District 5 met to consider seceding

from the national organization. After a tie vote, they decided to refer the matter to the miners themselves. District 5 did not officially disband, but thousands left the organization because of the cancellation of the eight-hour campaign.

9. NATIONAL Trade Assembly 135 of the KOL. The assembly remained affiliated with the UMWA.

A Circular Issued by the
Executive Council of the AFL

New York, June 1st, 1891.

To the Organized Wage-Workers of America:

Fellow-Workers: —

It becomes our painful duty to officially inform you what you undoubtedly already informally know, that the United Mine Workers have receded from their position and declared the eight-hour demand of the coal miners off.

In making this announcement to you in this way, it is necessary that you should be placed in possession of all the information in connection with, and how far we were informed of the movement, and what led up to the decision of the miners' officials. Hence to clearly understand this statement it is necessary to recount a few facts:

In accordance with the instructions of the Boston Convention of the American Federation of Labor,[1] the Executive Council in the early part of 1890 issued blank circulars to all affiliated National and International Unions, in which they were asked to state their numerical and financial strength, their ability and willingness to make the demand for the enforcement of the eight-hour workday, and their desire to be the trade selected by the Executive Council for the attainment of that object for their fellow-craftsmen, so that our best efforts could be concentrated upon that trade.

Among the Unions answering and giving the best evidence of a desire, preparation and willingness, were the carpenters and the coal miners. Both organizations had declared at their previously held conventions their determination to make the move May 1st, 1890. In accordance with the statements made and the prospects then appearing to the Executive Council, the carpenters were selected to make the movement first, and the coal miners were informed of that fact, and that their trade was selected to make the demand immediately after the movement of the carpenters. To this the miners acquiesced.

With what success the carpenters' movement for eight hours of 1890 was crowned, what concessions were gained for workers of other trades through our movement, it is unnecessary to mention here. Suffice by saying that it was entirely satisfactory to all concerned, and that notwithstanding all the efforts of enemies—interested, jealous or ignorant—to belittle the struggle and its results, the success is ours, the benefits of improved conditions belong to the toilers, and the honor will be accorded by the historical development of the labor movement to those who deserve it.

At the Detroit Convention of the American Federation of Labor, held last December, the eight-hour movement of the past year was reviewed, and resolved that the lines laid down, *i.e.,* to concentrate the efforts of organized labor upon the attainment of a given point was the one best calculated to promote the interests of the toiling masses. Hence the determination to continue the movement for the achievement of the eight-hour workday.

The delegates of the coal miners opposed the report of the Special Committee which had this subject under advisement, upon the ground that it left the selection of the trade to make the demand to the Executive Council. They expressed a fear that the Executive Council might select some other trade. They insisted that the Convention select the trade at once, and that the coal miners be the trade selected. It was urged by the miners' delegates that they had just come from the K. of L. Convention, and had there received assurances of co-operation and assistance for the eight-hour movement of their craft.[2] Is it surprising that such statements of their preparation and eagerness to enter the contest prevailed upon the Convention? It will be observed that the A.F. of L. neither "ordered" a strike of the miners—did not allure them into a "desperate struggle to injure" them; but on the contrary, if there existed any "duplicity" it was not practiced by the officers or the Convention of the American Federation of Labor.

Immediately after the Convention circulars were issued to the wage-workers appealing to them to make a great effort for the miners; to save their money for May 1st. The President was authorized to and made a trip through the country to arouse all to the active support of the miners' eight-hour movement, and in every place visited financial support was pledged, both publicly as well [as] officially at Union meetings. Never in the history of Labor's struggles in America was there such evidence of practical assistance as was plainly in view for the miners had they made the demand.

When the miners held their convention in February, at Columbus, they resolved to insist upon the eight-hour day. At their conference with the Mine Operators, at Pittsburgh, in April, they parted and the conference broke up because the miners refused to recede from their demand for eight hours being the recognized limit of the day's work on and after May 1st, 1891.

Can anyone doubt our honest belief that the miners were really in earnest in their declarations?

But during all this period the strike in the Connelsville coke region was pending, and it is necessary to call attention to some facts in connection with this strike in order to understand the subsequent events. The strike was against a scale of wages, the question of hours never being part of the demand until after the disagreement upon the price list and some time after the declaration of the strike.

The miners' officials requested the Executive Council of the American Federation of Labor to meet them and the General Executive Board of the Knights of Labor (whom they also requested to be on hand) at Pittsburgh, Pa., on March 31st. We immediately complied and were in attendance, but the officers of the K. of L. (to which order the miners also belong) were not, nor did they deign to give any reason for their absence. At that meeting, only thirty days before May 1st, the entire situation was gone over, and not the slightest intimation was given that they contemplated giving up the contest. We were asked to endorse a circular in aid of the coke strike, which we did, though, to be candid, very reluctantly, for we knew that the thought of organized labor was centered on the eight-hour movement of the miners of May 1st, and that no amount of special pleading could have changed or diverted their support to a side or premature issue.

On April 17 the miners' officials sent a representative to us to request a donation of $2,500 to aid the coke workers' strike. We held that as the money paid by the organizations to the Federation was for the sole purpose of the miners' strike of May 1st we could not comply with their request. Then the sum was asked as a loan. The representative of the miners stated that they had a fund of about $35,000, but were prohibited by their constitution from expending it for the coke workers, as they were not entitled to benefit. We agreed that the United Mine Workers of America should advance the $2,500 to the striking coke workers, and we guaranteed that the same would be paid by us on May 1st, 1891, on *condition that the miners make the demand for the enforcement of the eight-hour workday on that date.*

It might be asked what our purpose was in making that condition. First, let us say that we desired to maintain our good faith with those who contributed and proposed contributing their money for a specific purpose, and, second, that from many coal mining centres came the information that the officers of the K. of L. were conducting a secret and systematic agitation, through their emissaries, to work upon the fears of the miners, predicting certain defeat, discouraging them in every way, and urging them not to make the move. These tactics are further borne out by the fact that, not only was their official journal severely silent about a movement in which their members were (supposed) about to be engaged, but hailed with delight the announcement that it had been abandoned; abused and insulted everyone whose credulity had been played upon and finally rounding off their hostility to the movement by their chief officer declaring that he had "*No time to bother with the wage question.*"

The first official intimation that the miners' eight-hour movement was declared "off," we received on the morning of May 1st, 1891, the very morning the movement was to be made. Had we known, or could have spoken authoritatively earlier, we would not have allowed the organized wage-workers to look for a movement that would not move.

We have withheld this statement until now for the reason that the coke workers were engaged in their strike, and we did not desire to say one word that could be distorted or used against them in their struggle.

We have not a word of unkindness to say against the officers of United Mine Workers for declaring the movement off. They probably could not act in any other way than in accordance with the feeling of uncertainty and insecurity brought about by the enemies to the movement.

The wage-workers of America, yes, of the whole world, will know where to place the blame and hold the traitors to the cause of labor responsible.

Notwithstanding the disappointment to the earnest workers in the cause of labor and to the wage-earning masses, who have come to look to May 1st of each year to strike a link from off their shackles; as the day upon which a brighter light is shed, until finally in the full light of noon of labor's cause it shall stand out in all its glory free, emancipated, we shall continue in the course laid down—giving battle to labor's enemies in whatever garb they may appear.

Close up your ranks. Organize, educate and agitate. Eight hours and victory.

Fraternally yours,   Samuel Gompers, President,
P. J. McGuire, 1st Vice-President,
Wm. A. Carney,[3] 2d Vice-President,
John B. Lennon, Treasurer,
Chris. Evans, Secretary.
Executive Council   American Federation of Labor.

PDSr, Terence Vincent Powderly Papers, DCU.

1. The AFL held its fourth annual convention in Boston, Dec. 10-14, 1889.

2. The KOL General Assembly, which met in Denver, Nov. 11-20, 1890, took no official action on the eight-hour movement, but miners' representatives believed the Knights had given them assurances of support for their eight-hour campaign.

3. William A. CARNEY, a Pittsburgh iron mill rougher and member of Monongahela Valley Lodge 53 of the National Amalgamated Association of Iron and Steel Workers (NAAISW), was vice-president of NAAISW District 1 (1890-95) and second vice-president of the AFL (1891-93).

An Excerpt from a News Account of an Address at the 1891 Convention of the Boot and Shoe Workers' International Union of America[1]

[June 2, 1891]

BOUND HAND AND FOOT.

. . .

The convention was quite anxious to hear President Gompers, whose advent into the hall had been greeted with applause, which broke out in great volume when he arose to speak.

In opening he said:

"If any doubts that the trade-union movement is the natural organization of the wage-worker let him apply the one simple rule, the one plain statement that the conditions of wage-workers and his continually conflicting interest are the first essentials of attention.

"There are a number of people who have an objection to the word 'class' as applied to our American form of government. It is urged that because one may change from one class to another that it is an argument against the existence of a class. Then the chattel slaves never constituted a class, as occasionally they bought their freedom.

["]As conditions are today the shoemaker is bound hand and foot to his or her class.

"What is the remedy?

"The remedy is in your own hands. I see in the organization of the Boot and Shoe Workers' International Union one of the most encouraging hopes for the future.

"If the shoemakers constitute a class, I maintain that the trade union is their natural organization, and all other forms of organization is for them simply a false light or beacon hung out to lure the unwary on the rocks.["]

After counselling the delegates to be aggressive in their policy, Mr. Gompers continued:

"I think the Boot and Shoe Workers' International Union could declare that at some future time, say within the next two years, that it proposes to enforce the eight-hour work day. (Great applause.)

"Improve your organization. Make your dues to your local unions even higher. Some may think it will frighten away members,[2] but if it did it would only be for a time, and you would have such a strong organization on such permanent foundations that you would soon see the wisdom of such a course."

. . .

Boston Daily Globe, June 2, 1891.

1. The convention took place in Boston, June 1-5, 1891.

2. For example, an article in the *People*, reprinted from the *Age of Labor*, maintained that "the great expense of membership" was one of the principal factors discouraging workers from joining unions. "The cheaper a thing is the more of it will be sold," the paper argued. "The benefits of organization should come at the lowest possible price" (Nov. 20, 1892).

To George Perkins[1]

[June 1891]

APPEALS OF UNIONS 90 AND 141,[2] NEW YORK CITY.

. . .

REPLY OF THE SECOND VICE-PRESIDENT.

. . .

New York, June 12, 1891.

Dear Sir:

Upon the appeal of Union No. 141 against the decision of the Executive Board, I desire to say that in my judgment it is inconsistent for the Cigar Makers' International Union to protest against a continuance of the obnoxious tenement-house system of making cigars, if we are to allow members working in tenement-houses. There can be no question that cigar makers who work in tenement-houses may become members of the International Union, but they must leave the tenement-houses as soon as they join. Members who violate the law and the fundamental principles for which the organization contends, must be made to comply with the law, or disconnect themselves with the organization.

Fraternally yours,   Samuel Gompers,
Second Vice-President.

PLSr, *Cigar Makers' Official Journal,* June 1891.

1. George William PERKINS was first vice-president of the CMIU from 1885 to 1891 and president of the union from 1891 to 1926.

2. In October 1890 local 90 proposed an amendment to the CMIU constitution that would allow locals in certain prescribed cases to strike prior to receiving permission from the international president. Strasser, in tabulating the votes from locals on this amendment, refused to allow votes from those members of locals 90 and 141 who worked in tenement-house factories. After the CMIU Executive Board sustained Strasser's ruling in early June 1891, local 141 unsuccessfully appealed the decision to a vote of the general membership.

An Excerpt from a News Account of a Banquet Following the Founding Convention of the International Machinists' Union of America

[June 28, 1891]

A LABOR BANQUET.

At the conclusion of their labors last Wednesday evening, the Machinists held a banquet in this city at 85 East 4th st., to celebrate the birth of their National Union. . . .

It was near midnight when Thomas Allen,[1] who acted as toastmaster, rapped for order and introduced President Samuel Gompers, who answered the toast, "The American Federation of Labor." Mr. Gompers said that after dinner speeches were usually of a joking nature, but he would not joke and would not flatter. The preamble adopted by the machinists to the effect that the strongest union was unable to cope with capital unless it also resorted to independent political action, he characterized as a false step. Labor was now much better off than ever before; whoever said it was not, stated what was not true. Much was being said about "new trades unionism"[2] to show that it identified the political with the economic struggle; whoever said so was ignorant; "new trades unionism" stood where he stood; it was broad enough to take in all shades of opinion. If the machinists thought as their preamble indicated, why did they organize a union at all?

. . .

People (New York), June 28, 1891.

1. Thomas Allen was a New York City machinist.

2. During the period of recovery after the depression of the mid-1880s, unskilled laborers in Great Britain formed new unions and existing organizations of skilled workers expanded. A number of these organizations turned to socialists for leadership and to the state as an ally. These developments were termed the "new trade unionism"; they were epitomized in the London dock workers' strike of 1889.

At the 1890 AFL convention, SLP leader Lucien Sanial used the British example to demonstrate the potential for a similar movement in the United States, unifying trade unions with the SLP. In response, SG argued that socialist trade union leaders in Britain had, in fact, not sought to unite their unions with their party; instead, he maintained, they had pursued political and trade union activities in a parallel but separate manner. He insisted that the trade unions should pursue their political demands without tying themselves to any particular party, including the SLP. Throughout the early 1890s, however, SLP leaders continued to advocate a new trade unionism that would ally labor's political and economic efforts, uniting the socialist and trade union movements.

From Josiah Dyer[1]

Granite Cutters' National Union of
the United States of America[2]
Concord, N.H., July 10, 1891

Dear Sir and Brother:—

In reply to your enquiry I do not now recall any city that has passed such an ordinance as you mention and have been making enquiries but cannot find anyone who can give me any information of any city having passed such an ordinance.

If you succeed in getting any information on the subject will you oblige me by letting me know also.

Hoping this will find you in good health, and that now you are on the road to be a Grandfather[3] your head will not get bald, or your teeth fall out, as we generally associate a GRANDFATHER with being quite an old man, but you are not so very old to be having your children married away, mine have not begun yet to leave their daddy.

I see that you are into it again with Terry Powderly. I guess you two won't die happy unless you can hit at each other, eh!

Remember me to Chris. Evans and all enquiring friends.

Yours Fraternally and in F.L. and T.   Josiah B. Dyer.

TLS, Granite Cutters' National Union Records, reel 140, *AFL Records*.

1. Josiah Bennett DYER was secretary of the Granite Cutters' International Union from 1878 to 1880, and of the Granite Cutters' National Union, as it was renamed, from 1880 until 1895.

2. The GRANITE Cutters' National Union of the United States of America.

3. Henrietta Mitchell, daughter of Rose Gompers and Samuel Mitchell, was born in 1892.

To Josiah Dyer

July 16th. [189]1.

Mr. Josiah B. Dyer,
Sec. Granite Cutters Nat. Union
98 N. Main St. Concord, N.H.
Dear Sir and Brother:—

I am in receipt of your kind favor of the 10th. inst. for which many thanks.

I am in request of the information in reference to the ordinances [for][1] by the Stone Masons of Denver.[2] I did not know where to apply for the information other than from the officers of the Nat. organizations and thought you were in possession of it. However, if any news on the matter comes my way you may rest assured that I shall take pleasure in acquainting you with it; and call reciprocity. Could you ask through the Journal?[3]

I desire to repeat the query made to you some time ago, namely, that were the Executive Council of the American Federation of Labor to appropriate the amount of per capita tax and the assessments due by your Nat. Union, as an assistance towards the nine hour strike that your fellow-craftsmen were engaged in, would your Nat. Union become again affiliated?

I kindly suggest that you bring this matter to the notice of the Executive Committee of your Nat. Union.

I cannot help the dispute with Mr. Powderly. The man that strikes at the trade unions, aims his blow at me, and I will never allow either he or any one else to attack them either as an open enemy, or as a pseudo friend without being rebuked at my hands.

By the way you need not think me so venerable because I am a father-in-law and a prospective grandfather. Although your children have not yet begun to "leave their daddy," and of course by reason of that you consider yourself quite a boy, I will challenge you to half a mile run either on foot or on a bicycle for a purse to be put up by the California Athletic Club. Let me hear from you in reference to this challenge and I will show you who is old. Let "tides" in each other be our watchword, and we will hardly be such odd-fellows, as the world used to look upon us.

Our friend Evans joins me in sending best wishes and hoping to hear from you soon again I am,

Truly Yours   Saml Gompers.
President. American Federation of Labor.

TLpS, reel 5, vol. 6, p. 32, SG Letterbooks, DLC.

1. This word is written in the margin at this point.
2. Probably Stone Masons' International Union 1.
3. The *Granite Cutters' Journal.*

To Louis Klinger

July 18th. [189]1.

Mr. Louis F. Klinger,
Sec. Hod Carriers Pro. Union 5467 A.F. of L.
Green Tree Hotel, Broadway and 2nd St. E. St. Louis, Ill.
Dear Sir and Brother:—

I am in receipt of a letter informing me that your Union refuses to accept colored hod carriers as members on account of their color.

I should like you to inform me whether this is so, for if it is I have received an application for a charter from the colored hod carriers and I shall issue the charter to them.

I desire to add that if you will not accept them as members and the charter is issued to them, one of the conditions upon which the charter will be granted is that they must adopt the same working rules and rate of wages as prevails in your Union.[1]

Kindly give this matter your early attention and oblige,

Yours Fraternally   Saml Gompers.
President. American Federation of Labor.

TLpS, reel 5, vol. 6, p. 45, SG Letterbooks, DLC.

1. On July 24, 1891, SG issued a charter to Hod Carriers' Federal Labor Union 5491 of East St. Louis, Ill., on the condition that the local cooperate with Klinger's organization.

To John O'Brien[1]

July 29th. [189]1.

Mr. John O'Brien,
Pres. Federated Trades Council[2]
Portland, Oreg.
Dear Sir and Brother:—

I regret that circumstances beyond my control prevented an earlier reply to your last letter, because I regard the matter therein contained as of a highly important character.

One can scarcely begin to discuss the difficulties between the Nat. Brewers Union and the Brewers Union of the Pacific Coast without getting into interminable trouble, and I approach the subject with some degree of diffidence.

The Pacific Coast Union which was formerly connected with the National Union may have had cause for faultfinding with the administration of the affairs of the Nat. Union, but there is one act of which they have been guilty and which has led up to all the other troubles namely allowing themselves to be suspended from the Nat. Union for their refusal to pay an assessment. If they felt aggrieved or desired changes they could be best brought about by maintaining their good standing in the National Union. I think we all agree that though the Nat. Union may not have been able to give them much strength, they themselves could certainly not have become weakened by their connection with the National Union.

I am opposed to organizations encouraging employers in the violation of contracts entered into with workingmen, but you can very well see that a Nat. Union can only maintain its standing as a Nat. Union, when its local unions are all over the country, and the desire to extend its influences, and that is no doubt how No. 16 became organized, as well as the one at Portland,[3] the Executive, I suppose, hoping thereby to have the Journeymen Brewers flock to the standard of the National Union. We all know how this missed fire in San Francisco, and now an attempt is made in your city, with the results yet in doubt.

In this Brewers trouble I see more than is probably generally observed, and unless that matter is healed, and that very shortly, I fear that the Trade Union Movement of America will be divided into two distinct lines, one of the Pacific Coast, and the other of the remaining portions of the country, and it seriously pains me to think that I have not the power to force mutual concessions and thus heal the breach, and prevent the great injury to the interests of the toiling masses.

The trend of all movements, and of all Interests is to bring them closer together, it is the hope of intelligent workmen to bring the wage workers of the world into a closer alliance with each other to recognize the internationality of the labor movement, and the identity of the interests of the wage-workers of the world.

It is a painful and stinging blow to the advocates of these thoughts and hopes to find the organized workmen of America instead of unitedly co-operating to attain that end, themselves divided in their own country.

No man so thoroughly holds the key to the situation to prevent further calamities and can do greater good for the restoration of peaceful and harmonious relations, than Mr. Fuhrman. He might regard it as a humiliation to have the Pacific Coast Union in full fellowship with the Brewers Nat. Union upon the same conditions that other unions are attached to it but though those who know me are well aware of my dogged persistence in any contest with our common enemy, I think it shows the height of our character and the nobility of our manhood when we can make concessions for the attainment of a common good to our fellow-workers.

I do not share the howlings of distrust and suspicion of Mr. Fuhrman. I have seen him, spoken with him, spoken with others who have known him for years and those who know him best say that he is a conscientious, but impulsive man. That was the impression he also made upon me. I think if he were to see this subject in the light I do he would be great enough to rise to the occasion.

Will you kindly state the wages hours and other conditions of labor which the Local Union of the Nat. Union agreed upon with Weinhard?[4]

I heard from Mr. Tozier[5] about a week ago and I replied to him.

Sincerely hoping that the movement may be progressive and that success may attend our efforts, and that I may hear from you soon, I am,

Fraternally Yours   Saml Gompers.
President. American Federation of Labor.

N.B. You have my permission to make whatever use you desire of this letter for the purpose of promoting the [interests of?] our cause.

S. G.

TLpS, reel 5, vol. 6, pp. 75-76, SG Letterbooks, DLC.

1. John O'BRIEN, a Portland, Ore., printer, was president of the Portland Federated Trades Assembly (FTA) and president (1889-90, 1891-92) and vice-president (1890-91) of Multnomah International Typographical Union (ITU) 58 of Portland.

2. The Portland FTA organized in 1887.

3. In Portland most brewery workmen organized in branch 8 of the United Brewery

Workmen's Union of the Pacific Coast. The National Union of the United Brewery Workmen of the United States (NUUBW), however, attempted to organize a rival local there in 1891, an effort that ended with the conciliation of the two organizations at the AFL's convention in December 1891.

4. In May 1891 the Henry Weinhard Brewery of Portland insisted that all its employees join the NUUBW.

5. Albert Tozier, treasurer of the Portland FTA, was a printer and editor who served variously as corresponding secretary and member of the executive committee of ITU 58 between 1887 and 1893.

To P. J. McGuire

Aug. 4th. [189]1.

Mr. P. G. Mc-Guire,
124 N. 9th. St. Phila, Pa.
Dear Sir and Friend: —

Your favor of the 1st. inst. to hand and contents noted. Thanks for your prompt answer.

I desire to call your attention to the fact that the session of the American Social Science Association occurs on Sep. *2nd.*[1] and I hope that you will be able to arrange so that I can have the pleasure of your company and assistance there.

I doubt that I shall be able to go to Cincinnati for Labor Day in consequence of the receipt of a letter from Portland, surrendering their engagement of me so piteously that I have written to them to count upon my presence there on that date. I have not yet heard from them, but suppose that this settles it.

Thanks for your suggestions in reference to letter.[2] You will find the clipping you sent me enclosed together with a few copies of the "Correspondenzblatt."[3] Since they are the only copies we have I ask you to return them to complete the file of them in this office.

It affords me pleasure to note that the purposes of the S.L.P. are becoming clearer to the views of our members in the movement.

There is no doubt but what they intended to extend their control from the C.L.F. to the national movement, as represented by the American Federation of Labor. Let me give you an incident of that practice.

I suppose you know that immediately after the Detroit convention in spite of the advice of Morgan and others, and the promises of the N.Y. S.L.P. members that their Party should withdraw its representation from the C.L.F. they resolved to stand by that position and then proceeded to organize so-called Central Labor Federations in

Brooklyn and Jersey.[4] These were organized in opposition to the existing Central Labor Unions. They then decided upon holding joint meetings of these Central Labor Federations. The question of sending a delegate to Brussels from their joint organizations was discussed, referred to the individual unions and sections of the Party, and it was decided to send one delegate.

At the joint meeting when the delegate was to be elected with instructions from the S.L.P. they elected one, and after the election proceeded to elect the man who "would be elected as a delegate to the Brussels convention of the S.L.P." as a second delegate of the Central Labor Federations.[5]

You will thus see that they first overstepped the will of the Unions by electing two, and secondly by electing a man as their second delegate who had not yet been elected by the S.L.P. In other words they elected as their delegate any man that the S.L.P. might choose to elect.

Of course, that Mr. Sanial would be elected was generally supposed but not positively known. Talk of that ancient incident when the Roman had his horse nominated for Senator and elected by the people. They at least had something distinctive to vote for, but the illegal delegate whom these people voted for really had no existence.

Quite a movement has been going on of late among the S.L.P. members who are trade unionists, to have the Party withdraw their representation from the C.L.F.

On July 27th. the Party had a regular meeting at which the subject was discussed until a very late hour, and then by common consent the subject was dropped to be renewed the following Saturday evening at an adjourned meeting. The advocates of withdrawal left the meeting, and immediately after their departure resolutions were adopted declaring their purpose to "stick" and reelect the old delegates.

I cannot begin to tell you in a letter of all the intrigues and wire-pulling that has been going on among these people. They represent so few that they really amount to nothing in the Labor Movement, except that some people are frightened by the loudness of their brayings. As a matter of fact, they are not sincere socialists in the best acceptance of that term. They are partisans as dishonest as any of the old corrupt political parties, with the additional fault of a Pecksniffian demeanor of being "holier than thou."

Bob Dagan[6] was at the office a day or so ago and again called my attention to the fact that the K. of L. had sent two delegates to Brussels and urged upon me what he regards as the necessity of the Federation being represented there. He spoke of the fact that the last Int. Congress[7] had decided to have secretaries in each country for the purpose of conducting International correspondence. I suppose you know that I have been appointed to that position by them and have been doing that work.

He says that with our non-representation and the K. of L. being on the ground they will evidently walk off with that which although nothing but work and an empty honor, yet since the convention of the Federation has decided to call an Int. Labor Congress for Chicago in 1893 it is more than likely that we may be frozen out. The importance of electing a delegate to the Int. Labor Congress is not so much the question, but when we have taken the initiative, and to be possibly left out in the cold, is something deserving reconsideration.

I want you to give this subject your earnest thought and advise me on the matter.

I shall communicate with Mr. Linehan[8] as per your request.

Truly Yours. Saml Gompers.
President. American Federation of Labor.

N.B. For fully six weeks I have been in correspondence with Mr. F. U. Adams[9] of Chicago and have received a few letters from him. The last one I enclose for your perusal and advice. It seems that we cannot get the money from him just now. Whether it is not best to take his promissory note since it is likely that without it we may get nothing. We cannot get very much less from his note. Please return the letter after perusal.

S. G.

TLpS, reel 5, vol. 6, pp. 98-99, SG Letterbooks, DLC.

1. SG spoke to the American Social Science Association congress at Saratoga Springs, N.Y., Sept. 2, 1891, on "Trade Unions: Their Achievements, Methods, and Aims" (see "An Address before the American Social Science Association," Sept. 2, 1891, below).

2. Possibly a reference to the advice SG sought from McGuire on July 31, 1891, on preparing a communication to the 1891 session of the Second International, which met in Brussels, Aug. 16-22.

3. The *Correspondenzblatt*, the organ of the Generalkommission der Gewerkschaften Deutschlands (General Commission of German Trade Unions), was founded by Carl Legien in 1891.

4. The Jan. 25, 1891, meeting of the New York City Central Labor Federation (CLF) instructed its corresponding secretary to write to certain labor bodies in surrounding jurisdictions requesting each to change its name to include the words "Central Labor Federation" and to send representatives to a new joint board of such organizations. The United German Trades established the Brooklyn CLF in February 1891, about the same time that the Hudson County, N.J., CLF was founded, apparently by the Central Labor Union of Hudson County.

5. The New York CLF sent Lucien Sanial as one of its delegates to the Brussels conference. The other American socialist delegate was Rosenberg of Chicago. Abraham Cahan represented both the United Hebrew Trades and the Jewish section of

the SLP. The official minutes of the congress list only these three American delegates by name. As many as three others attended, but their names or affiliations are not listed.

6. Possibly Robert Degen, a journalist who worked for the *New Yorker Volkszeitung* in the early 1890s.

7. The founding congress of the Second International met in July 1889 in Paris.

8. James J. Linehan, a carpenter in 1891 and later a janitor, was a member of United Brotherhood of Carpenters and Joiners of America 1 of Chicago and secretary of the Trade and Labor Assembly of Chicago from 1891 to 1892 and president from 1893 to 1894.

9. Frederick Upham Adams was a Chicago journalist, author, and inventor. His articles in the *Chicago Tribune* on the problems of miners in Braidwood, Ill., during their strike in 1890 convinced SG and the AFL Executive Council to back his venture to photograph conditions in the coal mines with a loan of $200 in 1891. Adams failed to complete the work on this project, and throughout the 1890s SG was unsuccessful in recovering the loan despite persistent correspondence with Adams on the matter.

To Carl Legien[1]

Aug. 5th. [189]1.

Mr. C. Legien
Hamburg (St. Georg) An Der Koppel 79 I. Germany
Dear Comrade: —

I address you as a representative of the Trade Unions of Germany upon a matter of considerable importance.

The Convention of the American Federation of Labor directed me to forward their fraternal greetings, as well as an invitation to the delegates to the Brussels Convention requesting them to attend the International Labor Congress which we have called to be held in the city of Chicago in the United States in 1893, at the same time when the Government proposes to celebrate by a World's Exposition the 400th. anniversary of the discovery of America by Christopher Columbus.

I have sent a letter and invitation by mail to Monsieur Jean Volders,[2] Redacteur du "Peuple" Brussels, Belgium.

The reason of my writing this to you is that I have been informed that some effort might be made by some parties from this side of the Atlantic to suppress the letter. Enclosed please find a copy of the letter, and I trust that if you will be a representative to that Congress that you take it with you, and if the original is not read in due time, I request you to hand in the one enclosed; or should you not be a delegate I kindly ask you to place it in the hands of some representative Trade Unionist with the same request of him that I make of you.

I was very much impressed with the article upon "Strikes"[3] in the last issue of the "Correspondenzblatt" and intended to write in time for this mail, but find other business requiring my immediate attention, hence will postpone writing upon the article in question, for a few days.

Kindly asking you to comply with the request herein contained, and with assurances of my best wishes, I am,

Fraternally Yours   Saml Gompers.
President. American Federation of Labor.

TLpS, reel 5, vol. 6, p. 103, SG Letterbooks, DLC.

1. Carl LEGIEN was secretary (1890-1920) of the Generalkommission der Gewerkschaften Deutschlands (General Commission of German Trade Unions, subsequently the Allgemeiner Deutscher Gewerkschaftsbund [General German Federation of Trade Unions]) and editor (1891-1900) of its organ, the *Correspondenzblatt.*

2. Jean VOLDERS was editor of *Le Peuple,* organ of the Parti Ouvrier Belge (Belgian Workers' Party), and organizer of the Brussels congress of the Second International.

3. Various articles on strikes in the *Correspondenzblatt* during July took as a common theme the necessity for trade unions to have ample funds before engaging in them.

To Ernst Kurzenknabe[1]

Aug. 18th. [189]1.

Mr. Ernest Kurzenknaabe,
Sec. Journeymen Brewers Nat. Union of America.
171 Allen St. City.
Dear Sir and Brother:—

Your favor of the 12th. inst. came duly to hand and I laid the same before the Executive Council for their consideration.

Acting upon your intimation I telegraphed Mr. Furhman on Thursday to defer his answer until Saturday to your request for the Pacific Coast Brewery Workmen's Union to send a delegation to your St. Louis convention.[2] After the Council session on Friday I forwarded an urgent request by wire to Mr. Furhman for them to be represented at your convention.

Monday morning I received an answer from him stating that the invitation came entirely too late for them to take action as it would require a general vote of all their branches: in accordance wherewith it will be entirely impracticable for me to attend your convention since they will not be represented.

When I was in San Francisco and in conference with the Executive of the Pacific Coast Brewery Workmen's Union I used every honorable endeavor to have them make propositions for peace, and I was in great hopes that the propositions would be submitted to the members of your National Union and be accepted by them. I confess I was both chagrined and disappointed when I saw that the Executive Council of your National Union did not submit the propositions to be voted upon in the shape they were proposed, but added other conditions which nullified the original propositions.

You mention four propositions upon which the Pacific Coast Brewery Workmen's Union can rejoin the National Union, the last one, namely "the Pacific Coast can join only under one charter, that of Local Union 16" would not only be rejected by them, but engender so much bitterness of feeling that I deem it entirely inadvisable to forward it to them. I am sure it would only have a tendency to drive you further apart.

I beg to impress upon your mind, and sincerely hope that the convention will take some action in order to bring about peace between your National Union and the Brewery Workmen's Union of the Pacific Coast.

It is evident that one of the conditions upon which they will insist is that the headquarters of the National Union be transferred from New York to some other city.[3] Even in a letter received to-day from Oregon such an intimation is made.

I think peace can be brought about between the two organizations, and it certainly should be, by honest and earnest effort. There is certainly no humiliation in making concessions in order to bring about peace, and a thorough organization of men following a craft.

There are so many troubles in the Brewery trade, and the organized workingmen of other industries are called upon to such an extent to render aid to the organized Brewery Workmen that I am sure a feeling of disregard or indifference will be manifested by them unless the Journeymen Brewers themselves unite and make common cause.

I shall be pleased to go as far as possible to aid you in accomplishing that result, and earnestly hope it may be achieved. I earnestly hope the convention will take such action as will secure its achievement.

As per your request enclosed please find the original proposition made by the Brewery Workmen's Union.

Fraternally Yours   Saml Gompers.
President. American Federation of Labor.

TLpS, reel 5, vol. 6, pp. 141-42, SG Letterbooks, DLC.

1. Ernst KURZENKNABE was national secretary of the National Union of the United Brewery Workmen of the United States (NUUBW) from 1888 to 1899.

2. The NUUBW held its fifth convention in St. Louis, Aug. 23-27, 1891.

3. The NUUBW convention in Buffalo, N.Y., in April 1892 decided to move the national headquarters to St. Louis. The move took place in June 1892.

To Henry Eikhoff[1]

Aug. 20th. [189]1.

Mr. H. J. Eihkoff,
Sec. Metal Polishers Union 3702 A.F. of L.
Plymouth, Mich.
Dear Sir and Brother:—

Your favor of the 16th. inst. came duly to hand and contents noted.

I sent a number of letters to the Metal Polishers Unions affiliated with the American Federation of Labor with a view of helping in the organization of a National Union.

If the Committee of your Union is engaged in that work I shall be pleased to co-operate with them. The only question that I want your Committee to bear in mind is that when a convention for the formation of a National Union is held, it should be in some place convenient to all the Unions and since your Committee is but of a local character it might not have the desired influence upon the other local unions to induce them to send delegates to the convention.

As soon as I receive replies from more of the Unions I will forward them to you. Although they make no mention of the place I yet believe it would be most advisable to have the convention take place at the time and place where the next convention of the American Federation of Labor will be held, namely, Birmingham, Ala. It would be a double inducement for Unions to send delegates: one to attend the convention of the American Federation of Labor and the other for the formation of their National Union. Such a course was pursued last year with the Retail Clerks and Salesmen[2] and the Cooks and Waiters,[3] the local unions of which sent delegates to the A.F. of L. convention and in the interim of meetings formed their National Unions. Such I think could be advantageously repeated in your case.

Hoping that your Committee will take this matter into their early and favorable consideration and that I may hear from you as soon as convenient, I am,

Fraternally Yours   Saml Gompers.
President. American Federation of Labor.

TLpS, reel 5, vol. 6, p. 149, SG Letterbooks, DLC.

1. Henry J. EIKHOFF was a founder of the Metal Polishers', Buffers', and Platers'

International Union of North America at a convention held later in the year in Toledo, Ohio, and subsequently served as an officer of the organization.

2. The Retail CLERKS' National Protective Association of America.

3. While the WAITERS' and Bartenders' National Union was not founded until April 1891, August Delabar announced the formation of a "Waiters' National Union" at the AFL's 1890 convention (AFL, *Proceedings*, 1890, p. 20).

To Victor Delahaye[1]

Aug. 21st. [189]1.

Mons. Victor Delahaye
331 Rue Championnet Paris, France.
Dear Friend: —

It is such a long time since I have heard from you that I am not quite certain of reaching you by this letter, and I am anxious both to continue a correspondence with you, and to give and receive such information as will benefit the movement of labor in which we are both so much interested.

The Congress now being held in Brussels is of an important nature in itself, and although you may not be in a position at present to have any better information in Paris than I in America, it is nevertheless true that France is represented by a very much larger number of delegates and no doubt of a much more representative character of the organized working people than we are of America. In fact, the Trade Unions of this country are not at all represented there, and I am sure that though the men who attend it as delegates may have the best of intentions they represent only an insignificant minority of a few localities; hence if you can give me any information as a result of your mingling with the delegates after their return from Brussels, I shall be under renewed obligations to you.

There has been a slander circulated by the enemies of the Trade Union Movement of America that the American Federation of Labor has placed its seal of disapproval upon Socialism as a science, or a theory or even as a system of society for the future. Such I beg to assure you is not at all the case. What we have decided is that a Socialist Political Party, as a Political Party, cannot be represented in a Trade Union Congress, but that Socialists or working people entertaining any other theory are entirely upon an equality with all other working men, providing they are members of the Union of the trade, calling or profession that they follow. In other words, we maintain that a man can hardly be esteemed a Trade Unionist unless he is a member of his Trade Union.

With this I mail to your address a verbatim printed copy of the speeches upon that question discussed at the Detroit convention of the American Federation of Labor, together with the printed minutes of that convention for your perusal. If you desire to utilize them in the interest of our Movement I shall be pleased to forward you a few more copies.

Sincerely hoping that you are well, and that the Movement is progressing, and hoping to hear from you at your earliest convenience, I am,

Sincerely Yours   Saml Gompers.
President. American Federation of Labor

N.B. Kindly remember me to Mr. Keufer[2] of Typographical Union, and [other?] friends.

S. G.

TLpS, reel 5, vol. 6, pp. 152-53, SG Letterbooks, DLC.

1. Victor DELAHAYE was a French mechanic and socialist labor leader.
2. Auguste KEUFER was general secretary of the Fédération française des travailleurs du livre, the French typographical union, from 1885 to 1920.

To Bertha Palmer[1]

Sep. 1st. [1891]

Mrs. Potter-Palmer,
Pres. Board Lady Managers World's Fair,
Chicago, Ill.
Dear Madam:—

It is currently stated that the Board of Lady Managers is about to hold its meeting this coming week, and in all probability the question of classification will be a subject under discussion.

Permit me on behalf of the working men and women of this country under the banner of the American Federation of Labor to respectfully call your attention to the fact that in making the exposition it would be advisable to have a classification which will show the proportion of women['s] and children's work.

Let me quote a resolution adopted at our last convention upon the subject, and which is as follows:

"Resolved, That this Convention hereby express its disapproval of a separate exhibit of the productions of women at the World's Fair of 1893, and

["]Resolved, That we desire the adoption of some method of classification of exhibits as will plainly show the proportion of women's and children's labor in all products exhibited, and

["]Resolved, That the President of the American Federation of Labor be and is hereby instructed to forward this resolution to such officers of the World's Fair as may have control of the classification of the exhibits."

In the matter of this World's Fair it seems to us that those organized and authorized to speak in the name of the toiling masses of our country are entitled to some consideration in the exhibition of the products of labor's brawn and brain.[2]

Trusting that your Board will give this matter early and favorable consideration, I am,

Very Respectfully Yours   Saml Gompers
President. American Federation of Labor.

TLpS, reel 5, vol. 6, p. 182, SG Letterbooks, DLC.

1. Bertha Honoré Palmer (1849-1918) was chair of the World's Columbian Exposition's Board of Lady Managers. A prominent society figure, she was a supporter of the Women's Trade Union League, played an important role in organizing the Chicago millinery workers, and in 1893 became vice-president of the newly formed Chicago Civic Federation.

2. The Columbian Exposition displayed women's and children's work in separate buildings as well as interspersed in other exhibits throughout the grounds. The women's building contained handicrafts and artwork produced by women. The children's building functioned mainly as a nursery, kindergarten, and playground for the children of visitors to the exposition; it did, however, have exhibits on children's toys and books, work and play, as well as on child rearing.

To Thomas Mann

Sep. 2nd. [189]1.

Mr. Tom Mann,
Labor Commissioner
44 Parliament St. London, S.W. England
Dear Sir:—

I am in receipt of your favor of the 20th. inst. the contents of which I have noted with great interest.

Permit me to say that I have watched with much care such reports of the transactions of the Royal Commission on Labor[1] as the papers print but should esteem it a favor should you be enabled to forward any official account of the investigation as well as any comment you could find time to make. At any rate permit me to congratulate you and the organized working people of Great Britain upon the excellent defender of their rights they have in your choice as one of the commissioners.

Replying to your questions as nearly correctly as I can I desire to say:

1st. The membership of the American Federation of Labor is more than five hundred thousand (500,000). It is difficult to say what proportion of citizens to non citizens they consist of, but I should judge more than two thirds.

2nd. The attitude of the American Federation of Labor has been directed to the attainment of the Eight Hour workday by the efforts of the working people to secure it by adjustment with their employers and not from legal enactment for private employment. The attempt to secure a legal enactment for the Eight Hour workday has been directed for Government employes and trying to extend it to contractors on governmental work. In the state of Nebraska, however, a law has been passed constituting eight hours a day's work for all classes of mechanics, servants and laborers throughout the state, except those engaged in farm or domestic labor and providing a penalty of double pay to the mechanics, servants or laborers for any violation of the law, and an additional penalty of from 100 to $1.000.[2]

3rd. I do not know the membership nor the proportion of citizens in the Knights of Labor, and so far as their attitude on the movement to inaugurate the Eight Hour workday is concerned, I would add that it is ambiguous. They have it as one of the demands in their platform yet never take action to secure it and have really antagonized our movement in which we have been engaged for the past two years.

4th. Since the American Federation of Labor is purely a wage-workers' movement we have not attempted any concert of action with the Farmers' alliance since they practically are employing Farmers although our sympathies go out to them by [reason] of the [burdens?] they have to bear. Our efforts have rather been directed towards organizing the farm laborers with which I cannot say we have been successful up to the present time.

5th. Although there is an entente cordial between the Bro. of Locomotive Engineers,[3] Bro. of Railroad Locomotive Firemen,[4] Bro. of Railroad Trainmen,[5] Switchmen's Mutual Association[6] and Railroad Conductors[7] (they are National Trade Unions) and the A.F. of L. they are not affiliated with us. They have absolutely no connection with the K. of L.

6th. I should judge that the total number of adult males working on the Eight Hour System in the United States is about ten to twelve per cent.

These answers are subject to modification, but I think they are nearly correct.

The experience of employers and workmen alike who have either secured or conceded the Eight Hour workday accords that the claims made by the advocates of the Eight Hour System, that it is far more beneficial to all concerned, that it makes the toilers more independent and manly, that it improves not only their material and social well-being, but their moral and political condition and tends to raise the standard of excellence of all, nor does it destroy the business interests of the employers.

I was much pleased to learn that you had a visit from our friend Mr. Schulteis[8] and gleaned some information from him.

Sincerely trusting that your efforts may conduce to the welfare of the toilers of England, and incidentally those of the world, and that I may hear from you occasionally, I am,

Fraternally Yours　Saml Gompers
President. American Federation of Labor.

N.B. With this I mail to your address a copy of the report of the Special Committee on Eight Hours of our last convention, as well as a copy of the proceedings and a verbatim report of a discussion in which I took the liberty of mentioning your name among others. I commend it to your consideration and ask you for an opinion on it.

S. G.

TLpS, reel 5, vol. 6, pp. 184-85, SG Letterbooks, DLC.

1. The British government appointed the Royal Commission on Labour in 1891 to examine relations between capital and labor. Thomas Mann and six other labor representatives constituted a small minority of the body. It issued a report in 1894 endorsing the government's policy of neutrality in labor disputes and encouraging voluntary, non-binding arbitration through the Labour Department of the Board of Trade. The Commission's recommendations were the basis for the Conciliation Act of 1896.

2. Laws of 1891, chap. 54, enacted Jan. 6, 1891. The Nebraska supreme court ruled the law unconstitutional in 1894 on the grounds that it discriminated against certain classes of laborers and was an infringement of the principle of freedom of contract.

3. The Brotherhood of LOCOMOTIVE Engineers.

4. The Brotherhood of LOCOMOTIVE Firemen.

5. The Brotherhood of RAILROAD Trainmen.

6. The SWITCHMEN'S Mutual Aid Association of the United States of America.

7. The Order of RAILWAY Conductors of America.

8. Hermann J. Schulteis, a Washington, D.C., clerk, served on the U.S. Immigration Commission (1891-92) and wrote the commission's *Report on European Immigration to the United States* (Washington, D.C., 1893).

An Address before the American Social Science Association[1]

[September 2, 1891]

TRADE-UNIONS: THEIR ACHIEVEMENTS, METHODS, AND AIMS.

After eighteen hundred years the most eminent of the world's scholars have not hesitated to write "Explanations and Defences" of the Christian religion. The Trade Unionist need not therefore wonder that he, too, while defending a cause which dates back still further in the past, should be called upon again and again to give reasons for the faith within him, and reply to the new sceptics every generation produces. Long before Peter trod the streets of Rome or Paul addressed the people of Athens, the workers, the artisans of both Rome and Greece, had been forced into combinations.

At that day religion and politics were one: there was no line of separation beween Church and State. Slavery was the normal type of those who labored; yet, as civilization spread and cities rose, luxuries grew in demand, and with demand arose a new class, that of free artisans, skilled in all the arts of their various callings. But whether in combinations of the captured and doomed to slavery, or in protective associations of freemen, dire necessity alike compelled unity of action. The rapacity of the rich, the unbridled licentiousness and cruelty of the age, made the life of the toiler a dark and dismal one. Yet in spite of all threats and punishments, or rather because of them, the oppressed grew closer together, and silently whispered their grievances and their hopes. The history of the ancient guilds, their federation for mutual support, their pious care of the sick, and provision for the burial of the dead are matters well known, and which I need not here enter into.

In speaking of their aims, what I chiefly desire to emphasize is the fact that wherever a union of the toilers has come into existence it has arisen from a necessity to combat oppression. A free people never rebel. Before a man can become rebellious to existing circumstances, he must have grievances; and it is only when these eat into his soul, and goad him on to either desperation or retaliation, that concert of action is instinctively felt essential. Their aim was ever the same,—protection and mutual assistance under adverse conditions. But, it may be asked, if their aims are the same to-day as over two thousand years ago, wherein has there been any progress, if the producers of the world's wealth are still contending against injustice and combining to redress grievances?

The conditions are vastly changed from those of preceding centuries. In Christian lands chattel slavery has ceased. The taint of labor no longer carries with it legal servitude. Yet in what manner can Trade Unionism claim aught towards this achievement? In the first place, it can be confidently asserted that whatever tends to produce solidarity directly aids progress; for it is by the union of people for a common purpose, the subordination of personal to general aims, that a higher standard of social morality is attained, the sympathetic nature of man quickened, and the human brought into greater prominence over the selfish animal nature. The history of England and France illustrates in a marked degree the influence of Unions upon human progress. While England presents the battle-field where the guilds have uninterruptedly continued their warfare for centuries, and have done much to establish the sturdy independence of the toilers, France no less illustrates the influence of the spirit of industrialism.

When the first wild cry for the Crusades rang throughout Europe, civilization itself seemed to be in its midnight hour. The downfall of the Roman Empire, the repeated invasions of the Goth, Hun, and Vandal, the growing strength of Moor and Moslem, the constant wars of proud baronial lords, the abject condition of the serfs, the superstitious dread in high and low of all that indicated change, seemed to prophesy the fate of the empires of the East for the future of Europe. But the crusaders built wiser than they knew. As the exigencies of the later day brought emancipation to the black race in the South, so did it then to the serf. For centuries the serf had toiled in the same weary rut worn by his ancestors. Attached to the soil, and sold with it like the oxen he drove before the plough, unable to learn the state to which he belonged, his knowledge of the world was limited to the visible horizon. But in taking up the cross of the Crusade he became a freeman. For two centuries the contest was waged to rescue the Holy Land; and, though the Moslem remained in its possession, the battle was not lost. For during those two centuries there was a constant return of emancipated pilgrims,—men who had seen other lands, other civilizations, strange arts and luxuries of which they were hitherto ignorant. New desires, new wants arose; and in every city of France skilled artisans were called upon to supply them. Within the walled city, the Commune of France, against the rapacity of the feudal baron with his armed retainers were pitted the industrial organizations, whose very existence demanded peaceable conditions. There more than anywhere else was most clearly seen that struggle which characterizes progressive civilization, — on the one side, militant measures, relying upon the past, and, on the other, industrial measures, looking forward to the future. The King possessed but little real authority; but, allying his own cause with that of the artisans in these walled Communes (a strange alliance of king and toiler), the proud baron was over and again defeated, and the feudal tyranny supplanted.

As in earlier history the two opposing systems were slavery and trades-unionism, — the one compulsory servitude, the other voluntary co-operation, — so here we find the guilds strengthening the hands of order in the interest of peace.

Louis IX., Saint Louis as he is termed, in return for the aid thus rendered to the crown, whereby France was enabled to escape from the tyranny and horrors of feudal rule, formally recognized the Unions, and granted them privileges unknown in any other country. In short, it may be confidently asserted that the growth of French nationality, the solidifying of divergent interests, culminating in the Golden Age (as it is termed) of Louis XIV., was due chiefly to the organized artisans of that country. The student of history will not pause to consider whether such an alleged "Golden Age" was a perfect one or not, but he will realize the point I wish to emphasize: that the impetus given by the co-operation of king and guild tended to progress, annihilated feudal disorder, and furthered peaceful evolution.

On the one side, the past was represented by the mailed knight, intent on private revenge or plunder, carrying with him terror and desolation into countless homes: his only productive skill consisted in creating widows and orphans. On the other side, the future loomed up in the form of youthful Industry, to whom liberty and peace were as essential as air to lung-breathing animals. And yet but for organization these efforts would have been fruitless, and chaos and disorder would have remained. It is true that authority finally gained the upper hand, and forgot the debt of obligation due to these humble allies; but in the seed sown a spirit grew which culminated in the French Revolution, and has changed the face of the political and social world.

While this was accomplished by the French artisans through the causes and means mentioned, it must be conceded to the English that they made the most heroic and stubborn fight for industrial liberty. The laws in England for centuries continued so oppressive that even within scarcely more than a century the condition of Scottish miners was really that of serfdom. An author of repute states: "They were obliged to remain in the pit as long as the owner chose to keep them there; and they were actually sold, as part of the capital invested in the work. If they took work elsewhere, their master could always fetch them back, and flogged as thieves for having robbed him of their labor" (*Trant*[2]). The power of the justices to fix wages continued even so late as 1812. In the fourteenth century all organizations of workmen were prohibited as "conspiracies." In fact, less than a hundred years ago, until 1795, no workman could legally travel, in search of employment, out of his own parish. But restrictive laws and enactments to fix wages always end in failure. The day had passed when toilers could patiently submit. As W. T. Thornton[3] tersely says, "Men are seldom collected together in large masses without speedily discovering that union is strength; and men whose daily avocation obliged them to be constantly using, and by use to be constantly sharpening, their wits, were not likely to be backward in making this discovery." As a result of this determined opposition of the British workmen, Trade unions are now legal societies there, with due protection given to their funds, thus becoming constitutionally incorporated as institutions of that country.

To sum up their achievements in a sentence, we may briefly say, that, wherever the people enjoy most liberty, there Trade unions are most formidable. On the contrary, in those countries where long hours prevail, where poverty sits installed at the domestic hearthstone, where want and misery preside over the household economy, and hope is but a barren mockery and a dream, there the Trade union is not. And it is from these lands that our plutocratic adorers of abstract liberty seek to import "hands," numbering them with a tag, to supplant the labor of those whose brawn and muscle have won for them the liberty they delight to praise so vociferously on each recurring Fourth of July.

I have said that in those countries where economic and social misery abound and are the rule Trade unions do not exist. Permit me to add that, as in physical life the germs require natural conditions to their full development, so in the economic struggle for better and more humane conditions of life, the first seeds of discontent must make themselves manifest. In other words, a spirit of greater independence and awakening intelligence is essentially prerequisite to the organization of the Trade-union.

But their methods are revolutionary, we are told. Yes, in a sense they are. To-day, as in the past, unity of action is the result of necessity. Conditions have changed, it is true; but the fight must still be waged, though it be on other grounds. The religious and political issues of the past no longer enter into the contest, but year by year the issue is more clearly seen to be purely an economic one. The workman no longer tolerates religious dissension in his craft guild: to do so would be to thresh past century straw. The devout and undevout meet together, without knowing each other's religious preferences. In the modern Union religion is a matter of conscience, which each must settle for himself, acting upon his own responsibility. But trade matters, questions of wages, hours, working rules (which, by the way, when enforced without or against the voice or consent of the toilers, are more tyrannical and bear worse upon him than all the laws of country or State), and other conditions of labor involve a common interest, and upon these accord is found. Political issues, purely as such, likewise find the Union barren ground for sowing. There has been a steady growing conviction among organized toilers that political aims cannot settle economic demands. In spite of present efforts to unite the toilers of the land, both in factory and farm, upon a platform of political demands, I think I am right in asserting that the Unions—as such— will not be found committing themselves to any such programme. Individual members in large numbers undoubtedly will, but it will be as citizens rather than trade unionists.

And I may be here pardoned for a digression in connection with opposing methods in organizing toilers. One hundred years ago nothing was more common than bitter animosity between trades: battles between the journeymen of one and those of another were of frequent occurrence in the streets of London and Paris. Self-preservation was instinctively felt to be protection of trade privilege. To-day how different is the situation! Increased personal liberty has widened human fellowship; and, in the Federations of Labor here and abroad, the interests of the whole are seen to be best subserved in the welfare of each. In our country the general support given to the carpenters in their struggle for shorter hours is an example,—an instance, which that splendid body of independent toilers will more than cheerfully reciprocate to whichever of their allied brethren will next assume the banner at the front. Nor need we rely on this movement that the carpenters have made or other trades may make, as an example of the solidarity of feeling and concert of action resulting from the separately organized Unions. Every day, in city, town, and village, the same spirit and action are manifested in instances of heroic and temporary self-sacrifice that are made to advance the interests of those working at one trade,—in the hope, yes, the knowledge, that by such assistance the best interests of the entire grand army of labor are promoted.

On the other hand, we are met with a siren song which, promising an "Ideal" (some might say Idealistic) organization, virtually disrupts trade lines and destroys autonomous action, by subordinating independence to obedience to central authority. As Trade Unionists, we know nothing of mixed unions: we ask, in the warfare for greater industrial independence, that each combatant march under his own banner, where united action is final and obligatory upon those who may be selected to lead. In short, we oppose all effort to introduce militant measures issuing from the centre outward, and favor voluntary organization, preserving the autonomy of each trade. In other words we prefer action to promises, deeds to words.

In the half-hour allotted to me it is impossible to present more than a general outline of a subject that is more important in its bearing and influences on human progress than all other questions combined. Yet, at the risk of preventing myself from the opportunity of a better presentation of our cause, I feel it incumbent upon me to briefly refer to the question of strikes.

Generally, the view is held that strikes form the sum total of the efforts and results of the Trade-union movement, when, as a matter of fact, a strike is but one of the manifestations of it. A strike necessarily exhibiting an antagonism, and being a public act, it attracts general attention, and, whether successful in attaining the purpose for which it was inaugurated or otherwise, a judgment is formed: it is praised or condemned according to the result. But should strikes be condemned by thinking people? Together with those who love their fellow-men and who endeavor to aid in the solution of this great labor question, I believe that strikes should be avoided whenever and wherever possible. I ask myself, however, and I ask you, Will denunciation of strikes prevent them? Should the workers suffer their already scant means to be curtailed? Would you advise them to bear all the taskmaster's oppression, his insults and injustices, without protest? Shall the natural desire for improvement in his social and economic condition be curbed upon the only ground that he is a wealth-producer, — a worker? I say, No, — a thousand times No! Rather would we suffer the pangs of hunger for a time, when we are convinced that our temporary pain will give us at least a little relief from the overbearing tyranny, and a better opportunity to help in the struggle for amelioration in the condition and final emancipation of the toiling masses. Thanks to our trades unions, however, through the accumulation of a good fund in our treasuries, we need not enter into a strike as often as we otherwise would be compelled to, in order to resist oppression or secure improved conditions; nor need we suffer the pangs of hunger when engaged in a strike.

Strikes, as I have said, are but one of the manifestations—ay, only the outward manifestations—of the Trades union movement. Inquire from corporations and employers generally. Apply for the information from the Bureaus of Labor Statistics or the Trade unions, and, with strange accord, answers will come that the greatest work is accomplished, and that matters of wages, hours, rules, and other conditions of labor, are secured without resort to strikes. These concessions, wrested from the employing and capitalistic class every day, are ever going on, unheeded and unheralded, and form the great evolutionary force that builds up and develops a sturdy and a nobler manhood.

I have used the word "combatants." Such, indeed, we are, in all that the word implies. Against us we find arrayed a host guarded by special privilege, buttressed by legalized trusts, fed by streams of legalized monopolists, picketed by gangs of legalized "Pinkertons," and having in reserve thousands of embryo employers who, under the name of "Militia," are organized, uniformed, and armed for the sole purpose of holding the discontented in subservient bondage to iniquitous conditions. Already in many States the skirmish lines have met, again illustrating the fundamental fact of all progressive civilization: that the battle formerly drawn between religious and political opponents is, in our time, to be fought to a finish upon purely economic grounds. And in these sporadic skirmishes we again face old foes in new uniforms; the oppressor relying upon militant measures, which differ only in kind from those maintained by his mediaeval prototype, the male baronial lord, — while the oppressed, forced by adverse circumstance to unite for self-protection, calmly present a solid front, and refuse to do their enemies' bidding.

Combatants? Yes, self-defence is ever a virtue, and only such acts as are forced upon us do we accept; but it is a contest in which the Industrial Army knows no surrender. It is needless to dilate upon the time-worn calumny that we are opposing Capital. On the contrary, we only regret that Capital is so hedged in with monopolistic privilege, utilized to oppress, that the toiler is forced into economic subjection to its legalized holders. Trusting to the valiant spirit of the Industrial Army, a spirit born of the everlasting *Zeitgeist,* — the genius of the age, — knowing that we are carrying the standard for which men in all ages have suffered exile, imprisonment, and death by rack and stake and gibbet, — we still press on, holding a higher vantage-ground than ever in the past, and determined to "fight it out on this line" till the last enemy of industrial freedom is routed, and economic emancipation secured to a free and independent people, who, knowing their rights, will dare defend them against lords of either high or low degree.

While mistakes may be made and too often hasty action taken, as is ever the case in great contests, it is not our duty to carry aid and comfort to the enemy by prematurely condemning our overzealous videttes. The struggle, as I have tried to show, is not of to-day only, but the bequest of time; and in taking up the burden laid upon us we should ever, while protecting our present interests, have the glorious vision of the future which even the present organization of the American Federation of Labor but dimly outlines.

Finally, unity of action we have; determination and grit have been manifested; fixity of purpose is our bond of federated union. What more do we require? Nothing but to maintain the same zeal and an intensified earnestness in the knowledge of the justice and ultimate success of our common cause, when

> Each man finds his own in all men's good,
> And all men work in noble brotherhood.

Then, paraphrasing the words of a popular play,

> The World is Ours.

Journal of Social Science 28 (Oct. 1891):40-47.

1. The 1891 convention of the American Social Science Association took place in Saratoga Springs, N.Y., Aug. 31-Sept. 4.

2. William Trant, *Trade Unions, Their Origin and Objects, Influence and Efficacy* (1884; reprint ed., Washington, D.C., 1903), p. 9.

3. William Thomas Thornton was a British civil servant and author who spent most of his career as an administrator of public works in India. The quotation is from his book *On Labour, Its Wrongful Claims and Rightful Dues, Its Actual Present and Possible Future* (2d ed., 1870, p. 172), in which Thornton proposed replacing the adversarial relation of capital and labor with a society based on cooperation.

To Elizabeth Morgan[1]

Sep. 10th. [189]1.

Mrs. T. J. Morgan,
Box 67 Woodlawn Park, Ill.
Dear Madam:—

Your favor of the 6th. inst. enclosing circular came duly to hand, and I assure you I read the contents of both with much pleasure. They evidence sincerity and energy which deserve and I hope will result in success.

You ask me to express an idea as to how best to organize the women wage-workers. To be very frank with you I think that the ideas of organization are about as well shared by you as myself. I think however, that there is one mistake made by a number of people even though they may have the best of intentions. I cannot enter into an amplification of the idea I have in view, but can merely give it an outline.

Most people who start out with the idea of organizing women desire to do it wholesale, and my experience is that while a number of them may be organized, the elements of permanency and success are lacking for the same reason that many organizations fail among men. I believe the same causes in the one operate in the other namely, the failure of the projectors for women's organizations to recognize the absolute necessity of making each Union protective in its character. In other words, that the members of the Union should be required to pay higher dues into the Union, to receive a considerable benefit from it and thus enlist the material interests of the members in the Union; not so much for the sake of this material interest but for the sake of keeping them in the Union. When that is once secured progress can be made in any direction to the interests of labor.

If you can concentrate your efforts in organizing one trade of working women upon such a basis, some tangible result will have been accomplished, and as you know nothing succeeds so well as success it will be the means of inspiring confidence among the women wage-workers in the beneficent effects of organization.

I trust you will believe that I have nothing but the best of motives in making the above suggestion. At any rate you can give it that consideration you think it deserves.

I am very much interested in the matter of the investigation you have made of the sweat shops of your city,[2] and look forward to a perusal of your report with pleasure.

Asking you to write as frequently as convenient, and with earnest good wishes, I am,

Fraternally Yours   Saml Gompers.

TLpS, reel 5, vol. 6, p. 213, SG Letterbooks, DLC.

1. Elizabeth Chambers MORGAN was a founder in 1888 of AFL Ladies' Federal Labor Union 2703 and of the Illinois Women's Alliance.

2. In August 1891 the Trade and Labor Assembly of Chicago established a committee consisting of Michael Madden, Elizabeth Morgan, and Mark J. Mitchell to investigate the clothing industry sweatshops. Morgan wrote the twenty-four-page report the committee issued on Sept. 6 (*The New Slavery: Investigation into the Sweating System as Applied to the Manufacturing of Wearing Apparel*), describing unsanitary, overcrowded working conditions and calling for enforcement of the city's child labor laws and sanitary inspection ordinances.

To James Tillman[1]

Sep. 12th. [189]1.

Mr. J. F. Tillman,
Sec. Supreme Executive Board National Farmer's Alliance and Industrial Union.
239 N. Capital St. Washington, D.C.
Dear Sir:—

Your valued favor of the 5th. inst. notifying me of the Session to be held on the 17th. of Nov. at Indianapolis, Ind.[2] and informing me that you have assigned a part to me for the discussion of the principles connected with the economic reform of your movement came duly to hand.

I am mindful of the great questions you mention and beg to assure you that your movement has my fullest sympathy.

In the organization of the American Federation of Labor however, the President cannot act upon his own responsibility. He is subject at all times to the direction of its conventions and since the subject matter of co-operation with your Alliance has never come before the convention nor has an invitation been received by them for any such purpose, it seems to me that it would be committing the organization to a movement upon which it has not had an opportunity to have a discussion and render a decision. Our affiliated organizations, the great National and International Trade Unions of America are extremely careful that their rights and prerogatives should not be assumed by any person attempting to speak in their names unless they have first been consulted hence I believe you will fully appreciate the position in which I am placed, and I kindly ask you to cancel my name from the assignment of any part you proposed for me at your Nov. session.

Permit me to inform you that the next convention of the American Federation of Labor will take place Dec. 14th. 1891 at Birmingham, Ala. at which time I should be pleased to hear from you or in fact any time previous thereto at this office.

With renewed assurances of my sympathy for your movement, I am,

> Very Respectfully Yours   Saml Gompers.
> President. American Federation of Labor.

TLpS, reel 5, vol. 6, p. 221, SG Letterbooks, DLC.

1. James Fountain Tillman, a Tennessee farmer, was secretary of the Supreme Executive Council of the National Farmers' Alliance and Industrial Union (NFAIU).

2. The Supreme Executive Council of the NFAIU and the Farmers' Mutual Benefit Association met in Indianapolis, Nov. 17-21, 1891.

From August Delabar

Office of the International Secretary
Journeymen Bakers' & Confectioners' International Union of America
New York, Sept 17 1891

Dear Sir & Bro

I would request you to take stepts to have the Birmingham Ala people to Organize the bakers before the next convention else we must all Consum Scab bread, (genuin Scab bread) because all the men formely belongd to our Int Union but left us,[1] if not enough can be induced they should get one or two shops to Join union 17[2] Mobile Ala, i have sent several request to diferent people in B. but no reply. and if nothing is done i shall insist that no delegade is alowd to eat eather bread or cake *pies encluted* give this you etention at once.

Yours Fraternally   Aug Delabar
Int Secy

PS. Sey Evans if G. is already gone please etent to it yourselv Rochester circulare[3] i thing not neeted — our men is got the best of the K of L already

ALS, Journeymen Bakers' and Confectioners' International Union Records, reel 138, *AFL Records.*

1. Journeymen Bakers' National Union 73 operated in Birmingham, Ala., between 1888 and 1890.

2. Journeymen Bakers' and Confectioners' International Union (JBCIU) 17.

3. In September 1891, the bakers of the large firm of Culross Brothers Bakery in Rochester, N.Y., went on strike demanding union wages. The firm hired strikebreakers who organized into a KOL assembly. During September the JBCIU issued 5,000 copies of a circular endorsed by the AFL presenting its side of the difficulty.

To John Kirchner

Sep. 21st. [189]1

Mr. John Kirchner,
2606 Darien St. Phila, Pa.
Dear Friend: —

Your favor came duly to hand and I assure you the perusal of its contents caused me a severe pang. The memory of our many battles both side by side and on opposite sides of the house in the conventions of the Cigarmakers Int. Union being conspicuous parts of them. It would be useless for me to attempt to say anything to you in reference to the influence of our efforts to place the C.M.I.U. upon a sure footing and sound basis, yes and proud position it enjoys to-day. You know it as well as I do and among the many regrets I have for your present misfortune is the one that I shall not have the proud privilege of having you battling side by side with me to raise it a pinnacle higher in the struggle for economic and social progress and emancipation. Probably you more than any one else knows exactly my feelings, thoughts and impulses in the labor movement for I have confided in you when I have refused to utter a word to others. Even the men who now seek to aim their most bitter shafts at me little know how much I have done and am doing to help on the crystallization of that movement and result we hold so dear. Their continued antagonism shall not in the least prevent my best energies being devoted in that direction, if not as President of the American Federation of Labor, then probably as one in the ranks instead of leader of the toilers in the grand army of labor.

I shall miss you very much at the convention but you can depend upon me that I shall endeavor to assuage any feeling that may be manifested against you.

Our friend Mc-Guire informs me that you have kept your promise thus far and made a good impression by your abstinence at the Labor Day[1] demonstration in Phila. I do earnestly hope that you will stand firmly by your excellent resolve and feel confident that your persistence in that course will rally around you a host of friends, in numbers probably unknown to you.

I shall endeavor to comply with the request contained in one of your former letters and asking to be remembered to Mrs. Kirchner,[2] our friends and requesting you to write occasionally, I am,

Your Friend,   Saml Gompers

TLpS, reel 5, vol. 6, p. 235, SG Letterbooks, DLC.

1. It can be argued that the American holiday of Labor Day grew out of a parade and celebration sponsored by the New York City Central Labor Union (CLU) on Sept. 5, 1882. The idea soon spread. In 1884 the FOTLU proposed that a national labor day be celebrated each year on the first Monday in September, and George K. Lloyd of the New York City CLU introduced a resolution on the subject at the 1884 KOL convention; by 1885 several cities had official Labor Day celebrations. In 1887 Oregon became the first state to pass a law establishing the first Monday in September as Labor Day. Other states soon followed suit; the Pennsylvania law dates from 1889. A federal law in 1894 made Labor Day an official holiday for the District of Columbia,

the territories, and for federal workers, which for all practical purposes established it as a national holiday.

2. Maggie B. Kirchner was a dressmaker in Philadelphia.

To William Dillon[1]

Nov. 10th. [189]1

Mr. Wm. J. Dillon,
Sec. American Flint Glass Workers Nat. Union
18 Excelsior Block Pittsburgh, Pa.
Dear Sir and Friend: —

Mr. Chas. F. Reichers[2] Sec. of the United Garment Workers Nat. Union of America[3] called at this office Monday and showed me a letter received from you in reference to the efforts being made to compel Lippman and Sons, as well as Todd, Sullivan and Baldwin to make no discrimination against trade unionists.[4]

I have written heretofore as to what I regard to be right in the matter of the action necessary to be taken to bring these two firms to their senses and fair dealing towards the Garment Workers, and I only desire to add in connection with the same matter that the Knights of Labor are dependent upon the co-operation of Trade Unions to boycott Trade Union workmen, and if left to their own resources will soon be compelled to give up their war upon the trade unions.

In that letter however, you refer to matters which vitally interest me, namely that an officer of 231 K. of L.[5] has said that the United Garment Workers of America procured their charter from this office through fraudulent means. I appreciate the fact that you declared your disbelief in any such statement, and I beg to assure you that there is no foundation for it in fact.

A convention of the United Garment Workers was held from the 12th to the 18th. of April 1891.[6] There were fifty-four (54) delegates in attendance. Mr. Chris. Evans, Secretary of the Federation attended there as a representative of the Federation, and Mr. John B. Lennon, Sec. of the Journeymen Tailors Nat. Union of America[7] was in almost constant attendance, and being one vitally interested he should know. Upon the close of their convention (Apr. 18th.) they applied to this office for a charter. I communicated with the Sec. of the Journeymen Tailors Nat. Union and received his consent to the issuance of the charter which was issued May 4th. I believe you will see from this that due care was exercised and that the attempt by the K. of L. men to even question the validity of the issuance of the charter is only intended to discredit a bona fide Trade Union in the eyes of trade unionists. This in itself ought to be sufficient evidence of the maliciousness and untrustworthiness of the statements emanating from these people.

You say further that they claim to have forwarded papers to this office leaving the entire matter of dispute in the hands of the Executive Council of the A.F. of L. for [decision?]. This is in keeping with their other statements. There is not a [word?] of truth in it.

Will you kindly show this letter to Mr. Carney when you get a chance. It may serve to give him some information upon the same rumors which may have reached his ears, in connection with the United Garment Workers.

With kindest wishes for the prosperity of our movement and hoping to hear from you at your earliest convenience, I am,

Fraternally Yours　Saml Gompers.

President. American Federation of Labor.

TLpS, reel 5, vol. 6, pp. 433-34, SG Letterbooks, DLC.

1. William J. DILLON was secretary of the American Flint Glass Workers' Union of North America from 1886 to 1893.

2. Charles F. REICHERS of New York City was one of the founders in 1891 of the United Garment Workers of America (UGWA) and served as its general secretary (1891-95) and president (1895-96).

3. The United GARMENT Workers of America.

4. In the early months of 1891, the KOL boycotted the New York City garment firm of Todd, Sullivan, and Baldwin in a successful attempt to exclude trade unionists affiliated with the AFL. During the year the KOL secured similar exclusive jurisdiction at L. Lippmann and Sons. One of the first actions of the newly formed UGWA was to boycott both firms. Prior to the AFL convention in December 1891, Todd, Sullivan, and Baldwin signed an agreement to employ an equal number of workers from each of the contending labor organizations. The AFL convention endorsed a boycott against L. Lippmann and Sons, and that firm signed a similar agreement on Jan. 30, 1892.

5. KOL Garment Cutters' National Trade Assembly 231 organized in 1888.

6. The convention was held Apr. 12-15 in New York City.

7. The Journeymen TAILORS' Union of America.

To Dora Sullivan[1]

Nov. 10th. [189]1.

Miss Dora Sullivan,
Genl. Organizer A.F. of L.
87 Hoosick St. Troy, N.Y.
Dear Sister:—

Your favor of the 8th. inst. including application for the charter for the Collar, Cuff and Shirt Starchers Union No. 5588[2] of your city came duly to hand, and the document has been issued and mailed to your address, the receipt and letter of notification having been forwarded to Miss Margaret English,[3] the Secretary of the Union.

In issuing the charter to the Union I do so with some apprehension for I have usually found it impractical to issue charters to unions in the midst of any struggle that they may be engaged in. In departing from this rule I do so more to express my sympathy with the girls in their strike,[4] and I kindly ask you to impress that fact upon their minds when you install their Union. That they may win is my earnest wish.

It appears that the movement is not based upon ignorance to crush out the machine, but to protest against the machine being used to crush out the lives of the girls, and in this position all fair-minded people must accede that you are right.

In forwarding me the name of manufacturers and the brands that they manufacture, it would also be advisable to give some kind of a list of their jobbers and those doing a direct business with them.

I kindly ask you to install the Union at your earliest convenience after the receipt of this notification, and with kind wishes for the movement and the success of the Union, I am,

Fraternally Yours   Saml Gompers.
President. American Federation of Labor.

TLpS, reel 5, vol. 6, p. 436, SG Letterbooks, DLC.

1. Dora Sullivan, president of AFL Collar, Cuff, and Shirt Starchers' Union (CCSSU) 5577 of Troy, N.Y., became an AFL general organizer in 1891.

2. Actually 5577.

3. Margaret English was the secretary of CCSSU 5577.

4. On Nov. 2, 1891, women organized in CCSSU 5577 and employed by Miller, Hall, and Hartwell of Troy, N.Y., struck against 50 to 60 percent reductions in wages accompanying the introduction of the McKay Starching Machine. The 1891 AFL convention in Birmingham, Ala., placed a boycott on the products of the firm. The strike spread to two other Troy companies in January 1892, and in February the New York State Board of Mediation and Arbitration began investigating the dispute. The board dropped its investigation after the manufacturers successfully introduced strikebreakers.

The New York City Central Labor Federation to the Workingmen of New York

New York, Nov. 14, 1891.

IN REPLY TO GOMPERS.

Fellow Workingmen:—

You all know that Samuel Gompers has for more than a year been engaged in desperate attempts to destroy the Central Labor Federation of New York, even at the risk of developing antagonisms calculated to imperil the existences of local and national unions.

You all know the motives and object of that unscrupulous schemer. The organizations represented in this body had nipped in the bud his aspirations to political self-aggrandizement as the candidate of a boodle party. When he came to beg their indorsement of his nomination for the New York Senate by a Democratic faction of this city, they plainly told him that while they considered political action of an independent labor character the necessary complement of economic organization, they held that no man elevated by his fellow wage workers to the high post of duty which he, Gompers, chanced to occupy, should thus prostitute it to the old corrupt political parties under any pretext whatever. But when they emphasized their position by officially recognizing the only labor party in existence and admitting its delegates to seats in their central body, this contemptible office-seeker, reeking all over with the filth of boodle politics, retaliated by refusing that body a charter of the A.F. of L., for the reason, sufficiently ludicrous on his tongue, that no politics of any sort should be allowed in trade unions.

The Detroit Convention followed. You all know its outcome and effect. Although sustained by a majority which had been previously instructed by constituents industriously prejudiced against the C.L.F. and the S.L.P., Gompers found himself there antagonized by an imposing minority. And when he returned to New York, he found himself practically alone among the organized wage workers of his own city, that he but opposed and slandered at Detroit. He, President of the American Federation of Labor, had become here a pompous nonentity, unable to cut any figure in the labor movement of the American metropolis.

It must be granted that the position in which Gompers had placed himself was not only uncomfortable but intolerable. It was a position in which he could not decently face another convention of the American Federation of Labor, especially after his tremendous fiasco in the eight hour movement of the miners. How to extricate himself by obtaining here a following at any cost, naturally became his constant preoccupation, and the resources of intrigue that an unscrupulous politician can summon in desperate straits were drawn upon to the fullest extent of the means afforded by his high office.

First of all he undertook, with some success, to play the Conservatives and the Anarchists against the Socialists. His chief agent in the execution of this plan was a certain Henry Weissmann,[1] recently imported from the Pacific Coast, that his experience as a sand lot demagogue, and his opportunities as the newly appointed editor of the Bakers' Journal, fitted admirably for the disgusting task assigned to him. In the hands of Weissmann, the General Secretary of the Bakers' Union[2] proved a man of very soft paste, that could be worked out of his then Socialistic crust into some indefinite "pure and simple" trade unionist, and then finally hardened by strong heat into an enemy of the party that had repeatedly trusted and honored him. The wonderful somersault of August Delabar, under the whip of Weissmann, is sufficiently described in the circular recently issued by Bakers' Union No. 93,[3] and need not be here the subject of further comment.

Encouraged by this first defection, Gompers' next step was the formation of a third central body; a scheme which he had already concocted previous to the Detroit Convention, but which he then strenuously denied having originated or even entertained, when called upon for explanation in a committee of that convention. This new central body, which its founders grandiloquently baptized the New York Federation of Labor,[4] was first composed of the few bakers' unions that Weissmann and Delabar had under their thumbs, in addition to Gompers' own Cigarmakers' Union No. 144.

In order to give it an appearance of numerical strength, several disbanded organizations, existing only on paper—such as the Shoemakers[5] of Simon Gompers[6] and the Paperhangers No. 182[7]—besides the Clothing Cutters,[8] that Harry White[9] assumed to represent without authority, were immediately admitted. In that shape it promptly received from Gompers a charter of the A.F. of L.

Of course, such a "central body," so manifestly intended as a wedge for splitting the Central Labor Federation, could not be recognized by us as a bona fide organization. While a few honest unions had been drawn into it by misrepresentation or prejudice, it was plainly under the control of men intent upon ruling or ruining the labor movement in New York city—men ready to do any amount of union wrecking that might be required for the accomplishment of their selfish, personal ends.

Had there been any possible doubt of this, the next event in the evolution of the conspiracy would have exposed it in its ugly nudity.

Weissman and Delabar had used all their rope among the bakers. Now came Kurzenknabe, general Secretary of the Brewers' National Union.

This Kurzenknabe is neither a socialist, nor an anarchist, nor a trade unionist. He is Kurzenknabe pure and simple, for Kurzenknabe first, last and all the time. With hands strengthened by the boycott upon the pool breweries, which the United Central Labor Federations alone enforced in New York, Brooklyn and Hudson Co., he held by the throat the journeymen employed in union establishments, where he was recognized by bosses and foremen as the mighty being into whose hands the United Federations and the S.L.P. were supposed to have unreservedly placed their power. Fear of incurring his displeasure kept most of the poor wage working brewers in abject submission and but few dared to oppose or even discuss in their union any act or proposition stamped with the mark of his approval. Repeatedly he had been urged to use his opportunities for strenthening the kindred organizations of beer drivers, firemen and engineers, but all in vain. On the contrary, by his order the officers of Union No. 1,[10] for instance, declared the Greenville brewery a union concern, although none of the workmen employed there, with the exception of the "inside hands," were organized, and although the act of recognition was an usurpation, by the local officers, of powers that belonged to the local executive. The Brooklyn Central Labor Federation remonstrated, as it had an unquestionable right to do. For the protection of trades affiliated with it and entitled to its consideration, it resolved that the brewers should enter with the bosses into no contract without first submitting its contents. But although both the local and the national executives of the brewers took a similar stand, Kurzenknabe sustained the action of Union No. 1 in the Brewers' Journal and denounced the resolution of the Brooklyn C.L.F. as "a machination of certain leaders."

Similar was the case of the Grawer's Brewery, which the Brooklyn C.L.F. refused to recognize because scab carpenters were employed there. Kurzenknabe and his man Huber[11] called this "fanaticism." The latter tried to put through a resolution against the C.L.F., and although no final vote was taken upon it he published it as "adopted."

Such acts of scabism speak for themselves. We might indefinitely extend the list of injuries done to organized labor by this lazy despot, Kurzenknabe, whose apathy proved a stumbling block at every step in any effort made by the friends of the journeymen brewers to regain for their trade the high standing which it once held in this city. His conduct had aroused indignation and he began to fear that he might not be re-elected General Secretary. Gompers saw his opportunity, and tendered his aid on certain conditions. Kurzenknabe was to stab the Central Labor Federations—the only friends of the brewers—by getting the National Executive Board of his organization to recognize the "third central body," upon the ground that the body in question held a charter of the American Federation of Labor.

Having accomplished this feat, Kurzenknabe turned to Brewers' Union No. 1 and demanded from it a similar recognition. There he met with a stronger opposition than he had expected. A minority of clear-sighted men, among whom were the delegates of the union to the New York C.L.F., and numbering most of those who had displayed activity in the organization of the brewers, exposed and denounced in fit terms the dastardly scheme of Gompers and his tool. Kurzenknabe retorted in his usual way. He forced the recognition through by intimidating the less independent majority and threatened his opponents with expulsion. Not content with words he intrigued with the bosses to obtain, under pain of dismissal from the breweries where they were employed, the abject submission of the men who had shown that they dared to have an opinion of their own.

The New York C.L.F. was in duty bound to protect those men. To let Kurzenknabe wreak his vengeance upon them, to let him turn them—good and tried union workers as they were—into scabs or tramps, would have been the height of cowardice and infamy. But it desired also, above all things, to prevent the split among the brewers, which the union-wrecking process of its enemies seemed to render inevitable. And so, when the faithful men of Union No. 1, in order to avoid expulsion, formed a union of their own,[12] the C.L.F. admitted them to representation, but instructed them to apply for a charter of their national organization. In the meantime it notified their bosses that their dismissal would be resented by the only bodies of organized labor to which union breweries were indebted for the enforcement of the boycott upon pool beer; not that the raising of this boycott was ever contemplated—as Gompers lyingly proclaims in his circular[13]—but that a boycott might be placed upon any of the breweries which would dismiss good union men at the dictation of Kurzenknabe:

Fellow Workingmen:—We have placed before you, as briefly as we could, the facts in the pending conflict between an old corrupt trade-unionism, so-called, as represented by Gompers and his satellites, and the New Trade Unionism of America as represented by the United Central Labor Federations—a trade unionism in which the economic and political forces of labor shall be united into one honest movement for the emancipation of the working class.

Gompers' "policy"—if such may be called the intricate web of an unprincipled and egotistic schemer, pandering to ignorance for the sake of position—can deceive no one whose sense of right is not blunted by corruption or obscured by prejudice.

What he will now do is self-evident.

He will go next month before the Birmingham Convention of the American Federation of Labor with the monstrous claim, which no one on the floor of that convention may be sufficiently informed to effectually dispute, that the New York C.L.F. has of itself gone to pieces; that its disruption was brought about by the admission therein of the Socialist Labor party, to which he objected so wisely last year and the fatal consequences of which he predicted with the inspiration of a Jeremiah; that from its ruins emerged a bona fide central body, with a charter of the A.F. of L. and originated by the very organizations (Bakers and Brewers) which last year had been most blinded by designing individuals—Socialist politicians, enemies of organized labor, union wreckers, etc. — but which had since then perceived the wisdom, the statesmanship, the unselfishness of his course. He will then demand, "In the interest of harmony," that an end be put to the machinations of the "Socialist rascals"—who still keep up a show of resistance as if they never knew when they were beaten—by ordering every union affiliated with the A.F. of L. to sever its connection with the C.L.F. and to enter the new central body.

It is superfluous to say that in such a body "no politics of any sort" will be permitted. "Pure and simple trade unionism"—with its narrow view of the mighty conflict between Capital and Labor, its daily fights for a little more bread, its small victories and its great defeats, and especially with its fundamental principle of liberty, that it is the sacred right of every union man to become a political scab on election day—is "good enough" for the workingmen.

The Central Labor Federation.

People (New York), Nov. 15, 1891.

1. Henry WEISMANN was editor of the *Bakers' Journal* and the *Deutsch-Amerikanische Bäcker-Zeitung*, the organs of the Journeymen Bakers' and Confectioners' International Union of America (JBCIU), from 1891 to 1895, and was editor of the combined dual-language *Bakers' Journal and Deutsch-Amerikanische Bäcker-Zeitung* and international secretary of the JBCIU from 1895 to 1897.

2. August Delabar.

3. The circular, issued by JBCIU 93 of New York City, was published in the Oct. 11, 1891, issue of the *People*. It supported a proposal to fire Henry Weismann as editor

of the JBCIU journals because of his campaign against the SLP and the New York City Central Labor Federation.

4. The New York (City) Federation of Labor (NYFL) was organized in August 1891 by several New York City unions including United Garment Workers of America (UGWA) 4, CMIU 144, German-American Typographia 7, and JBCIU 7, with the object of unifying labor in the city independent of party politics. It received a charter from the AFL in September 1891. In July 1892 organizations affiliated with the NYFL and the New York City Central Labor Union united in a new Central Labor Union with a platform that excluded party politics.

5. Probably local 117 of the Boot and Shoe Workers' International Union.

6. Simon GOMPERS, SG's uncle, was a shoemaker.

7. Brotherhood of Painters' and Decorators' Union of America 182 of New York City.

8. The New York City Clothing Cutters' Union, local 4 of the UGWA.

9. Henry WHITE was secretary (1891-92) of the NYFL. He was a founder in 1891 of the UGWA and an active member of the New York Clothing Cutters' Union that became UGWA 4.

10. National Union of the United Brewery Workmen of the United States (NUUBW) 1 of New York City.

11. Jacob Huber was secretary of the NUUBW 1.

12. The Journeymen Brewers' Union of New York.

13. A reference to SG's circular to the Trade Unions of New York, Nov. 6, 1891 (reel 5, vol. 6, pp. 420-21, SG Letterbooks, DLC).

To Abraham Spring

Nov. 20th. [189]1

Mr. Abraham Spring,
2006 6th. St. Seattle, Wash.
Dear Sir and Friend: —

I am in receipt of your favor of the 12th. inst. enclosing copy for the article[1] which I requested. Thus far I have been unable to read it carefully but from a casual glance at various parts am satisfied that it is an excellent and an able document. As soon as printed a few copies shall be forwarded to you.

I assure you that it will afford me extreme pleasure to continue our correspondence for there is nothing that suits me better than to either learn the views of others or to give my views to them upon the important subjects bearing upon our great movement. For that reason I kindly ask you to write often.

You ask me to advise you upon the feasibility of your sending on your plan for restricting immigration. I desire to say in reply that I shall esteem myself under obligations to you if you will do so. I promise you that the matter will receive due consideration. You can have time to write it, and if you can send it so that it will reach here by the 10th. inst. it will reach me before I leave for Birmingham. If you cannot send it in that time then direct it to Samuel Gompers Florence Hotel Birmingham, Ala.

In my report I shall make mention of the immigration question and if you have a plan for the restriction, or as you put it "sifting" it, it may go a far way in helping us out. My only suggestion to you upon the subject is to be as brief and concise as possible.

You speak of your lack of education and determination to improve. Of course you will give me credit for not being a flatterer, but you know that there are many in our ranks uneducated who can teach the "educated" very much that they lack in essentials. It is the advantages of schooling which so many of us lack. We have been educated in the hard school of practical life.

Sincerely hoping that you will send on the plan and that at any rate you will write, and with kindest wishes, I am,

Yours Truly   Saml Gompers.
President. American Federation of Labor.

Remember me kindly to Mr. Frincke[2] and to our other friends in [Seattle?].

S. G.

TLpS, reel 5, vol. 6, p. 458, SG Letterbooks, DLC.

1. Spring prepared a memorial to the U.S. Senate suggesting legislation to restrict the immigration of criminals and paupers. The memorial was presented to the Senate and printed in 1892 (U.S. Congress, Senate, Misc. Docs., no. 176, 52d Cong., 1st sess., 1891, vol. 5).

2. John W. Frinke, president of the Northwest Cigar Co., was a member of the welcoming committee of the Western Central Labor Union, which organized Gompers' stay in Seattle in March 1891.

To the Editor of the
Pittsburgh Commercial Gazette

Nov. 21st. [189]1.

Editor Commercial Gazette.
Pittsburgh, Pa.
Dear Sir:—

For some time past you have been publishing articles in reference to me, which I cannot pride myself upon their complimentary statements or allusions; however, since they express your opinions or possibly the opinions of others, I regard them in the nature of criticism and consider that entirely proper. In fact criticism favorable or otherwise, is something I always court.

In your issue of the 20th. however, you make a statement which is not criticism but an assertion and that assertion is not true.[1]

You say that I am "now industriously canvassing my (his) chances for re-election." This may be a small matter to you but it is not so to me. We all have our vulnerable spot, that is mine.

It has always been one of my proud moments to reflect upon the fact that never in my life have I, either directly or indirectly, written or verbally, requested or hinted to any one to nominate, or appoint to or to vote for me for any office, in or outside the labor organizations. I am not, nor is anyone else, making a canvass for votes for my re-election; nor even my "chances for re-election."

Should you publish any more harsh things about me or discover any more defects in me which would disqualify me for the presidency of the American Federation of Labor, please don't say that I am canvassing or will canvass for votes, for it is not and will not be true.

Very Respectfully Yours   Saml Gompers.

TLpS, reel 5, vol. 6, p. 471, SG Letterbooks, DLC.

1. "To Succeed Gompers," *Pittsburgh Commercial Gazette*, Nov. 20, 1891.

An Article in the *Washington Post*

[November 25, 1891.]

APPEAL FOR MUTINEERS

A forgotten story of crime, a mutiny at sea, involving murder, was revived yesterday by a delegation of labor union officials who called upon the President[1] to ask the pardon of two American seamen who for seventeen years have suffered the penalty of their rashness.

In May, 1875, E. W. Clark and George Miller killed Conredon E. Peterson,[2] mate of the schooner Jefferson Borden,[3] and have lain forgotten in prison at Tomlinson, Me., until the Seamen's Union[4] took up their case at the Detroit meeting last year and enlisted other powerful organizations in their behalf.

The Jefferson Borden was a schooner of 600 tons burden in the carrying trade, which sailed from New Orleans for Liverpool in May, 1875, with a cargo of produce. Her captain, William E. Peterson, had gained such a hard name for his ill-treatment of his men that it was only by employing subterfuges he could induce a crew to enlist. Before this voyage he had disguised his schooner by repainting her and decorating her with a new name. By these means he was able to ship a crew of four men, who discovered after they were out from land that they had been deceived in the amount of sail carried by the craft through the captain's next scheme of taking in his jibboom and not displaying it until out at sea. Every sailor knows that a schooner of 600 tons, bearing full sail, cannot be handily manned by a crew of four men before the mast.

In the best of weather the crew would have been overworked, but on this voyage severe gales were encountered almost from the first day out. To add to the discomfort of his men, the captain had a habit of knocking them about with belaying pins and other articles of nautical furniture, and on the slightest provocation would flog them with the "ninetails" or inflict that exquisite torture of stringing up by the thumbs. In addition to working all day and night and being knocked about the deck, the men received no food but the poorest quality known to the service, which would be entirely uneatable from a landsman's point of view. The schooner was unseaworthy, and barely weathered the gales of the first week. Salt water leaked into the water tanks, making the supply for drinking and cooking purposes unfit for use.

Maddened by their hardships, Clark and Miller formed a mutinous conspiracy with a third member of the crew, John Glew, a British sailor, and one morning attacked the officers on deck, intending to seize the ship and sail for the nearest port for water. In the melee some one hit the mate, Conredon Peterson, who was the captain's brother, with a belaying pin on the head, killing him almost instantly. The captain retreated to his cabin and from the window laid out each of the three mutineers upon the deck with wounds from his revolvers. None of them was killed, but all were so badly injured that they were put in irons by the captain and the single sailor who stood by him, and, after treatment in a London hospital, brought to Boston, where they were turned over to the United States authorities for trial on the charges of mutiny and murder. The three men were convicted, and the two Americans sentenced to be hanged, the sentence being remitted afterward to twenty years' imprisonment. The Briton got off with a ten years' sentence through the efforts of the English consul, who had interested his government in the case and secured the ablest lawyers to be had for the man's defense.

Samuel Gompers, of New York, president of the American Federation of Labor, acted as spokesman for the delegation, which was received by President Harrison at 10 o'clock yesterday morning. A previous interview with the President, which had been arranged months ago, was given up on account of the funeral of Secretary Windom,[5] which occurred on the date appointed for the interview. In his speech Mr. Gompers dwelt particularly on the many extenuating circumstances of the affair, and laid stress upon the fact that at the time of the trial the law debarred the men arraigned from testifying in their own behalf, and the only evidence introduced at the trial were the biased statements of Capt. Peterson and his wife, who was aboard the schooner.

The President received the delegation informally standing, with one foot on a chair and his hands in his trousers pockets. He spoke of the crime of piracy, which was usually of necessity attended with murder, as one of the darkest known to civilization, but promised to consider the case carefully with all its mitigating circumstances after it has passed through the routine of reference to the Attorney General and the district attorney and judge of the district in which the trial was held. The delegates were pleased with their interview, and with the President's genial manner. Coming out they stood on the walk and watched Secretary Blaine[6] with great interest as he walked briskly across to the State Department with a roll of papers under his arm.

The gentlemen composing the delegation were: Samuel Gompers, president of the American Federation of Labor; John F. O'Sullivan,[7] of Boston, president of the Seamen's Union; J. L. Kennedy,[8] president of the Columbia Typographical Union; and W. E. Shields,[9] S. J. Gompers,[10] F. H. Padgett,[11] of the same organization; John Lomax[12] and Gabriel Edmonston,[13] of the Carpenters' Brotherhood; J. T. Elliott, of Baltimore, secretary of the Brotherhood of Painters; and J. B. Schofield,[14] of the Plate Printers' Union.[15]

Washington Post, Nov. 25, 1891.

1. Benjamin Harrison.

2. Corydon Trask Patterson was the first mate on the *Jefferson Borden* and the brother of the ship's captain, William M. Patterson.

3. Ephraim W. Clark was one of three seamen who mutinied on Apr. 20, 1875, on board the *Jefferson Borden,* a cargo ship en route from New Orleans to London. Another American, George Miller, and a British seaman, John Clew, also participated in the mutiny, in which the first and second mates lost their lives. The mutineers contended that harsh conditions and the cruelty of Captain William M. Patterson provoked their unpremeditated actions. At their trial in Boston in October 1875 Miller and Clark were convicted of murder and sentenced to hang. Clew was tried for mutiny and sentenced to ten years imprisonment. The case attracted popular attention and sympathy in New England and a campaign began to save Clark and Miller. On Dec. 1, 1875, President Ulysses S. Grant commuted their sentence to life

imprisonment at Maine State Prison in Thomaston. At the AFL's 1890 convention the International Amalgamated Sailors' and Firemen's Union introduced a resolution calling upon the Federation to lead a campaign to secure a pardon. Over the subsequent years the AFL worked for the mutineers' release. Citing the case as an example of the harsh conditions endured by seamen and the unfairness of maritime law, SG wrote to members of Congress asking for their assistance. The Federation also circulated petitions urging a pardon. SG met with President Benjamin Harrison on Nov. 24, 1891, and Mar. 23, 1892, appealing unsuccessfully for executive clemency. In 1894 President Grover Cleveland also refused to pardon the seamen. Miller died in prison Dec. 1, 1894. On Nov. 18, 1903, President Theodore Roosevelt commuted Clark's sentence to expire on Nov. 20.

4. The International Amalgamated SAILORS' and Firemen's Union.

5. William Windom (1827-91), a Republican congressman (1859-69) and senator (1870-81, 1881-83) from Minnesota, served twice as secretary of the treasury (1881, 1889-91).

6. James G. Blaine, the secretary of state.

7. John F. O'SULLIVAN, a reporter and labor editor for the *Boston Globe*, was president (1891-1902) of the Atlantic Coast Seamen's Union.

8. John L. Kennedy, a Washington, D.C., printer, served as president of International Typographical Union (ITU) 101 (the Columbia Typographical Union) from 1890 to 1891.

9. William E. Shields, a Washington, D.C., printer, was active in ITU 101.

10. Samuel Julian GOMPERS, son of Samuel Gompers, moved to Washington, D.C., about 1887 where he worked as a printer, compositor, and clerk.

11. Frank H. Padgett, a Washington, D.C., printer, served as corresponding and recording secretary of ITU 101 from 1888 to 1895.

12. Probably Essex L. Lomax, a member of United Brotherhood of Carpenters and Joiners of America 531 of Washington, D.C.

13. Gabriel EDMONSTON was a founder and the first president of the Brotherhood of Carpenters and Joiners of America (1881-82) and from 1886 to 1888 served as treasurer of the AFL.

14. Probably Andrew B. Schofield, a Washington, D.C., plate printer.

15. Probably Plate Printers' Protective Union 5041 of Washington, D.C., an AFL affiliate.

To Friedrich Sorge[1]

Nov. 27th. [189]1.

Mr. F. A. Sorge,
Hoboken, N.J.
Dear Sir: —

Your kind favor of the 24th. inst. came duly to hand and replying thereto desire to say that I appreciate the promptness of your acknowledgment of the receipt of my letter and documents.

There is no necessity for undue haste in the return of the bound book. Any time before the 1st. of January will do; as that date is the end of my term of office and probably will be the induction of another into it, and if this should be so I would like to turn over all matters to my successor.

I am obliged to you for the promise to send me a copy of the article when published. Although it is difficult for me to read German script I read the print very readily. It is not only the personal interest that I take in the article you will write but opportunity may present itself for a translation and publication of the article in English.

Referring to my request for a visit and your explanation of the circumstances which prevent you from complying ought to have occurred to me before I had written. Permit me to say that at the first opportunity that presents itself I shall avail myself of your kind invitation and call upon you, and bring a copy of the letter I wrote to Mr. Engels.[2] I beg to assure you that I appreciate your kindness in writing to him for an explanation of his failure to acknowledge the receipt or reply to my letter.[3] For years and years I have honored the man and know his devotion to the cause of labor. An opinion from him would have had large weight with me and an expression of it would no doubt have had some influence in determining the action of the Socialist Party, particularly in New York. They are now in such desperate straits that they organize opposition Unions to those in existence and declare boycotts on the product of bona fide Trade Unions.

I anticipated what your answer would be on the question of the Socialist Party being represented, as a party, in the conventions of the Trade Unions. In my judgment no man who thinks soundly and clearly and who has any conception of the labor movement can consistently take any other course, and I would have been untrue to the trust reposed in me and false to my convictions were I not to have taken the stand I did.

Assuring you of my kindest wishes for good health, I am,

Sincerely Yours   Saml Gompers.
President. American Federation of Labor.

TLpS, reel 5, vol. 6, pp. 490-91, SG Letterbooks, DLC.

1. Friedrich Adolph SORGE, former general secretary (1872-74) of the International Workingmen's Association, worked in Hoboken, N.J., as a music teacher.

2. See "To Friedrich Engels," Jan. 9, 1891, above.

3. Engels wrote to Sorge on Jan. 6, 1892: "The story about Gompers is *as follows:* He wrote me and sent me detailed papers of his organization. I was out of town a

great deal at the time—in summer—and tremendously busy in-between. Nor was I at all clear about the matter; I thought *Iliacos extra peccatur muros et intra* [They sin inside and outside the Trojan walls]. Then it was said that Gompers would come to Brussels or over here, and so I thought I would settle the matter orally. Afterward, when he *didn't* come, I forgot about the matter. But I shall look up the documents and write him that I decline the role with thanks" (Karl Marx and Frederick Engels, *Letters to Americans, 1848-1895: A Selection*, ed. Alexander Trachtenberg [1953; reprint ed., New York, 1969], p. 240; brackets in Trachtenberg).

To Bernard Dugan[1]

Dec. 2nd. [189]1.

Mr. B. J. [Dugan]
696 Main St. Poughkeepsie, N.Y.
Dear Sir and Brother:—

Your favor of the 29th. inst. came duly to hand and contents noted.

The supplies you ordered have already been forwarded you as well as a receipt for $4.50 which you sent in payment for the same.

Replying to your question permit me to say that in my judgment it would be a mistake to start a Bro'd of Shirt Ironers as distinct from the Laundry Workers excluding the women workers. You must bear in mind the fact that employers of labor care very little whether the workers in a certain industry are men or women. What they are after, particularly is to get their work done cheap and unless you make friends of your women co-workers you will make enemies of them; and both antagonistic to each other you will be playing into the hands of your employers.

I would be pleased to aid you all in my power to form a National Union of Shirt Ironers and Laundry Workers, but it would be idle and fruitless in any direction that would exclude women workers.

Hoping you will give this matter your serious attention and that the subject matter will be discussed in the light indicated and that I may hear from you frequently, I am,

Fraternally Yours   Saml Gompers.

TLpS, reel 5, vol. 6, p. 523, SG Letterbooks, DLC.

1. Bernard J. Dugan was a Poughkeepsie ironer.

To Joseph Barondess[1]

Dec. 4th. [189]1.

Mr. Jos. Barondess
Toombs Prison City.
Dear Sir and Friend: —

Your favor of the 3rd. inst. came duly to hand and contents noted.

In reply permit me to say that the reasons you give for declining my efforts in your behalf may seem tangible to you, and if so they certainly are binding upon me. For your very kind and appreciative words in reference to my humble efforts in your behalf please accept my sincere gratitude. I have always preferred to do a kind act, rather than make all boasts as some do and whom you so thoroughly well describe in your letter.

When I called upon you in the Toombs you mentioned the names of certain persons who were hunting you down and acting as spies and detectives watching your every movement. I shall be under obligations to you if you will repeat them and also state to what associations of labor they belong, if any. They have slipped my memory, and I will appreciate it very much if you will give the desired information in reply to this.

I regret very much to learn that your family is suffering, and would be only too happy to do something for their relief if in my power. I await your suggestion in reference to it.

I suppose you are aware that the convention of the American Federation of Labor takes place on the 14th. inst. You can readily understand how busy I am in preparing my annual report which must be in the hands of the printer three or four days before I leave and that it takes nearly two days to travel to Birmingham, and also that we have an Executive Council meeting on the 13th. inst. in that city, hence I am not sure that I shall be able to call upon you before I leave, but shall try. If it is impossible, I shall call upon you immediately after my return to the city. I kindly ask you however, to bear up. You have right on your side; You have the courage to declare it, and I extend to you the best wishes and sincere consideration of

Yours Fraternally   Saml Gompers.
President. American Federation of Labor.

TLpS, reel 5, vol. 6, p. 527, SG Letterbooks, DLC.

1. Joseph BARONDESS was an organizer in 1890 of Operators' and Cloakmakers' Union 1. He was found guilty in May 1891 of accepting a $100 check from a firm as part of a strike settlement, despite his contention that he did not intend to use the money personally. The court sentenced him to twenty-one months in prison.

To Frederick Carr[1]

Dec. 8th. [189]1.

Mr. Fred J. Carr,
Sec. Central Labor Union[2]
Room 20 Drummond Block Toledo, O.
Dear Sir and Brother: —

Your favor of the 4th. inst. came duly to hand and contents noted.

Replying thereto permit me to say that your conception of the constitutional provision is perfectly correct, but if the Union in question will declare that they will endeavor to induce the Int. Association of Machinists to eliminate the clause in their constitution which maintains the color line, under these circumstances and upon application of your C.L.U. a charter will be issued to their organization. I think that that position ought to be taken by all working men.

Wage-workers like many others may not care to socially meet colored people, but as working men we are not justified in refusing them the right of the opportunity to organize for their common protection. Then again, if organizations do, we will only make enemies of them, and of necessity they will be antagonistic to our interests.

When I paid a visit to the last convention of that organization[3] held at Pittsburgh, a declaration was made that in all probability at their next convention action in the direction herein indicated will be taken, and I hope that it soon will be so that that organization may also be allied with the trade unions of this country under the banner of the American Federation of Labor.

The dues of the Central Labor Unions to the A.F. of L. is $25.00 per annum payable quarterly.

With sincere good wishes and hopes to hear from you soon and frequently, I am,

Fraternally Yours   Saml Gompers.
President. American Federation of Labor.

TLpS, reel 5, vol. 6, p. 536, SG Letterbooks, DLC.

1. Frederick J. Carr was a Toledo, Ohio, metal polisher.

2. The Central Labor Union of Toledo and Vicinity organized in 1881.

3. The third convention of the International Association of Machinists was held May 4-8, 1891.

Excerpts from News Accounts of the
1891 Convention of the AFL in Birmingham

[December 16, 1891]

LABOR'S COUNCIL

. . .

. . . Delegate Williams,[1] Pittsburg, obtained permission to address the convention on the subject of the long strike of printers at Pittsburg,[2] explaining that the strikers had spent $20,000. The delegate went into the details of the strike, telling how it was conducted. The leaders had been restrained by a lower court from stopping printers in the street or at hotels, or elsewhere, in the effort to prevent them from engaging in work. The case had been appealed to the state supreme court of Pennsylvania, and if the strikers lost there it would be taken to the supreme court of the United States. To make these appeals the strikers needed money, and the delegate moved that this convention donate $3,000 for that purpose.

Delegate Doherty[3] (Pittsburg), spoke at length upon the same subject, going into the minute details of the strike, saying that the printers of Pittsburg were not alone interested, but all the working men of Pennsylvania. They had started a movement in that state to put judges in the courts who would deal out justice to the people.

Delegate Harding,[4] Chicago, favored the appeal for the proposed donation.

Delegate Goldwater,[5] Chicago, opposed the grant on the ground that Pittsburg should be able to take care of herself, and that it would not be good finance or good policy generally to vote away to a local strike so large a sum.

Delegate Lennon,[6] New York, could not favor the grant, instancing the recent tailors' strike in New York, on which the local union had spent $50,000. One hundred of their men were now in the toils of the law for action in the strike.

Delegate Dold,[7] Aurora, also spoke against the grant. It would be a favor that could not be extended to other organizations, and no such distinction should be shown to Pittsburg.

Delegate Williams replied that it was not a Pittsburg strike alone; it was an international strike. They were broke now because they had been always liberal in helping their brethren elsewhere. They had, for example, spent $24,000 in one Chicago strike, and $12,000 in a Boston strike. This fight was a matter of life or death to them at Pittsburg.

Delegate McNeill,[8] Massachusetts, offered an amendment to the motion to the effect that the incoming executive board be empowered to use at its discretion the sum of $3000 for the purpose aimed at, the board to select the case to make a test of.

Delegate Doherty raised the point that the amendment was out of order, but the chair overruled him.

Delegate McBride,[9] Pennsylvania, favored the amendment. The executive board should be impowered to make a test case, and they could as well begin with the case of the Typographical union of Pittsburg.

Delegate Valesh,[10] St. Paul, opposed the motion and the amendment.

Delegate Foster,[11] Boston, felt that Pittsburg and the state of Pennsylvania should be able to take care of the matter. The strikers should have the moral support of this convention. He therefore offered as a substitute for what had gone before, the following resolution:

"Resolved, That the American Federation of Labor condemns in unmeasured terms the conspiracy laws of Pennsylvania, and the recent decision of the Alleghany county courts, which interfere with the rights of free speech."

Delegate Williams said they had moral support in Pittsburg till moral support was piled up to the ceiling.

Delegate Skeffington[12] of Boston said the Pennsylvania conspiracy laws were the worst in America. He did not favor the proposed grant.

Delegate Lloyd,[13] Boston, thought the case a general one and the grant should be made. We should do everything to prevent strikes, but when a strike was once entered into it should be made as easy for the men as possible. The fact was men were becoming afraid to strike. It was time a determined fight was made on the question of conspiracy.

Delegate Doherty was disagreeably surprised at the turn the discussion had taken. He wished the convention to understand that every trade unionist in western Pennsylvania was deeply interested in the strike at Pittsburg.

Delegate Harding, Chicago, thought that the original motion should be acted upon one way or another. The amendment and substitute should be voted down.

Delegate Shields[14] held the same views expressed by Delegate Harding.

President Gompers took the floor. Why go out of the regular order to propose this motion now? He saw no good reason for such action. The Pittsburg printers could not doubt his own sympathy was with them, but he could see no good that could be accomplished by the adoption of the resolution to donate money.

Delegate Williams raised the point of order that his was not a resolution, but a motion.

The point of order was sustained by the chair, First Vice-President McGuire[15] acting as presiding officer.

President Gompers could not see the advisability of granting this money. The question ought to come up after the appointment and action of the regular committee, and the convention had gotten down to regular business.

The chair ruled President Gompers out of order.

"Then I'll try to see if I can't speak in order," replied President Gompers.

Proceeding, he said that it was injudicious to finally settle this question at the moment. They should wait until we had settled the financial policy of the federation. They should not finally vote away so much money until it was seen whether the organizations would continue to pay their dues. He was a watch dog in this matter, and he appealed to the convention to be cautious. Executive officers had almost to go down on their knees and beg for the payment of dues.

There was a great deal of confusion and excitement at this juncture, several members being on their feet at the same time, demanding recognition.

President Gompers resumed his seat and the chair recognized Delegate Lennon, who moved that the whole matter be referred to the committee on resolutions, and this was done, by a vote of 40 yeas to 8 nays.

. . .

There was some significance in the way in which two or three delegates seemed to resent President Gompers' remarks about the proposed grant to the Pittsburg strike. It is said that there will be opposition to the re-election of Mr. Gompers. This information was first given out by the Pittsburg papers two or three weeks ago. So the inference is that the opposition comes from that quarter. Whether it will take definite shape, and what the result would be in such event, are matters of mere conjecture. If the delegates are talking about it they are talking amongst themselves, for no whisper of anything of the sort reaches the news gatherers at first hand. It is all outside talk and may not amount to anything.

Some of the delegates "talk back" at the president in a way which leaves the impression that they are not friendly to his interests. That is to be expected. It is always so where strong men are concerned, and President Gompers is unquestionably a strong man—a man of knowledge, force of character, dignity and conservatism, and he makes a capital presiding officer. To the observer he is easily the strongest man in the convention.

Delegate McNeil of Boston seems to be the favorite leader on the floor. In personal appearance, he recalls some pictures of Longfellow one has seen. He seems to be a man of education, and is a ready and skillful debater. But there are a number of able speakers and bright men in the convention, notably: McBride, McGuire, Williams, Doherty, Secretary Evans, Lennon and Goldwater.

. . .

Birmingham Age Herald, Dec. 16, 1891.

1. Owen A. Williams, an Allegheny City, Pa., printer and member of International Typographical Union (ITU) 7 of Pittsburgh, represented the ITU.

2. Members of ITU 7 and International Printing Pressmen's Union 13 of Pittsburgh began a seven-month strike on Oct. 1, 1891, seeking higher wages and a nine-hour day. On Dec. 2, their employer, Murdock, Kerr, and Co., secured an injunction from the Allegheny county court preventing Eugene Walker and twenty-seven other union printers from picketing and harassing strikebreakers. The AFL 1891 convention voted $3,000 to help provide legal assistance, but on Jan. 3, 1893, the Pennsylvania supreme court upheld the injunction. After the state supreme court denied the appeal, the AFL Executive Council decided not to take the case to the U.S. Supreme Court.

3. Jeremiah Doherty, who represented the National Amalgamated Association of Iron and Steel Workers (NAAISW), worked as a rougher in a Pittsburgh mill. He became corresponding representative of NAAISW Monongahela Lodge 27 in 1889, serving in that position as late as 1894. In November 1892 he ran unsuccessfully for the Pennsylvania state senate as a Democrat.

4. John C. HARDING, president of the Illinois State Federation of Labor from 1890 to 1892, represented the Trade and Labor Assembly of Chicago.

5. Samuel GOLDWATER, a representative of the CMIU, was a founder of the Chicago Trade and Labor Council, was twice president of the Detroit Trade and Labor Council, and helped organize the Michigan Federation of Labor.

6. John B. Lennon represented the Journeymen Tailors' Union of America.

7. Charles DOLD, a member of CMIU 41 of Aurora, Ill., was a delegate of the CMIU.

8. George McNeill represented Federal Labor Union 3873 of Boston.

9. John McBride of Columbus, Ohio, represented the United Mine Workers of America.

10. Frank Valesh, a representative of the CMIU, immigrated to the United States from Bohemia in 1874. He was a member of CMIU 98 of St. Paul and an organizer of the Excelsior Club of St. Paul, a social reform club. Valesh married labor reporter Eva McDonald in 1891. He served as a Minnesota deputy labor commissioner from 1891 to 1895 and was active in the St. Paul Trades and Labor Assembly in the mid-1890s. In 1898 he moved to Graceville, Minn., where he became a cigar manufacturer and apparently left the labor movement.

11. Frank K. Foster represented the Massachusetts State Federation of Labor.

12. Henry J. Skeffington represented the Boot and Shoe Workers' International Union.

13. Henry LLOYD, a member of United Brotherhood of Carpenters and Joiners of America (UBCJA) 33 of Boston, represented the Boston Central Labor Union.

14. Either William E. Shields who represented the ITU or William J. Shields who represented the UBCJA.

15. P. J. McGuire represented the UBCJA.

[December 17, 1891]

LABOR TALKS

. . .

On the call of the committees Chairman McNeill, Boston, from the special committee on the Pittsburg strike, rendered a report. He said the committee believed that as this case had come before the convention for the first time, and in view of the great interests involved, it should be referred to the executive council with power to act. He then read the majority report as follows:

["]Whereas, A judge in one of the courts of Pennsylvania has, in the judgment of this convention, exceeded the authority of the court and violated a principle of justice in enjoining union printers engaged in a contest to maintain and defend their interest as wageworkers who have committed no act involving a breach of the peace or violation of law, and

["]Whereas, In the judgment of this convention the court in this case exceeded its power and jurisdiction, which, if allowed to stand unchanged, will be a constant menace to the advancement and progress of the wageworkers as a class, and the people as a whole; therefore

["]Resolved, That the American Federation of Labor, in convention assembed, do hereby pronounce the edict of the said court to be an unjustifiable and illegal interference with the liberties guaranteed in the bill of rights.

["]Resolved, That we hereby direct the executive council of the American Federation of Labor to proceed to challenge the order of the court by carrying the case to the highest tribunal in the land, and the executive council are hereby empowered and directed to expend a sum not exceeding $3000 in the prosecution of the case referred to in order that justice may be done to the wageworkers and the rights of the people upheld.

["]Resolved, That in the event that the case is not carried up to the highest courts, the executive council may use such part or the whole of the above named sum to test the constitutionality of the conspiracy laws or of any proceedings in equity against affiliated unions or union men in any state of the union.

["]Resolved, That we call upon affiliated unions to co-operate with the executive council of the American Federation of Labor in this work.

["]E. L. Daley,[1]
["]Jere Doherty,
["]Geo. E. McNeill.["]

Delegate Valesh of St. Paul, introduced the minority report. It was as follows:

["]Whereas, Conspiracy laws appear on the statutes of many states, and of late years it appears evident that the courts persistently construe them in such a manner as to annul the most law-abiding efforts of labor organizations for a betterment of conditions, and

["]Whereas, Enjoinment proceedings and similar tactics are now employed to oppose strikes, rather than the former methods of physical force to suppress laborers, and

["]Whereas, We see in this perversion of the courts a most dangerous menace to the very existence of labor organizations, because it is evident that there is a concerted plan to make the enforcement of conspiracy laws an excuse for draining our treasuries and terrorizing our members so that the efficiency of the organizations will be destroyed; be it

["]Resolved, That the American Federation of Labor hereby tenders a solemn and emphatic protest against these unwarranted proceedings, and the executive board are empowered to take such steps for the repeal of such laws, and that it exercise its discretion in aiding unions in fighting enjoinment proceedings where the courts have encroached upon the rights of labor organizations affiliated with the American Federation of Labor.

["]Frank Valesh.["]

Delegate McNeill made an argument in favor of the majority report. He said that the convention should serve an injunction against the courts of Pennsylvania in favor of the people.

Delegate Valesh advocated the adoption of the minority report. He said to devote money to this one strike was unjust to others who were members of the federation.

Delegate Doherty, Pittsburg, once more advanced the argument that this was not in aid of the Pittsburg strikers, it was to make a test case in the courts.

Delegate Lernnon called for the previous question, but it was not ordered.

Delegate Daley, Lynn, defended the majority report, saying that the Pittsburg strikers did not expect to receive a penny from the grant proposed to be made.

Delegate McGuire, Pennsylvania, opposed the majority report. He said the trouble was that the workingmen did not cast their ballots for their own interests, and the greatest kindness that could be done them would be to compel them to vote. In conspiracy cases, the accused never had any chance in states where the majority of any one political party was large. If the organized wageworkers of Pennsylvania would throw 30,000 votes from the party now in power such conspiracy laws as that under discussion would never be enforced. Let us not be led away by sympathy.

Delegate Burtt,[2] Wheeling, favored the majority report, and so did Harding, Chicago, Boyer,[3] Omaha, Skeffington, Massachusetts. It was opposed by Mrs. McDonald-Valesh,[4] St. Paul, Dald, Aurora.

Delegate Goldwater, Detroit, called for the previous question, and the call was sustained.

President Gompers was about to put the question of adoption or rejection of the majority report, when he was asked to decide this point:

"If an organization was entitled to more than one delegate, and there was but one delegate present, would said delegate be permitted to cast the entire vote of his organization."

President Gompers answered that such one delegate would, in the absence of his colleagues, be allowed to cast the full vote of his organization.

At once, several delegates appealed from the decision of the chair.

Delegate Loehenberg[5] was called to the chair and President Gompers reviewed the subject briefly, citing his authority for the decision just made.

The appeal was then put to the house and the president was sustained by a vote of 29 to 28 on division. The temporary chairman announced the vote and left the chair, whereupon Delegate McGuire demanded the yeas and nays, but the decision having been given he moved to reconsider the vote by which the president was sustained, and on this motion demanded the yeas and nays. The motion was laid on the table, yeas 1032, nays 940. So the president was sustained. The question recurred on a motion to substitute the minority for the majority report, and the motion was lost, yeas 570, nays 1316.

The majority report was then adopted amidst loud applause.

. . .

Birmingham Age Herald, Dec. 17, 1891.

1. Edward L. DALEY represented the New England Lasters' Protective Union (after 1890 the Lasters' Protective Union of America), of which he was general secretary from 1885 to 1895.

2. Joseph H. Burt (variously Burtt), a glassworker from Wheeling, W.Va., and a member of American Flint Glass Workers' Union of North America (AFGWU) 53,

represented the AFGWU. He served as a general organizer for the AFL in the late 1880s and unsuccessfully challenged SG for the presidency of the AFL in 1891.

3. William C. Boyer, a printer from Omaha, Neb., represented the International Typographical Union (ITU). He served as president of ITU 190 of Omaha from 1892 to 1893.

4. Eva McDonald VALESH was manager of the industrial department of the *Minneapolis Tribune* and a state lecturer and treasurer for the Minnesota Farmers' Alliance. On SG's invitation she addressed the AFL convention on "Women's Work."

5. Abraham B. LOEBENBERG, a retail clerk from Indianapolis, represented the Retail Clerks' National Protective Association of America.

[December 18, 1891]

LABOR'S MEETING.

. . .

Delegate Miller[1] of Chicago, from the committee on grievances, stated that he had a report to make which concerned President Gompers. The president called Delegate Jones[2] to the chair.

Delegate Miller read a long statement, signed by the officers of a Federation of Labor of New York, bitterly attacking President Gompers;[3] charging him, amongst other offenses, with having sought the office of state senator from a section of the New York democracy, and working in the interest of boodlers; that he had entered into corrupt political agreements, thereby betraying the cause of labor, and that he was "covered all over with the slime of boodleism." The attack was exceedingly severe, and at times caused an outburst of laughter. When the reading of the bitter screed had been concluded, Delegate Miller offered the following report:

["]We, your committee on grievances, after a careful investigation relative to the circular spread broadcast by the Central Labor Federation, do declare said circular a malicious, scandalous and vituperative document, and is also a criminal libel of the most flagrant character; and we find that the direct charges made against President Gompers were disproved by indisputable testimony; that on the imputation, or indirect charges, the committee find that President Gompers consistently acted in the direct line of conservatism which he has so notably laid out and successfully followed in all matters pertaining to the welfare of the American Federation of Labor. Therefore your committee recommend the following resolution:

["]Resolved, That this federation in convention assembled does emphatically declare its faith in President Gompers as an honest, upright and earnest worker in the cause of labor, and that it absolutely believes him to be as far above bribery, political boodleism or corruption as the stars are above mother earth; and your committee further recommend that the incoming president be requested to use his best efforts towards strengthening and perfecting the organization known as the New York Federation of Labor affiliated with the American Federation of Labor.

> ["]George Cavanagh.[4]
> ["]James McGill.[5]
> ["]C. M. Currier.[6]
> ["]George G. Speyer.[7]
> ["]John Strigel.["][8]

The report was unanimously adopted by a rising vote, and with the greatest enthusiasm. It was the most interesting and significant event of the day; significant of the great confidence which the convention reposes in the able president of the federation, and to an outsider indicative that President Gompers will today be elected to succeed himself.

. . .

The committee on organization reported a resolution providing for a woman organizer to organize workingwomen, said organizer to work under the direction of the executive council and be paid $1200 a year and allowed expenses. The report was made by Mrs. Ida M. Vaneaten, New York, and it brought several delegates to their feet. It was argued that it meant an expenditure of at least $3600 a year, and that the federation should not enter lightly into an expenditure of that magnitude.

Vice-President McGuire said that the Knights of Labor attempted a scheme of that sort for three years, and it was a miserable failure.

After some discussion the report was amended so as to leave the matter at the discretion of the incoming executive council, with power to act as might be deemed best, and as amended the report was adopted.

Vice-President McGuire was in the chair at 4 o'clock, and a card was read to the convention from the local labor and trades' unions, inviting the delegates to an entertainment at Erwell's hall at night.

A delegate asked if the four colored delegates were expected to be present at that entertainment. President Gompers replied that it was originally proposed to have an entertainment in one of the hotels of the city, and he asked if the colored delegates would be invited. The reply was that they probably would not be. He then said that he would decline to go to any place to which all delegates were not invited.

Delegate Devore[9] of Birmingham then stated that the invitation was to the convention of the American Federation of Labor, and not to individuals. This was satisfactory; and at 4:10 o'clock Vice-President McGuire declared the convention adjourned.

· · ·

Birmingham Age Herald, Dec. 18, 1891.

1. The only grievance committee member from Chicago was Charles Currier. The printed convention proceedings indicate that George Cavanaugh read the report.

2. John P. Jones of North Lawrence, Ohio, represented the United Mine Workers of America (UMWA). During 1891, Jones served as president of UMWA District 6.

3. See "The New York City Central Labor Federation to the Workingmen of New York," Nov. 14, 1891, above.

4. George CAVANAUGH of New York City represented the American District of the Amalgamated Society of Carpenters and Joiners, of which he was secretary.

5. James McGILL, a Louisville, Ky., horse collar maker, represented the Horse Collar Makers' National Union, of which he was general president-secretary from 1889 to 1893.

6. Charles M. Currier, a Chicago musician, represented Chicago Musical Society 5454.

7. George J. Speyer, a New York City printer, represented the German-American Typographia.

8. John Strigel, a shoe laster, represented the Detroit Trade and Labor Council.

9. Morris H. DeVore, a Birmingham, Ala., iron molder, belonged to Iron Molders' Union of North America 130. He represented the Birmingham Trades Council.

[December 19, 1891]

THE OFFICERS

· · ·

A resolution recommending united political action, which had been offered by Delegate Lloyd of Boston, was reported adversely from the committee on resolutions.

Delegate Lloyd said the committee had evidently placed him amongst the army of cranks. He had not hoped to get his resolution through, but it was an attempt to carry out his convictions upon this important question.

Delegate Williams of Pittsburg cited one or two instances where political action by unions had been productive of great good to workingmen. Millionaires had money to spend in bringing about political results; workingmen had nothing but their votes.

Delegate Goldwater opposed the resolution, intimating that those who favored such action were ignorant of the real spirit of trade unionism.

Delegate Smead[1] said the resolution was not intended to plunge unions into politics, but to teach them how to think.

Delegate Daley, chairman of the committee reporting the resolution, protested against this waste of time.

The previous question was ordered, and the adverse report of the committee was adopted.

. . .

Quite a lively debate grew out of the formal report of the committee on the president's address. Reference was had to that part of the address dealing with the color line in the National Machinists' union, and stating what steps the president had taken towards eliminating the color line.

Delegate Skeffington submitted the report, which commended the several subjects dealt with, and explained at length the bearings of the report.

Delegate Sheilds[2] of Washington criticized rather unfavorably the president's action.

Delegate Todlenhausen[3] of Knoxville was called to the chair, and President Gompers replied to the criticism of the Washington delegate with great vigor and eloquence. He was the last man who would interfere with the autonomy of national organizations. He had been faithful as a union man; he was a union boy. He was now 41 years old, and he had belonged to his union twenty-seven years. It was a late day to question his motives. He never trimmed his sails to catch the favoring breezes of popular will. He cared less for his life than for his honor. But he thought delegates saw something beneath these criticisms.

This remark had reference, probably, to the opposition to Mr. Gompers for the re-election to the presidency.

The debate was joined in by Messrs. Delebar,[4] Jones, Harding, Lennon, Burtt, McGuire, Doherty and others.

Delegate Doherty reminded the convention that it had but a few moments before drawn the color line, in taking action against the Mongolians. If they were to be honest and act upon broad principles let them withdraw their action toward the Chinaman. They could not honestly draw the line against the Chinaman and not draw it against the negro.

The committee's report was adopted.

A question from Delegate Miller[5] of St. Louis brought out from President Gompers the statement that the American Federation of Labor did not seek to interfere as to the qualifications of members of affiliating unions. The president said, however, that so long as he was president he would refuse to grant a charter to any organization drawing the color line.

. . .

AFTERNOON SESSION.

Immediately after the reading of the minutes in the afternoon session Miss Ida M. Van Eaten, representing, without a vote, the workingwomen of New York, asked through a delegate the unanimous consent to make a statement as to the resolution respecting the employment of a woman organizer, which yesterday was referred to the incoming executive council.

Permission having been given, Miss Van Eaten proceeded to make a speech of ten minutes, in which she dealt somewhat severely with some delegates who had not been friendly to her resolution, referring especially to Vice-President McGuire's "rather brutal" conduct, to Delegate McNeill's "sarcastic reply" to one of her questions, and to Delegate Lennon as the representative of an organization which was willing to receive the "dues from women members, but unwilling to allow women a vote."

"That is false; that is untrue!" angrily replied Delegate Lennon, rising to his feet.

Miss Van Eaten was allowed to proceed until she was called to order for reflections on members, more especially Vice-president McGuire. When she had concluded her remarks, Delegate Lennon rose to a question of personal privilege. He himself had organized many workingwomen, for which he had never received any pay; and Miss Van Eaten had reflected unjustly upon his organization.

Delegate McNeill detailed what took place between himself and Miss Van Eaten when she informed him that her committee had agreed to ask the convention to provide for a woman organizer at a salary of $1200 a year with expenses. He told her that he didn't think the convention would indorse the plan. So far as the question of salary was concerned, Miss Van Eaten could take his place as an organizer, and his salary she was more than welcome to. He had been an organizer for many years, and had been in receipt of no pay for that duty.

Vice-President McGuire said Miss Van Eaten had gone out of her way to attack him. He had organized women himself, and expected to organize many more. He mentioned more than one organization with which Miss Van Eaten had been actively connected, and which had died under her ministrations.

. . .

Delegate Frank A. Kidd,[6] from the committee on rules, reported unfavorably a resolution introduced by Delegate Strigel of Detroit, prohibiting holders of political offices from acting as organizers; and the fact was brought out that the resolution was aimed at an inspector of sidewalks in Detroit, whom Delegate Goldwater characterized as one of the best organizers in the United States. The inspector's name is Robert Y. Ogg.

Delegate Harding said that while it might be true that the resolution was aimed at one man, the principle was right. Whenever a man accepted office from any political party he in a measure sold himself to that party.

Delegate Dold was strongly opposed to allowing politicians to get into the councils of the trades unions.

Delegate Foster thought the resolution the most remarkable one that had come before the convention. The test of a man was his fidelity to trade unionism, not his connection with a political party. He pointed out Delegates McNeill, Aug Miller,[7] Daley, and others present, all holding political office. McNeill is a commissioner of manual labor in Massachusetts, appointed by Governor Russell,[8] without pay. Aug Miller is a state senator of Missouri, and Daley represents Lynn in the legislature of Massachusetts.

Delegate Doherty said they had begun a movement in Pittsburg to do away with all the obstacles to the rights of trades unionism, and to do that they must go into politics.

Delegate Williams reminded the convention that Amos Cummings,[9] Senator Voorhees,[10] Senator Plumb[11] and Congressman Richardson[12] of Tennessee were formerly printers. They were politicians now, but they had been always true to their obligations to the International Typographical union.

Delegate Owen Miller said he had been sent to the Missouri senate by working people, and he cited a number of laws which he had been able to have enacted for the protection of men who work. He regretted these flings at politicians.

Delegate Strigel said that in point of fact if every politician was taken from this convention there would be very few left. He desired to go on record as not making war on the sidewalk inspector of Detroit.

Delegate McBride said that in the miners' movement, the miners had selected from their ranks men whom they have urged into politics. In Ohio, in 1883, they had in that state a number of laws that were a curse and oppression to the working people. He himself was the first miner to be elected to the Ohio legislature. The delegate then cited a number of wise laws and great reforms that had been brought about by the working people having their own representatives in the legislature. A similar state of facts was true of Indiana, Illinois and other states. An ex-speaker of the Ohio legislature was in 1884 swinging a miner's pick in the Hocking valley.

The convention concurred in the unfavorable report of the committee, Delegates Harding, Thomas I. Kidd,[13] Faulkner[14] and Dodd asking to be recorded in the negative.

. . .

Birmingham Age Herald, Dec. 19, 1891.

1. Franklin H. Smead, a Cleveland printer and member of International Typographical Union (ITU) 53, represented the Cleveland Central Labor Union.

2. William E. Shields represented the ITU.

3. August A. Todtenhausen, a Knoxville, Tenn., tailor and member of Journeymen Tailors' Union of America (JTUA) Branch 38, represented the JTUA. He was general district organizer for the JTUA's Fourth District, covering the southeastern states, from 1889 until 1891, and the JTUA's Tennessee state organizer from 1891 until 1894. In 1897 SG commissioned him as an AFL general organizer.

4. August Delabar represented the Journeymen Bakers' and Confectioners' International Union of America.

5. Owen MILLER, president of the National League of Musicians (1891-92, 1894-95), represented AFL Musicians' Mutual Benefit Association 5579 of St. Louis.

6. Frank A. Kidd, a Chicago printer, represented the ITU. He served as recording secretary and organizer for ITU 16 from 1892 to 1894.

7. Actually Owen Miller.

8. William Eustus Russell was a Cambridge lawyer and Democratic governor of Massachusetts from 1891 to 1894.

9. Amos Jay CUMMINGS, Democratic congressman from New York, was a member of ITU 6.

10. Daniel Wolsey Voorhees (1827-97), a Democrat from Indiana, served as a U.S. congressman (1861-66, 1869-73) and senator (1877-97).

11. Preston B. Plumb (1837-91) served as a Republican senator from Kansas from 1877 until his death.

12. James Daniel Richardson (1843-1914) of Tennessee was a Democratic congressman from 1885 to 1905.

13. Thomas Inglis KIDD of Denver represented the Machine Wood Workers' International Union, of which he was general secretary-treasurer (1890-95).

14. James E. Faulkner, a Denver cigarmaker, represented the Denver Trades and Labor Assembly.

To P. J. McGuire

Jan. 22nd. 1892

Mr. P. J. Mc-Guire
1st. Vice-President A.F. of L.
124 N. 9th St. Phila, Pa.
Dear Friend:—

Your favor of the 18th. inst. came duly to hand and I am pleased to learn that you will be with us on Feb. 1st. and 2nd. Notes have already been taken in order to take up the cases you refer to.

I would have stopped off at Phila. on my return but I learned that there was to be a great gathering at Haverhill in consequence of the exposition of Ed. Loughlin.[1] I suppose you heard that he had been a Pinkerton detective for the past twenty-five years and in the pay of the Shoe manufacturers of Haverhill to pry into the affairs of the Boot and Shoe Workers Int. Union and that about two years ago he became a member of the latter organization and was in daily correspondence with the manufacturers giving them the inside information how to neutralize any of their organized efforts. An urgent dispatch reached me and knowing that my presence there might do some good there and having finished my business at Pittsburgh, and knowing further that you would not be in Phila. until Tuesday I went direct to Boston—then to Haverhill and returned home yesterday. I am sure that my presence at the meeting will have some good effect and that the treachery of Loughlin will react upon the manufacturers.

While I regret having been unable to see you upon the return trip I believe that duty called me to attend to that most urgent case.

I arrived at Pittsburgh in good time, had a talk with the men interested and an interview with the lawyers which was resumed and continued for about four hours on Sunday.

There is no doubt in my mind but what both the lawyers[2] are well qualified to prosecute the case. I laid particular stress however in my interview upon getting their views as to the ultimate result. In other words whether if the case were brought up to the State Supreme Court and a decision in our favor were to be rendered, whether in their judgment that would apply to all cases in the future and prevent the issuance of injunctions to working people hereafter on strike. They maintain that that would be the status of such a decision, and I have just received letters from them recounting the history of the case and that is proposed to be accomplished.

I enclose the entire matter to you for the purpose of submitting it to our legal friend in Phila.[3] and to get his judgment on the matter. You will see in Patterson and Stillwagon's letter to me they speak of $3.000.00 as by no means an exorbitant fee. Let me know how that strikes you.

I wish you would see that great care is exercised in the handling of these papers and have them returned here at the earliest possible moment.

With sincere good wishes, I am,

Truly Yours   Saml Gompers.
President. American Federation of Labor.

N.B. Yesterday afternoon Mr. V. Williams[4] and President Adams[5] of Union #7 wired whether I could guarantee $650.00 immediately so that the Counsel (above named) could proceed to push the case to the Supreme Court. I answered that nothing definite could be promised until after the E.C. meeting Feb 1st.

S. G.

TLpS, reel 5, vol. 6, pp. 651-52, SG Letterbooks, DLC.

1. The Boot and Shoe Workers' International Union (BSWIU) and the Lasters' Protective Union of America held a protest meeting at the Haverhill, Mass., city hall on Jan. 18, 1892, following revelations that Edward Loughran, president of BSWIU 9 and vice-president of the Massachusetts Branch of the AFL, had been a Pinkerton detective for twenty-five years.

2. David F. Patterson and William C. Stillwagon, Pittsburgh attorneys.

3. Probably Frederick J. Lambert, a Philadelphia lawyer.

4. Victor Williams was a member of International Typographical Union (ITU) 16 of Chicago and an organizer for the ITU.

5. Elijah J. Adams was president of ITU 7 of Pittsburgh from 1891 to 1892.

A News Account of the Wedding of Sophia Dampf[1] and Samuel J. Gompers

[January 1892]

MARRIED.

Gompers—Dampf.

On Wednesday January 27, an interesting event took place in the marriage of Mr. Samuel Julian Gompers, son of Samuel Gompers, President of the American Federation of Labor, to Miss Sophia Dampf, daughter of Mr. Meyer Dampf, Secretary of Cigarmakers Union 144, the marriage ceremony being performed by the Rev. Dr. D. Lowenthal.[2] The event was highly interesting in consequence of the high standing of the parents of both the groom and bride in the circles of organized labor of the country. The ceremony and the reception brought together a very large gathering of the friends of both families, among the number being the following: Parents, Samuel Gompers and Sophia Gompers,[3] Myer Dampf and Rose Dampf. Bridesmaids, Celia Hyman, Eveline Senft, Maggie Carr and Rose Banner;[4] best man, Henry Dampf.[5] Mr.[6] and Mrs.[7] Louis Gompers, Mr.[8] and Mrs.[9] Alex Gompers, Mr.[10] and Mrs.[11] Henry Gompers, Mr.[12] and Mrs.[13] Simon Gompers, Mr.[14] and Mrs.[15] Jacob Gompers, Mr.[16] and Mrs.[17] Jacob Cohen, Mr. and Mrs. J. Julian, Mr. H. Gompers,[18] Mr. A. Gompers.[19] Mr. Simon Cohen,[20] Mr. Samuel Mitchel,[21] Mr. I. Dampf,[22]

Miss Mamie Dampf,[23] Mrs. M. Hyman,[24] Miss Mary Hyman, Mr.[25] and Mrs. Moses May, Mr. and Mrs. Chas. Brand, Mr.[26] and Mrs. I. Koeser, Mr. and Mrs. Herman Brand, Mr. and Mrs. Sigmund Brand, Mrs. Lux, Mr. and Mrs.[27] John Lennon, Mr.[28] and Mrs.[29] Geo. Bloch, Mr. Chris Evans, Miss H. H. Stoddard,[30] Mrs. J. Sandusky, Mr.[31] and Mrs. Paul Herman, Mr.[32] and Mrs. E. Bleek, Mr.[33] and Mrs.[34] Joseph Corper, Mrs. I. Hess,[35] Mr.[36] and Mrs.[37] N. Rosenstein, Mrs. T. Chadwick, Mr.[38] and Mrs. B. Coster, Mr.[39] and Mrs. Henry Wennik, Mr. and Mrs. H. Drucher, Mr.[40] and Mrs. J. Sarfaty, Mrs. Phillips, Mr.[41] and Mrs.[42] Lewis Banner, Mrs. A. Winkel,[43] Mrs. Rogalino, Miss Netty Rogalino, Mrs. Lelyvelt,[44] Miss Sadie Lelyvelt, Mrs. Carr, Miss Annie Clark, Miss Josephine Clark, Theresa Clark, Miss Rosie Lelyvelt,[45] Miss Betsy Lelyvelt,[46] Mrs. Mark Levy,[47] Mr. and Mrs. Joseph Vince, Mr. Lewis Wolder,[48] Mr. Geo. Pape, Mr. I. Matthysse,[49] Mr. R. E. Pinner,[50] Mr. C. G. Bloete,[51] Mr. M. Brown,[52] Mr. E. Bereutz, Mr. Charles Buchner,[53] Mr. James Carson, Mr. E. J. Arundel, Mr.[54] and Mrs.[55] S. Prince, Mr. H. F. Hallahan.[56]

At the close of the ceremony, and after receiving the congratulations of their friends, the happy couple left the house amid the shouts and good wishes of all. A shower of rice and other pleasant tokens of good-will were given and they then departed on the 3.20 train for Washington, D.C., where the young people will make their future home. The bride was the recipient of a very large number of beautiful and valuable gifts. The social feature was kept up until a very late hour in the evening when all departed in good cheer. Before dispersing a telegram was received announcing their safe arrival in Washington.

Unidentified New York City newspaper, Jan. 1892, Scrapbook 1, reel 24, *AFL Records.*

1. Sophia Dampf GOMPERS.
2. Probably Daniel Lowenthal, rabbi of B'nai Shalom in New York City.
3. Sophia Julian GOMPERS, SG's first wife.
4. Rose Banner was the daughter of Louis and Louisa Banner.
5. Henry Dampf, son of Meyer and Rose Dampf, became a bookbinder in New York City.
6. Louis GOMPERS, SG's brother, was a cigarmaker.
7. Sophia Bickstein Gompers.
8. Alexander GOMPERS (1857-1926), SG's brother, was a cigarmaker.
9. Rachel Bickstein Gompers.
10. Henry GOMPERS (b. 1853), SG's brother, was a cigarmaker.
11. Sarah Wennick Gompers.
12. Simon GOMPERS (1865-1953), SG's brother, was a sheet metal worker.
13. Leah Lopez Gompers.
14. Jacob GOMPERS, SG's brother, was a diamond polisher.
15. Sophia Spero Gompers.
16. Jacob Cohen was a New York City cigarmaker.

17. Fanny (Femmetje) Gompers COHEN, SG's aunt.

18. Henry Julian GOMPERS (1874-1938), son of SG and Sophia Gompers, became a granite cutter.

19. Either Abraham Julian GOMPERS (1876-1903), who became a cutter in the clothing industry, or Alexander Julian GOMPERS (1878-1947), who became a cigarmaker. Both were sons of SG and Sophia Gompers.

20. Possibly the son of Jacob and Fanny Cohen.

21. Samuel MITCHELL, the husband of SG's daughter Rose, became a letter carrier and postal clerk.

22. Isaac Dampf, the son of Meyer and Rose Dampf, became a clerk in a New York City shoe store.

23. Mamie (variously Mary) Dampf was the daughter of Meyer and Rose Dampf.

24. Possibly Mary Hyman of New York City.

25. Moses May was a New York City cigarmaker.

26. Possibly Ignatz Koeser, a New York City tailor.

27. Juna J. Allen Lennon.

28. George G. BLOCK was secretary of the Journeymen Bakers' National Union from 1886 to 1888, a founder of the New York City Central Labor Union (CLU), and a leader in the Henry George 1886 mayoralty campaign.

29. Mary Block.

30. H. H. Stodart, a New York City stenographer, worked in the AFL national office from 1890 to 1895. She was probably the Henrietta H. Stodart involved in organizing women stenographers and typewriters in New York City in 1891.

31. Paul Hermann, a New York City cigarmaker, was business manager of the Picket Publishing Association, which supported SG's first editorial venture, the *Picket*, in 1886.

32. Edward H. Blick, who assisted with correspondence in the AFL office in the 1880s, was a clerk in the AFL national office from 1890 to 1895.

33. Joseph Corper was a New York City cigarmaker.

34. Sarah Corper.

35. Possibly Rosa Hess of New York City.

36. Nathan Rosenstein was the president of CMIU 144 of New York City.

37. Rachel Rosenstein.

38. Probably Benjamin Coster, a New York City cigarmaker.

39. Henry Winnick was a member of CMIU 144.

40. Probably Joseph Sarfaty who was employed by the AFL national office as a clerk in December 1889.

41. Louis Banner was a member of CMIU 144.

42. Louisa Banner.

43. Possibly the wife of Abraham Winkel, a New York City cigarmaker.

44. Hariet Lelyveld was a Dutch immigrant living in New York City. She may have been related to the Lellyveld family that for a time shared a house with SG's family when he was growing up in London; several men named Lelyveld were members of CMIU 144.

45. Rosa Lelyveld, the daughter of Hariet Lelyveld.

46. Bessie Lelyveld, the daughter of Hariet Lelyveld.

47. Sarah Gompers LEVY, SG's aunt.

48. Louis Wolder was a New York City cigarmaker who served as president of CMIU 144 in 1884.

49. Probably Isaac Mattyeser, a member of CMIU 144.

50. Reuben E. PINNER was a cigarmaker.

51. Charles George BLOETE had held various offices in CMIU 144, the Amalgamated Trades and Labor Union of New York and Vicinity, and the New York City CLU. He was special agent of the New York Bureau of Labor Statistics from 1887 to 1904.

52. Morris Brown was member of CMIU 144.

53. Charles Buchner was secretary of CMIU 10 of New York City.

54. Samuel PRINCE was a cigar packer and a member of CMIU 251 of New York City.

55. Mary Prince.

56. H. F. Hallahan, who was assistant financial secretary and corresponding secretary of CMIU 144 in the early 1880s, was possibly Henry Florence Hallahan, a Brooklyn cigarmaker.

To Eva McDonald Valesh

Feb. 9th. 1892

Mrs. Eva Mc-Donald Valesh,
c/o Bureau of Labor Statistics
St. Paul, Minn.
Dear Madame: —

Your favor of the 4th. inst. came duly to hand and contents noted.

You ask me for my opinion as to the probability of the A.F. of L. going into politics.

Let me say that as a matter of fact our organization has been in politics from the moment of its inception, but as you are well aware there are different kinds of politics. Some people imagine that there is no such thing as politics unless an organization rushes headlong into the arena to nominate and vote for some one for the office of President of the United States or of town Constable. The politics of the American Federation of Labor is to secure labor measures through any political party using every one of them for the purposes of labor, but warning them to keep their hands off when they propose to use us.

The wage-workers are a distinct class from all other classes in society. They organize and struggle as a class in their trade unions to obtain improvements in their condition, so that the distinction between [the] working class and the other classes shall be diminished to a minimum and then can strike a blow for the emancipation of the disinherited wage-working class and thus abolish all classes based upon wealth or possessions.

I hope I have answered your question plainly. When you write the article for the "Arena" will you kindly see that a copy is sent to me.[1]

Reciprocating your kind wishes and asking to be remembered [to my other?] dear friend,

Fraternally Yours, Saml Gompers
President. American Federation of Labor.

TLpS, reel 6, vol. 7, p. 36, SG Letterbooks, DLC.

1. Eva McDonald Valesh, "The Strength and Weakness of the People's Movement," *Arena* 5 (1892):726-31.

To Edward Cherry[1]

Feb. 10th. 1892

Mr. Edward Cherry,
Genl. Organizer A.F. of L.
714 Washington St. Owasso, Mich.
Dear Sir and Brother:—

I am exceedingly pleased to learn from your letter the progress made in the movement in Owasso and the general favor with which the American Federation of Labor is greeted by our fellow-workers. The time is not far distant when all trade unions will see the advisability as well as the necessity of federating the interests of all to protect the interests of one and all. In other words that we shall live for the attainment of the principle, "one for all and all for one."

I beg to assure you that your very earnest words of commendation and your kind expressions of my efforts are earnestly appreciated.

I have been brought up in the hard, cold cruel school of the trade unions whose very existence demands that men who take a leading part in shaping its work shall be more than mere word mongers. Out of a life of forty-two years I have worked in the factory for twenty-six years and have never been outside of the union of my trade since I was fourteen years of age, and it is only within the past five years that I have held an office which has paid me a salary or even compensated me for my loss of time, while having a family dependent upon me for support. I have been a participant in labor's struggles in almost every form and have learned by hard experience at least some of the requirements that an officer of such an organization as the American Federation should possess. Our trade unions are democratic in character and recognize that the sovereignty of the members and a federation of the trade unions such as the A.F. of L. is, must depend for its success upon the good-will of every member in the ranks. In the performance of my duties I endeavor to encourage this feeling of the sovereignty of the individual member and yet the co-ordinating of all individuals for the common good of the whole.

I am not a trade unionist from mere choice or whim or for revenue. I am a trade unionist from rearing and conviction.

I ask your pardon for saying so much of myself in this letter, but your earnest words of commendation have impelled me to have you know me somewhat better than my usual correspondent.

No doubt you will also have received documents from Mr. O'dea[2] of the Bricklayers and Masons Int. Union[3] for I wrote to him as well as to Mr. Meyers, to send you a communication and documents.

With earnest good wishes, I am,

Saml Gompers
President. American Federation of Labor.

TLpS, reel 6, vol. 7, p. 50, SG Letterbooks, DLC.

1. Edward H. Cherry, a carpenter from Owosso, Mich., was an AFL general organizer between 1892 and 1894.
2. Thomas O'DEA was secretary of the Bricklayers' and Masons' International Union of America (1884-87 and 1888-1900).
3. The BRICKLAYERS' and Masons' International Union of America.

To Oliver Smith[1]

Feb. 10th. 1892

Mr. O. P. Smith,
Genl. Organizer A.F. of L.
5 Sycamore St. Logansport, Ind.
Dear Sir and Brother: —

Your favor of the 8th. inst. came duly to hand and contents noted.

In reply permit me to say that I am pleased to learn that your services are in such active demand by the working men of your city. It evidently shows a proper appreciation of your worth and ability to aid them.

It would be a most happy and important event to have the Farm Laborers organized as a Union of Farm Laborers and directly attached to the American Federation of Labor. I believe it needs but such a beginning to bring the Farm Laborers into an organization and to have them placed in a National Union of their own side by side with the other great trade unions of our country under the banner of the American Federation of Labor.

A Union of Farm Laborers exists in England[2] and it has done wonderful good in transforming the farm laborer of that country from a position of slavery and degradation to one of comparative independence and comfort. Not more than thirty years ago in England the farm laborers were employed one portion of the year and then during another they were cast upon the streets or upon the roads and because of their misery and poverty became paupers, thieves, highwaymen or poachers. The great thought among the ruling classes of England was how to have sufficient prisons to keep them in, but with the formation of a Farm Laborers Union wages were increased, the home of the farm laborer was made permanent and the prisons were emptied and transformed into school houses and meeting rooms.

It seems to me that it is high time that something in this direction should be done for the farm laborers of America. I am in hearty sympathy with the movement of the Farmers for their relief from the unjust exactions and discriminations by the corporations against them, but I think upon examination you will find as a rule that they are employers of farm laborers and that their treatment of their laborers is little better if not worse, than the employers of labor in the Industrial Centres.

I call your attention to my expressions in my report to the Detroit convention upon that subject. I urge you by all means within your power to earn that proud title of being the first organizer of the farm laborers of the United States upon the basis of the trade union.

With earnest hopes for your success and hoping to hear from you a little more frequently than I have of late, I am,

Fraternally Yours   Saml Gompers.
President. American Federation of Labor.

TLpS, reel 6, vol. 7, pp. 47, 49, SG Letterbooks, DLC.

1. Oliver P. Smith was an Irish-born cigarmaker and member of CMIU 215 of Logansport, Ind. In 1891 he was elected an organizer for the Indiana Federation of Trade and Labor Unions.

2. British farm laborers belonged to several unions in the early 1890s. The largest, the National Agricultural Labourers' Union (NALU), derived from an organization that Joseph Arch founded in Warwickshire in 1872 and that he revived in 1889; it claimed 15,000 members in 1891. Other important unions of agricultural workers were the Eastern Counties' Labour Federation, the Norfolk and Norwich Amalgamated Labourers' Union, and the London and Counties Labour League. Agricultural unions in Britain declined after 1892; the NALU went out of existence in 1895.

To P. J. McGuire

Feb. 11th. 1892

Mr. P. J. Mc-Guire,
Sec. U.B.C. and J. of A.
124 N. 9th St. Phila, Pa.
Dear Sir and Brother:—

It becomes my duty to inform you that the matters referred by your General Executive Board relating to the violations of the Eight Hour Law of Nebraska and the Semi Monthly Payment Law of Pennsylvania[1] were both laid before the Executive Council of the American Federation of Labor at its session held in this city on Feb. 1st. 2nd. and 3rd. when the following actions were taken upon the cases respectively.

In the matter of the violation of the Eight Hour Law of Nebraska the President was directed to place himself in communication with some of the representatives of the labor organizations of Lincoln for the purpose of securing evidence of violations of the Eight Hour Law of that State, and that upon a case suitably arranged a sum not exceeding two hundred ($200.00) dollars was appropriated to aid in the prosecution of the violators of the Law.

In the matter of the Semi Monthly Payment Law of Pennsylvania the Secretary was instructed to secure evidence of particular cases where the Law has been violated. In regard to that matter I kindly ask you to publish in the "Carpenter" a call upon the Trade Unions of Penna, to submit complaints to this office.

Can you suggest to me the name of some energetic staunch Union man in Butte Montana to whom I could issue a commission as organizer? There is some exceedingly important work necessary to be done in that part of the country and the suggesting of a name by you would be sufficient warrant for me to issue such a commission.

Earnestly hoping that you may have recovered your health and that your trip has been a successful one, I am,

Sincerely Yours   Saml Gompers.
President. American Federation of Labor.

N.B. Yours from Erie just to hand. Will reply & comply later.

S. G.

TLpS, reel 6, vol. 7, p. 52, SG Letterbooks, DLC.

1. In 1887 Pennsylvania enacted a law (Laws of 1887, no. 121) requiring semi-monthly payment of wages in lawful U.S. currency for workers in mining and manufacturing. Four years later the act was strengthened (Laws of 1891, no. 71) by improving enforcement and invalidating private agreements allowing other than semi-

monthly payment. In 1892 several Pennsylvania unions sought the AFL's help in enforcing the law, and the Executive Council agreed to sponsor a test case. The law was declared unconstitutional in 1895.

To George Perkins

Feb. 16th. 1892

Mr. Geo. W. Perkins,
Pres. C.M.I.U. of A.
Fitch Institute, Buffalo, N.Y.
Dear Sir and Friend: —

A few months ago there was published in the Cigarmakers official Journal[1] a decision of the Supreme Court of the State of N.Y. on the injunction proceedings against the striking Cigarmakers of Binghamton, N.Y.

If you could forward me a copy or two of that journal I should esteem it a favor as it may aid us in the case we now have pending in the Supreme Court of Pennsylvania.[2] I should also like to obtain a copy of the brief of the Attorneys for the Cigarmakers in the case. Can you procure it for me or will it be necessary for me to apply direct?

I am under the impression that the Secretary of the Union at Binghamton[3] could make a copy, or if that is inadvisable a copy of the brief could be had from the Attorneys themselves forwarding it to this office from which a copy could be made here and theirs returned to them.

Asking you to pardon me for the trouble I am putting you to and feeling you will go as far as you can to aid me in the matter, I am,

Sincerely Yours   Saml Gompers.
President. American Federation of Labor.

TLpS, reel 6, vol. 7, p. 64, SG Letterbooks, DLC.

1. The *Cigar Makers' Official Journal* of December 1891.
2. See "Excerpts from News Accounts of the 1891 Convention of the AFL in Birmingham," Dec. 16, 1891, n. 2, above.
3. There were two CMIU locals in Binghamton, N.Y.: local 16 (handworkers), John J. Kenefick, corresponding secretary, and local 218 (rollers and bunch makers), Thomas Sweeney, secretary.

To Joseph Suchanek[1]

Feb. 29th. 1892

Mr. J. F. Suchanek,
Genl. Organizer A.F. of L.
125 Washington St. South Bend, Ind.
Dear Sir and Brother:—

The certificates of affiliation for Carriage and Wagon Laborers' Union 5635 and Teamsters and Draymen's Union No. 5637 are mailed to your address with this, and I kindly ask you to install the members at your earliest convenience.

Replying to your question permit me to say that the local unions or central organizations affiliated with the American Federation of Labor pay no strike assessment and consequently are not entitled to the receipt of benefits from that quarter. I have urged the local unions to do all they possibly can to establish some kind of a defence fund in their unions, and since it is our purpose to bring about a national union of all the trades and callings as soon as possible, it would almost be a folly to attempt to undertake to pay a strike benefit to the local unions of different trades when we would have so little opportunity of judging as to the conditions prevailing to regulate strikes and other trade troubles. Then again, it might prove exceedingly difficult to form national unions from the local unions which would be entitled to a strike benefit, without belonging to a national union. A scheme was suggested a year or so ago, but finally it was deemed inadvisable.

There is no doubt but what you are right in connection with the Carriage Workers, but it would be improper to make the stand in view of the position assumed by the Bro'd. of Painters and Decorators. If they claim jurisdiction, it would be impractical for you to dispute it.

I recognize that it requires no words on my part to persuade you to continue in your work despite the antagonism of weak-kneed union men who see a danger in the organization of their fellow wage-workers of other trades and callings. Instead of blaming or ridiculing you they should give you all the encouragement and assistance possible. With the work you are doing I am satisfied you will have the gratification of seeing South Bend one of the best organized cities in the country.

Last week I was in Chicago and returned passing through South Bend. Had I known that the train passed your city I should have wired you for the purpose of meeting me if it was only for the pleasure of talking to you for the two minutes that the train stopped.

Trusting that success may crown your every effort and with kindest wishes, I am,

Fraternally Yours   Saml Gompers.
President American Federation of Labor.

N.B. I enclose to you a list of the names of the Carriage and Wagon Laborers unions as per your request.

S. G.

TLpS, reel 6, vol. 7, pp. 96-97, SG Letterbooks, DLC.

1. Joseph F. Suchanek was a member of CMIU 221 in South Bend, Ind.

To P. J. McGuire

March 3rd. 1892

Mr. P. J. Mc-Guire,
Sec. U.B.C. and J. of A.
124 N. 9th St. Phila. Pa.
Dear Sir and Brother:—

Replying to your favor of Feb. 29th. permit me to say that in both the instances you call attention to this office has not been at fault. The Sash, Door and Blind Workers Union No. 5150 was organized July 9th. 1890 by one of the active members[1] of the Chicago unions of the United Brotherhood of Carpenters and Joiners and the application for the charter was forwarded by him to this office, and in the case of the Stair Builders union of New York City[2] the charter was granted by reason of the recommendation [of] an active member of the Carpenters District Council in the City of New York. In the latter case however, the charter has been recalled more than three weeks ago.

Upon the completion of this letter I shall write to the S.D. and B. Workers Union and endeavor to accomplish their transfer with the least possible friction and in the most fraternal spirit.[3] We have no other union of the kind you mention affiliated with the American Federation of Labor.

Acting upon the complaint contained in the paper of Mr. Wm. H. Kliver[4] President of the U.B. complaining of the treatment by the Superintendent of Construction[5] and the discrimination against Union men, I deemed it advisable in consideration of the importance of the subject matter and the large amount of work involved, to go to

Chicago to investigate the matter and to endeavor to secure the change if the complaint were true.

In company with Mr. H.J. Skeffington I went with Mr. Linnahan[6] of the United Brotherhood and called upon Mr. Lyman T. Gage[7] who is one of the most responsible men in the World's Columbian Exposition scheme. I laid the entire subject matter of complaint before him and he furnished me with a letter to Mr. Wm. T. Baker[8] President of the Exposition Company of which the enclosed is a copy. This letter is the substance of his statement to me. Throughout he disavowed any knowledge of the allegations made against the Directory[9] or its agents. I called upon Mr. Baker and received a letter of a similar character to the Superintendent of Construction Mr. Burnham who took down my complaint and then dictated a letter to the superintendent of the buildings on the grounds, Mr. Geraldine[10] and he promised to make the investigation.

Upon the following day I visited the grounds and had an interview with Mr. Geraldine in which the entire subject matter was gone over. Mr. Geraldine denied the allegations so far as the Directory or its agents were concerned. He disclaimed that the Eight Hour rule was violated except in one or two instances, and then the Contractors were called to account and the violation was discontinued. He stated that the only cases in which work was permitted more than Eight hours a day was when it was absolutely essential to the safety of the construction or work which it was absolutely essential to continue in for the safety of the property, and that then the Directory and himself had insisted that the men be paid time and a half, but that these were very rare occurrences.

I made inquiry as to the method of obtaining employment and could discover no means by which a discrimination could be made against Union men except the one that whereas the Union wage of the Chicago Carpenters is thirty-five cents per hour, some of the Contractors in truth only pay twenty-five cents per hour (which of course is discrimination enough). You will bear in mind however, that in the conferences between the Directory and the Representatives of labor an agreement was reached that the Eight Hour workday should govern the construction of the buildings (except in cases of extreme necessity), but the question of a minimum rate of wages as well as the question of the employment of Union men exclusively were not agreed upon. In other words, these were left open questions upon which the Directory refused to take positive grounds for the reason that they had let the work out to Contractors.

It seems to me that the entire trouble arises from the fact of the indiscriminate and joint employment of Union and non-union men and the friction which such conditions usually bring.

Mr. Geraldine as well as every other representative of the Directory expressed themselves in favor of the organizations of labor, but declared that as representatives of all classes of people, they were not in a position to discriminate against non-union workmen and to use their positions to force them into the Union. They had no objections however, to non-union men joining the Union. The matter of wages was a subject for adjudication between the workmen and the contractors.

Much stress was laid by Mr. Geraldine upon what he alleged to be the ungentlemanly conduct of one or two men who acted as the representatives of the Carpenters Union and the variation of statements made by both of them to him, and in their statements to the Union and to the men on the works. He claims that the cause of the whole dispute lies in this fact.

It seems to me from my investigation that if there has been any discrimination or any grounds upon which the complaint is based, that my visit will have the effect of its discontinuance, and that it certainly was beyond the knowledge of Mr. Geraldine and the Directory.

While at Chicago I had frequent conversations with a number of the representative Carpenters and found that an awful state of dissatisfaction exists with the administration of affairs. It would take too long to enumerate all the causes of complaint, but both sides agree that a visit from you to Chicago is essential to set matters straight. Of one fact I feel assured that unless something is done and that done soon, a rupture in the Carpenters unions connected with the Brotherhood is sure to follow.

This morning's "Volkszeitung" (March 3rd.) states that the Cabinetmakers in Downey's shop have joined with the Brotherhood Carpenters of this city to secure the $3.50 day and the abolition of the furnishing of large tools by the men. In other words, the men have kept faith with you and the representatives of the U.B. I earnestly hope that the trouble may be settled to the satisfaction of all concerned and thus prove a harbinger for co-operative effort for the establishment of the Eight Hour Workday for the Cabinetmakers and the maintenance of Union wages and rules for all.[11]

It is likely you may be enabled to use part of Mr. Gage's letter for publication in the "Carpenter" thus giving information in an official way to the Carpenters of Chicago. In connection with this subject I should also mention that Mr. Burnham stated to me that wherever and whenever the Eight Hour rule was violated, it would be proper for the Carpenters Unions of Chicago to make specific charges to him naming the Contractors and the dates.

Hoping that you have arrived safe, and with kindest wishes, I am,
Fraternally Yours   Saml Gompers
President. American Federation of Labor.

TLpS, reel 6, vol. 7, pp. 106-8, SG Letterbooks, DLC.

1. Sash, Door, and Blind Workers' Union 5150 was directly affiliated with the AFL. Its organizer may have been Joseph Roubik, a laborer in Chicago.

2. SG issued a charter to the New York Brotherhood of Stair Builders on Jan. 11, 1892, as AFL union 5616, but recalled it on Feb. 8, 1892, after learning of the existence of the United Order of American Stair Builders (UOASB). He asked the UOASB to invite the members of the New York Brotherhood to join the United Order.

3. SG wrote to Frank Kohout, the secretary of union 5150, on Mar. 14, 1892 (reel 6, vol. 7, p. 132, SG Letterbooks, DLC), and suggested that it should be placed under the jurisdiction of the United Brotherhood of Carpenters and Joiners of America (UBCJA).

4. William H. KLIVER, a Chicago carpenter, was president of the UBCJA from 1890 to 1892.

5. Daniel Hudson Burnham, a prominent Chicago architect, was in charge of construction and maintenance at the World's Columbian Exposition from 1890, assuming the title of director of works in October 1892.

6. James J. Linehan.

7. Lyman Judson GAGE was a Chicago banker and a member of the board of directors of the World's Columbian Exposition.

8. William Taylor Baker, a Chicago merchant and president of the Chicago Board of Trade, was president of the board of directors of the World's Columbian Exposition between 1891 and 1892. He was a founder and president (1895-97) of the Chicago Civic Federation.

9. The board of directors of the World's Columbian Exposition Corporation, the body established to organize, plan, and direct the world's fair.

10. Dion Geraldine, a civil engineer, was general superintendent and oversaw construction of the World's Columbian Exposition from 1891 to 1892.

11. On Feb. 15, 1892, the board of walking delegates of the UBCJA in New York City asked building contractor John Downey to dismiss seventy-eight cabinetmakers who, the board contended, were doing carpentry work for lower wages than UBCJA members. The contractor refused to accede to this demand, as did the cabinetmakers who were members of International Furniture Workers' Union of America 7 of New York. As a result about 1,000 workers of various building trades went on strike at construction sites throughout the city in late February. After a two-week strike a compromise was reached allowing cabinetmakers to remain at work at the carpenters' wage of $3.50 for an eight-hour day.

To Milton Farnham

March 10th. 1892.

Mr. M. G. Farnham,
Genl. Organizer A.F. of L.
144 Meek St. Indianapolis, Ind.
Dear Sir and Brother:—

Your favor of recent date came duly to hand, but owing to my absence from the city an earlier reply was impossible.

In compliance with your request I mail to you a copy of the constitution of the Barbers Int. Union.[1]

In reference to that portion of your letter about a member of the Union who insists upon opening the meetings of the Union with prayer, permit me to say that unless that is the unanimous desire of the members of the Union this practice must cease. Tolerance of religious belief, or non-belief is inherent in the Unions and we have no right to permit the conscience of any man being shocked either for or against religion in the meetings of our Unions.

For the past few days the newspapers give no accounts of the struggle of the Street Car Employes.[2] Can you give me any information in reference to it? All during the trouble the Union has not written or given any information to this office.

Trusting that they may have succeeded in their efforts and with kindest wishes and hoping to hear from you, I am,

Fraternally Yours   Saml Gompers.

TLpS, reel 6, vol. 7, p. 126, SG Letterbooks, DLC.

1. The Journeymen Barbers' International Union of America.

2. On Feb. 21, 1892, employees of the Citizens' Railroad Co. of Indianapolis, under the leadership of an organization known as the Brotherhood of Street-car Conductors, Motormen, and Car-drivers, went on strike protesting the dismissal of two workers and asking for higher wages. After a brief period under receivership the railroad agreed to a settlement on Mar. 11 honoring most of the union's demands.

To Elizabeth Morgan

New York, March 11th. 1892.

Mrs. T. J. Morgan,
6235 Madison Ave. Woodlawn Park, Ill.
Dear Madam:—

Your favor of the 9th. inst. with application for a charter for a Shoe Operators Pro. Union of Chicago came duly to hand and I have forwarded the application together with the $5.00 to Mr. H. J. Skef-fington, Genl. Sec. of the Boot and Shoe Workers Int. Union 325 Washington St. Boston, Mass.

Of course you understand that the Shoe Operators naturally come under the jurisdiction of the Boot and Shoe Workers Int. Union and it was necessary for me to forward the application as I have.

I am exceedingly pleased to learn that your efforts to organize have been in a measure, crowned with success and hope you will impress upon the minds of these girls the necessity of standing by the Union regardless of the result of their present contest.[1] My experience has been that when people have been organized while they were engaged in a trade difficulty the Union has lasted but a very short time after the trouble ended either way. I would also request you to impress upon their minds that they cannot depend upon any financial assistance from their Nat. Union in their present difficulty as a result of their organizing.

I was very interested in the clipping you sent giving an account of the meeting and ask you to earnestly convey to the girls my sincere wish that success may crown their efforts for justice and right, and that the only way to secure them is by and through thorough organization.

With kindest wishes and hoping to hear from you as frequently as convenient, I am,

Fraternally Yours   Saml Gompers.
President. American Federation of Labor.

TLS, Thomas J. and Elizabeth C. Morgan Collection, IU-HS.

1. In mid-February 1892 seventy male lasters, members of the Boot and Shoe Workers' International Union (BSWIU), struck against the Chicago shoe firm of Selz, Schwab, and Co. to protest a reduction in wages attending the introduction of new machinery. After negotiating a settlement on Feb. 26, the lasters went out again the following day because their employer refused to dismiss seven nonunion men hired during the strike. On Mar. 2 several hundred additional men joined the walkout, followed by about 250 women on Mar. 3. They demanded settlement of grievances, particularly related to company-imposed fines. The previously nonunion workers organized themselves and requested aid from the BSWIU. During the next two months the women refused company offers to rehire all women strikers, because it was unwilling to extend the same offer to the men. The strike ended on May 25, with the company restoring the old scale of wages and taking back all the women and all but three or four of the men.

To Roswell Flower[1]

March [17?]. 1892

Hon. Roswell P. Flower.
Governor of the State of New York.
Albany N.Y.
Dear Sir:—

Referring to our interview of this week permit me to say that I have received quite a number of endorsements from all sections of the state in favor of your appointment of Mr. James McKim[2] as Chief Factory Inspector. These with others which I expect, will be forwarded to you in the course of a few days; and together with those already in your hands will, I am sure, show the best endorsement any man could receive for any office.

The position in question was created by the Legislature at the instance of organized labor and Mr. McKim has their endorsement for that position. My interest in the matter is not in the nature of seeking office for myself or friends. The present incumbent is looked upon with disfavor by organized labor, we have no confidence in his ability, honesty or sincerity and we know that he has not enforced the laws. For these reasons and many others we insist upon the appointment of some other man and we respectfully suggest the one we have chosen as our representative for that office.

Very Respectfully Yours.   Saml Gompers.
President. American Federation of Labor.

TLpS, reel 6, vol. 7, p. 148, SG Letterbooks, DLC.

1. Roswell Pettibone Flower (1835-99), a New York City businessman whose career involved him in railroads, banking, and brokerage, was a Tammany Hall Democrat. He served as a U.S. congressman (1881-83 and 1889-91) and governor of New York (1892-95).

2. James McKim, a New York City walking delegate of the United Brotherhood of Carpenters and Joiners of America, was not appointed chief factory inspector. James Connolly retained the position until 1895.

To John Elliott

March 22nd. 1892.

Mr. John T. Elliott,
Sec. Bro'd. Painters and Decorators of America
1314 N. Fulton Ave. Baltimore, Md.
Dear Sir and Brother:

I am in receipt of your letter and postal card and would have answered earlier but found it almost impossible. Even by the time this reaches you I shall have already passed through your city on to Washington and hope that I shall have the pleasure of meeting you there. As I informed you our friend Mc-Guire will be part of the delegation.[1] I need not say how much pleasure it would give us to have you in our company and unless we see you there, and can make it at all possible we shall probably stop over for an hour or so at Baltimore on our return trip.

In reference to your suggestion about having Washington as the head-quarters for all the National organizations including the American Federation of Labor, let me say that while I agree with you entirely on the project, yet as a matter of fact I shall rather be disinclined to move from the city where I have spent the major portion of my life, and you can readily understand that if I were to advocate such a scheme, it would be necessary to set the example by advocating the removal of the office to Washington at the earliest possible moment. I can see all the advantages you mention, and while I am willing to do anything in the interest of our movement, I am free to say that I would very much dislike to move from even that modern Sodom and Gomorrah—New York City. Under such circumstances, I think it would be better for the A.F. of L. to have some other man as President. However, we can talk this over when we meet.

I regret to learn that matter you write about Behrens,[2] for as a matter of fact I thought he was better than that. It is true I did not have much confidence in the man as to his self-sacrifices in the interest of labor, but I never imagined he would sink so low as to prove a defaulter to the Union.

Earnestly hoping that the Bro'd. as well as all other trade unions may exceed in success the most sanguine expectations of their devotees I am,

Fraternally Yours   Saml Gompers.
President. American Federation of Labor.

TLpS, reel 6, vol. 7, p. 172, SG Letterbooks, DLC.

1. SG and the delegation met with President Harrison on Mar. 23, 1892, to urge executive clemency for the *Jefferson Borden* mutineers.
2. Probably Jacob Behrens, who represented Baltimore CMIU 1 in the Baltimore Federation of Labor.

To George Roesch

March 28th. 1892.

Hon. Geo. F. Roesch,
Chairman &c.
Dear Sir: —

I regret very deeply that a previously arranged agitation tour on behalf of the American Federation of Labor prevents my attendance at the hearing to-day on the Bill, giving the "right of free meeting in public parks and squares of New York City."[1]

The object of the Bill has my fullest sympathy and support. It is in my opinion, a measure of the greatest importance to all labor organizations and they have long felt defrauded of their constitutional right by being deprived of it. It is a privilege fully enjoyed by the people of monarchical England and even in many of our own large cities.

So long as the people are compelled to hire expensive halls for the purpose of public meetings, they are denied the right of free speech [in] the most effective manner possible.

The purity and continuance of popular government depends largely upon the facilities for popular meetings and discussions, and it is therefore obviously the advantage of every community to encourage, in every way possible, the discussion of public questions. But instead of doing this, the city of New York discourages discussion in the most effective manner possible, viz., by practically forbidding the holding of open-air meetings and thus forcing citizens, who can ill afford it, to pay hall rent for the right of meeting and discussion.

This Bill has the unanimous support of organized labor, the members of which now demand that the parks, which they have paid for and support be made free to them for public assemblage, which shall not be interrupted by the authorities save when it can be shown that the ordinary traffic of city is seriously incommoded thereby.

Very Respectfully Yours   Saml Gompers.
President American Federation of Labor.

TLpS, reel 6, vol. 7, pp. 189-90, SG Letterbooks, DLC.

1. The New York senate passed the bill on Mar. 30, 1892, and sent it to the assembly, which failed to take action on the measure.

To William Brown[1]

April 18th. 1892.

Hon. William L. Brown,
Senate Chamber, Albany, N.Y.
Dear Sir: —

It is with extreme pleasure that we learn that the Assembly of the State of N.Y. has passed the Bill granting the suffrage to women citizens.[2] It is a step in the right direction, and one that will not only be of great benefit to advancing civilization, but it is also a rare opportunity for the people of the State of N.Y. to have the honor of emancipating woman from the injustice of being governed by laws in which she has had no voice, either directly or indirectly.

I earnestly hope that you will exert your influence both by voice and vote, to secure the enactment of the Assembly Bill upon that subject.

> Very Respectfully Yours   Saml Gompers.
> President. American Federation of Labor.

TLpS, reel 6, vol. 7, p. 270, SG Letterbooks, DLC.

1. William Lee Brown, a New York City journalist, was the Democratic state senator from the New York fifth district from 1890 to 1893.
2. On Apr. 15, 1892, the assembly passed bill no. 1335, "An Act to Confer upon Taxable Citizens of the State of New York the Right of Suffrage Regardless of Sex." It apparently did not pass the state senate.

To Mary Kenney[1]

April 28th. 1892.

Miss Mary E. Kenney,
Associate Organizer A.F. of L.
335 S. Halstead St. Chicago, Ill.
Dear Sister: —

It is quite a time now since I have heard from you, but that has not prevented me from having in mind the subject matter upon which we conversed. I submitted a proposition to the Executive Council to have an organizer appointed for Women workers, and suggested your name for that position, and I have been authorized by them to act in the matter.

I am sure that there would be considerable work for you to start in with in N.Y. city. I think a week could be well put in for that purpose to start with, and then spending a few weeks among the Laundry Workers in the interior of the State, which would at the same time leave you plenty of time for rest and recreation, then returning to this city and remaining here a few weeks. In all probability we would hear such good results from your work, that I have great hopes that we might be enabled to have you work as general organizer for a long time to come. After a little has been done round here you could no doubt gradually wend your way Westward.

In asking you to take this matter under advisement I beg leave to suggest that you will submit the probable expenses and also the amount of compensation you would care to work for in this capacity in the interest of the women wage-workers. There is no desire on our part to be parsimonious, but with the limited and small revenue that the American Federation of Labor receives from its affiliated Unions, it is necessary to be exceedingly economical, while at the same time entirely willing to pay fair for work done.

A few weeks ago I had the pleasure of a visit to the College Settlement[2] and heard a lecture delivered by a very interesting gentleman, and in conversation with some of the ladies there, your name was freely a part of it and by no means uncomplimentary to you.

Trusting that the movement in Chicago is progressing and with kindest wishes and hoping to hear from you soon, I am,

Fraternally Yours   Saml Gompers
President American Federation of Labor.

TLpS, reel 6, vol. 7, p. 309, SG Letterbooks, DLC.

1. Mary Kenney (O'SULLIVAN) served as the AFL's first national organizer of women workers from May through September 1892.

2. The College Settlement, located in New York City, was founded in 1889 by alumnae of Smith College for the purpose of promoting social service to the poor by educated women.

To Ida Keys[1]

April 28th. 1892.

Miss Ida Keys,
14 N. East St. Indianapolis, Ind.
Dear Sister:—

Replying to your favor of the 25th. inst. permit me to say that I appreciate your intentions very much and desire to encourage your enterprise of starting a co-operative laundry. As regards the photograph you ask, I desire to say that while I appreciate the compliment, I cannot allow the use of it for such a purpose. It smacks too much of that fetish hero worship which it is the purpose of our movement to do away with.

Since the members of your Cooperative Laundry are all trade unionists why not use the label of the American Federation of Labor? One could be placed on each package of Laundry work sent out. Affixed you will find some sample labels together with price list of them.

With kindest wishes and hoping to hear from you upon receipt of this, I am,

Fraternally Yours   Saml Gompers.
President. American Federation of Labor.

TLpS, reel 6, vol. 7, p. 334, SG Letterbooks, DLC.

1. Secretary of Laundry Workers' Union 5254, an AFL affiliate, Ida B. Keys helped organize the Union Co-operative Laundry in Indianapolis.

To Hugh Grant

April 29th. 1892.

Hon. Hugh J. Grant,
Mayor of New York City.
City Hall, New York City.
Dear Sir:—

I have the honor to acknowledge the receipt of your favor of the 26th. inst. appointing me as one of the Committee of One Hundred for the purpose of making arrangement for the celebration in the City of New York of the 400th. Anniversary of the discovery of America. In reply I desire to say that I accept the position and appreciate highly the honor conferred by the appointment.

Permit me to assure you Sir, that I shall endeavor to perform my duty as a member of the Committee, to the best of my ability and shall attend the meeting called for the 3rd. of May.

Very Respectfully Yours   Saml Gompers.
President American Federation of Labor.

TLpS, reel 6, vol. 7, p. 311, SG Letterbooks, DLC.

An Excerpt from an Article in the *Cleveland Citizen*

New York, May 3. [1892]

FROM NEW YORK.

The Executive Council of the American Federation of Labor has finished its session, which has been an unusually long one and a number of important matters were acted upon. The principal question before the Council was the selection of a trade to make a move for eight hours, and it was decided not to make public the organization selected until everything was ready to make the demand with a degree of success. Owing to the publicity given to the proposed miners' strike last year the efforts of organized labor were defeated before the time arrived to make the stand, and it was for this reason that the Birmingham convention decided to leave the selection entirely in the hands of the Executive Council. The Council has also pursued a wise course in keeping the matter a secret until the time arrives to act. Many of the unions affiliated requested to be selected to carry on the battle for eight hours, and it is thought by some that the International Typographical Union, which convenes in Philadelphia in June,[1] has been awarded the honor, but this is merely conjecture, as members of the Council refuse to divulge the trade that will make the struggle.

A report was received from Chicago showing that union rates were being paid upon the Fair buildings, and that the eight-hour workday prevailed. It was decided to send a circular to all parts of the world warning working people against going to Chicago in search of work, as there are already 30,000 unemployed workingmen in that city.

The Council also decided to petition Congress not to close the fair on Sundays.[2]

An amendment to the Oates bill[3] limiting immigration will be proposed to exempt political refugees.

Mrs. Mary E. Kenny, of Chicago, received the appointment to organize workingwomen, and George L. Norton,[4] a member of the St.

Louis colored dock laborers' organization,[5] has been appointed organizer of the colored people of the South.

. . .

Cleveland Citizen, May 7, 1892.

1. The International Typographical Union held its 1892 convention in Philadelphia
June 13-18. The delegates voted to demand the nine-hour day and established a
defense fund for that purpose through a special assessment.

2. The congressional authorization for a coin commemorating the world's fair,
passed Aug. 5, 1892, stipulated that the fair close on Sundays (U.S. *Statutes at Large,*
27: 389-90). Despite this, the fair's managers kept the fair open on Sundays on a
technicality, and the superior court of Cook County approved the Sunday openings
in June 1893.

3. Congress took no action on the bill (H.R. 12, 52d Cong., 1st sess., 1892),
introduced by William Calvin Oates (Democrat, Ala.), to regulate immigration and
amend the naturalization laws.

4. George L. NORTON, secretary of St. Louis Marine Firemen's Protective Union
(MFPU) 5464, became an AFL general organizer in 1891 and in May 1892 conducted
a month-long organizing campaign among black workers along the Ohio and Mississippi rivers.

5. MFPU 5464 of St. Louis was chartered by the AFL in May 1891.

To Dora Sullivan

May 4th. 1892.

Miss Dora Sullivan,
Pres. Collar, Cuff and Shirt Starchers Union 5577 A.F. of L.
87 Hoosick St. Troy, N.Y.
Dear Sister:—

Your favor of the 2nd. inst. was placed before the Sub-Committee
of the Executive Council of the American Federation of Labor at its
session held in this office to-day,[1] and taking into consideration the
two facts you mention, that your Union has not had a meeting since
the receipt of the notice of the 28th. inst. and the further fact that
your Union is not in a financial condition to warrant the expenditure
of the money which would be involved by having witnesses attend a
hearing in the city of New York, we have concluded to appoint two
well known, earnest and impartial members of Unions to proceed to
Troy, and make an investigation of the entire matter, and report to
the Executive Council of the American Federation of Labor the result
of their findings.[2] That Committee will commence its sittings and
hearing on Friday evening May 6th. 1892 at seven o'clock at the

American House, Troy, N.Y. The names of the members of the Committee I shall inform you of by wire.

You will have your witnesses and such testimony that you desire to adduce present at the time and place mentioned, as well as all the Financial Secretary's and Recording Secretary's as well as Treasurer's books, for the examination of the Committee.

You ask for a specific statement of the matter to be investigated. It is as follows:

You made application to this office for an endorsement of a boycott by the Executive Council of the American Federation of Labor on the product of Miller, Hall and Hartwell, upon the ground that a device had been introduced in starching which was not an invention nor could properly be called a machine, but merely introduced for the purpose of reducing the wages of the Starchers.

The Laundry Workers[3] allege that the boycott was never officially asked for by your Union, that a majority of the members of your Union were totally unaware that any such application was to be made, that the wages of Starchers working on the starching machines have not been reduced from the rate of wages received by Starchers before the introduction of the machine, that your despatch to the convention of the American Federation of Labor was not based upon truth, that notwithstanding that you have induced both the Executive Council and the convention of the American Federation of Labor to place a boycott on Miller, Hall and Hartwell's goods you did so upon a misstatement of the facts in the case, and that you permit the members of your Union to work for said firm; that the girls who made affidavit certifying to a reduction of their wages, by reason of the introduction of the starching machine did so under a misapprehension, and that they now acknowledge that error, and that in consequence of the above, the boycott upon said firm is unjust.

You say that you will have a meeting of your Union on May 5th. at 8 P.M. This letter will reach you before that time, and it can be placed before your members so that you may be prepared to act at the time stated for the hearing.

Let me repeat what I stated in my letter of the 28th. There is no desire to do an injustice to your organization, but this matter is of such grave importance that delay will not be tolerated.

Fraternally Yours   Saml Gompers.
President American Federation of Labor.

TLpS, reel 6, vol. 7, pp. 340-41, SG Letterbooks, DLC.

1. The AFL's 1891 convention placed a boycott on the firm of Miller, Hall, and Hartwell of Troy, N.Y., in response to an application by AFL Collar, Cuff, and Shirt

Starchers' Union (CCSSU) 5577 (see "To Dora Sullivan," Nov. 10, 1891, n. 4, above). In mid-April 1892 AFL Laundry Workers' Union 5358 of Troy asked the AFL to lift its boycott. An AFL Executive Council subcommittee scheduled hearings on the matter for Apr. 28, but delayed them on the request of CCSSU 5577.

2. See "To the Executive Council of the AFL," May 23, 1892, below.

3. The AFL chartered Laundry Workers' Union 5358 of Troy, N.Y., in March 1891.

To John Daisy

May 6th. 1892.

Mr. John Daisy,
Sec. Pavers and Rammermen's Union No. 5611 A.F. of L.
119 E. Houston St. N.Y. City.
Dear Sir and Brother: —

My attention has been called to the fact that the Paving Cutters Union of the United States[1] is now engaged in a contest with their employers Association.[2] The latter are making an effort to force yearly contracts with the Union to begin in mid winter instead of as heretofore in the Spring.

You can readily understand that at that period of the year as a rule the workmen are in the worst position of any other time of the year to make agreements and that they would be placed at a great disadvantage thereby, hence the advisability and necessity of maintaining the present Spring contract agreement system.

I write this for your information and to further advise that it would be entirely improper for the members of your Union to go against the interests of the striking Paving Cutters.

Believing that you will act upon the principles of unionism and hoping to hear from you in connection with this subject at your earliest possible convenience, I am,

Fraternally Yours   Saml Gompers.
President. American Federation of Labor.

TLpS, reel 6, vol. 7, p. 363, SG Letterbooks, DLC.

1. The PAVING Cutters' Union of the United States and Canada.

2. In the spring of 1892 the Granite Manufacturers' Association (GMA) of New England demanded that the Paving Cutters' Union of the United States and Canada, the Granite Cutters' National Union of the United States of America, and the Quarrymen's National Union of the United States of America agree to change the date for the negotiation of the industry scale of prices from May 1 to Jan. 1. The unions objected to holding negotiations during the slow winter season and rejected the demand, leading the GMA to lock out some 20,000 union members over the first

two weeks of May. The lockout affected as many as 30,000 other stone workers throughout the Northeast who struck in sympathy. SG assured Paving Cutters' secretary James Grant that New York City pavers and rammermen directly affiliated with the AFL would cooperate with his union, while KOL stoneworkers in District Assembly 49 struck in support of the locked out workers. The less skilled quarrymen returned to work on their employers' terms by the end of the summer whereas the pavers turned to contract work. The Granite Cutters and the GMA established a framework for settlement on Sept. 10 by agreeing to maintain the current bill of prices until March 1895 and requiring three months' notice of a desire to renegotiate prices. On this basis all affected locals appear to have negotiated an end to the lockout by late December.

To the Delegates at the 1892 Convention[1] of the International Association of Machinists

May 7th [1892]

To the Delegates to the Convention of the International Machinists Union.

Sirs and Brothers: —

When you honored me by your invitation to address your last Convention at Pittsburgh, Pa. a great opportunity was presented, of which I took advantage and believe clearly demonstrated the necessity of a closer co-operation and federation of the trade unions of our country in order that the interests of our fellow wage-workers may be protected and promoted. Then I called attention, and I desire to emphasize it now, that under the banner of the American Federation of Labor there is no right that any trade union possesses which it would surrender by becoming affiliated with us. The autonomy of each are maintained, in other words, while exerting the greatest amount of influence as federated bodies of the wage-working class, the identity of no union is lost.

Of course in your organization, that constitutional provision declaring against the black man is still retained. I think upon mature consideration it will appear plainly upon the surface that the declaration detracts from your organization what it would otherwise be entitled to and receive, the co-operation and good-will of the wage working class that it would enjoy, while at the same time it cannot for a moment be imagined to obtain you any advantage whatsoever.

After my remarks to the delegates at the last convention most of them in conversation with me declared that had they had the opportunity of listening to my argument before the constitution was finally adopted, they no doubt would have made a change there and then. They assured me that it would be made at your present convention. Need I say how anxiously I await the news that this common sense, manly action will be taken and that with it will come your declaration to unite heart and hand with the trade unionists of America in the American Federation of Labor.

That your convention may be harmonious and successful is my earnest wish.

Fraternally Yours   Saml Gompers.
President American Federation of Labor.

TLpS, reel 6, vol. 7, p. 362, SG Letterbooks, DLC.

1. The International Association of Machinists held its fourth annual convention in Chicago, May 2-12, 1892. The union did not drop the "color line" from its constitution until its 1895 convention.

To William Luchtenberg

May 9th. 1892.

Mr. W. H. Luchtenburg,
Sec. Teamsters Union 5337 A.F. of L.
835 S. Front St. Columbus, O.
Dear Sir and Brother:—

I am in receipt of a letter in which it is alleged that unfair and improper discrimination is being made against members of your Union by reason of the fact that they are colored.

Permit me to say that I have no personal or official knowledge of this fact except the statements that I refer to, and I kindly call your attention to the fact that the American Federation of Labor positively places its stamp of disapproval upon such attempt. If the colored man will only act as a man, he ought to be encouraged in that effort rather than otherwise. Every man who works for wages and desires to help his brothers as well as himself to maintain their right and their manhood should be granted an opportunity of becoming members of the Union and every other benefit and privilege that is accorded to a Union man, regardless of whether he be white or black.

I earnestly hope that the statement made to me is not based upon truth, but if it is, I trust you will eliminate it from the consideration

of your organization and in either event to advise me of the true
status of the case at your earliest convenience and oblige,

Yours Fraternally   Saml Gompers.

President. American Federation of Labor.

TLpS, reel 6, vol. 7, p. 370, SG Letterbooks, DLC.

To William Prescott[1]

May 11th. 1892.

Mr. W. B. Prescott,
Pres. Int. Typographical Union
59 Vance Block, Indianapolis, Ind.
Dear Sir and Brother: —

Your favor of the 5th. inst. stating that the forthcoming convention
of the I.T.U. will undoubtedly consider and act upon the question of
a reduction in the hours of labor and inquiring what financial assistance the A.F. of L. could give in the event of the movement being
made, came duly to hand.

In reply thereto permit me to say that that is an exceedingly difficult
question to answer. You are aware that it is within the province of
the Executive Council to levy an assessment of two cents per week
for five consecutive weeks upon each organization affiliated to the
Federation for every member they have in affiliated unions. The sum
that that would yield together with a few thousand dollars in the
treasury would be all that the A.F. of L. could raise from assessments,
but of course that levy would have to be authorized by the Executive
Council of the American Federation of Labor.

When I wrote to you last month I desired to have some information
in order to lay it before the meeting of our Council who might then
be in a position to have a tangible proposition before them.

Last year when all thought was concentrated upon the contemplated
movement of the Miners for the Eight Hour workday we not only
would have been enabled to raise a large assessment fund but the
public mind, particularly that of the wage-workers, had been wrought
up to a pitch of enthusiasm that would certainly have resulted in an
exceedingly large fund being raised for them. When however, they
abruptly abandoned the movement, I am frank enough to admit, that
it caused quite a reaction as well as consternation among and in the
ranks of organized labor, and that in all probability it will be some
time before anything like the same kind of interest and concentration

of effort can again be brought about. However, I have no doubt at all in my mind but that should the I.T.U. at the coming convention decide upon taking action the Federation will do all that lies in its power to help it. How far the financial aid will go is more than I can tell at present, and I do not wish to make a statement to you that would lead you into a fancied security which could not be maintained.

Let me call your attention further to the fact that the Executive Council instead of making direct donations of money within the past year to affiliated organizations engaged in disputes with their employers have preferred to make loans of money to organizations to tide them over in their struggles, and which have been in some instances have been already repaid and in others will be paid at the times stipulated. Several thousands of dollars have already been loaned to organizations within the past few months under this system.

In all probability I shall spend a few days in Philadelphia during your convention and shall then be in a position to consult with you, your colleagues or committees upon this or any other subject affecting the I.T.U. and the A.F. of L.

I am glad to have been of some service to you in the Bookbinders matter[2] and I trust that the time is not far distant when all in the printing trade will be organized under the banner of the I.T.U.

Trusting that your convention may be entirely successful, and that I may hear from you, and with kindest wishes, I am,

Fraternally Yours Saml Gompers.
President. American Federation of Labor.

TLpS, reel 6, vol. 7, pp. 386-87, SG Letterbooks, DLC.

1. William Blair PRESCOTT served as president of the International Typographical Union (ITU) from 1891 to 1898.
2. Bookbinders seceded from the ITU in 1892 and joined with independent bookbinders' unions to form the International Brotherhood of BOOKBINDERS.

To Karl Wagner

May 13th. 1892.

Mr. Karl H. Wagner,
Genl. Organizer A.F. of L.
504 Charles St. Marietta, O.
Dear Sir and Brother: —
Your favor of the 11th. inst. came duly to hand and contents noted.

Permit me to answer your questions in the order in which you put them.

1st. The age of wage-workers becoming members of Federal Labor Unions under the American Federation of Labor is a matter for the Federal Labor Unions themselves to decide, but I should say however, that none under the age of eighteen years should be admitted unless in the cases of young persons who had already become journeymen.

2nd. The manual of common procedure is intended exclusively for the use of the members of the American Federation of Labor, and not for any person who is not or cannot become a member. The component parts of the American Federation of Labor are the trade unions of which hundreds of thousands of our fellow wage-workers of the Catholic religion are members, hence there can be no question as to the right of Catholic workmen to belong to them.

3rd. The trade unions composing the American Federation of Labor are not secret societies at all, and certainly not in the sense in which the Priesthood regards that term.

Replying to the other portion of your letter permit me to say that I shall address communications to the organizations you refer to.

Trusting that this explanation will be satisfactory and with kindest wishes, I am,

Fraternally Yours   Saml Gompers.
President American Federation of Labor.

TLpS, reel 6, vol. 7, p. 400, SG Letterbooks, DLC.

To George Norton

May 16th. 1892.

Mr. Geo. L. Norton,
Genl. Organizer A.F. of L.
2. S. Front St. New Orleans, La.
Dear Sir and Brother:—

I am in receipt of a letter from Mr. Ed. J. Donnegan,[1] Sec. of Car Drivers Union 5490 A.F. of L. of New Orleans in which he asks whether you have any authority to dictate any course for his Union, and I have been impelled by a sense of the situation and my duty to send him a letter[2] a copy of which you will find herein enclosed, and

I ask you to accept it as a guide in your work organizing in New Orleans and other places that you may visit as the special and general organizer for the American Federation of Labor.

It is necessary to address you upon a subject which is of an exceedingly delicate nature and one which probably it will hurt me more to speak of than you even to read, for you must be aware of the fact that so far as I am concerned I never have made distinction between the white and the black man in the matter of our identity of interests and the necessity of organizing the bringing them together in one fold, but you are no doubt aware of the feeling and race prejudices existing in the South and that it will take some time before it can be abated.

For that reason I would suggest that wherever there are white laborers who have any objection to your organizing them, then leave them to the efforts of the organizers of their respective localities. If I believed for a moment that the race prejudice could be overcome I would certainly extend your authority to all, but I am satisfied that any other course than the one suggested would only intensify the feeling and bring about results opposite to what we may desire and hope for.

You sent me a despatch to withhold the issuance of a charter to a Marine Firemen's Union in New Orleans,[3] and the following day I received an application for a charter from a Marine and Stationary Firemen's Union of that city. Ordinarily I should have issued the charter, and I now ask you to please state what objections you propose to interpose against the issuance of the charter?

Anxiously awaiting for a report and reply at your earliest possible convenience, I am,

Fraternally Yours Saml Gompers.

President American Federation of Labor.

TLpS, reel 6, vol. 7, p. 409, SG Letterbooks, DLC.

1. Edward J. Donegan was an AFL organizer in New Orleans.

2. SG informed Donegan on May 16, 1892, that Norton had been appointed general organizer for the Ohio and Mississippi river valleys but that his authority did not extend over Donegan's union or any other existing organizations. He asked Donegan to cooperate with Norton (reel 6, vol. 7, p. 408, SG Letterbooks, DLC).

3. SG chartered Marine and Stationary Firemen's Union 5707 of New Orleans on May 18, 1892.

To George Norton

May 17th. 1892.

Mr. Geo. L. Norton,
Genl. Organizer A.F. of L.
2 S. Front St. New Orleans, La.
Dear Sir and Brother:—

I am just in receipt of your favor of the 14th. inst. the contents of which are carefully noted.

In reply thereto permit me to say that Mr. John M. Callahan[1] is the organizer for the city of New Orleans. He was appointed April 22nd. 1892. When I wrote you that we had no organizer in that city it was true but since that time Mr. Callahan's name was suggested to me by organized labor and a commission was issued to him, but I regret that I had not yet received your letter when the one of yesterday was written you, not that I have any reason to complain of what I have written, but because I could have somewhat amplified it. The letters I received from the Car Drivers just mention the very circumstance to which I refer in my letter to you. The race prejudice exists to such an extent that it seems it were better under the circumstances, to give the white men and the colored men the opportunity of organizing separate unions rather than to have them not organize at all. It is only when men begin to organize that they also begin to realize that their interests are much more closely allied regardless of color, nationality, religious or other prejudices.

It is because of this that I wrote you in the strain that I did yesterday, and it hurt me very much to be compelled to ask you to exercise greater discretion and not run counter to the men who have these prejudices, and possibly in that way obviate rather than intensify the feeling of bitterness.

In any Union which has sufficiently advanced in their conception of the identity of the interests of labor regardless of color, you are fully authorized to proceed, but in those cases where it would hurt yourself, the colored workmen, the white workmen, as well as the general interests of the American Federation of Labor, I kindly suggest to you to be very discreet and allow our agitation and time to work the desired changes.

Since you leave the matter of the application which was received for a Marine and Stationary Firemen's Union discretionary with me, I shall issue the charter to them.

Permit me to further suggest the advisability of your calling upon Mr. Callahan and talking the situation over in the light of the statements I have made to you and will make to him. I think that if you would come to a clearer understanding with each other, much could be accomplished, but rather than have a conflict I would ask you to devote your efforts to the workers engaged in and about the Marine service on land and water.

With kindest wishes and hoping to hear from you frequently, I am,

Fraternally Yours   Saml Gompers.
President. American Federation of Labor.

TLpS, reel 6, vol. 7, pp. 416-17, SG Letterbooks, DLC.

1. John M. Callaghan, a cotton screwman in New Orleans, was an AFL general organizer in 1892. A member of Screwmen's Benevolent Association 1, he was one of the five committee members from the Amalgamated Council of Labor Organizations who directed the New Orleans general strike in early November 1892.

To John McBride

May 18th. 1892.

Mr. John Mc-Bride,
Pres. United Mine Workers of America
Clinton Bldg. Columbus, O.
Dear Sir and Brother: —

I am in receipt of a letter from Mr. Jas. L. Jones,[1] rooms 27-28 Burr Bldg. Scranton, Pa. our general organizer for that city. He mentions the fact that consternation prevails among the K. of L. of that city at the thought that you have a local union under the direct jurisdiction of the U.M.W. of A. instead of D.A. 16,[2] and that there is a concerted effort among some of the active men in that order to counteract the growing influences of trade unions, and particularly the jurisdiction of your Nat. Union. He also suggests that great good can be accomplished among the mine workers, if a Miner were appointed to go among them and agitate for organization upon trade union lines. He adds that whatever feeling there is for organization is in this direction, and that under no circumstances is it possible for the K. of L. to bring them together.

I earnestly hope that you will be able to give this matter your early attention. Having been in Scranton recently,[3] I am satisfied that what he says is based upon truth. A number of Miners with whom I conversed while there were anxious for organization and were enthusiastic for the United Mine Workers.

It affords me more pleasure than I can express to learn of the growth of the U.M.W. of A. under your administration and I assure you that I am anxious to be of some service, if I can be.

The Miners whom I met at Scranton are members, I believe, of Union 128 and they urged me to pay a visit to their region in the course of a month for a few days. Let me hear your views upon that.

Our friend Chris.[4] wrote to you about a man by the name of Julius Angelo.[5] I think that he is capable of good work among the Italians, Hungarians, Slavs, Poles, French and Germans. He speaks all these languages, and in my judgment could do good work. Unless he hears from you in a few days he will ship around the world. He is a furrier by trade and has been on strike for nearly three months. Rather than go to work as an unfair man, he will go to sea.

With kindest wishes to you, Pat.[6] and other friends, in all of which Chris. joins, I am,

Truly Yours   Saml Gompers.
President. American Federation of Labor.

TLpS, reel 6, vol. 7, p. 427, SG Letterbooks, DLC.

1. James Louis Jones was a Scranton painter.
2. KOL District Assembly (DA) 16 of Scranton, Pa., originally organized as DA 5 in June 1877. Because another DA 5 organized about the same time in Raymond City, W.Va., the Scranton organization became DA 16 in 1878.
3. SG visited Scranton on May 2, 1892.
4. Probably Chris Evans.
5. Julius Angelo was a member of the furriers' union in New York City, possibly part of the Furriers' Union of the United States of America and Canada that the AFL chartered on May 3, 1892.
6. Probably Patrick McBryde.

From James Riggs[1]

Car Drivers, Motor Men and Conductors'
Brotherhood, No. 5162, A.F. of L.
Indianapolis, Ind. May 20th 1892

Dear Sir—and Brother.

I am in receipt of a copy of the Detroit Street Ry Geazette[2] which contains a letter from you in which you request the Unions to select the most suitable time and place for calling a convention of the Street Car men.[3] Our Union have received no letter and consequently are late in sending in our report. However it is better late than never. Any time will suit us. But the place is what we are after Not because our union is located here but that every thing is in our favor. There is no city in the United States has as good railroad facilities. There is no city in the United States that is as thoroughly organized as our city (even the teamsters and shovelers are "in it["]). Am looking for the Boot Blacks next? We are prepaired to entertain the delegates in subpurb style. We are more centrally located than any other city, and it does seem to me that in justice to all Unions that Indianapolis is certainly the proper place to hold the convention. I have talked to Bro Gruelle[4] and Loebenburg and several other labor leaders here and all join with me in thinking that Indianapolis fills the bill in every particular. We have another reason which is above all others, and that is that we have a tyrant as President[5] urged on by equally as mean subordinates, and we are going to have serious trouble and a great deal of it, in order to maintain our Union. And by having the convention here might have a tendency toward quieting them down.

Hoping Brother Gompers that you will give this matter your best consideration

I am Fraternally Yours. J. P. Riggs
Cor. Sec.

ALS, Street Car Employees' Association Records, reel 142, *AFL Records.*

1. James P. Riggs, an Indianapolis streetcar conductor, was secretary of AFL Car Drivers', Conductors', and Motormen's Union (CDCMU) 5162. On Sept. 14, 1892, the founding convention of the Amalgamated Association of Street Railway Employes of America (AASREA) elected him national secretary, but the following evening he resigned.

2. Probably the local newspaper of Street Car Employes' Association 5391 of Detroit.

3. The 1891 AFL convention instructed SG to call a national convention of street railway employees for the purpose of establishing a national union. The AASREA held its founding convention in Indianapolis, Sept. 12-15, 1892.

4. Thomas M. GRUELLE, editor and publisher of the Indianapolis *Labor Signal* (1887-94), was president of the Indianapolis Central Labor Union (1889-92) and of the Indiana Federation of Trade and Labor Unions (1891-93), and an AFL general organizer (1891-94).

5. Probably a reference to Martin Dugan, a streetcar conductor elected president of CDCMU 5162 in January 1892.

To the Executive Council of the AFL

May 23rd. 1892.

To the Executive Council of the A.F. of L.

Fellow-Workmen: —

Pursuant to the resolution of the Council a Committee consisting of Mr. Henry Emrich[1] and Mr. Dan. Harris[2] proceeded to Troy, N.Y. for the purpose of investigating the justification for the placing of a boycott on the product of Miller, Hall and Hartwell. The Committee was treated contemptuously by the Collar, Cuff and Shirt Starchers Union and being desirous that no undue haste should prompt us into acting impulsively the same two gentlemen were again sent to Troy, N.Y. for the purpose of investigating the matter. Let me say that correspondence was had with the Sec. and Pres. of the Union in question and a telegram received at this office stating "that the Union would meet the Committee."

When the Committee presented themselves at the meeting room they were ordered out of the room, their request for an opportunity of five minutes to explain their position either before or during the meeting was denied them. They asked whether the Union would consent to an investigation and were promised an answer to be sent to them at their stopping place, the American House, Troy, N.Y. The Committee waited there until two o'clock the following afternoon and no information was vouchsafed them of any kind, nor did any representative of the Union come near them. It appears that the President, Miss Dora Sullivan by some means or another exercises her will as the supreme law of the organization, and that upon two occasions when spoken to, the members expressed their willingness to have the boycott and its maintenance investigated.

In pursuance of the resolution of the Council and in the event of the refusal of the Union to submit to the investigation, that the subject matter of the revocation of the charter of said Union be submitted to the Executive Council, I herewith submit to you the proposition whether under the circumstances the charter of Union 5577 should not be revoked for insubordination and violation of the obligation and principles of unionism.

Kindly return your vote upon this proposition at your earliest convenience.[3]

In view of the fact that no investigation has as yet been had tending to show whether the boycott upon Miller, Hall and Hartwell is justifiable or otherwise, that question is left in abeyance until further information has been received. Should the Executive Council vote to revoke the charter of Union No. 5577 I will give the Collar, Cuff and Shirt Starchers who desire to be loyal to the American Federation of Labor an opportunity of reorganizing their Union under a charter from the American Federation of Labor.

I beg to assure you that everything has been done consistent with the honor and dignity of the A.F. of L. and with the best interests of labor in order to arrive at a proper solution of this difficulty; with the influences surrounding the lady above referred to that has been impossible, every consideration has been shown her and the A.F. of L. would certainly lose in respect in the eyes of all organized labor if we did not insist upon the reasonable requests made by the Executive Council for the investigation to be complied with and submitted to.

Trusting to hear from you as soon as possible and with kindest wishes, I am,

Fraternally Yours   Saml Gompers.
President. American Federation of Labor.

TLpS, reel 6, vol. 7, pp. 442-43, SG Letterbooks, DLC.

1. Henry EMRICH served as secretary of the International Furniture Workers' Union of America between 1882 and 1891 and was treasurer of the AFL in 1888 and 1889.

2. Daniel HARRIS was president of the New York State Workingmen's Assembly from 1892 to 1897.

3. SG revoked Dora Sullivan's commission on May 24, and the AFL apparently withdrew the charter of AFL Collar, Cuff, and Shirt Starchers' Union 5577.

To John Callaghan

May 24th. 1892.

Mr. John M. Callahan,
Genl. Organizer A.F. of L.
76 Felecity Street, New Orleans, La.
Dear Sir and Brother:—

I am in receipt of your favor of the 15th, but having been out of the city for several days it has been impossible to reply earlier.

In reply thereto permit me to say that the Executive Council recognizing the importance of having Mr. Norton make an effort to organize the men on the Ohio and Mississippi rivers who ply their trade on land and water immediately connected with that traffic appointed Mr. Norton as special organizer. There was no idea nor thought of superseding you nor any other local organizer either in New Orleans or any other place that Mr. Norton may visit, but being a colored man and a man of fair ability and sincere, we believed his influence among his own people would be greater than any other for the purpose of organization. There is one thing that I am free to admit should have been done and that is to notify you that he would visit New Orleans. The omission of that notification to you was not done with the intention of slighting you in the smallest degree, and judging from your own letter as well as the information received from other sources in reference to you, I am not only gratified but proud of your co-operation in our great work and that you have accepted a commission as general organizer for the American Federation of Labor. You may rest assured that you have my entire confidence and respect and I only hope that I shall be in a position to aid you in furthering the work you have on hand.

As you will know before this the charter for the Firemen's Union has already been forwarded to you with the request that you install the Union.

I regret that Mr. Norton has not called upon you the second time as per his promise and shall make inquiries why he failed to do so.

Earnestly hoping that this explanation will be satisfactory and that you will continue to work in the great cause of labor and the toilers emancipation and that I may hear from you soon and frequently, I am,

Fraternally Yours   Saml Gompers.
President. American Federation of Labor.

TLpS, reel 6, vol. 7, p. 445, SG Letterbooks, DLC.

To Charles Miller

May 25th. 1892.

Mr. C. S. Miller,
General Manager Plymouth Rock Pants Co.
25 Eliot St. Boston, Mass.
Dear Sir: —
I am in receipt of your favor of the 19th. inst. the contents of which are carefully noted.

I have submitted your letter to the Secretary of the Journeymen Tailors Nat. Union of America Mr. John B. Lennon who makes the following reply to my letter of inquiry:

New York May 24th. 1892.

Samuel Gompers, Prest. A.F. of Labor.
Dear Sir and Bro: —
Your letter with enclosure received by you from the Plymouth Rock at hand, in reply I would say,

First, I do not know if their Cutters belong to the K. of L. or not.

Second, I do know that none of their Tailors belong to our Union. I am informed that a very few belong to the Garment Workers Unions.

Third, During the past 18 months repeated efforts have been made by myself and by our Unions in Boston to induce the Firm to unionize their place, but we have been met with nothing but excuses and postponements until patience has ceased in their case to be a virtue.

The Plymouth Rock Pants Co. are above and beyond all other Firms in the U.S. of the greatest detriment to the members of our Union, with branches in many cities where we have unions they have no work made there but send it all to Boston to be made by Scabs, at prices not one half as much as where the work is sold. We demand that at least their work shall be made by *Union* people, members of our Union, in order that we may have some control over a firm that is working constant injury to hundreds of our loyal members. Their talk about clean work shops may be true, but it does not cover the fact that it is *not* a *Union* Shop. If they are so anxious to grant a nine hour workday let them show their sincerity by starting in that direction with a Union shop. We have no intention of stopping their method of work but we do intend, that said method shall be conducted in some degree on lines laid down by our Union. When they are ready to settle our Union is ready to do them full justice, and I am sure there will be no conflict between our Union and the Garment Workers that will in any way interfere with reaching a proper settlement, when they are ready. The last time our Committee waited on the firm about three weeks ago they told our Committee that they wanted a fight with us.

We are therefore trying to accommodate them, and will so continue as long as fight is what they want.

Yours Truly John B. Lennon.
Gen. Sec. J.T.U. of A.

I beg to add that there is now pending before the Executive Council of the American Federation of Labor a proposition to endorse the boycott[1] upon the Plymouth Rock Pants Co. product and that your letter will be submitted to the Council for their consideration in connection with the subject matter.

From what I can learn it is not the intention of the Journeymen Tailors Int. Union as well as the United Garment Workers of America to interfere with your factory system, but insist that if your Co. proposes to advertise its friendliness to organized labor, your business should be conducted under Union rules and have some better claim than a non-union establishment.

Very Respectfully Yours   Saml Gompers.
President. American Federation of Labor

TLpS, reel 6, vol. 7, pp. 459-60, SG Letterbooks, DLC.

1. Clothing cutters belonging to United Garment Workers of America (UGWA) 1 and Journeymen Tailors' Union of America (JTUA) 12 employed by the Plymouth Rock Pants Co. in Boston struck on May 9, 1892, protesting wage rates and hours and demanding union recognition. In late May the UGWA and the JTUA jointly declared a boycott against the company's products. On June 10 all parties accepted an agreement raising wages, granting union recognition, and authorizing the use of the UGWA label on Plymouth Rock goods.

To Henry Skeffington

June 13th. 1892.

Mr. Harry J. Skeffington,
Sec. Boot and Shoe Workers Int. Union
325 Washington St. Boston, Mass.
Dear Sir and Friend:—

Enclosed please find a note which was left at this office for you the party leaving it expecting that you would call here.

There is a subject I desired to speak to you about when I saw you in Philadelphia and desired to bring before your convention.[1] Having found it already adjourned, I wish to submit it now.

Miss Mary E. Kenney of Chicago has been appointed the General Organizer for the American Federation of Labor and has been in N.Y. city about two weeks. The thought occurred to me that she might be of some assistance in organizing women's unions connected with your trade in the East. From what I know and see of her I know she is well qualified to perform the duties of such an office. Would you like to have her spend a few weeks in your trade? If you do, I am sure she will gladly consent to do so. Of course it is understood that you will bear her traveling and incidental expenses. If I thought other than good results would be obtained from her services I would not recommend this course. I am sure money could not be used to better advantage than to secure her services for a time at least.

Earnestly hoping that you will give this matter your early consideration and that I may hear from you soon, I am,

Fraternally Yours   Saml Gompers.
President American Federation of Labor.

TLpS, reel 6, vol. 7, p. 496, SG Letterbooks, DLC.

1. The Boot and Shoe Workers' International Union held its fourth annual convention in Philadelphia, June 6-9, 1892.

To Henry Glyn[1]

June 23rd [189]2.

Mr. Harry Glyn.
Sec'y. American Branch. Socialist Labor Party
206. East 51st Street. New York City.
Dear Sir:—

I am in receipt of your favor of the 22nd inst in which you ask me to debate before your Branch, with a representative thereof, the question "Whether Trades-Unionism pure and simple, or the new Trades-Unionism ie Trades Unionism fortified by *independent politics,* is the better for the worker". In reply permit me to say [that] it is evident that you with several others have been misled as to my position upon this question, caused no doubt by the wilful misrepresentation of me by the very men whose names you mentioned you ask me to meet. Can you point out a single utterance of mine in which I oppose *independent political action by the Trade Unions?* I am sure that you will have your labor for your pains should you undertake to find one. Your mistake or are uninformed as to the stand I take upon the Trade Unions and their political action. It seems that the maxim there are none so blind as those who will not see holds good in this case as others. Cannot a member of the Socialist Labor Party discover a contrast between *trade Union independent political action and Socialist Party action?* I doubt that reasonable men can be confused by sophistry into believing that they are synonymous.

But contradictory and erroneous notions prevail as to what the new trade unionism really stands for and portends [which?] is manifest from the fact that you find it necessary to give your definition of it. As a trade unionist I see progress and development on all hands, trade unions included; and what you term new trade-unionism is naught but what thoughtful and consistent union men have for years hoped and struggled for.

You compliment me by saying that my "untiring energy in the cause of labor is well known". in connection with this permit me [to] say that my duties so engross my time that I could only consent to a debate upon a well defined subject and when the interests of labor would be furthered. I desire to add that in my judgement neither of the two conditions prevail.

Very Respectfully Yours,   Saml Gompers.

ALpS, reel 6, vol. 7, pp. 546-47, SG Letterbooks, DLC.

1. Henry Glyn, a New York City bookkeeper, was an SLP nominee for minor New York City offices in the 1891 and 1892 elections.

To the Executive Council of the AFL

June 27th. 1892.

To the Executive Council of the A.F. of L.
Fellow-Workmen: —

Mr. P. J. Mc-Guire, 1st. Vice-President of the A.F. of L. calls attention to the fact that the K. of L. are endeavoring to allure trade unionists by promises of position, and that in some instances whole organizations have been turned over to that body because trade unions have not been in the field to defend our form of organization. He therefore suggests the advisability of the Executive Council authorizing the appointment of an organizer in Chicago, Boston, Philadelphia, New York and other places for specific periods, their loss of time and expenses to be borne by the A.F. of L.

Kindly vote whether this proposition shall be approved.[1]

In the case of Phila. he suggests the appointment of a member of Carpenters Union No. 8 Mr. Wm. F. Eberhart and offers on behalf of the United Bro'd. of Carpenters and Joiners to pay one half of the expenses for one month. He estimates the total expense for that period to be between $90.00 and $100.00 for both the A.F. of L. and the U.B.

Please communicate your vote upon this proposition also[2] at your earliest convenience and oblige,

Fraternally Yours   Saml Gompers.
President. American Federation of Labor.

TLpS, reel 6, vol. 7, p. 563, SG Letterbooks, DLC.

1. The AFL Executive Council approved McGuire's plan.

2. William F. Eberhardt, financial secretary of United Brotherhood of Carpenters and Joiners of America 8 of Philadelphia, served as an AFL organizer for one month during the summer of 1892.

To Perry Taylor

June 30th. 1892.

Mr. Perry D. Taylor,
23 Hancock St. Watertown, N.Y.
Dear Sir:—

Your favor of the 29th. came duly to hand and contents noted.

You speak of the fact that you do not wish to take the responsibility of starting a Union of Papermakers in your city because it might interfere in some way between you and your employer.

I regret that you should take such a peculiar view of the request made, for I have yet to learn of a fair-minded employer who would object to an organization of his working people, and your expression does seem so much like a man willing to bend his head in order to receive the slave's yoke.

Of course if the hours of your labor are so reasonable, if your wages are so fair, the treatment of your employer so just and your prospects for the future so bright that you do not need the protection of an organization with your fellow Papermakers, then your position is proper; otherwise, it is anything but that.

You say further that one of the reasons that you are not popular with the Papermakers of Watertown is that they go to the saloons and drink strong drinks and you do not. As a consistent abstainer I should think you would endeavor to do something to raise your fellow workers from such miserable conditions and to cure them from their bad habits. It may not be known to you, but let me assure you that it is a fact that there has been no factor, question or movement which has so weaned the workingmen from the drinking habit than the organizations of labor.

I should be pleased to hear from you further and urgently impress upon your mind the advisability as well as necessity of buckling on the armor of labor and to stand shoulder to shoulder with your fellow workers to defend, protect and promote the interests of all.

Very Respectfully Yours   Saml Gompers.
President. American Federation of Labor.

TLpS, reel 6, vol. 7, p. 581, SG Letterbooks, DLC.

William A. Carney (George Meany
Memorial Archives, AFL-CIO).

Mahlon M. Garland, 1896 (*Eight-
Hour Herald* [Chicago]).

Troops at Homestead, Pa., 1892 (DLC).

Tennessee miners during their strike, 1892 (*Harper's Weekly*).

DRIVING RIOTERS AWAY FROM WALHALLA HALL.

Wild Scene in the Street as the Result of Lack of Employment and Food and of the
Frenzied Promptings of Anarchistic Speakers—The Mob Chased by
the Police and Finally Dispersed.

The riot at Walhalla Hall, New York City, Aug. 17, 1893 (*New York Herald*).

The homeless taking refuge in Chicago's City Hall during the winter of 1893-94 (*Harper's Weekly*).

Jacob S. Coxey's Commonweal Army leaving Brightwood camp, Washington, D.C., May 1, 1894 (*Frank Leslie's Illustrated Weekly*).

HARPER'S WEEKLY

A JOURNAL OF CIVILIZATION

Vol. XXXVIII.—No. 1951.
Copyright, 1894, by Harper & Brothers.
All Rights Reserved.

NEW YORK, SATURDAY, MAY 12, 1894

TEN CENTS A COPY.
FOUR DOLLARS A YEAR.

"The Original 'Coxey Army,' " 1894 (*Harper's Weekly*).

Joseph Barondess, 1906 (George Meany Memorial Archives, AFL-CIO).

Eugene V. Debs, 1894 (*Harper's Weekly*).

Peter S. Grosscup, 1894 (*Harper's Weekly*).

Carroll D. Wright, 1894 (*Frank Leslie's Illustrated Weekly*).

"The Condition of the Laboring Man at Pullman," 1894 (*Chicago Labor*).

CALLED ALL RIGHT, BUT THEY ANSWERED "NAY, NAY."

Glendower Sovereign—" I can call spirits from the vasty deep!"
Hotspur Gompers—" Why, so can I, or so can any man;
But will they come when you do call for them?"—*Shatspeare's Henry IV., first part, Act III.*

A cartoon of Samuel Gompers and James Sovereign considering a general strike to support the Pullman workers, 1894 (*Chicago Tribune*).

The Labor Upheavals of 1892

In the summer and fall of 1892 a series of bitter strikes riveted national attention. In early July striking members of the National Amalgamated Association of Iron and Steel Workers, one of the largest and most powerful unions in the United States, clashed with the Carnegie Steel Co.'s private army of Pinkerton guards at Homestead, Pennsylvania.[1] Days later, a three-month-old strike at Coeur d'Alene, Idaho, erupted in violence when a mining facility was blown up and miners drove strikebreakers out of the region.[2] In mid-August railroad switchmen in Buffalo, New York, struck to demand enforcement of the state's ten-hour law, halting the movement of freight on the Lehigh Valley, the Erie, and the Buffalo Creek railroads,[3] and miners in Tennessee expelled hundreds of leased convict laborers and fought state troops sent in to quell the disturbance.[4] Finally, in November black and white workers of many trades in New Orleans joined forces and virtually shut down the city in a general strike, demanding union recognition and the preferential union shop.[5] If these strikes demonstrated the potency of economic organization, they also illustrated the decisive power of corporations and manufacturers' associations when backed by state and federal power, both military and judicial.

Gompers called attention to this powerful combination in his report to the 1892 AFL convention in Philadelphia. "In each of these labor struggles the employers, the corporations, have simply made a request and the armed forces of the States and the United States were at their bidding."[6] Although company spokesmen and local law enforcement officers usually cited strike-related violence to justify their calls for troops, the military played more than a peacekeeping role. Once they arrived, the troops were used not only to protect property, but also to assist in the introduction of strikebreakers and facilitate the resumption of production. By further frustrating the strikers' efforts, they served more often to provoke, not prevent, violence.

The utilization of governmental force to achieve corporate ends was perhaps most apparent at Homestead. Although strikers and other residents had battled Pinkerton guards on July 6, it was not until July 10 that Pennsylvania's Governor Robert Pattison called out the state militia, which arrived two days later. Scorning the friendly overtures

185

of union leaders who had maintained peace in the town for the previous several days, the troops escorted strikebreakers into the Carnegie mills, enabling production to resume on a limited basis by mid-month. The troops called in following violent episodes in Coeur d'Alene, Buffalo, and Tennessee played similar roles. Even in New Orleans, where the general strike proceeded peacefully, the state militia was mobilized, lending further credence to the notion that "peacekeeping" was not the military's sole function in these strikes.

Labor leaders in all these cases decried the outbreaks of violence, but they also condemned the use of troops. Further, they blamed employers for instigating the violence, citing, for example, the Carnegie company's original use of Pinkerton agents as the root of all later troubles at Homestead. As the *National Labor Tribune* put it, "That company made so practical [a] suggestion of blood as a method that it is not surprising the odor has been wafted all over the country."[7]

A second common feature of these strikes, in addition to the military intervention used to suppress them, was the introduction of legal proceedings against the strikers and their leaders. At Homestead, over 200 were arrested on a variety of grounds. In Coeur d'Alene almost 600 arrests were made, requiring the construction of stockades to hold the prisoners. Mass arrests also took place in Tennessee, where state troops held over 500 miners as "prisoners of war." At one point, even the state's commissioner of labor and his assistant were arrested. In New Orleans, the city's Board of Trade brought suit in federal circuit court against forty-four officials of the Workingmen's Amalgamated Council, charging them with violating the Sherman Antitrust Act in calling the general strike. The suit confirmed Gompers' concern, upon the passage of the act in 1890, that it would be used against unions, and prefigured its use against Eugene Debs and the American Railway Union during the Pullman strike in 1894. Generally, the charges stemming from these events ran the gamut from inciting riot through destruction of property, manslaughter, and murder, although at Homestead a novel attempt was made to define the strikers' actions as treason against the state of Pennsylvania. The AFL contributed financially to the legal defense of those arrested in Coeur d'Alene and Tennessee, and its largest expenditures were made in behalf of the Homestead defendants. Most of those arrested were eventually released—charges against them were dropped, they were acquitted, or their convictions were reversed.

Although these strikes and their resolution tested the limits of economic organization, Gompers denied that labor had met with total defeat in 1892. "It is not true," he said, "that the economic effort has been a failure, nor that the usefulness of the economic organizations is at an end. . . . the very fact that the monopolistic and capitalist class having assumed the aggressive, and after defeating the toilers in several contests, the wage workers of our country have maintained their organizations is the best proof of the power, influence and permanency of the trade unions."[8]

Notes

1. To the Executive Council of the AFL, July 7, 1892, n. 1.
2. To John O'Brien, Aug. 22, 1892, n. 2.
3. Ibid., n. 3.
4. Ibid., n. 4.
5. To John Callaghan, Nov. 21, 1892, n. 1.
6. AFL, *Proceedings*, 1892, p. 11.
7. *National Labor Tribune*, Aug. 20, 1892.
8. AFL, *Proceedings*, 1892, pp. 12-13.

To the Executive Council of the AFL

July 7th. [189]2

To [the] Executive Council of the A.F. of L.

Fellow-Workmen: —

You are already acquainted with the struggle now being waged by the members of the Amalgamated Association of Iron and Steel Workers against the wholesale reduction of wages, in some instances amounting to nearly 40%, offered by the Carnegie Company at Homestead, Pa.[1]

Yesterday an effort was made by the Co. to land an organized band of nearly 300 Pinkerton detectives, and with them a number of black sheep with the evident purpose of supplanting the labor of the men who have their homes and everything near and dear to them in that town, by imported and degraded laborers. The men on strike protested against the landing of this hired band, and were fired upon. They returned the attack and a number of battles took place, in some instances lasting over an hour, being renewed for the whole day.

It is reported at this office that there were nearly twenty-five killed and about sixty wounded. The battle ended with the Pinkerton men (who were in barges) surrendering to the strikers. They were then sent to hospitals out of town to be cared for. This office has been in constant communication with the general officers of the Amalgamated Association, and I have just been advised that an effort is being made to secure workmen in New York, Brooklyn and other places, and I have been requested to see that the Labor Agencies are watched, in consequence whereof I have delegated Mr. Daniel Harris to secure a number of unionists to picket the labor agencies in the places named in order to persuade workmen not to go to Pittsburgh to take the places of the strikers.

There has been no time to consult the E.C. upon this matter as urgency was necessary. I trust however, that you will advise me whether the course pursued meets your approval.

It seems to me that if the officers of the Amalgamated Association deem such a course advisable, the E.C. should hold a meeting at Pittsburgh or Homestead at the earliest possible moment. I would therefore kindly ask you whether you favor the E.C. holding a session at Pittsburgh, Pa. at ten o'clock Tuesday morning July 12th. Kindly wire your vote upon this proposition[2] upon receipt of this and oblige,

Yours Fraternally   Saml Gompers.
President. American Federation of Labor.

TLpS, reel 6, vol. 7, p. 597, SG Letterbooks, DLC.

1. On June 24, 1892, contract negotiations between the Carnegie Steel Co. and the eight lodges of the National Amalgamated Association of Iron and Steel Workers (NAAISW) in Homestead, Pa., each representing specific skilled crafts within different departments in the mills, broke down over company proposals to reduce wages and extend the expiration date of the contract from July to January. The company closed down its operations in Homestead by July 1, and the NAAISW, with support of unorganized mechanics and day laborers, struck to keep the mills closed. On July 6, 300 Pinkerton detectives hired by the company to guard the plant during the strike attempted to land at Homestead from two barges on the Monongahela River. Strikers and other Homestead citizens repulsed the landing attempts with gunfire, explosives, and fire. Two detectives and six Homesteaders died that day, while others suffered wounds, some of which proved fatal. Members of the Homestead NAAISW advisory committee arranged the surrender of the detectives and their removal from the borough, and the committee then took control of the town and the Carnegie facilities. On July 12 Pennsylvania National Guardsmen arrived in Homestead on orders from Governor Robert Pattison. They remained until Oct. 13, helping bring in new workers for the mills. On Nov. 18, members of the NAAISW lodges voted to release the Laborers' and Mechanics' committee from its obligation to support the strike, and on Nov. 20 a mass meeting of NAAISW members called off the strike. The workers returned on the company's terms; many were blacklisted throughout the iron and steel industry.

2. At the request of NAAISW President William Weihe, the AFL Executive Council did not hold the meeting.

An Excerpt from an Article in the *New York Sun*

[July 7, 1892]

LABOR LEADERS HERE DISTURBED.

The news of the riots at Homestead greatly disturbed the labor unions here. President Samuel Gompers of the American Federation of Labor, who has been out of town for some time, returned yesterday afternoon, and was at once besieged by reporters. The Amalgamated Association of Iron and Steel Workers, to which the strikers at the Carnegie Steel Works belong, is affiliated with the American Federation of Labor, and William A. Carney, the leading spirit in the Amalgamated Association, is a member of the Executive Committee of the Federation. Mr. Gompers appeared to be greatly agitated over the news from Homestead.

"I received this telegram," he said, holding out a paper, "which was the first news I had of the riot until I read the newspapers. It came from the headquarters of the Amalgamated Association of Iron and Steel Workers at Pittsburgh and reads, 'Bloodshed at Homestead, caused by Pinkertonism.' As soon as I read this I foresaw the deplorable consequences of the employment of Pinkerton men. This conflict has been provoked without cause by the employers. The men recognized some time ago the importance of the changes in the methods of the production of iron and steel by the introduction of new labor-saving machinery and were willing to submit to a reduction in their wages. When such a sweeping reduction as 40 per cent. was proposed, however, it meant starvation. The strike of the men was a protest against pauperization. Notwithstanding all this, however, the men conducted themselves peaceably until the Pinkerton men were introduced. The Pinkerton men meant a horde of Hungarians and Poles to take the places of the strikers. It must be remembered that many of the workers in Homestead own their own homes, built by the savings of years of faithful labor. The Sheriff at Homestead must have had the Pinkerton men engaged when the workers came and offered to protect the property. I consider this advent of mercenary cutthroats in the light of an invasion. The Pinkerton men are not officials, they are not citizens even, but are gathered up from the very scum of the earth."

Mr. Gompers did not think a boycott would be necessary for some time. The Amalgamated Association, he said, was one of the strongest organizations in America. It had a membership of 46,000, of whom 29,000 were in Alleghany county, and a well-filled treasury. When assistance was necessary it would be given. He had observed for some time back a movement among certain capitalists to down organized labor, but they would find it a big contract.

"As to this Homestead affair," he concluded, "I am sorry about it. I am, as every one who knows me believes, a conservative man, but I am tempted to say, in the light of what has occurred, that if people are to be slowly starved to death it is better to die a heroic death."

The Homestead trouble was discussed by the Board of Walking Delegates yesterday. John H. O'Connell,[1] the Master Workman of District Assembly 49, said to a reporter:

"I think this is the time when all central bodies should sink their petty differences, and I believe 49 and the Knights generally would unite in a boycott against the Carnegie productions if necessary. This is a very critical time. It looks to me exactly as if the same combination of circumstances existed as existed during the disastrous railroad strikes of 1876-7, when $30,000,000 worth of property was destroyed."

. . .

New York Sun, July 7, 1892.

1. John H. O'Connell, a New York City cigarmaker, was a representative of District Assembly 49 to the KOL's 1892 General Assembly.

To William Weihe[1]

July 11th. [189]2

Mr. Wm. Weihe,
Pres. A.A. of I. and S.W. of A.
Dear Sir and Brother:—

Your telegram of yesterday advising that the Executive Council should not hold a meeting at Homestead on this date came duly to hand and I have notified the members of our Council of that fact. If at any time you believe the Council should meet at Pittsburgh or any other place, kindly inform me by mail or wire and I shall have the members at any place at the earliest possible moment.

I saw by yesterday's papers that Gov. Pattison[2] has ordered the Militia to Homestead. It seems to me that at last the minions of capital have influenced him from the path of duty and right. If Gov. Pattison believes he had no justification for sending troops to Homestead last Wednesday when Sheriff Mc-Cleary[3] asked him to do so, he certainly could not have had any cause to send them now when everything is quiet and peaceful at Homestead, no lives endangered nor property imperilled.

The responsibilities now bearing upon you are of the weightiest kind and I know that your judgment can be relied upon, and for that reason I abstain from gratuitously offering any advice in this critical situation. All I can say to you is, that if you think my services can be of any benefit to the cause of the men on strike, I am yours to command.

Sincerely wishing that the cause of labor, home and liberty may triumph over injustice, wrong and avarice, I am,

Fraternally Yours   Saml Gompers.
President. American Federation of Labor.

TLpS, reel 6, vol. 7, p. 609, SG Letterbooks, DLC.

1. William WEIHE was president of the National Amalgamated Association of Iron and Steel Workers from 1884 to 1892.

2. Robert Emory Pattison, a Democratic lawyer from Philadelphia, served as governor of Pennsylvania from 1883 to 1887 and from 1891 to 1895.

3. William H. McCleary, a Republican, was sheriff of Allegheny Co., Pa., from 1891 through 1893. At the time of the attempted landing of Pinkerton detectives at Homestead on July 6, 1892, McCleary requested aid from Governor Pattison. The governor instructed him to use local resources to restore order. The sheriff, however, was unable to hire enough deputies for the job, and the governor ordered in the National Guard on July 10.

To George Iden[1]

July 15th. [189]2

Mr. Geo. Iden,
Newark, O.
Dear Sir and Brother: —

I am in receipt of your kind favor of the 13th. in which you ask my opinion as to the best method of avoiding disputes in the future such as is now taking place at Homestead, and ask further whether compulsory arbitration would not be a means. You add that you desire my views for the purpose of formulating them into legislation next Winter in the Ohio Legislature.

I regret that owing to a great rush of business it is just now impossible to reply at length or to go into details for the justification of my position. First, let me say then that I am unalterably opposed to compulsory arbitration. In the economic struggle for improved conditions there is no basis to start from for successful arbitration in all cases. It would require a different basis for each industry and that basis is attained or established in none. As a matter of fact we can only hope to secure arbitration when the wage-workers of a given industry are fairly or well organized. Arbitration on the field of labor can only be secured with the hope of justice being meted out to it, when the toilers in an industry are not only organized but in a position to defend and protect their rights. Then employers will be more chary to take advantage of the rights of their employes, and give better opportunities to the wage-workers to secure justice, improvement and amelioration in their condition.

I think that the struggles of labor cannot be obviated in the future. They may be reduced to a minimum. What we want as wage-workers is a free field with every opportunity to carry on our work of organization. The Pinkertons and their kind should be abolished. It should be made a penal offence for employers or corporations to refuse a wage-worker employment because of his membership in a labor organization and so should a blacklist be punishable by law. The hours of labor for women and children should be regulated by law and not over eight hours per day. Children under fourteen years of age should be compelled to attend school. Employers should be made liable for injury or accidents to their employes the same as [any?] other persons in the community, and the co-employe provision of the old law should be eliminated. Factory, mill, mine, shop and store inspection should be secured and with a few other measures of like nature, I have no doubt but what the working people of our cou[ntry] will be enabled to carry out their own salvation, their enemies to [. . .] but they are the expressions of the results of my observation, and if it does not appear too egotistical to say, my convictions of what is and is yet to come.

I have gone further into this matter than I anticipated I would when starting this letter, and I hope it may aid you in formulating some measures in the interest of our cause. Permit me to assure you that if I can be of further service to you in any way, it will be a pleasure for me to comply to the best of my ability.

Hoping that we may succeed in our efforts to organize and more thoroughly fraternize the toilers of our country so that they may be in a better position to fortify themselves in the struggle for their rights, their liberties and their homes, I am,

Fraternally Yours   Saml Gompers.
President. American Federation of Labor.

TLpS, reel 6, vol. 7, pp. 628-29, SG Letterbooks, DLC.

1. George Iden, a clerk for the Baltimore and Ohio Railroad, was secretary of Federal Labor Union 5368 of Newark, Ohio. He represented the fifteenth and six-teenth districts in the Ohio state senate from 1892 to 1895.

To Abraham Spring

July 15th. [189]2

Mr. Abe Spring,
2006 6th. St. Seattle, Wash.
Dear Sir and Friend:—

Your kind and interesting favor of the 7th. inst. came duly to hand, and I assure you that I perused its contents with mingled feelings of pleasure and sadness; pleasure to have heard from you as well as of the fair condition of the labor movement, as well as your commend-ation of my efforts in the work to promote our great cause, sadness at the pang it gave you to see the events of today and find their prototype in the last century. Yes my friend it has come to this that the wage-workers are defending their lives, their homes, their fire-sides, and their liberties against a pretorian guard hired and fitted out to kill for the purpose of wringing a few more dollars out of the flesh and blood of the wealth producers. I too regret the loss of life and the shedding of blood, but to me it is, and it should be to the thinking men, a premonition of what is yet to come. Sometimes my heart almost sinks at the thought of what we in our day may yet witness as the results of the overweaning greed of the corporate and capitalist class.

The wage-workers can do naught but continue to organize and to contend for the right to life, liberty and the pursuit of happiness. They cannot avoid it if they would, and they dare not if they could. Civilization, progress demands of them that they should stand true to their principles, their manhood and maintain the liberties we possess while contending for the greater freedom yet to come.

I have no doubt that the conflict in its bitterest form can be avoided if we can only gather the wage-workers of our country to organize and to realize their position, for the more firmly we are cemented in the bonds of fraternity the more completely will we demonstrate to the employing class that it is to the advantage of all when fair conditions prevail and concessions to the growing demands of the people are made.

In my judgment it is the greatest humanitarian and civilizing work we can do when we devote out entire energies to the organization and education of our fellow toilers.

In the matter of my visit to the West of which you speak, I desire to say that I am still of the opinion that for the reasons given in my last letter, it would be entirely inadvisable for me to go West for a time.[1] I hope that we shall continue to correspond upon this and other subjects in the interest of all and assure you that I always look to the receipt of your letters with pleasurable expectancy.

I shall write to Senator Chandler[2] and ask for a few copies of your article upon the Immigration Question.[3]

Hoping to be remembered to our fellow unionists of Seattle and with kindest wishes, I am,

Fraternally Yours   Saml Gompers
President. American Federation of Labor.

TLpS, reel 6, vol. 7, pp. 626-27, SG Letterbooks, DLC.

1. On June 30, 1892, SG wrote Spring that to avoid becoming embroiled in the political campaign, he would not travel to the West that year. Further, SG expected that during much of 1893 he would be busy preparing for the International Labor Congress to be held in conjunction with the World's Columbian Exposition in Chicago (reel 6, vol. 7, pp. 586-87, SG Letterbooks, DLC).

2. William Eaton Chandler (1835-1917) was a Republican U.S. senator from New Hampshire from 1887-1901.

3. "A Memorial by Abe. Spring Suggesting Certain Legislation to Restrict the Immigration of Criminals and Paupers from Foreign Countries" (U.S. Congress, Senate, Misc. Docs., no. 176, 52d Cong., 1st sess., 1891, vol. 5).

To Charles Foster[1]

July 18th. [189]2

Hon. Chas. Foster,
Secretary of the Treasury,
Washington, D.C.
Dear Sir:—

Information of a most authentic character has reached me that within the past ten days the number of Iron and Steel Workers who have arrived in this country from various ports has been entirely in excess over those who have arrived here at any time in years past, and inasmuch as there is a labor difficulty in the Iron and Steel Industry at Homestead, Pa. it seems more than a coincidence.

Most of those who arrive give Chicago as their place of destination, but it has been stated to me that the Immigrants land in New York, Philadelphia and Baltimore, go to Chicago and are held there with the expectation of being shipped to Homestead to take the places of the American Iron and Steel Workers now engaged in controversy with the Carnegie, Phipps and Co. concern.

In conversation to-day with one who has an opportunity of observation I learned that there are not a sufficient number of men earnestly devoted to the enforcement of the Alien Contract Labor Law[2] on duty at Ellis Island, and since your office gives you such large discretionary powers I trust you will increase the force now stationed at this port of entry for the enforcement of a law enacted to protect the American wage-workers from the cupidity of avaricious employers.

Should you feel inclined to accept my offer I shall esteem it a pleasure to detail one or two men to aid in the enforcement of the Law designed and enacted to prevent the American workman from being pauperized. While the enforcement of this Law requires constant vigilance, it seems to me that the present moment calls for additional and prompt effort to prevent it sinking into ridicule and contempt.

Trusting that you will give this your early and favorable consideration, and hoping to hear from you in reference thereto at your earliest convenience,[3] I am,

Very Respectfully Yours   Saml Gompers.
President. American Federation of Labor.

TLpS, reel 6, vol. 7, pp. 637-38, SG Letterbooks, DLC.

1. Charles Foster, an Ohio banker and former Republican congressman and governor, was secretary of the treasury from 1891 to 1893.
2. In 1885 Congress passed the Foran Act (U.S. *Statutes at Large*, 23: 332-33),

which prohibited the importation of contract labor with the exception of workers in new industries, relatives or personal friends of immigrants living in the United States, and such other groups as artists, lecturers, singers, actors, and servants. Congress made no provision for the act's enforcement until 1887, however, when it authorized the deportation of illegal contract laborers and provided for a very limited inspection of immigrants at ports of entry.

3. Foster referred Gompers to John B. Weber, commissioner of immigration at Ellis Island. After meeting with Weber in July 1892, Gompers nominated two men, Elisha H. McAnnich of Pennsylvania and Charles Rosenkranz of New York, and on Aug. 15 the Department of the Treasury appointed McAnnich to serve as immigrant inspector.

To Harry Kreeft[1]

July 20th. [189]2

Mr. Harry Kreift,
Sec. Pen and Pocket Knife Grinders & Finishers Nat. Union.[2]
Box 205 Northfield, Conn.
Dear Sir and Brother: —

I am in receipt of a letter from Mr. Wm. Wagstaff[3] general secretary of the Spring Knifemakers Pro. Union of America,[4] Box 697 New Brittain, Conn. in which he asks whether his organization can become part of the American Federation of Labor, and unless there is any objection raised by your organization I shall issue a charter to them when they apply.

I desire to say that I mentioned a subject to him which occurred to me and which I desire to repeat to you. The fact of the matter is that it seems to me that both your organization and the Spring Knifemakers Nat. Union are so closely allied in interests that there ought to be one national union of both. This would reduce the expenses and at same time make a greater and better working body. The members in each trade are not so large as to make two thriving national Unions, while in one the interests of all could be better served, protected and advanced.

I stated in my letter to Mr. Wagstaff, and I now repeat to you, that I am not sufficiently informed upon the details of your respective trades as to make me positive that the Unions should be amalgamated, with distinctive locals for distinctive trades under the one national head. That is the way it appears to me it could be arranged. Probably at your next convention, the matter might be discussed, and committees from both Unions meet for the purpose of securing the amalgamation if it is practical and advisable.

I expected to hear from you in reference to the difficulty you mentioned having with the Company.[5] I hope that you have succeeded in accomplishing your end or that you will in the near future.

Earnestly hoping to hear from you soon, I am,

Fraternally Yours   Saml Gompers.
President. American Federation of Labor.

TLpS, reel 6, vol. 7, p. 642, SG Letterbooks, DLC.

1. Probably Harry Kreeft, a knife grinder in Litchfield, Conn.

2. The Pen and Pocket KNIFE Grinders' and Finishers' National Union of America.

3. Either William Wagstaff (b. 1860) or his father William (b. 1828), cutters in Southington, Conn.

4. The Spring KNIFE Makers' National Protective Union of America.

5. SG referred to a knife grinders' strike at a Miller Brothers factory in writing to Kreeft on Oct. 25, 1892.

To Frank Rist[1]

July 21st. [189]2

Mr. Frank L. Rist,
c/o "Evening Post" Cincinnati, O.
Dear Sir and Brother: —

Your favor of the 19th. came duly to hand and I am obliged to you for the information you give. I prefer however to make a separate reply to one part of the subject matter contained therein.

You say that you are elected as a delegate to the Pittsburgh conference[2] and that you desire to act in accordance with the principles and policy of the A.F. of L. while there. Now as a matter of fact it is necessary to call your attention to how this matter all originated.

At the International Labor Congress in Paris in 1889 it was decided to have Secretaries in each country for the purpose of international communication upon important subjects of labor. I was communicated with and acted in that capacity by common consent. In 1891 at the Int. Congress held at Brussels the name of their organization was entirely changed to an International Socialist Congress. The invitation from the American Federation of Labor sent them by me per order of our Detroit convention was entirely ignored, owing as I am informed, to the influence of the representatives of the Socialist Labor Party of New York, and their Congress then decided to hold another in 1893 in one of the European countries (I forget now which, but believe Switzerland),[3] and at the end of the Congress a delegate from the N.Y. S.L.P. secured the passage of a quasi endorsement for the latter to hold some kind of Congress in 1893 at Chicago.

The question of an Int. Labor Secretaryship in each country was decided to be continued. When the S.L.P. delegates returned they found very little could be done in securing any following for the purpose of calling an Int. Labor Congress to rival the one called by the American Federation of Labor, and under the guise of preparing for the selection of an Int. Secretary of Labor used that as an ostensible purpose for the more subtle one of booming their project of calling an Int. Labor Congress.

I ask you whether for a moment you imagine that a sane man would call a conference of the organizations of labor of the country for the mere purpose of selecting a man to act as a secretary, to conduct correspondence with foreign countries if there was nothing more behind it. The hidden purpose is as I say, to endeavor to do something which shall destroy or neutralize the prestige of [the] American Federation of Labor in the effort to call an Int. Labor Congress.

Since you are going there it would [be] well to keep this matter in mind for I am sure there are other organizations who will send delegates under the same misapprehension. If you go, I would advise that you secure a copy of the "call" for the Conference and to see to it that they do not violate the terms of the call. So [far] as the personnel of the party to be selected as the Secretary, let me say that I have no personal wishes except that I only hope that the trade unionists that will be there see to it that a bona fide trade unionist is voted for by them.

In speaking as I do I do not wish you to understand for a moment that I am looking for the position, or want it, or even would consent to take it, for I positively could not attend to it. You know me, but others may imagine that I am declining a position that there is possibly no likelihood of its being tendered to me, and from the complexion of what I believe the delegates will be, I feel assured that it will not be tendered to me. I only write this to you so that you may understand that I do not want the position, and that it is not the seeking of it which prompts me to write as I do.

As a trade unionist I expect, as I know you will act in the interest of our great movement.

Trusting that this explanation will be [a] satisfactory reply to your question, and with kindest wishes, I am,

Fraternally Yours   Saml Gompers.
President. American Federation of Labor.

TLpS, reel 6, vol. 7, pp. 651-52, SG Letterbooks, DLC.

1. Frank L. RIST, a Cincinnati printer and AFL organizer, was a leader of International Typographical Union 3 and the Cincinnati Central Labor Council (CLC), and was the founder and editor (1892-1918) of the CLC's organ, the *Chronicle*.

2. The international labor congress in Brussels in August 1891 adopted a resolution calling for the establishment of national correspondence committees in every country to exchange information on the conflict between labor and capital. At a meeting called by Lucien Sanial and Henry Kuhn of the SLP in Pittsburgh, July 27-28, 1892, delegates from labor and socialist organizations established an American correspondence bureau. Frank Rist attended the meeting as a representative of the Cincinnati CLC. Trade union delegates insisted that the bureau be independent of political organizations, and the meeting adopted a resolution emphasizing that the bureau's sole purpose was to provide information "of a purely and exclusively labor character" (*United Mine Workers' Journal*, Aug. 4, 1892).

3. The Second International held its third congress in Zurich, Switzerland, Aug. 6-12, 1893.

From William Cogan and Charles Carroll[1]

New York July 28 [18]92

Dear Sir

the Carnegie Company are hiring men to go to Homestead in this city Bricklayers Pipe fitters and riveters they are going from this city today at 6 PM. six O Clock from foot of Cortlandt St this city all fare and expenses paid they are hired at the employment office Cor of 8th St 756 Broadway

from two of the men who were hired to go as bricklayers

William Cogan
Charles Carroll

ALS, Bricklayers' and Masons' International Union Records, reel 139, *AFL Records*.

1. Charles Carroll was a New York City bricklayer; Cogan was probably William P. Cogan, a New York City carpenter. The AFL hired them to procure work through one of the New York employment agencies hiring men to go to Homestead as strikebreakers. After signing on with the agency, they attempted to dissuade the agency's other employees from leaving for Homestead. When Chris Evans received the communication from the two men, he immediately wired the information to William Weihe in Pittsburgh.

An Article by Samuel Gompers in
the *North American Review*

[July 1892]

ORGANIZED LABOR IN THE CAMPAIGN.

It is with some trepidation that I begin writing this article, for while it may be true that I have as good opportunities as any other man in the country of conjecturing the probable action of the workingmen of America, and particularly those affiliated with the American Federation of Labor in the coming Presidential campaign, I am certain that my article will please but very few. I have had to say and write some things in my more than twenty-five years' connection with the labor movement for which I have incurred the displeasure of some very earnest, though, in my opinion, mistaken men who differ with our movement and myself, as one of its representatives, as to methods, but not as to the ultimate end and aim of the social, economic and political struggle of the toiling masses.

I feel sure that this production will in nowise tend to lessen this difference of opinion, but if it will tend to give a clearer understanding to a number of friends and foes as to what the trade unions really are; that their methods are within the range of reason; that their work is being crowned with success as far as conditions will permit; that they are the natural organization of the wage-earning masses; and that it is their mission to secure the amelioration as well as the emancipation of labor—then I shall feel my conscience eased, and be amply rewarded, in venturing to write an article upon the probable action of the American Federation of Labor in the coming Presidential campaign.

Why should its attitude be different in the coming Presidential campaign from what it has been in the past? In what way does the coming campaign differ from those of 1876, 1880, 1884 or 1888? Is there any particular principle involved in the party issues in which the wage-workers have a deep or keen interest? There is indeed none.

Was there any real improvement or deterioration in the condition of the working people, as a result of the changes, when Mr. Cleveland succeeded the late Mr. Arthur,[1] or when Mr. Harrison succeeded Mr. Cleveland? I think not, and I feel satisfied that I will not lose my reputation as a "prophet" if I venture to predict that, so far as the wage-workers are concerned, it will matter little if President Harrison or some other Republican on the one side, or any member of the Democratic party on the other, should be elected to succeed the present incumbent, or even should the People's Party succeed (though I doubt that they even entertain the belief that they will succeed) in electing their candidate to the Presidency.

The members of the organizations affiliated with the Federation will no doubt, in a large measure, as citizens, vote for the candidate of the party of their own political predilections. But the number is ever on the increase who disenthral themselves from partisan voting and exercise their franchise to reward or chastise those parties and candidates, that deserve either their friendship or resentment. With us it is not a question of parties or men; it is a question of measures.

That there exists a feeling of dissatisfaction with, and bitter antagonism to, both the Republican and Democratic parties is not to be gainsaid. Broken promises to labor, insincere, half-hearted support and even antagonism of legislation in the interest of the toilers on the one hand, and the alacrity and devotion with which the interests of the corporations and the wealth-possessing class are nurtured, protected and advanced on the other, have had their effect, and the result is that many toilers have forever severed their connection with the old parties. That the number will continue to grow larger year by year I have not the slightest doubt. To me this party defection of the wage-workers is one of the signs of the dawn of a healthier public opinion, a sturdier manhood and independence, and a promise to maintain the liberties that the people now enjoy, as well as to ever struggle on to attain that happy goal towards which, throughout its entire history, the human family have been perpetually pushing forward.

But in leaving old parties, to whom, to what shall former Democratic or Republican workmen turn? To the People's Party? Are such changes and improvements promised there that the workers can with any degree of assurance throw in their political fortunes with that party? Of course, acting upon the principle "of all evils choose the least," they will more generally cooperate with the People's Party than with any similar party heretofore gracing the Presidential political arena.

As a matter of fact, however, to support the People's Party under the belief that it is a *labor* party is to act under misapprehension. It is not and cannot, in the nature of its make-up, be a labor party, or even one in which the wage-workers will find their haven. Composed, as the People's Party is, mainly of *employing* farmers without any regard to the interests of the *employed* farmers of the country districts or the mechanics and laborers of the industrial centres, there must of necessity be a divergence of purposes, methods, and interests.

In speaking thus frankly of the composition of the People's Party there is no desire to belittle the efforts of its members, or even to withhold the sympathy due them in their agitation to remedy the wrongs which they suffer from corporate power and avarice; on the contrary, the fullest measure of sympathy and all possible encouragement should and will be given them; for they are doing excellent work in directing public attention to the dangers which threaten the body politic of the republic. But, returning to the consideration of the entire cooperation or amalgamation of the wage-workers' organizations with the People's Party, I am persuaded that all who are more than superficial observers, or who are keen students of the past struggles of the proletariat of all countries, will with one accord unite in declaring the union impossible, because it is unnatural. Let me add that, before there can be any hope of the unification of labor's forces of the field, farm, factory, and workshop, the people who work on and in them for wages must be organized to protect *their* interests against those who pay them wages for that work.

Then, if as an organization, the American Federation of Labor will take no official part in the coming Presidential campaign of a partizan character, it may, with a fair degree of reason, be asked what we will do? Some have asked whether we will have a candidate of our own in the field. I can answer both by saying that, apart from the acts already referred to above, we shall maintain as a body a masterly inactivity. As organized trade-unionists, we have had some experience with a Presidential candidate, and in campaigns of our own, the lessons of which have not been forgotten by us.

It may not be generally known that in 1872 the organized workingmen of the country placed a candidate in nomination for the Presidency of the United States. The National Labor Union,[2] the immediate predecessor and parent of the Federation, at its convention of that year, held in Columbus, O., selected the late David Davis,[3] of Illinois, as its standard bearer. So far as the nomination was concerned, quite a degree of success was attained. A candidate was placed in the field, but it was at the cost of the life of the organization. Another convention of the National Labor Union was never held after that. Indeed, so great was the reaction among the organized workingmen against this departure, and so thoroughly had they lost confidence in a general organization of a national character, that, despite all efforts to induce them to be represented in a national convention, defeat and disappointment were the result until 1881, when the Federation was called into existence.

Since its organization the American Federation of Labor has kept in mind two facts: first, the lamentable experience of its predecessor; and second, that, in the struggle for improved conditions and emancipation for the toilers, what is wanted is the organization of the wage-workers, not on "party" lines, but on the lines of their class interests.

As an organization, the American Federation of Labor is not in harmony either with the existing or projected political parties. So deep-seated is the conviction in this matter that, long ago, it was decided to hold the conventions of the Federation *after* the elections. Thus freed from party bias and campaign crimination, these gatherings have been in a position to declare for general principles, and to judge impartially upon the merits or demerits of each party, holding each to an accountability for its perfidy to the promises made to the working people, and at the same time keeping clear and distinct the economic character of the organization. By our non-political partisan [non-partisan political] character as an organization, we tacitly declare that political liberty with[out] economic independence is illusory and deceptive, and that only in so far as we gain economic independence can our political liberty become tangible and important. This may sound like political heresy, but it is economic truth.

As time goes on we discern that the organized workingmen place less reliance upon the help offered by others, and it is a spark upon the altar of progress that they have learned to more firmly depend upon their own efforts to secure those changes and improvements which are theirs by right.

Of course it must not be imagined that we have no interest in the political affairs of our country; on the contrary, we believe that it is our mission to gather the vast numbers of the wealth-producers, agricultural, industrial, and commercial, into a grand army of organized labor, and, by our struggles for improved conditions and emancipation, instil into the minds of the workers a keener appreciation of their true position in society and of their economic, political and social duties and rights as citizens and workers. Every advantage gained in the economic condition of the wage-workers must necessarily have its political and social effect, not only upon themselves but upon the whole people. Hence for the present, at least, nearly all our efforts are concentrated upon the field as indicated above.

Many may find fault in our refraining from directly entering the political arena by the nomination of candidates for national and State offices and will point to results in England and other countries for our emulation. In considering this question it must be borne in mind that the *bona-fide* labor movement, as expressed in the trades-unions of America, is much younger, both in years and experience, than it is abroad, and that the element of time is an important factor for the rank and file to mature that confidence in the wisdom and honesty of their leaders, which is as necessary a pre-requisite to the party entering the field of politics, as it has been in that of economics.

Whatever has been gained for the toilers in our country has been the achievement of the trades-unions, and it would be most unwise, not to say anything harsher, to abandon the organization, position and methods of past success to fly "to others we know not of." More than half of the battle of labor has already been won. No really intelligent man to-day disputes the claims of labor. The stage of ridicule is happily past; the era of reason has taken its place; and what is now needed is the means and the power to enforce our claim. To that end we are marshalling our forces, and we will demonstrate to the world that the demands and struggles of the toiling masses, while ostensibly and immediately concerned with their own improvement and emancipation, will develop the possibilities, grandeur and true nobility of the human family.

Having mapped out our course, the members of the American Federation of Labor can look on the coming Presidential campaign with a degree of equanimity not often attained by the average citizen. The excitement and turmoil, criminations and recriminations will not rend our organization asunder, as it has done so many others; and during it all, and when the blare of trumpets has died away, and the "spell-binders" have received their rewards, the American Federation of Labor will still be found plodding along, doing noble battle in the struggle for the uplifting of the toiling masses.

North American Review 155 (July 1892): 91-96.

1. Chester A. Arthur (1830-86) was vice-president of the United States from March to September 1881 and president from 1881 to 1885.

2. The National Labor Union (NLU) organized in Baltimore in August 1866 at a convention composed primarily of delegates from local unions, city central labor bodies, and eight-hour leagues. Under this name from 1866 to 1872, and as the Industrial Congress from 1873 to 1875, it was essentially a series of annual congresses for the formulating of labor-reform demands. Among those demands were the adoption of the eight-hour day, the establishment of cooperatives, organization of trade unions, reform in the currency, banking, and tax systems, and the creation of a U.S. department of labor.

3. David Davis (1815-86) of Bloomington, Ill., was a U.S. Supreme Court justice from 1862 to 1877. A convention in Columbus, Ohio, Feb. 21-22, 1872, sponsored by the NLU, nominated Davis for the presidency of the United States under the banner of the National Labor Reform party. Davis withdrew his candidacy, however, after failing to receive the endorsement of the Liberal Republican party.

To Clarence Connolly[1]

Aug. 8th. [189]2

Mr. C. P. Connolly,
Sec. Trades and Labor Union[2]
Mermod-Jaccard Bldg. (room 419) St. Louis, Mo.
Dear Sir and Brother: —

Having in mind the subject matter that the Committee from the Trades and Labor Union presented to me, and also your communication upon the subject of the annulment or revocation of the commission as general organizer to Mr. A. S. Leitch,[3] I desire to say that I investigated it and heard all parties in interest, and after mature consideration have concluded to revoke the commissions of all the organizers located at St. Louis, and to adopt a different method for the organizers located in your city.[4] The method I refer to is as follows:

That the Trades and Labor Union select one man to whom a commission from this office shall be issued as general organizer for St. Louis, and to also select four additional names to whom commissions shall be issued as assistant organizers. In selecting the names for the assistant organizers I trust you will have in mind and consult the wishes of those local unions which have no National Union of their trade in existence.

It should require no assurance that I have endeavored and shall endeavor to advance the best interest of our movement not only for any particular locality but for our whole country.

In my judgment the differences that have existed in the past have been more imaginary than real among the active workers in the labor cause of St. Louis, and if there were a little more mutual toleration of each others' views a better feeling would prevail and greater success attend the efforts of all.

I ask you to act upon the above suggestion in reference to the organizers at your earliest possible convenience as I write this the first letter after my return from your city, my visit to which I hope has been instrumental in doing some good to our great movement.

With kindest wishes to all, I am,

Fraternally Yours   Saml Gompers.
President. American Federation of Labor.

N.B. I have sent a copy of this letter to each of our organizers in St. Louis with an explanatory note.

TLpS, reel 6, vol. 7, p. 709, SG Letterbooks, DLC.

1. Clarence P. Connolly was a St. Louis printer and member of International Typographical Union 8.

2. The St. Louis Central Trades and Labor Union (CTLU) was founded in 1887.

3. Andrew S. Leitch was a printer, editor, and labor organizer active in St. Louis and New York in the late 1880s and 1890s. In St. Louis he published the *Union Record* (1890-94), was superintendent of the St. Louis Labor Press Association (1895-96), and was an AFL general organizer (1892).

4. When leaders of the St. Louis CTLU met with SG during his visit to the city in early August 1892, they accused Leitch of not acting in the best interests of labor in St. Louis and asked SG to revoke his organizer's commission. SG decided to install a new system of appointing AFL organizers in the city, hoping to "remove a great deal of the objection now entertained by the Trades and Labor Union to having an organizer independent of their body" (SG to Leitch, Aug. 8, 1892, reel 6, vol. 7, p. 710, SG Letterbooks, DLC).

An Article in the *Pittsburgh Dispatch*

[August 14, 1892]

A CALL FOR AID FROM HOMESTEAD.

The Executive Council of the American Federation of Labor finished its work in connection with the Homestead affair at the Duquesne Hotel last evening.[1] After the mass meeting in the village was over the council returned to the hotel and completed the circular on the situation which is intended for the American people, and will be sent broadcast all over the land.

President Gompers, Secretary Chris Evans and P. J. McGuire returned to New York on the fast line. They expressed themselves as well pleased with what had been done. Mr. McGuire said the meeting at Homestead was the largest ever held in the town, and the people there are greatly encouraged. The officers feel that the circular will correct all false impressions, and result in liberal contributions for the Homestead people. Mr. Gompers said the written statement covered the ground and he had nothing further to add. He remarked that trade in general had recovered a little, but he talked as if the outlook was not any too bright.

THE SIGNERS OF THE CIRCULAR.

The circular concludes by requesting all contributors to send their money to President Wiehe or Acting Chairman Thomas J. Crawford.[2] The document is signed by President Samuel J. Gompers, P. J. McGuire, President of the Carpenters' Brotherhood; John B. Lennon, Secretary of the Tailors' Union; Secretary Chris Evans, as the Executive Committee of the Federation; President Wiehe, President-elect Garland[3] and Secretary Steve Madden,[4] for the Amalgamated Association, and Hugh O'Donnell,[5] Burgess McLuckie,[6] Thomas J. Crawford and David Lynch,[7] for the Advisory Committee. The circular follows:

["]Seldom in the history of our country have we witnessed the lines of battle so closely drawn upon the field of labor as it is witnessed at Homestead. The Carnegie Steel Company, one of the most gigantic monopolies of the age, has undertaken to reduce the wages of their employes from 10 to 40 per cent. In their desperation and avarice they hired and brought 300 armed mercenaries, Pinkerton detectives, to Homestead to invade the homes of the men who created the millions that the Carnegies now possess. Under cover of the Pinkertons the company endeavored to introduce a pauperized and degraded set of laborers to supplant our fellow American workmen. The contest with the Pinkertons and its results are well known.["]

THE CLAIM AS TO HIGH WAGES.

["]It is not true that the men are receiving the high wages generally supposed, nor do a large number own their homes. We have made a careful investigation, and find that just before the lockout there were 3,421 employed in the mills. Of this number there were 13 whose wages averaged about $7.50 per day; 46 averaged between $5 and $7 per day; 54 averaged from $4 to $5 per day; 1,178 averaged from $1.68 to $2.50 per day, and 1,623 received 14 cents per hour or less, and further we find so many erroneous and false statements have been published as to the causes for which the men are nobly contending, their conduct during the struggle, the present situation and the prospect of victory that we feel called upon to issue this statement to the American public.

["]From 8 to 10 per cent own their homes, and about 15 per cent more have homes under mortgage; the remainder pay rent and a number of these have been evicted by the Carnegies. It is not true that the men are only defending the wages of the higher priced workmen. It is in defense of the 14-cents-per-hour men as much as any other that the Homestead workmen are making their gallant fight.

["]The cunning, calculating company proposed that the scale should terminate when the cold blasts of winter penetrate with biting severity. The company desired to place the men in the disadvantageous position of negotiating with them upon a new scale in January instead of as formerly in July.["]

Not Getting Skilled Workmen.

["]Notwithstanding the military forces of the State of Pennsylvania have been under arms at Homestead for nearly five weeks, and the country has been ransacked to find beings so low as to hire themselves to the company, there are less than 600 persons in the mill, and less than a dozen skilled workmen who can perform the work required. The situation is such we confidently assert that at no time during the struggle were the prospects of victory as bright as they are now. What the men in this contest need is your substantial support as well as your sympathy. The poorer paid men in Homestead and other Carnegie mills where men are now out to help their brothers at Homestead, are the ones who need your immediate help, and money is required to maintain their manhood, honor and interest. Every worker and liberty-loving citizen should contribute to the financial support of the brave men who to-day occupy the position of the advance guard of the labor movement of America.

["]The struggle at Homestead represents the issue between freedom and slavery, progress and reaction, and must be maintained until the workmen have some fair measure of recognition from the Carnegies. We assure you that every dollar contributed will be devoted to the men engaged in this contest. An effective system of relief has been organized, with proper safeguards, and every cent will be economically expended and rigidly accounted for. We also advise all working men not to come to Homestead or Pittsburg for employment until the pending dispute with the Carnegie Steel Company is settled.["]

The Address of President Gompers.

The mass meeting in the afternoon aroused all latent enthusiasm among the locked-out men, and 1,500 who crowded into the rink cheered themselves hoarse over the encouraging utterances of the leaders of the American Federation of Labor. Last night confidence in victory prevailed alone. The meeting was called to order by Acting Chairman Thomas Crawford, of the Advisory Committee. Jerry Dougherty[8] was appointed Chairman, and William McConegley,[9] Secretary. President Gompers was introduced amid applause. He said:

["]One scarcely knows how to begin an address to his fellow workingmen under the circumstances which surround you in Homestead to-day. We find men who dare to do that which they believe and know to be right in defense of their homes, their wives and children, and what they believe to be in defense of their fellow citizens of these United States. I say that this is a peculiar situation where citizens meet under the guns of the military of this proud State of Pennsylvania.

["]The Carnegie Company owns immense plants. They have introduced wonderful machinery, it is true, but they also possess an enormous monopoly of steel billets, and they want to introduce a scale based upon a minimum of prices for steel billets, which they control. I am informed that the men consented to a large reduction, but the firm wanted to reach men who might make $6 a day, but they do not want to call attention to men working for $1.14 a day. They do not want to call attention to the squalor and misery of those men. No, but they spread such rosy reports that instead of seeing the hovels, which I have seen, one would imagine every one lived in a palace. The steel workers have made a Carnegie possible. Mr. Frick signalized his advancement to the proud position which he has by issuing his edict saying, 'I will brook no interference from people who do not obey my order.'["]

THE INTRODUCTION OF THE PINKERTONS.

["]I ask if any autocrat could assume a more dictatorial attitude. You Homestead steelworkers, if there is a rosebush blooming it is your work; if there is anything under the sun which shines upon you, which makes Homestead valuable, it is your work. You refused to bow down to this wonderful autocrat, and the first answer he gave you was to send that band of hirelings into this peaceful community to force you to bow down to him, and ultimately drive you from your peaceful homes. I know not who fired the first shot on that memorable morning of the 6th of July, but I do know that the hearts of the great American people beat in unison and in sympathy with the brave men of Homestead. I am a man of peace and I love peace, but I am like that great man, Patrick Henry, I stand as an American citizen and say: 'Give me liberty or give me death.'

["]Animals cannot exist without food and water, and the true American citizen cannot live without his liberty. The attempts of Frick to bring two boatloads of vagabonds into Homestead was the death knell of the interference of Pinkerton detectives with the rights of organized labor. I do not indorse the attempt on Frick's life.[10] It certainly did our cause no good.["]

ATTACKING THE POCKETBOOK.

["]I do not think it does any good to harm even a hair on the head of such men. It is better to touch their pocketbooks, and I think that you will agree with me when I say that the Carnegie Company's pocketbook is being touched pretty hard just now.["]

Mr. Gompers severely criticised Secretary Lovejoy,[11] calling him, among other things, "a telephonic voluble crank, who talks without motion, and doesn't care or know what he says." He continued:

["]I hear that Lovejoy has said that if the Federation declares a boycott on Carnegie production the officers will be arrested for conspiracy. Now, I don't want to pose before you as an idle boaster and I certainly don't care to go to jail, but I do say this to you: If the American Federation believes that it will aid your cause to declare a boycott on Carnegie goods, I promise you that when that time arrives I will come within the borders of this great State of Pennsylvania and declare it to the world.

["]Above all don't lose your temper. Continue as you have been doing in waging your fight under a curtain of apparent masterly inactivity, and last of all and more important of all, don't work for Carnegie until he comes to your terms.["]

THE SPEECH OF SECRETARY MCGUIRE.

When Mr. Gompers sat down, P. J. McGuire, Secretary of the Brotherhood of Carpenters and Joiners of America, was introduced. He said among other things—that the battle on the Homestead river front was to his mind the Lexington of the labor movement, and that in the end it might also prove to be the Yorktown of the campaign, and that Carnegie and all of his kind would be forced to surrender. After commenting in caustic terms on the presence and behavior of the militia and the methods of the associate of the company, Mr. McGuire concluded his speech with these words:

["]It is a bad thing to whistle when going through a graveyard to keep your spirits up, but Secretary Lovejoy does it to the Queen's taste. The mill looks like a graveyard and the furnaces are crematories for 'scabs.'["]

John B. Lennon, Christopher E. Evans and William A. Carney made brief addresses. They were listened to attentively, but the speeches of Gompers and McGuire kindled the most enthusiasm.

Pittsburgh Dispatch, Aug. 14, 1892.

1. The AFL Executive Council met in Pittsburgh, Aug. 12-13, 1892.

2. Thomas J. Crawford, a Homestead steelworker, was vice-chairman of the Homestead advisory committee of the National Amalgamated Association of Iron and Steel Workers (NAAISW) from its inception on June 29, 1892. He became chairman in early September after authorities jailed the original chairman, Hugh O'Donnell. Later that month Crawford was charged with aggravated riot, conspiracy, and treason, charges that were all eventually dropped. He resigned from the committee on Nov. 19, leaving Homestead to take a job at a Uniontown, Pa., mill.

3. Mahlon Morris GARLAND was assistant president of the NAAISW from 1890

until November 1892, when he became the union's president. He served in that office until 1898.

4. Stephen MADDEN was secretary of the NAAISW from 1890 to 1892.

5. Hugh O'Donnell, a Homestead heater and member of NAAISW William Roberts Lodge 125, was elected chairman of the Homestead advisory committee when it was established on June 29, 1892. He resigned the position in early September when he was held without bail on charges of conspiracy, aggravated riot, treason, and two counts of murder. After being acquitted on one of the murder charges in February 1893, he was released on bail; all other charges against him were eventually dropped.

6. John McLuckie, an assistant roller and a member of both the NAAISW and of the Homestead advisory committee, was serving his second term as burgess of the borough of Homestead. In September 1892 he was charged with aggravated riot, conspiracy, treason, and two counts of murder related to the July 6 confrontation. He remained free on bail and all charges against him were subsequently dropped; nevertheless, he resigned his position as burgess on Oct. 31.

7. David Lynch, a heater and chairman of NAAISW Thomas Marlow Lodge 56 of Homestead, was elected to the Homestead advisory committee on June 29, 1892. In September he was charged with conspiracy and treason, though the charges were eventually dropped. In November he ran unsuccessfully for the Pennsylvania legislature as a Democrat from the sixth district. He subsequently served on the Homestead relief and defense committee that operated through March 1893.

8. Probably Jeremiah Doherty.

9. William F. McConegly, a gauger and member of NAAISW Armor Lodge 54, was a member of the Homestead advisory committee. In September 1892 he was one of the strike leaders charged with conspiracy and treason; the charges were subsequently dropped.

10. On July 23, 1892, Alexander Berkman, a Russian anarchist, forced his way into Henry Clay Frick's office in Pittsburgh's Carnegie Building, and shot and stabbed him. Frick returned to work two weeks later. On Sept. 19 Berkman was convicted and sentenced to twenty-two years imprisonment.

11. Francis Thomas Fletcher Lovejoy was secretary of the Carnegie Steel Co.

To Gabriel Edmonston

New York, Aug. 18th. 1892

Mr. G. Edmonston,
805 11th. St. N.W. Washington, D.C.
Dear Friend:—

Your favor of the 11th. came to my house during my absence at Homestead and I take this the earliest opportunity to reply.

I only have one copy of the souvenir and that is a bound one for the use of this office, but have written to P. J. requesting him to send you a copy and also one to Sam. When you receive it after reading the other matter I want you to take a glance at the article I have written in it on the question of "High Dues,"[1] and let me know your opinion of it.

I saw your photo and think it an excellent one. Won't you favor me with the original from which that was taken. I want it for my album.

I read the sketch of your life in the souvenir and of course the old rebel yell is in it "the light is still out for the repentent sinner" and even in the last hour we will take you into the fold of unionists.

I doubt my ability to come on during the G.A.R. meeting[2] as in all probability I shall be in Louisiana about that time. Will you please tell me the date upon which the meeting opens and also ascertain at what rate the G.A.R. return tickets from Indianapolis are likely to be sold at.

I am glad your taste for a good smoke is being cultivated. Plug uglies too often tried by you was indeed depraving not only to yourself but to every one associated with you.

By the way supposing you would make a trip with me to Indianapolis and New Orleans in Sept. If you do we may be enabled to take a trip on the Mississippi river from New Orleans to St. Louis lasting five or six days. This would be my first actual vacation and I am anxious for a few days to be away from the world. Let me know in reference to this.

I am much gratified to know that Sam and Sophia are getting along so nicely and I know that it also pleases you.

Did you read my article in the July number of the North American Review.[3] If you get a chance take a look at it in one of the libraries.

Did I send you a souvenir of our last convention. I have a few left and will send you one if you haven't seen it.

Asking to be remembered to our friends and with kindest wishes, I am

Truly Yours   Saml Gompers.

Don't fail to answer soon.

TLpS, Papers of Gabriel Edmonston, reel 1, *AFL Records.*

1. An article by SG entitled "An Argument in Favor of Higher Dues in Trades Unions" appeared in the *Official Handbook of the United Brotherhood of Carpenters and Joiners of America, 1892,* pp. 47-49.

2. Probably the Sept. 21, 1892, Indianapolis reunion of Union soldiers under the auspices of the Grand Army of the Republic.

3. See "An Article by Samuel Gompers in the *North American Review,*" July 1892, above.

To John O'Brien

Aug. 22nd. [189]2

Mr. John O'Brien
c/o Oregonian Office Portland, Oreg.
Dear Sir and Friend: —

I am in receipt of your interesting favor of the 8th. inst. the contents of which are carefully noted.

In reply I desire to say that while I can readily understand you cannot give the time you desire in furthering the great cause represented by the labor movement, yet I know that with or without a commission you will always do that which lies in your power to advance it.

I should have issued a commission to Mr. Grimes[1] but he has removed to Springfield, Ill. and in all probability will be active in that section of the country. I had the pleasure of meeting him a few weeks ago at St. Louis where he was a delegate to the convention of the United Brotherhood of Carpenters and Joiners of America.

I have endeavored to keep informed of the Coeur trouble,[2] but all the Associated and United Press accounts I know are garbled and colored in the interest of the Mine owners. I saw a statement in the hands of a friend of mine published in some paper on the Coast and issued by one of the organizations which gave the entire matter in its true light from labor's standpoint. I should like to be in possession of the paper if possible. I only had the chance to give it a glance by reason of the hasty departure of the party having the paper. Is it possible for you to secure it for me? You may know to which I refer.

Since your writing we can add Buffalo[3] and Tennessee[4] to Homestead and Coeur D'Alene where the equal rights of labor is denied to that of the wealth possessors. Organized labor is not in a position to stand a crucial test and you may rest assured that there will be a movement of the capitalists and their hirelings and hangers on all along the line and it will require the greatest effort of every right thinking man to prevent disintegration of the united forces of labor and a consequent demoralization and reaction. What is most needed now and will be for months to come is that the men who think clear and feel true to the cause shall not be mealymouthed in the discussion, demands and aspirations of the toiling masses. The future may find them in a position to stand the venomous attacks of the capitalistic classes, but that ought not to deviate us from what we know to be our duty. If we have the courage of our convictions to do as suggested, we will [do] better work in withstanding the onslaughts against our organizations and always assuming the aggressive rather than being placed in the contemptible and uncomfortable position of the defensive.

It will not be possible for me to attend the convention at Seattle[5] and I was really unaware of the fact of its being held so soon. If I had the date I should gladly write to them.

I hope that the organizations on the Coast will be more generally represented at the conventions of the American Federation of Labor and I am pleased to note what you say of the representation of the Portland Unions at Philadelphia next December.[6]

Trusting that the future may be brighter for you, and with kindest wishes, I am,

Sincerely Yours   Saml Gompers.
President. American Federation of Labor.

TLpS, reel 6, vol. 7, pp. 777-78, SG Letterbooks, DLC.

1. James F. Grimes moved from Portland, Ore., to Springfield, Ill., where he joined United Brotherhood of Carpenters and Joiners of America 16 in 1893. He subsequently moved to Houston, Tex., and became an AFL organizer in 1896.

2. During the first months of 1892 members of the Mine Owners' Protective Association of the Coeur d'Alene lead and silver mining region of Idaho shut down their mines and mills to protest an increase in railroad freight rates. With the reinstitution of the old rates, they agreed to reopen the mines on or before April 1, but at a lower wage scale. The Miners' Union of Coeur d'Alene, a central organization representing four local unions, objected, and the miners refused to return to work. When striking miners prevented four strikebreakers from working, the U.S. circuit court for the District of Idaho issued restraining injunctions in early May, and, during the next months, the mine owners brought in additional strikebreakers under armed guard. On July 11, inspired by the steelworkers' struggle at Homestead, Pa., and angered at the discovery of a Pinkerton spy, armed miners drove these men out of the region and seized two mines; a number of men were killed. A concentrating mill at the Frisco mine was blown up during the battle.

Governor Norman B. Willey called out the National Guard on July 11 and placed Shoshone Co., Idaho, under martial law on July 13. On his request, President Benjamin Harrison dispatched federal troops to the area on July 12; they arrived on July 14 and 15. During the next five days they arrested about 600 miners and sympathizers, holding many of them in makeshift stockades. Hundreds were indicted. In trials between August 1892 and March 1893, thirteen were convicted of contempt of court and four of conspiracy. The 1892 AFL convention appropriated $500 for the miners' defense and called for a congressional investigation. In the meantime the mines reopened with nonunion workers under military protection, and during the fall union men returned to work. Martial law ended on Nov. 19. On Mar. 6, 1893, the U.S. Supreme Court reversed the conspiracy convictions, and the courts then lifted the remaining indictments and released those still in custody.

3. Under the leadership of Switchmen's Mutual Aid Association (SMAA) Lodge 39, the switchmen on the Lehigh Valley, the Erie, and the Buffalo Creek railroads struck on Aug. 12, 1892, demanding the enforcement of New York state's ten-hour law. The strikers were initially successful in halting the movement of freight, but on

Aug. 15 a number of railroad cars were burned and the New York state militia was called in; they arrived on Aug. 18. The switchmen on the New York Central and Nickel Plate lines then joined the strike in sympathy. On Aug. 24 Frank Sweeney, grand master of the SMAA, met with the chief officers of the Brotherhood of Railroad Trainmen, the Brotherhood of Locomotive Firemen, and the Order of Railway Conductors of America, in an unsuccessful attempt to begin a general strike. The switchmen's strike collapsed the following day.

4. The uprising of Tennessee miners in the summer of 1892 developed against a backdrop of miner resistance to the Tennessee Coal, Iron, and Railroad Co.'s convict leasing contract with the state. In July 1891 miners had attempted to solve the problem by political means after a major confrontation over convict labor at the company's Briceville mines. In that incident, the company employed convict labor following the refusal of KOL miners to work under a new contract that prohibited strikes and required miners to utilize company check-weighman rather than their own. Local citizens and miners forcibly sent the convict laborers back to Knoxville. The state militia returned the convicts to the mines only to see them evicted again from Briceville as well as from Coal Creek, where Tennessee Coal subleased convicts to the Knoxville Iron Co. Miners allowed the convicts to return when Governor John P. Buchanan interceded and promised to call a special session of the legislature to consider repealing the convict labor system. The legislature, however, refused to abandon the leasing system, and a court subsequently upheld the company's contract with the state.

In August 1892 miners in Tracy City, Oliver Springs, Inman, and Coal Creek renewed their struggle against the company's use of convicts as full-time workers while free miners worked only half time. They seized the convict laborers and sent them away by train; the state militia returned the convicts and arrested several hundred miners. The 1892 AFL convention appropriated $500 toward their defense. Some of the defendants eventually received fines or prison sentences. Intermittent resistance continued throughout Tennessee, however, until the company's contract with the state terminated in 1896.

5. Probably a meeting of the Council of Federated Trades of the Pacific Coast, originally scheduled for Sept. 19, 1892, but postponed until June 5, 1893.

6. The 1892 AFL convention met Dec. 12-17 in Philadelphia.

To Lyman Gage

Aug. 29th [189]2

Hon. Lyman J. Gage,
Chicago, Ill.
Dear Sir:—

It was impossible to give you the estimate before I left Chicago, of what I believed the expenses would be for a few men to go to Europe in the interest of the International Labor Congress, owing to the many things I had to attend to while in your city, and the necessity for my returning here at the earliest possible moment. I do so now, and trust you will give the matter your early attention in order that the question can be definitely settled.

In my opinion it will require five men to devote their entire time until the early Spring of '93; two of them to devote their entire attention to England, Scotland, Ireland and Wales; one to France, Switzerland and probably Belgium; one to Germany, Austria and possibly Belgium or Holland; and one to Spain, Italy and Cuba. Either or all of these men may be compelled to visit other countries, and I certainly should like to arrange it so that one of them could start for Australia. If it were possible to secure representation ever so small from our Embryo Republic of the Far West it would redound to our credit and add much zest both to the Exposition, our Congress, and last but not least, our Country.

There would be a large amount of work necessary to be done by way of correspondence and additional clerical help, which in my opinion together with the travelling expenses would involve a total cost of not less than ten thousand ($10.000) dollars.

During our conversation I stated that in consequence of the time elapsing between our former conversation and the last that the necessity for so large a sum did not exist, but upon maturer thought I am forced to the conclusion that the sum of $10.000 will be necessary as at first calculated. Some months ago a lesser number of men could have performed the work. Now, in consequence of the time lost, additional men will be required to perform the work.

I am sure that if a proper appreciation exists as to the value of an International Labor Congress there will be no fault found upon the score of the money involved. While it may be a fact that the Congresses in the arts and sciences may be of general value, yet to the thinking portion of humanity the thought presses on our minds that there is but one actual living issue in which humanity is more largely interested than any other, and that is the Labor Question. To have a Congress representative in its character of the struggles, hopes and aspirations of the workers of the world would add dignity and importance to our Exposition, [and?] to our country.

There is no necessity of arguing this question with you, for I am aware that you conceive and appreciate its importance. I only ask now that you will have this question determined at the earliest possible time, so that we may be enabled to have our plans ready and prosecute the work with vigor.

Very Truly Yours   Saml Gompers.
President. American Federation of Labor.

TLpS, reel 6, vol. 7, pp. 788-89, SG Letterbooks, DLC.

To Thomas Crawford

Aug. 30th. [189]2

Mr. Thos. J. Crawford,
Box 196 Homestead, Pa.
Dear Sir and Brother:—

The enclosed letter came to this office during my absence in the West and I was unable to give it earlier attention.

From a perusal of it you will see that Mr. Frick makes some very damaging statements in reference to the men who received the highest pay while working for the Carnegie Co. I am confident that his statements have no foundation in fact, but I have promised Messrs. Funk and Wagnalls[1] that I would refer the letter to you and that you would make an answer to it, and that when you forward your answer to me I will add such comments as I think advisable or necessary.

I know the general attitude of such men as Frick when they discuss the actions of workingmen who dare maintain their rights and I have had several occasions to expose the falsity and fallacy of their utterances. I earnestly hope that you will give this matter your early and careful consideration and reply thereto at your earliest convenience sending your letter here.

Let me call your attention to the fact that Funk and Wagnalls are the Editors of "The Voice" the Prohibition Organ and very much interested in labor questions, and I am sure they will publish our statements in contradiction to those of Mr. Frick. In sending your answer to me please return Messrs. Funk and Wagnalls' letter.

I saw in the papers this morning that you and a number of men have again been arrested for conspiracy and aggravated riot, but yet the good work goes on and I am gratified to learn that the ranks of the Homestead Steel men and fellow-workers are unbroken and their courage undaunted.

In your letter to Secretary Evans you mention that there have been some envelopes without circulars. I mail to your address with this about 100 of them so that they can be enclosed. Should you need any additional they will be promptly forwarded. Those envelopes marked city were evidently intended to be for New York city. If you will have the words "New York" added to the address it will supply the deficiency.

In all probability you have heard that the meeting at which Mr. O'Donnell spoke in this city was quite a fizzle.[2] I am not surprised at all, for with the exception of Dr. Mc-Glynn[3] every New York man who appeared upon the platform at that meeting has been discredited in the ranks of organized labor. While Mr. O'Donnell was in New York he did not deign to place himself in connection with the labor men of this city who are in touch with the organized workers. Those with whom he was in company could not muster a "Corporal's Guard" at the meeting, and he has had his fizzle for his pains. You remember that when he started how faithfully he promised me to call at this office when in New York, and as a matter of fact he never showed himself. So far as I am personally concerned it makes very little difference, but it does seem peculiar for a man to come East representing a noble struggling Trade Union, instead of allying himself with his fellow unionists avoiding them and allowing himself to be made the tool of persons who are Union wreckers. However, Mr. O'Donnell's lack of judgment or fraternal conduct will in nowise deter us from performing the full measure of our duty to our Homestead struggling brothers, whom we will endeavor to aid to complete success and victory.

Kindly give the above matters, particularly the enclosed letter, your early attention and oblige,

Yours Fraternally   Saml Gompers.
President. American Federation of Labor.

TLpS, reel 6, vol. 7, pp. 792-93, SG Letterbooks, DLC.

1. Isaac Kaufman Funk and Adam Willis Wagnalls, publishers, were founders and partners in the Funk and Wagnalls Co. of New York City.

2. Hugh O'Donnell addressed a meeting, sponsored by KOL district assemblies 49, 197, and 253, at Cooper Union on Aug. 25, 1892.

3. Edward McGlynn, a New York-born Catholic priest, was an outspoken supporter of the single tax and the first president of the Anti-Poverty Society.

To William Weihe

Sept. 8th. [189]2

Mr. Wm. Weihe,
Prest. A.A. of I. and S.W. of A.
512 Smithfield St. Pittsburgh, Pa.
Dear Sir and Brother:—

Yesterday Mr. Mc-Gonigle secretary of the Advisory Committee of the Homestead Strikers called at this office on his way home. Messrs. Lennon, Evans, and myself had a general conversation upon the present situation of the Homestead struggle. He assured us that the conditions were very bright for the men, but expressed the belief that more ought to be done in the way of securing financial assistance for those not entitled to benefit from the A.A.

As a result of our conversation it was deemed advisable to make the following suggestion to you, that six or eight men from Homestead who are qualified to give in a plain matter of fact way a clear statement of the conditions and the present situation should be appointed to visit the Industrial Centres and take in a radius of from 50 to 200 miles, spending a few weeks in these localities and visiting the Unions at their meetings. They should be provided with credentials signed by yourself and the Secretary of the A.A., the Chairman and Secretary of the Advisory Committee and the Secretary and President of the A.F. of L.

We feel satisfied that if this course is pursued much of the interest manifested a few weeks ago might be revived in favor of the Homestead men and a great deal more assistance received than is now given.

You are no doubt aware that the unfortunate strike of the Switchmen at Buffalo and its result overshadowed the Homestead contest in the public eye. As a consequence I think something should be done to revive the interest and to convey the knowledge suppressed by the Press of the country that the contest at Homestead is still on with the chances good for victory.

I hope you will give this matter your early attention and advise me as to the course you desire to pursue in the matter.[1]

With kindest wishes, I am,

Fraternally Yours   Saml Gompers.
President. American Federation of Labor.

TLpS, reel 6, vol. 7, p. 821, SG Letterbooks, DLC.

1. There is no direct indication that Weihe took up SG's suggestion, though the following month SG and Chris Evans endorsed the credentials of committees that were raising money for the Homestead strikers.

To Mary Kenney

Sept. 12th. [189]2

Miss Mary E. Kenney,
259 Commercial St. Boston, Mass.
Dear Sister: —

I assume that I am indebted to you for the copy of the Boston "Globe" containing a report of the Labor Day celebration.[1] I am pleased to see that it was a great success and that you were a conspicuous participant therein. Other than that, we have not received any report from you as to what has been done since you have been in and around Boston, and I would kindly ask you to make such a report. Then again, I believe that you can be of greater service for a few weeks around Troy.

Last week I was in Philadelphia and had a conference with the Shirt Ironers and they are also anxious to have you go there if even only for a short time to aid in the organization of the Laundry Workers in a Union of that trade. There is also a wide field there among the Textile Workers.

I earnestly hope that you are having as good a time as possible and that your work is successful.

Before leaving the East write, and if your presence there is more necessary there for the present I shall interpose no objection. At any rate, you need not leave there unless you hear from me again, that is, if you deem it advisable to remain there longer.

I leave this afternoon (the 10th. inst.)[2] for Indianapolis and Milwaukee and will not return to New York before the 19th.

With kindest wishes and asking to be remembered to our friends, I am,

Fraternally Yours   Saml Gompers.
President. American Federation of Labor.

TLpS, reel 6, vol. 7, p. 841, SG Letterbooks, DLC.

1. The *Boston Daily Globe*, Sept. 6, 1892.
2. This letter was dictated on Sept. 10 and typed on Sept. 12.

To John McBride

Sept. 12th. [189]2

Mr. John Mc-Bride,
Prest. United Mine Workers of America,
Clinton Bldg. Columbus, O.
Dear Sir and Friend: —

I am in receipt of an interesting letter from our general organizer Mr. A. Todenhausen of Knoxville, Tenn. whom you will probably remember as a delegate to the Birmingham convention of the A.F. of L.

In his letter he calls attention to the fact that the Miners of Tennessee who rose in revolt against the Convict Lease System after being so outrageously treated by the Legislature of that State and the condemnation and denunciation that is continually being poured upon the heads of the Miners. He says that there is clear proof that the Miners did not kill some of the men in the posses, but that it was evidently through the bungling of their own associates who were thoroughly inexperienced. The Miners he says occupied the mountains, while the Sheriff's posses were in the ravine, and that the bullets by which some of the men were killed took an upward course and that it would be a physical impossibility for men occupying the position that the Miners did to have shot the officers in that way.

Mr. Todenhausen calls attention to the fact that it is essential that these men now imprisoned and under indictment shall be ably defended; that two lawyers have already been retained, but that the funds to pay them are lacking. He says that they are nearly all members of your Nat. organization and he appeals to us to see that they are provided with money in order to defend the men.

I have promised him that I would write you upon the subject and let him know the course we propose to pursue. I am sure that the case in question is one that appeals not only to our sense of unionism, but calls upon us to do something in order to prevent the corporations and their hirelings from hounding our men into prisons and upon the scaffold, so that they may destroy our unions and have our fellow toilers under their iron heel.

I hope you will take this matter under advisement and let me know what decision has been arrived at.

With kindest wishes and hoping to hear from you soon, I am,

Fraternally Yours   Saml Gompers.
President. American Federation of Labor.

TLpS, reel 6, vol. 7, p. 845, SG Letterbooks, DLC.

To P. J. McGuire

Sept. 12th. [189]2

Mr. P. J. Mc-Guire,
Sec'y. U.B.C. and J. of A.
124 N. 9th. St. Phila, Pa.
Dear Sir and Brother:—

The subject matter of the complaint forwarded by the General Executive Board of the U.B. in the matter of the violation of the Eight Hour Law in the State of Indiana has been decided upon, and I am authorized to say that the Executive Council of the A.F. of L.

has approved the application and decided that a sum not exceeding two hundred and fifty ($250.00) dollars shall be appropriated towards defraying the expenses in a test case[1] to be made in the Courts of that State.

I kindly ask you to advise me as to the most advisable course to pursue in reference to this action so that such parts of the sum decided upon may be placed in the possession of the parties having the case in hand. Will you be the medium of communication between the Union there or will you give us the address so that direct communication may be opened up with them?

Sincerely hoping that we may soon be successful in enforcing the Law and with kindest wishes, I am,

Fraternally Yours   Saml Gompers.
President. American Federation of Labor.

TLpS, reel 6, vol. 7, p. 840, SG Letterbooks, DLC.

1. United Brotherhood of Carpenters and Joiners of America 652 of Elwood, Ind., pursued prosecution of contractor E. R. Coxen for violations of the state eight-hour law (Laws of 1889, chap. 80). Coxen pleaded guilty before the case came to trial.

To Thomas Mann

Sept. 21st. [189]2

Mr. Tom. Mann,
82 Malmesbury Road, Bow, London, E. England.
My Dear Sir and Brother:—

I am in receipt of your favor of the 6th. inst. the contents of which are noted.

When Mr. Goeffrey Draye Secretary of the Royal Commission on Labor arrives here I shall deem it not only my duty but a pleasure to comply with your request and to aid him by all means within my power in ascertaining the information he is desirous of obtaining.[1]

During a tour of the country about two months ago a letter from you reached this office asking for information in reference to our Trade Unions and their distinctive features. I had just begun to prepare my answer when the great struggle at Homestead, Pa. occurred and within a short time thereafter the Railroad Switchmen's strike at Buffalo, N.Y. As a consequence I have been so thoroughly engaged that it was an absolute impossibility to finish the letter except by dealing in generalities and then ending it abruptly. Such is not my fashion of doing business and I preferred to await an opportunity when I could answer fully and to the point.

No doubt I shall have the pleasure of meeting Mr. Draye and when I do I shall make up in my attention to him for the failure to write. If Mr. Draye has not left England by the time this reaches you will you kindly ask him to advise me in reference to the time of his contemplated arrival here.

It was my intention previous to the meeting of the British Trade Union Congress[2] to have a representative trade unionist to go from here and be in attendance at the Glasgow meeting,[3] but in this I was very much disappointed. The object I had in view was to extend a formal invitation to the Trade Unionists of Great Britain to be represented at an International Labor Congress to be held in the city of Chicago during the holding of the World's Columbian Exposition celebrating the 400th. anniversary of the discovery of America.

The newspapers reported that the Congress adopted a resolution recommending to the Trade Unions of Great Britain to have as large a number as possible visit our Exposition. Do you not think it possible that the trade unionists who may visit the Exposition can be delegated by their respective Unions to attend our Congress? Of course I saw that your recent Congress resolved that an International Congress[4] be held some time during the coming year to discuss and act upon the Eight Hour Movement and that taken together with the one called for Switzerland may stand in the way to the fulfillment of this desire. If Trade Unionists will visit the United States it seems to me that nothing can be lost by their being delegated to represent their Unions in the Int. Labor Congress which will be the first one held upon American soil.

Last year Mr. Walter Thos. Mills[5] of Chicago presented an informal invitation at New Castle.[6] I have written to the Hon. Chas. Fenwick,[7] Secretary of the Parliamentary Committee on this matter more than a year ago and since then up to the present time have failed to elicit a reply from him.*[8]

I can readily understand how busy a man you must necessarily be, but I ask you to give me your views upon this subject and urge you to take as deep an interest in it as you possibly can.

With kindest wishes to you and to our fellow unionists of Great Britain and trusting that the dawn of a better day for the toiling masses is near at hand, I am, with fraternal good wishes,

Sincerely Yours   Saml Gompers.
President. American Federation of Labor.

* Today's mail brings the news that Mr. Fenwick laid my invitation I

sent you before this years congress. Can you inform me what [decision was made?] on it?

S. G.

T and ALpS, reel 6, vol. 7, pp. 890-92, SG Letterbooks, DLC.

1. As part of an effort to gather information for a series of reports on labor in foreign countries, Geoffrey Drage, secretary of Great Britain's Royal Commission on Labour, visited the United States in the fall of 1892.

2. The TRADES Union Congress of Great Britain (TUC).

3. The TUC held its 1892 meeting in Glasgow, Sept. 5-10.

4. The TUC resolved that its parliamentary committee convene an international congress in 1893 to discuss the eight-hour day. It subsequently abandoned the undertaking.

5. Walter Thomas Mills, a Chicago businessman, was chairman of the World's Congress Auxiliary (WCA) committee arranging an international congress on labor in conjunction with the World's Columbian Exposition. In 1891 he served as a special commissioner to Great Britain for the WCA.

6. The 1891 TUC meeting was held in Newcastle-upon-Tyne, Sept. 7-12.

7. Charles Fenwick (1850-1918), British miners' leader and Member of Parliament, joined the Northumberland Miners' Association in 1863, eventually becoming a trustee. He was a delegate to the TUC in 1884 and the following year was elected as a liberal Member of Parliament, holding his seat until his death. He served as a delegate to the Paris International Workingmen's Congress in 1889 and was secretary of the Parliamentary Committee and General Council of the TUC from 1890 to 1894.

8. Nov. 21 and 27, 1891, reel 5, vol. 6, pp. 467 and 492, SG Letterbooks, DLC.

To Edward Daley

Sept. 28th. [189]2

Mr. Ed. L. Daley,
Sec. Lasters Pro. Union of America,
620 Atlantic Ave. Boston, Mass.
Dear Sir and Brother:—

Your favor of the 26th. came duly to hand and contents noted.

You ask me for my opinion upon the operations of the Mc-Kinley Bill[1] and whether wages have been increased by reason thereof.

Let me say in reply that while I do not know the purpose you have in making the inquiry it is indicated in your postcript when you request me to state whether I have any objection to having my views made public. In my judgment the object is to have my reply published and in all probability used as a Campaign Document for either one of the two great Political Parties with the view of influencing voters for either of their tickets.

I am never loath to express an opinion or a conviction, but I have decided objections to be brought into the political campaigns of either of the Parties. I am a Union man and an officer of the Federation of Trade Unions of this country. Our organization has studiously avoided the discussion of questions that could be construed to be of a political partisan character, and I have too high an appreciation of that tacit injunction to violate it in this or any other political campaign.

If this question involved a question of labor instead of as it does a question of commerce I should be only too pleased to answer your question at this or any other time, but since the question of the Tariff can not and will not be decided regardless of the successful aspirant for the office in 1892, I believe that an answer to your question to be more appropriate and in keeping with the principles and policy of the American Federation of Labor, should be given after November 8th. 1892. A reminder at that time will, I assure you, receive a full and comprehensive reply.

I beg of you not to consider this letter written in any facetious frame of mind or from any purpose other than to maintain the strict neutrality of the American Federation of Labor as an organization, upon a question with which it has absolutely no business.

With kindest wishes to you and our friends in the movement and hoping to hear from you soon and frequently, I am,

Truly Yours   Saml Gompers.

TLpS, reel 6, vol. 7, p. 925, SG Letterbooks, DLC.

1. The McKinley Tariff Act of 1890 (U.S. *Statutes at Large*, 26: 567-625) represented a substantial increase in protective duties.

To Samuel Goldwater

Oct. 3rd. [189]2

Mr. Samuel Goldwater,
Genl. Organizer A.F. of L.
146 21st. St. Detroit, Mich.
Dear Friend:—

I suppose you deem it strange that I have not written you since I left Indianapolis, more especially after sending you the despatch requesting you to wire your views to the Detroit delegation to the Indianapolis convention of the Street Car Men, upon the action which had been taken declaring that they would form an independent National Union.[1] I believe you are entitled to some explanation and take this first opportunity to give it.

You are aware that the local unions of Street Car Men were undoubtedly brought into existence by our active unionists and organizers. You also know the contests that were made by and in the interest of the Street Car Men for shorter hours of labor, higher wages, improved conditions and the right to organize or participate in [unions], by the unionists throughout the various parts of the country. It is needless for me to say that had it not been for the trade unionists outside of the Street Car Men the former would have been defeated all along the line. As a matter of fact, whatever they have achieved in the line of improvement is due to the combined efforts of the unionists.

Profiting by the example and recognizing the assistance given the Street Car Employes the men of that calling began to organize all over the country on the Trade Union basis. At the last convention of the American Federation of Labor I was directed to call a convention of all Street Car Employes for the purpose of forming a National Union from among their number. I lost no opportunity nor spared any expense in order to make that convention a success. The organizers and trade unionists co-operated nobly with me so much so that when the convention was held at Indianapolis 50 delegates were present representing about 22 different cities. They saw that I went to Indianapolis especially for the purpose of assisting in the formation of the organization.

I called the convention to order; the greetings on all sides were most fraternal but I did not participate in their social festivities. On the Tuesday morning after the Committee on credentials report had been adopted in accordance with trade union principles I surrendered all authority to them, they electing their own officers. I remained with them during the session and in the afternoon was called upon by a Committee having an important matter in hand, and during my absence that afternoon the resolution was adopted declaring that they would maintain an independent attitude from the American Federation of Labor. To say that they would be independent as a National organization from the K. of L. is supremely ridiculous since there were not more than three or four K. of L. assemblies represented.

When I went to the convention the following morning entirely ignorant of what had transpired, I gave them the best possible advice upon questions arising, even at one time upon their own resolution inviting me to do so. Imagine my surprise when during the noon recess I learned for the first time from a Newspaper Reporter that they had adopted a resolution to be "independent." This action had aroused the indignation of every known unionist and believing that the Detroit delegation could influence a change, I wired you requesting you to despatch to them your views upon the subject. It had no effect however, for they persisted in their act.

Messrs. Gruelle and Loebenbeg one the Prest. of the Indiana State Branch[2] of the American Federation of Labor and general organizer of the A.F. of L. the other the organizer of the Retail Clerks Nat. Association endeavored to secure a hearing for the purpose of showing them the error that had been committed, but they were bluntly and discourteously refused a hearing. It was then that I determined that it became my duty to appear again before the convention and express my views upon the subject. Let me say parenthetically that the election of officers had taken place and the order of the Executive designated, that Mr. Webster[3] of Toledo had been selected as President and Mr. Riggs of Indianapolis as Secretary, Indianapolis being chosen as the head quarters.

Wednesday afternoon or Thursday morning Mr. Law[4] with another member of the Detroit delegation called upon me at the hotel expressing their disgust at everything that had taken place and particularly at the action of the convention in refusing to affiliate with the A.F. of L. Mr. Law asked me how many local unions it would require to form a National Union of Street Car Men and to receive a charter from the A.F. of L., the National Union to be independent of the one just formed. I told him that I disapproved of the idea of having two rival organizations of the same calling and urged him rather to use whatever influence he had in the convention to secure a change of this action.

It was on Thursday I called upon the convention and explained to them the error of their act. It is idle to attempt to recount here w[hat] I stated to them then for I believe I addressed them for more than half an hour. I called attention to the fact that their so-called independence was antagonistic to trade union principles and detrimental to their own interests; that it was a message of their own impotency to the Railroad corporations; that they had refused the alliance with the organizations that had secured for them their victories; that independence in the labor movement was a non-union man's argument; that the National Union had the legal, but had no more moral right to remain outside of the family of trade unions of the country, than the wage-workers have to remain outside of the Union of their trade or calling. I left them then only Mr. Husted attempting, before I closed, to palliate by glittering generalities and the expression of good will towards me for their conduct.

I repudiated their expressions of good will towards myself while they administered a rebuke to their friends and organizers. No one else attempted in my presence to defend their action. My words to the convention have already been verified, for in several parts of the country the Railroad corporations have taken them at their word and attacked them on all sides.

I am in receipt of telegrams from Youngstown, O. saying that the Companies there have made war upon the organization,[5] and they are now clamoring for me to come on. You know that since they have their National Union and their own National officers that I cannot come on and act for them unless it would be at the request of their National Officers. If I did without their authority it would in all probability bring about a conflict of authority, and I have thus far not received a request from their National Officers to act.

I should not be surprised if they receive an attack all along the line and that which it has taken years of effort and much expense to create and achieve may be destroyed through their own foolhardiness and shortsighted policy.

Through some action the officers who were elected first resigned, and Messrs. Law and Manuel[6] were elected President and Secretary respectively and the head quarters changed to Detroit. Through an indirect agency I have received a circular issued by these gentlemen in which they speak of the trade unionists represented at the convention amounting to about 4000, and the delegates representing the K. of L. representing more than 7000 members. The figures I have reason to know are not based upon facts, but even if the delegates representing the trade unions had resolved upon forming their National Union and affiliating with the American Federation of Labor they would certainly have influenced the K. of L. Assemblies to join their national organization. The trend and tendency is in that direction, and no locality could withstand it.

I see Mr. Law is now perfectly satisfied with the National organization. His disgust has disappeared since his conversation with me in the hotel. To what that change of mind is attributable, I believe he could better explain himself.

Let me say that notwithstanding their wrong I shall not only do nothing antagonistic to them, but do all that I possibly can to aid every effort they may make to make the National Union a success, confident that time will demonstrate their error and that it will be rectified.

I hope you will pardon this long recital of circumstances, but I deemed it my duty to notify you thereof.

To-day I shall write to Mr. Law in connection with the trouble in Youngstown and you have my liberty to show him or any other sincere unionist this letter. I only ask you in the interest of our movement that it shall not be given to the Press. There may be wrongs committed against the labor movement, but we have no right to make them a matter of public gossip for our enemies to feed upon.

With kindest wishes to you and our friends and hoping to hear from you upon receipt of this as well as a little more frequently than in the past, I am,

Sincerely Yours   Saml Gompers
President. American Federation of Labor.

TLpS, reel 6, vol. 7, pp. 929-32, SG Letterbooks, DLC.

1. The Amalgamated Association of STREET Railway Employes of America (AAS-REA).

2. Organized Sept. 9, 1885, the Indiana Federation of Trade and Labor Unions officially changed its name to the Indiana State Federation of Labor in 1897.

3. Actually Joel E. Husted, a conductor from Toledo, who represented AFL Electric Street Car Employes' Union 5450 at the convention. He was elected president of the new union on Sept. 14, 1892, but resigned the office the next evening after a dispute involving the location of the union's headquarters.

4. William J. LAW was president of the AASREA from 1892 to 1893.

5. AFL Motormen's, Conductors', and Drivers' Union 5550 of Youngstown, Ohio, was one of the organizations that participated in the founding of the AASREA.

6. Joseph C. MANUEL was secretary of the AASREA from 1892 to 1893.

To Charles Tuttle

Oct. 18th. [189]2

Professor Chas. A. Tuttle,
Associate Prof. of Political Economy,
Amherst College, Amherst, Mass.
Dear Sir:

I have the honor to acknowledge the receipt of your favor of the 7th. inst. and regret exceedingly my inability to reply earlier.

In reply to your question permit me to say that there is no doubt much of the restlessness, discontent and source of hardship to the working class of our country is due to the fact that their employment is so insecure and intermittent. It is due in a large measure to the inventions and improvements in the methods and processes of production, but more frequently to the effort of the employing class to reduce wages, increase hours and thus diminish the consumptive powers of the workers and as a necessary consequence tends to curtail the production (employment) of other workers.

It is a common custom more particularly in the unorganized trades and callings for employers to force and compel the workers to toil both day and late in the evening during the short season of the year, notwithstanding that there may be hundreds in that same occupation unemployed. The season is rushed and concentrated in the shortest possible time and "shut downs" follow immediately thereafter and continue for a long period. Time and again during this said "busy season" wages have been reduced. I should be pleased to give you further detailed information and data, but find myself considerably crowded with work pressing upon me.

With this I mail to your address a few pamphlets which will give you further information upon the subject. At another time I should be pleased to go into further details.

Assuring you that I appreciate your kind expressions commending the work we are doing to ameliorate the condition of our fellow-workers, and thanking you for the interest you manifest in our cause, I have the honor to subscribe myself,

Very Respectfully Yours   Saml Gompers.
President. American Federation of Labor.

TLpS, reel 6, vol. 8, p. 18, SG Letterbooks, DLC.

To Henry Blair

Oct. 24th. [189]2

Hon. Henry W. Blair,
Concord, N.H.
Dear Sir and Friend: —

Your favor of recent date came duly to hand, but owing to my absence from the city and a vastly accumulated mail an earlier reply was impossible.

It seems almost superfluous for me to say that I am pleased to learn that you are a candidate for Congress and sincerely express the hope that my pleasure will be enhanced by your election.

I have been actively engaged in the labor movement for more than twenty-five years, but have never known of a man being more thoroughly and systematically abused by the newspaper press than you were and for no other reason than that you dared defend the working people of our country as well as voice their hopes and aspirations.

I exceedingly regret that I am placed in a position which practically makes it impossible for me to go into your District and take part in the canvass and by that means contribute to your election, but I earnestly trust that the working men of your District will do their duty by themselves in standing by you.

Very Truly Yours   Saml Gompers
President. American Federation of Labor.

TLpS, reel 6, vol. 8, p. 29, SG Letterbooks, DLC.

An Article in the *Pittsburgh Dispatch*

[November 6, 1892]

ADVICE ASKED FOR.

The Executive Council of the American Federation of Labor met in this city yesterday. It consisted of President Samuel Gompers, Secretary Chris Evans and Treasurer John B. Lennon. They arrived on an early train from New York City, and went immediately to the headquarters of the Amalgamated Association. They went into consultation with the officers of that organization, and discussed the Homestead strike and the present condition of affairs until noon.

In the afternoon, in company with ex-President Wm. Weighe and other officials of the association, they went to Homestead and addressed the locked-out men at their usual Saturday meeting. On their return to this city another conference was held with the Amalgamated officials. They left for New York on the evening train.

Sizing up the Situation.

The officers of the Federation of Labor had come here on a special invitation of the Amalgamated Association to confer and size up the situation, and if possible adopt some means of bringing the present struggle to a close. The relations of the Amalgamated Association and Federation have been of the friendliest during the present struggle and they have been acting conjointly to bring the Homestead fight to a successful close.

President Gompers when asked last night as to the object of his visit and the probable result of the conference between the officers of the two organizations, said: "I am simply here to look over the ground and see if there is any change in the lockout at Homestead. There is no significance to be attached to the visit, and we have only the power to advise and recommend what is considered as the best course to be pursued. I was warmly received at Homestead, and there expressed my views on the situation, so that it is needless to repeat them here. I found little apparent change from my former visit, and must say the men are making a remarkable fight. Each one seems to be actuated with sufficient determination to never give in.["]

No Change of Programme Adopted.

"No. I do not think there will be any change of plan adopted as a result of the conference to-day. The men deny that there have been any desertions, and I had to take their word, as I was not on the ground long enough to find out, but from appearances there are no indications of any returning to work. Should the men working in any of the departments return it would be a serious blow to the others who are bravely holding out. The mechanics are said to be considering the advisability of going back to work, but I do not think they will.

"As to the effect of the finishers forming a new union,[1] I am inclined to think the movement will fall through. As it is, they are pursuing a very peculiar course to say the least, in trying to secede at this time. They have never notified the old order that they were going to leave it. Then again, why didn't they wait until the end of the time when the present scale would expire, and go about the formation of a union in a manly way? But I have too much confidence in the loyalty of the men to the Amalgamated to believe that they will leave it now. Should they do so, however, and the finishers form a separate union that would be successful, it would be a blow to organized labor, as both would surely lose by the move. Men work against their own interest to separate at the present time, and my wish would be that they stay together.["]

Doesn't Like the Treason Charges.

"I find, however, that the men are keenly feeling the way they are being treated in the cases against them. They do not find fault with the law, but in the way it is being administered. I consider the cases of treason[2] a travesty on justice, and if it were not for their serious nature would be inclined to treat them lightly. But it seems the most will be made of the cases, and [they] are giving the Homestead men some trouble. I find this to be evident and as the time draws near I believe it will be more so."

Mr. Gompers refused to discuss politics, saying that the Federation was a non-partisan political body and that he did not want to say anything on the subject.

In the conference the declaring of a boycott on the product of the Carnegie mills was discussed, but no action was taken. The opinion of some of the members present was expressed afterward, and they believed that no boycott would be declared. Though no decisive action was apparently agreed upon, the conference is considered as significant. What move will be made next is not known, but it is probable that something will be done in a short time that will bring this long drawn struggle to a close.

Pittsburgh Dispatch, Nov. 6, 1892.

1. On Oct. 29, 1892, a group of finishers from Pittsburgh and Youngstown, Ohio, seceded from the National Amalgamated Association of Iron and Steel Workers (NAAISW) and formed the Finishers' Union of Iron and Steel Workers of the United States (also known as the National Union of Iron and Steel Workers of the United States). The finishers were dissatisfied with the new wage scale negotiated by the Amalgamated and were concerned about becoming involved in further strikes. The new union never gained general support and lasted only a few years.

2. On Sept. 30, 1892, a grand jury, under instructions from Chief Justice Edward Paxson of the Pennsylvania supreme court, brought treason charges under the Crimes Act of 1860 against the thirty-five members of the Homestead NAAISW advisory committee. These charges were all eventually dropped.

To P. J. McGuire

Nov. 9th. [189]2

Mr. P. J. Mc-Guire,
124 N. 9th. St. Phila, Pa.
Dear Sir and Friend: —

Your favor of the 8th. inst. came duly to hand and contents noted.

It was my intention on my way home to stop over and have a talk with you at Phila. but I received information which necessitated my coming right on.

When we were in Pittsburgh last it was explained to us that the reason the Officers of the Amalgamated Association were indefinite in their telegraphic communication was due to the order of the Supreme Court upon the telegraph companies to produce all telegrams passing between any of the officers of the Association and any other person referring in the slightest degree to Homestead. As a consequence when the despatches from Mr. Garland were received that fact was in mind and we recognized that Mr. Garland was a careful man and would not send for us unnecessarily.

When we got to Pittsburgh there was a conference between the Advisory Committees of Homestead, Beaver Falls and the 29th. and 33rd. St. Mills[1] and the Executive Officers of the A.A., and the subject was sprung upon us of placing a boycott upon the Carnegie product.

The matter was thoroughly discussed and, in the presence of all, the officers of the Amalgamated Association declared that they believed a boycott inadvisable inasmuch as it would require their own Union men to refuse to work the product of any of the Carnegie mills which would reach the members of the A.A. that it would be difficult to know where this would end and might bring about an entire lockout in their trade.

These sentiments were expressed late in the afternoon and it was in the morning that I sent the telegram to you asking for your consent to put your name to any documents the Council might desire to issue. The conference was adjourned and we went to Homestead to address the men. It was resumed after our return and kept up to the last moment for us to catch the train. When we left the A.A. officials had not yet decided whether they would or would not apply for the placing of a boycott, hence you will see that there was no necessity for the issuance of any documents. When I called at the office yesterday I found a letter from Mr. Garland and Killgallon,[2] a copy[3] of which I sent to you to-day.

In compliance with your request I wired you [that] Friday would be agreeable to me to meet you and the Committee on Entertainment[4] as well as participate in the conference over the Kirchner matter.[5] In all probability I shall come on the 4:00 P.M. train due 6:05 at Phila. and will come right to your office from the train.

Upon the completion of this letter I shall write to Mr. Barnes[6] and ask him to have a Committee of the Union at your office at about 8:00 o'clock. Can you so arrange matters as to have the Committee on Entertainment meet us about 7:00 o'clock?

With kindest wishes and trusting this will be satisfactory, I am,

Fraternally Yours   Saml Gompers.
President. American Federation of Labor.

TLpS, reel 6, vol. 8, pp. 82-83, SG Letterbooks, DLC.

1. On July 14, 1892, eight lodges of the National Amalgamated Association of Iron and Steel Workers (NAAISW) at the Carnegie Steel Co.'s Beaver Falls, Pa., Mills and the Upper (29th St.) and Lower (33d St.) Union Mills in Pittsburgh initiated a sympathy strike in support of the Homestead strikers. After the Beaver Falls workers voted to return to work on Nov. 19, most of those strikers regained their old positions, although the strike had destroyed the NAAISW lodges of which they were members. The strike at the Union Mills, marked by periodic violence against strikebreakers, continued until Aug. 14, 1893, and also resulted in the disbanding of the local NAAISW lodges.

2. John C. KILGALLAN served as national secretary (1892-95) and secretary-treasurer (1895-97) of the NAAISW.

3. Garland and Kilgallan wrote to SG on Nov. 5, 1892 (reel 6, vol. 8, p. 80, SG

Letterbooks, DLC), informing him that the advisory committee of the NAAISW had decided against boycotting materials manufactured by the Carnegie Steel Co.

4. The committee on entertainment for the upcoming AFL convention.

5. Possibly a reference to Kirchner's misappropriation of Philadelphia CMIU 100's funds.

6. John Mahlon BARNES, secretary of CMIU 100 of Philadelphia (1891-93, 1897-1900), also served during the 1890s as corresponding secretary of the Philadelphia Central Committee of the SLP and as an organizer for the Philadelphia American Branch of the SLP.

To Harry Ives[1]

Nov. 10th [189]2

Mr. H. M. Ives,
Genl. Organizer A.F. of L.
1821 Van Buren St. Topeka, Kan.
Dear Sir and Brother: —

Your favors came duly to hand and contents noted.

Replying to your question permit me to say that the subject matter of which you write I believe ought to be left to local option, although I am strongly of the opinion that it is essential for us to do all we possibly can in order to eliminate the consideration of a color line in the labor organizations of the country. If we fail to organize and recognize the colored wage-workers we cannot blame them very well if they accept our challenge of enmity and do all they can to frustrate our purposes. If we fail to make friends of them, the employing class won't be so shortsighted, and play them against us. Thus if common humanity will not prompt us to have their co-operation, an enlightened self-interest should.

So far as the policy of the National movement is concerned, at least that has been decided by the conventions of the A.F. of L. by their elimination of the color line in the ranks of organized labor. While it may be impractical for us at present to make a declaration, I believe it would be more advisable to evade the question than to openly place ourselves in antagonism to it.

The Tin, Sheet, Iron and Cornice Workers Nat. Association[2] is affiliated and I believe that the Union that you may organize of the Tin Sheet Metal Workers should be attached to the National Association mentioned. I should be pleased if you succeed in the effort to have you send the applications through this office.

With kindest wishes and hoping to hear from you soon and frequently, I am,

Fraternally Yours   Saml Gompers.
President. American Federation of Labor.

TLpS, reel 6, vol. 8, p. 86, SG Letterbooks, DLC.

1. In 1892 and 1893 Harry M. Ives served as president of the short-lived Kansas
State Federation of Labor and in 1893 he worked as an organizer for the AFL.
    2. The Tin, Sheet Iron, and Cornice Workers' International Association.

An Article in the *National Labor Tribune*

[November 12, 1892]

HURRAH FOR HOMESTEAD!

The regular weekly meeting at Homestead rink was held on Saturday, Nov. 5, and was unusually well attended. The national officers
of the American Federation of Labor were present and met with
cordial welcome. George Hatfield[1] presided, with Harry Boyer[2] as
secretary. Samuel Gompers, president of the Federation of Labor, was
introduced as the first speaker. As he stepped before the audience a
unanimous burst of applause greeted him and continued for several
minutes. The genial president bowed acknowledgments, and with the
restoration of quiet spoke as follows:

"Men of Homestead, three weeks have passed since my former visit
to your midst. The dire predictions then made and repeated with
greater vehemency recently that the men were now ready to surrender
to whatever terms the Carnegie firm might wish to offer, has been
given the lie by your presence here to-day. It has been stated in the
public press that the Amalgamated Association was keeping you from
the mill. I am personally acquainted with the officials of the Association
and know they are all honorable men and the imputation is false.
When the struggle commenced it was not a question with the Amalgamated Association. They did not declare that you should leave the
mill, but it was by a unanimous vote on your part. When the Carnegie
people made their offer which you did not consider a sufficient re-
compense for your labor you quit in a body. It seemed the idea of
the firm to throw down the gauntlet to organized labor, and it was
a question of now or a year hence. Now after a struggle of four
months I will [not] ask you to surrender to the company (cries No!
No!). It is now a question of your standing together to the end and

the Carnegie firm must in the end be forced to recognize organized labor. By what right does any company lay down a rule that their employees must surrender their right to organize as a condition of employment. They say they give you employment. I say it is by your labor they are able to stand in the position of employer. They do not live on ozone, nor float through the air as zephyrs. They live like other human beings, or at least should, but there are many of them [who] live and act like beasts. The great question that agitates the civilized world is—how much shall the wage worker receive for his labor and how much shall the capitalist retain for his profit. The wage worker produces all the wealth of the country and has grown tired providing all and receiving comparatively nothing. To-day the struggle is on with Carnegie, to-morrow with another, and so long as the capitalist tries to deprive his employees of what they should justly receive so long will these struggles continue.

"There is an inherited right that men were wont to improve their condition, and whenever capital tries to deprive their employees of their just rights there will be unending strife between them. I doubt if ever a body of workingmen were offered a wholesale reduction in wages that they gracefully submitted, and I defy any person to show me where more frequent and sweeping reductions have occurred than with you men at Homestead. When this last reduction was declared you tried every just means to effect a settlement. Negotiations were declared off with the air of an autocrat by that man Frick. For months previous he had been negotiating to bring this band of cut throats of July 6 to try and force you at the point of the bayonet to go back to work. This failing, you were arrested on every known charge in the calendar to try and break your spirit. The constitution of our country declared that oppression of a subject is unjustified, and you were so treated when excessive bail was exacted in the charges you were arrested upon. Your leaders were arrested, and now three of them languish in jail. (A voice—They will get out on July 16.) On the other hand, we see these people arrested on similar charges at your instigation liberated on liberal bail. In all cases, unfortunately, discrimination is shown between the poor and the rich. If a laborer comes to this country with three suits of clothes in his trunk, one will be allowed to come in free and the other two he will have to pay duty upon. But if a 'dude' comes here with three trunks filled with wearing apparel he is allowed to bring them in without duty, as it is classed such an amount of apparel is necessary for one in his station of life. This is the policy pursued, unjust as it is, but when it comes that two men are charged with the same offense justice should be shown them, and their respective positions and ability to give bail should be fully considered."

Mr. Gompers then adverted to the shooting of Mr. Frick by Berkman,[3] and expressed his doubts that he had been shot at all. Continuing he said: "At this time, when the sympathies of the country were turned toward the supposed dying capitalist riddled with bullets, there was a young man[4] here in camp who said, when he heard of the shooting, 'he did not feel sorry.' His colonel treated him, for this expression, as no soldier has ever before been treated in the history of the civilized world. It is true, in cases of mutiny the offender was shot, but it was not just that Iams was punished four hours after this offense was committed. When this man sought redress before the courts can you wonder at his claim being ignored with a judge[5] upon the bench who insulted the jury because they did not bring in a verdict quicker?[6] How dare a judge speak to men his peers in every way in a question of such vital interest? Do you think for a moment, with such a judge on the bench, you can expect justice for the members of your advisory committee under indictment? I say if you want justice you must be up and doing. Many crimes have been committed in justice's name, but no matter how long we may suffer, justice we demand and justice we will have. (Continued cheers.) Another question that confronts me is the recent action of the finishers. I want to talk to these men. If they looked to their own interests they would undo everything they have done. With Homestead out on strike, Lawrenceville and Beaver Falls, and all contending for a right, you see men turn upon them and shoot them in the back, it is the highest treachery. Suppose they succeed, as they say they will, in their efforts, what does it mean? Your forces divided. It has ever been the effort of the enemy to divide the opposing forces. If this man who started this secession movement does not come back into the old Association he will be known the whole world over as the second Carey.[7] I hope these men will see the error of their ways, but you of Homestead stand together by the men who have sacrificed themselves for your interest, no matter how the battle may turn."

Mr. Gompers was cheered to the echo, and was followed by Chris. Evans, secretary of the A.F. of L., formerly a notably useful officer of the United Mine Workers. He complimented the men upon their steadfast stand for their rights, and touched up the finishers for their desertion from the Amalgamated Association, styling them as secessionists. He said he believed in law and order and the upholding of law, but when the laws of the country or state are inimical to the workingman the sooner they are obliterated the better.

John B. Lennon, treasurer of A.F. of L., followed in a brief address.

He stated that the present contest had done more for the human race than any event since the French revolution. "It has awakened thought," said he, "among the wage workers of the civilized globe to their needs, and they are seeking the mutual protection of their rights in organization." He concluded by saying that the only solution of the labor problem rested upon education of the masses. Ex-President Weihe, of the Amalgamated Association, was the next speaker. He was treated to an ovation from the audience, and was made the lion of the hour. He said: "It certainly should be gratifying to me, at the end of my term of office, to see the men of Homestead so united and harmonious in the ranks of organized labor. Could a strike be continued successfully without an organization? The split that has sprung up in our ranks I hope will see their error. You all know that the policy of the employers is to treat with their men without an organization back of them. The organization that has been established in the iron and steel mills has been a benefit to your interests. It has been truly said that the strike in the Carnegie mills has brought the question of labor forcibly upon the country at large. Then will be a time of reckoning. We know what injustice you have been subjected to. The acts in the beginning of this struggle were not due to you. These strifes will continue as long as the present laws of Pennsylvania stand. But I know when the next legislature meets in Harrisburg there will be an effort made to protect the rights of all men equally. You know, as iron workers, you cannot get a fair day's wages for a fair day's work without organization. For that reason I say hold fast one to the other, and when the time comes, if it ever does come, that you will be forced to surrender, act as a body for the benefit of all and not for the few. You know all the declarations of the company, that they were able to start the mills without you. But have they done it? They have scoured the country for men, and after four months they are not proving a success. But you, the old men, are the ones they want and are looking for. True, they have changed the management, but with the intention of throwing fire-brands into your lines, but have they succeeded? It is necessary for iron and steel workers to be organized in one body. You know previous to the formation of the Amalgamated Association in 1876 the various branches of the trade were organized in distinctive bodies, and what was the result? The employers would attack one branch and give the others work. As soon as they gained a victory over these they would attack each in turn, and what was the result? They had the men at their mercy. I say that those who are deserting us at the present time are doing themselves an irreparable injury, not only to the iron and steel workers, but themselves, and I say upon their shoulders will rest the responsibility of the present struggle at Homestead in the future. If the men here are not receiving the needed support who are the responsible parties but those who are deserting you in this hour of your need? men who have been benefitted by the organization for years.["] Mr. Weihe concluded by urging upon the men to observe the laws and not give any cause to lose the sympathy of the country, which they now possess.

Treasurer Lennon was followed by Mike Sotock, a Polack, who addressed his countrymen in their native tongue, and his remarks were greeted with frequent applause.

David Lynch, of the Advisory Board, closed the addresses amid a greeting that was personally complimentary. Among other things he said: "We find us here on another Saturday and another Saturday finds us here united as ever. I hope many another Saturday will find us in the same united body until our rights are conceded by the Carnegie firm. The firm has expended every effort and subterfuge to break our ranks. During the past week we have seen their latest scheme. They claimed that a body of the strikers was going back to work. These few men who are going back were never with us, and we are better off without them. The only honorable means for us is to stand together and win or lose. I for one will never go back unless we win. (Cheers.) These people can't run the mill without us. One man, even if he is the head of a department, cannot make a pound of steel without you, and see that none of you follow him in this direction. There has been a class of men, not members of the Amalgamated Association, who were not affected by the strike and could have remained at work and not be classed as 'scabs.' But they came out with us in sympathy for a just cause, and now if they were to return they would be stigmatized as 'scabs.' "

Thus closed a representative Homestead meeting of the men who are so bravely fighting a good fight, and whose self-sacrificing defense of principle will go into the history of labor's struggles for the right as a notable development of the noblest side of human nature.

National Labor Tribune (Pittsburgh), Nov. 12, 1892.

1. George Hatfield was active as a public speaker for the National Amalgamated Association of Iron and Steel Workers (NAAISW) in 1892.

2. Probably Harry Bayne, a hooker and member of NAAISW William T. Roberts Lodge 125, of Homestead, Pa. As a member of the Homestead advisory committee he was charged in September 1892 with riot, conspiracy, and treason, charges that were eventually dropped.

3. Alexander Berkman. See "An Article in the *Pittsburgh Dispatch*," Aug. 14, 1892, n. 10, above.

4. William L. Iams, a Pittsburgh salesman, served as a private in Company K of

the Tenth Regiment of the Pennsylvania National Guard during its occupation of Homestead.

5. William D. Porter was a judge on the court of common pleas in Pittsburgh.

6. When Iams refused to apologize for his remarks, Guard officers strung him up by his thumbs for twenty to thirty minutes and the next day dishonorably discharged him and drummed him out of camp in tattered clothing with his head half shaved. He brought suit against three former officers in October 1892, but the following month a jury acquitted them after twenty-one hours of deliberation.

7. John D. Carey, a Pittsburgh iron heater and former leader in NAAISW Equity Lodge 47, was named president of the short-lived Finishers' Union of Iron and Steel Workers of the United States. SG was probably comparing him to James Carey, a leader of the Fenian splinter group known as the Invincibles, who was involved in the assassinations of Chief Secretary Lord Frederick Cavendish and Under Secretary Thomas Burke in Phoenix Park, Dublin, on May 6, 1882. Following the so-called Phoenix Park murders, Carey testified against his former associates; his evidence led to the conviction and execution of five of the principals. He was murdered by a fellow Invincible in 1883.

To John Callaghan

Nov. 21st. [189]2

Mr. John M. Callaghan,
Genl. Organizer A.F. of L.
76 Felicity St. New Orleans, La.
Dear Sir and Brother: —

I assure you that I use no idle words when I say that I was exceedingly interested in reading the contents of your letter of the 13th. inst. and want to now frankly say that I am under deep obligations to you for giving me so comprehensive a view of the recent movement in your city.

You must indeed have had an awful amount of obstacles to overcome but more particularly at those points where your advice was adopted and where the officers entrusted with its execution failed or refused to perform their duty. Indeed I am gratified to know that you took such an active interest in the movement for I am satisfied without it a crushing and gigantic blow of defeat would have been dealt organized labor in New Orleans. As it is, a step in advance has been gained. Nothing which the working men of New Orleans enjoyed before the strike has been taken from them now, and quite a number have as you report obtained large and substantial concessions in the shape of wages, hours of labor and other conditions.[1]

A correspondent states that Mr. Leonard[2] acted very peculiarly during the strike. Was it he who called the men off from their work after the order to return was generally given? If you can give me any information upon this subject I shall be pleased to have you do so.

To me the movement in New Orleans was a very bright ray of hope for the future of organized labor and convinces me that the advantage which every other element fails to succeed in falls to the mission of organized labor. Never in the history of the world was such an exhibition, where with all the prejudices existing against the black man, when the white wage-workers of New Orleans would sacrifice their means of livelihood to defend and protect their colored fellow wage workers. With one fell swoop the economic barrier of color was broken down. Under the circumstances I regard the movement as a very healthy sign of the times and one which speaks well for the future of organized labor in the "New South," about which politicians prate so much and mean so little.

I have kept what I now want to say to the end of my letter. It is in reference to your resignation as general organizer for the American Federation of Labor. Of course I have taken the matters you suggest into consideration and it is by no means an easy matter to brave both family and affianced Bride, nor would I have the hardihood to attempt to influence you under the circumstances. If you insist upon the acceptance of your resignation I have no alternative but to acquiesce in your decision, but it pains me to think that our official relations will cease, and that which is of far more importance, that the organized workingmen will not receive the full benefit of your deliberate and good judgment and sterling tenacity of purpose. With men organizing in the South, their natural impetuous disposition I believed that the near future needed a man of your temperament and character, not only to aid them in their work but by your personality and influence advise them to pursue that course best calculated to lead to permanent and beneficial results. With your ability at the service of the organized working people of New Orleans, it is an outrage that they did not avail themselves of the opportunity presented by employing you so that you may be independent from looking for work at your trade.

I do not say this to in any way influence you to look for what is generally termed a "Labor position," but in order that the wage-workers themselves may positively at all times avail themselves of your services without detriment or serious loss to you. At any rate, may I ask you to correspond with this office as frequently as convenient? After hearing from you again, I shall adopt your suggestion of writing to the gentleman you mention.

I shall regret very much if some of the New Orleans Unions are not represented at the A.F. of L. convention.

Sincerely hoping that your future may be bright and successful and with kindest wishes, I am,

Fraternally Yours   Saml Gompers
President. American Federation of Labor.

TLpS, reel 6, vol. 8, pp. 114-15, SG Letterbooks, DLC.

1. In early November 1892 workers in New Orleans paralyzed the city's commerce for three days in a general strike that united them across race and skill lines. On Oct. 24 between 2,000 and 3,000 members of three directly affiliated AFL local unions— Warehousemen's and Packers' Protective Union 5800, Round Freight Teamsters' and Loaders' Union 5813, and Scalesmen's Union 5869 (the "Triple Alliance")—walked off their jobs demanding a ten-hour day, wage increases, overtime pay, and the preferential closed shop. The board of trade offered to recognize the white scalesmen and packers, but not the black teamsters. The Amalgamated Council of Labor Organizations (ACLO), generally referred to as the Workingmen's Amalgamated Council (WAC), conducting the strike for the unions, rejected the board's offer. After the collapse of further negotiations, the WAC initiated a general strike on Nov. 8, involving between 20,000 and 40,000 workers, belonging to some forty-two unions and the Building Laborers' Council and representing at least half of the city's organized crafts. The participating unions demanded recognition and the preferential closed shop, as well as favorable resolution of the Triple Alliance strike. Striking unions included locals of AFL national or international affiliates, as well as many directly affiliated locals, the Federation having issued at least thirty-five charters to New Orleans locals in 1892 alone. At least one KOL assembly also participated, although the Knights officially condemned the strike. None of the city's cotton trade unions went out.

Although the WAC offered to arbitrate every issue except union recognition, the board of trade on Nov. 10 filed suit in federal circuit court against forty-four union officials for violating the Sherman Antitrust Act and persuaded Governor Murphy J. Foster to call out the state militia, offering to provide $100,000 to defray the cost of the mobilization. The unions' negotiators subsequently held a series of meetings with the governor and reached a settlement on Nov. 11 that ended the general strike. It provided for arbitration of the Triple Alliance's wage and hour demands within forty-eight hours, resulting in a ruling in the workers' favor. Other unions also gained higher wages and reduced hours because of the strike. The settlement, however, conceded the employers' right to bargain directly with individual workers and did not insist on either union recognition or the preferential closed shop, major objectives of the general strike. The employers agreed not to discriminate against union members and promised to restore strikers to their positions if they were unfilled. Many unionists nevertheless lost their jobs, while those who regained them often had to accept less favorable terms. In March 1893 the federal court issued an injunction in the antitrust case against the unions' leaders even though the strike was over. Although some of the city's unions increased their membership during the strike and new ones were formed, the strike weakened the AFL in New Orleans, as many of the charters issued by the Federation in 1891 and 1892 were returned and few new ones were sent out; moreover, it exacerbated divisions between skilled and unskilled as well as between black and white workers.

2. James Leonard, a printer and member of International Typographical Union (ITU) 17, was both president of the New Orleans ACLO and deputy organizer for

the ITU for Louisiana in 1892 and 1893. He ran unsuccessfully for Congress on the Independent Workingmen's Political Club ticket in 1894. He was elected first president of the New Orleans Central Trades and Labor Council at its founding in 1899 and became a salaried general organizer for the AFL the same year.

To Andrew Leitch

Nov. 28th. [189]2

Mr. A. S. Leitch,
418 S. 4th. St. St. Louis, Mo.
Dear Sir and Brother: —

I am indeed obliged to you for the clippings you sent in the past two weeks, and I read them with as much interest as it was possible to summon to what you truly describe as a tame affair.

I am sure that your efforts to hold the Clerks off for a week and our joint efforts in getting Mr. Loebenberg at the subsequent meeting checked the K. of L. game to capture another Union. If they, the K of L., had succeeded it would have meant hauling another body of men down a yawning abyss of misery and despair. At least now the Clerks have their destinies in their own hands and can struggle with their brothers to accomplish the purposes for which they organized. Instead of those with whom they are associating acting the parasite upon them, their associates will reimburse them to a greater extent for any money expended or effort made in the labor movement.

I am glad that you have had an opportunity of talking with some of the officers of the K. of L. It only requires a keen insight into the character of the men as well as a fair knowledge of the underlying principles and purposes of the labor movement to recognize the K. of L. officers as "oily talkers and bitter enemies of trade unions unmitigated liars and treacherous." I have known them for years to be that. Promises made with apparent candor broken relentlessly and the very opposite policy pursued. For a long time I have not even deigned to notice them, for I believed that the time would soon come to pass when they would disappear entirely from the field of labor and join either the Bourgeoisie or Kleinburglichen class. They are drifting in this direction already and I am sure my judgment in this matter will not prove incorrect.

The very fact that they have failed to capture the Clerks Union and their attempt to resuscitate the old Clerks Assembly in East St. Louis[1] in order to antagonize the Union they failed to capture, and the bargaining they proposed to enter into with one of the store proprietors exhibits clearly what these men are in the movement for. Certainly for no good to say the least.

I read your notice of your convention in the "Union Record" and assure you that I could not help smiling at the biting sarcasm, and plain truth. I hope for the best from the Phila. convention.

With kind wishes and hoping to hear from you soon, I am,

Fraternally Yours Saml Gompers.

TLpS, reel 6, vol. 8, p. 137, SG Letterbooks, DLC.

1. Probably KOL Local Assembly 767 of East St. Louis, Ill., also known as the Queen City Clerks' Assembly, which issued a call through the *Journal of the Knights of Labor* in July 1892 for the formation of a national trade assembly of clerks. The call was apparently unsuccessful. In November delegates to the KOL general assembly held in St. Louis met with East St. Louis salesmen to discuss their concerns.

To P. J. McGuire

Nov. 28th. [189]2

Mr. P. G. Mc-Guire,
124 N. 9th. St. Phila, Pa.
Dear Friend Mc-Guire: —

Since writing my letter this morning the thought has occurred to me that the invitation to Congressman Elect Henry W. Blair might be taken to give our convention a certain political coloring, and inasmuch as Congressman and our fellow unionist Amos J. Cummings has always endeavored to do what he could to advance the cause of labor, it would be a graceful compliment to ask him to read a paper before the convention upon an important topic, such for instances as the Immigration Question (He will without doubt be Chairman of the Committee on Immigration of the Next House of Representatives), while at the same time it would neutralize the political coloring.[1]

Give me your advice upon this subject at once and oblige,

Yours Sincerely Saml Gompers.
President. American Federation of Labor.

TLpS, reel 6, vol. 8, p. 136, SG Letterbooks, DLC.

1. Henry W. Blair addressed the 1892 AFL convention on Dec. 14. Amos Cummings sent a communication that was read to the convention.

To Eugene Debs[1]

Nov. 29th. [189]2

Mr. Eugene V. Debs,
Terre Haute, Ind.
My Dear Debs: —

I am in receipt of your favors of recent date and owe you an apology for not responding earlier. Need I assure you that had it been possible for me to reply earlier that I would have done so? I feel satisfied you will take it for granted.

I esteemed it a privilege to extend an invitation to you to address the delegates to the Philadelphia convention of the American Federation of Labor. That you cannot accept it gives me sincere regret, but I assure you it is heightened by the fact that you are not enjoying good health.

The few to whom I communicated my purpose of inviting you to address our delegates were simply delighted at the idea, and subsequent to my sending you the letter a number of others suggested the idea of my sending an invitation to you, among others, our old friend P. J. Mc-Guire.

I earnestly hope that you may soon be convalescent and be robust for the great mission beyond doubt you are to fulfil in this great labor movement.

By an oversight I was evidently led into the error that your official connection with the Bro'd. of Locomotive Firemen had entirely been severed, but I am pleased to learn that you are still directing the "Magazine."

In reference to the article you ask me to write let me say that I shall endeavor to comply with your request. Of course you understand that just about this time I am considerably crowded with work, but shall do the best I can under the circumstances.

I kindly ask you to send me a good photo. of yourself as soon as possible, as I desire to place it with the photos. of the officers of all the Nat. and Int. Unions of the country in a frame to remain in the office of the A.F. of L.

Will you also kindly give me the name and address of the secretary of the new organization of Railroad Conductors,[2] as well as its technical name, upon receipt of this, and oblige,

Yours Sincerely   Saml Gompers.
President. American Federation of Labor.

TLpS, reel 6, vol. 8, p. 144, SG Letterbooks, DLC.

1. Eugene Victor DEBS was grand secretary and treasurer of the Brotherhood of Locomotive Firemen (1880-92) and editor of the *Firemen's Magazine* (retitled the *Locomotive Firemen's Magazine* in 1886) from 1880 to 1894. He founded the American Railway Union in 1893 and served as its president.

2. SG may be referring to the Order of Railway Conductors, which under its own name absorbed the rival Brotherhood of Railway Conductors in October 1891.

To G. W. Fairchild

Dec. 9th. [189]2

Mr. G. W. Fairchild,
Sec. Teamsters' and Draymen's Union 5637 A.F. of L.
Cedar Heights, South Bend, Ind.
Dear Sir:—

Since the organization of your Union it has been one source of constant dispute not only in the local labor movement of South Bend but also with the general movement and correspondence with this office.

In the first instance an error was made in having you organize a union and affiliated with the American Federation of Labor. A reference to the constitution will show that the Union affiliated with the A.F. of L. should be wage-workers. I learn that a number of your members are employers of labor and that not only are they employers but even antagonize an effort on the part of the wage working Teamsters and Draymen to become members of the Union.

Believing that the principles of the Trade Union Movement should be upheld and that they are not upheld when an antagonism to organization is manifested by employers of labor such as is the case in your Union, I hereby direct and order that the members of your Union who own more than one dray or one wagon or employ other Teamsters and Draymen be required to leave the Union on or before Dec. 20th. since they are employers of labor, that if this is complied with you may grant these owners of teams cards which should entitle them to return to the Union as members at any time in the future when they do not own more than one dray or wagon or employ help. If they are employing Union men there is no reason why they should not receive some certificate certifying to that fact and entitling them to the patronage of organized labor and its friends.

Unless the above order is complied with on or before the above date and notice thereof received at this office on or before the 22nd. day of Dec. the charter to Union 5637 will be revoked.

I assure you that this decision is not intended to be harsh nor to injure. We are organized to aid our fellow workers and to advance the cause of labor. We have no objection to fair minded employers, but we can not allow them to organize in violation of the general labor movement for the purpose of antagonizing existing organizations and turning to the detriment of our cause.

Trusting that you will [comply] with the above request within the time specified, I [am,]

TLp, reel 6, vol. 8, p. 182, SG Letterbooks, DLC.

To Andrew Leitch

Dec. 9th. [189]2

Mr. A. S. Leitch,
418 S. 4th. St. St. Louis, Mo.
Dear Sir and Brother:—

I am in receipt of your favor of the 4th. inst. and I read its contents with interest and I am free to say that I certainly agree with you in the expression of your thought that delegates to any body, should be chosen by the members in their sovereign individual capacity. This thought is not new with me. I believe that the officers of National organizations should also be elected by the popular vote of the entire membership of the National Unions rather than through their delegates at conventions.

As far back as '83 I proposed the election of officers and delegates of the Cigar Makers Int. Union by the popular vote and at the convention of that organization in '91 succeeded in having it adopted.[1] I am as much opposed as you are to "inner circles" practically electing a candidate to an office. I am opposed to caucuses of any character and never in my life participated in one.

It was because I thought a false impression might be made by your article in the "Record" that I asked you for your expression of opinion upon, or rather an explanation of it. I doubt however, that the election of delegates by any underhanded scheme obtains to any extent. In fact, I know of none, but if it should exist in any one case it is reprehensible and should be exposed and the parties to it denounced.

I regret that you include me (by inference me) in "the failure, so far, of the two large labor organizations and its leaders to grasp the idea of a progressive movement." I am free to confess that the term "progressive movement" is to me an indefinite expression. I believe

I know the ultimate ends and aims as well as result of present struggles and I have never failed to give expression to and avow them, but I have always been impressed with the belief that it was our duty to arouse a spirit of independence, to instill in the hearts and minds of the toilers that it was essential to promote and protect their class interests in order to reach and elevate the entire human family; that any tangible action that will lead them to take the aggressive in the contest to solidify their ranks, to crystalize their thoughts and to concentrate their efforts was a "progressive movement." I have faith that when these tactics are followed and the work in this direction accomplished that the wage workers will find the full means of emancipation. That I have ever declared this I will repeat in my report and recommendation to the conve[ntion. I] want you and I to continue our correspondence, a free expression of opinion between us will I am satisfied do us both good.

If the circumstances are as you say in reference to the Street Car Men's organizations, namely, that the leaders were Pinkertons it is rather a good thing that they went out of existence, only an eye should be kept upon the men who were the leaders so that they may not surreptitiously force themselves into the movement.

It is news to me that the Trade and Labor Assembly propose getting out a paper under the auspices of the Trade and Labor Unions.

With kindest wishes and hoping to hear from you whenever convenient, I am,

Fraternally Yours   Saml Gompers.
President. American Federation of Labor.

TLpS, reel 6, vol. 8, pp. 172-73, SG Letterbooks, DLC.

1. The CMIU convention in Indianapolis, Sept. 21-Oct. 6, 1891, approved a constitutional amendment to elect international officers by a general vote of the members rather than by the vote of the convention delegates. The CMIU reported in January 1892 that a membership referendum had approved the amendment.

Excerpts from News Accounts of the 1892 Convention of the AFL in Philadelphia

[December 14, 1892]

"HOMESTEAD DAY"

. . .

AFTERNOON SESSION.

After the roll call the first business of the afternoon session was the submittal of the following resolution by the Committee on President's Report:

"Inasmuch as our Executive Council has designated this day as 'Homestead Day,'[1] and as the people of our country are invited to contribute a portion of their earnings of this day for the proper defence of those of our fellow-unionists of Homestead now imprisoned and indicted for the assertion of their manhood rights and noble resistance to the onslaught of organized capital, and, as the American Federation of Labor have taken the initiative in this matter, therefore your committee beg leave to suggest that the day should be appropriately observed by this Convention, and recommend that the sum of $1000 be donated from the funds of the Federation for the purpose therein stated."

Delegate Wiseman[2] moved to amend the resolution by adding that the delegates to the Convention make a collection for the same purpose.

Treasurer John B. Lennon[3] did not think it politic for the Federation to make appropriation for the purpose designated, and urged that the money should come from the voluntary contributions of working men throughout the country.

Delegate Campbell[4] argued that the people of Homestead were the best judges of how the money given them could be best applied. If the money be taken from the treasury of the Federation it will be the same as if coming from the pockets of the working men.

Delegate P. J. McGuire[5] was opposed to both the amendment and the substitute. The appropriation, he said, ought to be given to the Amalgamated Association, to use it as it may deem best. Many of the delegates had not come prepared to give as much as they would care to and the proper method would be to have them lay the matter before their respective organizations.

Delegate Penna[6] saw no impropriety in raising a collection among the members of the Convention, and he hoped the amendment would be adopted.

A further amendment was offered by Delegate Morgan[7] that $500 be donated for the relief of the unorganized men who went on strike at Homestead out of sympathy with the union men.

This amendment was decided not in order.

Delegate Weihe,[8] of the Amalgamated Association of Iron and Steel Workers, was called upon and stated that the non-organized men who had gone out on strike in sympathy with the union men had been given support by the Association during the entire period of the lockout. He instanced the number of men who had not been taken back to employment as most in need of assistance.

The amendment to the resolution and a substitute offered for it by Delegate Valesh[9] were defeated by decisive majorities, and the original resolution was unanimously adopted.

THE COEUR D'ALENE MINERS.

Nearly three hours were consumed in a debate over the renewal of Delegate Morgan's motion to appropriate $500 to the relief of the unorganized men at Homestead who went out on strike because of sympathy with the union men. After much discussion a motion to postpone the consideration of the motion prevailed.

Then it was reconsidered, and again the motion to postpone was carried, but through his persistency Delegate P. J. McGuire was successful in having the roll called. This resulted in a small majority against postponement. Those favoring postponement then withdrew their opposition, and Delegate Morgan's motion was carried unanimously.

Flattered by his success, Delegate McGuire made a motion to appropriate $500 to the defence fund of the Coeur d'Alene miners. This was carried with but a few dissenting votes.

THE STRIKING MINERS IN TENNESSEE.

Delegate Todtenhauser[10] was not so successful, however, in his motion to appropriate $500 to the defence fund of the Tennessee miners, which aroused the vigorous opposition of Delegates Foster,[11] McCarthy,[12] Valesh, Goldwater[13] and Elderken,[14] who argued that donating money for such purposes was not within the province of the Federation, which had not the funds to give to all such calls as may be made upon it. The motion was warmly supported by Delegate Skeffington.[15]

A WOMAN PRESIDING.

During the debate, President Gompers called to the chair Mrs. Mary E. Kenney,[16] of Chicago, the only woman delegate in the Convention. This act evoked loud applause, and Mrs. Kenney presided with womanly grace, yet sufficient firmness, and a surprising knowledge of parliamentary forms.

FOR AND AGAINST THE MOTION.

In order to give Delegate Penna an opportunity to advocate Delegate Todtenhausen's motion, the time for adjournment, which had been fixed at 5 o'clock, was extended, and the speaker related his experiences among the striking miners of Tennessee, and made an urgent appeal for their recognition by the Federation in a substantial manner.

Delegate Wiseman spoke against the motion, contending that the Federation was not in a position to appropriate money for such a purpose.

President Gompers contended that, after what had been done in the Homestead and Coeur d'Alene questions, the appropriating of $500 more or $500 less was not of much importance. Before the money is appropriated it ought to be put into the treasury. It was not the province of the Federation to give money to non-union men who take no measures to protect themselves against their oppressors. The Federation should support its members, and do it in such a manner as to show all workingmen that it is their interest to join the ranks of organized labor. But why, he asked, should this indiscriminate giving of aid be adopted. It will be placing a premium on non-unionism and be discouraging to the men and women who have fought labor's battles under the banner of the Federation. If aid is to be given, the colored men in New Orleans who are affiliated with the Federation, and who fought for shorter hours and increased wages, ought to be helped. The color line has been obliterated by the labor unions. Other men, white and black, not organized, went on strike out of sympathy with these colored men.

Delegate Lenehan[17] said the question of whether the workingmen who have struck for their rights and need aid belong to the Federation or not ought not to influence the Federation so far as to refuse them assistance.

Delegate Jennings[18] held that, even if the Federation had [not] done wrong by appropriating sums to the Homestead men, Union men and the Couer d'Alene miners, it should put a stop to such practices before the treasury is depleted.

Delegate John J. Daily[19] argued that, as capital was employing new methods in its warfare against labor, so should labor resort to new means to advance the cause of the workingman everywhere, and one of the best means was to help those who are fighting for their rights.

Delegate McBride[20] told of the beneficent results of the fight against the convict lease system in Tennessee, and urged the adoption of the motion.

Delegate Foster moved to refer the pending motion to the Committee on Resolutions, but his motion was defeated.

Delegate Bandlow[21] moved the previous question, and Delegate Todtenhausen's motion was carried, only a few votes being cast against it.

. . .

Philadelphia Public Ledger, Dec. 14, 1892.

1. On Nov. 15, 1892, the AFL Executive Council issued an appeal, cosigned by Mahlon M. Garland and the Homestead Advisory Committee, designating Dec. 13, 1892, as "Homestead Day."

2. Henry Weismann represented the Journeymen Bakers' and Confectioners' International Union of America.

3. John B. Lennon represented the Journeymen Tailors' Union of America (JTUA).

4. Two delegates named Campbell attended the convention. R. M. Campbell, a printer and member of International Typographical Union (ITU) 11 of Memphis, Tenn., was an ITU delegate. James A. Campbell was secretary of AFL Hod Carriers' Union 5487 of Charleston, W.Va., which he represented at the convention.

5. P. J. McGuire represented the United Brotherhood of Carpenters and Joiners of America (UBCJA).

6. Philip H. PENNA was vice-president of the United Mine Workers of America (UMWA) from 1891 to 1895 and its delegate to the AFL convention.

7. Thomas J. Morgan represented the International Machinists' Union of America.

8. William Weihe.

9. Frank Valesh represented the CMIU.

10. August Todtenhausen represented the JTUA.

11. Frank K. Foster represented AFL Tackmakers' Protective Union 4007 of Boston, Mass.

12. Francis H. McCarthy, a member of Boston CMIU 97, represented the Boston Central Labor Union (CLU).

13. Samuel Goldwater represented the CMIU.

14. Thomas J. ELDERKIN, a delegate of the Trade and Labor Assembly of Chicago, was a leader in the Lake Seamen's Benevolent Association in Chicago and general secretary (1892-99) of the National Seamen's Union (after 1895 the International Seamen's Union of America).

15. Henry J. Skeffington represented the Boot and Shoe Workers' International Union.

16. Kenney represented AFL Shirtmakers' Protective Union 5652 of Chicago, Ill.

17. James J. Linehan represented the UBCJA.

18. James F. Jennings was a Dorchester, Mass., piano polisher. He represented AFL Piano Varnishers' and Polishers' Union 5908 of Boston, Mass.

19. James J. DALY of New York City represented the Mosaic and Encaustic Tile Layers and Trade National Union. He served as general president of that organization in the early 1890s.

20. John McBride represented the UMWA.

21. Robert BANDLOW, manager of the *Cleveland Citizen* from 1891 to 1910, represented the Cleveland CLU; he was that organization's secretary from the late 1880s to 1893 and its president from 1893 to 1894.

DISCUSSED BY THE AMERICAN FEDERATION OF LABOR.

. . .

MILITIA AND THE PINKERTONS.

The most important matter considered during the day, and the one which caused the most spirited debate, was the following report from the special committee of nine:

"The special committee of nine, to whom was referred the several resolutions bearing upon the employment of militia and irregular armed bodies, and also the standing army of the United States, in the recent labor troubles, beg leave to report that the said committee had the subject matter in connection with the several resolutions referred to it under careful consideration, and find that the power designed to rest with the masses of the people, as expressed in the Constitution of the National and State Governments and the statute laws for the protection of life and property, and to carefully guard the rights and liberties of the people, have been diverted from the purposes of their authors, and that the masses have lost the powers guaranteed them, and that those powers have been usurped by large corporations. The calling out of the militia and national troops, as well as irregular armed bodies, has been done on the solicitation and instigation of corporations. Since the recent uses to which troops have been subject has been brought about by allowing the people unchallenged to surrender their powers, we therefore believe that herein lies the vital point of our grievances. And in order to keep, maintain and perpetuate our rights, we recommend, in accordance with the demands of the numerous resolutions upon the subject, the following propositions for your consideration:

"That the American Federation of Labor and its affiliated bodies demand of their respective legislatures the enactment of laws embracing one of the following propositions which, in their judgment, may seem the most advantageous:

"First. They shall create a Board of Commissioners, to be elected by the people, consisting of as many members as there are Congressional districts in the State. Each member shall be elected by the Congressional district in which he resides. The said Board of Commissioners, after investigation of the difficulties, shall, in conjunction with the Governor, have sole power to call out the militia in cases of labor troubles or strikes.

"Second. That in cases of labor difficulties it shall be unlawful for the Governor to call out the militia for the suppression of the same, except upon a petition signed by at least one-fourth of the qualified voters of the county wherein the troubles may exist.

"We further recommend, as a remedy for the employment of Pinkerton or other armed forces, that we demand the enactment of laws by the several States of the Union prohibiting non-residents from serving as peace officers.

"We recommend the American Federation of Labor, and its affiliated bodies, to refuse to permit any member to enlist in the National Guard of any State, and that the members now enlisted be requested to withdraw as soon as they can lawfully do so, unless one or the other of the propositions herein offered are embodied in the State laws."

The report was vigorously attacked by Delegate Iden,[1] who said it was a reflection alike upon the patriotism of the workingman and the members of the National Guard. "Men have a right to strike, but strikers have no right," he declared, "to resort to lawlessness. When the Sheriff found his authority to enforce the laws defied, it was right to call upon the militia. It was more to the interest of the workingmen to preserve peace than to that of the rich, because anarchy means disaster to the poor. The remedy for the present condition of things is at the polls."

Delegate Lennon spoke in the same strain and was followed by Delegate O'Brien,[2] who said he had served four years and a half in the Union army during the civil war and his patriotism could not be attacked, but while he did not defend the lawless acts of the strikers at Coeur D'Alene and other places, he did protest against the equally lawless acts of the men, who, with the assistance of the militia, oppressed and fought the men battling for their manhood. The report of the committee, he said, did not condemn the President, the Governor of this or any other State, nor the regular army or the militia, but did denounce the misuse of the latter in strikes and lock outs.

Delegate Carney[3] said the workingmen of Homestead were as patriotic and peaceable citizens as could be found anywhere. From January 1st to July 1st of this year only three arrests had been made — two for drunkenness and one for assault and battery. Lawlessness was precipitated there by the bringing of the unwashed horde of Pinkertons. He claimed that the purpose for which the militia was organized was prostituted in bringing them to Homestead to put blacklegs and scabs into the places occupied by these patriotic and peaceable citizens. Pittsburg and Philadelphia send to Harrisburg men who prove wall flowers, chair warmers and space fillers, and to this course may be traced the legislation against the interests of the working man.

He asserted that some members of the militia at Homestead offered to doff their military uniforms and don that of the "scab" and "black-leg," to take the places of the locked-out men.

Delegates Wiseman and McBride contended that the militia have no place in labor troubles.

Delegate Foster opposed the recommendation of the committee, contending that, if the militia is made an instrument of oppression, the masses can promptly and completely right the wrong by filling the legislative, executive and judicial departments of the National and State Governments with men who will enact laws and interpret and enforce them in justice to all classes.

Delegate Marden[4] said that the fault was not with the militia, but with the working people themselves. He was a member of the militia in 1861 which fought for the preservation of the Government. Had it not been for the militia the delegates would not now be in session in Independence Hall. Every State and Territory ought to have the same laws as are in force in Massachusetts and Ohio which prevent the importation or employment of the Pinkerton or other bodies of men not recognized by the law in labor troubles.

· · ·

DISCUSSING THE MILITIA.

The question then recurred to the report of the special committee on militia and miners' troubles. Thomas J. Morgan arose and said that he agreed with the committee so far as the preamble was concerned, but he disagreed with their judgment as to the suggested laws. The report admitted that the present laws amply protect the safety and happiness of the people, and yet suggested changes. The trouble is that there has been a transfer of power from the people to corporations, because of the indifference of the people. Mr. Morgan, therefore, moved that the suggestions of the committee be struck out and the following substituted:

"That the force necessary to the proper constitutional use of the militia lies in labor representation in the Legislature and administrative departments of the respective States; hence we urge the working classes to see to it that members and friends of the working classes, and not the agents of monopoly, shall command the military and other departments of our State and National Government."

A number of seconders were heard, but P. J. McGuire was recognized. He spoke strongly in favor of the substitute. The people can get control of the militia by the use of the ballot on election day. They can get control of the Governor and of the Legislature. There ought to be more working men in the militia and not so many "dudes and bank clerks." The speaker was himself formerly a member of the New York Militia. The National Guard of the city of Paris proclaimed the commune and prepared the way for the present French republic.

A vote was taken, amid loud cries of "Question," and but two votes were recorded against the substitute. The report was then adopted unanimously as amended.

. . .

FAVORING A DEFENSE FUND.

Charles Dold,[5] for the Committee on Sinking Fund, presented a lengthy report, of which the following was the substance: Recommending the establishment of a sinking or defense fund of $500,000; that a pro rata assessment therefore be levied; that affiliated organizations shall be notified in August, by the Executive Council, of the amounts they are liable for; that assessments shall be based on membership in July reports; that the fixed amounts shall be paid by January 1, 1894; that any body failing to pay shall stand suspended; that after exhausting its own treasury, an affiliated body, which has paid up all assessments, can apply for $5 per week from the fund for each member on strike or locked out; that the sinking fund shall never fall below $300,000, extra assessments being levied when necessary; that after aid has been given from the fund for four weeks to one body of men, a vote as to its continuance shall be held in all affiliated organizations; and that if the vote is adverse to the striking or locked out men, assistance to them shall cease four weeks after such announcement is made.

On motion of Mr. Lapperd,[6] it was determined to take up the report seriatim. Mr. Dold spoke strongly in favor of the first section, declaring the need of a defence fund, the speaker taking the line that the methods of capital have changed and money must be fought with money. Messrs. McIntyre[7] and O'Brien thought that the matter was too momentous to be decided offhand. They doubted whether the convention could create such a fund without a vote of all affiliated bodies. Many of the unions now had elaborate financial schemes. Messrs. Payne,[8] Murray,[9] Nathan[10] and others spoke on the matter, when Mr. Morgan moved that the matter be referred to the incoming Executive Council to formulate a plan of defence fund in all its details and submit the same for a vote to all affiliated bodies. Mr. McCarthy moved as an amendment that the report be referred back to the committee. A general discussion followed, many contending that the affair should be settled at once. Mr. McCarthy's amendment, however, was lost, and Mr. Morgan's motion prevailed.

. . .

Philadelphia Public Ledger, Dec. 17, 1892.

1. George Iden represented Federal Labor Union (FLU) 5368 of Newark, Ohio.

2. John O'Brien represented the Portland, Ore., Federated Trades Assembly.

3. William A. Carney represented the National Amalgamated Association of Iron and Steel Workers.

4. William Henry MARDEN was general treasurer of the Lasters' Protective Union of America and represented that organization at this convention.

5. Charles Dold represented the CMIU.

6. John LAPPARD, a Chicago currier, represented the United Brotherhood of Tanners and Curriers of America.

7. Peter J. McIntyre, a printer, was a member of International Typographical Union (ITU) 49 of Denver, Colo; he was an ITU delegate at the convention.

8. George W. Payne represented the American Flint Glass Workers' Union (AFGWU) and was a member of AFGWU 18 in Millville, N.J.

9. Edward W. Murray, a Phillips, Wis., lumberman, was the secretary of AFL FLU 5704 and its delegate to the convention.

10. Abel L. Nathan represented the Pueblo Trades Assembly, Pueblo, Colo., of which he was secretary.

[December 18, 1892]

THE CONVENTION OF THE AMERICAN FEDERATION OF LABOR ADJOURNS.

. . .

GOVERNMENT OWNERSHIP OF TELEGRAPH LINES.

A breezy discussion followed the introduction of a resolution declaring belief in Government ownership of telegraphs and telephones. Mr. Morgan moved to amend so that the resolution would read: "We reaffirm our belief in the Government's ownership of telegraphs and telephones, and that all means of transportation and communication and means of production should be owned and controlled by the Government." Mr. McGuire opposed the amendment, on the ground that it was visionary, and liable to split the Federation. Mr. Carney took the same ground. He thought if the Federation wanted too many things at the same time, it would get nothing. Mr. Cessna[1] attacked the ownership of coal mines by railroad companies. He thought, if put on the same basis as the postal service, the Government's ownership of telegraphs, telephones and railroads is perfectly feasible.

The vote on the amendment was taken and it was apparently lost. "Roll call" was demanded, but the necessary nine seconders were not heard, and the President decided that it could not be had. This ruling brought several delegates to their feet, including Mr. Morgan, the Socialistic leader. Mr. Linehan arose and with some heat, said he favored roll call. "We'll show him," said he, "that the great majority of the delegates are opposed to his Socialistic doctrines, and he will be unable to go around the country and say he was arbitrarily shut off by the President." The roll call showed 958 votes for and 1627 votes against the amendment. The original resolution then passed.[2]

. . .

COMPULSORY ARBITRATION.

A resolution favoring the passage of a compulsory arbitration law by Congress, reported without a recommendation by the committee, occasioned a lengthy debate. Mr. O'Brien opposed the passage of the resolution, because, in the preamble, it was stated "arbitration is the only method of settling disputes." Mr. McCarthy moved that the resolution be referred to the Executive Council. Ed. L. Daley[3] amended that the resolution be printed and sent to the various affiliated bodies, so that the delegates to next year's convention may be instructed how to vote.

Mr. Weissman opposed the reference. The Convention was perfectly able to settle the matter. The passage of the law would place another weapon in the hands of the capitalistic classes who now control the Government and own the Courts and police, as against men's individual rights.

Mr. McBride said he introduced the resolution merely to create discussion. He assailed the constant statement that the capitalistic classes owned the Government, and that workingmen had individual rights paramount to everything, and men who make such statements do not belong to this country, nor in Labor Unions.

Mr. Foster said the resolution was another step in the direction of State Socialism.

Mr. Valesh offered as a substitute a resolution declaring that the Federation recognizes as one of its "basic" principles, compulsory arbitration, while recognizing, at the same time, its inefficiency when the workingmen are not organized.

Mr. McGuire thought that the resolution smacked of the Elizabethan age. If the Government makes arbitration, why should it not also regulate wages and the hours of labor? The powers that now direct the militia against strikers would then use the Board of Compulsory Arbitration. The carpenters favored arbitration, but not compulsory arbitration. Mr. Penna said if compulsory arbitration had been in force, there would now be no memories of Homestead. Mr. Morgan said the opposition to compulsory education and arbitration and the Government ownership of railroads and telephones came from men who are real anarchists, for they distrust and oppose government. Individual liberty, said he, harnessed children to carts in coal mines; closed schools when profit could be made from the pupils and sent rotten ships to sea to get insurance—until organized government stepped in and stopped it all. Mr. Linehan offered the resolution because it was the direction of drawing the line between employer and employe too tight and of dividing the people into two classes arrayed against each other. Mr. Goldwater, of Detroit, said compulsory arbitration would be a dangerous experiment, and quoted the city he represents, where nearly every large industry is owned and controlled by the two United States Senators. Mr. Gompers said the words compulsion and arbitration are antagonistic terms. If it existed employers could take the initiative; offer to make reductions, and as arbitration is comprised, wages would gradually fall. James J. Daley contended for striking in preference to arbitration. Mr. Sesner, the tall representative of the Farmers' laborers,[4] who, organized less than two years, number 48,000, said the men could take the initiative and ask continually for advances. Mr. Miller[5] told of when electrical workers struck against a reduction at the Thomson-Houston works in St. Louis, and won, receiving an advance instead of a reduction. Mr. Duncan[6] said compulsory arbitration would have been beneficial to the granite cutters when on strike. Messrs. Crawford,[7] Bandlow, White[8] and Carney also took part in the discussion, which was closed finally by a motion of the previous question. Mr. Valesh's substitute was adopted.

· · ·

Philadelphia Public Ledger, Dec. 18, 1892.

1. Probably William Cessna, a Jacksonville, Fla., businessman and delegate representing Federal Labor Union 5607.

2. The convention proceedings recorded the vote on Morgan's amendment as 559 to 1,615. What then passed was an amended version of the original resolution. The original resolution read "Resolved, That the A.F. of L. hereby reaffirm its position in favor of the government ownership of telegraph and telephone systems." It was amended to add the words "railroad and transportation" (AFL, *Proceedings,* 1892, p. 39).

3. Edward L. Daley represented the Lasters' Protective Union of America.

4. Probably Alonzo B. Crouse who represented AFL Farm Laborers' Protective Union 5873 of Bellaire, Ohio.

5. Henry MILLER, a St. Louis electrician, was grand president of the National Brotherhood of Electrical Workers from 1891 to 1893, and represented the union at this convention.

6. James DUNCAN was a leader in the Baltimore branch of the Granite Cutters' National Union of the United States of America. He represented the Baltimore Federation of Labor, of which he was president from 1890 to 1892.

7. J. A. Crawford, a Bryant, Ill., miner, was a member of United Mine Workers of America (UMWA) District 12 and represented the UMWA.

8. Henry White represented the United Garment Workers of America.

To Mr. Hacker

Dec. 21st. [189]2

Mr. Hacker,
c/o Phila, "Tageblatt"
613 Callowhill St. Phila, Pa.
My Dear Sir:—

I have your favor of the 18th. inst. in reference to the votes of the delegates of the Brewers Union. The same will be compared with our official tally list and inquired into in order to see that the matter will be fully and accurately recorded. In the printing of the tally lists an error occurred crediting the delegates of the Brewers Union with only 20 votes each instead of 40 each, but in each tally list where any vote was taken upon the roll call, the correction was made by Secretary Evans crediting each of the delegates of the Brewers Union with 40 votes. Thus I think you will find the vote fully recorded. At any rate; I thank you for your kindness in calling my attention to the matter.*

Permit me to thank you also for your congratulations on my reelection to the Presidency of the American Federation of Labor and to assure you of my appreciation of the compliment implied. You express the hope that the time may not be far distant when you will find me "in the ranks of the Party." In answer let me say that while I have no words of dissent to use to the "Party" you evidently refer to, I must still declare that I prefer to be in the organization cf the working classes than any "party." The most conservative as well as the most radical, theoretical and practical workers agree that the emancipation of the working classes must be achieved by the working classes themselves. I fail to find an expression anywhere where it is declared to be a working class "Party." However, we need not quarrel upon that score so long as we are sincere and devoted to the true interests of labor each in our own sphere and contribute our efforts to the amelioration in the condition and final emancipation of labor.

Very Truly Yours   Saml Gompers
President. American Federation of Labor

* Upon examination of the poll list I find the votes credited to the

Brewers Union delegates 40 each and this totals as declared at the convention.

TLpS, reel 6, vol. 8, p. 208, SG Letterbooks, DLC.

From Ben Terrell[1]

Washington, D.C. Dec. 21, 1892.

Dear Sir: —

It has been with much interest and pleasure that I have watched the proceedings of your late meeting at Philadelphia.

I was disappointed in not having you with us at St. Louis last February,[2] and have been told by Mr. J. F. Tillman, that he had received a letter from you in which you seemed to think that you had not been invited to a participation in the deliberations of the industrial organizations who met for the purpose of council at that time. I sent a circular letter to all the presidents of National industrial organizations and do not see why you should not have received yours, and supposed that you had done so, until informed of the position taken in your letter to him.

I write Mr. Powderly of the Knights of Labor and Mr. Stelle[3] of the F.M.B.A.[4] today, asking them to meet Mr. Loucks,[5] President of the Farmers' Alliance, and myself, at this place on the 5th. of January. In view of the recent heated political campaign, and the tendencies of our orders to participate in politics, I deem that it will be to the advantage of the industrial organizations and the good of the country generally, that we should consult in regard to matters that I deem of great and pressing importance. I am sure that good results will follow such a meeting, and after consultation, it may be deemed expedient for us to issue an address taking position for our orders in regard to the different political parties. In my judgment we should form no entangling alliances with any of them, but solely educate in the science of politics and leave our membership to occupy the position of a free citizen of this country, demanding that he be allowed to worship his God and exercise his franchise after the dictates of his own conscience. Right now in the incipiency of this movement of industrial reform, we should look well to the preservation of our organizations, separate and distinct from any party complications.

Hoping to hear from you favorably,[6] and meet you on the 5th. of January, I am,

Yours Fraternally   Ben Terrell,
Pres. C. of I.O.

TLpSr, AFL Executive Council Vote Books, reel 8, *AFL Records.*

1. Ben Terrell, a Texas farmer active in the state's Farmers' Alliance, was elected national lecturer of the National Farmers' Alliance and Co-operative Union (NFACU) at its founding in 1887 and remained in that position in the NFACU's successor organization, the National Farmers' Alliance and Industrial Union of America (NFAIU). Elected president of the Confederation of Industrial Organizations (COIO) in 1891, he favored nonpartisan political action. He was defeated for permanent chairman of the COIO in St. Louis in 1892 by third-party advocate Leonidas Lafayette Polk.

2. The COIO met Feb. 22-24, 1892, in St. Louis; the conference issued the call for the first presidential nominating convention of the People's party.

3. John P. Stelle, an Illinois farmer and teacher, was elected secretary of the Farmers' Mutual Benefit Association (FMBA) in 1887, serving through the early 1890s when the organization experienced a rapid decline. He established the *Progressive Farmer* in 1888, and in 1892 made it an organ of the People's party.

4. The FMBA was founded in southern Illinois in 1883 and had spread to six states by 1890. Mainly concentrated in Illinois and Indiana, it engaged in cooperative marketing and buying. After unsuccessful efforts in the political campaigns of 1890 and 1891, the organization declined precipitously; it maintained only scattered local lodges by the following year.

5. Henry L. Loucks, a South Dakota farmer and president of the South Dakota Farmers' Alliance, served as president of the NFAIU from 1892 to 1894.

6. SG wrote Terrell on Dec. 24, 1892, that the AFL Executive Council would consider the question of the Federation's sending a representative to the January meeting. "I agree with the view you express," Gompers commented; "we want no entangling alliances with any political party and that our organizations can best serve their purposes by remaining separate and distinct from party complications" (reel 6, vol. 8, p. 220, SG Letterbooks, DLC). The Executive Council apparently rejected the proposal.

To the Executive Council of the AFL

New York, Jan. 6th. 1893.

To the Executive Council of the A.F. of L.
Fellow-Workmen:—

I am just in receipt of a letter from Messrs. Patterson and Stillwagon the Attorneys in the Printers Injunction case of Murdock & Kerr vs. Eugene Walker et. al. They enclose a certified copy of the decision of the Supreme Court of Pennsylvania, which affirms the decree of the Court of Common Pleas and endorses the opinion of the Judge of said Court.

In accordance with the agreement the balance due these Attorneys ($850.00) has been forwarded to them.

From the conferences of Messrs. Mc-Guire, Lennon and Myself with Attorney Lambert of Phila. last Summer we were clearly shown how erroneous and defective the papers were drawn in this case. The manner in which the papers were drawn and the result of the case certainly justify the action taken by us at the Birmingham convention of the A.F. of L. It is another case where passion and enthusiasm gained a temporary advantage over reason, with a point scored against labor.

In accordance with the decision rendered, in cases of labor dispute in Pennsylvania an injunction is easily obtained to restrain both strikers and their friends named and unnamed restraining them "from gathering about plaintiff's (employer's) place of business and from following the workingmen employed by plaintiff, or who may hereafter be employed, to and from their work and gathering about the boardinghouses of said workmen." This simply and in plainer language means that an attempt of workmen to follow other workmen who may have taken strikers' places for the purpose of persuading them by argument to leave their work would be guilty of a violation of the injunction and could be arrested and thrown into prison for contempt.

It seems to me advisable that the case under consideration should not be prosecuted any further, since the papers are beyond doubt improperly drawn and defective inasmuch as existing law was not even quoted in many instances in the appeal, nor acquired rights depended upon.

I would suggest that either a friendly case should be brought about before the Court of Penna. with an injunction issued and argued upon the merits of its continuance and permanency, and if decided against us and it be carried to the various Courts without a single right being waived, I feel certain that the decision of the Supreme Court will be overturned and by that same body.

Kindly give me an expression of your opinion upon this subject at your earliest convenience and oblige,[1]

Yours Fraternally   Saml Gompers.
President. American Federation of Labor.

N.B. Attorney Patterson has been engaged by the prosecution as private attorney by the Carnegie Company to prosecute the Homestead men.

S. G.

TLpS, AFL Executive Council Vote Books, reel 8, *AFL Records.*

1. See "Labor's Council," Dec. 16, 1891, n. 2, in "Excerpts from News Accounts of the 1891 Convention of the AFL in Birmingham," above.

To Mahlon Garland

Jan. 13th. [189]3

Mr. M. M. Garland,
Prest. A.A. of I. and S.W. of A.
512 Smithfield St. Pittsburgh, Pa.
Dear Sir and Brother: —

In response to our call for Homestead Day apart from the money forwarded by the organizations to your office and Homestead direct, we have received several thousand dollars. This money you are aware as our call indicated, is to be devoted towards the defense of the men of Homestead.

At the convention when this subject was under consideration the delegates indicated their desire that the American Federation of Labor should have its especial Counsel for the men. When I make mention of this of course I hope you will not infer that it is either the purpose or desire of the delegates or the officers of the A.F. of L. to have Counsel who would not be in accord, or in opposition to the wishes of either the Amalgamated Association of Iron and Steel Workers or even the indicted men. As a matter of fact both these facts will have to receive our first consideration and you may rely that nothing will be done without the consent or against the will of your Association and the men.

Just previous to the convention I received a letter from Mr. Frank Valesh of St. Paul, Minn. and when I saw him at the convention at Philadelphia he repeated in substance what he had written to me and is to the following effect: that the trade unions of the North West felt that when they subscribed a few thousand dollars towards defraying the expenses of Messrs. Ergo[1] and Irwin[2] to take part in the defense of the men they did all they could do, and that in all likelihood they would be unable to continue. I am informed that Messrs. Ergo and Irwin volunteered their services and that the money paid them by the Unions of the North West was merely for expenses in preparation, traveling &c.

From information received I am led to believe that both these gentlemen aided materially in defending and securing the acquittal of Mr. Critchlow,[3] and if it meets with your views and those of the men, I will communicate with Messrs. Irwin and Ergo direct, or through the organizations of Sioux City and St. Paul asking them whether they will continue their services and efforts in behalf of the men under indictment, and the A.F. of L. to pay their expenses.

I wish you would consult your colleagues in the [trade?] as well as the men in prison and under indictment and let me know your views upon it at your earliest convenience. In the course of a week or two the Executive Council of the A.F. of L. will hold a meeting and I should very much like to be enabled to place your answer before them and thus enable us to take decisive action upon the matter.[4]

With kindest wishes to you and office friends, and hoping to hear from you soon and frequently, I am,

Fraternally Yours   Saml Gompers.
President. American Federation of Labor.

TLpS, reel 6, vol. 8, pp. 301-2, SG Letterbooks, DLC.

1. George W. Argo, a Sioux City, Iowa, lawyer.
2. William W. Erwin was a St. Paul, Minn., criminal lawyer active in the populist movement.
3. Sylvester Critchlow, a resident of Homestead, Pa., was arrested on July 18, 1892, on charges of murdering two men—one of them a Pinkerton detective—on July 6. Other charges were later brought against him as well. On Nov. 23 he was acquitted of one murder charge. He remained in jail until the following February, however, pending disposition of the other charges.
4. The AFL Executive Council authorized the payment of a $2,000 retainer to Erwin.

From Bernard Koenen[1]

Secretary
Int'l Furniture Workers Union of America[2]
Brooklyn, Jan. 14th 1893

Dear Sir and Brother

Complying with your desire to have a statement of circumstances which in our judgment should warrant the Executive Council in cancelling the loan of $1500 00/100 which we have received from you, I will say in the first plase our total indebtedness is to large to get [out] of it within the next three or four years to come. It amounts yet to about 20,000 Dollars. This is a hindrance almost to great to fill our position among the Trade Unions in regard to agitation and extension of our organization; it condemns us to stagnation and very likely retrogression. Our Int'l Union had to deal with fights for 9 hours in Baltimore Philadelphia Boston St. Louis Cleveland Chicago and Cincinnati, besides this with a lockout in Evansville, strikes in San

Francisco Indianapolis Brooklyn Milwaukee and Newark, all within 20 months.[3]

The movement in the 4 first named cities was successful, Chicago has gained but little and in Cincinnati the decision is still pending. The upholsterers in Cleveland had to submit.

The situation as a whole was realy satisfactory, if the 8 hour strike in New York City[4] had not been inaugurated. I hardly need to repeat the circumstances which induced our Union NY and others to make the demand. It is well known in our circle and especially Mr. McGuire as a member of your council is well informed of the fact that the carpenters have pushed our unions ever since they themselves were working 8 hours. It was as well to meet the carpenters desire, as to get the advantage of the 8 hour workday that caused the demand to be made and the carpenters in return promised their full assistance. Mr. McGuire himselfs emphasised this in a meeting of Union NY two weeks previous to the begining of the strike.

The cabinetmakers as the leading part and made confident by these assurances, did not hesitate and were very hopeful to win.

Now you may say, they could have terminated the strike and lockout which latter it was to a great extent, long before the expences ran up to more than 60,000 Dollars, but, as the situation then stood they were bound to try the utmost and calculating that the carpenters might at last come to recognize that their own interests were at stake, they kept up hope and strike until they were compelled to give it up with the great indebtedness, disappointed and disgusted alike.

It is undeniable that locals of the Brotherhood (an affilited organization) are largely responsible for the indebtedness having become so unbearably high. Considering this, together with the fact that our locals have always liberally contributed to assist labor in any contest against capital and the poor and helpless position we now find ourselves in, we think it but just and fair and in the interest of the Federation as well as our own to have the loan cancelled.

It would go a great way to harmonize the antagonistic feeling now prevailing among the furniture workers against the carpenters of New York City and produce faith towards the American Federation of Labor.

Hoping for an earnest and favorable consideration.[5]

I remain yours Fraternally   Bern. Koenen
Secry.

ALS, International Furniture Workers' Union of America Records, reel 140, *AFL Records.*

1. Bernard KOENEN was a Brooklyn cabinetmaker and a member of International Furniture Workers' Union of America (IFWU) 7 of New York City. He was corresponding secretary of the IFWU (1891-92), its recording secretary (1893-95), and editor of the union's journal (1891-95). In 1893 he was the SLP's nominee for Brooklyn alderman at large.

2. The International FURNITURE Workers' Union of America.

3. In October 1890 the convention of the IFWU empowered the organization's Executive Committee to initiate a campaign for the eight-hour day and to levy assessments for its support. The ten-hour day was the general rule in the trade in most cities at the time, and while the union did launch some eight-hour movements in cities already working nine-hour days, the agitation centered on achieving a general nine-hour day. Rather than call a concerted national strike, the IFWU attempted to impose nine hours gradually by confronting one firm or city at a time. Results were uneven, with some firms conceding nine hours and others waging bitter battles against the union with some success.

4. Members of six New York City locals of the IFWU struck on Apr. 4, 1892, to reduce their hours from nine to eight per day. Local 7 (cabinetmakers) reported that its strike was an attempt to match the reduction achieved by carpenters in their successful eight-hour campaign in 1890. While woodcarvers, machine workers, and varnishers struck in sympathy, local 7 complained that locals of the United Brotherhood of Carpenters and Joiners, which had encouraged the cabinetmakers to strike in the first place, not only ignored calls for support by the building trades' Board of Walking Delegates but openly sided with employers. Local 7 also protested that KOL District Assembly 253 provided replacements for striking cabinetmakers. After determined resistance by the Furniture Manufacturers' Association, the cabinetmakers called off their strike on July 8. Some furniture workers' locals continued to strike until September before abandoning the effort.

5. The AFL Executive Council extended the loan to the IFWU. The 1893 AFL convention cancelled all loans for strike assistance granted prior to Jan. 1, 1893.

From William Marden

Lasters' Protective Union of America[1]
Boston, Mass. Jan. 23rd 1893

Dear Sir & Brother;—

Enclosed please find clippings from the Boston Papers which if you haven't seen will I think be of interest to you Especially that part that refers to the A.F of L. You can see that the K of L are up to their Old Game fighting Trades Unions, (under the cloak of Scab Manufacturers) you will also see that sneak of a G.M.W. Powderly is in the fight, but hasn't the Courage to show his hand to the public, but as of old has his tools do the dirty work.[2] This fight against the L.P.U. and the A.F of L was brought about by a dirty ward politician by the name of M. J. Bishop[3] who publishes a paper by the name of *The Index*, which has a circulation of about 300, is an officer of Dist 30 K of L,[4] the district that Scabbed it on the Lasters in the Worcester county fight of the Shoemakers in 1887, after we paid out over $7000. to their members to keep them from scabbing it upon themselves. I would like to hear from you on this matter and will send you any further information you may want.

Fraternally Yours   W. H. Marden

TLSr, Lasters' Protective Union Records, reel 141, *AFL Records.*

1. The LASTERS' Protective Union of America (LPUA).

2. Competition among unions in the shoe industry during the early 1890s influenced the prolonged dispute between lasters and Bouvé, Crawford, and Co. of Brockton, Mass. The LPUA, the Boot and Shoe Workers' International Union (BSWIU), the New England Cutters' Union (NECU, also known as the Cutters' National Union), and KOL National Trade Assembly (NTA) 216 met in late 1891 in an unsuccessful attempt to adopt a united shoe label for the industry. While the LPUA, BSWIU, and NECU adopted a common blue label, NTA 216 continued to use the KOL yellow label. When lasters at Bouvé, Crawford, and Co. walked out on Dec. 3, 1891, in a disagreement over production quotas and wages, the KOL declined to lend its support to the strikers. The AFL's 1891 convention placed a boycott on the firm, which was operating with nonunion workers, but in January 1893 KOL District Assembly (DA) 30 of Massachusetts announced that it had lifted this boycott, together with one enforced by the LPUA, with the apparent support of the KOL's general officers. It was not until March 1895 that the LPUA and the firm settled the dispute, leading the AFL and the LPUA to end their boycotts. In April 1895 the LPUA, BSWIU, and NTA 216 united as the Boot and Shoe Workers' Union, adopting a single label, which the AFL endorsed in December 1895.

3. Michael J. BISHOP was KOL general worthy foreman (1893-96), secretary-treasurer of KOL DA 30 (1893) and of the Massachusetts KOL state assembly (1893-94), and editor of the *Weekly Index* (1892-94).

4. KOL DA 30 was established in 1879.

To William Marden

Jan. 24th. [1893]

Mr. Wm. Marden,
Treas. Lasters Pro. Union
620 Atlantic Ave. Boston, Mass.
Dear Sir and Brother:—

I am in receipt of your favor of the 23rd. enclosing clippings for which I am extremely obliged to you.

Yes, I have noted the cowardly and unfair acts of Powderly together with some of his henchmen in Massachusetts. It is a repetition of what they have done heretofore but I am inclined to the belief that their latest acts sound more like shrieks from drowning men than ability to do anything tangible. Of course it cannot be gainsaid that a few men can do more harm than a much larger number can do good, but really the days of usefulness of the K. of L. (if they ever had any) are certainly gone by.

What do you think of a concentrated effort by some of the unionists throughout New England, somewhat after the old revivals? I feel certain that it would more than offset the evil designs of the Powderlys and the Bishops.

Yes, the Fleischmann yeast has been boycotted by the Journeymen Bakers and Confectioners Int'l. Union for the past four years, and endorsed nearly that length of time by the American Federation of Labor. In all likelihood we would have brought that firm to terms some time ago were it not for the treachery of the K. of L. officers. The action of D.A. 30 in the Bouve-Crawford boycott is the same trick in the shoe trade as their action with Fleischmanns in the baking trade.[1]

Give me an expression of opinion upon my suggestion. I haven't any doubt but what the trade union movement will prosper despite all the antagonism of its enemies, whether of the "K nights, or K apitalists, or K orporations."

Remember me kindly to our friend Daly and our other comrades and accept the kindest wishes for yourself and write soon, to,

Yours Fraternally   Saml Gompers.
President. American Federation of Labor.

TLpS, reel 6, vol. 8, p. 334, SG Letterbooks, DLC.

1. The Journeymen Bakers' and Confectioners' International Union (JBCIU) and the AFL placed a boycott on Charles Fleischmann's compressed yeast firm, Fleischmann and Co., in 1889 on the basis of the JBCIU's contention that Fleischmann had a business interest in his brother's Vienna Bakery, with which the union had a dispute. In May 1890 the Bakers accused KOL District Assembly 220 of aiding Fleischmann in Brooklyn in his campaign to have the boycott lifted. The JBCIU ended its boycott of Fleischmann and Co. in April 1893, with Fleischmann recognizing the international union and the union admitting its error in boycotting the yeast manufacturer. The AFL lifted its boycott at the end of May. See *The Early Years of the AFL*, pp. 417-18, n. 1.

To John Weber[1]

Jan. 31st. [1893]

Col. Weber,
Commissioner of Immigration,
Ellis Island, N.Y.
Dear Sir: —

Information reaches me that there is a systematic shipping of Swedes in violation of the Alien Contract Labor Law by the Vermont Marble Company of Rutland, Vt.

My informants believe that the members of that Company, United States Senator Redfield Proctor,[2] and his son Fletcher D. Proctor[3] are so influential that they are above the law. I hope that if there is a violation of the Alien Contract Labor Law in this instance you may be enabled to detect it and demonstrate to our friends that this influence has no power in your Department.

A short while ago I was informed that some of the men in your office whose duty it is to watch and board incoming vessels have thoroughly neglected their duties by reason of absence from their posts.

If you were to make a rigid examination and ask each subordinate you would unquestionably arrive at the truth of this statement.

In making this complaint to you I do not do so for the purpose of having it ventilated through the press or any other way, or even to cause the dismissal of the men I have in mind. I do believe however, that an investigation would demonstrate this neglect of duty and an admonition from you bring about the desired result.

With kindest wishes and hoping to hear from you in connection with this matter, I am,

Fraternally Yours   Saml Gompers.
President. American Federation of Labor.

TLpS, reel 6, vol. 8, p. 358, SG Letterbooks, DLC.

1. John B. Weber (1842-1926) was a Republican congressman from New York from 1885 to 1889 and commissioner of immigration at Ellis Island from 1890 to 1893. He chaired the U.S. Immigration Commission in 1891.

2. Redfield Proctor (1831-1908), former president of the Vermont Marble Co., Vermont state representative (1867-68, 1888), state senator (1874), lieutenant governor (1876-78), and governor (1878-80), was the U.S. secretary of war from 1889 to 1891 and a U.S. senator from Vermont from 1891 until his death.

3. Fletcher Dutton Proctor (1860-1911), president of the Vermont Marble Co., was a member of the Vermont state senate (1892) and house of representatives (1890, 1900, 1904), and governor of the state (1906-8).

From William Duncan[1]

No. 202 Seldon Ave. Detroit, February 3rd. 1893.

Dear Sir:

On January 31st. there appeared in one of our morning papers a criticism on a paper I sent to the Trades Council[2] of this city, in which it was stated that wages of workingmen had decreased within the past few years. The paper said I was in error for wages had advanced rather than declined.

The statement I made was based on information received from mechanics and laborers in this city, with whom I had conversed on this subject, and delegates to various national organizations.

It would be gratifying if you will be kind enough to give me the result of your observation as to the present price of labor as compared with ten or fifteen years ago.

I believe there is no one better posted in this regard than yourself.

Hoping to be favored with an early answer, I remain

Very truly yours,   Wm Duncan

TLS, Granite Cutters' National Union Records, reel 140, *AFL Records.*

1. William Duncan of Detroit was a U.S. immigration inspector.
2. The Detroit Trade and Labor Council.

To J. C. Bean[1]

Feb. 6th. [1893]

Mr. J. C. Bean,
Bellaire, O.
Dear Sir and Brother: —

Your favor of the 31st. came duly to hand and upon your acquiescence I have forwarded both your letters to Mr. John Mc-Bride,[2] accompanying them with a letter of mine summarizing and explaining the position you have taken.

In view of the fact that the employing Farmers have antagonized every effort made by you and your colleagues to organize the Farm hands, it would be inconsistent on your part had you not objected to the enemies of your organization sitting with you in an organization which is intended to protect and promote your interests. Men in the labor movement should be required to make their choice of going with one or the other party to a contest and since the contest is made by the employing Farmers against the organization of the Farm Laborers sincere unionists should cut loose from said employers organizations.

Could not something be done to organize Farm hands in other parts? Are you not acquainted with some farm hands to whom I could write and send documents, or would not some intelligent active farm laborer, a thorough believer in unionism, be willing to go to other parts for the purpose of working and at the same time organizing his fellow farm laborers? If he would do Farm work, while at the same time doing some organizing, he would be earning wages, and possibly a little financial assistance from the A.F. of L. would help him to do good work in the interest of the movement.

I wish you would take this under consideration with your colleagues and let me have an expression of opinion upon it.

With kindest wishes and hopes for success in the near future, I am,

Fraternally yours   Saml Gompers.
President. American Federation of Labor.

TLpS, reel 6, vol. 8, p. 373, SG Letterbooks, DLC.

1. J. C. Bean was secretary of AFL Farm Laborers' Protective Union 5873 of Bellaire, Ohio.
2. Feb. 6, 1893, reel 6, vol. 8, p. 372, SG Letterbooks, DLC.

To Albert Cox[1]

Feb. 7th. [1893]

Mr. A. E. Cox,
Sec. L.U. 78 C.M.I.U. of A.
Box 216 Hornellsville, N.Y.
Dear Sir and Brother:—

Your favor of the 4th. inst. came duly to hand and contents noted.

In reply permit me to say that it affords me pleasure to learn the interest taken by the Union in reference to the coming Constitutional Convention in this State.[2]

Of course if we could secure that recognition on the probable winning ticket for labor men, it would be an excellent thing, but I am inclined to the belief that it is more than likely that neither the Democratic nor the Republican Party will put a labor man upon its ticket for delegates at large.

Under the Law they are both sure of having their delegates at large elected and they need not fear defeat. So far as the work in the various Districts is concerned, that is more feasible and likely to meet with success.

I wish we could talk the matter over instead of making it a subject of correspondence. No doubt much better results could be obtained, and a concert of action established. However, the opening up of the correspondence makes the matter much easier, and in all probability there will be a conference this coming Summer when the subject can be freely gone into.

It would be well to have your Committee continue and work up a sentiment throughout the State upon the subject, you commencing in your own town. The coming Convention will be an opportunity not often presented and should be taken advantage of.

With kind wishes and trusting this explanation will be satisfactory, I am,

Fraternally Yours   Saml Gompers
President. American Federation of Labor.

TLpS, reel 6, vol. 8, p. 378, SG Letterbooks, DLC.

1. Albert E. Cox.

2. The New York constitutional convention met intermittently between May 8 and Sept. 29, 1894. Among the proposals from SG and other labor leaders considered by the convention were amendments for city home rule, the referendum, abolition of convict labor, restriction on the use of conspiracy laws, and employer liability. In all, the convention considered some 400 amendments and recommended thirty-three, all of which were ratified in the November 1894 general election. The principal changes involved a reorganization of the judiciary and a reduction of legislative interference in the affairs of cities.

To William Duncan

Feb. 7th. [1893]

Mr. Wm. Duncan,
202 Selden Ave. Detroit, Mich.
Dear Sir and Brother:—

Your favor of the 3rd. inst. asking me whether you are correct in the statement that wages of working men had decreased in the United States within the past few years has been duly received.

You do me the honor of saying that you believe there is no one better posted in this regard than myself. I cannot positively say whether you are correct in this estimation of me, but whether you are correct or not I must certainly say that I entirely disagree with the view you have taken of the matter.

It does not require much investigation to prove the fact that wages of workingmen have increased within the past decade, and not only that, but that the purchasing power of wages has increased. To deny these facts is to declare not only the labor movement but our civilization a failure, that intelligence has not increased, become more general, that there is a lesser conception of the rights and duties of the masses than there was. No friend Duncan, you are mistaken; wages of workingmen have not decreased.

With kindest wishes and trusting this explanation will be satisfactory and that I may hear from you soon, I am,

Fraternally Yours   Saml Gompers
President. American Federation of Labor.

TLpS, reel 6, vol. 8, p. 382, SG Letterbooks, DLC.

To George Norton

Feb. 7th. [1893]

Mr. Geo. L. Norton,
Sec. Marine Firemen's Pro. Union 5464 A.F. of L.
3 N. Levee St. St. Louis, Mo.
Dear Sir and Brother:—

Your favor of the 3rd. came duly to hand and contents carefully noted.

In reply permit me to say that the new P.W.[1] was sent out yesterday afternoon. There have been a few which were sent out with a letter, but I refer to the general sending out of the P.W.

You say that there is some talk of the color line being drawn in the American Federation of Labor, and I state to you that that is an utter untruth immaterial by whom circulated. I never heard the subject mooted by any one and our record has been made up upon that subject. There are positively two National trade unions which we could get simply by asking them, but we refuse them admission only because they draw the color line.

The suspicion is unjust to the men who have incurred hostility because they dared speak for the equal rights of the black and white men and their equal recognition in the organizations of labor.

I am surprised that you should even for a moment harbor the thought that such a feeling prevails. At our convention not even one vote could be mustered to draw the color line. With you and all sincere men I condemn the attempts on the part of certain people who are in our movement simply to advance their own personal, financial and political interests. It becomes our duty to do all that we possibly can to help the honest men to maintain the purity of our organizations and movement.

With kind wishes and trusting this explanation will be satisfactory, and hoping to hear from you soon and frequently, I am,

Fraternally Yours   Saml Gompers
President. American Federation of Labor.

TLpS, reel 6, vol. 8, p. 386, SG Letterbooks, DLC.

1. Password.

To Harry Ives

Feb. 10th. [1893]

Mr. H. M. Ives,
Prest. Kansas State Branch A.F. of L.[1]
1821 Van Buren St. Topeka, Kan.
Dear Sir and Brother: —

Your favor of the 4th. came duly to hand, and I desire to say that though the Governor[2] seems disinclined to appoint you as Commissioner of Labor he is possibly doing labor a better service and that is by retaining you as President of the State Federation.

I am sure that while it may not advance your own interests as well, the wage-workers will have the full advantage and benefit of your action, advice and co-operation with them. However much you may have desired to do for the wage-workers of Kansas, had you received the appointment, delicacy if not practicability, would have prevented you from doing all that you desired, hence after all I am inclined to look upon Governor Lewellen's refusal to appoint you as a blessing in disguise. He certainly must be a peculiar man to imagine that the trade unions will allow their members to be abused 364 days in the year, and turn in and vote for their abusers on the 365th. — Election Day.

The beginning of this week Gen. Weaver[3] delivered a lecture here and we had quite a talk until nearly two o'clock in the morning. He also called at this office upon the following day when we discussed a number of matters in connection with the labor movement and the "People's Party." I expressed myself very plainly to him as to our attitude and he fully concurred with my views of organization for less hours being essential for every reform movement to uplift the toiling masses.

I do hope that the Bureaus of labor will not degenerate into a partisan adjunct to the regular machines to grind out partisan literature. If they go that way it is more than likely that a sentiment will develop demanding their abolition, and there is no denying that the Bureaus are doing good work as a rule, disseminating correct knowledge upon the condition of affairs in the labor world.

I shall look forward with pleasure to reading the proceedings of the State Federation and am glad to learn that they were so successful as you mention them to have been.

With kindest wishes and hoping to hear from you soon and frequently, I am,

Fraternally Yours   Saml Gompers.
President. [American Federation of Labor.]

TLpS, reel 6, vol. 8, p. 399, SG Letterbooks, DLC.

1. The Kansas State Federation of Labor was formed in 1890 and chartered by the AFL in 1892.

2. Lorenzo Dow Lewelling, a businessman and authority on penal reform, was elected governor of Kansas in 1892 on the People's party ticket, serving from 1893 to 1895. SG wrote to Lewelling on Jan. 3, 1893, recommending Ives's appointment as commissioner of the Bureau of Labor Statistics.

3. James Baird Weaver (1893-1912), an Iowa lawyer and Civil War general, was a former congressman elected on the tickets of the Greenback party (1879-81) and Democratic and Greenback-Labor parties (1885-89). He ran unsuccessfully for the presidency as a candidate of the National Greenback party in 1880 and the People's party in 1892.

To James Johnson[1]

Feb. 17, [1893]

Mr. J. S. Johnson,
Treas. Penna. State Branch A.F. of L.[2]
254 Jackson St. Allegheny, Pa.
Dear Sir:—

I am in receipt of a letter[3] from Mr. Robert Watchorn,[4] Chief Inspector of Factories of Pennsylvania, in which he calls attention to a number of amendments that have been introduced in the legislature for the improvement of the Factory Act of your state.[5] He says he has been called upon very frequently by the organizations of Penna. for the enforcement of the Law, and that he has endeavored to perform it to the best of his ability, but he finds the law decidedly defective in many particulars. The amendments which have been introduced in brief are as follows:

1st. Ten hours labor in any day, nor for a longer period than sixty hours any week.

2nd. Providing for the affidavit of parent or guardian as to the date and place of birth of child employed, or having no parent or guardian the affidavit of child itself.

3rd. Having the age limit of children to be employed in factories to be fixed at 14 years instead of twelve as now prevails.

4th. Factories or shops shall post regularly the number of hours required each day of the employes.

5th. Giving authority for the publication of a large number of the reports of the Factory Inspector's Department.

6th. Giving the Factory Inspector power and authority to appoint twelve additional deputy inspectors.

7th. Giving the Factory Inspector authority to incur expenditures for the enforcement of the law not to exceed $4000.00.

8th. Requiring the owner or superintendent of each factory to report all accidents or serious injury done to persons, to the Factory Inspector.

9th. To provide for suitable wash and dressing rooms and water closets and where opposite sexes are employed to provide separate places for their convenience.

10th. For the inspection of fire escapes and providing for better sanitary conditions in factories and workshops.

Though they may not be all that we may desire yet they are decidedly a great improvement on what now exists, and it is more than likely that it will be necessary to try and obtain what we can get rather than to make demands to obtain larger concessions and fail entirely in our effort.

I would suggest that you issue a circular to all the Unions in Pennsylvania urging upon them both the necessity and the advisability of visiting and writing to both the members of the Assembly and Senate in their respective Districts, and to insist that they favor the passage of the amendments referred to.

Let me call your attention to the fact that Massachusetts has 30 factory inspectors, New York 18 with an amendment now prevailing seeking an increase of the number to 30,[6] Ohio has 15 and Penna. only seven one of whom is a clerk in the office.

While we are all engaged in the movement to uplift the masses of our people, there is none that so strongly appeals to our sense of justice as well as calculated to promote our interests as the one of protecting the young and innocent children from the greed of avarice. I trust that you will give this matter your earnest, favorable and prompt attention and advise me what action you propose and will take.

Assuring you of my co-operation in any way within my power to further the adoption of these amendments, I am,

Fraternally Yours   Saml Gompers.
President. American Federation of Labor.

N.B. I do not know the names or addresses of the President[7] or Secretary of your State Branch hence I kindly ask you to send this letter to either one of them and informing me how and where I can reach them.

S. G.

TLpS, reel 6, vol. 8, pp. 429-30, SG Letterbooks, DLC.

1. James S. Johnson, an Allegheny, Pa., machinist, was a member of Machine Woodworkers' International Union 20 of Allegheny and secretary-treasurer of the Pennsylvania Federation of Labor (PFL).

2. The PFL organized in 1890.

3. Feb. 16, 1893, Files of the Office of the President, General Correspondence, reel 59, *AFL Records.*

4. Robert WATCHORN, who as chief clerk to Pennsylvania Governor Robert Pattison helped secure passage of the 1893 amendments to the Pennsylvania factory inspection law, served as the first chief factory inspector of Pennsylvania from 1893 to 1895.

5. The Pennsylvania factory inspection law (Laws of 1889, no. 235) set a minimum age of twelve for employment, prohibited anyone under the age of sixteen from working more than sixty hours per week, created an office of factory inspector, and established safety and sanitary regulations for factories and mercantile establishments. The state legislature amended the act in 1893 (Laws of 1893, no. 244) along the lines proposed by Watchorn, with several modifications. It set the age limit for child employment at thirteen and prohibited those under sixteen from working more than twelve hours a day or sixty per week.

6. The New York state legislature amended the factory laws in 1893 to provide for twenty-four deputy factory inspectors, not more than ten of whom were to be women (Laws of 1893, chap. 173).

7. Elmer Ellsworth GREENAWALT, a member of CMIU 257 of Lancaster, Pa., was president of the PFL.

To Thomas Elderkin

Feb. 23, [1893]

Mr. T. J. Elderkin,
Genl. Sec. Treas. National Seamen's Union of America[1]
47-49 W. Lake St. Chicago, Ill.
Dear Sir and Brother: —

I have the honor to acknowledge the receipt of your favor of the 21st.[2] and beg to assure you that it afforded me extreme pleasure to be the recipient of your letter as well as the information it contains.

It is needless to say that I feel an intense interest in the organization of the Seamen of America. I have ever felt that the men who go down to the sea in ships were entitled to share not only the sympathy but the active co-operation of every man who believes in the elevation of the human character and the amelioration of the conditions surrounding their occupation. Heretofore I have given considerable of my time and efforts in this direction and will go to any length within my power to still further assist in this great work.

You have no doubt learned that we have been unsuccessful in our efforts to secure a pardon for the two men who were so brutally treated and provoked to mutiny on the Jefferson Borden. President Harrison expressed himself that he believed there was no good grounds for exercising executive clemency at this time in the cases of these two men. How a man with any heart and brain could arrive at such a conclusion seems difficult to comprehend. You may depend however, that I shall not lax in my efforts with the incoming President[3] in order to move him to grant a pardon to Clark and Miller.

Mr. Jas. Mc-Laren of the Pacific Coast has been in this city a few weeks[4] and is making some headway in organizing the Seamen here although it is exceedingly difficult and hard work. On leaving here he will proceed to your convention.[5]

By the way, will you give me some information as to the exact date and place of your meeting? It may be likely that I shall have some communication to make, and if I have, I should like to know exactly how and when I can communicate with you.

In my judgment I think the action proposed to be taken to have the National Union affiliate with the American Federation of Labor is in line with the best interests of all concerned. You know that by becoming affiliated there is no right that you now possess that would be forfeited as a National Union, and it certainly would bring the wage-workers of our country into closer touch with each other to

work on and on in the great movement for reform and final emancipation.

You need never fear of wearying me by your communications. I
am pleased to hear from you at any time, and particularly on the
questions affecting the industrial masses of America.

Wishing the convention every success and asking to be remembered
to our fellow unionists, I am,

Fraternally Yours   Saml Gompers.
President. American Federation of Labor.

TLpS, reel 6, vol. 8, pp. 443-44, SG Letterbooks, DLC.

1. The National SEAMEN'S Union of America (NSUA).

2. National Seamen's Union Records, reel 142, *AFL Records.*

3. Grover Cleveland.

4. James McLaren, organizer for the NSUA, was organizing in the Northeast
between December 1892 and March 1893. He was in New York City from mid-
February through March.

5. The second annual convention of the NSUA was held in New Orleans, Apr. 18-
20, 1893.

To Harry Ives

Feb. 23, [1893]

Mr. H. M. Ives,
Prest. Kansas State Branch A.F. of L.
1821 Van Buren St. Topeka, Kan.
Dear Sir and Brother:—

Your favor of the 18th. received and the contents read with much
interest.

The same frame of mind, I often find myself in, as you describe
yourself to be in in [. . .] discussing the trade union and strike question
with our populist friends. They simply do not understand and are
woefully ignorant upon the underlying principles, tactics and operations of the trade unions. The strikes that are won, the advantages
that are gained every hour and minute of the day by the wage-workers
and which are unnoticed and unheralded, escape the notice of the
men who superficially examine into the laws of our present societary
conditions.

It is exactly as you say, they want to prevent the men who have a
little property from becoming wage-earners, and while I sympathize
with the wrongs from which this class of men suffer, yet it seems to
me to be inevitable by the operations of concentrated wealth that

they will soon be forced into either one of the two classes of society, the large employers and possessors of wealth or else the great army of wage workers. I say that I have sympathy with those who have a little land and a little house burdened by mortgage, but I am compelled by my observation as well as knowledge, to expend the largest sum of my sympathy on those who have neither land nor house to mortgage.

No doubt your chances for the Commissionership have suffered by reason of your outspoken declaration in this regard. I am sure I could get more cheap notoriety by a lesser degree of persistency in this line of thought and action, and thus avoid the antagonism of men strong in the belief that I am wrong and who regard the trade unions as but a hindrance to what they believe to be more radical changes.

I am glad of the information you give me in reference to the situation of the House of Representatives. The reports from there borrow any color according to the political partisan newspapers, and since we have no People's Party organ here it is difficult to obtain their version. Your letter, as an evident sympathizer with their movement, throws additional light upon the subject.

I regret that Mr. Johnson[1] was forced out of the State by the means you refer to. It certainly should have no effect upon the legislature. It is the old trick resorted to time and again.

When the 12 hour Law was pending in the Legislature of Massachusetts the employes were forced to sign a petition against it. The same occurred with the 11 Hour Law, the 10 Hour Law[2] and when the 58 Hour Bill[3] was about to be passed the employes were again forced to sign petitions against it, but when on July 2nd. last the Law went into operation there was such an outpouring and jubilee at Fall River as I never yet witnessed before in my life. It has been the practice of corporations and unfair employers to always resort to contemptible tactics of this character.

With kind wishes and hoping to hear from you soon, I am,

Fraternally Yours   Saml Gompers
President. American Federation of Labor.

TLpS, reel 6, vol. 8, pp. 439-40, SG Letterbooks, DLC.

1. William Lee Andrew JOHNSON of Kansas City, Kans., served as vice-president of the National Brotherhood of Boiler Makers of the United States of America (1892-93) and grand president of the International Brotherhood of Boiler Makers and Iron Ship Builders of America (1893-97). He and at least seventy-five other boilermakers in shops of the Atchison, Topeka, and Santa Fe Railroad who lost their jobs claimed it was in retribution for their refusal to sign a petition to the Kansas state legislature opposing a bill for the weekly payment of wages.

2. The Massachusetts state legislature rejected a bill in 1850 that would gradually

have lowered the hours of labor first to eleven per day and then to ten. In 1853 the legislature turned down a ten-hour bill, but manufacturers voluntarily adopted an eleven-hour day the same year.

3. The Massachusetts 58-hour law applied to women and minors employed in manufacturing or mechanical work (Laws of 1892, chap. 357).

To the Executive Council of the AFL

New York, Feb. 28th. 1893.

To the Executive Council of the A.F. of L.

Colleagues: —

In pursuance to instructions the conference between the Musicians Unions of Baltimore,[1] the officers of the National League of Musicians[2] and the undersigned, met at the Eutah House Baltimore, Md. Feb. 26th.

After allowing all parties to expend whatever bad feeling they were possessed of and fully placing the responsibility of the previous misunderstandings, in a conciliatory spirit the committees of both organizations met and urged on by the officers of the National League of Musicians and myself, finally agreed upon a basis of settlement of all disputes and an amalgamation of both organizations under the National League and a charter from the American Federation of Labor. The agreement arrived at is subject to ratification by both local organizations, but from the attitude of the conference committees and the resolution that in the meantime the musicians of both organizations would play with each other's bands, it is evident that there is little if any, danger of the failure of our effort.[3]

On Monday I went to Washington and interested myself in the Car Coupler Bill[4] which was to be called up under a suspension of the rules requiring a two thirds vote. By the friends of the Bill I was informed of the grave danger of its failure to receive this vote, and immediately procured a list of doubtful members and am pleased to say that the Bill passed by more than the required two thirds vote, 184 ayes and 85 nays. The Bill now goes to the President for his signature, and since he recommended a measure of this character in his Message to Congress it is difficult to see how he can avoid signing it. This matter is of such importance, not only so far as the Bill in itself is concerned, but as to its precedent in legislation of this character by the National Government, that I deem it my duty to officially advise you thereof.

Don't fail to be in attendance Sunday Morning March 5th. and oblige,

Yours Fraternally   Saml Gompers.
President. American Federation of Labor.

TLpS, AFL Executive Council Vote Books, reel 8, *AFL Records.*

1. There were two rival musicians' unions in Baltimore, the Musicians' Protective Union of Baltimore (MPUB; National League of Musicians of America 17), and the Musical Union of Baltimore (MUB).
2. The National League of MUSICIANS of America.
3. The MUB rejected the amalgamation plan, and in June 1893 the AFL issued a charter to the MPUB.
4. The Safety Appliance Act (U.S. *Statutes at Large*, 27: 531-32), which became law Mar. 2, 1893, required railroads engaged in interstate commerce to equip their trains with automatic couplers and power brakes by Jan. 1, 1898.

To Jerome Jones[1]

March 8, [1893]

Mr. Jerome Jones,
Genl. Organizer A.F. of L.
Cor. Stevenson Ave. and Wetmore Sts. Nashville, Tenn.
Dear Sir and Brother:—

Replying to your favor of the 6th. permit me to say that it affords me pleasure to learn that success is crowning your efforts in the organization of our fellow toilers.

In the matter of the Laundry Girls the thought occurred to me that it would be advisable if they were to adopt the policy pursued in many other cities where the Laundry girls have organized and become attached to the American Federation of Labor, namely, for them to use the A.F. of L. label to be placed upon the packages of goods sent out that have been laundried in shops employing exclusively Union members and granting Union conditions.

I affix hereto a copy of the A.F. of L. label and since they are sold at so reasonable a figure (see enclosed price list) they would not be very expensive to the organization, and yet give the opportunity to the organized wage workers and sympathizers with our movement, to encourage by their patronage the employment of Union girls.

I looked through the "Journal of Labor" of Feb. 26th. and March 3rd and failed to find any editorial under the caption of "Colored Labor." I note what you say upon the subject of colored labor however, in your letter, and I am in entire accord with those sentiments. It isn't a question of social or even any other kind of equality that need be recognized in the organization of the colored wage workers into Unions. It is one of absolute necessity.

If the colored man is not permitted to organize, if he is not given the opportunity to protect and defend his interests, if a chance is not given him by which he could uplift his condition, the inevitable result must follow, that he will sink down lower and lower in his economic condition and in his conception of his rights as a worker and finally find himself an absolute dependent, (worse than chattel slavery) in the hands of unfair and unscrupulous employers.

If our fellow white wage workers will not allow the colored worker to co-operate with him, he will necessarily cling to the other hand (that of the employer) who also smites him, but at least recognizes his right to work. If we do not make friends of the colored men they will of necessity be justified in proving themselves our enemies, and they will be utilized upon every occasion to frustrate our every effort for economic, social and political improvement.

If humanity does not prompt us to recognize these facts, then an enlightened self-interest certainly should.

I am not at all surprised in view of the cases that you mention, that many of our fellow workers in the Building Trades are still compelled to work ten hours a day. It is only surprising that they are not working longer hours and even at lower wages. I wish the slogan would come forth among the toilers of the South, working men organize regardless of color; organize to protect yourselves, to defend yourselves, to gain those conditions and improvements which are yours by right.

From the above you will see that I am in entire sympathy with the attitude you have assumed upon this question, one that I have always believed in and hope will soon be realized and accomplished.

With kindest wishes and hoping to hear from you as frequently as convenient, I am,

Fraternally Yours   Saml Gompers.
President. American Federation of Labor.

TLpS, reel 6, vol. 8, pp. 476-77, SG Letterbooks, DLC.

1. Jerome JONES, a printer, reporter, and newspaper editor, was a member of International Typographical Union 20 in Nashville, Tenn., and an AFL organizer.

To Thomas Morgan

March 10, [1893]

Mr. T. J. Morgan,
6239 Madison Ave. Chicago, Ill.

Dear Sir and Brother: —

I exceedingly regret that illness kept me from the office, and that is the reason why I was unable to reply by mail in time to reach your meeting Saturday the 11th. inst.[1] giving an expression of my opinion upon the subject matter of wider scope of education for our children in the public schools.

At the outset let me call attention to the fact that there is not one man or woman who loves liberty and humanity in America, but who always points to the public schools of our country as the bulwark of American freedom. If that is so, and I have no hesitancy in acquiescing in that statement, then it seems to me that the natural consequence follows that it behooves us to do all that we possibly can to secure an education broad and comprehensive for every child in America.

Either we will have to bear the expense of rearing intelligent boys and girls, or we will have to bear the penalty for our failure and niggardly policy by an increase in the number of paupers, criminals, &c.

It always seemed to me that the expenditures of money by the people for the education of their children was one to which no expenditure could be put to better use. It brings its reward in a thousand and one ways, and apart from its advantages, away above and beyond it comes the consideration, it is just, it is right.

Until a child is fourteen years of age — the factory, the work shop should be closed to it, the school room, play ground and sunshine should be open to them, and instead of gloom, ignorance and misery, gladness, hope and a brighter future should be the channel to which the thoughts of the young should be directed.

With kind wishes and hoping this explanation will be satisfactory, I am,

Fraternally Yours   Saml Gompers.
President. American Federation of Labor.

TLpS, reel 6, vol. 8, p. 481, SG Letterbooks, DLC.

1. On the basis of a resolution by Morgan, the Trade and Labor Assembly of Chicago hosted a meeting on Mar. 11, 1893, to discuss the place of special or so-called fad studies, including music and art, in the public school curriculum. Numerous labor representatives, educators, and professionals attended. After the close of the meeting, Morgan presented a telegram from SG supporting special studies and noting

that "there is nothing too good for the children of the masses to learn in the public schools" (Mar. 12, 1893, *Chicago Inter Ocean*).

An Article by Samuel Gompers in the *Labor Signal*

New York, March 13. [1893]

IMMIGRATION EVILS.

The question of immigration, like all others of a reformatory character in the past few decades, was first broached and agitated by organized wageworkers.

I distinctly remember when a little more than a dozen years ago the immigration question was first finding occasional expression in the labor organizations that I heard a member, who had left the Emerald Isle scarcely three years, denounce the evils the toilers suffer from immigration.

From that time the thought occurred to me that there is something more in this world than philosophy and philanthropy which prompts the people to advocate measures of a reformatory character.

When the first demand was made by the wageworkers that the immigration of Chinese should be entirely stopped, a wild cry went up from those people who always believe in "letting well enough alone," regardless of how the so-called "well enough" may injure and ultimately destroy our own people. Constitutional objections were raised and solemn treaty stipulations thrust across the path in the desire to prevent the inauguration of that law which is now nearly universally regarded as justifiable and necessary.

All during the years of agitation of the proposition to prevent unfair employers and soulless corporations from entering into contracts with workers in foreign countries to emigrate to and work in this the charges of demagogy, ignorance, selfishness and Know Nothingism were laid at our door, but here again the thought that time and necessity make more converts than reason is strengthened by what happened a few months ago.

King cholera makes his appearance in some foreign cities, a major portion of our country's "Four Hundred" are kept at quarantine a few days, and from one end of swelldom to the other an effeminate and hysterical shriek can be heard to close out every "demd forwenner, aw, wather, emigrant, dontcherknow," and every one of our unsophisticated friends joins in the shout, believing that in the total inhibition of all immigration lies the solution of the economic and social problem, the panacea for all our ills.

We do not wish to erect a Chinese wall around these United States. We want every man and woman who comes here of his or her own volition. We want that energy and zeal infused in the blood of the people of our nation which prompt those leaving home, kindred and fond ties behind to battle along with those in (to them) a new country for improved conditions.

But when we find a condition of affairs confronting us such as the very conservative commissioner of labor, Hon. Carroll D. Wright,[1] reported, that nigh on 2,000,000 wageworkers are unable to find employment, we are compelled to look the conditions squarely in the face and endeavor to solve the problem by rational and humane methods.

There is not an industry in our country today in which there is not a large excess of workers. The mines, mills, factories, workshops and farm lands are overcrowded with men and women vainly asking for an opportunity to earn their bread by the sweat of their brows.

For the year ending June 30, 1890, there were 455,302 immigrants who landed upon our shores. Of this number there were 44,540 skilled workmen and 135,360 unskilled workmen or laborers, the remainder being women and children. For the year ending June 30, 1891, there were 555,496 immigrants, 55,000 of whom were skilled workmen and 148,000 unskilled workmen or laborers.

Imagine this force of over 1,000,000 in two years coming into our country with nearly 2,000,000 unemployed. While I do not attempt to make any one believe that this million of immigrants added the same number to the unemployed, yet I think that none will gainsay they have largely added to it.

Those who advocate a better regulation and greater restriction of immigrants often advocate widely different measures, some of which are not only unjust, but inhuman.

I believe that the same and better results can be accomplished without doing any one an injustice or even repudiating our oft declared sentiment that "westward the course of empire takes its way."

Nor do I advocate a restriction of immigration only from a selfish and narrow policy that is often adduced in advocating this measure. In my report to the Birmingham convention of the American Federation of Labor,[2] speaking upon the subject of immigration, I said: "We see artificial famines in some of the older countries caused by the vast holdings of the titled wealthy class. While the masses starve the tyrannical autocrats and effete monarchs bolster up their miserable dynasties by forcing immigration, while their willing tools furnish the means to aid the discontented and hungry out of their respective countries, and as they cannot go to many other countries in Europe, and owing to the laxity of public spirit and a recognition of the dangers that threaten us, they are literally 'dumped upon our shores.' There are societies formed for that special purpose who forward at least 10,000 immigrants each month. And, again, the ship companies, by the wiles known to the cunning speculator, improperly stimulate unnecessary and unhealthy immigration.[3] Quite recently, spurred on by organized labor, a better effort is made to enforce the law.

"There are ways and means by which, without bigotry, narrowness and a spirit of Know Nothingism, these wrongs can be remedied, and they can and should be formulated.[4]

"I view the immigration problem not from the mere selfish standpoint of our own protection, but I am persuaded that it not only tends to destroy the independence, progress and advancement of our people, but also is an efficient means by which the effete institutions of some of the European countries are perpetuated, and thus economical, political and social reforms postponed or avoided."

Since I penned these lines I am more fully persuaded than ever of the justice and force and truth of these utterances.

If the toilers of the older world were more largely concerned in improvements of their conditions rather than the hope of escaping from them as a last resort, the powers that rule them would soon be compelled to acquiesce in the demands of a popular uprising which would be inevitable and overpowering.

If the conditions of the workers in other countries were improved, the incentive to emigrate to ours would be lessened. Improvements in the material, social and political condition of the people of Europe and Asia could not take place without correspondingly benefiting the whole human family regardless of their geographical location. I would suggest as a means to better regulate and restrict immigration the following:

First—That the government of the United States should designate one particular officer, to be appointed by the president, who would be responsible for the proper enforcement of all immigration laws, and that appointments of all officers in the department be made by this responsible officer.

Second—That this responsible officer (name him commissioner or superintendent of immigration if you will) should be a man well known to be in sympathy with the spirit of the law and be a member in good standing of one of the organizations advocating the passage and enforcement of the immigration laws.

Third—That all subordinate officers at all ports and borders should be appointed, regardless of their political affiliations, who are known to be in sympathy with the law and who are members in good standing of the labor organizations of the country.

Fourth — A sufficient force of immigration inspectors should be appointed.

Fifth — That ship companies should be prohibited from issuing in this country tickets for passage from foreign ports to this, except to excursionists.

Sixth — That agents in the cities and towns of foreign countries should be required to furnish our consuls with a certificate describing the material condition and moral character and the actual status of each person who purchases a ticket from him, and that if the certificate is found to be based upon false information the immigrant should be returned and no person to whom this ship agent shall thereafter sell a ticket shall be admitted into the country. By way of explanation I would say that this would force ticket agents to be careful in the issuance of tickets and to furnish all information, or a failure to comply with the conditions would practically be a revocation of his license to continue the business.

Seventh — The United States should prescribe the amount of air and room space to which each passenger shall be entitled in every ship, the air and room space to be such as is scientifically demonstrated to be commensurate with health and decency. This provision in itself would largely reduce the number brought by each vessel and necessarily increase the cost of passage.

Eighth — No unmarried illiterate adult should be admitted. No illiterate male adult should be admitted.

Ninth — The law allowing the return of immigrants who come here in violation of the contract labor law after one year should be amended so as to extend to the time when they actually become citizens of the United States, during all of which time the employer or corporation who or which brought the contract laborer to this country should be amenable to its penalties.

Tenth — A more scientific means of quarantine should be inaugurated, and the power of the president fully and freely exercised whenever the exigencies may require a temporary but total cessation of immigration.

Eleventh — A continuous and permanent movement should be inaugurated and encouraged to reduce the hours of labor of those who work too long hours, so that the large masses which are now unemployed can find work to do, and those who would come here under the regulations and restrictions above referred to would find easy assimilation.

There is no doubt in my mind but that even the propositions I suggest, if enacted into law, would prove themselves inadequate unless the men who are intrusted with the enforcement of its provisions would be in entire accord with them and sustained not only by the popular will, but the mighty force of executive power. At any rate, if these suggestions were acted upon in good faith, and experience would show how far changes would be required, these could be supplied from time to time.

The interests of the workers of all countries are identical. We know that necessity is the mother of organization as well as of invention. If the wealth producers wherever located were to organize, these evils of which we now complain would soon be remedied, the brotherhood of man established and the dream of the poet realized.

> Till the war drum throbb'd no longer and the
> battleflags were furl'd
> In the parliament of man, the federation of
> the world.

Samuel Gompers.

Labor Signal (Indianapolis), Mar. 17, 1893.

1. Carroll Davidson WRIGHT was commissioner of the U.S. Bureau of Labor from 1885 to 1905.

2. AFL, *Proceedings*, 1891, p. 15.

3. SG omitted here the following text: "Then again, the great corporations which, in violation of the law, enter into written and implied contracts for servile labor to crowd and compete with the employed, and large masses of unemployed working people of our country. To crown the wrong some of the officers of the United States Government charged with the enforcement of the law to prevent improper immigration, showed a lack of sympathy with the law, connived at its violation, and sought to bring the whole law and the spirit of the law into utter ridicule and contempt" (ibid.).

4. SG omitted here the following text: "One officer of the general government should have undivided authority and be held responsible for the enforcement of the law" (ibid.).

To Hermann Schulteis

March 28, [1893]

Mr. H. J. Schulties,
923 H. St. N.W. Washington, D.C.
Dear Sir and Friend:—

Your favor of the 22nd. would have received earlier attention were it not for the fact of my absence from the city on business connected with the American Federation of Labor.

You say that you heard that I was not treated as I should have been by Secretary Carlisle[1] when I was in Washington.

I do not know how such a report reached you, for as a matter of fact there is no truth in it, except so far that an incident occurred from which your informant may have drawn his inference.

You are aware that the Executive Council of the American Federation of Labor held a session and conference in Washington last week. A gentleman known to have intimate relations with the administration informed one of the members of our Council that organized labor as such, would have no influence with the administration. This taken in connection with a publication in the press of the country a day previous to the same effect, was sufficient to prevent our calling upon the President and Secretary even if we contemplated so doing.[2]

You can readily understand that while I exercise my functions and duties as a citizen, I have little, if any, business with either the President or Secretary Carlisle, in that capacity. I do however, represent hundreds of thousands of working men and women organized for their common protection and for the welfare of the people as a whole, and in that representative capacity I desired to have the privilege of a conference both with the President and Secretary Carlisle. If, however, I was to be regarded as acting in my private capacity as a citizen, I fail to see the advantage of my calling upon either of them.

Neither the American Federation of Labor as an organization, nor its officers are hunting for office for themselves or their adherents. The Immigration, the Alien Contract Labor and several other laws which were enacted through the efforts of our organizations should at least have men to execute them who are known to be in sympathy with those laws and in the appointment of men to fill those positions it certainly seems but reasonable that the views of the Executive Officers should be consulted and met.

I note what you say in reference to the appointments already made and proposed.

With kind wishes and hoping to hear from you as frequently as convenient, I am,

Sincerely Yours
[Preside]nt.

TLp, reel 7, vol. 9, p. 3, SG Letterbooks, DLC.

1. John G. Carlisle of Kentucky (1835-1910), a former Democratic congressman (1877-90) and U.S. senator (1890-93), was secretary of the treasury from 1893 to 1897.

2. The AFL Executive Council, which met Mar. 19, 1893, in Washington, D.C., directed SG to correspond with Carlisle urging enforcement of the immigration law.

To Peter Breen[1]

Mr. Peter Breen,
Box 529 Butte City, Mont.
Dear Sir and Brother:—

I have the honor to acknowledge the receipt of your favor of the 23rd. and beg to assure you that both its receipt and its perusal gave me considerable pleasure.

It breathes the spirit of manhood, courage and independence and yet no bravado. Many of our fellow toilers in the North, West and East fully appreciate the situation the Miners of Coeur D'Alene had to meet in their struggle last Summer. The large body of the people however, have failed to comprehend the situation. We find a repetition of it in many parts where sycophantic judges have demonstrated themselves to be willing tools to corporate wealth.

We see the orders issued by judges Ricks, Taft,[2] Billings[3] and Law-rence.[4] It is certainly more than a mere coincidence that these orders should have been issued so close upon each other, and I have declared both by letter and in interviews that it is my opinion that there is some agreement or tacit understanding to strike a blow at organized labor. That these efforts will prove futile and unavailing I am more than satisfied.

If judicial decrees were the means by which progress could be prevented or the freer exercise of labor's rights, we would never even occupy the vantage ground we now have. The aristocracy of England and the other countries as well as in America, have always found some willing judge to clothe any tyranny with their judicial ermine. Men were disfigured, branded, sent to prisons and hanged for daring to stand up for their rights and the rights of their fellows, and in spite of all opposition and antagonism or repressive measures the wage-workers have continued to organize and more thoroughly or-ganize, despite it all.

I view this recent movement on the part of corporations and judges as an aggressive act on their part. Much will depend upon the im-mediate outcome by the attitude assumed by the toiling masses of the United States.

If we cringe before the corporations and are afraid to meet the issues, without doubt it will be some years before labor's voice can dare be heard or we may be in a position to raise our heads. I believe we should not be cowed by demonstrations to thwart our purposes and to deprive us of our rights. On the contrary, now more than ever does it become our duty to face the conditions presented, and by our pertinacity in the maintainance of the justice of our cause imbue courage and self-reliance among the workers and bring dismay to our enemies.

With you I believe that unity is an essential to the achievement of our purposes, and I beg to assure you that I strive with all the power I command, to accomplish that end.

We appreciate the fact that the small amount the American Federation of Labor appropriated towards the defense fund of the men of Coeur D'Alene was but a small drop in the bucketful required, yet it was given as a evidence of our principles and sentiment, and it is gratifying to know, that it was accepted in that spirit.

It does not often occur that a man who is many times a millionaire will so freely come forward both with his influence and money, to stand by the cause of justice and right as the man you refer to did at Coeur D'Alene. You do not mention his name, and under the peculiar circumstances I am most curious to learn it.[5]

With kindest wishes to yourself and to our friends in the movement and trusting that every success will crown the efforts of the toilers of America, and asking you to communicate with me occasionally, I am,

Sincerely and Fraternally Yours   Saml Gompers
President. American Federation of Labor.

TLpS, reel 7, vol. 9, pp. 7-8, SG Letterbooks, DLC.

1. Peter Breen was a member of the Butte miners' union. He was elected as a Democrat to the Montana state legislature in 1890 and was serving as district master workman of KOL District Assembly 98 in 1892. Breen was arrested in August 1892 on murder charges stemming from the Coeur d'Alene mining strike. The charges were dropped on Mar. 28, 1893. He subsequently became a labor lawyer.

2. After a series of unsuccessful meetings between representatives of the railroad brotherhoods and the management of the Toledo, Ann Arbor, and Northern Michigan Railroad dating from 1891, engineers and firemen struck on Mar. 8, 1893, to demand a wage increase and union recognition. The company in turn began replacing union members with nonunion workers. Peter M. Arthur, grand chief of the Brotherhood of Locomotive Engineers (BLE), invoked the Brotherhood's rule 12, requiring engineers on adjoining lines to boycott the cars of the struck railroad. On Mar. 11 Augustus J. Ricks, U.S. district judge for the Northern District of Ohio, enjoined connecting railroads from refusing to handle the Toledo's cars in interstate commerce, and the boycott was lifted. Following unsuccessful mediation efforts by Ohio Railroad Commissioner William Kirkby, the boycott was resumed. William Howard Taft, U.S. circuit judge for the Sixth District (Ohio), issued another injunction on Mar. 17. The following day Arthur withdrew the BLE's boycott, effectively ending the strike. The company refused to reemploy any members of the BLE. On Apr. 3 Taft ruled that the BLE's rule 12 constituted an illegal conspiracy under the Interstate Commerce Act.

3. On Mar. 25, 1893, Judge Edward C. Billings of the U.S. circuit court for the Eastern District of Louisiana ruled that New Orleans merchants were entitled to

judicial protection and relief from the effects of the New Orleans general strike of 1892. Billings maintained that the strike was a conspiracy in restraint of trade as enjoined under the Interstate Commerce Act.

4. On Mar. 29, 1893, Abraham Riker Lawrence, a justice of the New York supreme court, heard a motion by the Clothing Manufacturers' Association (CMA) to enjoin a boycott of its firms by the United Garment Workers of America (UGWA) and the AFL. He granted the union a week's adjournment on the condition that no further boycott circulars were distributed in the interim. On Apr. 5 UGWA officers along with SG appeared before Supreme Court Judge George Carter Barrett, who denied the CMA's request for an injunction. On Nov. 10 Justice George Landon Ingraham of the New York supreme court granted the CMA's request for an injunction, over-ruling Barrett's decision. In April 1894, however, a three-judge panel of the court overturned Ingraham's ruling.

5. Probably a reference to Marcus Daly of the Anaconda Copper Mining Co., who apparently provided a $10,000 cash bond for Breen when he was arrested in October 1892 on charges connected to the Coeur d'Alene strike.

An Excerpt from an Article in the *New York World*

[April 1, 1893]

GOMPERS URGES THEM ON.

. . .

. . . There was much enthusiasm at yesterday's meeting of the locked-out men[1] in Beethoven Hall, in East Fifth street. Samuel Gompers made a fiery speech denouncing the Knights of Labor, which was received with applause and cheers.

He spoke at length about the boycott and reiterated his former statements that the Federation considered it the most valuable weapon it possessed and intended to keep on using it.

"Even conceding, which I do not, that boycotting is wrong," said he, "what is the present attitude of the manufacturers in trying to force men out of unions so they may crush them? Judges Ricks and Tafft in their decisions have declared that men have no right to stop work when they want to. Judge Ricks has decided that they must work whether they want to or not. Suppose they refuse? What then? Why, they are guilty of contempt of court. To punish them for that, they are put in jail. Then they can't do any work anyway. So the Judge's order defeats his own purpose. Men are no longer chattels to be bought and sold. The men of America are free and we must have the manhood to defend the principle.

"Even if Judge Lawrence is upheld by the Supreme Court of the United States, his decision can't be enforced. No power on earth can prevent the boycott. Boycott is simply a new term for an old fact. What is the great Protective Tariff but a boycott on European manufacturers? You can't stop people from boycotting till a law is passed to force men to buy just such goods. You can't prevent my talking so long as I have a tongue, and just so long will I be able to tell my friends who my enemies are, and ask them not to deal with them.

"Now as to the K. of L. They are the buccaneers of the labor movement. All they are trying to do is to feather their own nests," said Mr. Gompers.

"The lockout has demonstrated one fact, and that is that only 110 of the workmen in the association's shops are Knights of Labor. I met a manufacturer last night and he told me that he liked the Knights of Labor better than the Federation because it was cheaper to pay one or more leaders of the Knights of Labor a few hundred or even a few thousand dollars than to pay better wages all around, which was what the Federation men demand. Boycotts were often put on for no earthly reason, and taken off on payment of a few hundred dollars or so."

. . .

New York World, Apr. 1, 1893.

1. In January 1893 members of United Garment Workers of America (UGWA) Clothing Cutters' Union 4 of New York City struck Sinsheimer, Levenson, and Co., demanding an agreement on wages, hours, holidays, and hiring. The Clothing Manufacturers' Association (CMA) then stepped in and attempted to negotiate an agreement to cover all CMA firms; the strikers returned to work pending the outcome. At the same time, the CMA opened negotiations with local assemblies of KOL National Trade Assembly (NTA) 231. The UGWA and the CMA reached an agreement in late February; the CMA presented it to the KOL locals for their endorsement as well, but the Knights rejected it. The UGWA then demanded the addition of a new provision in the agreement giving priority in hiring to UGWA members. When the CMA refused, the UGWA renewed its strike at Sinsheimer on Mar. 16 and subsequently instituted a boycott of the firm with support from the AFL.

When the CMA threatened to lock out UGWA members, NTA 231 announced it would provide KOL cutters in their place. On Mar. 25 CMA firms locked out some 800 to 900 UGWA cutters, and an equal number of other workers walked off the job in sympathy with the UGWA; thousands of tailors depended upon these cutters for their own employment. Some KOL members refused to work, but others took the places of UGWA cutters. When the UGWA extended its boycott to all the participating firms on Mar. 27, the CMA obtained temporary injunctions against the AFL's and the UGWA's boycotts; these injunctions were dissolved by court action, however, on Apr. 5.

On Apr. 12 six CMA leaders were arrested on the UGWA's charges of conspiracy for instituting the lockout. The arrests came only hours before negotiations were to begin under the auspices of the AFL and the New York State Board of Mediation and Arbitration. Released on parole, the CMA leaders proceeded with the negotiations, and the two sides reached an agreement on Apr. 20 (see "Excerpts from a Report on the Mediation of the New York City Clothing Cutters' Strike," Apr. 12-20, 1893, below). UGWA cutters returned to work on Apr. 24 with the understanding that differences at individual shops would be settled by an arbitration board of CMA and UGWA members. By the end of May, however, these differences still remained, and the UGWA claimed that the CMA had not reinstated all the locked-out men as agreed. In June a grand jury dismissed the conspiracy charges against the CMA leaders.

To the Executive Council of the AFL

New York, April 4, 1893

To the Executive Council of the A.F. of L.

Fellow-Workmen: —

Saturday morning April 1st. I was served with copies of two complaints entered by the members of the Clothing Manufacturers Association, and two injunctions restraining the American Federation of Labor from in any way advising or assisting the locked out Clothing Cutters or Garment Workers, and also restraining the A.F. of L. from issuing any circular which will interfere with the trade of the plaintiffs.

At a conference it was found necessary to retain counsel to appear in Court and to make answer for and on behalf of the American Federation of Labor. The restraining order is made returnable at eleven o'clock Wednesday morning April 5th. In company with Mr. John B. Lennon Treas. of the A.F. of L. we secured the services of Mr. J. W. Goff[1] a very able attorney. The general retainer was $250.00, Mr. Goff saying that he would act fairly by us and that he expected us to act honorably by him.

I feel convinced that he will not be exorbitant in his charges upon us. Incidentally Mr. Lennon and I heard while in the office of Mr. Goff that he had been sought to be retained by the other side.

Since the retention of Mr. Goff, Col. George W. Hart[2] has volunteered his services in our behalf and Judge T. J. Mackey[3] has also volunteered his services.

I kindly ask you to vote upon the proposition to confirm the action in retaining Mr. Goff to defend and represent the American Federation of Labor.[4]

If there are any suggestions that any member of the Council desires to make in this matter I trust that he will freely do so.

With kind wishes, I am,

Fraternally Yours   Saml Gompers.
President. American Federation of Labor.

TLpS, AFL Executive Council Vote Books, reel 8, *AFL Records.*

1. John W. Goff was a New York City lawyer.
2. Probably Colonel George H. Hart, a New York City lawyer and legal advisor to SG.
3. Thomas J. Mackey was a New York City lawyer.
4. The AFL Executive Council approved the retention of Goff as legal counsel.

A Translation of an Excerpt from an Article in the *New Yorker Volkszeitung*

[April 9, 1893]

COURAGEOUS IN BATTLE.

Under the auspices of the American Federation of Labor, an impressive mass meeting was held yesterday evening at Cooper Institute. The meeting had been called to express the support of the working people to the locked-out cutters and, at the same time, to criticize the unjust judicial decisions that have recently been handed down by the courts against the workers. It was a great meeting. Almost every seat in the huge hall was taken and at least 2500 people were present. Christ. Evans, the secretary of the American Federation of Labor, opened the meeting with a speech in which he emphasized that the locked-out cutters deserved the support of the workers of New York City. Evans expressed the hope that the cutters' lockout would contribute to the greater unification of the workers of New York. Following this, Daniel Harris, the president of the state branch of the American Federation, was elected chairman, Christ. Evans, English secretary, and Henry Emrich, German secretary. Among the vice-presidents of the meeting were: Alexander Jonas,[1] John Swinton,[2] Sam. Gompers, Rudolf Modest,[3] Charles Rosencranz, Geo. McVey,[4] Geo. K. Lloyd,[5] James Archibald,[6] A. Cahan,[7] M. Dampf, J. B. Lennon, and others. Harris emphasized in his speech that without organizations the workers would be at the mercy of the manufacturers. He noted particularly that the United Clothing Manufacturers represented, according to their own figures, 50 million dollars of capital, and had resolved to destroy the cutters' union, but that the working people would not allow this. "The workers of this country," said Harris, "are now confronted with the question: 'to be or not to be.' The workers of the United States must be reminded to consider whether they are going to let themselves be oppressed by the united capitalists with the aid of the courts."

Chas. Reichers, the secretary of the United Garment Workers, was then introduced as the first speaker. He explained the causes that had led to the cutters' lockout, and emphasized that the manufacturers had staged it to break the union. The speaker sharply criticized the actions of the Knights of Labor, and said that the manufacturers had wanted to destroy the Knights in 1886. But now, he said, one can see the charade; the Knights of Labor are helping the manufacturers. Reichers denied the charge that the Garment Workers in Rochester took the jobs of the Knights who had struck there.[8] In his address the speaker mentioned that on Monday the tailors would stop work in the shops and the contractors would close their workplaces so that they could not employ any scabs.

"If the cutters stand together," said Reichers, "as single-minded as they have been in the past, the victory cannot fail to come."

Samuel Gompers, the president of the American Federation of Labor, was the next speaker. He was greeted with great applause. First, Gompers criticized in no uncertain terms the actions of Assemblyman Butts,[9] who had stated in a speech at the assembly during the debates on the conspiracy law[10] that he (Gompers) was a professional agitator, who only stirred up trouble in order to draw his fat salary. The speaker stated that he could not say how much money, earned through his corrupt practices, Butts had in his pocket when he was giving a speech against the anti-conspiracy law. Gompers then thoroughly critiqued the recent judicial decisions against the workers. "For several months now we have been confronted with conditions," the speaker said, "that give us plenty to think about. We saw a supreme court justice from the state of Pennsylvania who described workers in Homestead, members of the Iron and Steel Workers' Association, as traitors, because they defended their homes, their families, and the constitution of the United States. Shortly after this decision, this Chief Justice Paxon resigned from office in order to act as receiver for the Reading Railroad. He was only able to get this lucrative position because of the corrupt services that he had rendered to the capitalists. And the other judicial decisions followed the famous decision of Chief Justice Paxon. Justices Ricks and Taft ruled that workers do not have the right to leave their jobs. They issued injunctions against the workers. Some people say the decisions were based on the 'Interstate

Commerce Law,'[11] but the lawmakers never intended this law to be used against the workers. There was a time when a worker was not allowed to leave his job. He was branded if he ran away from his master and hanged if he repeated this 'crime.' In those days, a worker was a serf, but those days are past. We are living in the year 1893. Slavery, which prevailed in the past, cannot be brought back by judicial decisions." Gompers emphasized that strikes could not be prevented by the decisions of the courts. At the end of his address he criticized the actions of the clothing manufacturers here, and emphasized that these bosses own palaces while the people who are being exploited by the manufacturers live and have to work in cramped rooms. The speaker encouraged those present to support the locked-out cutters with every means. . . .

. . .

New Yorker Volkzeitung, Apr. 9, 1893. Translated from the German by Patrick McGrath.

1. Alexander JONAS was a member of the editorial board of the *New Yorker Volkszeitung.*

2. John SWINTON published the influential New York City labor reform newspaper *John Swinton's Paper* between October 1883 and August 1887.

3. Rudolph Modest (variously Modiste) was a member of New York City CMIU 90. He ran for political office on the SLP ticket in 1891 and was active on a number of committees of the New York City Central Labor Federation (CLF) in 1892 and 1893.

4. George H. McVEY, a Brooklyn pianomaker, was treasurer of the New York City CLF between 1892 and 1894.

5. George K. Lloyd, a smith, was recording secretary of the New York City Central Labor Union (CLU) in 1891 and 1892.

6. James Patrick ARCHIBALD was an officer in the New York City CLU and its successor, the Central Federated Union, from 1882 to 1904, with the exception of one year.

7. Abraham CAHAN was the editor of the *Arbeiter Tseitung* (*Arbeiter Zeitung*) in New York from 1891 to 1894.

8. On Mar. 7, 1891, twenty-one Rochester, N.Y., firms belonging to the newly organized Clothiers' Exchange locked out some 350 clothing cutters belonging to the KOL, setting off a month-long strike that affected some 15,000 to 20,000 garment workers. The employers were attempting to weaken the influence of KOL local assemblies and KOL National Trade Assembly 231 (the United Clothing Cutters, Trimmers, and Tailors of North America), an influence reflected in work rules interfering with the use of apprentices and overtime work, a union shop policy, and the effective use of boycotts. The Clothiers' Exchange accumulated a large fund to protect member firms against further boycotts, forced workers to renounce allegiance to the KOL, and had national and local union leaders arrested on conspiracy and extortion charges. A back-to-work movement led to the collapse of the strike in early April.

During the strike by the United Garment Workers of America (UGWA) in New York City in 1893, some KOL leaders claimed that UGWA members had taken the jobs of Knights during the Rochester strike. In retaliation, most Knights in New York

City continued to work and some filled the positions of locked-out UGWA members. While KOL workers composed only a small portion of New York City cutters, and not all Knights went along with this retaliatory strategy, the continued employment of Knights as well as nonunionists in jobs formerly held by UGWA members became a major point of contention in settling the dispute.

9. Arthur C. Butts was a Democratic assemblyman from New York City (1893-94, 1896).

10. The New York conspiracy law, revised in 1881 (Laws of 1881, chap. 676), made the use of force, threats, or intimidation to interfere with the trade, calling, or property of another, an illegal conspiracy, though allowing peaceable assembly and cooperation to advance or maintain wage rates. State and local officials successfully invoked the conspiracy law on numerous occasions against labor leaders involved in strikes, boycotts, picketing, and similar activities. A bill legalizing union boycotts and peaceful efforts to persuade workers to strike passed the New York assembly on Apr. 18, 1894, but was not approved by the state senate.

11. The Interstate Commerce Act of 1887 (U.S. *Statutes at Large*, 24: 379-87) established the Interstate Commerce Commission to regulate railways engaged in interstate commerce. It made provisions governing rates charged for services and prohibited rebates, drawbacks, discriminatory charges, and pooling.

To John McBride

April 10, [1893]

Mr. John McBride,
Prest. United Mine Workers of America,
53 Clinton Bldg. Columbus, O.
Dear Sir and Brother: —

For quite a time I have been in correspondence with our general organizer Mr. John Kirby[1] of Fremont, Colo. He has succeeded in organizing a number of Unions, among others the Miners.

In each of my letters I have urged that they become attached to the United Mine Workers of America, but when our organizer has laid the matter before the men they simply rejected both the offer and the conditions and insisted that they would organize unions throughout the State and as each one was organized, become attached to the American Federation of Labor direct, intending to form a State Organization of Miners.

It is needless to say that I have frowned down upon this and have used all the persuasive power at my command to urge them to direct their organization to the proper channel. In one of the last letters received they say, that unless they can come in directly under the A.F. of L. they will remain independent from the A.F. of L. as well as the United Mine Workers of America or in fact any other alliance.

When these letters came, our friend Evans and myself consulted upon the matter and we determined to lay it before you for your consideration and do so now. Since these men seem so determined not to become attached to the U.M.W. of A. would it be advisable to allow them to remain independent and outside of the influence and spirit permeating our movement[? Would] it not be advisable to humor them for a while, that is to say, to allow them to receive a charter from the A.F. of L. and in the course of a year or so bring every power to bear upon them to join and [become] attached to the U.M.W. of A. There have been a number of circumstances where this course has been pursued in other trades, of course always first receiving the consent of the officers of the National Union of the trade in interest.[2]

[I trust?] you will give this matter your early attention and advise [me] of the decisions you arrive at upon the subject.

You have no doubt seen the decision rendered by Judge Barrett[3] in [the injunction?] proceedings brought before his court by the Clothing Manufacturers Association to restrain, both the American Federation of Labor and the United Garment Workers of America from sending out circulars [on this matter?] While it is not an entire refutation and repudiation of Judges Ricks, Taft and Billings it is sufficient at least in this measure act as an offset and is encouraging.

Trusting that your convention[4] may be entirely successful and that the organization may continue to grow and prosper, and with kindest personal wishes to you and colleagues and hoping to hear from you at your earliest convenience, I am,

Fraternally Yours   Saml Gompers.
President. American Federation of Labor.

TLpS, reel 7, vol. 9, pp. 28-29, SG Letterbooks, DLC.

1. Possibly the John Kirby who served as an AFL district organizer in Ouray, Colo., in the late 1890s.

2. There is no evidence that the miners affiliated directly with the AFL in this period.

3. See "To Peter Breen," Mar. 31, 1893, n. 4, above.

4. The 1893 convention of the United Mine Workers of America met at Columbus, Ohio, Apr. 11-13.

Samuel Gompers and the Arbitration
of Labor Disputes

Throughout the last half of the nineteenth century, labor leaders, employers, and public officials attempted to establish formal procedures to resolve industrial disputes without resort to strikes and lockouts. Contemporaries referred to these procedures in general as "arbitration." Included under this term were settlements achieved through "conciliation," which meant the resolution of disputes by the interested parties themselves, "mediation," where the disputants were brought together by a third party for the purpose of conciliation, or "arbitration" in a more specific sense, that is, settlements reached through authoritative decisions of a third party. As the meaning of these terms evolved, so too did the AFL's position on them.

When Samuel Gompers testified before the New York Bureau of Statistics of Labor in 1885, he acknowledged this overlapping and perhaps confusing terminology. Referring to the "arbitration committees" appointed by unions to negotiate with their employers, he acknowledged that "this I speak of is hardly arbitration—it is conciliation." Similarly, when he called for "compulsory arbitration" at these hearings, the compulsion he sought was one that would require employers to negotiate with unions and their representatives. As he put it, "Where one side would desire to have arbitration and the other refused, I would have the law compulsory."[1] It was this conception of arbitration, with the state functioning as a mediator between the disputants, that Gompers and the New York State Workingmen's Assembly supported when they lobbied for the establishment of the New York Board of Mediation and Arbitration in 1885 and 1886.

Labor's support for state arbitration efforts in the 1880s, however, gave way to misgivings in the 1890s. As early as 1888, when the New York Board of Mediation and Arbitration called for compulsory arbitration, it was already clear that the "compulsory" component meant not simply the mandatory collective bargaining that Gompers had envisioned, but, in addition, could involve the required acceptance of decisions made by state arbitrators. Faced with growing evidence of judicial hostility toward labor, Gompers and other labor leaders feared opening yet another arena of labor relations to state interfer-

303

ence and began to take firm stands against this kind of compulsory arbitration. Speaking before the AFL's 1894 convention in Denver, Gompers insisted that "disputes between the workers and employers may be generally adjusted by arbitration, but if they are, it will only come when the workers are better organized, when their power and their rights have received greater recognition. The first step must be organization, the second conciliation, and the next possibly, arbitration, but compulsory arbitration—never."[2]

If Gompers opposed compulsory arbitration as the term had come to be used in the 1890s, he nevertheless continued to campaign for his earlier position and actively participated in mediation and conciliation efforts. He took part in efforts to mediate strikes and grievances during his trips around the country,[3] but probably played the role of mediator even more frequently in New York City. Although documentation of these activities is rare, Gompers' participation in the negotiations surrounding the settlement of the United Garment Workers strike in 1893 was recorded in the proceedings of the New York State Board of Mediation and Arbitration. Not only does this document demonstrate the conflicting notions of mediation, arbitration, and conciliation among the participants, but it also provides a detailed picture of Gompers' role as a negotiator and an advocate of what later became known as collective bargaining.

Notes

1. New York Bureau of Statistics of Labor, *Third Annual Report* (Albany, 1886), p. 450.

2. AFL, *Proceedings*, 1894, p. 15.

3. See, for example, "To the Executive Council of the AFL," May 17, 1893, below, decribing Gompers' efforts in negotiations between workers and the Liggett and Meyers Tobacco Co. and the Drummond Tobacco Co. of St. Louis. SG reported to the 1894 AFL convention that over the course of the year "in a large number of instances the services of the members of the Executive Council were secured by affiliated organizations in conferences with employers to adjust trade disputes; it is pleasing to add that in most cases the arrangements were mutually satisfactory" (AFL, *Proceedings*, 1894, p. 16).

Excerpts from a Report on the Mediation of the New York City Clothing Cutters' Strike

[April 12, 1893]

The first meeting was held at the Madison Avenue Hotel, April 12, 1893, at 8.30 o'clock p.m. The meeting was called to order by Mr. Gompers, who stated the object of the conference.

On motion, Commissioner Feeney[1] was elected chairman of the meeting.

Following is a report of the conference:

Mr. White.[2] — On behalf of the United Garment Workers of America, the committee request that, prior to further negotiations being conducted looking to a solution and an adjustment of the present difficulties existing, the Clothing Manufacturers' Association should declare the present lockout at an end, and the conditions prevailing prior to the lockout to exist pending the negotiations.

Mr. Hochstadter.[3] — On the part of the Manufacturers' Association it is useless for us to entertain that suggestion, because it would only entail delay and because the executive committee of the Clothing Manufacturers' Association are here ready to proceed to a settlement of the difficulties.

Mr. Hornthal[4] then offered the following proposition:

"We recognize the right of men to affiliate with trade unions, if they so desire, and their right to be represented in any differences between employers and employes by such representatives as they may select.

"We recognize the right of any man to refrain from affiliating with any trade organization. In the selection of employes we will not discriminate against any men by reason of their affiliations or non-affiliations."

The proposition of Mr. Hornthal was rejected by the garment workers and the following counter proposition was offered by Mr. Zuber:[5]

"We insist that the shops shall be union shops, but especially declare that we do not ask the Clothing Manufacturers' Association to discriminate against any organization of labor in the employment or discharge of men."

Mr. Reichers.[6] — Some of the members of the Clothing Manufacturers' Association believe that I am entirely opposed to a settlement of any kind. But I thought probably, by advancing this proposition, that it might smooth out matters. If rejected by the manufacturers it remains as before, but I believe that probably both parties might be satisfied if we had no agreement at all; no written agreement. We did not seek an agreement in the first place. I want to make my statement clearly understood; we did not seek an agreement with the manufacturers' association; we never asked the manufacturers' association for one until the subject was broached by them.

. . .

Mr. Gompers. — For the purpose of having your proposition come properly before the manufacturers' association, or, rather, their executive committee, for consideration just now, do you make the proposition that, in view of the failure to thus far agree as to the terms of settlement of the present difficulties, the lockout be declared at an end, and that no written agreement be entered into, and that the men return to work?

Mr. Reichers. — This is my proposition: That, in view of the failure to thus far agree as to the terms of settlement of the present difficulties, the lockout be declared at an end and that no written agreement be entered into, and that the men return to work.

Mr. Zuber. — This proposition of Mr. Reichers was unauthorized by the rest of the executive committee.

. . .

Mr. Zacharias.[7] — After deliberating for two hours we can not come to an understanding. We have resolved either to have no agreement or have a union agreement. One or the other must be decided, or we will withdraw.

Mr. Gompers. — I would like the members of your association to take some formal action upon the proposition made by the executive committee of the United Garment Workers. I would like then to take some formal action.

. . .

Mr. Hochstadter. — The manufacturers' association reject the proposition, and reject it for this reason, that it would simply be going over in the next few months the same trouble we had the last three months, and that the gentlemen have other business to attend to besides attending meetings and joining in conferences when they see exactly the same road to travel. It is disagreeable and can not be agreed upon.

. . .

Mr. Gompers. — Acting in the capacity of mediators in this matter, as members of the executive council of the American Federation of Labor, in consultation with Mr. Feeney, of the State Board of Arbitration, we have formulated something which we propose, with the hope that it will be accepted, believing, as we do, it to be fair and in the spirit of mutual concession.

We have taken the first section of the old agreement, or rather the proposed agreement,[8] between the Clothing Manufacturers' Association and the United Garment Workers and have taken the proposition of Mr. Hornthal, and, without any material change, have proposed it as an addition to section one of the agreement. We have stricken out the words, "if they so desire," as being superfluous and unnecessary. We have also stricken out the second declaration as being superfluous and unnecessary, since the first declaration carries the second with it. The section would therefore read, as stated in the agreement, or in the proposed agreement, with this addition: "The Clothing Manufacturers' Association recognizes the right of men to affiliate with trade unions and their right to be represented in any differences between employers and employes by such representatives as they may select. In the selection of employes we will not discriminate against any men by reason of their affiliations."

The second proposition we make is: "That the members of the manufacturers' association having agreements with the United Garment Workers of America shall maintain the terms of said agreements until the time of the expiration of the same."

We believe that the proposition we make is conciliatory in spirit, and made with an earnest desire to see the present difficulties settled. In the body of the agreement there are other measures and matters which were partially or entirely agreed upon and which could be made the basis of further agreements. We recommend that our proposition be adopted and that the lockout be declared at an end.

Mr. Hochstadter. — As I understand this proposition, it is made by the executive council of the Federation of Labor, acting in the capacity of mediators, and Mr. Feeney, on the part of the State Board of Arbitration, as a basis of a proposed agreement to take the place of the preamble to the agreement which was under way at the time these difficulties arose, and that the first clause would then read as follows: "Whereas, the United Garment Workers of America, affiliated with the American Federation of Labor, deem it to the interest of cutters and trimmers that they should be members in good standing of some recognized labor organization, and the Clothing Manufacturers' Association of New York is in accord with the United Garment Workers of America, to the extent that membership in a labor organization, honestly and discreetly conducted, is to be commended; and,

"Whereas, the association favors any proper measures on the part of such unions to increase their membership, the association agrees that it will instruct its members, at all proper times, to recommend honest and conservative organizations of labor. And the Clothing Manufacturers' Association recognizes the right of men to affiliate with trade unions and their right to be represented in any differences between employers and employes by such representatives as they may select.

"In the selection of employes the Clothing Manufacturers' Association will not discriminate against any men by reason of their affiliations.

"The members of the manufacturers' association having agreements with the United Garment Workers of America shall maintain the terms of said agreements until the expiration of the same."

What will be the status of the other members of the association as to an agreement? What is the idea of the executive council with regard to the other members of the association?

Mr. Gompers.— The agreement, I understand, would remain.

Mr. Hochstadter.— Then you suggest that an agreement practically the same as was signed shall be amended so far as suggested and the balance to stand as it is, with the additional clause that that agreement shall not apply to the manufacturers who already have made agreements, but they shall conduct their business under individual agreements with the United Garment Workers?

Mr. Gompers.— Until the expiration of their agreements.

Mr. Hochstadter. . . . The only member of our committee who has such a contract is willing to live up to it, if our organization deems it wise for him to do so, but without the consent of the other houses we can not consent to such a proposition. The committee thinks it unwise to have two sorts of agreements under which the members of our association should work. Whatever agreement we make we think should be an agreement for every member of our association. If it is good enough for the balance of us it ought to be good enough for those who have already made contracts, and if you do not make that an important question as to those contracts being carried out, taking into consideration that they have only a few months to run, and make one and the same agreement, it would be easier to effect an agreement binding on every member of the association. I don't say, speaking for the committee, that we reject that proposition, but we can not agree to the contract for individual houses, but the association can make a contract for all. So that, if you can see your way clear to rescind the proposition, so far as those few houses are concerned, it would make it easier for us to come to a settlement. It would be easier in matter of time. It can't be very important when you consider the short time they have to run, and can't be a particular thing when the most important member expresses himself willing to carry out that agreement. But as I said before, there is that difficulty, that we will be obliged to ask the other members whether the agreements are agreeable to them, and if the matter is not insisted on, we could finish our agreement.

Mr. Gompers. — We regret that it is important. We believe that when there is an agreement between a firm of employers and an association of workmen, that that contract ought to be lived up to, and it does not vitiate the condition of an agreement. We only ask that those agreements shall be lived up to until the expiration of the time for which they were made. I am quite desirous of having this matter settled to-night; but since this matter has been dragging along, the difficulty has lasted now nearly three weeks, a question of a day is unimportant. You men, as merchants, employers, may have time during the day; the men representing the garment workers are locked out; they lose no time during the day. The executive council of the Federation of Labor will lay all their business aside and meet you, if necessary, during the day; say that to-morrow at 1 o'clock, sharp, we will meet at some place more convenient to our business down town, more adjacent to it, and there conclude the business we have in hand. In the meantime it will give you an opportunity of consulting the other seven firms who have agreements with the United Garment Workers.

· · ·

Mr. Mendelson.[9] — We have discussed this matter on the lines that it is agreeable to the garment workers. I don't want to ask an expression of their opinion, unless the council of the Federation of Labor think it advisable to go into that.

Mr. Gompers. — The matter was referred, by the nature of the application of the United Garment Workers, for approval of the executive council, and for the sustaining of their position. By the nature of the application, under the laws, the matter has been placed practically in our hands. So long as there was a possibility of the manufacturers' association committee and the executive committee of the United Garment Workers to agree or to discuss points of agreement, we did not desire to exercise any of the functions and duties devolving upon us by reason of the matter having been placed in our hands and by which we obtain jurisdiction. When that failed, it became our duty to take charge of the matter, and I have no hesitation in saying that any agreement made by your committee and the executive council will be signed and adhered to by the officers of the United Garment Workers.

· · ·

[April 13, 1893]

. . .

Mr. Gompers. — I would like to request an authoritative statement from Mr. Hochstadter, or any other authorized member of the executive board of the Clothing Manufacturers' Association, as to their attitude upon the acceptance or rejection of that part of the agreement offered last evening or this morning before we adjourned.

Mr. Hochstadter. — The answer of the executive committee of the manufacturers' association to the proposition of the council of the American Federation, as to the two clauses which were suggested as a basis of agreement, is that they agree in substance to the first of those clauses and that they reject the clause which refers to agreements or contracts which had previously been made between members of our association and the garment workers.

Mr. Gompers. — My colleagues and myself, in endeavoring to bring about this conference, hoped and expected that peace would result from it. We are fully and keenly aware of and appreciate the serious condition prevailing in the clothing trade. We desire to act the part of mediators, but it must not be imagined, even for a moment, that we came here for the purpose of yielding everything. If there can be peace it will be good, but it must be peace with honor. If there is not peace with honor, I, as one, would advise the men who are associated under the banner of the American Federation of Labor to be defeated in battle. I would rather, as a man and as an executive officer of the organization that I have the keen pleasure and honor of representing, to go down with my banner flying than to have it trailed in the dust.

Last evening, during the course of the discussion, our friend, Mr. Hochstadter, representing the manufacturers' association, said there must be sincerity of purpose, and, by indirection, intimated that a suggestion made by one of the members representing the United Garment Workers of America was hardly sincere. There must be a cardinal principle recognized, and that is that a contract entered into between man and man, or man and an association, or between association and association, should be lived up to truthfully, faithfully and honorably. We do not yet give up hope of arriving at an amicable adjustment, and I say now that we do not recede from the position, but will temporarily withdraw that proposition to which the committee of the manufacturers' association object, and suggest that we proceed to the other conditions and points upon which there is a possibility of agreement, and then renew the question again. If, during the course of our deliberations, we can arrive at an understanding or agreement which is honorable to both parties, it is possible that that may be yielded, but until other conditions of the agreement are arrived at and settled we are willing to withdraw that proposition.

Mr. Hochstadter. — I have been deeply impressed with the remarks made by our friend in reference to his desire for a peaceful and amicable outcome of our difficulty, and I do not yield to him in the intensity of that desire nor in the sincerity of our purpose of arranging a satisfactory agreement as between ourselves and our employes. At the same time I must be free to confess that in proceedings of this kind sentiment should not be considered; that we came here as business men, at a great sacrifice of time, most of us without any selfish purpose, all of us, I was going to say, without any selfish purpose, and all of us without any possible benefit to be derived from any agreement which may be entered into. I know that almost all the houses represented here in the executive committee are not such houses against whom can be brought a single cause of complaint. As regards the question as to the condition of the men employed by the gentlemen who are represented here, or by firms represented here, there can be, in all fairness, no cause for complaint.

No workingman that I know of, no trade that I have any knowledge of, is in a better condition than the trade which is represented here by the Garment Workers of America. They are housed in the best premises in the city of New York. The rooms in the houses where they are occupied are the best, the best lighted, the best heated; it is pleasantest in the winter and in summer; their hours are short and they have holidays frequently; and there is nothing they can expect to win, because their conditions are satisfactory. But sometimes there is a principle involved as regards employers and employes. We can not be expected and can not be asked to come here day after day and sacrifice ourselves for any purpose when we can not see any practical result. I don't want it to appear that other conditions may prevail which will ultimately make this of minor importance. We are representatives of the Clothing Manufacturers' Association and we are assured that these annoyances referred to are the result of the contracts which were entered into. Consequently, this position which we have taken with the federation is made with all sincerity. The clause is objectionable. There are hundreds of reasons outside of the statements that the contracts were forced, no matter how complacently. They have expressed that they were forced as with a pistol. These contracts are the cause of all difficulty in the way of establishing an agreement. They of themselves are of no importance. One can be avoided in two weeks; at most they will all be ended in a short while. These are my sentiments and are reasons why I must object to the withdrawal of this clause and discussion now. I don't wish to be peremptory; I don't wish to bring about a breaking up of this conference. Time must be considered. There can be no outcome if this is made a sine qua non. I trust, in view of what I have said, they will see the wisdom of withdrawing what I have expressed is of no great importance.

. . .

Mr. Gompers.—I regret very much that the gentlemen of the manufacturers' association should assume that position, that there can be no agreement with this proposition laying in abeyance. It would appear as if the desire was to break up negotiations right here. Though that may not be the desire, it would appear so to one uninterested. I want to say my proposition was to temporarily withdraw. Of course, even formally withdrawing it does not deprive us of the right of introducing it at any other stage of the proceeding. Why not permit the withdrawal and consideration of it until later? For instance, if there is an agreement which would be satisfactory to all parties, and the representatives of the garment workers could say: "Well, under the circumstances, we will allow the proposition to fall by reason of the general agreement arrived at." I think, however, that no loss of position, no surrender of a right, is asked on the part of the representatives of the manufacturers' association. Supposing we say we withdraw it, that would not deprive us of the privilege of renewing the proposition. The matter of mere verbal maneuvering should not be important.

Mr. Hochstadter.—I admit the statement made by Mr. Gompers is quite correct. There is nothing in the situation which would make it incumbent on them, or either side, not to withdraw it. My object is to convince the other side positively, and without any shadow of a doubt, so far as this side is concerned, whatever the agreement may be, that it must be an agreement of the association; and having accomplished that I have no objection to the withdrawal of that proposition, and, of course, they will note that it will be with the object in view of coming to an agreement as to everybody.

. . .

Mr. Gompers.—I should say that the proposition I made having been acquiesced in, we go to the next point. I have in view the fact of the time of the representatives of the manufacturers' association, and I also have in view the time of the representatives of the United Garment Workers, which they ought to devote to the management of their interests, and I also want to say that the time of the executive council of the Federation of Labor is of some value, and, without stating the sacrifices of any one, I would state it is valuable to others if not to us. I would, therefore, suggest that we proceed to a consideration of the next point.

Commissioner Feeney then read the second clause of the original agreement.[10]

Mr. White.—The manufacturers' association have locked out not only the cutters and trimmers, but the examiners. Consequently I think the rate of wages should be made with them also. They also are human beings. I submit, on behalf of my colleagues, that the standard rate of wages for examiners be fifteen dollars, as a minimum.

Mr. Evans.[11]—I have no desire to discuss the question, but I want to try to place this conference in a position that it understand itself as to what it has done. So far we have had the first proposition. As you get along, every proposition should be read, after amended, in the form as amended, and then adopted by the conference; then go to the next. I think you should have the stenographer read the first clause, as amended, and so on through all, and have the conference agree, and then adopt as a whole afterwards.

Mr. Hornthal.—I am afraid the gentlemen who are here, the manufacturers, do not know anything of the manufacturing department of the clothing business; they are all office men. The rate of wages, as fixed in the agreement, was agreed upon after consultation with members who understood that branch. I know nothing about it, so far as the wages of the examiners are concerned. While we are perfectly willing to put in examiners in the agreement, I think the amount they are to receive should be left blank until we have had an opportunity to learn what they are getting to-day. You understand all the Federation men were locked out, whether examiners, men who picked up work, or whatever they were, all were included; but I don't see why this clause entirely should be adopted. I think I have spoken to the members of the association, and while they have objected, as I stated, the demand controls the wages. If you do adopt this, and I believe the sentiment of the association is to adopt it, there will be no trouble about the price. I understand every house has different sorts of examiners. In one house bushelmen, in another house a tailor will do the work; each house runs different men for this purpose. This question has just been suggested. The executive committee think, because of these facts, we could not tell what an examiner was. This subject has been spoken over, and in the agreement, I think, the examiner was left out because the examiners could not be placed in the list of the manufacturing department.

Mr. Reichers.—I would like to say some houses employ as many as fifteen examiners. We admit right here before you that the wages are very different. In some houses they pay thirteen dollars, some fourteen dollars, some fifteen dollars. I know examiners that get twenty dollars. Some houses, when they have a great deal of work, have separate bushelmen and examiners, and each does separate work. However, examiners and bushelmen ought to be included in this. I don't say the price should be fixed to-day; but after you get your necessary information from your representative, your working partner, the chances are you will very materially differ in prices, and let us from those prices create a minimum.

Mr. Gompers. — May I ask a question in connection with this matter? The question is predicated upon a statement made by some manufacturers, that, in some establishments, there are persons employed who do the examining and do bushelmen's work and other work. In view of that would it not be advisable to say, instead of the provision, as proposed to be put in at the end of that section, "examiners or persons employed exclusively as examiners, their wages shall be so and so much minimum," so as to cover the point of the condition of such houses as do not employ persons as examiners exclusively?

Mr. Reichers. — In some houses one man does both examining and busheling.

Mr. Zuber. — As to the question of examiners and bushelmen, so far as fixing minimum wages is concerned, it seems to me best to let the matter go by the board for the present. The manufacturers confess they are most office men. Let them get the statistics, and probably then some conclusion can be arrived at.

Mr. White. — The manufacturers accept the proposition to fix a minumum rate of wages for examiners, and we will arrange that afterwards.

Mr. Marx.[12] — That question could only lead to endless trouble because no man could fix the line of demarkation of an examiner. Some receive half pay of regular examiners. Why should he be classed as an examiner? It is a question that is very intricate.

. . .

Mr. Hochstadter. . . . In the interest of those we employ, regardless of the fact whether they are union or non-union men, I am personally in favor of high wages; but in the interest of the men, I object to the insertion of a minimum rate of wages, and I do that fearlessly because I mean it for the best interests of everybody, and I do it because for peace in the future it had better be eliminated. You can not make a manufacturer see that a man is worth twenty dollars, if he is worth only eighteen dollars. There will be a way and there has been such a way, where men who were bound to accept twenty dollars, have been obliged to do things in an underhand way and pretend to receive twenty dollars. The natural consequence which will follow is that no man shall receive less than twenty dollars. It would also follow from that statement that he should not receive more than twenty dollars, because if he should not receive less than twenty dollars, regardless of the fact of his skill, why should he receive more than twenty dollars? But he does receive more. Why and how? When he is competent; when his services are worth more, you can not prevent any individual improving himself, and they will get more because skilled labor is worth its price. With what sense of justice can you request a member of your organization, or if a member of no organization, to give up his employment if employment is offered him at a price which he and the employer can agree upon? You can not make an agreement of this kind. Your organization does not control all the clothing houses in America. You drive men on the street without the prospect of any work; you hamper the conditions of the trade in every possible way; you drive a certain element to another place. If they get more than twenty dollars, it is because of their skill; if less, because of the lack of skill. It hampers everybody. Every skillful man, including those here, will not and does not work for twenty dollars. The condition of trade is such that they are called for and obtain and get more than the ordinary rate of wages. Others are just as old men, have just as many dependent upon them, are just as anxious to obtain employment as skilled men. We should make this clause, if we make any, a question dependent on the condition of trade and their surroundings.

. . .

Mr. Reichers. — I think the gentleman on the opposite side is imbued to-day with entirely too much sentiment. He knows himself that a man whom he would have to pay less than twenty dollars he would not have on his floor, because his rent is too high, unless he keeps the man for charity. I say if a man is a clothing cutter and knows his business, he is going to belong to the union every time, and that the mechanics are locked out to-day the manufacturers must admit. Furthermore, I claim that the minimum rate of wages is never going to hurt their business. In fact it will compel every competitor in trade to sell his garments at something similar to the figures you are selling at. You know there are manufacturers a few blocks from you who have not such lofts as you have, and are paying their people only twelve dollars or fourteen dollars, who are manufacturing the same class of garments you are. Here is Mr. Rosenberg; he manufactures a cheap grade of goods, and he wants only good men, because he uses a great deal of space, and if he is to be a direct competitor of men who pay only twelve dollars or fourteen dollars (and I can show you where they get fifty dollars for the purpose of taking men to work), I say, where he is in competition with such men, that a minimum rate of wages is to his interest.

Mr. Gompers. — I want to say something in reference to the minimum rate of wages. I think there is an entirely mistaken notion prevailing among the gentlemen. I will accept the statement of Mr. Hochstadter that his desire is to do the very best he can and knows how to do for his men and men who work for other houses, and take his statement and Mr. Hornthal's to that effect. I say the minimum rate of wages is in their interest and is a protection for every fair inclined employer against the cupidity of his competitor. Go to all the industries that you will and you will find that employers almost invariably, so far as the organizations of labor are concerned in the establishment of a minimum rate of wages, say that it prevents the undercutting in that particular. They enter with their capital in the markets of the world on a level and upon an equality. None have an advantage over the other, except that they may purchase larger quantities and possibly thereby obtain a lesser rate. But, so far as wages are concerned, if there is not an establishment of a minimum rate, it depends upon the generosity of the employers. It is the antithesis of generosity; it is the antithesis of fair dealing. I submit that, upon my hypothesis, you must consent that the establishment of a minimum rate of wages is to your advantage.

You don't want to have the clothing trade pass upon who is the meanest of the manufacturers; you don't want to have the rate or lack of rate established upon one who desires to take an unfair advantage of his competitor in business; and you don't want the tendency of wages to be downward, because I believe it is agreed by all the community that in a country where low wages prevail prosperity does not prevail. It is only in a country or community where the highest wages are paid that prosperity prevails. And the organized effort of the working people is, if not to raise, at least to maintain a minimum rate of wages, and the efforts of organized employers and organized workmen should be to maintain rather than deteriorate this state of affairs.

Mr. Marx. — I would like to say that I have listened to Mr. Gompers particularly with great interest and care because I wanted to hear a good exposition of that principle that no man who could not earn twenty dollars as a cutter had any right to live. Now, if the proposition were that we were to limit the maximum to the latter sum I would say we were wrong. Let the cutter make all he possibly can make. We are in favor of high wages for selfish purposes, and that selfish purpose is that every dollar paid out comes back to us. I am speaking for the smaller manufacturers. They are not satisfied to let the men who can not make twenty dollars a week starve. They think it wrong to throw them in the poor-house. Unfortunately there are such men. Mr. Reichers has stated that they work in some houses for twelve dollars or fourteen dollars. It may seem at first blush that they were being oppressed by the employers, but if you look further you will find the reason that they do not get more is because they are unable to earn more; they have not the brains; they are slower; nature has been hard on them; and I claim it is un-American to say, "If you can not earn twenty dollars you must go to the poor-house." I speak for the smaller manufacturers. I wish to say that in regard to competition we, according to the statement, would be the sufferers, the manufacturers who pay full pay, whose men receive full pay in the shops; they are the men who would be the sufferers; but the workmen working in their shops would not suffer. I would like to ask a question whether they really believe that a workman who works for smaller pay in certain shops is able to turn out as good work as the man who works in a shop and gets higher wages, and the same quantity.

Mr. Gompers. — This is not a matter of opinion with me. If it were I should easily be changed, my view might be modified; but if I may be permitted to say something which I hope will not be considered boastingly, I have given this matter a lifetime study, and it is a matter of conviction, forced upon me by study and by conditions and experience, rather than expressions of mere opinion that might occur and suit itself to mere circumstances and expendencies. The men who work in some of those establishments referred to and who obtain fourteen dollars or fifteen dollars a week, he asks whether they do as good work and whether they do as much. As a rule they do not do as much; as a rule they are not as competent; but I want to say that that rule is not because they are incompetent, not because they can not do that work; it is because they receive low wages, and you will find that in those houses, those establishments, whether in your trade or in any other, it is the maxim among business men that the highest priced labor is the best labor. You will find that in every trade, wherever wages have been increased, the competency and the efficiency of the labor has increased in even a greater ratio than the wages increased. Let me say that it does not depend so much upon trade. During the era of prosperity coming right after the panic of 1877 to 1880 and 1883, from 1881 to 1887, there had been an era of prosperity, and all along the line of industry and commerce the workers began to move, and in a very few years there was an increase of wages. In all industries except one in this country was there a rise of wages, and that one exception was the business in and around

Cohoes, N.Y.; and in the midst of that prosperity, in the midst of the greatest production of cotton and wool that ever existed in this country, notwithstanding the fact that there was not an operator out of work, they were compelled to submit, and the only reason was because they had no organization.[13] I want to say (I hope it won't be taken facetiously) I know that the Knights of Labor, in their agreement with the manufacturers' association, have no statement of rate of wages, or the understanding is there is no minimum rate of wages. I would suggest that the men who are not competent to receive this money, the minimum rate of wages, rather than have them, let them join the Knights of Labor, and if there be no agreement as to wages, they will be under their supervision. I believe that we have discussed this question pretty well and have gone over it very well, and I think we can come to a settlement now and proceed to the consummation and end it; and let us greet each other in the spirit of fairness and fellowship.

Mr. Hochstadter. — The suggestion made by the last speaker would indicate a way out of the difficulty for such men who are cutters in the city of New York who are not able to command a minimum rate of wages that the garment workers see fit to place. It comes rather unexpectedly and suddenly, and I want to take it all in before I accept the situation. I think if the gentleman's ideas were followed along, so that a cutter who could not find employment at that minimum rate should exercise his right to leave that organization and to affiliate with some other organization or no organization, it would be a way out of the difficulty for that particular kind; and I don't see any objection, except the law which would prevent the employer from giving him work. It has that merit that it shows a way out for the men that we have been referring to. It has an objection in this, that our arrangements with the workingmen who are now represented here by the Federation of Labor should be exactly the same arrangements we make with everybody, whether represented here or at any other time. It seems unfair to take advantage of the others. However, before pressing that second clause to a vote, if I understand the intention, I should like a moment's consideration of the matter before it is put to a vote, with my colleagues, to see what their opinion is in the matter. I take it for granted that it shall be a matter of public notoriety or general information that only members of the Federation confine themselves to twenty dollars or over, and others shall exercise their own judgment. I think it an unfortunate position, but I accept it, and think it will necessarily weaken that association, and induce manufacturers and perhaps unscrupulous ones to point out a way of getting cheaper labor.

Mr. Gompers. — I would say there is not anything I have ever said that I ever had cause to regret. I may confess that I usually think what I say and know the full import of it. I say the representatives of the United Garment Workers of America are looking for the protection of their own men. If incidentally others are benefited, that is their purpose also, but primarily the members of that association. I say, if my friend Hochstadter thinks I have placed my colleagues in an inconvenient position, I believe we are right and think the position I have stated is agreeable to us, and we will take every opportunity of making it known.

Mr. Reichers. — The reason why this clause was laid over was on account of examiners.

Mr. Mendelson. — We fully went over that point with the gentlemen, and when we agreed upon this basis of wages we intended to carry it out. With the examiners it can not be carried out.

Mr. Gompers. — Is it an understanding that the committee of three, as provided by both sides, shall meet within thirty days from the ratification of the agreement and consider the question of examiners?

Mr. Marx. — In view of the spirit of peace that has prevailed, I am willing, on behalf of the manufacturers' association, to forego the principle which it might involve, and in the interest of peace I propose that the second clause of this agreement stand and that the third clause be crossed off. There is one word to be added, "incompetency," and therefore I propose that the second clause be adopted and the third clause eliminated.

The second clause was thereupon adopted.

. . .[14]

[April 14, 1893]

. . .

Mr. Hochstadter. — Under the circumstances, I think that the chair is proceeding in a proper way, and I move that the Clothing Manufacturers' Association agree, immediately upon the ratification of this agreement, to declare the lockout at an end, and the shops of the respective members of the association open for employment to the members of the United Garment Workers of America, and that all vacancies that exist (I speak without consultation and subject to correction), or that may exist during a period which I don't care to specify without consultation, shall be filled, upon application, by members of that organization.

Mr. White. — Our members have been discharged through a concerted movement by the manufacturers' association, of course, without consultation, as far as we are concerned. They were thrown on the streets through no act of ours; on the contrary, because we refused to do something. I claim that, inasmuch as they have caused this systematic lockout of our members, in order to place matters as they were before, they are obliged to take back every single individual into his respective position, and those who took the places in the meanwhile should leave. I think this fair. It will be utterly impossible, at the present, even to induce our members to go back to work, knowing the positions were taken advantage of in the meanwhile by strangers. The manufacturers' association knows the custom of the labor organizations; how utterly impossible it will be for a body of men to go to work, knowing their positions were taken by others; they will not go back individually; they can go back as one man. They were locked out as such and must go back the same way.

Mr. Gompers. — The proposition of Mr. Hochstadter has been discussed by Mr. White. I would suggest, in the interest of time and arrival at a conclusion, that Mr. White or some other member of the United Garment Workers' committee would formulate a proposition. They have propositions opposite each other, and we can then see what can be done, instead of criticism.

. . .

Mr. Reichers. . . . I present the following proposition: "All employes locked out on March 25, 1893, are to be reinstated in their former positions within three days after signing of this agreement, and all employes engaged since the above date by any member of the association shall be discharged in the meantime."

Mr. White. — I simply wish to supplement the remarks made by Mr. Reichers. It is absolutely final, without the possibility even of arbitration, that our men will not go back to work as long as a single individual in any shop in the association remains who took their place. That is absolutely final, and arbitration is unnecessary. That is recognized as a principle of every labor organization, and I don't know where an exception has been made to it, unless it was the defeat of a labor organization. That is the only exception ever made to it, when they admitted defeat.

Mr. Gompers. — I am informed that there have been Knights of Labor who have gone from one shop to another since this lockout occurred. If I can understand correctly, there is no objection to these Knights of Labor proceeding back to the shop from which they went and to be worked with by members of the United Garment Workers, in those shops which they left and will return to. These people who have been engaged, and were either Knights of Labor or members of the Federation of Labor, since the lockout, these are the parties referred to.

Mr. White.—I object to this.

Mr. Gompers.—I would like to know what the position of the manufacturers' association is on this subject, and I should very much dislike to see that this conference would fail upon that point; but I must say, for my colleagues and myself, that it seems to us that the proposition of Mr. Reichers is a proper one. You will see that there is no effort, no object, nor is there anything withheld, nor is there any animus against the Knights of Labor or people who were employed in the shops previous to the lockout and who remained; but if the lockout is to be declared off, it practically means that you should bring the situation back to the time when the lockout occurred. I think that is the fair and proper way. I think the position of the committee of the garment workers on that point is one which can not be receded from. If they are to go to work as individuals then they will go back as individuals, but only after they have been beaten. They are not beaten yet; that I think is admitted. There are two opposite factions or contestants up to the present time, and thus far I think it will be conceded that there has been no evidence of desertion on the part of the United Garment Workers. The contest is waged with as much vigor, with as much earnestness and with as much chance for ultimate success as were in sight on the first day the lockout occurred, but we came here and have concluded the terms of an agreement, and this is really a mere matter of detail to the manufacturers, but it is one which strikes at the very root of our organization. If there was anything harsh imposed there might be grounds for modification; there might be grounds on which my colleagues might intervene and say: "You have gone too far; it is inadvisable to insist on what you ask"; but this proposition, moderate as it is, I think ought to be accepted by you.

Let me say, further, you have heard it remarked by others as well as myself, that this agreement is subject to ratification. Not only do we fear that the position is one which is justified, but I want to call your attention to the fact that, by reason of the necessity for ratification of the agreement, each member would feel as if the blow was meant for him. And if the committee themselves would consent to the proposition as offered by Mr. Hochstadter, the members, feeling themselves each one as if he himself were placed in the position of being left out in the streets, would result in the unanimous rejection of the agreement by them. You can see this yourselves, if you will only place yourself in the position of the locked-out men, and who are expected to vote that either one of them or any one of them, shall be left out of consideration in this settlement, shall be left out of employment. If the trade does not warrant their continuous employment, the same rule would prevail as has always prevailed, and the employer would be a bad business man and would without doubt be considered as committing commercial and business suicide by employing men without having work for them. That must be admitted. That is not disputed or denied. I don't want to lash myself into an enthusiastic address, but I say this to you, that there is every evidence of an opportunity for arriving at an amicable adjustment of the differences, and possibly bringing about lasting peace between the manufacturers and the garment workers, and it is likely to lead after this year to such conference or renewal of agreements by which the trade can go on uninterruptedly, and the manufacturers can enter into business without fear of difficulties arising. If you agree, you are laying a foundation for future and greater prosperity in your industry than you or we may know of. But I do say, in the interest of peace, in your own interest as well as the garment workers, that this should be conceded, and then go on with the work of prosecuting the industry by your joint efforts and make it what it is and what it is possible to be.

. . .

Mr. Hochstadter.—We were about to hear a proposition in reference to a certain phase of the situation which has not yet been stated. I think we ought to know that phase of the situation, as to the status of the Knights of Labor who have been transferred, so to speak, to other shops.

Mr. White.—I would like to explain. We have reliable information and assurances that some Knights of Labor remained at work in some of the shops, while other Knights of Labor were unscrupulous enough to go to other shops. We have assurances that the Knights of Labor will not work with those. Those people had nothing to complain of; they were at work, and in order to further demoralize our organization they took places in other shops that were in distress. Now, even Knights of Labor will leave the shops if they go back, and you will have evidence of this. We consider them even worse than other men; we can not possibly take them into consideration whatsoever; we look upon them as blacker than ever. So far as we are concerned, we look at them as worse than others because they are open and declared enemies. The other men who took our places in many cases are unfortunate, and in many cases not mechanics, and wanted an opportunity to learn the trade.

. . .

Mr. Hochstadter.—The situation grows a little more difficult than it seemed to us. The action of the Knights of Labor is not such as to induce us to discuss it here, nor do we feel called upon to justify their movements or what they have done since this lockout took place. We must act in accordance with the situation as we find it at present. It is a matter of fact that in many shops of the manufacturers' constituency there is quite a number of tranferred knights. If the position taken by the garment workers is receded from, as regards their being willing to work in such shops as the men may happen to be from, the situation might be somewhat simpler, but until we get an absolute opinion either in one direction or another, the matter assumes a very difficult character. . . .

. . .

. . . The fear that has been expressed of not obtaining employment for locked-out men is very probably a groundless one. There is a sufficient demand for the employment of the mechanics and of good mechanics, as most of them are, to justify me in saying there is no difficulty in finding employment for every locked-out man. In point of fact, one of our prosperous manufacturers, who is a member of the executive committee, would be ready in a few days to employ half the locked-out men, 200 of them, and give them the wages as agreed upon. That is impossible at the present time, but the fact remains that within a few days employment could be found for half the locked-out men. So that, so far as that is concerned, there will be no danger of lack of employment. The method of returning is of course a very important matter and a matter that deeply concerns both sides to the controversy, but more especially the garment workers. . . . Now, if I understand it, the men who are willing to accept this agreement will not agree on two conditions. They will not return in a body if Knights of Labor occupy the positions they held prior to the lockout. Secondly, they will not return in a body to shops where these Knights of Labor would return to their original employment. These are two conditions on which the workingmen will not return in a body. It forces the manufacturers into this position, that before they can make any arrangement as to the return of the men who are now locked out it will be incumbent on us to discharge the Knights of Labor wherever they may be. That, it must be admitted, is simply impossible without the willingness of the manufacturers to engage in another dispute similar to the one now in controversy.

While I admit that I notice a desire of these gentlemen to make an arrangement that might possibly come to an agreeable conclusion, they concede that it is a physical impossibility; and before we go on to endeavor to convince ourselves that the position which we announce is not a proper one, this particular state of affairs must be receded from by the garment workers or we must agree to it. I propose, for the sake of finding out just where we stand, that it shall be agreed, as to any arrangement that is made, that the Knights of Labor shall not be disturbed from their employment.

Mr. Reichers. — Does the speaker realize that all these different complications occurred or had arisen on account of something which he has done, but had no right to do? You had no reason to lock out a number of men who never did you any injury. My proposition is that all employes locked out on March 25, 1893, are to be reinstated in their former positions within three days after the signing of this agreement, and all employes engaged since the above date by any member of the association shall be discharged in the meantime. I am willing to add: "No Knight of Labor who left a position in any house to take a postion in another should be reinstated."

Mr. Gompers. — We have consulted and have drawn up the following as a substitute for the foregoing propositions which have been presented by both sides: "All employes locked out on March 25, 1893, by the manufacturers' association shall be reinstated in their former positions within three days after the signing of this agreement, and the status, number and personnel of all employes (who were so locked out) shall be restored to the condition prior to March 25, 1893."

Let me say, before handing this for consideration, that we have sought to eliminate any expression to which exception could be taken and have reduced it down to the smallest number of words we could employ to cover what was desired. Let me say, in connection with this matter, that the manufacturers' association ought to consider that one of the main features which has always been sought by organizations of labor, in agreeing with employers, is for the establishment of a recognition of the union. I have no instance in my mind, covering a participation in labor movements in America for twenty-five years, where an agreement has been entered into with an employer or employers' association, unless the result of that agreement was the recognition of an establishment as being a union establishment. This is the first one that I am aware of. It is a very large concession to be made by the members of the United Garment Workers. I want to add this, and what seems to me to be a very important consideration, probably if the United Garment Workers were not to have an agreement with the manufacturers' association (a written agreement) that they might not possibly or probably even insist on that point and allow the future to develop and do what they desire; but they have entered into an agreement, or an agreement is about to be entered into, certain stipulations; in an agreement, at least, men can not go back as individuals. They agree as an organization with you, and as an organization they must go back to work, and the parties who have been employed since this lockout shall be discharged. Practically that is what it means. But you will observe that it also states that the status, number and personnel shall be restored to that which prevailed March 25, 1893. In other words, it concedes the point that Mr. Hochstadter has made, but without so stating; first, because it is inadvisable to state so. To concede it is inadvisable. We believe that in this direction it is as far as can we go. We want peace; the members of the United Garment Workers, together with the American Federation of Labor, have made concessions, quite a number of them, have modified demands, have pared down what was insisted upon to a large degree, gone as far as we can go, and we hope it will be accepted, so that this difficulty, as it may be called, may be obviated.

Mr. Hochstadter. — That proposition is not an unfair proposition, and under ordinary circumstances there should be no objection to it, because it contains the essence of what is fair, but with all the desire the other side may have to do what is fair and just for the purpose of arriving at a conclusion, a man can not be expected to accomplish impossibilities, and in so far as that proposition would involve the performance of impossibilities, I on behalf of the manufacturers must object to it in so far as that and no further. It is a physical impossibility to accomplish the provisions of that resolution, because there is not the amount of work in some particular shops that would enable each member to carry out the intention; whereas, in the aggregate it could be accomplished. For instance, my firm has not employed since the lockout a single individual; we have not added a single individual to our working force. Those discharged that day and a few who were transferred or transferred themselves to other shops, reduced our force twenty odd, I think; since which time we have not changed our working force. We did not because we didn't want to. The fact remains that we have not added a single one. I speak of this because I am entirely familiar with that establishment, and, as a friend of mine stated this morning and again just now, he is in the same position. It would be impossible for us to employ the same number of men as we did at the time of the lockout. I did not wish to allude to this. What is desired can be accomplished, but the manner of accomplishment is impossible.

With that statement the resolution would be acceptable, with a slight amendment which would not in the least change the circumstances that prevent the employment of the locked-out men. If you were to add to the resolution a proviso, "the needs of the establishment warranting it," it would be very readily agreed to; thereby not compelling such houses as have not the necessity for so many employes to employ them. Again, as I stated, there are houses that would be willing not only to take the number of men, but a great many more, so that they can all receive employment.

. . .

Mr. White. — Even let us suppose that there is not sufficient work for all those who were locked out, they could be re-employed Monday morning. Can it not be arranged so that the men can be employed the first week and laid off the next week? If not sufficient work for the entire force, can it not be obviated by the manufacturers placing the entire force at work and the next week have them laid off? We can not possibly explain to any single individual in our association the reason why he was not employed. Some of these houses only had a few men at work during the whole difficulty, and I know many of these houses will have to run double time and do night work. I know they will be willing to do that. I don't see any reason for it.

. . .

Mr. Hornthal. — I can readily see the proposition made by Mr. White would be simply untenable, for two reasons; the first reason would be, we then will be charged with discriminating against garment workers. I locked out eighteen men; I take back eighteen men at the end of the week and discharge these. Mr. White or Mr. Reichers will come to me and say, "Why don't you discharge those other men?" The charge will come back home to me that I am discriminating against the garment workers, which I should not have done. . . .

. . .

Mr. Hochstadter. — The manufacturers' association submit this as a substitute: "That upon the signing of the agreement, or immediately thereafter, the employes shall apply to the various shops from which they were discharged, and the employers shall, as far as their requirements will permit, employ such men. But in case the condition of the trade in any firm will not justify the employment of all locked-out men, they shall be furnished employment by other members of the association, so far as that is possible, and such men shall have the first opportunity for re-employment in the houses from which they were locked out."

Mr. Zuber. — I want to say this can not be entertained; it is altogether out of the question.

Mr. Gompers. — I believe I catch the drift and the intent of the counter proposition offered by Mr. Hochstadter, on behalf of the manufacturers, and it means simply that those who have taken the places of the locked out men are to be retained, and the members of the United Garment Workers of America who have been locked out are to make application for their situations, to both of which Mr. Hochstadter signifies an affirmative answer. That proposition is not acceptable. I was under the impression that we could arrive at some settlement of this matter upon a basis consistent with some degree of honor on the part of the United Garment Workers, on the part of the employes, and on the part of the American Federation of Labor; but if that is consistent, I must say that it is not acceptable; it can not be accepted. If the locked-out garment cutters must return to work with those who have been employed by the manufacturers' association since the lockout has occurred, they will do so when they have been beaten. If the members of the garment cutters' union are to make application for work as individuals they will do so, but only when they are beaten. That has not yet occurred. I want to say that the offer you have made possibly may be taken as a basis; might be amended in a way to bring the conflicting opinions nearer to each other; but it is the very antithesis of the proposition submitted by the garment workers, and between them there is a chasm which can not be overcome. If they say the men are to come back as individuals they will do so only when the organization is disrupted; they will come back then only and when they are hungry enough to seek work.

. . .

Mr. Hochstadter. — So far as the manufacturers are concerned, they have nothing more to say, nothing further to add. The only thing that has occurred during the conference was to strengthen my conviction which I expressed, so far as employment is concerned. I have been requested to pledge myself that there will be sufficient work for all the locked-out men in houses of the association, but I don't care to pledge myself.

Mr. Zuber. — I want to ask whether those who have taken the places of our members who were locked out are to be returned to the positions they held, if the lockout is declared off?

Mr. Hochstadter. — I have no objection to answering the question. It is the positive determination of the members of the Clothing Manufacturers' Association that the men who have been employed since the time of the lockout shall not be discharged, except for cause or want of employment.

Mr. Gompers. — I see nothing that we can do any further. Since that declaration of Mr. Hochstadter I can not see for the life of me

how the United Garment Workers can consent to such an arrangement, nor can I get my colleagues to advise them to accept it.

. . .

[April 20, 1893]

. . .

Mr. Hochstadter. . . . This question of discharging men, which is
primarily the object of the proposition that was brought from the
other side, is a question which not only affects our shops individually,
or the manufacturers, each individually, but it affects a principle that
interests the entire community, and it is a principle that has been
discussed again and again in every difficulty of this kind, and has
always been and always will be a source of trouble. The men who,
either from being locked out or from striking for some particular
grievance, in settling questions are invariably confronted with the
problem as to how and when men shall be released from their situations, and, as a matter of course, they are anxious to do or ought
to do all possible things to bring them back in their situations with
as little difficulty and as little humiliation as possible. Naturally, after
an agreement has been made with the men, all men who are innocent
should, on account of the agreement, be reinstated, and there should
be no further hardship on account of the difficulty, whatever it may
have been. Anybody can see that that is the first desire on the part
of the leaders of the discharged men or striking employes. At the
same time, men who are leaders must deal with the situation as they
find it. If it is possible to accomplish their first desires, their most
natural desires, they would be unfit for their positions if they failed
to make the strongest possible fight for that particular object; but, if
in the course of their discussion, it appears to be utterly impossible
to accomplish what they desire, wise men, even if they are striking
men, must do the best they possibly can, not for their particular factory
but for the particular good of everybody connected with them and
whose interests they have at heart.

It was said here, at the last conference, that there never was a
difficulty terminated where it was not made an absolute condition
that the striking men or locked-out men must be reinstated, excepting
when the entire movement was defeated, when, of course, the men
were obliged, under the circumstances, to go back to work under the
best terms that the employers would be satisfied to give them. We
take it that that is not the situation to-day, nor do we wish it to be
considered as a defeat for either one or the other party. We acknowledge that before either one or the other is ultimately defeated, great

hardship, both on one side and the other, will be experienced, and it is the desire of the manufacturers that those hardships shall be avoided, if possible.

In endeavoring to bring about an arrangement of that kind, it must be conceded that something must be done, both on one side and the other, to obtain a termination. If either one side or the other adhered positively to the terms and conditions exacted, it would be a miracle if the matter could be quickly terminated. Now, we accept that condition of affairs, and we understand that if we desire to terminate this matter it is impossible that we shall carry out to the letter everything that we believe the manufacturers are entitled to, and we believe, at the same time, if there is a sincere desire on the part of the garment workers to terminate the matter, that they must acknowledge that it is impossible to carry out to the letter everything they demand. The demands made for the purpose of terminating this situation are twofold; one would not be satisfactory to the locked-out men without the other, and the same position was announced by the manufacturers' association. The two resolutions show what these demands are. One is that every man who was employed since the lockout must be discharged and every man locked out must be reinstated. That is a bald statement of facts, and, so far as that demand is concerned, we must say that it is impossible of being accomplished. At the same time we do not believe and do not think because of that impossibility there is no solution of the difficulty, and it is our desire that there shall be a solution, and for the purpose of bringing back as soon as possible the men who are out of employment to their former positions. It is a physical impossibility, as I said before and I repeat it now, to bring back every man in the position he occupied prior to the lockout. That impossibility arises from various causes, one of which is that there are men employed, and situations must be vacant before the men can be re-employed. In reference to that matter we must again take the position that we took on the day the conference broke up. We must again say, in behalf of those who have engaged men, and which men are now occupying situations which were vacated, doing their duty and doing it properly, that the employer can not, with justice to his own ideas of what is right and proper, acknowledge the right of any man with whom he has had a difference to demand a change in the situation to such an extent as to require the discharge of these men; and in that we are not altogether alone. There has been a great deal of feeling in the strike that is now on at Ann Arbor; a great deal of animosity and a great deal of trouble in reference to whatever that situation is, which, after a great many hardships on both sides, no doubt seems to be now in the way of adjustment. The papers this morning indicate that the differences that have arisen have in a great measure been arranged; but exactly the same difference that stares us in the face to-day is confronted by the two parties to that contest in the west. The dispatches, this morning, say that the general manager of the Toledo road[15] sees his way very clear to a termination of the situation, and the two parties are in conference; but the demand that the men who have been employed be discharged stands in their way. They will not discharge them. This is not an isolated case. The same difficulty is there; they may not settle; in the course of time the men may gain their point. The probabilities are that the longer the termination of the settlement is delayed the more difficult it will be for the employes to obtain employment. The situation is the same here, with the exception that instead of the men striking they have been, to a large extent, locked out. The more delay the more difficulty there will be in arranging to take in the men who are now out of employment. I acknowledge that it is a hardship; that it is a difficulty which the leaders are bound to face, and it is for them to say to what extent they can face the men and acknowledge whatever they have gained in this contest has been sufficient. Loss has been sustained; loss of employment for a certain number of men whose places have been filled. I said at the last conference, and I repeat it again, without intending to have it considered as a threat or an inducement to terminate the situation, but as statement of fact, that the situation in New York, as far as the locked-out men are concerned, is not improving in that direction, and the situations that were ready for them on Monday, after we terminated the conference, are not ready for them to-day. There will be less for them next week; there will be less next year. The other side may listen to this impatiently, but at the same time we say this only for the purpose of bringing them to the same conservative frame of mind that we are in ourselves. We are anxious for the sake of our men, for whose interests we always have regard, we are anxious for our own sake that these matters shall be terminated as soon as possible. We both have the same interest. We must give way to each other as far as possible, if we have any desire whatever to come to an understanding; and with that in view I beg the other side to reconsider the position they took. . . .

Now, I have said about this matter, as moderately as I could, what I have, to induce the gentlemen to realize the position we are in and not require us to do these impossible things. It altogether depends on the spirit in which they receive it. If they are determined to maintain their position and we are determined, as we are, to maintain ours, it is impossible to come to an understanding. We are anxious to come to an understanding; we trust the other side are anxious.

And in view of the desires we have, let us talk about this matter in the spirit in which I have tried to treat it, and see if we can not reach a conclusion.

Mr. Gompers. — I am hardly in a position to speak authoritatively for the men who represent the United Garment Workers. I am free to say that I have listened with a great deal of interest to what Mr. Hochstadter has said. He makes a point in reference to the Ann Arbor strike and the negotiations now pending or reported as pending between the Brotherhood of Locomotive Engineers and Mr. Ashley, of the Ann Arbor railroad, and he very properly makes the distinction that in that case it was a strike and in this case it is a lockout; but in making the distinction he does not seem to give the distinction the importance due it. We believe that as a rule, whether in strikes or whether in lockouts, it is a matter which must receive that serious consideration which Mr. Hochstadter called attention to. It is a problem that always confronts the employes and the employers. But we occupy a unique position here for this reason, and a reason that I have already called attention to. If, for instance, the manufacturers' association would not contemplate a written agreement with the cutters, then it might be an open question; but you see that these men going back and asking for their places, some of them getting them, others not getting them, practically they return to the shops as individuals, when, as a matter of fact, you have entered into an agreement with them as an association. It is paradoxical. Not only that, they seemed to me to be the very antithesis of each other. I believe I understand the intimation, if I may be permitted to use that term, expressed by Mr. Hochstadter in reference to men now employed in shops and who supplant some of the men who were locked out. And if I understand the intention correctly, or the intimation, it is that in the natural course of trade or the business relations between the firms in their cutting deparments, it would naturally tend toward having the best men in their employ; and, since it is conceded that the cutters who were locked out are the best workmen in the trade, naturally it would tend toward their re-employment and the regaining of their old places, even at the cost of discharging the men gradually. I will say this to you, gentlemen, that, if there was no agreement, it might possibly be that the men could accept that; but I again wish to impress on your mind the fact that they have an agreement with you. If you declare the lockout at an end, it will be that the future engagements and relations between the manufacturers' association and the United Garment Workers will be on the basis of a written agreement, and I again say to you that a written agreement, on the basis of the possibility of some men getting to work and others not, is an inconsistency, to say the least.

There is one thing I want to reply to, Mr. Hochstadter's remark, particularly, when he spoke of wise men who are leaders and should consider the questions confronting them and deal with them as such. But Mr. Hochstadter will remember the term leaders, and more especially of associations composed of trade unions, of which the garment workers are organized and the Federation are organized, is the very opposite of that old idea of leadership. No leader or officer, known by any name, can, or dare, issue orders. It is not within his power; he is shorn of that privilege, and we think very rightly and justly, and to the interest of all concerned. It must always be understood that when in a conference the men who represent the United Garment Workers are not the leaders, but are mouth-pieces and spokesmen; they have no right or power to make agreements, and irrespective of what they agree to, it is subject to adjudication by the men themselves. Of course, this may be new to the clothing trade; it is not, however, in other trades. And I am sure if the manufacturers will come to an agreement and honorable settlement, they will find that they will deal with an organization, subject to the action of the organization, and that no man as an individual or as an officer can attempt to enter into an agreement which binds the people to certain conditions without their consent, and that the agreement will be calculated to advance the interests of both parties. If I understand the statement of Mr. Hochstadter, it is practically a reiteration of the proposition that the manufacturers made last week when we adjourned. I should prefer that the representatives of the union, in interest, would give an answer to that. If they accede to it, then, of course, we can go right ahead; if they do not, I have a suggestion to make, which I would like to have discussed, but which I think would be premature to state now.

Mr. Zuber. — I suppose I understood Mr. Gompers right. He wishes an answer from the members of the garment workers. We can hardly answer any differently than a repetition of our former answer, for the simple reason that we recognize, and the manufacturers recognize the fact that the proposition they make must be submitted to the men. If it were said that the men should apply for work, and if vacancies existed they would obtain employment, and those who can not find employment with the houses must do the best they can, each man will consider himself as being the one who will be rejected, and vote against the agreement. Consequently, it would be useless to consider the matter in that form. That is practically our answer.

. . .

Mr. White. . . . Our men were locked out in a body, and consequently those who were employed during the time the men were locked out certainly have no business there if this matter is settled. Almost the identical agreement which the manufacturers tried to induce us to accept is being attempted to be forced on us. Of course, I realize the manufacturers would score a great victory if we permitted those who took the places of the locked-out men to remain. It would go in the papers that we receded from our position because we modified the first clause. Under such circumstances, if the manufacturers are going to have a victory, they might as well force us into defeat without our signing away our rights and power, virtually throwing down our arms and accepting the worst position which could befall us.

Mr. Hochstadter. — The last speaker has demonstrated just what we fear, that, instead of looking for an amicable and proper termination of this difficulty, to use an ordinary expression, they are playing to the galleries. What the public will think and what the papers will say actuate them to a large extent. Of course, that is only human, but it ought not to be a serious consideration with men who have interests of other people at stake. . . .

Mr. Reichers. . . . As far as speaking to the galleries is concerned, I would like Mr. Hochstadter to understand we have a declaration of principles in our constitution, and it is a principal point that when men are locked out they must have the option to go back as they were locked out. We have nothing to gain by this, as I understand. We are not playing for applause from the gallery. It is immaterial to me whether the men decide to go back or decide to stay out. They sent us here to make the best arrangement for them that we possibly could, and after we have done that, we are supposed to go to them with the best arrangements we could make, and it is then optional for them to accept them or not. And if we endeavor to get the best we can it is simply our bounden duty to do so and simply to do our level best.

Mr. Gompers. — I don't know to what measure I am entitled to the compliment paid me by my friend Mr. Hochstadter, but I can say that my colleagues are trying to get the best they can for the purpose of aiding the men with whom I am associated. In the conference I have endeavored, with my colleagues, to act the part of mediator if I could, and you will see that I at one time asked the chairman, who is a member of the State Board of Arbitration and Mediation, to arrange some common point which we could recommend to our conference as the basis of a settlement. That is still our purpose, that is our purpose ever.

. . .

Now I come to the thought which I had proposed to suggest. There is such a wide difference between the two propositions pending that, from a mere discussion of them, there seems to be no possibility of arriving at an understanding. They are as widely different as the two poles. I would suggest, therefore, that the executive committee of the manufacturers' association select one man, one of their number, and that the United Garment Workers select one of their number, and these two endeavor to arrive at an understanding and report it to this conference, the conference in the meantime to take a recess for fifteen minutes or half an hour. It is likely that the committee could agree. If they can agree, I think they ought to. And as I said last week, and I think I repeatedly said, so long as there is a chance of agreement, either one of us ought to exert ourselves to obtain that end. If the committee of two report to this conference, and there may still be a division, possibly we can not do anything. If we can not, let us understand it as soon as possible, so that the time of the manufacturers and my colleagues and myself, and I want to say, last but not least, the chairman of this conference, Mr. Feeney, may not be wasted.

The garment workers appointed Mr. Smith as their representative, the manufacturers appointed Mr. Mendelson, and Commissioner Feeney was requested to act on the committee with them.

A recess was then taken till 8.30 o'clock p.m., at which time the committee presented its report.

Mr. Hochstadter.—I move that the report of the committee be adopted, as far as it has been agreed upon, and the clause that is in dispute be stricken out, or rather, the private agreement. The document itself, it seems to me, as far as I can see, is complete enough without going into the matter any further. It may be necessary to leave something to the fairmindedness of the parties to the agreement, because it would not be politic to put it all down in the agreement. I don't like the idea of a private agreement; it makes trouble; it is apt to lead to a misunderstanding, and when it comes to be enforced it is in the discretion of somebody. This discretion might not be properly used. I don't believe in private agreements. I think we ought to make an agreement, one that we can enter into and carry out and make a public matter of, and the document, as far as agreed upon by the members of the committee, seems to me to contain all that is necessary. And since there is a difference as to the other clause, it will be simple enough to strike it out.

Mr. Smith.—I want to call Mr. Hochstadter's attention to this: I was willing this private agreement should be held by Mr. Feeney, and I think Mr. Feeney will use all proper discretion.

Mr. Hornthal.—I am in accord with Mr. Hochstadter. I believe in having everything above board. It is only by reason of agreements concocted in the dark that trouble arises. I don't believe in those things and I am not so weak, nor so foolish, as you may call it, as to be afraid to stand up and acknowledge one way or another. We acknowledge by the instrument prepared by Mr. Feeney, Mr. Mendelson and Mr. Smith, that we will take the men as federation men, in the shops from which they were discharged, and where we can't take men back in these same shops by reason of circumstances which have occurred, to wit, the employment of others to do their work, we will provide places for them. I am not afraid to go to the public and say we had to concede certain things for the purpose of an adjustment of this matter, and whether the public say that the clothing men have been beaten or the United Garment Workers have been beaten, would not bother me. I have never heralded one way or another, although it has been said to-day that the president of the Clothing Manufacturers' Association heralded complete victory. I think, in order to prevent any question, if you will read the papers and not believe all that you read, you will be all right. I wish to say that I disclaim all statements in the press, and especially as to who is victorious and who not. I am willing it should go to the world that we concede that the men should come back as federation men, and where it is impossible to re-employ them in the same shops from which they were locked out, that we agree to place them somewhere else. That is a concession. To-day our shops are not open to any federation men. I am willing to have this go on record. I don't believe in leaving a matter of this kind in the hands of any one party. No distrust is meant to Mr. Feeney, but people may disagree, and if there is a disagreement, which might occur, we would be all blamed. It would be said we are a pretty set of people; we make one agreement and mean another. I believe an honest agreement to be wisest. I believe they can accept our assurance rather than an agreement. We have acknowledged we have a great many incompetent men; we want to get rid of some as soon as we can. I am not ashamed to say that a great many men taken on within the last two weeks, as the other side have said, and as I will admit, and I will say that for many members of the manufacturers' association, as a rule, are a class of people we want to get rid of as soon as we can. I believe that in ten days or two or three weeks, most of these men will be dropped out by reason of their incompetency. I have men who were locked out who were with me for ten or fifteen years; and I am sorry that they are away. I am going to get them back; I am going to keep them; and I want to get rid of these other men, who prove themselves incompetent, as soon as I can get rid of them. I have taken on seven or eight men. I know I am going to get rid of half of them, certainly within the next few weeks. Although a suit has been brought against me by one of the men for $25,000, I am going to take him back too. We want to get rid of most of the men taken on. Those men who came from other shops were loaned from one to the other shop, and I am willing to state publicly that they were loaned from one shop to another. For instance, they were loaned by Mr. Brown to Mr. Jones and others, and it is understood these men are to go back as soon as the difficulty is over. I am certain at the end of a week or so some of the firms who loaned their men to another shop will demand their return. All these difficulties will right themselves within a week or two, I think, and I can say, as president of the Clothing Manufacturers' Association, that that is the understanding. The men thus loaned are to go back to the shops and all things will right themselves. I don't believe in private agreements. A word is passed, and then Mr. White will have to make an explanation to Mr. Jones, and I may have to make an explanation to somebody of the association. The result is we will differ and explanations pro and con will have to be made. The people will think there is something behind this. Let us rather have a little trust in each other than make any of these underhand agreements which, if they come out, will reflect discredit on me, on Mr. Gompers and also on Mr. Feeney. I believe in doing these things squarely and fairly. That is the best way, and matters will come out right in the end.

Mr. Gompers. — The executive committee of the United Garment Workers have conferred with the officers of the American Federation of Labor upon the proposition agreed to by the committee, and in connection also with the statements made by Mr. Hornthal, the conference having lasted quite a time. We have had quite a number of them and, in the beginning, whether we were justified or not, it is more than likely that both sides may have viewed the purposes of the other with some degree of suspicion as to their sincerity in the effort to arrive at an amicable adjustment. As the conferences have grown and we have learned each other better, and weighed the statements of each other with a greater degree of care, I think that suspicion may have fallen away and given way to a degree of confidence in each other's sincerity and respect for each other's words.

In view of the very frank statement of Mr. Hornthal, president of the association, as to the intention of the members of the manufacturers' association, we were very much impressed with its tone and its apparent sincerity. We believe that there is a desire to carry out the contract and understanding in the spirit as well as to the letter. In view of these facts, we have advised the members of the executive committee of the United Garment Workers, and they have acquiesced in our decision to accept the agreement.

We are also of the opinion that a plain understanding is possibly better than any secret agreement, of and for which both parties may be accused of insincerity. What this understanding is is plain to every man. You want your own men back; you want your competent men, and men who have served you for years and perform their work to your satisfaction, and to the comfort of all concerned.

We believe that we have entered upon the last, or very nearly the last, obstacle to an agreement, and I, with considerable pleasure, say to you that the proposition is accepted by us.

The proposition is as follows:

"The locked-out men to be employed by the firms who discharged them within three days after the signing of the agreement.

"If the condition of trade in any particular shop does not warrant the continuance in employment of all the men, they shall be provided with places in shops of other members of the Clothing Manufacturers' Association at equally good wages.

"No opposition shall be made by any member of the United Garment Workers of America to working in the respective shops to which they may go.

"The manufacturers shall not discharge any men by reason of the recent differences; but this shall not interfere with the rights of the manufacturers to discharge men for other causes."

Mr. Hochstadter. — It affords me a great deal of pleasure to find that the continuous labors of the members of this conference are at last rewarded with some measure of success, and that the outcome has been so acceptable to both sides. The agreement as it now stands, and which is the result of this conference, is so plain that it can scarcely be misunderstood by anybody.

. . .

I think I have clearly stated our views. I don't want to say much in conclusion, but I can scarcely refrain from adding to what I have said, and to what I have said so frequently and so nicely, as my friend says, that in all this matter we have acted as spokesmen of the association. I have not had in the slightest degree any personal feeling in what I have said against anybody on the other side or in behalf of anybody on my side. I have done what I have done from a sense of duty, which I will do again, and which I never can regret. But I am more than thankful that the result has probably been to cement a little closer the men in our employ to ourselves.

I thank you for the courtesy shown to me in this conference and hope the results will justify what we have done.

Commissioner Feeney. — It is understood this agreement as presented has been adopted.

Mr. White. — The next thing would be for both sides to agree upon a public statement to be made about the settlement of this affair, in order that it can be explained that it is a mutual compromise.

Mr. Evans. — While I believe that it would be wisdom to use a great deal of discretion as to what should be presented to the public, yet I am inclined to think that it would be advisable for a committee of one from each side to agree on a statement, and make it in as few words as possible. The reporters, of course, are here, and, as we have already come to a conclusion, and a very satisfactory one at that (which, by the way, I am very pleased to note), you will remember that this is a question which is not confined only to New York city, but extends throughout the entire country at the present time, and the trouble between the clothing manufacturers of New York city and the United Garment Workers is a question that a great many are interested in, and I think that a plain statement, in as few words as possible, should be agreed upon before you adjourn.

I want to say that I have attended a large number of conferences between employers and employes. I have seen some very complicated questions arise between the two parties, and I don't know that on any occasion have I felt better than I do to-night to think that, after spending the time we have together, after each party presenting its views in the best manner possible, we have arrived at a settlement; and I trust that from this time forward the fact that we have met together will have a tendency to establish a better feeling between the United Garment Workers and the manufacturers of New York city, that will be of lasting benefit to both parties interested.

Commissioner Feeney. — If the manufacturers think that the proper course, I think it well to declare the lockout at an end.

Mr. Hornthal. — I have several resolutions which I wish to offer.

"The resolutions adopted by a meeting of the executive committee of the Clothing Manufacturers' Association of March eighteenth shall be rescinded."

"All circular letters that have been issued by the United Garment Workers of America and kindred organizations in reference to the members of the Clothing Manufacturers' Association, shall be nullified."

"All strikes heretofore inaugurated by the United Garment Workers of America in shops of members of the Clothing Manufacturers' Association, shall be declared off.'"

"All legal proceedings, whether civil or criminal, heretofore begun by either association or individual members thereof against each other or against either of its members shall be discontinued, without costs to either party; the criminal proceedings to be referred to the respective attorneys for lawful abandonment.'"

The foregoing resolutions were adopted.

Mr. Gompers. — I think that the conference has been quite conspicuous for the spirit of fair dealing, and while there is not that full recognition of the union which we would have liked, we hope that, by the conduct of our members, by the spirit of fairness which will be manifested by our conducting the affairs of our association, it will commend itself to the manufacturers, and that it will commend itself to all employers as well as to the employes, and that before very long there will be accorded a full recognition of each other's corporate interests as organizations, as unions to deal with each other in that way, to have committees representing both your own interests, and with due regard for the interests of the employes on the one hand, and the employers on the other, that you may meet annually and consider the various questions that may arise and may require adjudication. I am satisfied that when that is carried out, then the height of the prosperity of the clothing industry will be attained. I am satisfied that no reasonable employer will have occasion to complain, with any degree of justification, of the conduct of the United Garment Workers. It is an organization primarily instituted for the benefit of employes. It is a combination to protect but not to injure. It proposes not to tear down, but to build up. There is no man or set of men that it seeks to overthrow. It does seek to enthrone their fellows so that their interests will be protected; so that their rights may be conceded. Their ability as workmen will warrant fair treatment at the hands of the manufacturers' association. I am free to say that the statement made by Mr. Hornthal, as president of the association, prior to the adoption of the committee's report, largely contributed towards this end. It was open and firm and did him, as well as the association, credit. It did us credit and honor. I am free to say to you that it did largely influence us to arrive at the result we did, and to accept the proposition, as we believed, as we now believe, that if the agreement and understanding is carried out in that spirit, there will be no cause for dissension. And I want to repeat, that, so far as the courtesy extended to my colleagues at the hands of the manufacturers' association or members of the manufacturers' association, is concerned, they have my grateful acknowledgment, and I am not accustomed to say anything that sounds pretty merely for the sake of its sounding pretty; and I want, also, here to extend my acknowledgment of the very marked impartiality and earnestness that has marked the course of our chairman, Mr. Feeney; that I hope that this will not be the last of his successes as a member of the State Board of Arbitration; and to the members of the United Garment Workers' committee, I extend my congratulations.[16]

. . .

Board of Mediation and Arbitration of the State of New York, *Seventh Annual Report* (Albany, 1894), pp. 89-91, 94-99, 106-13, 115-22, 131-32, 134-39, 143-48, 150-51, 155, 158-65, 168-76, 178-81.

1. Edward Feeney was editor (1892-93) of the *Brooklyn Citizen* and a commissioner (1893-95) of the New York State Board of Mediation and Arbitration.

2. Henry White.

3. Albert F. Hochstadter, of the clothing firm of Alfred Benjamin and Co., was treasurer of the Clothing Manufacturers' Association (CMA).

4. Lewis M. Hornthal, a clothier, was president of Weisman and Co. and of the CMA.

5. John J. Zuber was a member of Brooklyn Clothing Cutters' Union 5.

6. Charles F. Reichers.

7. Benjamin Zacharias was one of the union representatives.

8. That is, the tentative agreement negotiated between the CMA and the United Garment Workers of America (UGWA) in January and February 1893.

9. Herman S. Mendelsohn, of the clothing firm of Banner Brothers and Co., was vice-president of the CMA.

10. This clause stipulated the wages to be paid cloth shear cutters, machine or knife cutters, and lining cutters or trimmers.

11. Chris Evans was a representative of the AFL.

12. Mr. Marx was a representative of the CMA.

13. Probably a reference to the textile strike at Harmony Mills in Cohoes, N.Y., in 1882.

14. The discussion and subsequent ratification of the remaining sections of the tentative agreement negotiated in early 1893 are not included in the present volume. These dealt with the employment of apprentices, hours, paid holidays, arbitration of differences relating to the agreement, discrimination by contracting tailors against UGWA members, and the resolution of complaints by the UGWA against CMA firms. The document also provided for the continuation of existing contracts between the union and individual association manufacturers.

15. Henry W. Ashley was the general manager of the Toledo, Ann Arbor, and Northern Michigan Railroad.

16. Although many union cutters returned to work, the UGWA maintained that the CMA did not reinstate all of the locked-out men.

From James Duncan

Office of Secretary
Federation of Labor.[1]
Baltimore, April 14th 1893

Dear Sir

I have today received from Bro. George Mitchell Secretary of the Westerly[2] Branch G.C.N.U. a letter in reply to a recent communication of mine reminding him of the Matter of a place for your Son[3] to finish his Apprenticeship. He says he is not sure of your address so he asks me to write to you least his letter to you may not reach you.

I am happy to say that he has Succeeded in getting a place for him from Mr James Gourley Supt. of the Rhode Island Granite Works. He had some difficulty in getting a place as the large firms dont want any apprenctices and the small firms have all the apprentices mentioned in their agreement. The "Rhode Island" Granite firm is a very large concern handling all kinds of work therefore a splendid place for a young man to gain a full knowledge of the intricacies of the Trade. They do both Building and Monumental Work and find a ready market for their product, while in traveling throughout the country after a young man becomes a journeyman the name of a Westerly R.I. training is a credential anywhere. The firm do not care for apprentices as the most of their work requires experience and although Mr Gourley refused at first to give his word to take him he did so at Mr Mitchells solicitation, and concluded by saying he would take him and if he proved to be of any account and wished to advance himself he would give him all the chance any young man could get. So I think everything will be all right and the object you had in mentioning the matter to me will be fully fulfilled.

The sooner he gets there the better now and by serving a year from now he will be a journeyman next year in a very good season of the year. He will find no difficulty in getting there I think and I wish him God Speed in his endeavour. The firm is the same that cut the work for the Equitable Building in New York and many other large buildings there and are now doing the New Congressional Library job for Washington D.C. in Concord N.H. —

Will be glad to hear you are finally very successful in your attempt to settle the trouble in New York City.[4]

Yours Fraternally   James Duncan.

Bro. Mitchells address is 16 spruce Street Westerly R.I.

Mitchell thinks your son will be put to work piece work and that the company may pay him the journeymans Bill which will give him a chance to make fair pay—

J D

ALS, Granite Cutters' National Union Records, reel 140, *AFL Records.*

1. The Baltimore Federation of Labor.
2. Westerly, R.I.
3. Henry J. Gompers.
4. Probably a reference to the clothing cutters' lockout in New York City.

To the Executive Council of the AFL

New York, April 26, 1893.

To the Executive Council of the A.F. of. L.
Fellow-Workmen:—

During the Course of the week Mr. Ashley[1] now associated with Mr. Kenney[2] in the publication of the weekly paper "American Industries" called here and the meeting of the Executive Council at Washington recently was spoken of. Incidentally he mentioned that the officers of the present administration expected a call from us and there was some disappointment at our failure to call upon them.

I had an interview subsequently with Mr. Kenney and explained to him the intimation we received at Washington "that organized labor could expect no favors at the hands of the present administration" and that that was the reason why we did not call. Mr. Kenney expresses himself to the effect that if any intimation of that character was given it must have resulted from a misapprehension. He suggested that I call upon the President, the Secretary of State[3] and possibly the Secretary of the Treasury upon matters connected with legislation as well as the appointment of persons by these officers for the enforcement of laws enacted in the interest of labor.

I am disinclined to go upon this mission unaccompanied by at least one member of the Executive Council and for that reason offer the following alternative propositions. 1st. That one member of the Executive Council and the President proceed to Washington at the earliest possible moment for the purposes above stated the member of the Council to be elected by the Council itself. 2nd. That the entire Council be summoned to meet at Washington.

It is respectfully suggested to the members of the Council that the communications emanating from this office should be regarded as confidential.

Kindly return your vote[4] upon the above propositions at your earliest convenience and oblige,

Yours Fraternally   Saml Gompers.
President. American Federation of Labor.

TLpS, AFL Executive Council Vote Books, reel 8, *AFL Records.*

1. Alfred Ashley was associate editor of *American Industries,* a New York City publication devoted to tariff reform and labor issues. He had also edited the *Building Trades Record* and worked as a reporter for the *New York World.* He had previously been a carpenter and a member of the New York City Board of Walking Delegates.

2. Horace Kenney was the editor of *American Industries.*

3. Walter Quintin Gresham (1832-95), a Republican lawyer from Indiana, served as U.S. secretary of state from March 1893 until his death.

4. On Oct. 23, 1893, the AFL Executive Council met with federal officials including Attorney General Richard Olney and Secretary of the Treasury John Carlisle to urge enforcement of the eight-hour law and the Geary Act, and the pardoning of the defendants in the *Jefferson Borden* mutiny case.

To the Executive Council of the AFL

New York, May 17, 1893.

To the Executive Council of the A.F. of L.
Fellow-Workmen:—

I beg leave to submit the following report of my trip to the West. As per instructions of the Philadelphia convention I visited the convention of the International Machinists Association[1] as well as having had a number of conferences with the officers and delegates to that body. The convention was fully aware that I would appear at its afternoon session of Thursday May 4th. and on the morning of that session prior to my appearance with unseemly haste they had already decided adversely upon striking out the color line in their constitution.

I was well received and the A.F. of L. commended, but a feeling prevails among the delegates that since the organization originated in the South and the race prejudice existed to so large a degree there, the local unions would secede from the International Association should the word "white" be stricken out.

At St. Louis I met a committee from the Tobacco Workers Union #5778[2] by appointment. They were adverse to the opening of negotiations with the Liggett and Meyers Tobacco Company by themselves or through me. I subsequently persuaded them that it was the most advisable course to pursue. Four conferences were held with the firm, and in the meantime I requested and obtained from the Trades and Labor Union of St. Louis the appointment of a committee to act in conjunction with us in the conferences. On Friday afternoon an agreement was reached of which the enclosed is a copy.[3]

I take this opportunity of congratulating both the Executive Council and the A.F. of L. upon what is a splendid victory of a trouble existing more than seven years. By way of explanation I should add that at the time referred to the firm locked out 49 men in a certain department substituting women and girls' labor therefor from that date until the day of the agreement.

Kindly vote upon the ratification of the agreement at your earliest convenience.

With the President[4] of the Trades and Labor Union and subsequently a committee of the Carpenters Council of St. Louis I had a number of conferences with the Drummond Tobacco Company for the purpose of settling the differences existing between them.[5] When I left St. Louis on the evening of the 12th. the matter was in a fair way of adjustment. As soon as I hear from them I shall report the result to you.

The convention to organize the Broom Makers[6] into a National Union was successful and a start has been made with fair prospects of the organization growing in numbers and influence. They have decided to become affiliated with the A.F. of L.

I had a number of conferences with the officers of the National and International Trade Unions as well as local unions.

Mr. Ernest Kurzenknaabe Secretary of the Brewery Workmen's National Union stated that the object he had in view in having the Executive Council ratify the proposed contract with the employing brewers of St. Louis was to impress them with the importance that the organization received the moral support in their demands of the A.F. of L. as well as the K. of L. You have a copy of the request. Please advise me whether you vote in favor of its endorsement.[7]

After I reached St. Louis I was invited to address a meeting of tailors and Garment Workers on Wed. evening May 10th. My name had been announced to address it before I reached that city. Although having three meetings to attend to that evening one commencing at six o'clock the Tobacco Workers, the Garment Workers at eight and the Trades and Labor Union of St. Louis, I got there as soon as I could.

It has been publicly reported[8] that I was hissed and denounced at the meeting. Let me say that a few Garment Workers responded to the call for the meeting and were there with a few K. of L. members, organized a gang to interrupt and disturb the meeting, and the newspapers report the fact that had I not been there and both by discretion and determination a physical encounter could not have been prevented. I addressed the meeting and against the organized effort succeeded in addressing those present for nearly an hour.

When Mr. Madeira[9] a local member was introduced to speak it seemed as if all restraint upon the organized turbulence had loosened. I assumed the chair and again commanded order. At twenty minutes after ten I left the hall without any adverse demonstration whatever and then attended the meeting of the Trades and Labor Union. If there was any manifestation against me at that meeting it must have taken place after I left. Had I so desired it would have been only necessary to request the 200 delegates and unionists who were in attendance at the meeting of the Trades and Labor Union in the hall on the opposite corner of the street to have adjourned their meeting and come over to the hall and thus overawe the contemptible conduct of the few K. of L.

At the meeting of the Trades and Labor Union where I went as the representative of the A.F. of L. I was cordially and fraternally received and the best of feeling expressed for our movement by that body.

The movement in St. Louis is in excellent condition. In view of the published reports I deemed it my duty to recount these few facts in connection with the meeting of the Garment Workers referred to.

The convention or conference called by the Blacksmiths[10] at Philadelphia May 15th. was not successful, but few having responded to the call. Mr. John C. Knight[11] general secretary of the Blacksmiths International Union was present and the few delegates who were there entered into the conference and in all likelihood the organization he represents will at its next convention decide to affiliate with the A.F. of L. and the Blacksmiths local unions now directly affiliated with us will become attached to the International Union.

Kindly asking you to return your votes upon the two propositions submitted above, and with kindest wishes, I am,

> Fraternally Yours   Saml Gompers.
> President. American Federation of Labor.

TLpS, AFL Executive Council Vote Books, reel 8, *AFL Records.*

1. The International Association of Machinists held its fifth annual convention in Indianapolis, May 1-10, 1893.

2. AFL Tobacco Workers' Union 5778 of St. Louis was chartered in July 1892.

3. The agreement stipulated that the Liggett and Myers Tobacco Co. would give preference in hiring to union men and maintain a union shop.

4. Frank Von der Fehr was a member of CMIU 44 of St. Louis.

5. The 1892 AFL convention endorsed a boycott of the Drummond Tobacco Co. initiated by the carpenters' council of St. Louis because the company would not agree

to employ union labor exclusively in the construction of warehouses and other build-ings. The AFL lifted the boycott in May 1893 after the company agreed to hire only union labor.

6. Delegates from AFL federal labor unions organized the International BROOM Makers' Union in Chicago on May 9, 1893.

7. The Executive Council apparently took no action on the matter of the contract, which was signed May 24, 1893, by the Brewers' and Maltsters' Union 6 of St. Louis and the Brewers' Association.

8. *St. Louis Globe Democrat,* May 11, 1893.

9. Probably Adolph Madera, a St. Louis cigarmaker.

10. The International Brotherhood of BLACKSMITHS.

11. John C. Knight (d. 1895?) of St. Louis served as grand secretary and treasurer of the International Brotherhood of Blacksmiths in the early 1890s.

To J. F. Chopper

May 19, [1893]

Mr. J. F. Chopper,
15 Block S. Pueblo, Col.
Dear Sir:—

I am in receipt of your favor of the 13th. and am indeed surprised at what must be a pretence of ignorance upon a matter which is so generally known.

I repeat what I stated in my previous letter that the entire Treaty[1] between the United States Government and the Czar of Russia has not been officially made public but a few of the provisions have been, and they indicate quite plainly that any man who will advocate a system of government for Russia as we have here would be arrested, and since he could not obtain a pass-port from the authorities of Russia would endeavor to secure one by other means in order to escape to the United States, our Government would be compelled under the provisions of the Treaty to return him to the tender mercies of the greatest autocrat and tyrant ever called upon to reign over a people.

I certainly agree with you that the United States should not be made the dumping ground for the purpose of receiving the output of the jails and prisons of the whole world, and I think upon a little investigation you could certainly convince yourself that I have made quite as much endeavor as you know to prevent this wholesale un-restricted and undesirable immigration, but I think it is certainly an unjust imputation on your part to say that because men dare love liberty that for that reason they are disreputable and criminal.

Some of the men who have engaged in the Revolution of '48, in[deed] many, have occupied High positions even in the Cabinet of the United States Government. In the Chartist Movement of England for manhood and universal suffrage and equal rights, a number of the best men of that country were forced to seek an asylum here. Some of the most notable and active friends of the movement for Ireland's freedom and Home Rule Government have attained distinction in the land of our country acting in the capacity of diplomatic representatives at foreign governments. In fact one could go through the whole gamut of the active participants for a larger degree of freedom for a people, and find that instead of their [act?]ing as you by indication stigmatize them, they are justified in receiving and enjoying the asylum and protection of the American people.

A treaty is supposed to be reciprocal in its nature. Can you for a moment imagine an American fleeing to Russia for either freedom or [liber]ty? In a word you were asked to to lend a hand in aiding the cause of the poor and downtrodden. If you prefer to withhold that, that is your privilege, but please make an exception in that regard, of,

Yours Very Respectfully   Saml Gompers.
President. American Federation of Labor.

TLpS, reel 7, vol. 9, pp. 118-19, SG Letterbooks, DLC.

1. A Russo-American extradition treaty, signed in 1887, came up for Senate approval in 1893. Americans engaged in a public debate over the treaty, with supporters contending that the growing unrest in the United States was the result of admitting Russian political refugees. Opponents, many of whom were concerned about Russian domestic persecution, asserted that the treaty would end American asylum for political offenders. Despite a flood of petitions in protest the Senate ratified the treaty.

To D. F. Gahan[1]

June 1, [1893]

Mr. D. F. Gahan,
Prest. Elgin Watchmakers Union 5504
253 Orange St. Elgin, Ill.
Dear Sir and Brother:—

Your favor of the 28th. came duly to hand and contents noted.

In it you say that the membership in your Union is decreasing by the displacement of men by women and that the women so employed are receiving from 40 to 50% less in wages than that which is paid to the men retained or was paid to the men displaced, and you ask whether the moral support of the American Federation of Labor will be extended to you in case of a contest. You mention the fact that a boycott against the Company would be an effective weapon to prevent this injustice.

In reply permit me to say that it is both improper as well as unwise to make any contest upon a movement by which women are introduced into a trade, although it would be perfectly proper to make a protest against the reduction of wages paid to women or men.

If it is the desire of your Union to prevent an injustice of the kind mentioned, and you believe that the A.F. of L. could aid you by the placing of a boycott upon the Elgin Watch Manufacturers, it would be necessary for your Union to make a formal application to the A.F. of L. for that purpose, stating the grounds upon which the application is sought.

I should add that it would be simply folly to struggle against the introduction of successful machinery in a trade.

With kind wishes and hoping this explanation will be satisfactory, I am,

Fraternally Yours   Saml Gompers.
President. American Federation of Labor.

TLpS, reel 7, vol. 9, p. 163, SG Letterbooks, DLC.

1. D. F. Gahan was secretary (1891-92) and president (1893) of AFL Elgin Watchmakers' Union 5504.

To Charles Fenwick

June 22, [1893]

Hon. Chas. Fenwick,
Sec. Trade Union Congress Parliamentary Committee,
119 Buckingham St. Strand, London, Eng.
Dear Sir:—

I have the honor to acknowledge the receipt of your favor of the 5th. inst. the contents of which are carefully noted.

Replying to your question permit me to say that the convention of the American Federation of Labor held at Philadelphia, Pa. Dec. 12th. 1892 decided to abandon the holding of an International Labor Congress, at Chicago in 1893.

The reason which impelled the convention to this course was that the Trade Union Congress of Glasgow decided to call an International

Labor Congress to be held in London during this year for discussion and action upon the Eight Hour question. Then, again, as you know another Congress is about to be held in Zurich in 1893. The delegates to our convention believed that with these two congresses it would have been out of the question for European delegates to come to Chicago and preferred abandonment to a fiasco.

I am free to say that had we known that the call of your last Congress would have been abandoned and also that there would have been a good attendance (as my correspondence now indicates) we would never have departed from the original project of holding an International Labor Congress. Our entire action in the matter however, was governed by what we believed to be the best interests of the wage-workers of all countries.

I mail to your address with this a printed copy of the proceedings of our Philadelphia convention which contains the report of the Committee, as well as my own upon this subject.

It would be but proper to add that the Directory of the World's Columbian Exposition have called, what they term, an International Labor Congress; where a number of men from all parts of the world have been invited to read papers. This Congress therefore is not a body composed of delegates elected by trade or labor societies, but merely, as stated, are invited to prepare, read and discuss, without taking action, upon the various phases of the labor question and the labor movement.

From what I can learn there will be quite a number of active men in the labor movement of Europe at Chicago during the Exposition and in attendance at the Congress, and I wish, if you have the opportunity, that you would acquaint those contemplating coming, with my earnest desire to make their stay as pleasant as possible and to place every convenience at their disposition for the attainment of any information they may desire.

I would suggest that our correspondence might continue in order that any matter of interest occurring in either country could be communicated to each other in a fraternal and official manner.

With kindest wishes to yourself and the labor movement of Great Britain, I am,

Very Truly Yours   Saml Gompers.
President. American Federation of Labor.

TLpS, reel 7, vol. 9, pp. 195-97, SG Letterbooks, DLC.

To John Altgeld[1]

New York June 27. [189]3.

Hon. John P. Altgeld.
Govenor of Illinois.
Springfield, Ill.
In the name of more than half million american wage workers I
sincerely thank you for extending justice to and pardoning Fielden,
Schwab and Neebe.[2]

Samuel Gompers.
President. American Federation of Labor.

ALpS, reel 7, vol. 9, p. 203, SG Letterbooks, DLC.

1. John Peter ALTGELD was the Democratic governor of Illinois from 1893 to
1897.
2. Samuel FIELDEN, Oscar W. NEEBE, and Michael SCHWAB were the three surviving
Haymarket defendants.

To George Norton

June 27, [1893]

Mr. Geo. L. Norton,
Sec. Marine Firemen's Union 5464 A.F. of L.
4 N. Levee St. St. Louis, Mo.
Dear Sir and Brother: —

I have received a letter from the Secretary of Marine Firemen's
Union 5626[1] making complaint against your Union for conduct un-
becoming Union men. The complaint made is as follows:

"The Marine Firemen #6 of St. Louis A.F. of L. would like to hear
your instructions in regard to colored M.F.U. in this city. They claimed
they would hold out for last season's wages; when it came to the point
they took boats from us at $5.00 per month less. Is this unionism or
not?

["]Now in regard to this matter the colored Union #1 has used us
for a tool to uphold wages and they took the work from us for less
money. Would like to hear from you immediately."

I kindly ask you to make answer to the above complaint at your
earliest convenience. I sincerely hope that some misapprehension prevails as to the matter, for I dislike to believe that men organized to

improve their own condition as well as that of their fellow workmen, would act in an unfair manner.

With kind wishes and hoping to hear from you at your earliest convenience, I am,

Fraternally Yours   Saml Gompers.
President. American Federation of Labor.

TLpS, reel 7, vol. 9, p. 221, SG Letterbooks, DLC.

1. Andrew W. Schrick.

To the Executive Council of the AFL

July 6, [189]3.

To The Executive Council of the A.F. of L.
Fellow-Workmen: —

In compliance with the instructions of the last convention of the A.F. of L. I drafted a plan for a Sinking Fund for the American Federation of Labor.

This was submitted to the last meeting of the Executive Council and it was resolved that a copy be forwarded to each member of the Council for the purpose of making such changes, amendments or additions as they in their judgment may deem necessary, each member of the Council forwarding his copy with such changes to this office.

I enclose to you herein a copy of the plan and respectfully request you to comply with the resolution of the Executive Council at your earliest convenience, and oblige,

Yours Fraternally   Saml Gompers.
President. American Federation of Labor.
[Enclosure]

AMERICAN FEDERATION OF LABOR SINKING FUND.

1st. A Sinking Fund of $500.000 is hereby established which shall be known as the American Federation of Labor Sinking Fund.

2nd. The organizations affiliated with the American Federation of Labor shall within sixty days from the ratification of this article forward to the Secretary of the American Federation of Labor the sum of twenty-five cents for each member in good standing in such affiliated organizations, and every three months thereafter a like sum of twenty-five cents for each member shall be paid and forwarded, as in this section provided.

3rd. As soon as the sum of $600.000 shall have been received at the office of the American Federation of Labor in pursuance to the provisions of this article, the affiliated organizations shall be notified by the Secretary of the American Federation of Labor that the limit of said fund has been reached, and that the assessments shall be discontinued and not renewed until the expenditures as hereinafter provided shall reduce the sinking fund to $500.000. When this latter figure has been reached by reason of expenditures in defence of and for the protection of affiliated organizations engaged in labor disputes, the Executive Council of the A.F. of L. shall order through the President of the A.F. of L. a resumption of the payments by the affiliated organizations of the twenty-five cents for each member in good standing, such payments to be made within thirty days from the date of the issuance of such an order and be repeated every three months thereafter until the fund hereinbefore mentioned shall reach the sum of $600.000.

4th. Organizations affiliated with the A.F. of L. failing to pay either or all of the assessments provided for in this article within the time specified, shall be suspended from the A.F. of L. and shall not be permitted to continue its affiliation.

5th. No organization shall be entitled to the benefits provided in this article until the same shall have been in regular affiliation and in good standing with the A.F. of L. for at least six months.

6th. Any organization becoming suspended from the A.F. of L. as provided in this article may become reaffiliated with it after payment in full of all assessments levied by this article and which such organization may have been indebted to the A.F. of L. at the time of its suspension, such organizations not to be entitled to the benefits of said fund until six months after reaffiliation.

7th. Any affiliated organization becoming involved in a labor dispute which has been approved by the Executive Council of the A.F. of L. shall be entitled to receive from the fund created by this article the sum of four dollars ($4.00) per week for each member of such organization engaged in said difficulty.

8th. Any affiliated organization desirous of receiving the benefits herein prescribed shall through their executive officers make a full and complete report to the Executive Council of the American Federation of Labor, and if the said application be approved by the Council the payment of the benefits herein provided shall commence on the fourth week after said difficulty has been inaugurated.

9th. The fund hereby created shall be deposited by the members of the Executive Council in at least five different banks in the name and as trustees of the American Federation of Labor.[1]

TLpS and TDp, reel 7, vol. 9, pp. 251-54, SG Letterbooks, DLC.

1. The AFL Executive Council decided not to attempt to establish the sinking fund because of the depression that began in 1893.

To William Owen[1]

July 10, [1893]

Mr. W. C. Owen,
317 New High St. Los Angeles, Cal.
Dear Sir: —

I am in receipt of your favor of the 30th. and can truly say that I was very much pleased not only perusing its contents but to hear from you. Our friend Weissman stated that he had received a letter from you and I was much pleased in reading it in the Bakers' Journal.[2]

Referring to what you say about the Socialist Labor Party of New York and its mirage the C.L.F. of New York, I think you place altogether too much importance upon them. As a matter of fact they have absolutely no influence upon the labor movement of the country and cannot reach its members.

Their attempt to compel the wage-workers to vote the S.L.P. ticket after their failure ought to brand them as scabs, has not only failed to accomplish the desired end, but it has to a very great extent proven a boomerang. You can readily understand how small its effect must be when the Brewers Unions which were believed to be tied hand and foot to this unfair doctrine have repudiated it entirely. The Journeymen Bakers National Union which was believed to have been fed upon it spurned it entirely, and tore it out root and all not only in form but as even a part of its constitution and declaration of principles.

There is quite another thing which these S.L.P. men are trying which would be far greater in its consequences to bring destruction upon their unions. The organizations of the so-called "Hebrew" trade unions[3] is creating a schism which I fear will have evil consequences upon some portions of the movement. For this reason many of these hebrews who never having been privileged to organize before, and instead of getting their first knowledge of organization in the unions, mingling with the working men in those trades of other religions and nationalities, are organizing in unions of their "religion" rather than of their trade.

It seems to me that sooner or later this will create a counter movement against them, and it will not only take on an economic but a religious phase antagonistic to theirs.

These so-called Hebrew trade unions are fostered and encouraged by men who claim to be socialists. For one who is sincere in the movement and knows whereof he speaks, as well as having a conception of the historical struggles and the tendencies of the labor movement it is painful and distressing.

Does it not strike you as peculiar that men who claim to be free in religious matters, socialists, should encourage anything to divide people in organizations on religious grounds, thus perpetuating ignorance and necessarily hostility?

Somehow or other I have a faith in the "law of compensation" and for those who are responsible for these divisions and antagonism there must come a day of reckoning. When that day comes you may rest assured something hard will drop. The workingmen in America are a long suffering and patient people, but when they once perceive that men through ignorance, malice or to serve their own ends, have come between them and their goal, they simply put them out of the way.

The trade unions stand for the justice, protection as well as liberty of the worker. They deny the right of their employers to dictate to them how their franchise will be used, and I feel certain that that which they deny their employers they will not yield to others who have not and cannot have power over them. Even if they had the power, it would soon be rebelled against and overthrown.

Of course we are struggling now under adverse conditions and every anti-Union spouter seems to roll his antagonism as a sweet morsel under his tongue. To hold our men together, to maintain the unions and to prepare for the first dawn of a brighter day is our first duty. When that day comes (and it will not be long I am sure) you will find the anti-unionists "shut up."

I feel interested at what you say that you have opportunities to disseminate correct ideas upon our movement, and that you will utilize them so far as your present condition will permit.

I sincerely hope that you are getting along fairly and that I may hear from you occasionally.

Very Respectfully Yours   Saml Gompers.
President. American Federation of Labor.

TLpS, reel 7, vol. 9, pp. 272-73, SG Letterbooks, DLC.

1. William C. Owen was a leading West Coast promoter of the Nationalist movement based upon the utopian socialist ideas of Edward Bellamy.

2. In its July 8, 1893, issue, the *Bakers' Journal* published a letter from Owen asserting that the confiscation and redistribution of property were the first principles of every form of socialism, including Nationalism. The letter was written in response to an article in the *New Nation* of May 27 entitled "Nationalism and Confiscation," which maintained that the Nationalists did not really espouse confiscation.

3. In October 1888 the SLP's Yiddish-speaking branch 8 and Russian-speaking branch 17 in New York City met with three small Jewish unions to form the United Hebrew Trades (UHT). The new organization worked to organize Jewish workers into unions, eventually playing a prominent role in establishing the United Garment Workers of America and the International Ladies' Garment Workers' Union, among others. In October 1890 the UHT called a conference that created the short-lived Hebrew Labor Federation of the United States and Canada. In December 1895 it was one of the founding organizations of the Socialist Trade and Labor Alliance (STLA), of which it became District Alliance 2 in February 1896. Many of its constituent unions remained affiliated with the AFL, however, and in September 1897 the United Brotherhood of Cloakmakers helped form the Federated Hebrew Trades of Greater New York (FHT) in opposition to District Alliance 2. In December 1899 the UHT left the STLA and amalgamated with the FHT.

To Frank Rist

July 10, [1893]

Mr. Frank L. Rist,
room 14 Fisher Block, 259 Walnut St. Cincinnati, O.
Dear Sir and Brother:—

Your favor of the 2nd. came duly to hand and contents noted.

I am free to say that I am fully impressed with the importance of the statement you make, yet I think it is a mistake to abandon a Labor Day parade and demonstration. I would not care how short a route was selected for the workingmen to go over, yet they ought not to give up their parade.

Of course, walking of itself is not an educator, but the parade on Labor Day is a protest against wrong, and an educator to many thousands of men who will read of the buoyant spirit and the manly bearing of the toilers in their march.

Then again, while a festival will be scarcely noticed in the press a parade through the streets must be, and if it is not fairly treated in the press many of the workers who will see the parade will necessarily be disappointed. As a business question then the newspapers would be compelled to give it attention. However, since you have decided upon the subject this year it may be too late to alter the programme, and I would not wish you to alter it if the matter has been fully decided upon. I merely mention this for the future.

I should add that there is something to contemplate in the parades of the toiling masses taking place all over the country at the same time. The festival could take place at any rate and have speakers address the assembled toilers.

You ask me to suggest the names of two good men with national reputations to address your meeting. I believe you are aware that there will be quite a number of men who will go to Chicago and I have some misgivings that they would leave there on Labor Day for any other city. However you may write to the man who is regarded as the classical orator in the labor movement, Frank K. Foster, 134 Harrison Ave. Boston, Mass. Thos. Wisdom,[1] 114 Grace St. Pittsburgh, Pa. or Mr. John Mc-Bride, 53 Clinton Bldg. Columbus, O. It is more than likely that a number of men whom I could otherwise suggest, will this year be at the city of the World's Fair.

I hope you have received and acted upon my letters in reference to the Dayton affair.[2]

With kind wishes, I am,

Fraternally Yours   Saml Gompers.
President.

TLpS, reel 7, vol. 9, p. 270, SG Letterbooks, DLC.

1. Thomas J. WISDOM was second vice-president of the Iron Molders' Union of North America (IMUNA) from 1890 to 1895.

2. The Metal Polishers', Buffers', and Platers' International Union applied in June 1893 for a boycott upon the products of the Western Wheel Co., whose employees were on strike over wage cuts. SG, believing that the company was located in Dayton, Ohio, asked Rist to investigate and try to adjust the differences. Upon discovering that the company was located in Chicago, he made a similar request to William C. Pomeroy.

To David Watkins

July 17, [1893]

Mr. David Watkins,
Sec. Rail Mill Helpers' Union 6049
112 W. 8th. St. New Albany, Ind.
Dear Sir and Brother: —

Your favor of the 14th. came duly to hand and I have given the subject matter therein contained careful thought.

Replying thereto permit me to say that there is really no scale yet adopted by the Rail Mill Helpers, although I shall endeavor to obtain further information upon that subject and communicate it to you as soon as received.

I mail to your address with this a copy of the constitution of the A.F. of L. as well as copies of a few local organizations which you may use as a basis for your Union.

What you mention in reference to the white and colored men in the Mill is a very serious question and one that cannot be lightly gone over. It is useless to deny the fact that there is a great amount of race prejudice still existing among white workmen, and it is well for us to keep this fact in mind.

Those who know me know that I have and am still doing all I possibly can to create a better feeling and judgment upon this subject. I believe that nothing can so effectually eliminate and overcome this prejudice so thoroughly as the organization of our fellow-workers both white and black.

Inasmuch, however, as that prejudice still exists, and that many white workmen will not belong to the same local organization with black men, and will not meet with them as members of the same local union, it might be more advantageous to go to work gradually to accomplish the desired end. In other words, have the Union of white men organized, and have the Union of colored men organized also, both unions to work in unison and harmony to accomplish the desired end.

It is useless to be simply trying to ram our heads through stone walls; recognizing the conditions which exist is the best way we can secure the organization of all in a way which must ultimately bring about a unity of feeling and action among all toilers.

Trusting you will give this matter your earnest consideration and that the suggestions may be accepted in the spirit of candor and fraternity in which they are tendered, I am,

Fraternally Yours   Saml Gompers.
President.

TLpS, reel 7, vol. 9, p. 290, SG Letterbooks, DLC.

To Thomas Elderkin

July 20, [1893]

Mr. T. J. Elderkin,
Sec. Entertainment Comm. Labor Day Parade Trades
 and Labor Assembly & Building Trades Council,[1]
47-49 W. Lake St. Chicago, Ill.
Dear Sir and Brother: —

I am in receipt of your favor of the 17th. inst. the contents of which are carefully noted.

In reply permit me to say that there certainly must be some mistake somewhere for I know of no invitation which I have extended to Governor Altgeld to address a meeting at the World's Fair either on Labor Day or any other day. In fact, I have issued no invitations thus far to any one to address labor demonstrations for Labor Day. If any one has invited Gov. Altgeld in my name, they have certainly done so without my consent or authority, and in fact against my wishes.

In a letter to Bro. Wm. C. Pomeroy,[2] our general organizer for Chicago I took occasion to say that since there has been a failure of agreement between the Committee of the Trades and Labor Assembly and the World's Fair Directory for the Labor Day festival, I will not only do nothing to mar the success of the Trades and Labor arrangements, but would aid its efforts by all means within my power.[3]

In my judgment it would be quite a compliment to the labor organizations to have Gov. Altgeld address the Trades and Labor festival participants, and at the same time would be a grateful acknowledgment to him for his manly, just and honorable action in pardoning Neebe, Fielden and Schawb. When the press and the capitalist class unite in howling down a man for a just act, it is time that the organized intelligent masses of labor should rally around and support him in every way within reason. You may say to Gov. Altgeld, and I should be pleased in having you communicate it to him, that if he has been invited to address any assemblage on Labor Day at the World's Fair grounds in my name, he has been imposed upon, and you can say further that it would afford me keen pleasure to meet him at labor's gathering at Kuhn's Park Sept. 4th. 1893.[4]

With kind wishes and trusting this explanation will be satisfactory, I am,

Fraternally Yours   Saml Gompers.
President. American Federation of Labor.

TLpS, reel 7, vol. 9, p. 298, SG Letterbooks, DLC.

1. The Chicago Building Trades Council was organized in 1890.

2. William Curtis POMEROY of Chicago was the editor of the *Purveyor*, the journal of the Hotel and Restaurant Employees' National Alliance (1893-94), and was an AFL organizer (1893-94, 1896).

3. SG wrote Pomeroy on July 10, 1893, that since the World's Fair Directory "compels all arrangements for that day on our part to be outside of the Fair grounds and brings on an appearance of antagonism which is unpleasant," that he would refuse to speak at the World's Fair on Labor Day (reel 7, vol. 9, p. 260, SG Letterbooks, DLC).

4. SG also wrote to George Schilling, commissioner of the Illinois Bureau of Labor Statistics, on July 21, 1893, asking him to relay a similar message to the governor. Altgeld spoke at the labor day picnic of the Trade and Labor Assembly of Chicago on Sept. 4, as did SG, who praised the governor for his pardoning of the Haymarket defendants.

To Charles Bestel

July 21, [1893]

Mr. Chas. F. Bestel,
Genl. Organizer A.F. of L.
Box 308 Muncie, Ind.
Dear Sir and Brother:—

Your favor of the 18th. came duly to hand and contents noted.

In it you say that a stranger arrived in your town lately and being a member of a Federal Labor Union obtained admission in the Federal Labor Union of Muncie[1] and then claimed to have a grip of the hand authorized by the A.F. of L. You ask whether the statement of the party is founded upon fact.

In answer let me say that it is not. The A.F. of L. thus far has had no grip of the hand nor any signs other than those mentioned in the manual of common procedure, and that is intended as more of a fraternal greeting than anything else. The wage-workers of our country are engaged in too serious a work to be losing time for the study of maneuvers of the hand and pantomimic signs. By the way let me ask had the stranger you refer to beside his card of membership a traveling card and did he have the regular P.W? Your Union should be careful as to whom it admits to membership. Of course any one coming with a clear card should be admitted.

There is in existence an Association known as the Amalgamated Association of Street Railway Employes of America with head quarters at Detroit. The name and address of the Secretary are Mr. W. J. Law, 7 Telegraph Block, Detroit, Mich. I shall see that you receive documents giving the required information for the formation of a local union of Motormen conductors of street railway employes etc.

The condition of trade you mention existing in Muncie prevails to a greater or lesser extent all over the country. It is due to well defined causes and which it is necessary for the toiling masses of our country to bravely face. I am sure that had our fellow workers heeded the warnings and advice so often given them that in times of peace prepare for difficulties, they would not find themselves in the plight they now are. It would have been much more convenient, helpful and advantageous to have contributed high dues to the Union while work was plentiful and fairly remunerative in order to defend and protect our interests now. My advice to the workingmen is under all circumstances to stand by the Union. Although we may not be able to gain many advantages now, yet if we fail to maintain our organizations we will prove like clay in the hands of the potter to be molded in any shape; in other words we will be helpless to protect ourselves from the selfishness and greed of the moneyed classes and unfair employers.

If on the other hand, we stand by our Unions we shall in the largest measure defeat the attempts to reduce our wages, lengthen our hours of labor and the imposition of unfair conditions, while at the same time the maintenance of our unions will place us in a position to take advantage of the first sign of revived business and industries.

Sincerely hoping that the men will prove themselves true to the Union in order to be true to themselves, their families and their fellow workmen, I am, with kindest wishes,

Fraternally Yours　Saml Gompers.
President. American Federation of Labor.

TLpS, reel 7, vol. 9, pp. 299-300, SG Letterbooks, DLC.

1. The AFL chartered the Muncie, Ind., federal labor union in March 1893.

To the Executive Council of the AFL

New York, Aug. 7, 1893.

To the Executive Council of the A.F. of L.
Fellow-Workmen: —

During a recent interview with Mr. Ed. F. Mc-Sweeney,[1] Assistant Commissioner of Immigration at the port of New York, he expressed his earnest desire to co-operate with the labor organizations of America for the enforcement of the Alien Contract Labor Law.

To do this effectually it would be necessary that he could place himself in immediate telegraphic communication with the secretaries of local organizations in case immigrants arriving at Ellis Island or at other ports of the country are suspected of being laborers coming here under contract (written or implied) and whose destination may be the localities in which labor disputes exist.

He says that there is no fund at the disposal of his Department which could be used for any such telegraphic purpose. He therefore suggests that the sum of $100.00 be placed by the A.F. of L. in the hands of a telegraphic company to pay for forwarding and receiving telegrams of the character above mentioned.

In connection with this it would be advisable if the suggestion of Mr. Mc-Sweeney is adopted, for the issuance of a circular by this office to all the Trades and Labor Unions of America asking them that in the event of any labor dispute occurring in their locality to com-municate the same to this office at once. This office could then com-municate the same to the Immigration Commissioners.

Kindly return your vote upon the following propositions:

1st. Shall the sum of $100.00 be deposited for the purpose indicated in this letter?[2]

2nd. Shall a circular as outlined above be issued?

Kindly return your vote upon these propositions at your earliest convenience, and oblige,

Yours Fraternally   Saml Gompers.
President. American Federation of Labor.

TLpS, AFL Executive Council Vote Books, reel 8, *AFL Records.*

1. Edward F. McSweeney was assistant commissioner of immigration at Ellis Island from 1893 to 1902.

2. The AFL Executive Council approved the appropriation.

To Francis Wood[1]

Aug. 10, [1893]

Mr. Francis N. Wood,
311 E. Main St. Decatur, Ill.
Dear Sir and Brother: —

I am in receipt of your interesting favor of the 4th. inst. and can truly say that I appreciate the situation as you describe it existing in Decatur.

I am most anxious to have your co-operation in our movement for

I firmly believe you can be of great service to it, but you can readily understand that it is essential for an organizer to be in accord with the movement in the locality of his jurisdiction. How is it possible for us to have any influence with the wage-workers of a city if the organizer does not possess the confidence of his fellow wage-workers?

I have no personal feeling in the matter, neither have I an axe to grind. My whole and sole purpose in issuing commissions and continuing men in the office of general organizers is that they shall be able to do some good for their fellow workers in the city, who at the same time has their confidence.

I make this suggestion to you. Have the men who desire your acting as general organizer broach the subject in their respective Unions, and then have the Unions endorse the request for your reappointment as organizer, and you may rest assured it will be complied with.

I believe you will agree with me that the above proposition is fair and one which if approved by the locals will give you greater prestige and influence for good than all else.

Can you give me any information what has become of Mr. W. G. Woods? He was at one time organizer for the A.F. of L. for Decatur and a member of the Typographical Union.[2] He left Decatur and went to New Bedford, became secretary of the local Typographical Union[3] there and absconded with their funds taking with him other property and leaving nothing but a very bad reputation behind. I should add that he was known in New Bedford under the name of B. F. Glidden.[4]

I have received a letter from Bro. John Alsbury requesting your appointment as general organizer, but since he gives no address at which I can reach him I kindly ask you, should you see him, to say that I acknowledge the receipt of his favor and repeat to him the suggestion that I make to you above.

With kind wishes and hoping to hear from you, I am,

Fraternally Yours   Saml Gompers.
President.

TLpS, reel 7, vol. 9, p. 370, SG Letterbooks, DLC.

1. Francis Newton Wood, a barber, had organized barbers and street railway employees in Decatur, Ill., in 1892 while serving as a general organizer for the AFL. SG revoked his commission in February 1893 on the request of the Decatur Federation of Labor.

2. International Typographical Union (ITU) 215 of Decatur.

3. ITU 276 of New Bedford, Mass.

4. Benjamin F. Glidden was secretary of ITU 276 from January to June, 1893.

Labor and the Depression of the 1890s

The American economy experienced a series of crises during the last three decades of the nineteenth century, the last and one of the most severe of which began with the financial panic of 1893. Although there was a temporary upturn in late 1895, a further decline followed in 1896 and the beginnings of recovery, in fact, were not apparent until well into 1897.

The sharp drop in the stock market in May 1893 precipitated the initial financial panic, but signs of a weakening economy had been evident for several months, foreshadowing the impending collapse of business activity nationwide. By the end of the year, some 500 banks and 16,000 businesses had failed. "Never before has there been such a sudden and striking cessation of industrial activity," the *Commercial and Financial Chronicle* noted, describing the failures that occurred in August alone. "Mills, factories, furnaces, mines nearly everywhere shut down in large numbers, and commerce and enterprise were arrested in an extraordinary degree . . . and hundreds of thousands of men thrown out of employment."[1] Although reliable national statistics were not collected during the depression, Richard T. Ely estimated that 2 million workers were unemployed by the fall of 1893, and Gompers put the figure at 3 million by year's end. At the height of the depression in June 1894 some 20 percent of the non-agricultural workforce was idle. Despite relatively stable wage rates, cutbacks in hours and production levels lowered earnings some 18 percent for non-farm workers between 1892 and 1894.

If statistics were hard to come by, evidence of destitution and despair mounted daily. Police in New York City, for example, estimated that 20,000 homeless walked the streets. In Chicago more than 100,000 were out of work and the homeless overflowed the corridors of City Hall where they had taken refuge. In Denver an influx of unemployed silver miners so overwhelmed the city that whole trainloads of men were sent east at no charge or at reduced rates.

A number of trade unions in larger cities—for example, the printers, cigarmakers, carpenters, and shoe workers—were able to provide assistance to their unemployed members, and existing charitable organizations, emergency relief committees, municipalities, and self-help advocates attempted to feed and clothe the needy. Programs ranged from the "Indianapolis Plan," which provided a dollar's worth of food for a day's labor, and Detroit's "Pingree Potato Scheme," which transformed vacant lots into garden plots for the poor, to Baltimore's "Friendly Inn," a private relief agency that sheltered the poor but also arranged work assignments for its inmates. Although these and similar plans offered short-term sustenance for the unemployed and served as models for other cities, they could neither reverse nor resolve the massive problems generated by widespread unemployment.

By the late summer of 1893, workers were demanding more comprehensive relief programs. Cloakmakers in New York City, for example, led by Joseph Barondess, met during the first week of August to arrange a "parade" of the unemployed and asked other unions to join them. On August 10, twenty-two New York City labor leaders, including Gompers, met at the office of the United Garment Workers to discuss appropriate action and, after a four-hour meeting, called a conference of all the city's trade unions for August 20.[2] Before that meeting could take place, however, unemployed workers in the garment district began holding daily mass meetings to keep the issue of unemployment before the public. When anarchists including Emma Goldman addressed these gatherings, the public grew increasingly alarmed and the press reported that radical rhetoric had inflamed "mobs" of "Hebrew immigrants" and fomented "riots."

Such notoriety induced Gompers to clarify his position on relief efforts. "Much injury can be done to a movement for the relief of the unemployed if it is not properly and intelligently directed," he cautioned on August 18, "and it can only be so directed by organized labor."[3] Two days later about a hundred representatives of New York City trade unions formed the Labor Conference for the Relief of the Unemployed (LCRU), which pledged itself to lobby local, state, and federal officials to develop a public works program and to back up those efforts with public demonstrations of support.[4] In addition, the LCRU held weekly meetings, organizing its own relief system and coordinating the efforts of the city's trade unions.

Workers in Chicago also called for more substantial relief efforts. In mid-August about 5,000 unemployed gathered at the Columbus Statue in Lake Front Park to listen to speeches in English, Polish, and German. Announcing that they had been "reduced to our present state by a few schemers who have misled us as a people through our representatives," the group resolved to demand municipal public works jobs. Such demonstrations, and the parades that usually followed, continued almost daily until a fight broke out between the protestors and the police. "I sympathize with the honest laborer," Mayor Carter

Harrison explained, "but I despise the professional labor disturber."[5] Just as in New York City, the disturbances were blamed on anarchists who had incited immigrant workers.

Late in August Samuel Gompers arrived in Chicago to address the International Labor Congress then in progress at the World's Fair. He remained in the city long enough to participate in a public demonstration held at Lake Front Park on August 30. Pointing out that labor wanted work, not soup houses, Gompers suggested that public works projects—including the improvement of country roads, rivers, and harbors, as well as the completion of the Nicaraguan canal— would provide the employment necessary to relieve social distress.

Gompers found public officials largely unresponsive to such appeals, however. In New York City he and other workingmen met with Mayor Thomas Gilroy on August 22, but the mayor argued that there was little he could do legally to create public works.[6] Gompers also wrote New York's Governor Roswell Flower, requesting him to meet with an LCRU committee to discuss calling the state legislature into special session, but the governor put him off.[7] In September Governor Flower enunciated the prevailing official opinion on such programs in a speech delivered at Syracuse. "In America the people support the government," he declared; "it is not the province of the government to support the people. Once recognize the principle that the government must supply public work for the unemployed, and there will be no end of official paternalism."[8]

Labor's call for public works did not subside, despite the fact that it continued to be largely ignored. The AFL's 1893 convention in Chicago, for example, adopted two resolutions on the subject proposed by Thomas Morgan. One asserted that "when the private employer cannot or will not give work the municipality, state or nation must." A second, while applauding "the humane efforts of private individuals to relieve the terrible distress of the unemployed," insisted nevertheless that "it is the province, duty and in the power of our city, state and national governments to give immediate and adequate relief." The convention also pledged AFL support for Jacob Coxey's "good roads" proposal. "What labor wants is not charity," Gompers told a mass meeting held during the convention; "it wants work."[9]

Although the severity of the depression sharpened Gompers' criticism of the economic system,[10] he was able to find some comfort in the fact that trade unions, which had been "mowed down and swept out of existence" by other panics, were now manifesting "not only the powers of resistance, but of stability and permanency."[11] The depression continued to worsen in 1894, however, and it was within the context of this overwhelming economic crisis and such manifestations of social unrest and discontent as Coxey's army, the Pullman strike, and the growing strength of the Populist party, that the Federation's affiliates took up consideration of the AFL's political program.

Notes

1. Quoted in Samuel Rezneck, "Unemployment, Unrest, and Relief in the United States during the Depression of 1893-97," *Journal of Political Economy* 61 (1953): 325.

2. See "A Committee of Trade Unionists to the Trade Unions of New York City," Aug. 11, 1893, below.

3. *New York Herald*, Aug. 19, 1893.

4. See "An Article in the *New York Sun*," Aug. 21, 1893, below.

5. Quoted in Carlos A. Schwantes, *Coxey's Army* (Lincoln, Neb., 1985), pp. 28-29.

6. See "An Excerpt from an Article in the *New York World*," Aug. 23, 1893, below.

7. See "To Roswell Flower," Aug. 24, 1893, below.

8. State of New York, *Public Papers of Roswell P. Flower, Governor, 1893* (Albany, 1894), p. 351.

9. AFL, *Proceedings*, 1893, p. 37; "Labor Leaders Talk," Dec. 14, 1893, below.

10. Speaking in Chicago, for example, Gompers said that "wherever a man or woman desiring to work, capable of work, cannot find the opportunity to work to sustain life and to obtain the necessaries of life, that system of society is rotten at its base and foundation, . . . is rooted in injustice, and . . . requires the earnest, the honest, the determined and unremitting effort of the toiling masses of our entire country and the world to supplant it by justice, fair dealing among men and mankind" ("Labor Leaders Talk," Dec. 14, 1893, below).

11. AFL, *Proceedings*, 1893, p. 12.

A Committee of Trade Unionists to the Trade Unions of New York City

Aug 11th [1893]

Dear Sir and Brother:—

At a conference held by a number of active men in the trade union movement of our city,[1] the industrial, commercial and financial condition of the country was discussed, as well as the question of organizing a demonstration of the unemployed of New York, and further to devise means for the relief of our fellow-workers. The conference appointed the undersigned committee to issue this address to the trade unions of New York City.

Your Union is therefore kindly requested to discuss the question of organizing such a demonstration as is above referred to, and to select three representatives of your Union to a conference to be held with the representatives of all other trade unions of the city of New York to be held at the International Labor Exchange 257 E. 10th. St. at two o'clock of the afternoon of Aug. 20th.

Whatever decision your Union may arrive at as to the advisability or non-advisability of such a demonstration, the discussion of means of relief for your fellow-workers should be sufficient to warrant you to select your representatives and have them in attendance at the conference.

We are in a maelstrom of an industrial depression which requires earnest and prompt action by the trade unions of New York.

Sincerely hoping you will comply with the above request and furnish your representatives with credentials, we are,

> Fraternally Yours   Daniel Harris, Cigar Makers Union;
>   Henry Weissman, Bakers Union,
>   James J. Murphy,[2] Typographical Union;
>   T. C. Walsh[3] Carpenters Union.
>   Jos. Barondess, Cloak Makers Union.
>   Samuel Gompers. Chairman of Conference.
>   Chris. Evans. Sec'y.   ″   ″

TLpSr, reel 7, vol. 9, p. 372, SG Letterbooks, DLC.

1. Aug. 10, 1893.

2. James J. Murphy was president of International Typographical Union 6 of New York City.

3. Thomas C. Walsh was secretary of the New York District Council of the United Brotherhood of Carpenters and Joiners of America.

To Auguste Keufer

Aug. 16, [1893]

Mr. A. Keufer,
Rue Jean Jacques Rousseau 35 Bourse Du Travail,[1]
Paris, France.
My Dear Comrade:—

Your favor of the 6th. of July was handed to me by Mr. Louis Vigoureux.[2] I have endeavored to treat him fairly and placed him in possession of information and on the train for more of it. He certainly has made rapid progress in speaking the English language and when he returns, should he do so, you will no doubt be surprised at his mastery of our tongue.

I am sure I can not account for the breaking off in our correspondence which was so happily begun and cordially continued for a number of years. Possibly, both, being overwhelmed with the business of the movement we have had little time to continue imparting information to each other.

You ask for a few details of the situation in America. No doubt the telegraphic and written correspondence published in the French papers has already given you an idea, but I am sure the truth has been withheld or only faintly outlined. There can be no doubt but what the bond holders, the usury class of the world is engaged upon an attempt upon the wealth producers, the people, but while this injustice is being practiced there is something far deeper lying at the bottom of the economic, industrial, commercial and financial troubles now upon us. One can not have even a vague idea of the immensity with which production has been carried on within the past few years in the United States and how it has been augmented. Steam is applied to everything except where electricity has been put in operation. Between these two forces applied to the production of wealth, the productivity of the worker has increased enormously.

The trade unions of America have been engaged in an effort to reduce the hours of labor, and we have been fairly successful in that, but it has been impossible to keep the movement in ratio with the great productivity of labor, hence the ability, or better the opportunity, of the wage-workers to keep pace in their consumptive power to their productive capacity has failed, and as a consequence, thousands aye, hundreds of thousands have been thrown out of employment, and the [terr]i[b]le work is still going on.

In several of our largest [centres?] monster demonstrations are being held and preparations for other demonstrations of the unemployed

[are] to be held. Even without these efforts on the part of the active men in the labor movement, in numerous instances the unemployed gather of their own volition without being asked to do it or requested by any one. Taking this together with the large increase of immigration and you can imagine a condition of affairs which is indeed appalling. The only redeeming feature in all this maelstrom of confusion is the fact that the wage workers are remaining true to the banner of their Unions. They recognize that as soon as they surrender these, their only means of defence, that their course will be downward at so rapid a pace as to almost completely overwhelm them and cast them down into an abyss of misery, poverty and despair.

There are some who believe that this period of depression through which we are passing now will be relieved in the course of a few weeks and that the legislation at Washington will settle the matter. I am constrained to say that I do not share this opinion, much as I could wish it were so. The evil is deeper rooted than can be affected by the legislation at our capital, and in my judgment though we may have a temporary breathing spell of relief we cannot emerge from this crisis within a year or more.

There are many other things which occur to me and which I should like to convey, but time and my duties in other directions forbid. Since I have given you just a mere glance at the conditions here, I should be pleased with a letter from you recounting the situation in France and as you view it in Europe. I should also be under additional obligations to you if you will kindly give me some information in reference to the closing by the Government of France of the Bourse Du Travail. The newspapers here say that it was because some of the Syndicat de Chambre refused to give the registry of the names of their members, and while this may be a fact it has caused me to believe that the Government certainly had some other intention than the mere ascertaining of these names, and that possibly it may have been the desire to be in league with the bourgeoisie of your country, or possibly to know the exact strength or weakness of the organizations, or even to use these lists for political purposes in the approaching elections. However, I should be pleased to hear from you upon the subject.

Before this reaches you our friend Victor Delahaye will have arrived in New York on his way to Chicago to read a few papers which he has prepared for the World's Columbian Exposition Auxiliary Labor Congress.

You remember in 1889 our friend Hugh Mc-Gregor[3] brought a letter from me to the International Labor Congress held in Paris in connection with the Paris Exposition. Mr. Mc-Gregor informed me I believe that you helped to translate the letter into the French language. You remember that letter was the first suggestion for the holding of a labor demonstration in all civilized countries on May 1st., and that that suggestion having been adopted by the Congress has since been made a European Labor Day demonstration on each recurring 1st. of May. Strange as it may seem, it is yet a fact, that I have not a copy of that letter and am anxious to have one. Will you kindly endeavor to obtain a copy of that letter for me and send it here immediately whether in the French language or the English. I can have it translated again if it is in French.[4]

With this I mail to your address a few documents which I ask you to accept with my compliments.

Sending you the best wishes of the organized wage-workers of America and trusting that the organizations of the wage-workers of France may continue uninterrupted, I am, with kindest regards,

Yours Sincerely Saml Gompers.
President. American Federation of Labor.

TLpS, reel 7, vol. 9, pp. 388-90, SG Letterbooks, DLC.

1. The Bourse du travail in Paris, founded in 1887, was the first of many government subsidized institutions that served as trade union meeting places and public labor exchanges. Minister of the Interior Dupuy closed the Paris Bourse on May Day of 1893 because a large number of the unions using it had failed to register themselves as required by law. It reopened in 1896 under a new constitution that divided control among representatives of the unions and the national and city governments.

2. Louis Vigouroux, a French journalist, attended the 1896 AFL convention as a representative of the school of agriculture of the University of Paris and the Musée social. The latter, established in 1894 as an institution to obtain and disseminate information on social issues, was attempting to gather information on labor movements in various countries.

3. Hugh McGREGOR served as SG's secretary during the late 1880s, directing the AFL office during the president's absence. He helped organize seamen on the Atlantic coast and between 1890 and 1892 served as secretary of the short-lived International Amalgamated Sailors' and Firemen's Union.

4. In his autobiography, SG recalled that he never obtained a copy of the letter.

To John O'Brien

Aug. 17, [1893]

Mr. John O'Brien,
Genl. Organizer A.F. of L.
c/o The "Oregonian" Portland, Oreg.
Dear Sir and Friend:—

I have your favor of the 11th. with enclosure, and I think it is the most practical thing you [can do?] in the issuance of the circular.[1]

There is one subject I should have preferred you to have omitted since to my mind it is more of a commercial question than an industrial one. However, no harm can come from it, and I am sure the circular will do a great amount of good in arousing the Unions of the Coast to be more generally and thoroughly represented than heretofore.

If we expect any reforms from legislative action or hope for a clearer conception on the part of the general public of the struggles, hopes and aspirations of organized labor, we will have to act more unitedly than heretofore. The wage-workers of the Pacific Coast apart from local questions, must of necessity come to the conclusion to co-operate with the general labor movement of the country. I recognize the great distance between us and the immense mountains that divide us, but oceans and mountains do not divide the capitalist class of the world, and at least in this if in nothing else, we should follow the precept and example they set us.

A formidable representation from the Coast at our convention at Chicago[2] would in itself be a demonstration as much as a representation in the convention.

I am obliged to you for the information you give in reference to the recent sky-rocket movement[3] headed by the anti-trade unionists you mention, and a similar result, as attended their pyrotechnic display, is the case elsewhere, under similar circumstances. After all, it is the unceasing plodding of the trade unions that makes its influence felt, which is permanent in its character and goes on despite the antagonism of pseudo friends and open enemies.

Thanks for the copy of the petition on the Chinese question.[4] It is excellently framed and in a happy and apt vein.

If you care to have us pay for the cost of printing and mailing circulars I will transmit check for the amount.

With kind wishes and hoping to hear from you at an early date, I am

Fraternally Yours Saml Gompers.
President. American Federation of Labor.

TLpS, reel 7, vol. 9, p. 395, SG Letterbooks, DLC.

1. This probably refers to the letter O'Brien sent to West Coast central labor unions and labor papers in August urging West Coast workers to send delegates to the AFL's 1893 convention to gain the Federation's support of Chinese exclusion.

2. The AFL's 1893 convention met in Chicago, Dec. 11-19.

3. This probably refers to events leading to the formation in July of the Central Labor Council of Portland as an alternative to the Portland Federated Trades Assembly, an AFL affiliate.

4. The Geary Act of 1892 (U.S. *Statutes at Large*, 27: 25-26) had extended the provisions of the Chinese Exclusion Act of 1882 to prohibit the immigration of Chinese

laborers to the United States for another ten years. It included a new provision requiring Chinese workers already in the United States to register within one year or face deportation. Most Chinese resisted registration pending a court test of the act's constitutionality, and, in the interim, the Cleveland administration did not enforce it. After the Supreme Court upheld the act's constitutionality in May 1893, Congress voted in November to extend the registration deadline for another six months.

During 1893 O'Brien took an active role in the campaign for enforcement of the Geary Act. Various western labor organizations sent resolutions to Congress in this period in support of enforcement, and there was apparently a petition to that effect as well. In 1894 a Sino-American treaty retained the practice of registration but nullified the terms of the 1888 Scott Exclusion Act by allowing Chinese workers to return to the United States if they had left wives, children, or parents in this country or owned property here worth $1,000 or more.

To Matthew O'Rourke[1]

Aug. 18, [1893]

Mr. M. J. O'Rourke,
233 Baltic St. Brooklyn, N.Y.
My Dear Sir:—

Your favors of the 4th. and 12th. both came duly to hand but like yourself having been indisposed and yet exceedingly busy with my work I have been unable to give them the attention they deserve. Even now I am so rushed with business of importance that my reply must necessarily be brief reserving much that I would otherwise say until you are convalescent and can make it convenient to call here and talk it over.

I was very much impressed with the statements contained in your letter. There is no question in my mind but that there exists a gigantic conspiracy not only among the money lenders of the United States but of the civilized world with the sole object in view to prey upon the people, that the wealth possessors are withholding the people's money in order by hook and by crook to defraud them I haven't the slightest doubt.

There is no hope that the newspapers will publish the truth in reference to these matters for as a rule they are either partners or beneficiaries of the schemes.

This is dictated on the 18th. and I shall tomorrow send a messenger with a note to the Editor of the "World" for the Mss. you say you left with him to be delivered to me or a messenger from me in case they do not publish it.

It is more than likely if we could arrange a time for an interview I could place you in communication with a number of gentlemen who could and would push a thorough investigation into the outstanding and unaccounted bonds of the City Government of which you speak.

Sincerely hoping that you are convalescing and hoping to hear from you at your earliest convenience, and arranging for an interview at a time mutually convenient, I am, with kindest wishes,

Very Respectfully Yours   Saml Gompers.
President. American Federation of Labor.

TLpS, reel 7, vol. 9, p. 402, SG Letterbooks, DLC.

1. Matthew Jephson O'Rourke, an author, had worked as a clerk in the New York City comptroller's office in the 1860s during the period that "Boss" William M. Tweed controlled the city government. In 1894 he claimed that Tweed and his accomplices had issued and sold millions of dollars worth of bogus bonds. O'Rourke believed it likely that such activities continued under subsequent comptrollers. A citizens' committee investigated the charges and filed two petitions before the state supreme court in December 1894 requesting an official investigation of the comptroller's office. The court denied the petitions on the grounds of insufficient evidence.

To Francis Thurber[1]

Aug. 18, [1893]

Mr. F. B. Thurber,
c/o Thurber Wyland and Company,
West Broadway & Reade St. N.Y. City.
My Dear Sir: —

I have the honor to acknowledge the receipt of your favor of the 17th. and have perused its contents with much interest.

You say that I can render a real service to the laboring men of our country by declaring strongly in favor of the repeal of the purchasing clause of the Sherman Silver Act,[2] and I assure you that it causes me no little regret that in this instance I am compelled to express a dissent from those arguments which you state in your letter.

The Sherman Law was not passed in the interest of silver nor in the interest of the laboring people of the country. It was enacted (as the author[3] himself declared) to prevent a Free Coinage Bill from passing Congress. With one so fully equipped to discuss the question of finance as you are, I feel almost abashed to adduce any arguments in contravention of any opinion expressed by you, but even at the risk of appearing presumptuous I ask you to consider the following few facts.

Silver was practically demonetized in 1873, and was again made an important part of our system of Currency in 1878. The last great panic commenced in 1873, immediately after the demonetization of Silver, the panic was practically ended in 1879, the Spring after the resumption of a Silver Currency. The panic has again recurred this year when we are again threatened with the demonetization of Silver.

To issue a Currency based upon Gold alone, would imply that the government must at all times keep in the Treasury, such a supply of that metal as would be sufficient to redeem any and all of its certificates or else these certificates be dishonored.

The supply of Gold is always limited, it would be possible for a few men of enormous wealth, to offer at any time such a number of Gold notes, demanding their full value in Gold, as would be sufficient to entirely deplete the Treasury of its Gold reserve.

In order to get back this reserve required either by usage or law, the government would be compelled to purchase from the holders of gold throughout the world, at whatever prices they could combine to dictate, such an amount as would again fill up the reserve. This might happen again and again not only in America, but in all countries having a Currency based upon Gold, with the inevitable result of raising the price of the metal.

The supply of Gold is limited, and at all times inadequate to the wants of the Country. The world's supply of that commodity cannot be increased by any act of legislation, though the legislation of any country may increase the demand for it.

Mark you I do not pretend to say that the cause of the panics was the demonetization of silver nor that its threatened demonetization today is the cause of our present industrial stagnation. The causes lie far deeper than the demonetization or remonetization of silver. The financial agitation of today and of years gone by were in my judgment contributory to the intensity of the stagnation and added to the burdens of the people.

In some time in the future I should be pleased to talk this matter over with you fully, and we could then discuss what we really believe the causes are which produce these economic and social phenomena called panics and which occur with a peculiar periodical regularity and precision even when the question of silver is not remotely related to it.

With assurances of my regard for you personally and for the opinions you may hold, and again expressing my regret that we disagree upon this subject, I am,

Very Respectfully Yours   Saml Gompers.
President. American Federation of Labor.

TLpS, reel 7, vol. 9, pp. 399-400, SG Letterbooks, DLC.

1. Francis B. Thurber was a prominent New York City merchant and lawyer. He played a major role in initiating and conducting the New York Hepburn Investigation of 1879 and took part in the establishment of the New York State Anti-Monopoly League, of which SG was a member, the New York State Railroad Commission, and the Interstate Commerce Commission.

2. The Sherman Silver Purchase Act of 1890 (U.S. *Statutes at Large*, 26: 289-90) required the Treasury to purchase 4.5 million ounces of silver per month, paying for it with legal tender Treasury notes redeemable in gold or silver coin. Silver advocates argued that this use of silver to expand the currency would promote inflation, raising wages and crop prices and making it easier for debtors to meet their obligations. The panic of 1893, however, created a large demand for the redemption in gold by the Treasury of silver coins and paper currency. The act was repealed Nov. 1, 1893, in order to restore confidence in the currency and end the drain of gold from the national reserves.

3. John Sherman (1823-1900), an Ohio Republican, was a U.S. congressman (1855-61), senator (1861-77, 1881-97), secretary of the treasury (1877-81), and secretary of state (1897-98).

To Edward Bemis[1]

Aug. 21, [1893]

Professor Edward W. Bemis,
University of Chicago, Chicago, Ill.
My Dear Sir:—

Your favor of the 3rd. inst. came duly to hand. I should have been glad to have responded earlier but owing to my being indisposed the earlier part of the month and a subsequent rush of work it was impossible to do so before. Even now my reply must be brief.

It is true that I had an extended conversation with the representative of the Baron Hirsch Trade School,[2] and I believe demonstrated even to his satisfaction that the trade school he represents as well as the other trade schools, are only working great injury to the interests of the American wage-worker. He certainly seemed so impressed with my arguments that he arranged for an interview with the executive[3] of the fund in this country and myself, but owing to the illness of the gentleman it had to be postponed. I expect it to take place in the near future.

The statements I made to you a few years ago in reference to the apprenticeship system applies to-day with equal if not greater force than they did then. It is not only ridiculous but positively wrong for the trade schools to continue in their practice turning out "botch" work men who are ready and willing at the end of their so-called "graduation" to take the places of American workmen far below the wages prevailing in the trade. With probably half or more of the toiling masses of our country unemployed, the continuance of the practice is tantamount to a crime.

I have not seen the blast against the trade unionists to which you may refer, but I know that all the anti-trade unionists find the present condition an admirable opportunity to vent their spleen and to give expression to their ignorance of both the great work performed by the trade unions in preventing a deterioration in the condition of the toiling masses.

Of course, now is scarcely the time when advances can be made, but I believe every thinking man will agree to the statement that were it not for the existence of the trade unions we would now witness not only wholesale reductions in wages far beyond that even suspected by many, and which if successfully enforced, would intensify the stagnation and multiply the misery a thousand-fold. I can say, however, that our organizations are very nearly holding their own, and to weather this storm which is now beating about our heads is the great task before us. When the returning era of prosperity comes whether it is in a month or a year you will find the trade unions emerging from this dark cloud of despair strong and aggressive, in the struggle for improved conditions for the toilers of America. Those who in the meantime have berated and abused the trade unions will hide their heads in shame at their false prophecies and their ridiculous notions.

I do not know that I shall have the opportunity of availing myself or the privilege and honor you extend to me of the hospitality of your home, but be that as it may, I know that I shall have much pleasure in renewing our cordial and friendly acquaintance.

With kindest wishes, I am,

Very Truly Yours   Saml Gompers.
President. American Federation of Labor.

TLpS, reel 7, vol. 9, pp. 410-11, SG Letterbooks, DLC.

1. Edward Webster Bemis, an economist and public utilities expert, was an associate professor of political economy at the University of Chicago.

2. The Baron de Hirsch Trade School opened in the spring of 1892 in New York City to train young Jewish immigrants in a trade.

3. Possibly Adolphus S. Solomons, superintendent of the Baron de Hirsch Fund from 1890 to 1903.

An Article in the *New York Sun*

[August 21, 1893]

GROPING FOR A PANACEA.

Eighty or ninety delegates from trade unions, mostly those affiliated with the American Federation of Labor, but some not, met yesterday afternoon at the International Labor Exchange, 257 East Tenth street, pursuant to a call sent out by Samuel Gompers and others. The meeting lasted almost five hours. Robert M. Campbell of Typographical Union No. 6 presided. Then formal resolutions were passed calling for the appointment of three committees. They say:

Resolved, That a committee of five be appointed by this conference to solicit the aid of the labor organizations of the employed workingmen and of the sympathizers with labor for contributions to aid the unemployed workingmen of this city.

Resolved, That a committee of five be appointed to call on the Mayor[1] and other authorities of this city and upon the Governor and other authorities of this State with a view to starting up and opening up new public works to provide employment for unemployed labor.

Joseph Barondess had this tacked on to the resolution:

And, be it further Resolved, That this same committee call on the Board of Civil Justices and request them to postpone evictions of unemployed workingmen for non-payment of rent until this crisis is over.

The third resolution, proposed by Mr. George E. McNeall of Boston, was:

Resolved, That a committee be appointed by this conference to draft an address to the public proclaiming the new economic gospel.

Joseph Barondess also got a resolution through denouncing the sweating system and asking the Legislature to pass a law wiping out the evil.

Samuel Gompers called the meeting to order. He said:

["]Fellow Unionists: This is one of the greatest crises in the history of our country. While in many epochs of the history of the United States there have been panics, with hundreds of thousands of people thrown out of employment, never before has 80 per cent. of the labor population of America sought honest livelihood without obtaining it. It may appear presumptuous on the part of any labor organization or any of its representatives to speak thus while Congress is in session discussing what it terms means of relief for the people, although we know that they are as far from the fundamental cause of the wrongs that exist as the sun is from the earth. Is the question Congress is now discussing at the root of the evil? No. It is merely contingent to it; merely intensifies it.

["]The present crisis is no fault of ours. The condition exists. We are not to blame, but the blame rests on the shoulders of the wealth possessors of this country. But placing the responsibility is one thing and to devise means to root out the evil is another. Many things have been suggested to relieve the unemployed. During the past week we have seen movements more forcible than elegant, more practical than advisable.[2] But have we any hope for relief by violating the laws of our country and our State? I am not here to condemn any overzealous labor movement but I ask you as labor men, as representatives of masses of toilers, to act wisely, coolly, determinedly, and practically. We called this meeting to immediately aid the starving. As for the Central Labor Federation, which excludes all who do not desire to label themselves, as for the Central Labor Union, which doesn't represent the workingmen of New York save for ulterior purposes, as for the Hebrew Trades (and nothing is more hurtful to the Hebrews as workingmen and to the general interests of labor than for workingmen to organize on a religious basis), as for all these, with such a condition how can a successful move be started unless by all?

["]But how can we get relief? Why, this city can begin almost immediately to build its rapid transit road, improve its streets, sewerage, wharfage and docks. This State can improve its roadways and deepen the Erie Canal. This national Government should build the Nicaragua Canal, should dredge the Mississippi and make one navigable ship canal from it to the Peninsula of Michigan. And apart from public improvements, the employing class, the corporations, instead of discharging half their help and increasing the hours of those employed, should divide the labor among all. And you who are employed should share in prosperity with your fellows and share in misery. But why should the man who steals and violates the law be sent to prison and to work while the honest man and his child starve?["]

Mr. Gompers then appointed Messrs. Walsh, Lemmler, Kaufman, Campbell, and Adler[3] a committee on credentials. While the committee was at work George E. McNeal, General Lecturer of the Federation of Labor, who was introduced by Mr. Gompers as a myriad-minded man, addressed the meeting. Mr. McNeall said:

["]They say speech is silver and silence is golden. If I could coin silence for the poor I'd close my mouth forever. But when we turn to the statesmen and ask for bread they give us a stone. While the clergy all over the land preach of bread for the hereafter why do they not give it to us now? Give us bread to-day. Not in charity, but deliver unto us that which we have produced and which is ours. But if you hold a demonstration do it in calmness and coolness. Be not hasty. The first thing this conference should do is to insist that the Government of this city shall take statistics of the unemployed within its limits, and then you should hold them up as evidence of the failure of the statesmanship of the controlling classes.["]

Victor Delahaye, the Frenchman who is on his way to the Labor Congress at Chicago, told how France had appropriated 2,000,000 francs to guarantee the payment of money advanced to the labor organizations there. He advised that labor in this country demand and bring about a similar action on the part of our Government. Chris Evans, Secretary of the American Federation, also spoke. He appealed to the conference to work to get bread at once, saying there were thousands of men in this city who have no idea where their next meal is coming from.

The report of the Committee on Credentials showed that twenty unions were represented. They were Cigar Makers' Unions Nos. 13,[4] 144, 10, 90, and 251; Typographical Unions Nos. 6, 317,[5] and 7; Garment Makers' Trades Council, Amalgamated Carpenters and Joiners, Carpet Makers' Council, Operators' and Cloakmakers' Union, United Cloak and Suit Cutters, Overcoat and Suit Makers No. 30, Chandelier Makers' Protective Union,[6] Carpenters' and Joiners' 468,[7] District Council No. 1, Carpenters and Joiners, Bakers Union No. 1,[8] German Waiters' Union, Executive Board of the Brotherhood of Tailors and United Garment Makers,[9] Brooklyn Operators' and Tailors' Union No. 27,[10] Operative Tailors' Union and Italian Branch of Cloakmakers.

Then began three hours of vehement discussion and emphatic speechmaking. Moses de Costa[11] of Cigar Makers' Union No. 13 plunged into a speech about the police.

"I witnessed the demonstration they called a riot in Grand street," he said, "and a more disgraceful scene I never saw. It was caused by the brutality of the police. Big, burly, brutal men clubbed innocent people. What we must do is to go down into our pockets and provide bread for the unemployed. Let us do it now. Let us also persuade the Government to open up the arid lands of the West. The War Department must provide rations if people are starving. And we will see them do it, as they did in 1873 and in 1857."

A man named Lindler[12] of Cigar Makers' Union 13 jumped up and shouted: "Make the Judges and their like, every man who gets over $1,200 a year, give half of their money to the poor."

Another cigar maker from Union No. 10 named Davis[13] said: "Bury the hatchet in these labor fights! Let all organizations, Hebrews too, get together. We are all hungry. Let us get work if we can. But McNeall said that instead of bread they give us a stone. Yes, and by and by they will give us bullets. Congress has sat for twelve days and done nothing but draw mileage. Let all of us cooperate, every workingman regardless of the organization to which he belongs.''

A man named Stewart said: "Yes, put your hands in your pockets!"

"There's nothing in the pockets," shouted a number of delegates.

Delegate Dauf[14] jumped up and said: "We are all talking! None of us has any practical plan. You don't know how to help the starving, and I don't know either.''

Delegate Kuntz of Cigar Makers' Union No. 10 said: "We should help each other. Let all workingmen help, be they called Socialists or what!''

"Politics is here!" shouted a voice. "Political scabs!" Prolonged cheers and counter yells greeted the mention of the Socialists. Gompers at once took the floor. He was very red in the face and said:

"I tell you that you cannot get the Central organizations together, not even on Labor Day. I'm full of opinions, I'm full of principles, I'm full of declarations, but they don't bring work to-day. I've heard the flings in regard to political scabs. If they are intended for any people in which I am concerned, I say I am no political scab. Let them roll under their tongues their flings. I dared to vote for Peter Cooper in 1876. I never truckled to Tammany or the Union League.[15] Instead of partisan interests we have class interests. Realize that and you will be better off.''

Henry Weisman followed Mr. Gompers. "I am known as an Anarchist!" he shouted, "and I do not deny it. Don't put the trades unions to the purposes of a charity organization. Let them stand dignified. I agree with Mr. Gompers, and I endorse any suggestions that will send to the Mayor, to the State, or to Washington a committee to present our rights, regardless of political flings here.''

Mr. Schaffer, a Socialist, exclaimed: "Let us march to Albany 100,000 strong and show the Legislature what their laws have done! Let us——''

But Secretary Thomas C. Walsh of the Brotherhood of Carpenters and Joiners interrupted him. Mr. Walsh is big, with a marvelous voice.

"Hold on!" he said. "While we sit here fiddling Rome is burning! We're only blowing off. It is ridiculous to hear this lot of guff. Marching to Albany! Umph! I was afraid the gentleman was going to say swim there. I say, let us go to our unions first for aid. They have money. If they won't give the aid, let them be damned! This is no time for speeches. We want money, not gas.''

Joseph Barondess followed Mr. Walsh.

"Workers, fellow workers, and detectives," he said, looking at Detective Lang of the the Fifth street station, the only policeman present; "We've been talking all the afternoon. I've got no wages for the past four weeks. I know what hunger means. What have you so-called radicals done to-day? What do you do on election day? The Democrats told you not to vote for Republicans."

Instantly there was a rumpus. Yells and cheers drowned Barondess's voice.

"I have the floor and I will be heard!" he shouted. "Social Democrats know that is true!"

"That's not true!" shouted Socialist Schaffer.

"What is to be done?" continued Barondess. "I respect all men of any party here to-day as workingmen. But when the question came up here as to what we could do men got up and preached their political gospels. I know that some men wouldn't go and parade unless their boss said so. Lo the glorious Jerusalem of United Hebrew Trade! But all else aside, get money. If the Pope from Rome sent $3,000,000 for the starving masses, take it. Take all the money offered. I move the appointment of a committee for that purpose."

Then followed the moving of the resolutions printed above. A man named Thomas objected to the resolution of Barondess in regard to requesting the Civil Justices to postpone action in eviction cases.

"Who are you?" asked Barondess of Thomas. "Who do you represent?"

"Thousands of non-union workmen," said Thomas.

The delegates howled. At length Mr. Gompers obtained a hearing for Thomas.

"It's against the law to ask the Civil Justices to do such a thing," said Thomas. "Ask the city to reimburse the landlords for the unemployed workingmen. The Justices will not do what you have asked."

"Yes they will," said Barondess. "They've done it already for me. And as for us asking the city to look out for the landlords, let the landlords look out for themselves. They have always done it, and can do it now."

The resolutions were passed without further discussion, save some advice from Mr. Gompers. The committee chosen to receive subscriptions and solicit aid were Joseph Barondess, Louis Walters,[16] George Middleton,[17] C. N. Adler, and James Doyle.[18] This committee will also confer directly with all labor unions to solicit their cooperation.

The committee to call on the Mayor and the State authorities is Samuel Gompers as adviser, Henry Weisman, Moses de Costa, Charles F. Reichers, Robert M. Campbell, and Henry White.

The committee to present the new economic gospel is George E.

McNeall, Samuel Gompers, Chris Evans, Joseph Barondess, Andrew Smith,[19] Henry White, and T. C. Walsh. It is not yet stated what the new gospel is.

Henry Weisman then said that he was convinced that certain delegates present could prevent further demonstrations like the one at Walhalla Hall. He moved that the conference go on record as disapproving of such demonstrations. Joseph Barondess immediately took issue. Weisman replied with an arraignment of Emma Goldman.[20]

"She harangued the people in Union square last night," he said, "with statements devoid of common sense. Men here can prevent that happening again."

The conference, Mr. Barondess willing, said that it hoped any more demonstrations would be omitted until after a big demonstration was held. The conference then adjourned to meet next Sunday at the same time and place.

New York Sun, Aug. 21, 1893.

1. Thomas F. Gilroy, a Tammany Democrat, was mayor of New York City from 1893 to 1894.

2. Street demonstrations of the unemployed began on the lower East Side of New York City on Aug. 16, 1893, and on the next day a crowd of about 5,000, consisting mostly of Jewish workers, converged on Walhalla Hall, filling the surrounding streets. When the proprietor refused to let the men use the beer hall as a meeting place, some workers broke into it and destroyed much of the interior. By the end of the day some twenty workers had been arrested. Meetings and rallies, punctuated by disputes between anarchists, socialists, and others, continued on subsequent days, including one at Union Square on Aug. 19 addressed by anarchist Emma Goldman. Subsequently police cracked down on anarchists by arresting their leaders and disrupting their meetings.

3. C. N. Adler, corresponding secretary of German-American Typographia 274 in New York City, served on standing committees of the New York City CLU in 1893.

4. CMIU 13 of New York City.

5. International Typographical Union 317, listed as a Hebrew local in New York City.

6. Chandelier Workers' Benevolent and Protective Union.

7. United Brotherhood of Carpenters and Joiners of America (UBCJA) 468 of New York City.

8. Journeymen Bakers' and Confectioners' Union 1 of New York City.

9. The United Garment Workers of America.

10. Actually Journeymen Tailors' Union of America 23 of Brooklyn.

11. Moses de Costa was a member of CMIU 13 of New York City and served on standing committees of the New York City CLU in 1892 and 1893.

12. Possibly Henry Lindner, a New York City cigarmaker.

13. Bernhard Davis.

14. Possibly Meyer Dampf.

15. Union leagues, also known as Loyal leagues, originated in the North during the Civil War, after Union forces suffered reverses in 1862. Designed to bolster morale

and support Lincoln's reelection, they initially promoted the establishment of a new Union party but eventually operated as part of the Republican party.

16. Probably Louis Wolder.

17. George W. Middleton.

18. James G. Doyle represented UBCJA 468 at the Brotherhood's 1896 convention.

19. Andrew J. Smith was a New York City carpenter.

20. Emma GOLDMAN was an anarchist and a union organizer in the clothing industry.

An Excerpt from an Article in the *New York World*

[August 23, 1893]

NO HALLS FOR REDS.

. . .

CALLING ON THE MAYOR.

The committee appointed at a meeting of the unemployed Sunday called upon Mayor Gilroy yesterday to see if something could not be done by the municipal authorities to furnish employment to those now idle. Samuel Gompers, President of the American Federation of Labor, was chairman of the committee. With him were Henry Weismann, of the National Bakers' Union; Moses De Costa, of Cigar Makers' Union 13; Charles F. Reichers, General Secretary of the Garment Makers' Union; Robert M. Campbell, of Typographical Union 6, and Henry White, of the Clothing Cutters' Union. Mr. Gompers said that the condition of the unemployed was heartrending and calamitous, and he thought the city could relieve this distress to a considerable degree by pushing public works already begun and inaugurating new enterprises. He said that in some of the trades fully 90 per cent. are now unemployed, but the Mayor interrupted him to say that he could hardly believe that statement. The situation was bad enough, however, he added, and he thought that every possible means should be exhausted to relieve the distress.

Continuing, Mr. Gompers said that the laboring people "preferred to keep within the law, but he thought it was safest and best for the municipal authorities to provide work for the unemployed."

"I don't know whether you mean that as a threat or not," said the Mayor, looking Mr. Gompers square in the eyes.

No Threat Intended.

"Oh, no, not at all," answered Mr. Gompers, "but no community can be entirely safe where a large body of the people are without employment."

"Well," said the Mayor, "every workingman who calls on me shall have a welcome and a hearing, so long as I am in this office; but I would have been unfaithful to my trust if I had not before this considered the situation of affairs which brings you here. Whatever I can do, either as a public officer or as a private citizen, to relieve the distress I am ready to do. But I cannot do that which is impossible under the law. In the matter of new improvements, $1,500,000 is being spent, and contracts for new sewers and other work in the annexed district have been let amounting to nearly $2,000,000. In addition, the Dock Board[1] has authority to expend $3,000,000 a year for four years in dock improvements. If your committee has any suggestions I am ready to hear them."

Baker Weissmann said that half the men in his trade were out of employment. Cigarmaker Moses DeCosta said that fully 90 per cent. in his trade were idle. He suggested that the city build a rapid-transit road.

"But we cannot do that until after the Legislature meets next January," said the Mayor. "Legislation is necessary before we can begin."

"Commissioner Andrews is discharging men instead of hiring more,"[2] said Mr. DeCosta.

"He has to cut down expenses," said the Mayor. "He would be liable to indictment and imprisonment if he exceeded his appropriation for the year."

"Then why is Mr. Brennan walking the streets a free man?"[3] triumphantly asked Mr. Gompers, and the Mayor looked worried.

"Ask the District-Attorney," he answered tartly.

Robert M. Campbell said that 30 per cent. of the printers were idle. "But we will go further than Mr. Gompers," he added. "We not only prefer to keep within the law, we insist that our members shall obey the law."

Mr. Gompers explained the workings of the Committee on Relief and besought Mr. Gilroy to do what he could to assist it. The Mayor promised to give the subject his immediate and earnest attention. He might make some announcements regarding measures for immediate relief a little later. He also promised to communicate with the heads of departments and to bring the matter up at the next meeting of the Board of Estimate.[4]

. . .

New York World, Aug. 23, 1893.

1. The New York City Department of Docks.
2. William S. Andrews, appointed commissioner of the New York City Department of Street Cleaning in July 1893, discharged several hundred men in August to cut expenses in the face of a large deficit in the department's budget.
3. Thomas S. Brennan resigned as the commissioner of the Department of Street Cleaning in July 1893, leaving a substantial deficit in the department's budget.
4. The New York City Board of Estimate and Apportionment.

To Roswell Flower

Aug. 24, [1893]

To the Hon. Roswell P. Flower,
Governor of the State of New York,
Watertown, N.Y.
Dear Sir: —

Pursuant to instructions of the Conference of organized labor of the city of New York for the Relief of the Unemployed, a Committee was authorized to wait upon you and urge you to call an extra session of the Legislature of this State with a view of authorizing and providing the prosecution of great public improvements to the end that the great works necessary to the success of our city may be completed, and at the same time relieve the great army of the unemployed of the City of New York.

It is not our purpose in this letter to urge the reasons for this step, but merely to request you to state a time when the Committee may have an opportunity of meeting you in the city of New York so that the ground upon which our request is based may be presented to you for your favorable consideration and action.[1]

Trusting that we may receive an early and favorable reply, I am,
Very Respectfully Yours   Saml Gompers.
For the Committee.

TLpS, reel 7, vol. 9, p. 417, SG Letterbooks, DLC.

1. Flower put off the proposed meeting and refused to call the legislature into special session, at the same time issuing public statements in opposition to the principle of government aid to the unemployed.

An Interview in the *New York World*

[August 28, 1893]

DUCEY[1] AND GOMPERS.

. . .

Samuel Gompers I saw at his desk in the headquarters of the Federation of Labor in Clinton place. He sat in his shirt sleeves hard at work reading reports and dictating letters. He had just received a telegram from Samuel Lesem[2] from Denver offering to send two carloads of potatoes and two carloads of flour to the hungry unemployed in New York. I suggested that the offer might be the expression of a Western desire to rebuke the New York goldbug. He thought it might, but was ready to receive such rebukes without limit. Mr. Gompers is a broad-shouldered man, with black hair, a strong face and very good, frank eyes. He is a direct, well-balanced man. I reminded him of the fact that some wise gentleman had said there was no distress in New York and asked him whether he could prove the contrary. He said:

"Over one hundred thousand men are out of work and are in need in New York. In two of the most important trades—the cigar-makers' and the clothing-makers'—80 or 90 per cent. of the men are out of work. This I know of my own knowledge. Among the cigar-makers various benefit funds exist which the men subscribe to at the rate of 25 cents per week.

"There is a benefit for those out of employment. Those applying for this benefit must report at headquarters every day and register. The hours for registering are so arranged that no man who has work can successfully figure as one of the unemployed. This registry proves what I have said regarding the number of men out of work. I prefer such statistics to any man's opinion. I have as good grounds for my assertions concerning the unemployed clothing-makers.

"Of the printers 30 per cent. are out of work. Among the bakers, usually the last to suffer in a panic, since all men must have bread, 50 per cent. are idle. The stone trade is practically shut down. The building trade has gone to pieces. Buildings are left half finished, among them Grant's tomb, for which the public subscribed the money, and schoolhouses on which work is delayed because the gentlemen who could order it to continue are in Europe or elsewhere out of town.

"To say that any such awful distress as this is customary is vicious untruth. The number of unemployed as compared with the usual state of affairs at this time of the year is multiplied by more than six.

"The pushing of public works should be insisted upon, but the conditions are so serious and the danger of famine so great that help, the distribution of food, charity—whatever it may be called—is urgently needed.

"I am aware of the limitations under which the Mayor suffers. When I went to him it was with a knowledge of his powers and to talk on municipal questions only. When we wish to ask for work requiring State legislation we shall go to the Governor and not to the Mayor. I have studied the question and know what the Mayor can do. I do not agree with the idea that public works are just so much taken from the pockets of the people. Public enterprises add to the wealth of the city, to the value of property, to the comfort of citizens and to the prosperity of workingmen.

"I will tell you frankly that I am a bimetallist and not in favor of the present repeal of the present Sherman law. I do not favor the Sherman law by any means, but I think it ought to be held as a hostage for free coinage. The act was passed as a trick by Sherman to prevent free coinage. It should be used to defeat the trick. To attribute present troubles to the Sherman act or to imagine that its repeal will right matters is the merest childishness.

"It is remarkable how conspicuous the causes of the real trouble are made by the absence of any reference to them at Washington.

"Here is the cause of the trouble: In the last twenty-five years the application of steam, the discovery and application of electricity and the subdivision of labor have increased the laborers' productive capacity fifty-fold.

"The consumption of products must rest with the masses. The power of consumption has not increased in proportion to the increase in the productive power. Stagnation has come as a consequence: after that the discharge of employees with the consequent decrease in the consumptive capacity, then more discharges, and so on indefinitely. The Sherman law is bad because it intensifies the disastrous conditions by adding to the lack of confidence."

Mr. Gompers believes that this nation alone, because of its powerful independent position, could successfully undertake the task of forcing the free coinage of silver upon the entire world. He believes that no nation is sufficiently independent of us to ignore us or sufficiently powerful to crush us financially, and that we ought to start in on the free-silver fight at once and alone if necessary.

Arthur Brisbane.[3]

New York World, Aug. 28, 1893.

1. The Reverend Thomas J. Ducey, pastor of St. Leo's Roman Catholic Church in New York City, was also interviewed.

2. Samuel Lesem was a Denver insurance agent.

3. Arthur Brisbane was managing editor of the *New York World* from 1890 to 1897, when he became editor of William Randolph Hearst's *New York Evening Journal.*

An Address before the International Labor Congress in Chicago

[August 28, 1893]

WHAT DOES LABOR WANT?

A legend of ancient Rome relates that while the capitol was building, there came one day to the tyrannical king Tarquin the Proud, a poor old woman, carrying nine books of prophecies of the Sibyl, which she offered to sell for three hundred pieces of gold. The king laughingly bade her go away, which she did; but after burning three of the books, she returned and asked the same price for the remaining six. Again treated with scorn, she retired, burnt three more of the volumes, and then came back demanding the same sum for the three which were left. Astonished at this conduct, the king consulted his wise men, who answered him that in those nine books, six of which had been lost, were contained the fate of the city and the Roman people.

To-day the marvellous Sibyl, who grows the grain, yet goes a-hungered; who weaves the silken robes of pride, yet goes threadbare; who mines the coal and precious ores, yet goes cold and penniless; who rears the gorgeous palaces, yet herds in noisome basements, she again appears. This old, yet ever young Sibyl, called labor, offers to modern society the fate of civilization. What is her demand? Modern society, the most complex organization yet evolved by the human race, is based on one simple fact, the practical separation of the capitalistic class from the great mass of the industrious.

If this separation were only that resulting from a differentiation in the functions of directions of industrial operations and their execution in detail then that separation would be regarded as real, direct progress. But the separation between the capitalistic class and the laboring mass is not so much a difference in industrial rank as it is a difference in social status, placing the laborers in a position involving a degradation of mind and body.

This distinction, scarcely noticeable in the United States before the previous generation, rapidly became more and more marked, increasing day by day, until at length, it has widened into a veritable chasm; economic, social and moral. On each side of this seemingly impassable chasm, we see the hostile camps of rich and poor. On one side, a class in possession of all the tools and means of labor; on the other, an immense mass begging for the opportunity to labor. In the mansion, the soft notes betokening ease and security; in the tenement the stifled wail of drudgery and poverty. The arrogance of the rich ever mounting in proportion to the debasement of the poor.

From across the chasm we hear the old familiar drone of the priests of Mammon called "Political Economists." The words of the song they sing are stolen from the vocabulary of science, but the chant itself is the old barbaric lay. It tells us that the present absolute domination of wealth is the result of material and invariable laws and counsels the laborers, whom they regard as ignorant and misguided, to patiently submit to the natural operations of the immutable law of "supply and demand." The laborers reply. They say that the political economists never learned sufficient science to know the difference between the operation of a natural law and the law on petty larceny. The day is past when the laborers could be cajoled or humbugged by the sacred chickens of the augers or by the bogus laws of the political economists.

The laborers know that there are few historic facts capable of more complete demonstration than those showing when and how the capitalists gained possession of the tools and opportunities of labor. They know that the capitalists gained their industrial monopoly by the infamous abuse of arbitrary power on the part of royal and federal potentates. They know that by the exercise of this arbitrary power a well established system of industry was overthrown and absolute power was placed in the hands of the selfish incompetents. They know that the only industrial qualifications possessed by these incompetents was the ability to purchase charters, giving the purchaser a monopoly of a certain trade in a specified city and that the price of such charters, the blood money of monopoly, was such paltry sums as forty shillings paid to the king or a few dollars to congressional (mis) representatives. They know that by the unscrupulous use of such monstrously unjust privileges, competent master workmen were deprived of their hard-earned rights to conduct business, and were driven into the ranks of journeymen; that the journeymen were disfranchised and that the endowment funds for the relief and support of sick and aged members of the guilds and Unions, the accumulation of generations, were confiscated. They know that thus did the capitalist class have its origin in force and fraud, shameless fraud, stooping so low in its abject meanness as to steal the Trade Union's sick, superannuated and burial funds.

The laborers well know how baseless is the claim made by the political economists that the subsequent development of the capitalist class was spontaneous and natural, for they know that the capitalists not content with a monopoly of industry enabling them to increase the price of products at will and reduce the wages of labor to a bare subsistence also procured legislation forbidding the disfranchised and plundered workmen from organizing in their own defense.

The laborers will never forget that the coalition and conspiracy laws, directed by the capitalists against the journeymen who had sublime fidelity and heroic courage to defend their natural rights to organization, punished them with slavery, torture and death. In short, the laborers know that the capitalist class had its origin in force and fraud, that it has maintained and extended its brutal sway more or less directly through the agency of specified legislation, most ferocious and barbarous, but always in cynical disregard of all law save its own arbitrary will.

The first things to be recognized in a review of the capitalistic system are that the possessors of the tools and means of labor have not used their power to organize industry so much as to organize domestic and international industrial war and that they have not used the means in their possession to produce utilities so much as to extract profits. The production of profits instead of the production of honest goods, being the primary and constant object of the capitalistic system. We have a waste of labor appalling in its recklessness and inhumanity, a misuse of capital that is really criminal and a social condition of cheerless drudgery and hopeless poverty, of sickening apprehension and fathomless degradation almost threatening the continuance of civilization.

The state of industrial anarchy produced by the capitalist system is first strongly illustrated in the existence of a class of wealthy social parasites; those who do no work, never did any work and never intend to work. This class of parasites devours incomes derived from many sources; from the stunted babies employed in the mills, mines and factories to the lessees of the gambling hells and the profits of fashionable brothels; from the lands which the labor of others has made valuable; from royalties on coal and other minerals beneath the surface and from rent of houses above the surface, the rent paying all cost of the houses many times over and the houses coming back to those who never paid for them.

Then we have the active capitalists; those engaged in business. This number must be divided into two classes; the first consisting of those legitimately using their capital in the production of utilities and honest goods. The second, those misusing their capital in the production of "bogus" imitations of luxuries; of adulterations and of useless goods, the miserable makeshifts specially produced for the consumption of underpaid workers. With this "bogus" class must be included not only the jerry builders and the shoddy clothiers, but also the quack doctors and the shyster lawyers, also the mass of insurance and other agents and middlemen. Coming to the laborers, we must regard them not only according to their technical divisions as agricultural, mechanical, commercial, literary and domestic, with numerous subdivisions, but also as economically divided into three classes, those engaged in the production of utilities, those engaged in all other pursuits and those constituting the general "reserve army" of labor.

The first economic division of laborers consisting mainly of agriculturalists, mechanics producing utilities and a very limited portion of those engaged in commerce. Upon this moiety devolves the task of supporting itself, the parasitic capitalists, the "bogus" capitalists, the workers engaged in ministering to the demands of the parasitic capitalists, the workers employed in the production of "bogus," and the immense reserve army of labor; also the army and navy, the police, the host of petty public functionaries; also the stragglers from the reserve army of labor, including the beggars, the paupers and those driven by want to crime.

We have seen that the possessors of the tools and means of industry have failed in establishing order in their own ranks as evidenced in the class of parasitic capitalists and a class of "bogus" capitalists, miserable counterfeiters, who rob the wealth producers of the just reward of honest work, while they degrade the workers by making them accomplices in their fabrications, then rob them by compelling them to buy the worthless goods they have fabricated and finally poisoning them with their adulterations.

While failing to protect society in its consumptive capacity, the capitalist class has shared and degraded society in its productive capacity.

It has accomplished this result by establishing alternating periods of renovating idleness and debilitating overwork, by undermining the very foundation of society, the family life of the workers, in reducing the wages of the adult male workers below the cost of family maintenance and then employing both sexes of all ages to compete against each other,

> Our fathers are praying for pauper pay,
> Our mothers with death's kiss are white;

> Our sons are the rich man's serfs by day,
> Our daughters his slaves by night,

and finally by refusing to recognize the workers in a corporate capacity, and by invoking the collusion of their dependents, the judges and the legislators, to place the organized workers outside the pale of the law.

Nevertheless in spite of all opposition, the Trade Unions have grown until they have become a power that none can hope to annihilate.

To-day modern society is beginning to regard the Trade Unions as the only hope of civilization; to regard them as the only power capable of evolving order out of the social-chaos. But will the Sibyl's demand be re-regarded or heeded before it is too late? Let us hope so. The Trade Unions having a thorough knowledge of the origin and development of the capitalist class entertain no desire for revenge or retaliation. The Trade Unions have deprecated the malevolent and unjust spirit with which they have had to contend in their protests and struggles against the abuse of the capitalist system, yet while seeking justice have not permitted their movement to become acrid by the desire of revenge. Their methods were always conservative, their steps evolutionary.

One of the greatest impediments to a better appreciation by the capitalists of the devoted efforts of the Trade Unions to establish harmony in the industrial relations, has been the perverted view taken by the capitalists in regarding their capital as essentially if not absolutely their own, whereas, the Trade Unions taking a more comprehensive and purer view, regard all capitals large and small, as the fruits of labor's economies and discoveries, inventions and institutions of many generations of laborers and capitalists, of theoreticians and practitioners, practically as indivisible as a living man.

Another impediment to the establishment of correct industrial relations has resulted from the vicious interference of the political economists with their unscientific analogy between commercial commodities and human labor. The falsity of their analogy was exposed in 1850 by a Parisian workman who was being examined before a commission appointed by the French government to inquire into the condition of the working people. One of the commissioners took occasion to impress upon their witness, that labor was merely a merchandise. The workman replied if "merchandise is not sold at one certain time, it can be sold at another, while if I do not sell my labor it is lost for all the world as well as myself; and as society lives only upon the results of labor, society is poorer to the whole extent of that which I have failed to produce."

The more intelligent will however before long begin to appreciate the transcendent importance of the voluntary organization of labor, will recognize the justice of the claims made by that organization and will become conscious that there is nothing therein contained or involved that would be derogatory to the real dignity and interest of all, to voluntarily and frankly concur in.

In order to understand the wants of labor it is essential to conceive the hypothesis upon which the claims are based, hence the necessity of presenting the foregoing.

What does labor want? It wants the earth and the fulness thereof. There is nothing too precious, there is nothing too beautiful, too lofty, too ennobling, unless it is within the scope and comprehension of labor's aspirations and wants. But to be more specific: The expressed demands of labor are first and foremost a reduction of the hours of daily labor to eight hours to-day, fewer to-morrow.

Is labor justified in making this demand? Let us examine the facts.

Within the past twenty-five years more inventions and discoveries have been made in the method of producing wealth than in the entire history of the world before. Steam power has been applied on the most extensive scale. The improvement of tools, the consequent division and sub-division of labor, the force of electricity, so little known a few years ago, is now applied to an enormous extent. As a result, the productivity of the toiler with these new improved machines and forces has increased so many fold as to completely overshadow the product of the joint masses of past ages. Every effort, every ingenious device has been utilized to cultivate the greater productivity of the worker.

The fact that in the end the toilers must be the great body of the consumers, has been given little or no consideration at all. The tendency to employ the machines continuously (the worker has been made part of the machines) and the direction has been in the line of endeavoring to make the wealth producers work longer hours.

On the other hand, the organized labor movement, the Trade Unions, have concentrated all their forces upon the movement to reduce the hours of daily toil not only as has been often said, to lighten the burdens of drudgery and severe toil, but also to give the great body of the people more time, more opportunity and more leisure in order to create and increase their consumptive power; in other words, to relieve the choked and glutted condition of industry and commerce.

The prosperity of a nation, the success of a people, the civilizing influence of our era, can always be measured by the comparative consuming power of a people.

If as it has often been said, cheap labor and long hours of toil are necessary to a country's prosperity, commercially and industrially, China should necessarily be at the height of civilization.

Millions of willing heads, hands and hearts are ready to frame and to fashion the fabrics and supply the necessities as well as the desires of the people. There are hundreds of thousands of our fellow men and women who cannot find the opportunity to employ their powers, their brain and brawn to satisfy their commonest and barest necessities to sustain life. In every city and town through this broad land of plenty, gaunt figures, hungry men and women with blanched faces and children having the mark of premature age and emaciated conditions indelibly impressed upon their countenances, stalk through the streets and highways. It does not require a philanthropist nor even a humanitarian to evidence deep concern or to give deep thought in order to arrive at the conclusion that in the midst of plenty, such results are both unnatural and wrong. The ordinary man may truly inquire why it is that the political economist answers our demand for work by saying that the law of supply and demand, from which they say there is no relief, regulates these conditions. Might we not say fails to regulate them?

The organized working men and women, the producers of the wealth of the world, declare that men, women and children with human brains and human hearts, should have a better consideration than inanimate and dormant things, usually known under the euphonious title of "Property." We maintain that it is both inhuman, barbaric and retrogressive to allow the members of the human family to suffer for want, while the very things that could and would contribute to their wants and comforts as well as to the advantage of the entire people, are allowed to decay.

We demand a reduction of the hours of labor which would give a due share of work and wages to the reserve army of labor and eliminate many of the worst abuses of the industrial system now filling our poor houses and jails. The movement for the reduction of the hours of labor is contemporaneous with the introduction of labor saving machinery and has been the most faithful of all reformatory attempts of modern times, since it has clearly revealed the power of the working people to realize an improved industrial system and raises the hope that we may yet be able to stem the tide of economic, social and moral degradations, robbing those who work of four-fifths of their natural wages and keeping the whole of society within a few months of destitution.

Labor demands and insists upon the exercise of the right to organize for self and mutual protection. The toilers want the abrogation of all laws discriminating against them in the exercise of those functions which make our organizations in the economic struggle a factor and not a farce.

That the lives and limbs of the wage-workers shall be regarded as sacred as those of all others of our fellow human beings; that an injury or destruction of either by reason of negligence or maliciousness of another, shall not leave him without redress simply because he is a wage worker. We demand equality before the law, in fact as well as in theory.

The right to appear by counsel guaranteed by the constitution of our country is one upon which labor is determined.

To prescribe narrower limits to the wage workers and urge as a special plea that right is accorded before the courts, is insufficient. The counsel of the toilers have earned their diplomas by sacrifices made and scars received in the battle for labor's rights rather than the mental acquirements of legends and musty precedents of semi-barbaric ages. The diplomas of labor's counsel are not written on parchment, they are engraved in heart and mind. The court our counsels file their briefs in and make their pleas for justice, right and equality in are the offices of the employers. The denial to labor of the right to be heard by counsel—their committees—is a violation of the spirit of a fundamental principle of our republic.

And by no means the least demand of the Trade Unions is for adequate wages.

The importance of this demand is not likely to be under-estimated. Adam Smith says: "It is but equity that they who feed, clothe and lodge the whole body of the people, should have such a share of the produce of their labor as to be themselves tolerably well fed, clothed and lodged." But the Trade Unions' demand is for better pay than [that] which Adam Smith deemed equitable. The Trade Unions taking normal conditions as its point of view, regards the workman as the producer of the wealth of the world and demands that wages (as long as the wage system may last), shall be sufficient to enable him to support his family in a manner consistent with existing civilization and all that is required for maintaining and improving physical and mental health and the self respect of human beings.

Render our lives while working as safe and healthful as modern science demonstrates it is possible. Give us better homes is just as potent a cry to-day as when Dickens voiced the yearnings of the people of a generation ago.

Save our children in their infancy from being forced into the mael-strom of wage slavery. See to it that they are not dwarfed in body and mind or brought to a premature death by early drudgery. Give them the sunshine of the school and playground instead of the factory, the mine and the workshop.

We want more school houses and less jails; more books and less arsenals; more learning and less vice; more constant work and less crime; more leisure and less greed; more justice and less revenge; in fact, more of the opportunities to cultivate our better natures, to make manhood more noble, womanhood more beautiful and childhood more happy and bright.

These in brief are the primary demands made by the Trade Unions in the name of labor.

These are the demands made by labor upon modern society and in their consideration is involved the fate of civilization. For:

> There is a moving of men like the sea in its might,
> The grand and resistless uprising of labor;
> The banner it carries is justice and right,
> It aims not the musket, it draws not the sabre.
> But the sound of its tread, o'er the graves of the dead,
> Shall startle the world and fill despots with dread;
> For 'tis sworn that the land of the Fathers shall be
> The home of the brave, and the land of the free.

What Does Labor Want? A Paper Read before the International Labor Congress, Chicago, Ill., September, 1893 (New York, n.d.).

An Excerpt from an Article in the *Chicago Inter Ocean*

[August 30, 1893]

HOW TO LEND AID.

. . . A reporter for *The Inter Ocean* yesterday put the question to a number of persons at the Labor Congress at Art institute.

"What do you recommend for the practical and speedy relief of the unemployed of Chicago assuming that there are 25,000 or more, and that everybody wants to help?"

Samuel Gompers, President American Federation, said: "I would first find out if any are in distress and relieve them first. Hungry people can neither reason nor work. Then I would use every possible channel to secure work. Public improvements should be pushed. The Chicago idea of business men and labor people joining forces in carrying on this work is especially a happy one. I have not studied the local situation in Chicago sufficiently to go into detail, but furnish bread first and then work, unless you can furnish the work first, in which case the people will furnish their own bread, which is much better."

. . .

Chicago Inter Ocean, Aug. 30, 1893.

A Translation of an Article in the *New Yorker Volkszeitung*

[September 17, 1893]

INVITED TO THE BANQUET.

At 8 o'clock a conference of the French delegates[1] was held at the Richeleu Hotel. Delegate Kugler[2] chaired. After the meeting had been opened, a committee arrived from the Central Labor Federation and the Socialist Labor Party. Among the members of this committee were Hugo Vogt, August Waldinger, Dan. De Leon,[3] Oppermann,[4] Chas. Wilson.[5] De Leon was the speaker for the committee. He declared in a lengthy speech that it was the duty of the committee to present the situation to the delegates as it is, so that they could make no mistake about the way things are here in the labor world. The speaker explained he had heard that all the French delegates were socialists, although they belonged to different groups. "You know, therefore," he continued, "that it is socialism that will bring about the emancipation of the workers. But here in America there are a great number of workers who do not understand this. The fault lies not with the workers, but with their leaders who make them believe that they need the help of the capitalists." The speaker noted especially that there were two general tendencies in the workers' movement here, one that believes, as the Central Labor Federation does, that it is necessary for the workers to fight at the ballot box and, when necessary, on the battlefield, and the other represented by Gompers. The speaker then explained the work of the leaders of the American Federation of Labor and mentioned that the treasurer of the Federation had declared it would be sophistry to say that antagonism existed between capital and labor. De Leon described Gompers' agitation and his behavior toward the socialists. He then said that the socialists had arranged a reception for the French comrades which, if possible, was to take place Tuesday evening, and that the French delegation was cordially invited. De Leon emphasized that the socialists and the members of the Central Labor Federation could not take part in a reception in which the representatives of the American Federation of Labor also participated. De Leon's speech was greeted with great applause.

One of the delegates then said that the situation was delicate, since the delegation wanted to be on friendly terms with all the unions. He emphasized that the delegation was composed of socialists, but certainly did not want to assume responsibility in this difficult situation.

Following this, Gompers appeared at the conference, and a French delegate asked that he state, since he would very much like to know, whether he was a socialist. Gompers then spoke at least three quarters of an hour. He said he was astounded when he heard that he had been accused of dishonesty. The delegates explained, however, that he had not been called dishonest by anyone. Gompers then expressed his astonishment that he was being asked what kind of socialist he was. The delegates, he continued, did not know him and could not act as judges in disagreements that had existed for years. The delegates had come to America for a special purpose, and could not stand in judgment over him. He explained at length that he had been in the labor movement since his childhood, and whoever accused him of playing into the hands of the capitalists was not speaking the truth. He had always fought for the proletariat and had been a member of a union since 1865. He then maintained that the people who were always accusing him didn't understand anything about socialism. "These people think," he said, "that it is necessary for the propaganda of socialism to destroy trade unions." With great pathos, he stated that different conditions existed in different countries, and that one must therefore use different methods. "I have never written or said anything against socialism," said Gompers. "There is in fact not one demand of the socialists that is not also put forward by the trade unionists and by me. As long as this system exists, the capitalists will continue to make profits. Once the profits stop, then this system will end too, and the cooperative system will be introduced." Gompers also spoke at length about his ideal of the socialist communal system, and emphasized that it would be a system based on industry and opposed to everything connected with business, a communal system in which the interest of the individual would be the interest of all. At the end of the speech he emphasized that he had spoken with members of the committee of socialists in order to make possible a single reception for the French delegates.

After these speeches there was a lengthy discussion. A member of the French delegation said they could not act as judges, that they were socialists but they were above all else defenders of unity. "In

France, too, we suffer from disunity," he said, "and we have seen there that the workers spend their best time fighting each other instead of the capitalists. If there is no other way, we will have to accept both invitations."

Following this, Gompers said he was still in favor of arranging a single reception. Then De Leon spoke. In a very fine speech he contradicted what Gompers had said. The discussion continued for quite some time. When the paper went to the presses at 1 o'clock, a decision still had not been made.

New Yorker Volkszeitung, Sept. 17, 1893. Translated from the German by Patrick McGrath.

1. The municipal council of the city of Paris sent a delegation of thirty-four workingmen and women to the 1893 Chicago World's Fair to examine the industrial exhibits and study the methods employed by the various trades. The group arrived in New York on Sept. 16, and remained there until Sept. 20.

2. Kugler was a Paris machinist.

3. Daniel DeLeon was the editor of the SLP's official organ *People* from 1891 until 1914, and the SLP's leading figure during that period.

4. Charles Oppermann, a furrier, served on various committees and as sergeant-at-arms of the New York City Central Labor Federation between 1892 and 1895, and in 1894 ran as an SLP candidate for the New York assembly.

5. Charles F. Wilson, a New York City rock driller, was a candidate for city and state offices on the SLP ticket between 1891 and 1893.

A Translation of an Article in the *New Yorker Volkszeitung*

[September 19, 1893]

FRANCE'S DELEGATES.

Yesterday the French delegates began to collect information about the working and living conditions of workers here. Some of them toured the tenement-house districts with a knowledgeable comrade, where they looked at the "sweat shops," while others visited the office of the American Federation of Labor, and there were informed about the activities of the unions and the organization of the Federation. Samuel Gompers gave the delegates the constitutions, official journals, and labels of the different unions that belong to the Federation, and also showed them how the officials of the Federation conduct its business. They were shown the charters, the applications for charters, and other forms, and they took detailed notes on all this information.

A number of delegates visited some of the larger factories during the day, and then viewed the Brooklyn Bridge and other sights.

In the evening all the delegates came together at the Kellner-Klub-haus. The American Federation had arranged a reception in honor of the delegates, and a large number of union representatives were present. The outside of the building was draped with American and French flags; the inside was also tastefully decorated with flags and garlands.

The French delegates appeared shortly before 10 o'clock, led by Samuel Gompers. The hall was packed when the event began. John J. McGuire introduced the president[1] of the National Alliance of Hotel and Restaurant Employees[2] as chairman, and after a cold supper had been served Gompers gave the welcoming speech. His remarks were in no way new. He said that the American workers supported the French proletarians in their struggle, and if anyone tried to make the French believe that the workers of the United States were not dedicated to progress, the delegates should regard such a statement with caution. "Workers in America have to fight against unique conditions," said the speaker, "which are quite different from those in other countries. If someone in France or in another country preaches revolution, he will not be considered an enemy of the country; there, if one organizes wageworkers with the purpose of revolutionizing the people, one is not condemned as an enemy of civilization." Gompers emphasized that the workers here consist of Spaniards, Englishmen, Frenchmen, Germans, and members of other nations, that the one does not trust the other, and that a person who fights for certain principles becomes the enemy of those who adhere to other beliefs. He then declared that he was neither radical nor conservative, that he was not pledged to any "ism" at all, but was "a member of his union, a member of the labor movement, that he would follow this movement, no matter where it might lead him." Gompers emphasized especially that he was an opponent of all [one-man] leadership, that he would rather be among the sansculottes of the workers than above the workers. Finally, he explained in his speech that in America, as in France, different groups existed within the labor movement. In Germany, he said, similar divisions exist; one finds Marxists there, Lassalleans, Progressives, Anarchists, Conservatives, and Radicals, while in England one finds members of the old and new trade unionism. But one thing was certain, he said, that all are striving to bring about the emancipation of the workers. The platform of the trades union, he said, was wide enough for radicals and conservatives.

After Gompers' speech, Edward Sykes,[3] a member of Cigar Makers' Union No. 144, performed a song, and then Delegate Barthelmy,[4] the delegate of the Paris food workers, read a speech in English in which he expressed the delegates' thanks for the reception.

William Weihe, John B. Lennon, and Christ. Evans also spoke. At the close of the reception the delegates were welcomed by the individual guests.

New Yorker Volkszeitung, Sept. 19, 1893. Translated from the German by Patrick McGrath.

1. John MEE was president of the Hotel and Restaurant Employees' National Alliance from 1893 to 1894.

2. The WAITERS' and Bartenders' National Union changed its name to the Hotel and Restaurant Employees' National Alliance in 1892.

3. Edward Sykes was a shopmate of SG's at the firm of Matthew Hutchinson after the cigarmakers' strike of 1877-78.

4. F. Barthelemy (variously Bartholemy) was secretary of the French National Academy of Cuisine.

To Samuel Bell[1]

Sept. 21, [1893]

Mr. S. H. Bell,
Sec. Comm. Intl. Typographical Union on Government
  Ownership and Control of Telegraphs etc.
423 G. St. N.W., Washington, D.C.
Dear Sir and Brother:—

I am in receipt of your favor of the 16th. inst. the contents of which are carefully noted, but I have been unable to give the matter earlier attention.

You are no doubt aware that the last convention of the American Federation of Labor, the same as many of its predecessors decided positively in favor of the Government ownership and control of all means of transportation and communication.[2]

In accordance with that resolution petitions have been sent broadcast throughout the country asking signatures of unionists and sympathizers so that the subject matter may be brought in one united petition to the attention of Congress. You may count positively upon my co-operation and I feel confident that I can rely upon that of your Committee to make manifest progress in the lines of agitation laid down.

May I ask you to continue the communication with this office so that we may clearly understand what course is being pursued by your

Committee and I shall freely communicate the same to you, what has and is being and will be done to push this matter.

Before this reaches you I shall be en route to Milwaukee to attend the convention of the Cigar Makers Intl. Union[3] returning about Oct. 6th. Should you desire to communicate with me in the meantime please address me care of Cigar Makers Intl. Union convention West Side Turn Hall, Milwaukee, Wis. and after that date to this office.

Fraternally Yours   Saml Gompers.
President. American Federation of Labor.

TLpS, reel 7, vol. 9, p. 467, SG Letterbooks, DLC.

1. Samuel H. Bell was a Washington, D.C., printer and member of International Typographical Union 101.

2. See "The Convention of the American Federation of Labor Adjourns," Dec. 18, 1892, n. 2, in "Excerpts from News Accounts of the 1892 Convention of the AFL in Philadelphia," above.

3. The convention of the CMIU met in Milwaukee, Sept. 25-Oct. 12, 1893.

To Isaac Cowen[1]

Sept. 21, [1893]

Mr. Isaac Cowan,
c/o Cleveland "Citizen" Cleveland, O.
Dear Sir and Brother:—

I am in receipt of your favor of the 18th. inst. enclosing a series of resolutions and propositions for making the Cleveland "Citizen" the official journal of the American Federation of Labor.[2]

There is no doubt in my mind but what the A.F. of L. should have an official journal. Whether based upon the scheme proposed or not is not and cannot be a subject for discussion at present. I would suggest that the delegate of your Central Labor Union[3] to the next convention of the American Federation of Labor to be held the second Monday in Dec. 1893 in the City of Chicago, Ill. be directed to bring the subject matter before the consideration of the delegates there assembled. Whatever action that body may take will be perfectly satisfactory to,

Yours Fraternally   Saml Gompers.
President. American Federation of Labor.

TLpS, reel 7, vol. 9, p. 464, SG Letterbooks, DLC.

1. Isaac Cowen, a machinist, was corresponding secretary for the Cleveland Central Labor Union (CLU).

2. The 1893 AFL convention considered a resolution from the Cleveland CLU to endorse the *Cleveland Citizen* as the AFL's official organ. The convention referred the proposal to the AFL Executive Council but also approved a separate resolution authorizing the Federation to issue its own monthly journal. In January 1894 the Executive Council decided that the two resolutions were incompatible and declined to endorse the *Cleveland Citizen.*

3. The Cleveland CLU, founded in 1887, superseded the Cleveland Trades and Labor Assembly.

An Article in the *People*

Milwaukee, Oct. 2 [1893]

THE CIGARMAKERS.

The Cigarmakers' Convention debated last Thursday the question of "Independent political Action." Besides Mr. Gompers, the leading speaker against the motion was Moses DeCosta of New York, a Republican heeler. The leading arguments for the motion were made by Mallon T. Barnes[1] of Philadelphia, and also by Bachman[2] of Union 65, Lynn, Mass., who said: ["]The workingmen, the masses, could be united soon enough for the political as well as for the economic struggle; it is, however, the leaders that prevent union; it is to their interest to move hand in hand with the capitalists."

The motion was finally defeated by 265 votes against 85.[3] The honest and progressive vote of 85 was a great gain upon the vote two years ago;[4] and when it is considered that it came mainly from the large unions, it represented a much larger proportion of the workers than would appear.

Next was the motion on a preamble that should join the economic and political movement. This too was lost; but the vote in favor was 135 against 212.[5] The tide of New Trade Unionism is rising, and will yet drown the rats.

People (New York), Oct. 8, 1893.

1. J. Mahlon Barnes.

2. A. J. Boshman represented three Massachusetts CMIU locals: 65 (Lynn), 151 (Waltham), and 324 (Gloucester).

3. The motion was on a preamble, introduced by E. Wolf of Brooklyn CMIU 132, that read: "Wage slavery being the outcome of our anarchistic industrial productive system, we believe it the duty of labor to organize in an economic organization as well as a separate political party, to ameliorate and emancipate with view of attaining the cooperative commonwealth" (CMIU, *Proceedings of the Twentieth Session of the Cigar Makers' International Union of America* [1893], p. 13). After a debate that lasted much of the day on Sept. 28, the convention voted down this preamble 83⅝ to 263⅜.

4. A reference to two preambles brought before the 1891 CMIU convention. One, introduced by Charles Drees of Tacoma, Wash., CMIU 113, was postponed indefinitely by a vote of 144 to 16. The other, offered by Frederick Schaefer of New York City CMIU 90, was withdrawn after its first section was defeated 51 to 220.

5. The preamble presented by A. F. Boyard of Victoria, B.C., CMIU 211 read: "Organization being necessary for the amelioration and emancipation of labor, we have organized the Cigar Makers' International Union of America, and recognize the fact that the final emancipation of labor can only be accomplished by the combined economic and political action of the wage workers" (CMIU, *Proceedings*, p. 13). It was turned down by a vote of 135⅔ to 212⅔.

To Josiah Dyer

Oct. 31, [1893]

Mr. Josiah B. Dyer,
Sec. Granite Cutters Nat. Union
98 Main St. Concord, N.H.
Dear Sir and Brother:—

Last week while in Washington the Executive Council of the American Federation of Labor called upon the heads of the various departments including Secretary Carlisle, the Attorney General[1] and the Assistant Supervising Architect[2] (the Chief[3] being out of the city at the time). From our effort we are decidedly of the opinion that it is better to secure executive action on the part of the Secretary of the Treasury than to depend upon either the Courts or new legislation.[4]

What is required is that you will ascertain the number of instances where the Eight Hour Law has been violated. Have the evidence forwarded to this office and you may rest assured that everything will be done in order to secure the enforcement of the law.

I repeat that the members of the Council were fully impressed with the belief that the law can be enforced, not only upon the buildings in course of construction but upon the material furnished. You do your part of the work herein outlined—and you may depend upon the Council doing its duty. We must take specific action to secure a decision, not from the Attorney General but from the executive departments which will in effect reverse the opinion of Attorney General Miller[5] and set the matter at rest. If we secure one department to act in accordance with our understanding of the law it will be much easier to secure the enforcement of the law by all the departments of the Government.

Kindly asking you to give this matter your immediate attention, and with kindest wishes to you and hopes for success, I am,

Fraternally Yours   Saml Gompers.
President. American Federation of Labor.

TLpS, reel 7, vol. 10, p. 4, SG Letterbooks, DLC.

1. Richard Olney (1835-1917), an attorney and Democrat from Massachusetts, served as U.S. attorney general from 1893 to 1895 and as U.S. secretary of state from 1895 to 1897.
2. H. C. McLean was assistant supervising architect and chief clerk in the federal supervising architect's office.
3. Willoughby J. Edbrooke.
4. Dyer had complained to SG concerning violations of the eight-hour law that Congress passed in August 1892 limiting to eight hours the work of construction laborers on public works (U.S. *Statutes at Large*, 27: 340). During the next two years SG tried unsuccessfully to document violations in order to strengthen his case for an enforcement order from Secretary of the Treasury John G. Carlisle. He received approval and funding from the AFL Executive Council for an apparently abortive plan to gather evidence by placing AFL agents at work sites where there were suspected violations and, for a time, he retained Henry Blair to prepare the presentation to Carlisle.
5. On Aug. 24, 1892, William Henry Harrison Miller (1840-1917), U.S. attorney general from 1889 to 1893, rendered an opinion that the 1892 eight-hour law applied only to those employed in the construction of public works and not to labor on the materials used in such projects.

To James O'Connell[1]

Nov. 3, [1893]

Mr. Jas. O'Connell,
Grand Master Machinist Intl. Association of Machinists
14 N. 9th. St. Richmond, Va.
My Dear Sir:—

I have the honor to acknowledge the receipt of your favor of the 1st. inst. the contents of which are carefully noted, and I beg to assure you that the perusal of the letter gratified me exceedingly, inasmuch as it indicated not only a fraternal spirit but what all thinking men must agree is an evidence of progress not only in one organization but along the whole line of the labor movement.

You say that in compliance with instructions from the convention of your International Association held at Indianapolis, a resolution will shortly be submitted to the referendum vote of the members whether the word "white" shall be stricken out from your constitution, and you ask me further if an affirmative vote is had upon that proposition whether I can give you any assurance that the division in the organizations of machinists will cease a[nd] be a thing of the past.

In order that a comprehensive answer may be given to your question it is necessary to recite briefly a few incidents which have occurred within the past five years.

The American Federation of Labor was instituted upon the idea that to the Union of the trade belongs absolute jurisdiction on all matters connected with that trade. That principle is just as applicable to your Association as to any other. The recognition of this cardinal principle, however, did not deny us the right of expressing the sentiments of trade unionism against any matter involving the general interests of the labor movement.

With a view of bringing the organized toilers of our country into closer communion with each other, and recognizing that your Association was outside the pale of the American Federation of Labor, I opened up a correspondence with one of your predecessors[2] with the object that the affiliation of your Intl. Association with the great trade unions of our country under the banner of the American Federation of Labor might be accomplished.

From that correspondence resulted the developed fact that an inherent weakness as well as the declaration of a wrong principle existed in the International Association. I sought to convey this fact to your predecessor as well as to the members of your organization, and I am pleased to say that from that time a steady progress has been gained until now the matter is to be decided by the membership, and I hope, affirmatively.

A number of Unions of machinists throughout the country were corresponding with me at the time and these organizations protested against becoming part of your Intl. Association so long as the objectionable feature was retained and the affiliation with the A.F. of L. had not been consummated.

At the Detroit convention of the A.F. of L. this spirit and thought took shape, namely, that your Association should be communicated with for the purpose of attaining the end expressed and desired, and a resolution adopted that in the event of a negative answer being given that the Machinists Unions outside of your Association should be invited to attend a conference for the purpose of discussing the situation.

It is a matter of general knowledge that I attended your convention held in Pittsburgh and that the questions were decided negatively. I had no alternative but to call a conference. When it was held I then addressed the assembled delegates who had decided to form the International Union.[3] There were two representatives of your Association present and they can verify what I say that it was a distinct understanding that as soon as your Intl. Association eliminated the word "white" from its constitution and became affiliated with the American Federation of Labor, that from that moment they would become part of your International Association and thereafter work in accord and harmony with it.

This is the situation today. It was a solemn compact and clear understanding and must be lived up to without evasion or reservation. I feel convinced that little or no antagonism would manifest itself against the achievement of unity and harmony among the machinists of our country providing the actions referred to are accomplished by your Association.

You may count on me positively to live up to the other statements I have made in connection with this entire matter.

It afforded me extreme pleasure to learn of the growth, and extension and beneficent influence of your Association, and I employ no idle words when I express the sincere hope that the time is near at hand when every machinist in the country will be under the banner of your Association and upon its folds may be written, progress, reform, protection and defense of all.

Again expressing the hope that the vote of the members may eliminate any measure tending towards retarding the full success of your Association, and the labor movement, and with kindest wishes, I am,

Fraternally Yours   Saml Gompers.
President. American Federation of Labor.

TLpS, reel 7, vol. 10, pp. 18-20, SG Letterbooks, DLC.

1. James O'CONNELL was grand master machinist of the International Association of Machinists from 1893 to 1911.

2. Thomas Wilson TALBOT was grand master machinist of the National Association of Machinists from 1889 to 1890.

3. The International Machinists' Union of America.

To Frank Notton[1]

Nov. 10, [1893]

Mr. Frank M. Nolton,
Genl. Organizer A.F. of L.
807 10th. Ave. Ashland, Wis.
Dear Sir and Brother:—

Your favor of the 6th. came duly to hand and contents noted.

I am pleased to learn that the wage-workers of your city take an active interest in the movement of labor for improved conditions, and that they seek to maintain their position by organization. In no other way can we hope to secure justice for ourselves and our fellow-workers.

There is one element I note with regret. It seems to me that religious organizations of whatever character should never be permitted to interfere with the growth of the organizations of labor. We have no antipathy or antagonism to religious organizations known by any name, but the more the wage-workers learn that their Unions should be kept free from religious influences the sooner the dawn of emancipation from the thraldom of wrong and injustice. The Protestant, the Catholic, the Jew and the free thinking unfair employers are all besmirched by the same tar. Religious professions or the absence of them count for naught when the question of the interests of the toiling masses are at stake. Their sole aim is to obtain labor at the lowest possible wage that the toilers are willing to work for and as a rule they do not ask what a man's religion is but how cheap and how long he will work.

It is positively ridiculous and suicidal for us as wage-workers to allow matters of religion to interfere with the progress and success of our movement. Every man should be permitted to pray at the altar he prefers without let or hindrance. Coming into the meeting of the Union the questions of labor's interests and the interests of our families and our fellow men should be uppermost in our minds. All other divisions and causes for antagonism and bickering should be left on the outside.

I earnestly hope that you will impress this upon the minds of our fellow wage-workers of Ashland, and advise me of the result.

With kind wishes and hoping to hear from you as frequently as convenient, I am,

Fraternally Yours   Saml Gompers.
President. American Federation of Labor.

TLpS, reel 7, vol. 10, p. 32, SG Letterbooks, DLC.

1. Frank M. Notton of Ashland, Wis., was a sign painter and general organizer for the AFL.

To Henry Spaeter[1]

Nov. 10, [1893]

Mr. Henry J. Spaeter,
13 Chestnut St. Belleville, Ill.
Dear Sir and Brother:—

Your favor of the 6th. came duly to hand and contents noted.

Replying thereto permit me to say that under the circumstances you mention it seems that nothing else could be done but to secure a charter for the members of your Union.[2] I think, however, that a serious mistake will be made if you are to be known by the name of "German" Hod Carriers Union. If that name would be proper, there is no reason why the Irish Hod Carriers Union, the Italian Hod Carriers Union etc. should not be formed and thus we would have workmen instead of organizing in bodies capable of effecting some advantage and good in their interests, continually bickering and antagonizing each other.

Under the circumstances you mention it may be wisest to organize a Union of Hod Carriers composed exclusively of white men, provided the spirit of fraternity is maintained, that is of trying to work in harmony with each other so that the interests of the Hod Carriers will not be jeopardized, and a charter could be issued to you as Hod Carriers Union with its number regularly designated by this office. Without calling yourselves either German Hod Carriers Union or white Hod Carriers Union the designation of your number would in itself be a sufficient distinguishing mark between the unions composed of white and black men.

If you will act upon this suggestion it can be carried out and unity maintained, while at the same time not flying in the face of the color prejudice.

I enclose to you herein a blank application which can be filled out should the Union decide to follow the course suggested.

With kindest wishes and hoping to hear from you at your earliest convenience, I am,

Fraternally Yours   Saml Gompers.
President. American Federation of Labor.

TLpS, reel 7, vol. 10, p. 33, SG Letterbooks, DLC.

1. Henry J. Spaeter was a Belleville, Ill., laborer.

2. The AFL chartered Hod Carriers' Protective Union 6237 of Belleville, Ill., in December 1893.

To the Board of Aldermen of New York City and County

[ca. Nov. 15, 1893]

To the Honorable the Board of Aldermen of the City and County of New York, Sitting as a board of County Canvassers to canvass the vote cast at the General Election held, November 7th, 1893.

Your Petitioner, Samuel Gompers, a citizen of the State of New York, and a duly qualified elector and voter therein, residing in the City and County of New York, and a Candidate [. . .] for the office of Delegate to the Constitutional Convention from the 9th Senate District of the City and County of New York, at the Election held November 7th, 1893, upon the affidavits of fraud herewith presented, claims that he was duly elected as such delegate at such election, and that had all the votes cast for him thereat been counted he would have appeared to be so elected upon the returns now before your honorable body, and he hereby requests that this Board adjourn the canvassing of the returns of the various Election Districts for said Election, contained in said 9th Senate District, of the votes cast for Delegates to said Constitutional Convention, for a reasonable time to enable your petitioner to obtain further evidences of fraud which he has been informed exists; and Your Petitioner hereby further protests against the canvassing of said returns as now presented to your honorable body, and demands an investigation of the charges of fraud in the election aforesaid, and in the returns of the votes cast for said Constitutional Delegates in said 9th Senate District; and Your Petitioner further requests a notification from your honorable body of the time and place which may be fixed for hearing the evidence and arguments as to said frauds, in order that he may be present thereat in person and by Counsel.

And your Petitioner further demands of your honorable Body that you canvass the votes cast for him as said Delegate to the Constitutional Convention for the 9th Senate District in the City of New York, and declare him by your return duly elected to such office, as he would have been so declared upon the returns made by the several inspectors of election, had not said votes been wrongfully counted.[1]

All of which is respectfully submitted.

Saml Gompers.

TLpS, Files of the Office of the President, General Correspondence, reel 59, *AFL Records.*

1. SG did not serve as a delegate to the New York constitutional convention.

To the Executive Council of the AFL

New York, Nov. 23, 1893.

To the Executive Council of the A.F. of L.

Fellow-Workmen: —

I am in receipt of a letter from Mr. H. J. Skeffington Secretary of the Boot and Shoe Workers Int'l. Union in which he calls attention to the fact that a number of local unions of Shoe Makers have called a convention to be held at Chicago during the coming week beginning Monday Nov. 27th. for the purpose of forming what they term the "Western Union of Shoe Makers."[1] It is a movement to secede from the International Union and to divide the organization of the shoe makers still further under different heads and in different camps.

Mr. Skeffington states that though he has been partially successful by correspondence in inducing a few Unions to refrain from participating in the convention which had previously favored so doing, yet he believes that an injury cannot be prevented unless he is there himself to head it off.

He calls attention to the fact that the strike of 2700 members of the International Union[2] has drained the funds, not only of the general organization but of every local, and that they have not a dollar which he can utilize for the purpose of defraying his expenses to go to Chicago and give this matter his immediate and personal attention. He therefore makes application for a loan of $250.00 to be returned within three months.

Secretary Evans, Treasurer Lennon and the undersigned had a consultation in reference to this matter, and decided that the application for a loan should not be considered, but inasmuch as the circumstances were well known to be as stated by Mr. Skeffington it became the duty of the Executive Council to aid in the prevention of a secession movement, when the same can possibly be accomplished by the expenditure of a part of our funds. Not desiring to take this matter in our own hands it was agreed that the following proposition should be submitted to the Executive Council.

That the sum of $150.00 be appropriated towards defraying the expenses of Mr. H. J. Skeffington or other representative of the Boot and Shoe Workers for the purpose of proceeding to the place where the convention is to be held, and to use his best efforts to prevent a schism in the organization of the Boot and Shoe Workers.[3]

Kindly return your vote upon the above proposition at your earliest convenience and oblige,

Yours Fraternally   Saml Gompers.
President.

N.B. Members of the E.C. residing out of N.Y. City will kindly return their vote by wire unprepaid.

S. G.

TLpS, AFL Executive Council Vote Books, reel 8, *AFL Records.*

1. In his letter of Oct. 21, 1893, to SG, Skeffington referred to the organization as the "Western Association of Shoemakers" and characterized its leaders as "Delegates to our recent Convention at Chicago" who "failed to have their own way there" (Boot and Shoe Workers' International Union Records, reel 139, *AFL Records*).

2. Pray, Small, and Co., boot and shoe manufacturers in Auburn, Me., locked out the female operatives in the company's stitching department on Aug. 1, 1893, after they refused to accept a wage reduction and sign individual contracts with the company to replace the contract previously negotiated for them by Boot and Shoe Workers' International Union (BSWIU) 21. By the end of the month six other shoe companies, who together with Pray and Small comprised the Auburn Shoe Manufacturers' Association, also instituted lockouts; BSWIU 21 then called out the remaining union members still employed in the seven shops. Members of the Lasters' Protective Union of America joined the walkout in September. Union mass meetings in Auburn and surrounding towns for a time dissuaded nonunionists from taking the jobs of the strikers. The Manufacturers' Association obtained a temporary injunction in October prohibiting unionists from distributing circulars or using other methods of discouraging workers from taking their places. By the end of November, using new workers, including Armenian immigrants, the firms had resumed nearly full production. The strikers were unsuccessful in attempts to establish a cooperative factory and by January 1894 employers had largely won the struggle, though many union members remained out indefinitely. The 1893 AFL convention authorized a boycott on Pray, Small, and Co. and, after a personal investigation by SG (see "To the Executive Council of the AFL," Feb. 5, 1894, below), the AFL Executive Council voted to implement the boycott.

3. The AFL Executive Council approved the proposal. SG also wrote a letter to Skeffington stating that he was opposed to further division among the shoe workers and urging him to go to Chicago to prevent "the consummation of so dastardly a scheme" (Nov. 23, 1893, reel 7, vol. 10, p. 70, SG Letterbooks, DLC). In a separate letter of the same date SG suggested Skeffington use his letter to promote unity.

To P. M. Arthur[1]

Nov. 28, [1893]

Mr. P. M. Arthur,
Grand Chief, Bro'd. of Locomotive Engineers,
Cleveland, O.
My Dear Sir:—

The press of the country publish a statement that General Superintendent White[2] of the Railway Mail Service of the United States has prepared a bill[3] and submitted it together with his report, to Post Master General Wilson S. Bissell,[4] who, it is said, will approve of the same and refer it to Congress.

The purport of the Bill is, I am informed, to regard a member of any railroad organization who shall, by reason of a dispute with any railroad Company, delay the transmission of the mails, by quitting work (strike) as outlaw, placed in the same category as a robber, to be brought before the Courts and tried for the alleged offence.

It seems to me that this would strike at the very root of the organizations of the railroad employes. In fact, it would be tantamount to a denial of the right of the workmen to seek redress for grievances, their right to quit the employment of the Company, and in another form reintroduce a system of serfdom abolished nearly a century ago.

The thought has occurred to me that the time has arrived when the railroad organizations should in no uncertain tones voice their sentiments, assert their rights and not allow a proposition which in its application must result in a denial of men's natural right to resist injustice and struggle for improved conditions.

In view of this state of affairs I have determined to bring this subject before the forthcoming convention of the American Federation of Labor and to obtain an expression of the sentiment of that body upon the matter.[5]

Would it not be advisable for a representative of your organization to meet a Committee of the A.F. of L. for the purpose of taking this subject under consideration. I commend this matter to you most earnestly, and respectfully ask you whether you could not make it convenient to be there in person, or if that is inconvenient, to appoint some officer or member of your Brotherhood to represent it in a conference with the A.F. of L. Committee.

The convention of the A.F. of L. will be held Dec. 11-16 1893 at the Common Council Chambers, (City Hall) Chicago, Ill., the headquarters of the Federation being at the Briggs House, cor. 5th. Ave. and Randolph St.

Fraternally Yours   Saml Gompers.
President. American Federation of Labor.

TLpS, reel 7, vol. 10, p. 84, SG Letterbooks, DLC.

1. Peter M. ARTHUR was grand chief engineer of the Brotherhood of Locomotive Engineers from 1874 until 1903.

2. James E. White served as general superintendent of the Division of Railway Mail Service of the U.S. Post Office Department from 1890 to 1907.

3. Several bills were introduced in Congress dealing with obstruction of the mails in the spring of 1894 but none became law.

4. Wilson Shannon Bissell served as U.S. postmaster general from 1893 to 1895.

5. In his message to the 1893 AFL convention, SG reported on his correspondence with the railroad brotherhoods concerning efforts to defeat a proposed bill to punish interference with mail trains. The committee on the president's report concurred in these efforts.

To John O'Sullivan

Nov. 28, [1893]

Mr. John F. O'Sullivan,
258 Commercial St. Boston, Mass.
Dear Sir and Brother:—

I am in receipt of your favor of the 27th. inst. the contents of which are carefully noted.

In reply permit me to say that I was much shocked at the revelations at Philadelphia.[1] As a matter of fact if Mr. Powderly has been as dishonest as Mr. Hayes[2] describes him and charges him with being, it at once stamps Hayes as being the worse man of the two. The fact that he remained silent all these years while this crookedness was going on and only waited until they quarelled before exposing their alleged joint wrong-doing, inculpates him beyond question. Then again, when Mr. Powderly was reelected how could Hayes consent to be a fellow officer with a man whom he charged with being thoroughly dishonest and unscrupulous, a forger and a perjurer.

You know that as a matter of fact Hayes has always been the greater antagonist to the trade unions of the two, was always bitter, vindictive and relentless. To be frank with you I much regret, not so much the fact of Mr. Powderly leaving the office of the Chief Executive of the Knights of Labor, but rather the manner in which he was forced to do so. All his years of work have not saved him from mental Liliputians and destructionists. It is a repetition of the old cry of Hosannah, followed by that of "crucify him."

At present there is nothing absolutely new going on around the office. Today I start for Schnectady and will return by Thursday and then shall have to apply myself strictly to getting out my report for the A.F. of L. convention.

Won't the "Globe" send either you or Willard[3] to Chicago.[4] I believe that we will have a very interesting convention. Matters of great importance will have to be decided there.

Many thanks for your kind suggestion and good wishes. Friend Evans joins me in kindest regards and in asking you to remember us to our friends in Boston.

Anticipating the pleasure of meeting you soon, I am,

Fraternally Yours   Saml Gompers
President. American Federation of Labor.

TLpSr, reel 7, vol. 10, p. 87, SG Letterbooks, DLC.

1. The KOL General Assembly met Nov. 14-28, 1893, in Philadelphia. General Secretary Treasurer John Hayes charged General Master Workman Terence Powderly with misuse of the Order's funds, general neglect and incompetence, and working with Republicans to sabotage the 1892 reelection campaign of Grover Cleveland. The assembly's finance committee exonerated Powderly and he won reelection. The General Assembly rejected Powderly's nominees for the General Executive Board, however. He tendered his resignation over the issue on Nov. 25, and, two days later, the delegates voted to accept his resignation.

2. John William HAYES was a member of the KOL General Executive Board from 1884 to 1916, serving as general secretary-treasurer from 1888 until 1902 and as the Knights' last general master workman from 1902 until the Order closed its central office in 1916.

3. Cyrus Field Willard was a labor editor for the *Boston Globe;* he was active in utopian socialist movements.

4. The *Boston Globe* carried coverage of the convention, without a by-line.

To Samuel Goldwater

Dec. 1, [1893]

Mr. Samuel Goldwater,
146 21st. St. Detroit, Mich.
My Dear Friend:—

Your favor of the 28th. came duly to hand, and I assure you that I was very much pleased to hear from you although I can truly say I regret you find yourself in the condition you do. I think you will accept it as a genuine expression of my wish that you may soon find remunerative employment, and that both beneficial and congenial.

Yes, I know the methods employed by some men calling themselves socialists. I have read and heard of wrong and even crimes committed in the name of freedom, but for men supposed to have an ideal, resorting to such contemptible and depraved methods as the so-called socialists do, is almost beyond belief.

So far as I am personally concerned they neither worry nor annoy me. The only element that disturbs me about them is that it would take time to convince our plain sailing every day unionists of the designs of these men, the same as it took a long time to expose the antagonism to trade unionism of the K. of L. That it will come I am sure, and when that day of awakening and reckoning arrives you will find such a cyclone strike these men that they will never again show their heads or pretend to speak in the name of labor.

You understand me, or at least you should, that I have not a word to say against socialists as such or socialism as a science or a theory but those in our country who prate loudest of their socialistic partisanship have rendered the greatest service to the capitalist class they were capable of in antagonizing the trade union movement.

I should certainly like to have seen you in Chicago and hope you will be able to arrange matters so as to be there, even though not as a delegate, then as a friend of our movement, and those assembled I feel sure will be pleased to see and greet you.

Maintain your stand by all means. You have both the intelligence as well as right on your side and in the end these must prevail.

Again expressing the hope that you may find work suitable to your taste and interests, and reciprocating your kind wishes for success, I am,

Sincerely Yours   Saml Gompers.
President. American Federation of Labor.

TLpS, reel 7, vol. 10, p. 94, SG Letterbooks, DLC.

To Woyt Losky[1]

Dec. 1, [1893]

Mr. Woyt Losky,
Sec. Hotel and Restaurant Employes Nat. Alliance,
428 N. 7th. St. Phila, Pa.
Dear Sir and Brother:—

Your favor of the 29th. came duly to hand and contents noted.

In it you say that some of the Unions attached to the National Alliance owe from six to nine months' dues, that by suspending such unions it would throw out a majority of the Executive Board and also some of the constitutional officers elected by the convention. You then ask the following questions:

1st. Can a minority of the Board legally suspend the majority by suspending their Unions?

2nd. By reinstatement of said Unions would such officers resume their offices?

You forward me a constitution of the National Alliance for my guidance on that matter. Both from it as well as from my experience in the labor movement, I should say that when your Executive Board in enforcing its constitution suspends a local it does not suspend the members of that local who are desirous of remaining true to the National Alliance, that is, in their loyalty as well as the payment of the required amounts that they may be indebted to the National Alliance. In other words, if a member or a number of members of a local union desire to maintain their relations with the N.A. and a majority of that local fails to live up to the constitutional requirements, the minority should not be deprivied of their rights to be in good standing and full fellowship with their National Union.

This seems to me to be an answer to both your questions. I would say in addition thereto that in view of the present industrial stagnation the officers of National trade unions should exercise some discretion before using extreme measures for the enforcement of the payment of taxes from local organizations whose members may have failed to pay by reason of lack of employment.

You have asked for an expression of opinion and it is given you kindly and fraternally, but without any desire on my part to have you rest under the impression that you are bound thereby.

With kindest wishes for success, I am,

Fraternally Yours   Saml Gompers.

President. American Federation of Labor.

TLpS, reel 7, vol. 10, p. 96, SG Letterbooks, DLC.

1. Woyt LOSKY was general secretary of the Hotel and Restaurant Employees' National Alliance from 1893 to 1896.

To Oliver Teall[1]

Dec. 5, [1893]

Mr. Oliver Sumner Teall,
60 Wall St. N.Y. City.
Dear Sir: —

In compliance with your suggestion to advise you finally as to my acceptance of your invitation to aid in a movement to start soup houses, etc. in the city of New York for the coming Winter, I am constrained to say that I must be excused from acting in that capacity.

What the workingmen of the city of New York and the country want is work, in order that they may be self-sustaining, not charity which tends to humiliate them and destroy their independence. Organized labor is engaged in a movement to secure justice for labor, not alms. You will therefore no doubt observe that holding these views it would be most inappropriate for me to participate in the work you suggest.

The toiling masses of our country are in no wise responsible for their lack of employment and their distress. The blame lies at the doors of the wealth possessors and the so-called "captains of industry" who have so ruthlessly and so incompetently brought about the present conditions. Let them endeavor to right the wrongs they have committed.

I feel convinced that the time will come, sooner or later, when the outraged people will demand a reckoning from those who have assumed economic and political control, and who have so flagrantly violated their trusts.

Very Respectfully Yours   Saml Gompers.
President. American Federation of Labor.

TLpS, reel 7, vol. 10, p. 105, SG Letterbooks, DLC.

1. Oliver Sumner Teall, a real estate investor active in the Republican party, was chairman of a volunteer committee attempting to organize a relief effort for the homeless and hungry in New York City.

Samuel Gompers with John Burns (left) and David Holmes, 1894 (ICHi-10460).

Thomas Mann, 1894 (*Harper's Weekly*).

Kier Hardie, 1894 (*Harper's Weekly*).

Elizabeth Chambers Morgan, 1894 (Thomas J. and Elizabeth C. Morgan Collection, IU-HS).

Thomas J. Morgan, 1890s (Thomas J. Morgan Collection, ICU).

Daniel DeLeon with his son, Solon, c. 1890 (SHSW-WHi [X3] 33796).

A socialist cartoon on the antagonism between the SLP and Samuel Gompers and Henry Weissmann, 1893. The caption read: "Weissmann: 'Hurry up Sammy. We thought to head her off, but she is gaining on us at a fearful rate. If we jump, we'll get hurt; and if we don't, we'll be crushed or killed.' " The wheels of the handcar are labeled "Alleged Peoples Party," "Republican Nominee Labor Champion," and "Labor Fakirs Endorsements"; the train is labeled "SLP New York 22000 votes" (*People* [New York]).

A cartoon criticizing Samuel Gompers' position on silver, 1894 (*Rocky Mountain News* [Denver]).

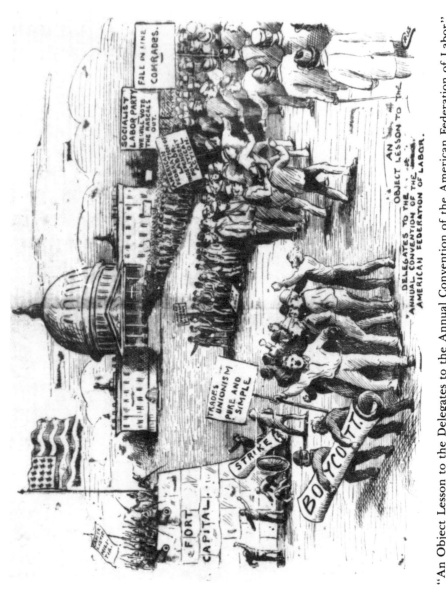

"An Object Lesson to the Delegates to the Annual Convention of the American Federation of Labor," December 1893 (*Chicago Labor*).

A cartoon commenting on the organization of the People's party at Cincinnati, May 1891 (*Judge*).

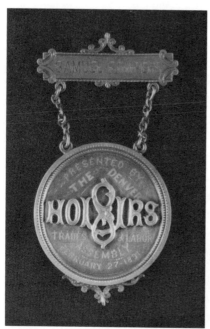

Eight-hour medal presented to Samuel Gompers by the Denver Trades and Labor Assembly, Feb. 27, 1891 (George Meany Memorial Archives, AFL-CIO).

Program of grand reception and ball given for Samuel Gompers by the Council of Federated Trades of the Pacific Coast, Mar. 14, 1891 (George Meany Memorial Archives, AFL-CIO).

· Grand Reception and Ball ·

· · Given Under the Auspices of the · ·

Council of Federated Trades of the Pacific Coast

· · In Honor of the Visit of · ·

Samuel Gompers
PRESIDENT AMERICAN FEDERATION OF LABOR

At Woodward's Gardens

Saturday Evening, March 14th

· · · 1891 · · ·

· Programme ·

1 Grand March and Lancers—*President Gompers*

2 Waltz—*American Federation of Labor*

3 Polka—*Our Visitors*

4 Schottische—*President Fuhrman*

5 York—*Sub-Federation*

6 Quadrille—*Lady Shoe-Fitters' Union*

7 Waltz—*All the Unions*

8 Polka—*Progress*

9 Schottische—*Prosperity*

10 Mazurka—*Organization*

11 Lancers—*Centralization*

12 Waltz—*Co-operation*

· Programme ·

13 Polka—*Arbitration*

14 La Marjolaine—*Good Will*

15 York—*To Victory*

16 Virginia Reel—*For the Old Folks*

17 Waltz—*Education*

18 Polka—*Rights of Labor*

19 Schottische—*Good Will of the Press*

20 Lancers—*Eight-Hour Movement*

21 York—*Labor Day*

22 Waltz—*Emancipation*

23 Quadrille—*To Our Friends*

24 Polka—*Council of Federated Trades*

A cartoon protesting the Sunday closing of the Chicago World's Fair, 1893. The caption read: "Workman—'For three long years Capitalism forced us to work every Sunday on the World's Fair, and the Church did not interfere; but now, having finished the work, we, the creators of the exposition, are not allowed on Sunday—our only day for rest and recreation—to look at the product of our toil.'" (*Labor* [St. Louis]).

Cover of the first issue of the *American Federationist,* March 1894.

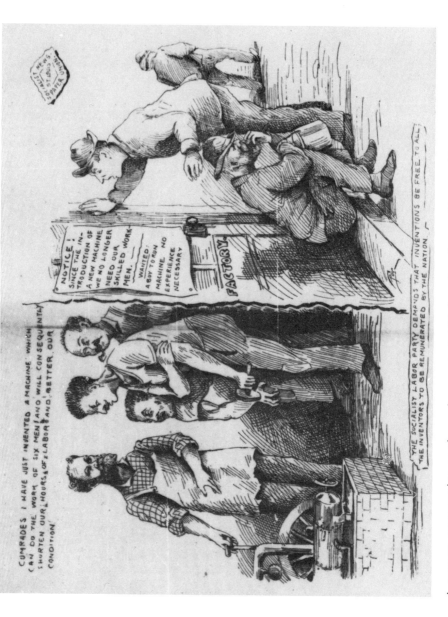

A cartoon commenting on the replacement of skilled workers by machinery, 1894 (*Chicago Labor*).

"Human nature, as described by Samuel F. Gompers, of the American Federation of Labor," 1894 (*Utica Saturday Globe*).

John McBride, 1895 (*Harper's Weekly*).

Samuel Gompers, 1894 (*Review of Reviews*).

The Political Program

When delegates to the AFL's Chicago convention took up consideration of resolution number 53 in December 1893, they reopened a longstanding debate on the question of independent political action and its relation to trade unionism. Motivated by the severe and still worsening economic depression and inspired by the Trades Union Congress of Great Britain's apparent embrace of an independent labor party, the resolution offered a "political program" that encompassed socialist, populist, and trade union demands and endorsed labor party politics "as an auxiliary to . . . economic action." Although convention delegates did not ratify the program as such, but voted simply to disseminate it to affiliates for their approval, their action seemed to signal a change in Federation policy. The convention's decision, labor journalist Eva McDonald Valesh reported, "was the most radical action ever taken by the A.F. of L."[1] The year-long debate that ensued, however, indicated that consensus on the question continued to elude the Federation.

Gompers encouraged all sides to debate the program in the pages of the *Federationist*. The question, in fact, dominated the very first issue of the journal, which appeared in March 1894. "I am satisfied that an independent labor party will be the outcome of the present movement in the A.F. of L. . . ," wrote Henry Weismann of the bakers' union, "but I am also convinced that its composition, its policy and its aims, will be in strict keeping with the sound Trade Union philosophy of the American Federation of Labor." Frank Foster, editor of the *Labor Leader* in Boston, disputed this notion. He argued that plank 10, which called for the collective ownership of the means of production and distribution, "means nothing more nor less than that the trade unions of America are to be simply annexes of the Socialistic Labor party." While Gompers did not comment directly in the *Federationist* on either the program as a whole or on plank 10, he clarified his position in an editorial. "In politics we shall be as we always have been, *independent*," he proclaimed. "Independent of all parties regardless under which name they may be known." In his view, economic organization was of primary importance, and voluntary political action a practical necessity.[2]

Thomas J. Morgan of the International Machinists' Union, an ardent proponent of a political labor party and, at this time, an active populist, recognized that plank 10 promised to alter significantly the direction of the labor movement. "Every other section is common place," he wrote in the *Federationist*, "but not so with number 10." This section of the platform, he stated forthrightly, "*is socialism* . . . and instead of concealing the fact, we would have your whole attention and thoughts directed to it, so that the vote may be the measure of your understanding and conviction." For Morgan, the collective ownership of the means of production meant that "the ownership of the iron and steel mills of the country shall be transferred from the Carnegies and the Fricks to the Amalgamated Association of Iron and Steel Workers."[3]

As the discussion of the program progressed, it evolved into a debate over trade unionism and its effectiveness in a changing economic world. Deteriorating social and economic conditions intensified this debate as high unemployment coupled with the increasing use of injunctions and coercive state power to break strikes tested the limits of "pure and simple" economic organization. Some workers contended that these new conditions required a "new trade unionism" based on political as well as economic power. "Strikes and boycotts have had their day," remarked James T. Kelly of the electrical workers' union, "and in the future organized labor must look for permanent advancement through education and the ballot." The journal of the American Flint Glass Workers maintained that it was "no use singing the praises of trades unions when everywhere there are idle men and women, and the strongest unions have lost their power of resistance against the monstrous combinations of modern capital." In the March issue of the *Federationist* Morgan chided those pure and simple unionists who dismissed plank 10 as "chasing rainbows," and he mocked their arguments in support of economic organization. "Better stay with the Carnegies, Fricks and such, nothing like our trusty weapons, the strike, boycott and political pull. See how we have reduced the hours of labor! See how we have raised our wages! See our success at Homestead, Buffalo, Cour d'elene, Tennessee! See the labor laws we have had placed on the statute books as a result of the political help we gave to candidates who were friends of labor! See how we overawe the State and federal courts! Aye, see the starving multitude, see the blind leading the blind, and the knaves (feasting) with the enemy."[4]

AFL Treasurer John B. Lennon rejected this criticism and insisted that "trade unions are by no means standing still either as to their demands for better conditions, nor as to the methods by which their objects shall be attained." Similarly, New York garment workers' leader

Henry White argued that real progress would be attained only as workers improved their standard of living through economic organization. "The effective use of the ballot which presupposes harmony of thought upon theoretical questions . . . has baffled the minds of the greatest of statesmen," he wrote. "Consequently a political movement to unite labor must spring necessarily from the primary movement of the trades unions."[5]

Although a number of AFL affiliates had already endorsed the program,[6] Gompers remained opposed to a political labor party, and in his presidential address to the AFL's 1894 convention he urged the delegates to "steer our ship of labor safe from that channel whose waters are strewn with shattered hopes and unions destroyed."[7] When the convention's discussion of the political program took place on Dec. 14 and 15, 1894, Gompers engaged a stenographer to record the debate, and the verbatim report thereby preserved was subsequently published by the Federation in pamphlet form.[8] After voting unanimously to consider the document section by section, the delegates deleted the preamble (1,345 to 861), accepted, with minor amendments, all but one of the planks, and added two new ones.[9] They rejected plank 10 (1,217 to 913), and substituted instead a plank calling for the abolition of the monopoly system of landholding. Finally, when asked to approve the amended platform as a whole (in a resolution substituted for the endorsement of political action), they refused to endorse it (735 to 1,173). This final vote resulted in confusion over the status of the planks that the convention had previously approved individually. The issue was not clarified until the following year, when the AFL's New York convention adopted them as its "legislative demands."[10]

Notes

1. AFL, *Proceedings*, 1893, p. 37; *Chicago Inter Ocean*, Dec. 17, 1893. The resolution initially proposed submitting the program "for the favorable consideration" of the affiliates. The word "favorable" was deleted by a vote of 1,253 to 1,182 (AFL, *Proceedings*, 1893, pp. 37-38). For the 1893 convention's consideration of the political program, see "New Labor Platform," Dec. 15, 1893, in "Excerpts from News Accounts of the 1893 Convention of the AFL in Chicago," below.

The AFL Executive Council, meeting shortly after the convention, voted to submit the program to the Federation's affiliates to "consider and vote upon each of the 10 [sic] propositions separately, and instruct their delegates [to the AFL's next convention] as to each proposition." In addition, the Council ordered the political platform to be printed monthly in the *American Federationist* throughout 1894 (AFL Executive Council Minutes, Jan. 15, 1894, reel 2, *AFL Records*. For SG's initial public reaction to the political program, see "An Article in the *New York Herald*," Jan. 7, 1894, below).

2. Henry Weismann, "The New and the Old," *American Federationist* 1 (Mar. 1894):

8; Frank K. Foster, "Labor Politics, Policies and Platforms," ibid., p. 6; [SG], "Salutatory," ibid., p. 10.

3. Thomas J. Morgan, "The Programme," ibid., p. 7.

4. James T. Kelly to the Editor of the *American Federationist*, ibid., p. 17; for the Flint Glass Workers' editorial see "An Article in the *People*, Mar. 18, 1894, below; Morgan, "The Programme," p. 7.

5. John B. Lennon, "Organized Labor Means Progress," *American Federationist* 1 (Sept. 1894): 142; Henry White, "Are Strikes Failures?" ibid., p. 143.

6. John R. Commons et al., *History of Labour in the United States*, 4 vols. (1918-35; reprint ed., New York, 1966), 2: 511; Philip S. Foner, *History of the Labor Movement in the United States*, vol. 2, *From the Founding of the A.F. of L. to the Emergence of American Imperialism*, 2d ed. (New York, 1975), p. 289.

7. AFL, *Proceedings*, 1894, p. 14. See "President Gompers' Report," Dec. 10, 1894, in "Excerpts from Accounts of the 1894 Convention of the AFL in Denver," below.

8. See "An Interesting Discussion on a Political Programme at the Denver Convention of the American Federation of Labor," Dec. 14-15, 1894, in "Excerpts from Accounts of the 1894 Convention of the AFL in Denver," below.

9. The two additional planks called for the repeal of conspiracy and penal laws and the "abolition of the monopoly privilege of issuing money" (AFL, *Proceedings*, 1894, p. 39).

10. AFL, *Proceedings*, 1895, p. 67.

Excerpts from News Accounts of the 1893 Convention of the AFL in Chicago

[December 12, 1893]

LABOR IN COUNCIL.

The American Federation of Labor began its thirteenth annual convention at 10 o'clock yesterday morning in the Council Chamber of the City Hall with 142 delegates present.

. . .

The next thing on the programme was an address of welcome in behalf of the labor unions of the city, which was delivered by W. C. Pomeroy,[1] Vice President of the Trade and Labor Assembly.

Mr. Pomeroy drew rather a gloomy picture of the condition of the wageworker of Chicago in his address. He said in part:

["]In the name of a hundred thousand idle men I bid you welcome. . . .

["]In the name of toil I welcome you within the gates of the mistress of the inland seas, where the palace shines bright in the ante-Christmas-tide and the hovel holds not a faggot to warm its freezing tenants.

["]In the name of those edifices erected to the glory of God, but whose doors at night are tightly closed to the freezing poor.

["]In the name of those ministers who fatten from the vineyards of God, meanwhile forgetting that God's children are hungry and have no place to lay their heads.

["]In the name of the fashionable congregation of the fashionable church in the fashionable suburb, where the palace, filled with warmth within, drops from the eaves the melting snows upon the frozen hovel where poverty hides its haggard soul on the very threshold of hypocrisy.

["]In the name of these things I bid you welcome.

["]In the name of the child slave whose young life is sacrificed on the altar of greed, I bid you welcome.

["]In the name of the seamstress in the sweater's den who perils honor to toil for bread, I bid you welcome.

["]In the name of the haggard sweater, himself a victim to greed, I bid you welcome.

["]In the name of the pillars of the sweating system, millionaires and deacons, whose souls are endangered by avarice for gold, I bid you welcome.

["]In the name of the wage slave whose sweat of blood is coined into golden ducats in the mint of mammon, I welcome you here.

["]In the name of our hospitals filled with homeless maimed.

["]In the name of our insane asylums filled with paupers crazed by care and crime.

["]In the name of our poorhouses filled to over flowing in a land of plenty.

["]In the name of our morgue and its outcast unknown dead.

["]In the name of that populous suburb, the potter's field, and its countless paupers' graves — in the name of all these I bid you welcome.

["]In the name of that homeless wanderer in this desert of stone and steel, that wayfarer whose wolfish hunger hounds him ever onward, whose sleepless eyes wildly seek shelter and slumber, whose hopeless heart lies leaden in his bosom, whose blank despair grows darker and darker every hour, whose brain grows faint for want of food, whose shivering, shrinking form grows sick at the sight of his own shrunken shadow, whose ambition is dead, whose hope is dead, whose heart is dead, whose soul is dead, whose dismal past is the background of a future whose horizon looms darkly above the grave; in short, that necessary product of American freedom and prosperity — the American tramp. In his name, and in the name of his million brothers of sorrow, I welcome you to the city whose motto is 'I will.'["]

. . .

Chicago Inter Ocean, Dec. 12, 1893.

1. William C. Pomeroy represented the Hotel and Restaurant Employees' National Alliance.

[December 13, 1893]

ALTGELD IS INVITED.

. . .

Then a committee representing the evangelical churches of Chicago asked to be heard. It consisted of the Rev. Dr. H. W. Thomas,[1] Dr. Arthur Edwards,[2] the Rev. Simeon Gilbert,[3] the Rev. O. P. Gifford,[4] the Rev. R. A. White,[5] Bishop Fallows,[6] the Rev. M. L. Williston,[7] Rabbi Brown,[8] and the Rev. Father Hatton. The Rev. Mr. Williston, as secretary of the committee, read the following:

["]At a meeting of ministers Monday afternoon, representing nearly every religious denomination in the city, assembled to consider the present extraordinary emergency in Chicago, a committee was appointed to present to your body the following expression of fraternal interest and fellowship, which was unanimously and enthusiastically adopted:

["]It was resolved that, in believing, as we are sure you also do, that love to God is proved by love to man, we earnestly desire a happy and satisfactory issue to the deliberations of your influential body on behalf of the millions of industrious men whom you represent, whose interests you have at heart, and whose faithful labor is a strong foundation stone beneath the temple of the national well being.

["]We also desire at all times, and most especially in this crisis of bitter trouble, to act with you in all practical ways in relieving the present distress and in promoting those high and worthy ends which you worthily seek.["]

Then a number of clergymen made short encouraging speeches.

President Gompers' Reply.

President Gompers said in reply:

["]The words of encouragement you give us we highly appreciate. For too many years have ministers of the gospel of all denominations used their power in the pulpit instead of along the line of humanity and progress in talking in the opposite direction. (Cheers.) Too long have the ministers talked not to workingmen, but down to them. (Cheers.) Our work is right and reaches the lowest. We go down to the dregs and raise them up to cleanliness and virtue and honor and their rights and so our work, as it is being better understood, will have the sympathy of all mankind. Concerning the nobility of God we propose to carry out 'Thy will be done on earth as it is in heaven.' (Cheers.) We want to go to heaven. Those who scarcely believe in a heaven say, if there is one, they want to go there. But we want a little of that heaven here. (Laughter and cheers.) If I read the signs of the times aright, we are going to get it. In the name of the great army of organized discontent in America, gentlemen, we thank you for your greeting.["] (Cheers.)

Dr. Thomas made a brief reply, then in a quiet, rather dramatic way extended his hand to Gompers, and with a hearty handshake bade him good-by and godspeed.

. . .

Chicago Tribune, Dec. 13, 1893.

1. Hiram W. Thomas was pastor of the Peoples' Church.
2. Arthur Edwards was the editor of the *Northwestern Christian Advocate,* a publication of the Methodist Episcopal Church.
3. Simeon Gilbert was associate editor of *Advance,* a publication associated with the Congregationalist Church.
4. Orrin P. Gifford was pastor of the Immanuel Baptist Church.
5. Rufus A. White was pastor of the Englewood Universalist Church.

6. Bishop Samuel Fallows was associated with St. Paul's Reformed Episcopal Church.
7. Martin L. Williston.
8. Dr. Edward B. M. Browne was rabbi of Congregation Emanuel.

[December 14, 1893]

WILL NOT ARBITRATE

After a spirited debate lasting over two hours the American Federation of Labor yesterday declared against the principle of arbitration in disputes between employers and employes.

The debate brought out some curious features in connection with the subject. As one of the delegates expressed it: "It seems like a severe comment on our boasted progress when the organized workingmen of America declare against the principle of arbitration at a time when one of the most conservative European governments has just declared in favor of the principle of compulsory arbitration." The speaker referred to the action of the English government in the coal miners' strike,[1] which has just been referred to a board of arbitration.

Yet the delegates to the convention seemed to be thoroughly posted on what they were doing, and the arguments showed that their action was not the result of any hasty conclusion, but of deep thought on the subject from a theoretical standpoint, backed up by considerable experience in the practical working out of the system.

In a general way the delegates who opposed the adoption of the resolution did so on the ground that compulsory arbitration as a general rule was not only impracticable, but, under existing circumstances, would work positive disadvantage to labor organizations and workingmen.

How the Question Came Up.

The question came up on the report of T. J. Morgan,[2] chairman of the committee on resolutions, on the following resolution, which was submitted for consideration in the programme of business:

["]*Whereas,* Labor is the creator of capital, we believe that labor should be placed on an equality with capital before the law, and

["]*Whereas,* Labor is compelled to treat or negotiate with the representatives of capital in fixing a price for labor, therefore be it

["]*Resolved,* That the Federation of Labor take the necessary steps through their president to formulate a bill and get the same before the different State Legislatures, making it obligatory on the part of corporations and the representatives of capital to treat and negotiate with the representatives of labor in conference or otherwise in the settlement of wages, disputes, and in other matters when their services are called for, and that we pledge our influence and votes irrespective of party to get the principles herein set forth incorporated into law.["]

The resolution was submitted by Delegate James Brettell,[3] of the Amalgamated Association of Iron and Steel Workers of the United States.

Chairman Morgan, in announcing the non-concurrence of the committee to which the resolution was referred, said the objection to it was its lack of an enforcing or compulsory clause. When the objection to the resolution took the ground of an objection to compulsory arbitration Mr. Brettell insisted that question was not raised in his resolution, but the delegates argued the question from that standpoint.

REPORT OF THE COMMITTEE REJECTED.

A motion to accept the report of the committee was lost by a vote of 24 to 47, which seemed to indicate that the convention was in favor of the resolution. But in the discussion which arose on a motion to adopt the resolution as submitted the opponents of the measure got the best of it to the extent of over 200 votes on a roll call of the organizations represented.

Delegate Lennon, of the Journeymen Tailors' Union, struck some of the hardest blows in opposition. He said compulsory arbitration was a misnomer to start with and carried a contradiction in itself. Arbitration, he insisted, was only possible under certain circumstances, and when those circumstances existed the dispute would naturally seek that means of settlement without the intervention of a statute to enforce it. On the other hand, with a compulsory statute, workingmen would find themselves called on to answer the demands of employers for reductions in wages oftener than they would invoke the law to secure advances. He predicted that compromise after compromise would be demanded by employers until the labor organization would be compromised out of existence.

Delegate Carney, of the iron and steel workers, was in favor of arbitration, and cited the case of the striking English coal miners.

DELEGATE WEISMANN IN OPPOSITION.

Delegate Weismann, of the Bakers' International Union, opposed the resolution because he believed it would tend to break down labor organizations by making the individual members careless about keeping up their unions under the belief that they could get their grievances righted through the agency of the board of arbitration. That idea would be all right provided absolutely fair and impartial men could be secured to sit as arbitrators, but he was not disposed to trust his cause to men who would surely be appointed to office through a political machine.

Delegate James J. Daly, of the tile layers,[4] had had experience in settling disputes by arbitration when Dr. McGlynn was one of the arbitrators. He claimed that the reverend doctor in spite of his great profession of friendship for the workingman had decided against the people for whom he professed such great interest, and that decision was so flagrantly unjust, Mr. Daly said, that it would only be necessary to state the case to any real friend of the workingman to bear out his assertion. Mr. Daly said the New York State Board of Labor Arbitration was a laughing stock wherever anything was known of its action. Nearly every delegate present had something to say upon the question and the opposition had decidedly the best of the argument all through.

HAS LONG BEEN AN IMPORTANT QUESTION.

The convention thus settled in the negative a question which has been argued more than any other connected with the labor problem — a question whose affirmative has been held by many of the ablest labor leaders to be the only solution of that vexed problem.

It is probable that President Gompers will get a raking over the coals today for having totally ignored the question of woman suffrage in his annual report to the convention. At the last convention a resolution was adopted pledging the Federation to the cause and instructing its officers to use all the powers vested in them to secure National enfranchisement for women. It is claimed that President Gompers had not injured his lungs shouting for the right of women to take part in politics as voters, but, on the contrary, has rather belittled the cause.

Miss Mary Kenney, who is one of the most active women in the local labor movement and who has done wonders in the way of organizing the workingwomen of Chicago and elsewhere, was promoter of the resolution adopted last year. She is after Mr. Gompers with a sharp stick and though not a delegate to the convention has many warm friends among the delegates who appreciate the practical work she has done for her toiling sisters and who believe the president was derelict in attempting to ignore a question of so much interest to women.

· · ·

Electioneering for the Offices.

The convention will elect officers tomorrow and a good deal of quiet electioneering went on all day for the several candidates for the respective offices. . . .

While there is considerable opposition to the selection of President Gompers, that opposition does not seem as yet to have crystallized on any particular candidate. The Western delegates, from whom this opposition mainly comes, are willing to compromise on any Eastern man, provided they can have the headquarters removed to Chicago, and if Mr. Gompers is beaten it will be through a combination of that sort.

The main objection to Mr. Gompers is on the ground that he has held the office long enough and that it would be good policy to make a change.

. . .

Chicago Inter Ocean, Dec. 14, 1893.

1. The Miners' Federation of Great Britain struck in June 1893, refusing to accept a wage cut of 25 percent. After efforts at conciliation by business and local political leaders had failed, Prime Minister William Gladstone arranged for an arbitration conference that ended the dispute on Nov. 17. The settlement turned the question of wages over to a board of conciliation.

2. Thomas J. Morgan represented the International Machinists' Union.

3. James BRETTELL of Mingo Junction, Ohio, represented the National Amalgamated Association of Iron and Steel Workers of the United States and was a member of local 22 of the organization's second district. He was third vice-president of the AFL from 1893 to 1894.

4. The Mosaic and Encaustic TILE Layers and Trade National Union.

[December 14, 1893]

LABOR LEADERS TALK

"They who would be free themselves must strike the blow," was the sentiment which prevailed and was spoken at the labor mass-meeting at Bricklayers' Hall, Peoria and West Monroe streets, last night. An audience of less than 200 assembled in response to the invitation of the Trade and Labor Assembly, the object being to give local trades unionists an opportunity of hearing the delegates in attendance upon the American Federation of Labor convention. The notice of the meeting was brief, but those who attended were enthusiastic supporters of the principles advocated by the speakers. Nearly every one in the hall wore a badge of some union or other.

As President of the Trade and Labor Assembly John McGrath[1] acted as Chairman. Seated with him upon the platform were many delegates from other cities and these leaders who were upon the list of speakers:

Samuel Gompers, New York; P. J. McGuire,[2] Philadelphia; Frank Foster,[3] Boston; John McBride,[4] Ohio; John Lennon, Philadelphia; Henry Weissman, New York; John McGlynn,[5] San Francisco; H. J. Skeffington,[6] Boston; Martin Fox;[7] Adolph Loeffler,[8] Tennessee; B. J. Kelly,[9] Pittsburg; Jerome Jones,[10] Nashville; William B. Prescott;[11] and James Duncan[12] of Baltimore.

Samuel Gompers' Address.

Chairman McGrath then said that he would introduce one who needed no introduction to the American people, "the Little Giant of the American Federation of Labor, Samuel Gompers." (Applause.) Mr. Gompers said:

["]'They who would be free themselves must strike the blow.' (Applause.) I do not resent the overtures that are made for organized labor. I do not repel the sympathy expressed for the hopes and the aspirations underlying the labor movement. On the contrary I welcome it as a ray of hope coming down out of a sky overcast with clouds. But now, as well as at any time in the history of the development of the human race, it is well to keep in mind that 'they who would be free themselves must strike the blow.' Look through the length and breadth of our country. Mark the fact that among hundreds of thousands of sturdy men, strong women with hearts that have only been chilled recently, you can see the pangs of hunger upon their faces. Mark the fact that in this era, the closing of the nineteenth century, when the mind and ingenuity of mankind have made it possible to produce the good and necessary things and the human family has made it easier than ever before that just because it is easier to produce these things society answers that that is the reason we must suffer.

["]I am free to admit that conditions of labor, as a rule, are better in our age than they were before. I am not one who declares that the whole struggle of the human family is one vast fallacy. On the contrary I recognize the great good that has been accomplished. I recognize the progress that has been made. I recognize the vantage ground obtained, but I say that we can by reason of the advance and progress made, we can see and discern clearer the wrongs that are inflicted upon our fellows and ourselves, and are determined to obliterate them from the affairs of man. (Applause.)

["]I lay this down as a proposition underlying the labor movement and upon which I think it can afford to stand or fall: That wherever a man or woman desiring to work, capable of work, cannot find the opportunity to work to sustain life and to obtain the necessaries of life, that system of society is rotten at its base and foundation (applause), that it is rooted in injustice, and that it requires the earnest, the honest, the determined and unremitting effort of the toiling masses of our entire country and the world to supplant it by justice, fair dealing among men and mankind. I am not unmindful of the elements with which we have to contend. I do not underestimate the powers which confront us and which antagonize us, nor do I overestimate their power and strength.["]

Power of Labor Organizations.

["]I do not underestimate the power and strength of our organizations of labor, nor do I overestimate them. I believe without egotism, and consider that I have a fair conception of what they are doing and what they can do. And in recognizing that fact I am free to admit that at times such as we are now in the midst of it is popular, it is the current thought, it is the fashionable thing to say that the trade unions are impotent to fight the contests of labor, and I, from an experience of nearly thirty years, and after a careful study of our movement, not only in the United States, but wherever the trade unions were formed, I say to you, my friends, that the trade unions now existing in the United States are factors which hold in check the avalanche of panic which has seized our country (applause), and intense as this panic is, fearful as the poverty which exists is, pained and hungry as many thousands of our fellow-workers are, it is almost stupendous to even imagine for a moment the conditions which would have prevailed and would prevail if our trade unions were not to act as the breakwater and the dam. (Applause.)

["]My friends, there are a number of people who at this time more than any other find it the best opportunity to hurl their antagonism and their epithets at the organizations of the trades unions. The fact that they maintain themselves; the fact that they stand as a solid body; the fact that the trades unions are capable of having a convention in the midst of these overwhelming—almost overwhelming conditions, such as are taking place, the American Federation in the City of Chicago, is the best answer to the carping critics and antagonists of the labor movement. (Applause.) I say to you, my friends, say that the trade unions are impotent or weak. I know where they are weak and where they could be made stronger, and it becomes our duty to try and make them stronger, and make their vulnerable points invulnerable. But I ask you, my friends, in the midst of this cyclone

that has been coming upon us for the last three months, the corporations and the Fair employers, and some who might think that they
are Fair employers, endeavoring to take advantage of labor and concentrating their efforts upon organized labor in antagonism.["]

THE LEHIGH VALLEY STRIKE.

["]An organization of railroad employes on the Lehigh Valley road
struck[13] and I am free to admit that everything that was demanded
by the Lehigh Valley railroad employes was not obtained, but the fact
that they revolutionized and rebelled, the fact that they rebelled
against the attempt of that company to force conditions down their
throats and to place new shackles upon their limbs, and the fact that
the men rebelled against these conditions and compelled one of the
most autocratic of corporations to say 'I will receive the committees
of your organization,' was the check. And so, as many of our friends
who may underestimate the value of the results in that battle do not
know the conditions which these men had to contend against and the
lasting benefit that they have conferred upon the toiling mass of our
country.

["]It served notice the same as the coal-miners' strike in England
served notice upon the miners and capitalists of England, beyond
which it was not safe to go. In the same way did the railroad organizations serve notice upon the corporations of the United States;
told them that there is a limit beyond which it is not safe to drive us.
(Applause.) And it has had a good effect upon the employing class in
general, and I know that it has in regard to the working people. The
men who are known as the captains of industry have demonstrated
by the fact of the thousands and hundreds of thousands of unemployed, willing toilers that their reign and rule has been a sad fallacy,
and that they are incompetent to be the captains.

["]I am certain, however, the work of organization, the work of
obtaining our rights must be gradual in its character and must conform
to the progress, the intelligence of our fellow-workers. The trade
unions are what we are. They represent our ideas, our views, our
intelligence, and they can be made exactly what we want to make
them. They are elastic in character. They are narrow as we are narrow-
minded; they are broad as we expand our views. And the organization
and the trade union is the concrete or the aggregate expression of
our aggregate intelligence and wants. When we say that the trade
unions are narrow, or that they are no good, we simply declare that
we each and every one of us, are narrow and no good. Now, more
than ever, is it necessary to stand true to the banner of trade unionism.

Now, more than ever, is it necessary to defend our position. And during our present industrial crisis our fight may be a defensive one, but hold on to the organization. Men who may be employed, men who may be earning small wages, hold on to the organization. You may be making sacrifices now, but you would be making greater sacrifices if you would leave the union.

["]The fact that the union exists is in itself a power and a factor which prevents the employing class from taking unfair and undue advantage of you. (Applause.) Even if that were the only consideration, but there are others, many others, one of which at least I desire to mention, is this: That if the unions, the trades unions were to be disbanded, if you were to leave your organizations, when the revival in industry should come around, when trade should take a boom, you would have no organizations to help you take advantage of the improved conditions, but you would have to lose six months or a year or longer in order to organize, while on the other hand if you maintain your organizations, and the revival in industry comes, you will be prepared to immediately take advantage of the improved conditions, and then not only get back that which has been taken from you, but so much more and more, and still more expanding our organizations, until we get all that we produce, the results of our labor, and emancipate the toiling masses. (Applause.)["]

APPEALS FOR ORGANIZATION.

["]There are many things to say. There are many of our friends here to say them. I have spoken to Chicago workingmen often. It is not a new thing for me to address you. I have not spoken possibly upon very many essential points, but I do urge and appeal to you, fellow-workmen, those who are not members of the union, to organize in your unions; those who are members, stand true to its fold and banner. Try to share the work that you have with those who have none at all; try to help make sacrifices in order that they may tide this struggle over. Carry them along as best you can, for I am sure if we do not we will simply be playing into the hands of our enemies.

["]The thought comes to me that a few months ago the Governor of the State of New York came to Chicago to the World's Fair, and being interviewed upon the matter of the relief of the workmen he said: 'Within ten days the wheel of industry will be whirling again and no trace of the industrial and financial crisis will be apparent.' I took occasion to say at a meeting after that wise declaration that if the Governor's statesmanship was not superior to his prophecy it must certainly be at a very low par, and that his reputation as a prophet was necessarily sacrificed. Just look at the conditions as they are. It makes strong men weep and strikes at the heart and very soul. We are grateful to those who are giving something, but what labor wants is not charity; it wants work. (Applause.) The right to work is an inherent right, for it means the right to live, and no man should have it in his power to deny the right of a man to live.["]

. . .

Chicago Tribune, Dec. 14, 1893.

1. John J. McGrath was a member of Bricklayers' and Masons' International Union of America 21 of Chicago.

2. P. J. McGuire was representing the United Brotherhood of Carpenters and Joiners of America at the AFL convention.

3. Frank K. Foster represented AFL Tack Makers' Protective Union 4007.

4. John McBride was a delegate of the United Mine Workers of America.

5. Michael M. McGlynn, a printer and member of International Typographical Union (ITU) 21, represented the San Francisco Labor Council. In 1894 he was the council's recording secretary; also that year he began publishing the *New Union* and, later, the *Voice of Labor.* In the late 1890s he was living in Los Angeles where he edited the *Labor World.*

6. Henry J. Skeffington was the delegate of the Boot and Shoe Workers' International Union of America at this convention.

7. Martin Fox was a representative of the Iron Molders' Union of North America. He was president of the union from 1890 to 1903.

8. E. Loefler represented AFL Piano Tuners' Protective Union 6231 of Nashville, Tenn.

9. Patrick J. Kelly, a glassblower from Butler, Pa., represented the American Flint Glass Workers' Union of North America (AFGWU) and was a member of AFGWU 77.

10. Jerome Jones was representing AFL Crispin Shoemakers' Union 6230.

11. William B. Prescott represented the ITU.

12. James Duncan was the delegate of the Baltimore Federation of Labor.

13. On Nov. 18, 1893, 1,800 railroad workers, including engineers, firemen, conductors, trainmen, and telegraphers, struck the Lehigh Valley Railroad. Leaders of the railroad brotherhoods called the strike after officers of the Lehigh refused to meet with them concerning the discharge of three members of the employees' committee of the Philadelphia and Reading Railroad, which the Lehigh had acquired. The company secured nonunion employees to operate its lines. On Dec. 6 the unions agreed to call off the strike in a settlement mediated by the boards of arbitration of New York and New Jersey, two states where the Lehigh had operations. By the agreement the company retained those of its new employees that it regarded as competent, but agreed to rehire former employees without prejudice to union membership and allow them to divide the available work among themselves until the business of the railroad made work-sharing unnecessary.

NEW LABOR PLATFORM

There was a contest in the American Federation of Labor convention yesterday between the conservative and socialistic delegates, regarding the adoption of the principles of the platform[1] to be submitted at the next annual convention.[2]

The conservatives came out ahead. The matter was the principal feature of the day's business. The committee on resolutions brought up for the consideration of the delegates a programme containing the fundamental principles of independent labor politics. A recommendation accompanied the report of the committee to the effect that the planks should be submitted to the favorable consideration of the labor organizations represented in the convention. Several hours were spent in debating the question. Those known to hold socialistic ideas expressed themselves as against the striking off of the word "favorable" as had been moved. The more conservative delegates favored it. The latter won their point and the report of the committee as amended was concurred in. It was left with the delegates to submit the platform to their constituents, who will vote upon the propositions seriatim.

· · ·

Chairman Morgan, of the committee on resolutions, submitted a programme for the nationalization of railways, mines, telegraphs, etc., as proposed by English economists as a basis for the political labor movement. A motion to have the matter presented to the organizations of the federation for the purpose of having their delegates instructed to vote upon it at the next convention of the federation received the support of a number of delegates and the disapproval of others. The platform has twelve planks in it, as follows: Compulsory education, direct legislation, a legal eight-hour work day, sanitary inspection of workshop, mine, and home; liability of employers for physical disability, abolition of contract labor in all public work, abolition of the sweating system, municipal ownership of street cars, electric light, and gas plants; nationalization of telegraphs, telephone, railways, and mines; collective ownership by the people of all means of production and distribution, the principle of referendum in all legislation.

It was moved to have the resolution taken up and voted upon seriatim.

MORGAN'S IDEA DEFEATED.

The delegates at once became interested in the proposition for a labor party platform and were not slow in expressing their views. Delegate Daley declared that he would not indorse a platform of the nature suggested because it contained anarchistic sentiments. Delegate W. J. Miller,[3] of the Massachusetts Typographical Union, advanced too far into partisan lines and was hissed by his colleagues. Representative Weiseman, the father of the resolution, arose to defend it. He declared that he had no desire to have the convention take a hasty action on the resolutions, but he desired to have the trades unions established on the basic principles of the labor movement. He wanted the delegates to refer the matter to their constituents for decision. He expressed himself as being in favor of independent political action by union men.

Delegate Morgan moved that the convention should go into a committee of the whole for the purpose of suspending the rules and giving more latitude in debate. He considered the question under discussion the most important that would be brought before the convention, and termed it "the connecting link between this country and the movement across the water." Delegate Fox, who assumed the chair at the invitation of President Gompers, promptly decided the motion to be out of order, because it had not been introduced before discussion began. An appeal was taken, but the chair was sustained.

CAUTION IS COUNSELED.

Debate followed on a motion to strike out the word "favorable" appended to the resolution by Mr. Morgan's committee. Delegate Foster, of Boston, asked the convention to be cautious in its deliberation on the subject. He was not in favor of having the doctrines recorded as having met the approval of the convention without first having the constituents pass upon it. He said that the most remarkable class of politicians he had ever seen were of the independent order. W. C. Pomeroy believed that independent political action of the laboring classes would result in the formation of an independent political party of the masses. "Ten thousand independent votes will swing the electoral vote of New York and Illinois," he said, "and 3,000 will do the same thing in New Jersey or Indiana. The independent vote will ultimately, if persisted in, swing the old parties into line with the principles of organized labor."

Representative Miller,[4] of the electrical workers, asserted that he had been in three conventions of the federation, in every one of which the independent political party came up and was killed in the debate. He thought the workingman could secure what he wanted at the ballot box.

"FAVORABLE" IS KNOCKED OUT.

A vote was taken at the afternoon session upon the motion to strike out the word "favorable," as had been recommended by the committee, in that clause which provided that the resolution should be submitted to the "favorable" consideration of the delegates' constituents. A calling of the roll showed that a total of 1,274 votes were in favor of striking out the word and 1,161 against.[5] The resolution as thus amended was then submitted to a vote, resulting in 2,244 votes favoring its adoption, with 67 against.

. . .

Chicago Inter Ocean, Dec. 15, 1893.

1. See "An Article in the *New York Herald*," Jan. 7, 1894, below.
2. The AFL held its 1894 convention in Denver, Dec. 10-18.
3. William Joseph Miller of Boston was a member of Boston Mailers' Union 1 of the International Typographical Union (ITU) and an ITU delegate at this convention.
4. Henry Miller represented the National Brotherhood of Electrical Workers.
5. The convention proceedings give the vote as 1,253 to 1,182.

[December 17, 1893]

GOMPERS IS ELECTED

Samuel Gompers was last night re-elected president of the American Federation of Labor for the twelfth consecutive time. The movement on the part of the Western delegates to bring the presidency of the federation from the East, where it has remained for a number of years, to the West, failed when the matter was submitted to a vote. John McBride, of the United Mine Workers' Union, from Ohio, was the candidate selected to take up the fight against President Gompers. The voting of the delegates as the roll was called showed that the contest was to be a close one. As the names of delegates were called their vote was recorded as in behalf of their organizations. It took several minutes for the secretary to count the votes. When announced it was as follows: Gompers, 1,314; McBride, 1,222; Gompers' majority, 92.

Election of officers was made an order of business at the evening session. Charles F. Beechers[1] placed Samuel Gompers in nomination. Thomas Elderkin, of the Seamen's National Union, Chicago, was called to the chair while the vote for president of the federation was being taken. Treasurer Lennon seconded the nomination of President Gompers. The name of John McBride was placed before the convention by T. H. Penna[2] and seconded by Richard Powers,[3] of Chicago. The names of P. J. Maguire, Frank K. Foster, and W. C. Pomeroy were introduced, but respectfully declined. Tremendous cheers greeted President Gompers as soon as the Secretary had made known his victory. He responded to the cries of "speech" with a brief address. He said:

PRESIDENT GOMPER'S SPEECH.

"I would, indeed, be bereft of feeling were I not moved by your manifestations, by your vote, by your renewed confidence. I want to say that years before I held a salaried office I was the victim of that abnormal wrong of child labor. I was forced into a factory when I was young, and I was a union man when I was a mere boy. As a wage-worker I have tried to be a union man in my every-day conduct in the factory and outside. I have tried to serve the labor movement as faithfully as I know how. Robbed of the means of an education no one feels keener than I the wrongs committed against the innocent children of the world. I can say to those who favor my election I never solicited, directly or indirectly, any man to vote for me. The men who voted for John McBride lose not one jot of my respect. I know his worth and appreciate the sentiment of the delegates who placed his name in nomination and made my election unanimous. The man who strikes at trade unions strikes at the heart of Sam Gompers. I make no pledges of what I shall do but I shall perform the duties of the office to the best of my ability and try to see that the banner of the American Federation of Labor is not trailed in the dust.["]

. . .

. . . A resolution introduced favoring the removal of the headquarters of the Federation from New York city further west called for no small amount of debate after the election of officers was disposed of. The city of Toledo, Ohio, was suggested as a central point for the new headquarters. President Gompers did not favor the resolution; in fact, he declared that if the resolution should pass the convention might accept his resignation. He declared that the work of his office would be impaired if a change should take place. A vote was taken on the question and the resolution was not adopted, the vote being 984 for, 1,483 against.[4]

. . .

No More Souvenirs.

The executive session was commenced at 2 o'clock and continued nearly four hours. When the matter of an executive session was first introduced it was stated that subjects were to be discussed in secrecy, it being considered inadvisable to make them public until the convention should arrive at some conclusion. It was rumored that charges had been made against President Gompers and the officers of the executive council concerning the receipts of a publication issued in the interests of the order. It was claimed that the federation, during the life of the publication, had not received a statement of receipts and expenditures.

After the subject matter had been properly placed before the convention President Gompers arose to defend himself and his fellow-workers on the executive council. Shades were placed before the glass doors leading to the council-room, the gallery was closed, and two policemen from the Central Station stood guard in the corridor to keep the crowd of visitors away from the doors. With these precautions taken the president of the federation answered to the accusations against him. He spoke for over an hour. He declared that there was no foundation for the charges, and that they had been brought up preceding the election of the officers of the federation with the idea of injuring him in his Presidential candidacy. Other delegates spoke exhaustively upon the resolution. A committee consisting of Delegates Carll,[5] Fox, Armstrong,[6] Elderkins, and Foster was appointed to weigh the evidence and make its report.

Mr. Gompers Vindicated.

The result was a complete vindication for those implicated. In reporting the committee placed its finding on record, which was in substance as follows:

["]We find that a souvenir of the federation has been contracted for by President Gompers, and the amount received for the same, we believe, has been expended by him for the interest of the federation. We recommend that in the future, however, no souvenir shall be issued. We further recommend that the president give to the convention a detailed statement of the receipts and expenditures in order that the fullest information on the subject be accorded to all delegates.[″][7]

. . .

Chicago Inter Ocean, Dec. 17, 1893.

1. Actually Charles F. Reichers who represented the United Garment Workers of America.

2. Philip H. Penna represented the United Mine Workers of America.

3. Richard POWERS represented the National Seamen's Union of America. He was president of the Lake Seamen's Union into the 1890s.

4. The convention proceedings report the vote as 980 to 1,483.

5. LeRoy Carl represented the United Brotherhood of Carpenters and Joiners of America (UBCJA). He was a member of UBCJA 453 of Auburn, N.Y.

6. Hamilton Armstrong represented the Denver Trades and Labor Assembly.

7. The convention adopted the committee's report and SG presented a full statement of the transactions.

[December 19, 1893]

WAS THERE A SCHEME?

. . .

Considerable discussion was provoked by the introduction of a resolution recommending the passage of a free-coinage bill by Congress at the ratio of 16 to 1 as one of the means of relieving the monetary stringency. A minority of the committee concurred in the report and it was adopted.

. . .

Chicago Inter Ocean, Dec. 19, 1893.

An Editorial in the *People*

[December 24, 1893]

The dry-rot has set in the American Federation of Labor. As an organization, the A.F. of L. is at best a cross between a wind-bag and a rope of sand; it has no cohesion, vitality or vigor worth mentioning. But whatever of these good things it might possibly have acquired under proper action, it can not now any more hope to get. Defeated at all points, thanks to its false tactics of pure and simpledom, it has not only stuck to them but it has re-affirmed the presidency of its incubus, the ignorant and perverse misleader of Labor—Samuel Gompers. Nor is this the worst. A numerically strong element, that wanted to overthrow him, could find no better candidate around whom to rally than the politician labor leader John McBride, a fellow who either is already out of a job, having pretty successfully wrecked the miners, or who expects to be soon out of his job, and would like to get a living out of the movement.

An organization that is put to such a Hobson's choice as Gompers, who declares the captitalists are entitled to their profits under the present system, and has no word of condemnation for his treasurer Lennon, who declares it is fallacy to claim there is any hostility between the employer and the employe, and John McBride, has no reason of being. In point of fact, it is deader than dead.

People (New York), Dec. 24, 1893.

To James Sovereign[1] and John Hayes

Jan. 4, [18]94.

Messrs. J. R. Sovereign and John W. Hayes,
General Master Workman & Gen'l. Secretary Treas. Knights of Labor,
Philadelphia, Pa.
Gentlemen: —

I have the honor to acknowlege the receipt of your favor of the 14th. inst.[2] conveying the substance of a resolution[3] adopted by the General Assembly of the Knights of Labor held in Philadelphia Nov. 14-28th. The same was laid before the Convention of the American Federation of Labor held in Chicago, Ill. Dec. 11-19th. and in compliance with the request therein contained, three representatives were appointed for the purpose of meeting and conferring with representatives of other National organizations as indicated in your letter.

The representatives selected on behalf of the American Federation of Labor are Mr. P. J. Mc-Guire, Frank K. Foster and Samuel Gompers, and having conferred in reference to the suggestion you make concerning the time and place of meeting, we have deemed it advisable to suggest that the first week in Feb. would be about the most convenient, and since Philadelphia is the head-quarters of your organization, as well as the residence of one of our colleagues, that that city be the place.

It affords me pleasure to be enabled to state that the fraternal spirit permeating your letter was very cordially received, and the request for the selection of the representatives, with alacrity agreed to.

Earnestly hoping that the conference may be productive of great good to the toiling masses of our country, I am, with great respect,

Yours Very Truly   Saml Gompers.
President. American Federation of Labor.

TLpS, reel 7, vol. 10, p. 129, SG Letterbooks, DLC.

1. James R. SOVEREIGN served as general master workman of the KOL from 1893 to 1897.

2. Printed in AFL, *Proceedings*, 1893, p. 54.

3. The 1893 KOL General Assembly passed a resolution calling for a conference of all trade unions to be held in the early part of 1894. After a preliminary meeting, called by Joseph R. Buchanan, was held in Philadelphia, Apr. 28-29, 1894, the conference met June 11 and 12 in St. Louis; attending were delegates from the AFL, KOL, National Farmers' Alliance and Industrial Union of America, United Green Glass Workers' Association of the United States and Canada, National Brotherhood of Electrical Workers of America, Brotherhood of Locomotive Engineers, Brotherhood of Locomotive Firemen, Brotherhood of Railroad Trainmen, and Order of Railway Conductors of America. The KOL presented six resolutions calling for an annual meeting of labor organizations, arbitration of disputes between labor organizations, a process of joint approval and support of strikes involving more than a thousand workers, mutual recognition of working cards, coordination where more than one local of a craft existed, and support for third party candidates—particularly those of the People's party. While the Farmers' Alliance and Railroad Trainmen delegates joined KOL representatives in support of these proposals, a thirteen to five majority rejected them in favor of the AFL's substitute resolutions defending the trade autonomy and political independence of unions and calling for the elimination of dual unionism. The delegates did agree to hold annual conventions beginning with one on Feb. 22, 1895, but these failed to materialize.

An Article in the *New York Herald*

[January 7, 1894]

STARTING A LABOR PARTY.

Ever since the beginning of the present industrial depression, and, indeed, for nearly a year before that, the chief topic of discussion in labor circles has been the demand for an independent political party of labor. The chief obstacle has been that labor was divided into two great factions and several smaller ones, and that great bitterness of feeling existed between these two divisions.

When the federation met in convention in Chicago a few weeks ago it was found that the cry for political action on independent lines had arisen among the delegates' constituents and that this sentiment was continually growing. The Committee on Resolutions was almost buried in resolutions bearing on the question. After much debate the following was adopted as best declaring the feeling of the delegates who were there to represent and legislate for about one million men:—

POLITICAL PROGRAMME.

Whereas the trade unionists of Great Britain have, by the light of experience and the logic of progress, adopted the principle of independent labor politics as an auxiliary to their economic action; and whereas such action has resulted in the most gratifying success; and whereas such independent labor politics are based upon the following programme, to wit:—

1. Compulsory education.
2. Direct legislation.
3. A legal eight hour work day.
4. Sanitary inspection of workshop, mine and home.
5. Liability of employers for injury to health, body or life.
6. The abolition of contract system in all public work.
7. The abolition of the sweating system.
8. The municipal ownership of street cars and gas and electric plants for public distribution of light, heat and power.
9. The nationalization of telegraphs, telephones, railroads and mines.
10. The collective ownership by the people of all means of production and distribution.
11. The principle of referendum in all legislation.

Therefore resolved, That this Convention hereby indorse this political action of our British comrades, and

Resolved, That this programme and basis of a political labor movement be and is hereby submitted for the favorable consideration of the labor organizations of America, with the request that their delegates to the next annual Convention of the American Federation of Labor be instructed on this most important subject.

The platform represents the labor of several days by the Committee on Resolutions and is the result of a careful consideration of all the suggestions made by the delegates. Even then the Convention further amended it by striking out the word "favorable" in the last clause, and thus submitting the platform on it own merits, without indorsement or objection from them, to their contituents.

The reason that this change was made was because the delegates felt that, though they indorsed the platform, the matter was of too great import to be settled by any representatives, but must be considered by the people themselves.

MODERATE SOCIALISM.

It will be seen on reading the platform that the tenth plank contains in a nutshell the whole essence of the socialist creed, and that the platform all through is that of moderate collectivism or socialism.

This platform has not been finally adopted yet, but there seems to be no doubt on the part of any of the well known labor leaders that it will be, and that a party will be in the process of formation long before the federation meets again in December to finally ratify the platform.

I talked with President Samuel Gompers regarding the prospects of the platform and the causes which led to such a radical departure from the traditions of the federation as its adoption.

"Do you think, Mr. Gompers," I asked, "that the example of England had much influence on the delegates at Chicago?"

"Yes, I do. The trades unions of England have had the benefit of longer experience and struggle, and their actions are closely watched by the men who are prominent in the labor movement here. England has been going through for some years what we are beginning to feel here and has been able to figure out what is needed. We have watched her and are ready to profit by her example. I believe that the present industrial depression will have the effect of turning the thoughts of the workingmen of America toward independent political action, and that such action will be on the lines laid down in the platform which the Convention referred to the individual organizations.

"Personally I approve of nearly everything in the platform, and so do most of the delegates who were in Chicago, and I believe it will be adopted by the organizations. It would not be fair for me to say now what changes I would make. That must be left to the people.

"I believe that the time has come for independent action on the part of organized labor. The industrial depression has been caused by a false system of economics, and can only be righted by such action. The introduction of improved machinery, the application of steam and electricity to manufacturing and the progress of invention, without a corresponding reduction in the hours of labor, have caused a great displacement of men, which produces what seems to be over-production, but is really underconsumption.["]

MUST ASSERT HIS MANHOOD.

"The laborer has been too long considered a mere tool for the enrichment of his masters. He must wake up and become a man in fact as well as in name. What we really want is a new 'bill of rights,' and that we must gain it through our own efforts.

"The people are now beginning to see how insincere and shallow the protestations of friendship from the old parties and politicians are, and that the time has come to take independent action."

Henry Weismann, who is the recognized leader of the more radical wing of the Federation of Labor, and is a pronounced socialist, though a bitter enemy of the socialist labor party machine, believes that the next year will see the greatest uprising of labor, in a political sense, that has ever taken place, and that it will not be purely local.

"At last," he said, "we have lifted the trade unions out of the narrow rut in which they were working into something higher and broader, and in doing it we have not endangered their existence."

Many other labor men with whom I talked expressed the same opinions, and all seemed to feel that the independent labor party of America would soon be an accomplished fact.

New York Herald, Jan. 7, 1894.

An Article by Samuel Gompers in the *New York World*

[January 14, 1894]

HOW TO HELP THE HUNGRY.

That the present number of unemployed, distressed and suffering is greater than has ever existed in the history of our country is beyond dispute. That more earnest attention is being given to the problem of how to "find a way out" than ever before cannot be denied. But a proper consideration of the subject of the unemployed workers and the means to their relief cannot find intelligent discussion unless the causes which have produced this condition of affairs and a fair estimate of the extent and number involved in the misery are understood.

It is variously estimated that the unemployed number between one million and three millions of wage-workers in the United States. When it is borne in mind that from one to five others are generally dependent for support upon this vast army of unemployed, one is only on the threshold of an appreciation of the maelstrom of poverty, misery and poignant distress in which our people are seething.

To the demand for work has now been wed the cry for bread. The astonishment of Mayor Gilroy at my statement to him a few months ago, "That it is safest and best for a community when its people are generally and remuneratively employed," has disappeared, and he, too, now acts upon the same hypothesis of what he then scornfully chose to regard as a threat.[1]

AN INDUSTRIAL ANOMALY.

The fields of our wonderful domain have blossomed with abundant harvests, beneath our feet is stored the wealth of ages for the needs of man. The cattle feed upon a thousand hills, and our massive forests, covering empires of States, crown the earth with glory. All nature smiles upon the abundance of prosperous peace. The sword of war is sheathed and pestilence has withdrawn its destroying hand. Invention has quickened production. Electricity and steam have conquered time and space, the hands of labor skilled in every craft answering the will of an intelligent, industrious, peace-loving people.

It is true that never before were the people in a position to so completely and easily produce all the articles and things which they require for their maintenance, and even to gratify every reasonable taste. I ask this question of the political economists, the men who weigh and measure the flesh and blood and human hearts of men, women and children upon the same scale and by the same rule that they weigh and measure a pound of pork — by what strange phenomenon, rule or law does a condition so anomalous exist, that because the ingenuity of man has rendered it easier to produce the necessaries of life, that, therefore, it is more difficult for a large portion of the people to live? A science which cannot find an explanation and suggest a remedy for such abnormal abominable conditions must be wofully deficient.

Of course, one can hear the old siren voice croaking "overproduction, overproduction." The student, the philosopher, the humanitarian are not and will not be satisfied with the answer. They want to know why people should want for the very things of which there is an "overproduction"; in other words, more than is wanted.

The millions of idle men and women of our day, the employed workers who find themselves hourly on the brink of joining the unemployed, the loved ones whose lives are dependent upon the wages of the breadwinners, all cry aloud in protest against a societary system which condemns them to poverty, hunger and despair simply because human intelligence has devised methods for producing more wealth than ever before in the history of man.

THE HOURS OF LABOR.

You cannot easily convince a man that because there is too much clothing he and his loved ones must go in rags. It is difficult to be persuaded that on account of there being too much corn, wheat, meat, &c., people must go hungry or starve; that they must be shelterless because there are too many houses. The political economists must amend their answer to this all-absorbing problem or stand convicted of insincerity or ignorance, of being apologists and special pleaders for a monstrous wrong.

The movement of the organized workers presents to the world a remedy for such a state of affairs—a remedy which does not depend upon a theory for its defense, but which experience has demonstrated to be efficacious. I refer to the movement to reduce the hours of labor.

Regardless of what its opponents may urge against this movement, the fact remains that it has the merit of withstanding all antagonism, and at every opportunity being made the most potent demand of the masses for their relief, progress and happiness. The only reasonable solution of the problem that is up for discussion, and, I hope, early settlement, the problem by which mankind in general and the toilers especially shall all be benefited and none injured by the never-ending, constant improvement in wealth-producing methods, is the movement to reduce the hours of labor. The general movement is usually known as the "eight-hour" movement, but as a matter of fact it should be remembered as the "shorter-hours" movement.

Fewer hours of daily labor means more constant employment the year round, and the workers more generally employed. Fewer hours portends new wants created, a constant pressure or levelling upward of the human family. Fewer hours means less idleness and more happiness; more work and more wealth for all; fewer jails, but more school-houses; a more comprehensive appreciation of the rights and duties of men, and the great motive power to give progress and civilization a constant, gradual and evolutionary impetus.

I feel quite sure that had the eight-hour movement, inaugurated by the American Federation of Labor a few years ago, received the co-operation of those it had a right to expect it from, and less antagonism of the capitalist class, the present awful industrial stagnation, with its attendant army of unemployed and consequent suffering, would have been averted, or certainly its effects would have been less severe.

Of course, the failure to act wisely in the past cannot have any effect upon the present or the future except as it may teach us to profit by the experience. The question then arises what should be done to afford immediate relief for the unemployed, as well as what will permanently make the recurrence of such panics impossible.

Propositions for Relief.

I have read all, or nearly all, the propositions for relief that have been urged within the past few months, as well as those which have been suggested in more normal periods for the past twenty-five years. I have endeavored to distinguish and separate the chaff from the wheat, and together with my own experience and judgment shall offer a few suggestions upon the subject.

It must be borne in mind that our body economic is suffering from a fearful malady, and that it is not merely a temporary disorder. For it is a matter of history that the poor we always have with us, and we shall always have the poor, with (or against) us so long as we shall permit a large portion of people to become poor through no fault of their own, but in consequence of unsound, incoherent, inhuman and unfraternal economic and social conditions.

Hence my suggestions shall not only be of that order simply to "tide over the present," but to be of a permanent benefit also, and tend to help along that long-looked-for goal when man's inhumanity to man shall be regarded as a relic of a past and barbaric age.

I shall not attempt to place my propositions in the order of their importance, and I should add that I am not at all sanguine that the most important will receive more than scant consideration from those who have it in their power to adopt them. On the contrary, judging from the past, I should say that the most practical and efficient of my suggestions will be rejected. They are too nearly in the right direction.

1. The Federal Government should improve the roads of the country over which it has jurisdiction. It is admitted by all that our country roads are the worst in any civilized nation.

2. The permanent improvement of the safeguards on the Mississippi River should be authorized and inaugurated by Congress.

3. Congress should begin the work of the two important shipping canals so necessary to the commerce of our country.

4. The bill introduced by the late Congressman Wright,[2] of Pennsylvania, during the panic of 1873-79 (I forget the exact time of its introduction), by which Congress authorized the loan of $2,000 at a low rate of interest to settlers upon Government land, the Government taking a first mortgage upon the property. The money to be devoted under its supervision to the erection of small homes, and helping the settler until the first crop has been harvested. The mortgage to be paid within twenty-five years. Thus the Government having a safe and paying investment and aiding thousands of its citizens to independence. This bill should be resuscitated and passed, although it

only received 22 votes at the time stated. The late Congressman S. S. Cox[3] was among the number who voted in its favor.

5. Work on an extended scale should be prosecuted on our rivers and harbors. I mean work, not merely appropriations for rivers which exist only in the imaginations of some Congressmen.

WORK ON PUBLIC ENTERPRISES.

6. Congress should authorize the Department of Labor to arrange for the reception of reports of the industrial situation in each industry as regularly as the weather reports are now made; and the issuance of say, weekly bulletins, giving accurate information upon this most important subject.

7. The Eight-Hour law should be thoroughly enforced.

8. The Legislature of the State should immediately set to work improving the roads.

9. Our Erie Canal could be deepened and widened, allowing entry to larger craft propelled by steam and electricity.

10. The labor of the inmates of our prisons and reformatories should be confined to their own support, and not be allowed either to supplant or come into competition with free citizens. (Is it not strange that work can always be found for prisoners; that industrial stagnations do not throw them out of employment, while citizens unconvicted of crime are yet condemned to idleness, hunger and possible starvation? But such is the order of our nineteenth-century civilization.)

11. The work on the State Capitol, State park, salt works and institutions should be prosecuted to completion.

12. The Legislature should authorize the city of New York to construct a system of rapid transit, which may be owned, controlled and operated by its citizens in their corporate capacity. The officials of this city should insist upon this authority, but should they fail to do so, the citizens should see to it that their officials do insist upon it.

13. The city government should erect sufficient school-houses for all children of school age, and not allow, as now, thousands of children to be turned away from school every year for lack of room.

14. The public parks authorized by law should be started at once and those existing improved.

15. Our improved system of docks should be extended and proceeded with.

16. The speedway should be sped along without delay (and without depriving the people of a view of the river).

17. The system of sewerage should be extended until it is general,

and for sanitary purposes all tenement-house "vaults" should be abolished and connected with the sewers at once.

18. New streets could be opened up in the uptown districts with advantage.

19. All work should be done directly for the national, State or municipal governments. This would eliminate the profit of contractors and allow the employment of more people and have better work performed for the money expended.

DUTY OF EMPLOYERS.

20. The plan of Mr. Washington for a voluntary contribution of money by all employed citizens, to be used in employing a number of the unemployed, is a good one as far as it can be carried out and should be encouraged. With him I would urge that, when employment is furnished, if you wish to help and relieve, and not intensify the present suffering, pay a fair standard wage. A lower rate is merely the incentive to reductions in wages of wage-workers in kindred trades and callings, reduces their power and opportunity for consumption and perpetuates the condition we are striving to emerge from.

21. Employers, both private and corporate, instead of discharging half their employees, should divide the work to be performed among all. It is far better, and would sooner end our industrial stagnation if all were employed, even at half time.

22. Upon the employed workers I would urge not only compliance with the last suggestion, but a most strenuous insistence upon their employers that the work to be done be divided among all. I know that as a rule the workers, particularly organized workers, have desired this, but they should use every means at their command to influence their employers to comply with it. They should bear in mind that there is a very narrow margin between themselves and the unemployed, and that very soon it might be their lot to be numbered among the latter, and then they would regard the employed worker as a very selfish being on account of his unwillingness to share the work with "his unemployed brother." The golden rule is not bad in labor as well as religion.

23. The movement to gradually and continually reduce the hours of labor must be prosecuted and carried to its logical result—a reduction commensurate with machinery improvements, keeping in mind the necessary increasing power of consumption and the requisite reserve labor for the production of more wealth. As long as there is a man or woman able to work, willing to work and who cannot find work, the hours of labor of those employed are too long.

As a rule, I am opposed to charity as a means to relieve economic ills, for it spoils the donor and humiliates the recipient. In view, however, of the present pressing need, I prefer to hold back adverse criticism just now, except that I am constrained to repeat an axiom of labor, "We want work, not charity."

What is the wonderful progress made by the human family to the hungry man? What is our civilization and advancement to the unemployed? To their view the whole past and present is one vast failure, and the future a blank. It should be remembered that an unemployed man, with all that that portends, is a sad, a demoralized man, or, as Carlyle[4] said, "A man willing to work and unable to find work, is, perhaps, the saddest sight that fortune's inequality exhibits under the sun."

It is indeed not to be wondered that in such a plight the workless recognize that they have a grievance against society, and make themselves a "nuisance" to their fellow-men. They have the "inalienable right to life, liberty and the pursuit of happiness," and such a declaration to a man with an empty stomach and his little ones suffering from cold and hunger is worse than a hollow mockery.

It is a question which is wisest, safest and best for every community— to find employment for the workless in a manner which will, while saving them, bring its full reward and return, or whether they shall be permitted to become demoralized, paupers, tramps or criminals, and supported as such by all.

I trust that none will think that I have gone too far in my suggestions for the relief of the unemployed, but, even if they should, I hope they will examine them carefully and read them in the light of experience, and the fearful conditions by which we are confronted. At all events I have the satisfaction and, pardon the conceit, the knowledge that I am right, and hope they will be put into practice.

In fancy I hear some one say, "Not all of them, now." I answer that they are based on truth and justice and in the end these must prevail.

Saml Gompers.

New York World, Jan. 14, 1894.

1. See "An Excerpt from an Article in the *New York World*," Aug. 23, 1893, above.

2. Hendrick B. Wright (1808-81), a Pennsylvania lawyer, was a Democratic representative to Congress (1853-55, 1861-63, 1877-81). He introduced a bill in 1877 (H.R. 10, 45th Cong., 1st sess.) to provide government loans of $500 to settlers of public lands, the loans carrying a 3 percent interest rate and repayable over ten years. The bill did not pass. Wright left the Democratic party in 1880 and ran unsuccessfully for reelection on the Greenback-Labor ticket.

3. Samuel S. Cox (1824-89), a lawyer, was a Democratic representative in Congress from Ohio (1857-65) and, subsequently, from New York (1869-85, 1886-89).

4. Thomas Carlyle.

To Alice Woodbridge[1]

Jan. 19 [18]94.

Miss Alice L. Woodbridge,
Sec. Working Women's Society
27 Clinton Place, N.Y. City.
My Dear Madam:—

I am in receipt of your favor of the 10th. instant with enclosures.

In reply to the same permit me to say that the Bill in reference to regulating the employment of women and children in commercial establishments[2] has had the consideration of the American Federation of Labor, and unquestionably the endorsement heretofore would hold good in this instance.

You may count upon whatever support I can give towards securing its passage. I would suggest, however, that you would place yourself in communication with Mr. Daniel Harris, President of the N.Y. State Branch of the A.F. of L. 332 E. 8th. St. N.Y. City, who has authority in matters pertaining to state legislation affecting labor. I am sure he will give you every assistance within his power.

Although I am in favor of the measure for the formation and maintenance of free public employment bureaus[3] (and I know of its success in Ohio) hence I should be pleased to personally aid you, I cannot however take official action upon the matter by reason of no decision having been arrived at upon the subject by the A.F. of L.

I believe them to be efficient in every respect, and though unable to give it that same support at present as I can the other Bill, yet I would not lose an opportunity of saying a good word in its favor.

This office cannot be the agency for the sale of tickets for any Fair, but if you will send two fifty cent tickets to me personally, I shall remit the amount for them.

Trusting that your efforts in both these directions may be successful, I am,

> Very Respectfully Yours　Saml Gompers.
> President. American Federation of Labor.

TLpS, reel 7, vol. 10, p. 178, SG Letterbooks, DLC.

1. Alice L. Woodbridge, a former stenographer and saleswomen, was secretary of the New York Working Women's Society.

2. See "To Martin McMahon," Feb. 9, 1891, n. 3, above.

3. A bill calling for the establishment of free public employment offices was introduced in the New York legislature in January 1894, but did not become law until 1896. The bill (Laws of 1896, chap. 982) required the commissioner of labor statistics to establish such offices in cities with populations over 1.5 million.

To the Executive Council of the AFL

New York, Jan. 20 [18]94.

To the Executive Council of the A.F. of L.

Fellow-Workmen: —

Enclosed you will please find a copy of a letter just received from the General Secretary of the United Garment Workers of America.

You will observe that the question is whether the Executive Council will make an appropriation of five hundred ($500.00) dollars from its funds for the purpose of carrying this case to the general term of the Supreme Court.

Kindly return your vote[1] upon the application at your earliest convenience. Members of the E.C. residing outside the city of New York will send on their vote upon the proposition by wire unprepaid.

Fraternally Yours   Saml Gompers.

President. American Federation of Labor.

N.B. The dispatch in Mr. R's letter asks him to call upon the Attorney at once.

S. G.

[Enclosure]

New York. Jan. 20, 1894.

Mr. Saml. Gompers,

Prest. Am. Fed. of Labor,

Dear Sir and Bro: —

Since receiving the resolution adopted by the Executive Council at its last session "That it would be impossible for the Council to appropriate 1500 dollars towards appealing from the decision of Justice Ingraham[2] in the case of Sinsheimer vs. The United Garment Workers" I immediately notified our Councilors of your decision explaining that under these circumstances it would be impossible for us to proceed with the case. That we the Garment Workers would as soon as possible pay the expense of what had been done up to the present on printing etc. as per our agreement.

Yesterday I received the enclosed telegram in answer to our letter. I complied with the request and received the following offer. If the Garment Workers are able to advance 500 dollars our Councilors Fromme Bros. are willing to stand all costs of trial and printing of entire case through the Supreme Court general term. This will carry us over for three or four months before decision can be rendered by which time if it should be against us we will be in a position to carry the case to the Court of Appeals ourselves.

Surely the members of the Executive Council understand that not alone are the Garment Workers threatened in this case, the welfare of every labor organization is at stake by this action and that we are simply the victims of circumstances, and that sooner or later would have come up and possibly at even greater expenses to the A.F. of L.

Further, if we do not take advantage of this opportunity a precedent will be established making it possible for employers on the slightest provocation or pretext to enjoin labor unions from following out their natural sources of protection.

We feel it our duty to make this last appeal to you the Executive Council of the A.F. of L. to take up this matter for us so it cannot be said we did not make every effort to prevent this blow against organized labor.

Fraternally   Chas. F. Reichers.
Genl. Sect'y.

TLpS and TLpSr, AFL Executive Council Vote Books, reel 8, *AFL Records.*

1. The AFL Executive Council voted against the appropriation because of the Federation's other financial obligations.
2. See "To Peter Breen," Mar. 31, 1893, n. 4, above.

To Charles Palmer[1]

Jan. 20 [18]94.

Mr. Chas. E. Palmer,
Sec. Bldg. Trades Committee
1442 Patapsco St. Baltimore, Md.
Dear Sir and Brother: —

I am in receipt of your favor of the 19th. instant the contents of which are carefully noted.

In reply thereto permit me to say that there is not a law upon the statutes of any State in the Union which is of the least practical benefit so far as employers' liability for accidents to employes is concerned, unless that liability would result practically from maliciousness on the part of employers.

Some time ago a fireman working in a steamship had one of the bags of coal break, come down and nearly kill him. Upon a suit in the Courts he obtained damages but the Steamship Company appealed to the Court of Appeals and that Court reversed the decision of the lower courts and practically rendered a decision nullifying every feature of the law.

It seems to me that it would be necessary to start all over again in securing some law making employers liable for accidents to employes unless caused through the negligence of the employes themselves. I hope soon to have such a measure framed that will cover the point in question.

With kind wishes and hoping this explanation will be satisfactory, I am,

Fraternally Yours   Saml Gompers.
President. American Federation of Labor.

TLpS, reel 7, vol. 10, p. 185, SG Letterbooks, DLC.

1. Charles E. Palmer, a bricklayer, was secretary of the Building Trades Section of the Baltimore Federation of Labor.

From Ernst Hemleben

920 Jackson st La Crosse Wis Jan 22th 1894

Dear Sir & Bro.

I would like to ask you, if you would please, and do me a small Favor. Which Pres. J. C. Meyers[1] Recommend me do you. For further information. In the first place is this. Is their shut a thing as a Cracker Baker Union. I would like like to start one. If I can do so. I have ask several. But they say it wont Work But still it nothing like trying

In the Cracker Factory were I am Working We have lots of trouble. Low, Wages. and no steady work. Were I now, if we had a union, We could demand steady work and probable more wages.

How to start a Union I dont know. Because their is only five, of us.

I would like to hear from you Soon. What Advise you have in that Respect.

I Remain Yours Fraternally   Ernst. Hemleben

ALS, Journeymen Bakers' and Confectioners' International Union Records, reel 138, *AFL Records.*

1. Probably John C. MEYERS, a St. Paul, Minn., barber, who served as president of the Journeymen Barbers' International Union of America from 1890 until 1894.

To George Malby[1]

Jan. 27, [18]94.

Hon. George R. Malby,
Speaker of the Assembly,
Assembly Chamber Albany, N.Y.
Dear Sir:—

From the proceedings of the Assembly I learn that a resolution[2] has been introduced and referred to the Ways and Means Committee which has for its purpose to abolish or consolidate several of the commissions of the various departments in the State of New York.

It is currently understood that the object aimed at is the consolidation or subordination of the Bureau of Labor Statistics, the Board of Mediation and Arbitration and the Factory Inspector's Department.[3]

If such is the case, I desire on behalf of the workingmen and women of this State as well as of the entire country, to enter my most solemn and emphatic protest against such action.

These Bureaus and Department were created at the instance of the organized workingmen and women of the State of N.Y. Nearly every State in the Union has followed the example of the N.Y. Legislature in regard to these matters, and now after the good that has been accomplished to do with these Bureaus what is currently reported the design is, is to declare them failures to the world, which in my opinion would not only be untrue but set in a reactionary and retrogressive movement.

If anything should be done in these matters at all, it should be to enlarge their scope of usefulness, to encourage their work and by no means to injure or handicap them.

I kindly ask you to submit this protest to the Assembly and refer it to the Committee having the subject matter in charge and oblige,

Yours Very Respectfully   Saml Gompers.
President. American Federation of Labor.

TLpS, reel 7, vol. 10, p. 194, SG Letterbooks, DLC.

1. George R. Malby, a Republican, was a member of the New York assembly from 1890 to 1895.

2. During 1894, the New York legislature considered proposals to consolidate or abolish various state commissions and offices to reduce waste and expenditures. It was not until 1901, however, that the Office of Factory Inspection, the Bureau of Labor Statistics, and the Board of Mediation and Arbitration became bureaus of a new Department of Labor (Laws of 1901, chap. 9).

3. The office of factory inspection was created by the New York legislature in the factory act of 1886 (Laws of 1886, chap. 409).

From Thomas Morgan

Office of General Organizer,
The International Machinists' Union of America.
Chicago Ills   Jan 31st 1894

Dear Comrade.

We respectfully notify you that the Local Typographical Unions of New York City in an alliance with the association of Machinists, have under penalty of discharge from Employment in Linotype Printing Offices, compelled six members of our Local Union No 2, to join the association and in this way aim to compell all our members employed or seeking employment in such offices to join the Association

Will you kindly inquire into this matter and inform me as to the jurisdiction of the AF of L in this particular violation of our Federal Compact by the local Typographical Unions.

Fraternally yours   T J Morgan
Gen Secretary

ALS, International Association of Machinists' Records, reel 141, *AFL Records.*

An Excerpt from a News Account of a Mass Meeting at Madison Square Garden

[January 31, 1894]

WORK, NOT CHARITY

Nearly 20,000 workingmen were in Madison Square Garden last night.[1] It was a mass meeting of the unemployed—probably the largest, most remarkable gathering of wage earners this country has ever known. This meeting was suggested by Dr. Stanton Coit,[2] of the Neighborhood Guild, at No. 26 Delancey street, and it was held under the auspices of eighty-three labor unions.

. . .

Many of the unions brought their flags. The first demonstration came when the flag of the United Clothing Cutters appeared. It was like the sound of hail upon a tin roof many times magnified—the sharp rattling musket fire, not of a regiment, but of an army. It drowned the huzzahs and shouts. There were the banners, too, of the Socialists. Among many other memorable things this meeting was remarkable for the struggle between the Socialists and Anarchists.

For a while it dominated everything else, and in the end was a victory for the Socialists.

. . .

SAMUEL GOMPERS HISSED.

When Samuel Gompers was introduced the cheering was drowned by caterwauls and hisses. The Socialists were making the fight against him. "Fellow-workingmen," he began. The jeering and hissing drowned his voice. He threw his head back until his heavy mane of hair rested on his shoulders. His swarthy face flushed. His maxillary muscles stood out in bunches on his cheeks. His eyes flashed. It was a critical time for the President of the American Federation of Labor. If it should go forth that a gathering of 20,000 workingmen hissed him from the platform, what would be his standing? It was one man against thousands. He strained his voice until it was like the hoarse braying of a bull.

"There is an old saying that those who would be free must themselves strike the blow."

Strange and inexplicable is the weather-vane temper of a great audience. That worn quotation quieted the crowd. It gained a hearing for Mr. Gompers. He went on passionately and earnestly until all opposition to him was quieted. It was a splendid victory, that of one man against so many.

. . .

New York World, Jan. 31, 1894.

1. The mass meeting, held on Jan. 30, 1894, was chaired by Stanton Coit and addressed by philanthropists and reformers as well as labor and socialist leaders. It adopted resolutions demanding relief programs. According to press accounts, the huge crowd became unmanageable during the meeting, nearly knocking over the speakers' platform and drowning out many of the orators with catcalls. By the time SG spoke, factional rows within the audience had nearly led to a riot, causing police to call in reinforcements in an attempt to control the crowd.

2. Stanton Coit was an Ohio-born activist in the London ethical society movement from 1888 until his death in 1897. He was a founder in 1886 of the Neighborhood Guild in New York City. Following the plan of Toynbee Hall in London, it gave university students the opportunity of working to improve the lives of the poor while living in a slum community. The Neighborhood Guild, a forerunner of the settlement house movement in the United States, became the University Settlement in 1891. It was active in organizing relief efforts for the poor and unemployed during the depression of the 1890s.

To Louis Schroeder

Feb. 2, [18]94.

Mr. Louis Schroeder,
505 E. Water St. Milwaukee, Wis.
Dear Sir and Brother: —

I am in receipt of your favor of the 20th. instant together with the application for a charter for a Central Labor Union in your city.

In reply permit me to say that the application does not come in due form, since it is not accompanied with the fee for the same, hence it does not come regularly before us as an application. However, I should say to you that the last convention of the American Federation of Labor adopted an amendment to the constitution providing that two charters could not be issued to two different central bodies in any one locality. You seem to have anticipated that as shown in your letter and state that you use these means in order that the subject matter of the action of the Federated Trades Council[1] should be brought to the attention of the Executive Council of the A.F. of L.

Permit me to say that you fall into an error when you say that the Federation has decided that central bodies shall take no political action. On the contrary, the Chicago convention decided to submit to the affiliated organizations the advisability of pursuing just such a course. In due time the programme will be submitted to the organizations and they are expected to instruct their delegates to the next convention of the A.F. of L. definitely upon that subject.

I earnestly deplore the dispute and contention which has arisen among the organized wage-workers of your city, for I regard it as particularly unfortunate in view of our present industrial crises. The entire enemies of the labor movement are using every possible means for the purpose of disrupting our organizations and destroying their influence and power in defence of the rights and interests of the working people.

In view of such a condition of affairs it would be well if we were to lay aside all differences of opinion and subordinate self, that the best interests of our fellow men and women may be protected and advanced. If the proper spirit prevails on both sides I am sure that harmony and unity can be accomplished. It is only when we fail to see the right, and are governed by our prejudices that dissensions arise which create divisions, preventing unity which leaves us in a defenceless position to have labor's enemies place the yoke upon our necks, shackles upon our limbs. Unless this matter is adjusted soon I feel certain that all will have cause to regret it.

The Executive Council of the A.F. of L. will not have a meeting for some time to come and before it takes place I hope unity will be restored in your ranks. However, at the first meeting of the Council the entire subject matter will be laid before them.[2]

With kind wishes and hoping to hear from you as the situation progresses, I am,

Fraternally Yours　Saml Gompers.
President. American Federation of Labor.

TLpS, reel 7, vol. 10, pp. 208-9, SG Letterbooks, DLC.

1. The Milwaukee Federated Trades Council was founded in 1887. For a discussion of the dispute within the Milwaukee labor movement, see "Michael Fallon and Samuel Godfrey to the Executive Council of the AFL," Apr. 11, 1894, below.

2. The AFL Executive Council discussed the matter at its Apr. 21, 1894, meeting, but took no action.

To the Executive Council of the AFL

New York, Feb. 5, [18]94.

REPORT OF PRESIDENT GOMPERS' VISIT
TO AUBURN, ME.

Early of last week a communication was sent by the Secretary[1] of the Joint Board of the Boot and Shoe Workers of Auburn, requesting the Secretary[2] of the Boot and Shoe Manufacturers Association of that city to call a meeting of the Association for the purpose of holding a conference with the undersigned.

Upon my arrival in Auburn a reply from Secretary Small was received stating that the Association though intending no discourtesy to the undersigned thought there was no necessity for a conference. I then wrote to Pray, Small and Company inquiring that inasmuch as it was the firm in which the trouble originated and from which it spread, whether they would not have a conference for the purpose of amicably adjusting existing differences. A negative was given to the request.

In the evening a great mass-meeting was held in which the men and women reiterated their intention to stand out until fairer conditions should be conceded by the manufacturers.

I made an investigation of the actual conditions and found them as follows:

1st. That trade is extremely bad in Auburn due to the general industrial stagnation, and to a diverting of the boot and shoe trade by reason of the contest; That there have been about 500 of the 2,300 who originally struck and were locked out who had returned to work; That the manufacturers have very irregular employment even for those who have returned; That the large mass and best boot and shoe workers are still out and have been so now for 25 weeks; That though deprivation and sacrifices are being borne and made the men and women will hold out provided they can get some support.

The General Secretary[3] and Assistant[4] of the organization expressed the belief that in the course of four or five weeks the shoe making trade must revive and that if the people can be sustained the manufacturers of Auburn would be compelled to concede fairer conditions.

It is necessary to add the four conditions that the Manufacturers Association imposes upon every one who seeks employment.

1st. That they shall not belong to a labor organization.

2nd. That they shall sign an individual contract.

3rd. That a week's notice must be given before any employe can quit work except under forfeiture of the week's wages, and that at the will of the employer if two or more should give notice of a week it shall be within the power of the employer to so notify the workmen to withdraw their notice. Failure to withdraw will act as a forfeiture of the wages.

4th. That ten per cent of the wages of the workmen will be withheld until $40.00 has been accumulated, and violation of a contract will result in a forfeiture of this amount over and above the week's wages.

These are the conditions as I found them but should be considered entirely separate from the application of the organization for financial assistance.[5]

TDp, AFL Executive Council Vote Books, reel 8, *AFL Records.*

1. Charles G. Burlington, a shoe cutter, was the secretary of the joint board.

2. L. Linn Small of Pray, Small, and Co. was elected secretary of the Auburn Shoe Manufacturers' Association in October 1893.

3. Henry J. Skeffington.

4. John D. DULLEA was assistant general secretary (1894) and later general secretary (1894-95) of the Boot and Shoe Workers' International Union (BSWIU).

5. The AFL Executive Council rejected the BSWIU's application for a $1,000 loan for the Auburn strikers but authorized an appeal for voluntary assistance through the *American Federationist.*

From Joseph Wood[1]

Corliss Association of Stationary Engineers of America
4349 Maffitt ave St. Louis, Feb 5th 1894

Dear Sr.

I am requested to as[k] for your opinion on the following case. we engineers have had a very hard struggle here in St Louis in trying to better our condition for the past two years, and it is only at this late day that we have seen any results from our labors we began to request the houses and factorys supposed to be union to employ union enginers the first place we made the request was leggitt and meyers tobacco Co. they issued orders for their engineers to join the union (they have 4) one of these was a member of our ass'n and we succeeded in geting the Chief Engineer to come in with us but one engineer working in their box factory joined one of our social organizations of engineers. as we are the only union of engineers in the city we protested and the firm insisted upon him joining a union the box makers of this factory have a union #6042[2] A.F. of L they offered to take him in their union. (a engineer with box makers) we protested againste this and made such a fuss they finally did not take him in. this man still refuses to come in our association claiming we made a fight on him to force him in our union and he will not join us. he later makes application in to the International machinsts union and is excepted. and shows a card from the machinests union A.F. of L. and his supertendent says that is all he wants. we have made complants against other houses and we find two other engineers who are going into the machinests union. what we want to know if they can do this thes men are following engineering for a livehood and are not working at the machinest trade. please understand this. a good engineer is usual a machinest also he does not have to be but he has advantages by being one but a machinest as a rule are not engineers and know nothing about engineering. thes men going into the machinest union is discouraging to us they also do it to try and break up our union a[s?] St Louis never had a engineers union untill untill I organized this association and as our association meets saturday I hope you will try if possible to have an answer by this time I trust I have explained the case fully to you but would be pleased to give you any further information you desire[3]

Resp   J. W Wood.
Engineers Union A.F. of L. #5658.

ALS, Corliss Association of Stationary Engineers' Records, reel 140, *AFL Records.*

1. Joseph W. Wood, a St. Louis engineer, was secretary of AFL Corliss Association Engineers of America 5658.

2. The AFL chartered Tobacco Boxmakers' Protective Union 6042 of St. Louis in May 1893.

3. On Mar. 2, 1894, SG wrote to Thomas J. Morgan, general secretary of the Machinists' International Union, noting what he regarded as the machinists' unfair position in this case.

To William[1] and Frank Hollister[2]

Feb. 6, [18]94.

Mr. W. C. Hollister and Bro.
148 Monroe St. Chicago, Ill.
Dear Sirs:—

Your several favors came duly to hand, and contents noted.

Replying thereto permit me to say that when your favor of the 19th reached here I was East engaged in work by direction of the Executive Council. I am free to say, however, that I am considerably surprised to think that you should have assumed by reason of not hearing from me at once that the American Federation of Labor had no control over the publication of Mr. Lloyd's[3] address.[4] In fact, as I understood it, the American Federation of Labor had full control of it.

I enclose to you herein a circular 10.000 of which were distributed to the Trade and Labor Unions of the country, and I had great hopes that a very large circulation would have been secured for the paper, apart from the original order given. Of course you can readily understand that your offer to sell single copies for two cents, and 15 for 25 cents places us in a very poor light before the working people and the public generally, while at the same time narrow down our opportunities for selling it. Is it not possible for you to make arrangements so as to sell the paper the same price as the A.F. of L., or have us have the exclusive right of their sales? In either event, you would have the printing of them.

By this same mail I write to our friend Lloyd making the same suggestion, and I earnestly hope that some satisfactory arrangements can be made.

I promised to write you in connection with another matter, but have been unable to do so up to the present moment. You say that from a remark made to you by a friend you were led to believe that I left Chicago under the impression that you had antagonized my reelection for the Presidency of the A.F. of L. and you say that if this is so, that it is a false impression.

Let me say to you in answer that whoever communicated that to you evidently fell into error. As a matter of fact I know of no one to whom I expressed an opinion either one way or another upon the subject, and if I had any impression at all in connection with it it certainly was that you favored my reelection.

You remember when I called at your office in the early part of Sept. and had a pleasant chat with you, your Brother, our friend Carroll[5] and others, when Mr. Carroll voluntarily stated to me that he had not heard of any opposition to my election, but if there was any I should communicate that fact to him and he would do all that he possibly could to further my success, I acted then as I have upon every occasion when my own personal interests are involved, and that is, I said nothing. As a matter of fact I never believed the subject of my election to the Presidency of the A.F. of L. or any other office in the labor movement was a proper subject for me to discuss with any one. If those who favored my election cared to say anything, they would have to espouse my cause either without any prompting or encouragement from me.

I may have mistaken notions in reference to matters of this character, but I assure you that I prefer defeat any time, than to either canvass for the office or to visit my ill will upon those who may oppose my candidacy, nor do I for a moment want you to believe that I am ungrateful or unmindful to those who may have exerted themselves in my behalf. On the contrary, I think I am deeply sensible of such services, and appreciate them far beyond measure of expression.

You will pardon me if I am compelled to decline to discuss the candidacy of the other gentleman you refer to and your attitude towards him. Taking it all in all, the entire subject was within your province, and I firmly believe you acted as your conscience dictated to you.

It should be needless to say that I thank you sincerely that I earned your good opinion sufficiently that you advocated my reelection, and to again assure you that your informant must have been mistaken.

With kindest wishes and asking you to remember me to our friends Carroll, Meyer[6] and others, I am,

Very Truly Yours   Saml Gompers.
President. American Federation of Labor.

TLpS, reel 7, vol. 10, pp. 235-36, SG Letterbooks, DLC.

1. William C. Hollister was a Chicago printer specializing in labor publications, including the *Eight-Hour Herald*.

2. Frank C. Hollister.

3. Henry Demarest LLOYD of Chicago was a noted social activist and reform writer.

4. The AFL published the address that Lloyd delivered at its 1893 convention (*The Safety of the Future Lies in Organized Labor* [Washington, D.C., 1893]), and the Hollisters' firm was preparing to republish it.

5. Michael J. Carroll of Chicago was the editor of the *Eight-Hour Herald* and a member of International Typographical Union 16. He belonged to the Executive Committee of the Chicago Civic Federation and was active in the Federation's efforts to secure legislation providing for arbitration of industrial disputes.

6. Probably H. B. Meyers, a publisher in the same building as the Hollisters' firm.

To Henry Blair

Feb. 7, [18]94.

Hon. Henry W. Blair,
House of Representatives, Washington, D.C.
Dear Sir and Friend: —

The Executive Council of the American Federation of Labor have determined that the opportunity should be given to Secretary Carlisle for an issuance of an order in reference to the Eight Hour Law of Aug. 1st. 1892.[1]

It seems to be extremely difficult to have some one make up a case in which an order can be asked from the Secretary of the Treasury. A few with whom I communicated upon the subject have said that "if the Department desires the information it could be easily ascertained by its officers." You know as well as I do, if not better, that it is that very thing which we have to overcome, that the Departments are not over anxious to make a case upon which they could base an order enforcing a law in the interest of labor, and particularly one limiting the hours.

I should like some time to have an opportunity to talk the matter over with you for an hour or so, and see whether a case could not be formally presented to the Secretary of the Treasury. I know that the employes who are working more than eight hours a day on Government work would very reluctantly, if at all, give testimony to the violation of the law, but if I knew of a few instances in which the law is being violated I would detail a few men to watch the works, and then they could of their own knowledge present affidavits to the violation of the law. I think this about the most practical method of overcoming the difficulty, and I ask you to consider it.

It is needless to say how much I appreciate the trouble you went to in having the copy of the contract[2] etc. in the eight hour matter prepared and sent me, but I found that the contract had already expired and the work performed.

Do you expect to come to this city any time within the next few weeks? If you do, and will drop me a note as to your coming, I will gladly meet you at any time and place convenient to you, or if you do not contemplate leaving Washington could we arrange a time in about two weeks when I could take a run down to Washington and discuss the matter with you. There is a subject in connection with this that I also desire to communicate at the same time.

Since Secretary Carlisle expressed himself at our interview so favorably as to his understanding of the Law, I am most anxious that something should be done in the near future by which we may be enabled to determine whether he will issue an order for its proper enforcement, or whether we shall be compelled to make a test case of it, or on the other hand whether additional legislation may be necessary.

With kindest wishes and hoping to hear from you at your earliest convenience, I am,

Very Truly Yours Saml Gompers.
President. American Federation of Labor.

TLpS, reel 7, vol. 10, pp. 240-41, SG Letterbooks, DLC.

1. See "To Josiah Dyer," Oct. 31, 1893, n. 4, above.
2. Blair had sent SG a copy of the government's contract with E. F. Gobel.

To J. C. Nolan[1]

Feb. 7, [18]94.

Mr. J. C. Nolan,
787 Cedar St. St. Paul, Minn.
Dear Sir and Brother: —

I am in receipt of your favor of the 31st. the contents of which have been given careful attention, and I beg to assure you that the perusal of its contents gave me pleasure as well as interested me very much.

It should go without saying that I regard the affiliation of the Bro'd. of Locomotive Engineers with the other great trade unions of America under the banner of the American Federation of Labor as not only desirable but essential. I have in mind not only the future of the A.F. of L. but the B. of L.E. as well. For years I have given the subject much thought and have lost no opportunity of impressing it upon the minds of the Engineers whenever I met them in meeting, or individually.

In my reports to several conventions I have made reports and recommendations upon the same subject. Even in my last report to the Chicago convention I did not fail in regard to this as you will see by a reference to the proceedings of said convention.

In my judgment the great mistake that the B. of L.E. have made is the policy of isolation it has pursued for so many years. Chief Arthur is accused by many of having an improper motive for his persistency in that policy. Notwithstanding the fact that I differ with him essentially upon that subject, I have too great a regard for the good work he has done in building up that grand organization to even for a moment harbor a suspicion that he is prompted by anything else than an honest, though mistaken policy.

The student of the struggles of the toiling masses, as well as the observer of current events, must, I think, observe that as the trend of the times is for a greater concentration of the wealth possessors, the employers of our country, it is necessary for our common protection and advancement that Unions of Labor both skilled and unskilled while maintaining their distinct trade lines should see to it that their rights and interests may not be encroached upon.

If the B. of L.E. in becoming affiliated with the American Federation of Labor were to lose its identity, its autonomy or independence, I should not only hesitate to recommend that course, but as a Union man myself I would not occupy the position I do as President of the A.F. of L. I would not have the Union of my trade, or of any trade lose either of these rights. In fact, I would not surrender them to any power on earth. The A.F. of L. makes no such requirement, in fact, it is contrary to its policy, and the fundamental principles upon which it is built.

One need merely inquire from our affiliated National or International Unions or brotherhoods, and he would soon learn that the distinctive character of each and all of the organizations is recognized and strictly enforced.

Then again, there are no burdensome taxes which the organization is required to bear nor onerous conditions against which to contend. We seek by our co-operation to strengthen the power and influence of our struggling brothers and sisters of labor, to give tone and character to the whole labor movement, to crystalize a better thought and a healthier public opinion upon the toilers efforts for an amelioration in their condition, and to secure the passage of such laws as will protect and promote the interests of all.

In that work all men should join hands, and I assure you that I most cordially welcome your efforts to accomplish this much desired purpose, and assure you that I will aid to the very best of my ability to the attainment of its success.

With this I mail to your address a number of documents to which I invite your attention as giving a clearer exposition of the purposes, the duties and the rights of affiliated unions.

With kindest wishes and hoping to hear from you frequently, I am,

Fraternally Yours   Saml Gompers.
President. American Federation of Labor.

TLpS, reel 7, vol. 10, pp. 244-45, SG Letterbooks, DLC.

1. J. C. Nolan was an engineer for the Great Northern Railroad.

To Harry Vrooman[1]

Feb. 16, [18]94.

Rev. Harry C. Vrooman,
31 Concord Ave. Cambridge, Mass.
My Dear Sir:—

I have the honor to acknowledge the receipt of your favor of the 7th. inst. and I am free to say that I welcome the effort that is about to be made by your organization[2] to unite the moral forces of our country for concerted action against the admitted evils of our time, and shall look forward to the papers published in "The Arena" with expectancy and shall no doubt read them with pleasure and benefit.

You ask me whether I would act as a member of your National Advisory Board, and I beg to assure you that it affords me pleasure to be able to accept the invitation. In accepting, however, it will be necessary for me to say that it will be impossible for me to write upon any subject outside of the duties of my office any time within the next month. If I can be of service thereafter to further the cause we are engaged in, I shall not only regard it as a duty but as a pleasure to comply.

Sincerely hoping that the effort may be entirely successful, I am,

Very Truly Yours   Saml Gompers.
President. American Federation of Labor.

TLpS, reel 7, vol. 10, p. 287, SG Letterbooks, DLC.

1. Harry Chase Vrooman was a minister at the Congregational Church in East Milton, Mass., and national secretary-treasurer of the Union for Practical Progress.

2. Founded in 1894, the Union for Practical Progress agitated against political corruption, child labor, intemperance, sweat shops, and the like. With some forty branches in Boston, Philadelphia, Baltimore, Providence, and elsewhere, the union focused on different problems each month, and utilized existing organizations and religious institutions to carry on its campaigns. SG served as a member of its national advisory board. The *Arena* served as a regular channel for the publication of material pertaining to the organization's program.

To Thomas O'Rielly

March 3, [18]94.

Mr. Thos. F. O'Rielly,
132 W. 96th St. N.Y. City.
Dear Sir:—

I have the honor to acknowledge the receipt of your favor of the 1st. inst. and in compliance with your request I mail to your address with this the pamphlets you name as well as a copy of the first issue of the "*American Federationist.*"

Replying to your question permit me to say that there never was a large representation of labor in the United States Congresses although several Union men were members of them. Today Amos J. Cummings and Mr. Gallagher[1] are members of the Typographical Union, Martin Foran[2] and Thos. F. Murch[3] were respectively members of the Coopers[4] and Granite Cutters Unions, also John Fehrenbach[5] of the Machinists.

The American workingmen have lagged considerably in securing representation of candidates from their own ranks in Congress. They have made much greater strides in being represented in the various legislatures.

In England there are 11 labor representatives in Parliament. In Germany there are 40 representatives of the Socialist Democratic Party.

These are as near the facts as I can give them to you offhand, and are nearly reliable.

With kind regards, I am,

Very Truly Yours   Saml Gompers.
President. American Federation of Labor.

TLpS, reel 7, vol. 10, p. 342, SG Letterbooks, DLC.

1. Jacob Harold Gallinger (1837-1918), a New Hampshire printer before becoming a physician, was a Republican congressman (1885-89) and senator (1891-1918).

2. Martin Ambrose FORAN was a Democratic congressman from Ohio from 1883 to 1889.

3. Thomas Henry MURCH of Maine was secretary of the Granite Cutters' International Union (1877-78) and a U.S. congressman from 1879 to 1883, elected on the Greenback-Labor ticket.

4. The COOPERS' International Union of North America.

5. John FEHRENBATCH was elected president of the International Machinists and Blacksmiths of North America in 1871 and 1872. He was elected to the Ohio legislature as a Republican in 1875, and served a single term.

To George Horn[1]

March 5, [1894]

Mr. Geo. L. Horn,
Sec. Bakers & Confectioners Intl. Union
9 Hilsendegan Block, Detroit, Mich.
Dear Sir and Brother:—

I am in receipt of your favor of the 1st. inst.[2] and am pleased to learn of the action taken in reference to the Bill for permitting trade union journals to be mailed as second class matter[3] and hope we may be successful in our effort.

Replying to your question permit me to say that the Chicago convention of the American Federation of Labor decided positively that no loans of money should be made from the funds of the A.F. of L. You will remember that there was in the neighborhood of $5.000 loaned to various organizations last year and in one bulk they were donated by the convention. The question of further loans was then reported upon, discussed and disposed of as stated.

In my judgment I desire to say that both actions were not conducive to the best results, as I believe that loans should be made; and you will remember that in my recommendations to the conventions of the past two years I advised such a course, nor do I believe it practical to donate them for that simply destroys the basis of our actions in these matters.

No doubt we shall have to depend upon the revival in industry and organization (which I hope will soon take place) for the introduction of our proposed Sinking Fund and then be in a better position to render that aid which many of our organizations are really in need of.

Regretting our inability to comply with your request,[4] and with kindest wishes, I am,

> Fraternally Yours   Saml Gompers.
> President. American Federation of Labor.

N.B. Let me have your opinion upon the *"American Federationist."*

> S. G.

TLpS, reel 7, vol. 10, p. 352, SG Letterbooks, DLC.

1. George L. HORN was secretary of the Journeymen Bakers' and Confectioners' International Union from 1892 until 1895.

2. Journeymen Bakers' and Confectioners' International Union Records, reel 138, *AFL Records.*

3. On Dec. 20, 1893, Republican Congressman Eugene Hainer of Nebraska introduced a bill (H.R. 4897, 53d Cong., 2d sess.) to allow periodicals issued by benevolent and fraternal societies to be mailed as second-class matter. The bill was referred to the Committee on Post Office and Post Roads where it received no further action.

4. Horn requested a $500 loan for his union from the AFL in the face of lockouts of his members in Chicago, Boston, and Columbia, Pa.

To Michael Raphael[1]

March 7, [1894]

Mr. M. Raphael,
118 York St. Brooklyn, N.Y.
Dear Sir and Brother:—

I am in receipt of your favor of the 5th. inst. stating that the Brooklyn Central Labor Union resolved to invite a representative of labor's interests to deliver an address on the subject of the Greater New York,[2] and the attitude organized labor should take towards that measure. You request me to accept the invitation to deliver such an address.

I am pleased to note, however, that you are aware of the fact that my duties are of so pressing a nature that it may be difficult for me to accept, in fact such is the case. Together with the duties I have heretofore performed as President of the American Federation of Labor I am also now required to give great attention as Editor to our Magazine the *"American Federationist,"* hence it would be utterly impossible for me to accept the invitation much as I would be pleased to say something interesting upon that subject.

In connection therewith let me say that apart from any consideration of local pride which such an enlarged city would instill, it seems to me that the labor movement of the greater New York would receive a great impetus from it. In some of the labor organizations both in New York and Brooklyn a difference in the wages, hours and other conditions exists among the workers of both cities. In several trades though equally organized, a difference in wages exists of from 25 to 50 cents per day and I am fully persuaded that with the accomplishment of the unity of the two cities there will be little if any difficulty in securing a uniformity.

This in itself will be of great advantage. Apart from this it would bring to our movement a greater concentration of effort and unity of purpose. Why not invite either, Dan. Harris, Ed. King,[3] F. W. Sullivan,[4] John R. O'Donnell[5] or some other equally capable man. I feel confident that some arrangement could be made by which they could appear from a certain date mutually agreeable and discuss this question.

Regretting my inability to accept the invitation at this time, and with best wishes, I am,

Fraternally Yours   Saml Gompers.
President. American Federation of Labor.

TLpS, reel 7, vol. 10, p. 357, SG Letterbooks, DLC.

1. Michael Raphael, a cigarmaker in Brooklyn, was secretary of CMIU 87 between 1890 and 1897.

2. On May 4, 1897, the state legislature passed the Greater New York Charter, which united the Bronx, Brooklyn, Manhattan, Richmond, and Queens into Greater New York effective Jan. 1, 1898.

3. Edward KING, a type founder, was active during the 1880s in the New York City Central Labor Union.

4. Possibly James William SULLIVAN, a New York City printer active in International Typographical Union 6, who represented the AFL's New York State Branch at the AFL's 1894 convention.

5. Possibly John R. O'Donnell, an editor of the *New York Evening Telegram.*

To Fusataro Takano[1]

March 9, [1894]

Mr. F. Takano,
Great Barrington, Mass.
Dear Sir:—

I am in receipt of your favor of the 6th. inst. the contents of which are carefully noted.

In reply permit me to say that I experienced more pleasure in the perusal of your letter than I have time, or opportunity, or possibly the ability to express. To my mind it appears that no growth or permanent good can come either to the workers of America, Japan or any other country without the essential factor to secure it, namely, organization. That you, after a stay of a few years in our country, have arrived at the same conclusions and propose on your return to Japan to do what you can to instill this thought upon your fellow countrymen, is an evidence to me that your time has been well spent here, and that you may be in truth a benefactor to your fellow countrymen and to the human family.

Truly as you say I cannot enter into a full discussion of this subject in a letter nor answer your questions as I believe they deserve to be, but the initial step to be taken by any people must of necessity be the right to coalesce, the right to organization. That right I am aware is not accorded to the subjects of the Japanese empire.

The workers should be organized in the unions of their respective trades and callings at the earliest possible time. That brings unity of feeling and action and instills in the hearts and minds the feeling and knowledge of interdependence, security and progress. The indiscriminate organization of workers regardless of their trades and callings is by no means to be compared in its stability and results to the organizations upon trade lines.

As per your request I mail a number of documents to you with this and commend them to your careful study.

Should you at any time be enabled to make a visit to this city and have an hour to spare, it would afford me pleasure to discuss this matter at length with you. In all likelihood a better understanding could be had than a mere correspondence could secure.

Again expressing my appreciation of your kind thoughts upon the organization of the Japanese workmen, and trusting that your effort may be entirely successful, I am,

Very Respectfully Yours   Saml Gompers.
President. American Federation of Labor.

TLpS, reel 7, vol. 10, p. 367, SG Letterbooks, DLC.

1. Fusataro TAKANO was a founder in San Francisco of the Shokkō Giyū-kai (Fraternal Society of Workers), a study group among Japanese immigrants concerned with applying American trade union methods to labor problems attending Japan's industrialization.

To David Lubin[1]

Mr. D. Lubin,
412 K. St. Sacramento, Cal.
Dear Sir:—

Both your favors of the 26th. and 27th. insts. came duly to hand the contents of which have been given careful consideration.

Replying thereto permit me to say that from the tenor of both your letters I am convinced that you misjudge my motives, do me an injustice and the cause you advocate serious injury.

When I wrote the Chairman[2] of the Committee on Promulgation of the Sacramento Federated Trades Council[3] suggesting the advertising columns of the "*American Federationist*" for a notice of your pamphlet[4] it was because I believed that would be a better means of reaching the attention of the working men of our country than by the issuance of a circular. Let me state to you that Mr. Higgins in his letter to me requested me to issue a circular to the labor organizations of the country advising them of the fact that upon application either to him or to you a copy of your pamphlet could be obtained gratuitously.

He offered to pay for the printing, mailing, postage etc. involved in the issuance of the circular. I suggested the columns of the "*American Federationist*" as being more advantageous to all concerned and likely to accomplish better results. How you get the notion from this suggestion that this would be a prostitution must be achieved through a process of reasoning I fail to comprehend.

If you had written an article upon the subject of your proposition and I had refused it publication in the Magazine and suggested that it be inserted as an advertisement, you would certainly have had good grounds of complaint, but having suggested the course I have, I repeat that it would have been advantageous to both and would have accomplished much better results.

To demonstrate to you that I am not opposed to your proposition I offer you the columns of the "*American Federationist*" to contribute an article upon the subject of your Proposition, asking only that it be confined to a reasonable length, say from 1.000 to 1200 words, and I would add that this offer is made to you freely without regard to whether you purchase any copies or not. The Magazine is for sale to those who wish to purchase it. Its columns are open only to those who have something to suggest in the interest of the toiling masses of our country and cannot be purchased or diverted to any other purpose.

Coming to the consideration of your Proposition let me say that many of your postulates are not only correct but self-evident. Beyond doubt a uniform rate of transportation of the farm products of our country would greatly tend towards improving the condition of all our people, but I submit to your candid consideration whether it would not be easier of attainment by the Government Ownership and Control of the railroads of our country. If the matter is the more feasible and practical way to the attainment of your Proposition, why not give that your support? It has already received the sanction of several conventions of the American Federation of Labor and is on the tapis for discussion and adjustment.

I should say that if you conclude to contribute an article to the Magazine as I suggest above, you need not, unless you please, take cognizance of my suggestion as to the Government ownership and control of railroads. You can discuss your Proposition in your own way.

You urge me and my colleagues to make your Proposition an especial study. Without appearing egotistical I desire to say to you that I have read your pamphlet and I think that I have fairly digested it, but I desire to remind you of the fact that we are but the executors of the will of our fellow unionists, and until they have endorsed the plan it is not within our province to propagate it to the exclusion of other measures upon which a conclusion has been reached.

In the beginning of this letter I say that you are doing your own cause an injury. Let me give you my reasons for so stating. There was probably not ten delegates to the Chicago convention of the American Federation of Labor whom you did not in some manner give offence to not the least of which was your unnecessary obtrusion of your views upon religious matters. In your letter of the 26th. you exhibit the same lack of judgment. Your religion or mine is a matter of your private concern and mine, one with which we are to be at peace with our own consciences. It is immaterial to me what you believe the mission of your co-religionists to be. The world is not concerned with my religion. You do not ask me to discuss your Proposition from the standpoint of my religion, or if you do you should not.

I am President of the American Federation of Labor, and so long as I hold that office I shall endeavor to perform the duties devolving upon me to the best of my ability and the highest conceptions I can form. It matters little to me at which altar you may pray. For myself, I would prefer to set my ideal of a man, as a man of honor and sincerely devoted to the amelioration of the condition of my fellows, and to contribute my mite towards their emancipation from all injustice and wrong.

You say that your chief glory is that you are a Jew. Mine is that I have a heart, a mind and a conscience, that I have struggled with my fellowmen and yearn to struggle on for a better day when the ridiculous divisions, questions which make man an enemy to man instead of his brother, shall be eliminated.

It is neither necessary to affirm or deny any religion or lack of it that I may have. It is neither your concern nor that of any one else. Jefferson placed this as a test of Americanism—"Is he honest, is he true, is he faithful to the Constitution?" I am willing that that test be applied to me so far as the labor movement of our country and the struggles of the people are concerned, and if I should come up to a fair conception of these requirements it should certainly satisfy even you.

That it is likely that I may not hold the position that I now occupy very long, I will not attempt to gainsay. There are others equally or more competent to hold it, fully as faithful, but at least when that time arrives I shall have the proud satisfaction, the great glory of my life, to know that I have done my best without regard to religious creed, political divisions, or previous conditions, and have given the best twenty-six years of my life to a cause which I regard as the highest, the noblest and the holiest the people of the world have ever been called upon to espouse.

You say that you have had the privilege of "equality, liberty, education and some means." You have been most fortunate. I have not had the advantage of any of these. I hope you will not deem it amiss if my purpose is to secure for my fellow workers the opportunities you have enjoyed, and of which I have been deprived.

Let me call your attention to one of the very unfair attitudes that you have assumed and one which if persisted in in other quarters must do your cause injury. On the envelope of your letter of the 26th. is marked "personal"; at the heading of your letter you mark it "private," and at its close you put this addenda, "While the letter is marked private I reserve the right to make *public* use of it whenever *I* may see fit so to do." You practically propose to enjoin secrecy and privacy upon me, and reserve to yourself the right to give it publicity. Permit me to say in connection herewith that you have my full permission to do just as you please with your letters and mine. I am not accustomed to receive private letters addressed to me as President of the American Federation of Labor, and I do not so regard them.

In closing I would add that this letter is written in the best of spirit, and I trust that you will so regard it.

That I may hear from you soon is the earnest wish of,

Yours Very Respectfully   Saml Gompers.
President. American Federation of Labor.

N.B. I shall forward a copy of this letter to Mr. Higgins.

S. G.

P.S. If you publish any part of your letters to me I trust that you will publish them entire. At any rate if you publish my reply I have a right to and do demand that it shall appear as written in full.

S. G.

TLpS, reel 7, vol. 10, p. 371-74, SG Letterbooks, DLC.

1. David Lubin, the owner of a Sacramento, Calif., dry goods store and of a mail order business, was a leading advocate of agricultural reform.

2. Probably John M. Higgins, who became a printer for the state of California.

3. As early as March 1890 the Sacramento Federated Trades Council existed as an organization of ten local unions affiliated with the Representative Council of the Federated Trades and Labor Organizations of the Pacific Coast.

4. Lubin's *A Novel Proposition* (Sacramento, 1893 and 1894), published in two parts as pamphlets, discussed the impact of transportation costs of agricultural commodities on farmers and workers. A segment of his discussion appeared under that title in the *American Federationist* (1 [May 1894]: 47-49, 54), in which Lubin proposed to use custom revenues to subsidize the shipping of agricultural staples abroad.

To George McMurphy[1]

March 16, [1894]

Mr. Geo. L. Mc-Murphy,
Box 761 Tacoma, Wash.
Dear Sir and Brother:—

Some little time ago you wrote to this office upon the matter of the Bill of the Hon. W. H. Doolittle[2] for the purpose of making a Commissioner of Labor of a cabinet officer, that Mr. Doolittle stated that the Commissioner was opposed to the measure and gave as his judgment that organized labor is also opposed to it.

I am free to say that I am not sure of the position that organized labor takes upon the subject since the matter has not been either discussed or decided. Some short time ago I had an interview with the present Commissioner and I am free to say that up to that time I was favorable to the proposition, but he convinced me to the contrary. The main point which gained my adhesion to his thought upon that subject was that if it was a cabinet position, the cabinet would always be changed, once, if not more than once in four years, and with every political change, the position would always be one which would be close to the political party in power. His position would be made a partisan political reward and not reward for actual merit or services rendered in the interest of the toiling masses.

A cabinet officer would be necessarily at the cabinet meetings and have the confidence of his colleagues, and you can readily understand that never would an opportunity come to a bona fide labor man, regardless of his politics. The partisan political consideration would be first and his interest in the labor problem last. I commend this to your earnest consideration. However, let me say that I should be pleased to have an expression of your views upon that subject.

Supposing you were to write an article for the "*American Federationist.*" I am sure it would be of interest and tend largely towards gaining an expression of opinion from the organized wage-workers of the country upon that subject.

I mail to you with this a copy of the Magazine and trust you will do whatever lies in your power to further its circulation in and around your city.

With kind wishes and hopes for success, I am,

Fraternally Yours   Saml Gompers.
President. American Federation of Labor.

TLpS, reel 7, vol. 10, p. 396, SG Letterbooks, DLC.

1. George L. McMurphy was a carpenter.
2. William Hall Doolittle (1848-1914), a Tacoma, Wash., lawyer, was a Republican congressman from 1893 to 1897. On Dec. 7, 1893, he unsuccessfully introduced a bill (H.R. 4514, 53d Cong., 2d sess.) to make the U.S. Department of Labor a cabinet level department.

An Article in the *People*

[March 18, 1894]

STRIKING THE NAIL ON THE HEAD.

The *National Glass Budget*, official organ of the American Flint Glass Workers' Union, gives the leading place to a criticism of *The Federationist*, the new monthly organ of the American Federation of Labor. In this article the lash is applied to the pure and simple Gompers crew with vigor and effect by one of the very organizations attached to the A.F. of L.

This is the article:

"We are in receipt of the first number of the *American Federationist*, published by the American Federation of Labor, 14 Clinton Place, New York, and deem this a proper opportunity to express our disappointment with the quality and essence of the matter presented in the opening number of volume 1. Typographically the number is neat and clean and worthy of the great cause it has espoused to champion.

"But when it comes to the real matter presented and the course outlined by Mr. Gompers, the editor, one who expected the clear ring of the most advanced thought upon economic questions cannot but be disappointed while searching the 19 pages of windy and wordy editorial and special matter. The political programme, now certainly the most important question before the members of the Federation as a whole, is placed upon the last page, without note or comment, and is thus strictly in keeping with Mr. Gompers' editorial promise, not to 'step too far in advance and not to be found lagging in the rear of the column,' but rather keep somewhere back in the middle or center of the moving hosts of labor, where it is more comfortable and safe, and where one is less likely to be struck by bullets from the enemy in front, or be jabbed or nabbed from behind, or scarred by enfilading fire from either side.

"One can call this anything under the sun, but it is not leadership. A triumphant army 'whose goal is human justice' requires flying banners and must have tattered ensigns, and it must have leaders who will have the courage to take their proper place at the head of the column; right where the poisoned arrows thickest fall.

"Perfectly in line with Gomperianism is also this other editorial declaration:

"[']In politics we shall be as we always have been, independent. Independent of all parties, regardless under which name they may be known.[']

"Mr. Gompers ought to know that there can to-day be no such thing as independent politics, any more than there can be independence in trades unionism. What would be thought of a mechanic who would say: 'As regards trades unions I shall be as I always have been, independent. Independent of all trades unions, regardless under what name they may be known.'

"Does Mr. Gompers recognize his face in the mirror? The mechanic who holds himself aloof from labor organizations on the weak and cowardly excuse of independence is a scab. What is a labor leader, who claims to be, and to have always been, independent in politics?

"Mr. Gompers tries to thus evade the real question now confronting the entire labor movement in the United States, and for this reason it is necessary 'to rub his nose into the ashes,' here and now, in sight of all the people, and upon the appearance of his initial number of *The Federationist.*

"The real question is not independent politics on the 'catch as catch can' style with a labor leader nominated on the capitalistic party tickets, a la Sam Gompers, Weissmann, McBryde,[1] Foster and McNeill, whereby the workers are kept divided among the Republican, Democratic, Populist, Prohibition and Single Tax parties, but whether labor shall cut loose from its semi-political, half sea-horse and half dog-face fakirs, traders and quacks and organize a separate, distinct political labor party, distinct from, independent of, and opposed to all other middle class reform or capitalistic boodle parties; and having for its central idea the abolition of wage slavery and all that hangs thereby or depends thereon as outlined in the platforms of the great proletarian movement in all the industrial countries, especially Germany, France, Belgium, England, Australia and to a less extent, but upon the same lines, by the Socialist Labor Class Party of the United States.

"Mr. Gompers knows that only through a great loss [mass] movement on such lines can we ever hope to cope with what he calls the 'powerful enemies to labor's interests, entrenched in legalized form, having the means to, and who will level their resources of civilization against us.'

"How else are we ever going to depose from their places of power those gigantic enemies of humanity, entrenched in legalized form, except through the ballot-box on labor class lines? Certainly not by voting this year for Gompers on the Republican, for Frank Foster on the Democratic next year and for McNeill on the Populist ticket whenever he can catch a nomination.

"We hope Mr. Gompers will come up front to better advantage in subsequent issues of the journal, which is capable of doing a vast amount of good for the American labor movement. It is nonsense to quote such nice little pieces of poetry as this:

> Whether you work by the piece or work by the day,
> Reducing your hours increases your pay,

to the the hundreds of thousands of men and women who would be only too glad to work long hours for very short pay if they could only get the chance. No use singing the praises of trades unions when everywhere there are idle men and women, and the strongest unions have lost their power of resistance against the monstrous combinations of modern capital, which can only be successfully resisted upon the political field by a great labor class movement of the protelariat, already making 55½ per cent. of our population and together with the middle class making 91 per cent. of the population, but who, both together, own 29 per cent. of the national wealth, while the millionaire and capitalist class make but 9 per cent. of the population and own 71 per cent. of the national wealth.

"The battle of labor against its exploiters must be fought out in the political arena, where the hosts of united labor can cast millions of ballots to the vanishing thousands of its capitalistic oppressors, and not by putting thousands of empty stomachs against the bayonets of the State controlled by the Carnegies, Fricks and Vanderbilts.

"Mr. Gompers and his pure and simple followers must wake up to the new condition of affairs which confront us, and come out of their antiquated close communion, paean singing, craftbound lodgeroom mummery, and get abreast of the times.

"But, in so far as the study of fossils is interesting, we commend the *American Federationist* to all who are interested in bric a brac and the veneration of the antique.

"If we had been consulted we could have furnished some modern ideas for the front page of the *Federationist*. Instead of the hand pick coal miner in the attitude of 'bearing in' we should have suggested a picture of the Lackner coal cutting machine in use in the modern mines, which displaces about 50 per cent. of skilled labor and bears in under coal 5 feet 8 inches; instead of the old fashioned 3 high rolls with their displaced 'heave ups' and roller, the Morgan continuous billet mill or the Jones rail mill, in which no human hand touches the steel product from the time the metal is charged in the blast furnace till it reaches the straightening machine and is loaded in the cars on the switch. A modern planer, band saw and steam hammer would also be more abreast of the times than the hand saw, the hand hammer and the primitive tools with which our remote ancestors plied their humble crafts.

"Instead of the motto: Omnia Labor Vincit, we would have suggested Ora et labora, or better yet, Ora pro nobis, or still better, O tempora! O mores!"

People (New York), Mar. 18, 1894.

1. John McBride.

To Jacob Coxey[1]

March 22, [1894]

Mr. J. S. Coxey,
Massillon, O.
Dear Sir and Friend: —

This will introduce to you Mr. I. D. Marshall[2] who has been appointed by the New York Press to report your march "On to Washington." I learn his instructions are, and I feel his disposition is, to write up the march candidly and fairly, and to give you a fair chance to have your side of the march presented to the American public.

Under the circumstances it seems to me that this is an exceptional opportunity, and one that you should be glad to take advantage of. I bespeak for Mr. Marshall your kind consideration, and trust that your movement may be peaceful and successful.

Very Truly Yours   Saml Gompers.

N.B. Regards to friend Browne.[3]

S. G.

TLpS, reel 7, vol. 10, p. 403, SG Letterbooks, DLC.

1. Jacob Sechler Coxey (1854-1951) was a successful Massillon, Ohio, businessman who owned a silica sand mill. A supporter of monetary and social reform, he led a march on Washington, D.C., in the spring of 1894 in an attempt to persuade Congress to finance a public works program for the unemployed. Beginning in Massillon with over a hundred followers on Mar. 25, the march drew further participants from all over the country and arrived in Washington on Apr. 29. It culminated in a confrontation on May 1 at the Capitol where police prevented Coxey from speaking, arrested his associates Carl Browne and Christopher Columbus Jones, and attacked the crowd that had gathered to watch; Coxey was subsequently also charged. The three were found guilty of carrying banners (small insignias that each had worn on his lapel) on the Capitol grounds; Coxey and Browne were also convicted of having walked on the grass.

2. Isaac D. Marshall was a New York City journalist.

3. Carl Browne (1849-1914), Coxey's close associate and advisor, conceived the idea of the march on Washington and was its chief marshal. Originally from Illinois, he settled in California where he worked, among other things, as a printer and political cartoonist and supported socialist and radical causes.

To George Perkins

March 22, [1894]

Mr. Geo W. Perkins,
Prest. C.M.I.U. of A.
39 Commerce Bldg. Chicago, Ill.
Dear Sir and Brother:—

I am in receipt of your favor from Washington. I am glad to learn that you are upon the ground working up the sentiment in favor of the cigar trade. I knew that your presence would bring a potent influence possessed by no one else upon the subject.

I knew it must have been an oversight or else in the crowding of the work that you omitted to say anything about the Magazine[1] in the journal, and accept your explanation in the spirit in which it [is] made. I feel convinced that you will do what you can in future issues and thank you for your promise upon the subject.

There is one thing I desire to emphasize. You need never fear my attitude on the trade union issue. Look through my editorials in No. 2. and I am satisfied it will disabuse the minds of any one as to my position. I have made too many fights and withstood too many on-slaughts in the past in defence of my conviction upon this subject to retreat at this late date. Of course, if I were convinced that my previous position was wrong [no] one would surrender from it more readily than I would, but with every day of my life I am becoming more fully satisfied that the trade unions are not only the organizations for the defence of labor today, but will be the machines by which eman-cipation will be secured, and is to-day the germ of the future state.

With kindest wishes, I am,

Fraternally Yours   Saml Gompers.
President. American Federation of Labor.

TLpS, reel 7, vol. 10, p. 405, SG Letterbooks, DLC.

1. The *American Federationist.*

To William Seubert[1]

March 30, [1894]

Mr. Wm. Seubert,
Sec. Brooklyn Labor Lyceum Association,[2]
949 Willoughby Ave. Brooklyn, N.Y.
Dear Sir:—

I have your favor of the 28th. inst. with enclosure, the same having been handed to me by Mr. Herzberg,[3] the contents of both of which have been duly noted.

Replying thereto permit me to say that your Committee view its relations to the Bar Tenders and Waiters organization[4] from a standpoint wholly untenable in the labor movement. Your Committee seem to take the position, that because the members composing your Association are in the main working men, that for that reason you should be accorded privileges and rights denied to other fair employers. Both the organizations as well as the ethics of the trade unions deny the right of the employer of labor when engaged in a contest with him and a settlement is reached that he shall have the power to declare and enforce the giving of employment to workmen regardless of which organization they may belong to. Such a right may be accorded to the employer when the workingmen are either weak or have been entirely defeated in a contest with him, but after a settlement is reached, when the Union is to be recognized, the union in question and having jurisdiction, is the one which usually insists upon exclusive employment by the defeated or fair-minded employer.

I do not know by what process of reasoning you are entirely actuated in the business of your Association, but I desire to call your attention to the fact that the National Trade Unions claim absolute jurisdiction in the matters affecting their respective trades and callings.

The Hotel and Restaurant Employes Nat. Alliance is the organization of the waiters, bar tenders etc. of the United States, and because there is some Picayunish local in Brooklyn that has been hostile to this National Alliance, gives your Association no moral right to give it recognition or to declare that you will give employment to the members of the National Alliance and to that local without discrimination.[5]

In too many instances employers hostile to labor make the same claim that your Association does in this matter. They too say they will not discriminate against Union labor. The fight of the Typographical Union on the "Staatszeitung"[6] two years ago was because Ottendorfer[7] made the same declaration.

There may be no doubt that your Association is organized for the purpose of benefitting the working people, but it seems to me you should not lose sight of the fact that when working men are employed by you, you are employers of labor and should be willing to accord to the union of your employes the same privileges and rights that every fair-minded employer concedes.

This matter has been hanging now for months. The Committee which called upon me last March 5th, promised to have a meeting of the Association summoned within two weeks from that date, and that has not been complied with, and now I find that a meeting has been called upon the date of your semi-annual meeting of your Association April 6th. I can only say that I earnestly hope that you will come to some conclusion and that, a favorable one upon that date.

Since this controversy has been on I have stood between the National Alliance and your Association, preventing the boycott application being endorsed or even voted upon. Much as I should dislike to be counseled to proceed in a hostile manner upon this subject I am free to say to you that unless some favorable action is taken by your meeting on the 8th. inst. and this office advised of it, I shall have no means of preventing the boycott taking its course.

Again assuring you that I sincerely hope you will make that course unnecessary, I am, with kindest wishes,

Yours Very Truly   Saml Gompers.
President. American Federation of Labor.

TLpS, reel 7, vol. 10, pp. 436-37, SG Letterbooks, DLC.

1. William Seubert, a Brooklyn cigar shop owner, ran for minor offices in Brooklyn on the SLP ticket from 1891 to 1893.

2. The Brooklyn Labor Lyceum, which was operated by the SLP, contained a meeting hall, library, basement saloon, and offices and employment bureaus of unions, most of them predominantly German.

3. Probably George Herzberg, secretary of German Waiters' Union 1 of New York City and a member of the New York City Central Labor Federation credential committee in 1892.

4. In November 1893 the Hotel and Restaurant Employees' National Alliance (HRENA) requested that the AFL boycott the Brooklyn Labor Lyceum on the grounds that the Lyceum discriminated against Alliance members because of their political affiliations (or lack of affiliation with the SLP) and would not comply with union rules in hiring waiters or bartenders. SG attempted unsuccessfully to mediate the dispute. Although the Lyceum and the HRENA failed to reach an accord, the AFL Executive Council did not approve the boycott.

5. The executive board of the HRENA, with which German Waiters' Union 1 had been affiliated, expelled the local in December 1893. This followed an incident in September in which members of the HRENA struck the Labor Lyceum for its refusal to sign a standard union contract, while members of the waiters' union took their

places. As a result of the Labor Lyceum dispute, New York unionists objected to the seating of George Herzberg at the Alliance's July 1894 convention.

6. In February 1892 members of German-American Typographia 7 of New York City went on strike against the *New Yorker Staats-Zeitung* because the management employed nonunion workers. In April the AFL approved a boycott on the paper. The strike ended unsuccessfully in September.

7. Oswald Ottendorfer was the editor and proprietor of the *New Yorker Staats-Zeitung.*

To Julius Friedman[1]

March 31, [1894]

Mr. Julius Friedmann,
Genl. Organizer A.F. of L.
803 Hickory St. St. Louis, Mo.
Dear Sir and Brother:—

Your favor of the 27th. together with application for charter for a Colored Musicians Union[2] has been duly received.

If the charter is granted by this office it will be necessary to grant it as a Musicians Union with its regular number. To put the word "colored" on their charter would be a recognition of the color line in our organization and one which must necessarily redound to our discredit and bring disadvantage. If they desire they can use the word "colored" in their intercourse with others, but in this office they must be known by the occupation and number of the Union and not by the color of their skins.

With kind wishes, I am,

Fraternally Yours   Saml Gompers.
President American Federation of Labor.

TLpS, reel 7, vol. 10, p. 445, SG Letterbooks, DLC.

1. Julius Friedman was a member of CMIU 44 of St. Louis.
2. In May 1894 the AFL chartered the Great Western Union of Musicians 6349 of St. Louis.

To William Chandler[1]

April 4, [1894]

Hon. W. E. Chandler,
Senate Chamber, Washington, D.C.
My Dear Sir: —

As one, who I know, is exceedingly interested in the Immigration question, I have the liberty of addressing you upon a matter which comes to me in such a way that I cannot ignore it.

Of course it is as well known to you as it is to me that the Steamship Companies which are interested in either evading the Immigration and Alien Contract Labor Laws, or having their provisions non enforced, have their (the Companies') lobbyists continually at work in Washington.

Through our friends and associates in Washington I learn that there is an attempt being made to cripple the efficient work done by the Immigration Commissioners at the port of New York, and that the particular official against whom the lobbyists seem to aim their shafts of opposition is Mr. Edward F. Mc-Sweeney.

I desire to say to you in all candor that organized labor had no connection in securing Mr. Mc-Sweeney's appointment, although he was closely associated with us for many years. I am sure his appointment met with general approval because of his well-known sympathy with the laws and the knowledge that he would carry them out both in letter and spirit.

Since his appointment Mr. Mc-Sweeney has given general satisfaction and has performed his duties to my own knowledge so as to merit the gratitude of all who are interested in maintaining the laws referred to, and we regard it as most unjust and unmerited that any effort should be made by any one to interfere in any manner with the prosecution of his good work. It is more than likely that the Steamship Companies and their lobby would be pleased to have some one in his position more pliable and susceptible to their influences.

Trusting that you will give this matter your earnest consideration and assuring you that it is prompted by the sole purpose of having the laws enforced in the interest of the American workingmen and the American people, I have the honor, Dear Sir, to remain

Very Truly Yours   Saml Gompers.
President. American Federation of Labor.

TLpS, reel 7, vol. 10, p. 447, SG Letterbooks, DLC.

1. William Eaton Chandler (1835-1917), a New Hampshire lawyer, was secretary of the navy from 1882 to 1885 and a Republican U.S. senator from 1887 to 1901.

To Adlai Stevenson[1]

New York. April 4th, 1894.

Hon. Adlai E. Stevenson,
Vice-President of the United States.
Senate Chamber, Washington, D.C.
Dear Sir: —

The newspapers of the country publish what purports to be the text of a Treaty[2] negotiated by the Secretary of State of the United States and the Minister of the Chinese Empire. It is further stated that this Treaty has been favorably reported to the Senate in Executive Session without amendment. Neither this report nor the published statements has been denied and every indication points to their trustworthiness, and my colleagues of the American Federation of Labor, as well as myself, assume them to be true.

To say that we are surprised and distressed that the administration of our country should negotiate a treaty of the character, practically surrendering to the Government of China rights which have been struggled for and achieved, is to say the least putting it mildly.

The Scott Exclusion Act[3] and the Geary Law were not passed in response to a maudlin sentiment nor a national antipathy. They were not passed as an experiment but as the result of sore trials and the absolute necessities of our people. They became laws not by reason of any kindness on the part of Congress, but rather at the earnest demand of the toiling masses of our country.

It is needless here to discuss the impossibility of the amalgamation or assimilation of the Chinese in America with our people. That has been so clearly demonstrated as to need no elucidation at my hands. That the immigration of Chinese into this country is undesirable and should be prohibited, is not only self-evident but is even admitted by the representative of the Chinese government in the proposed Treaty itself.

Experience has demonstrated however, that a wide divergence is clearly manifest between an expression of opinion on the part of the representatives of the Chinese Government and their action upon the subject matter of Chinese immigration.

I am sure that no Senator will need be convinced that if the provisions of the Scott and Geary Laws have in a measure been successfully evaded and violated by the Chinese in consequence of the elasticity of their consciences and their disregard for any oath or affirmation, that they will have no difficulty to "prove" that they have lawful wives, children or parents in the United States or "property therein in the value of $1.000.00 or debts of like amount." In fact the safe-guards of the present law by which the American people may be protected against the wholesale invasion of Chinese laborers, are swept aside by this proposed treaty.

It has taken years of education and experience for the United States Government to recover its absolute right to determine for itself its policy for the better protection of our people against the influx of the Chinese, and the proposed Treaty simply gives the right to the Chinese Government to interfere and question our domestic as well as foreign policy in dealing with this question.

At present an awful problem confronts us. The appalling sight is witnessed of millions of our fellow men and women actually idle and literally without the means of sustaining life. If at any other time the flood-gates of immigration should be opened, certainly in the presence of such an awful crisis wisdom, patriotism, statesmanship and humanity forbid the step.

The laws now upon our Statute Book in reference to Chinese immigration have been the result of due deliberation; and express the wants of our people. The proposed treaty has been negotiated in darkness and secrecy. The people are not aware that their rights are about to be invaded and their interests destroyed, or we would witness such an expression of determination on their part that would cause the Senate to pause before this new blight is placed upon them.

If you doubt the intensity of feeling and interest upon this subject, give official sanction to the publicity of this Treaty and time for the people to demonstrate their position upon it. You will then be convinced that apart from a few sentimentalists the American people are practically a unit against its ratification.

Public policy cannot be urged for secrecy in considering this treaty, nor can the interests of our people be promoted by its ratification.

In the name of more than half a million of organized working men and women of America, I enter my most solemn protest against the ratification of the Treaty by your Honorable Body, and earnestly hope it will be rejected.

Asking, Dear Sir, that you will submit this protest to the Senate, I have the honor to remain,

Yours Very Respectfully   Samuel Gompers.
President. American Federation of Labor.

TLpSr, reel 7, vol. 10, pp. 449-50, SG Letterbooks, DLC.

1. Adlai Stevenson was a Democratic congressman from Illinois (1875-77, 1879-81) and vice-president of the United States (1893-97).
2. The treaty, concluded on Mar. 17, 1894, was subsequently ratified and pro-

claimed on Dec. 8, 1894. For a description of this treaty and its relationship to the Geary Act of 1892, see "To John O'Brien," Aug. 17, 1893, n. 4, above.

3. The bill was introduced by Democratic Congressman William L. Scott of Pennsylvania and was signed into law Oct. 1, 1888 (U.S. *Statutes at Large*, 25: 504). It prohibited Chinese residents who left the United States from returning and cancelled the identity certificates allowing reentry that had been provided for under the Chinese Exclusion Act of 1882.

Michael Fallon[1] and Samuel Godfrey[2] to the Executive Council of the AFL

Recording and Corresponding Secretary.
The Industrial Council of Milwaukee.
385 Broadway. Milwaukee, Wis., April 11th, 1894

To the Executive Council of the A.F. of L.:
Gentlemen;

We, your petitioners, the Industrial Council of Milwaukee, desire to present to you a clear and concise statement of facts. Why we left the Federated Trades Council, and our reasons for forming a new central body. They are many and will be fully hereinafter set forth.

That there was always a lack of harmony in the old Council cannot be denied. At almost every meeting there were bitter factional fights, and the scenes enacted were a disgrace to organized labor. Instead of coming together and legislating for the benefit of the toiling masses, the delegates would engage in personalities in a most shameful manner. Things kept going from bad to worse as the Council grew, and finally, after the "Wisconsin Vorwaerts," a rabid socialistic sheet, was made the official organ against the wishes of the majority of unions affilliated, matters assumed a serious aspect and it was evident that a crisis was near at hand. That paper kept urging the German delegates to attend meetings and down the Irish, as every English speaking delegate was called. It was constantly fomenting trouble, and on several occasions had its allies prefer charges against members, and has in every manner possible tried to drive them out of the Council. — And for what reason? Simply because they dared to oppose their socialistic ideas and try and check their evil tendencies. Urged on by this paper, the radical element would at almost every meeting most shamefully insult the American flag, until it was almost impossible for a man who loved this country to retain his seat and not resent the insult, and on numerous occasions hand to hand conflicts were narrowly averted.

The funds of the Council were also being diverted to the use of a few members for their personal needs instead of being used for the upbuilding of organized labor, as it was intended for one of the delegates in particular was drawing on the funds at a lively rate, notwithstanding the protests of a few of the members.

Another very important reason for our withdrawing was the outrageous basis of representation. According to the new constitution (which was adopted by a small minority of the unions) (See Art. II, Sec. 1, Con.) a union was entitled to three delegates for the first 100 members and one delegate for every 50 thereafter, thus enabling three trades, namely: the Brewers (21), Carpenters (18) and Cigarmakers (9), by reason of their numerical strength, to control the legislation of the body. How absurd, three trades doing all the business for the thirty odd unions represented. That it was outrageous and absurd cannot be questioned. The unions that seceded protested against this unheard of and most unwise representation, but their protest was of no avail, and they simply had to stand it or git out.

Again, should a delegate from an English speaking union present a grievance, no matter how just it was, if the "gang" that ruled the Council opposed it that settled it. On the other hand, should they have a grievance, an unjust one at that, they would expect us to fall in line and assist them. Had it not been for the wise course pursued by the conservative element, when they were in the majority, these rabid socialists would have placed the Council under the ban of the law and in all probability have caused organized labor to suffer a severe set-back.

Another and a most important reason which caused the withdrawal of your petitioner from the Council was the entering of that body into politics. While we are not opposed to independent political action, Still we do not deem it proper until the National and International Bodies sanction it. They inserted in their constitution a very obnoxious clause (See Art. III, Sec. 9 Con.), which deprives a delegate of his personal liberty. That clause deprives a delegate, though he be a good union man and in every way qualified to fill any office in the gift of the Council, from being an officer, should he choose to vote as his conscience dictates. He must vote as the Council says, should they enter into a political fight. (The recent election in this city showed the desire of unions to go into politics and justified our objection. Out of a total of 52,000 votes cast the labor ticket received less than 4,000, notwithstanding the triple combination, composed of the Trades Council, Peoples Party and Socialistic Labor Party.)

The Council instead of attending purely to trades union matters has become a political headquarters. Although they were warned by a majority of the unions that much evil would result from such a move, the minority of unions, by reason of their large representation, did not heed the warning, but followed the advice of a few radicals who did not care what the outcome would be, men who were not trades unionists, men who had openly boasted that they would rule or ruin the Council, men who had urged the German delegates to withdraw from the Council, because, as they said, it was being run by the Irish.

But the climax came at last, when at the regular meeting of the Council, held Thursday, Nov. 16, 1893, the credentials of John E. Coughlin[3] from the Tanners and Curriers Union, No. 1,[4] were presented to the Council. Mr. Coughlin came with duly accredited credentials from his union. He had been a delegate previously and was an expresident of the Council, and enjoyed the reputation of being the best presiding officer the Council had ever had, although he was distasteful to the radical or Socialistic element.

On presentation his credentials were objected to by Delegate Hunger,[5] on the grounds that he was not an active member of his union, and that he had held a political office and was a democratic politician. By the way this Mr. Hunger has been the man to do all the dirty work for the "reds." In consequence of the objection and according to the constitution Mr. Coughlin's case was referred to the Executive Committee for investigation, although no direct charges had been brought against him. The Vorwaerts, the paper heretofore referred to, edited not by a trades unionist nor a member of the Council, but by a rabid Socialist,[6] who is opposed to trades unions on general principles, came out Thursday evening and warned all the socialists and radicals to be on hand and down this man Coughlin at any cost. The paper also heaped upon him an uncalled for tirade of personal and political abuse. In response to the socialistic organ all the radicals were on hand. Two-thirds of them could not talk English nor understand it, neither did they care whether they could or not, so long as they had read what the Vorwaerts had said.

When the matter came before the Executive Committee, all members not being present the board was equally divided on the question. It was then agreed to report the matter back without any recommendation and let the Council decide. Mr. Hunger, chairman of the committee, reported the case to the Council, and stated that in his opinion Mr. Coughlin could not now be seated, having since the deposit of his credentials gone into the saloon business. Heated discussion followed, the main front being whether the union or the Council had the power to decide what constituted active membership in a union, the whole matter hanging on the interpretation of the first clause of Sec. 2, Art. II, of the new constitution of the Council.

Mr. Coughlin was not given a chance to appear before the Executive Committee and defend himself, nor was his union officially notified of the objection, but it seems that this man Hunger constituted himself to be in the triple capacity of *accuser, judge* and *jury,* and, as we will further show, to your entire satisfaction, as an *act of revenge* on his part, Mr. Coughlin having brought in a first report against the union of which he (Mr. Hunger) is a member in the matter of a grievance that union had against the Volkszeitung, the paper of which the Vorwaerts is a successor.[7]

When the objections were made against Mr. Coughlin's admittance they were not made on the grounds of him being in the saloon business because he was not thinking of going into it at the time, But, however, the original charges were lost sight of and the saloon question was brought up. But common justice must prevail. The saloon question was given a hearing, although it was out of order at the time. The constitution of the Trades Council plainly says that all delegates must be active members of the unions they represent. It does not present to dictate to unions who shall and who shall not be active members. This would be out of the question as the unions have their national and international and their own local rules to go by. The Tanners and Curriers union said that Mr. Coughlin was an active member of the most active kind. In fact he organized the Tanners and Curriers union and is at present the president of their international organization.[8] He is a man whose unionism is of a national character. A man who has done more towards the upbuilding of organized labor in this city than perhaps any one else, who was but recently discharged by a tannery boss on the grounds that he was a union man, the foreman of the shop stating that his very presence seemed to enthuse the men into joining the union

Mr. Coughlin asked for the floor. Although there was some opposition to it he was granted his request. "He stated that the opposition was brought about through personal enmity. He claimed that some time ago this man Hunger from Typographia No. 10[9] was a delegate, in fact at the time that he (Coughlin) was president of the council. It was the desire of the socialists to make the Volkszeitung, now the Vorwaerts, the official organ of the Council. To this Mr. Coughlin objected on the grounds that the Volkszeitung was not a trades union paper. But, however, the majority ruled and the Volkszeitung was made the official organ. A short time after Typographia No. 10 had some difficulty with that paper, the German printers not being able, it was stated, to get their pay. Delegate Hunger brought the matter before the Council on behalf of his union and made a motion to have a committee appointed to wait upon the manager of that paper. Mr. Coughlin was appointed chairman of that committee. After investigating the case, although somewhat prejudiced against that paper, he exonorated the latter and reported that it was the union that was to blame for the trouble. Hunger took exceptions to the report of the committee, which exceptions were not sustained by the Council, and from that day on he ceased to be a delegate and did all in his power to damage the Council, starting the move by having his own union withdraw from it, which afterwards came back, and about five or six months ago returned Mr. Hunger as one of its delegates." When the union he represented withdrew from the Council this man Hunger caused to be published in the German printers official organ a very bitter attack on the Council, and tried to break up the organization by working up a feeling against the English speaking delegates, but it did no good at that time, and he waited for a chance for revenge on Mr. Coughlin, which came at last by objection to Mr. Coughlin's being seated in the Council, he (Hunger) knowing he had a majority to back him.

After a debate lasting over three hours, in which personalities were freely indulged in, and a personal encounter more forcible than otherwise seemed iminent, and after they had been made plainly aware that they were wrong and about to perpetrate a gross injustice against a fellow union man a vote was taken and resulted in the rejection of Mr. Coughlin's credentials.

In taking the vote upon the question as to whether Mr. Coughlin should be admitted as a delegate to the Council a very peculiar thing happened. At first a rising vote was taken and those voting in the affirmative numbered thirty-three, two separate counts being taken. When objection was made and the vote taken by roll call there were only twenty-five in the affirmative, a number of Mr. Coughlin's supporters having become disgusted with the proceedings, and as the hour was getting late, left the hall. Not being able to stand this thing any longer the following unions withdrew:—Cream City Typographical Union, No. 23,[10] Steam Fitters Union,[11] Steam Fitters' Helper's Union,[12] International Mason and Bricklayers Union,[13] Plumbers Union,[14] Plasterers Union, Electrical Workers Union,[15] Tanners and Curriers Union, No. 1, Tanners and Curriers Union, No. 3,[16] and quite a number of delegates and about one-half of the officers, all of whom resigned and have not been in the Council since.

That the refusal to seat Mr. Coughlin was made almost entirely on prejudice. Mr. Coughlin had been president of the Council, as before stated, was recognized as a staunch union man and no charge stood against him on any records of the Council or was made against him by any trades union represented in the Council, nor was there anything against his "individual character" to bar him from being seated. Prejudice because he would not yield to the political opinions of the majority of the Council, was the sole motive of those who opposed his admission, as was plainly apparent to all who heard the arguments of those opposed to him.

That the Council has no right to decide who shall represent a union as long as he has commited no overt act against the Council or any trades union, other than the union sending him as a delegate. The trades unions do not derive their powers from the Council but from their national or international unions and cannot cede any of this power to any central body such as the Federated Trades Council. The union having the power to withdraw its delegates at any time clearly gives it the power to its representatives.

It should be remembered that Mr. Coughlin was one of the striking tanners and as such had been blacklisted by the tanneries of the city. He had been out of work for over a year and through the influence of friends secured the appointment to take care of the state's exhibit at the World's Fair. Durring that time he never withdrew from his union and continued to hold the presidency of both the local and National Tanners' Unions, and while holding that position at the fair was re-elected president of the Tanners National Union, also their delegate to the A.F. of L. convention. When he returned to the city he again looked for work as a tanner, but the blacklist was still in force against him. Determined not to surrender his principles for the sake of a position he remained true to his union and looked about for work. After his credentials had been sent to the Council he entered the saloon business to enable him to support his family. Something he was unable to do at his trade.

It might be well to state right here that at the same meeting Mr. Coughlins credentials were objected to a Carpenter by the name of Eckelmann[17] was given a seat in the Council, notwithstanding he had been in the saloon business three or four months prior to that time. There was no objection to him, he being a radical socialist and one of their "gang." He voted against Mr. Coughlin.

Personal spite characterized the whole move, this was very apparent. This man Hunger has been a sort of disturbing element ever since he has been returned to the Council, and to him more than anyone else is due the responsibility of its disruption.

We also desire to bring to your notice the causes which led Mr. Coughlin to enter the political fight of 1892, in support of the Democratic ticket. Trouble had arisen between the Milwaukee Sentinel and Cream City Typographical Union, No. 23, and owing to the character of the subscribers of the paper it was believed that the best method of fighting the paper was on political lines. This plan was adopted and a mass meeting held to bring the matter before the laboring people of the city. At this meeting Mr. Coughlin made a brief address, but confined himself to a trades union view of the matter never touching on any of the political questions of the day. (Mr. Skeffington was also a speaker at that time, having been engaged by the Printers' Union). Another gentleman, at that time vice president of the Council, and at present a respected member of that body, made a political address on the same occasion and at another time delivered another address in the interior of the state in the interest of the same party. The latter's stand in the Council has never been questioned.

To further show you the inconsistency of the Council, we desire to mention the matter of the Musicians' Union.[18] Sometime ago that union, through the organizer of this state, made application for a charter to Mr. Gompers. It was refused on the grounds that a national organization of musicians was in existence and an application should be made to them. Notwithstanding this refusal the Council admitted their delegates to a seat in the Council and the State Federation[19] granted them a charter. Whereupon this same clique that caused Mr. Coughlin's rejection heaped upon Mr. Gompers a most unwarranted tirade of abuse and denunciation.

"Consistency thou art a jewel"

Another matter we desire to call your especial attention to is the organizing of the Lake Faring Mens' Union[20] by Messrs. Weber[21] and Dolan.[22] In doing so they have endeavored to break up the National Seamens' Union, which is represented in the A.F. of L. and also affiliated with the Federated Trades Council. This man Dolan is a saloon-keeper and belongs to no labor organization, has been a most bitter enemy of trades unions, and it has been stated on good authority is in league with the Vessel Owners Association. That man was given a seat in the Council, notwithstanding the seamen were already represented there, and clearly a violation of the Constitution of the Trades Council (See Sec. 3, Art. II.), and against a protest of the local Seamens' Union;[23] they also voted him a sum of money to assist in carrying on his work of organization. At one of the meetings of this new union a member from the old union asked them if they had a charter, and if so, when did they get it! He was promptly told to shut up or they would put him out. He then objected to their work of opposition, but was told to get out or they would cause him to be arrested.

That there was something radically wrong with the Council is evidenced by the fact that out of 75 unions in this city less than 40 were affilliated with it. And the reason why was on account of its radical socialistic tendencies.

There are numerous other reasons for taking the step we have, but we believe those given are ample to justify us in our action.

For the reasons given above we certainly have just cause for complaint, and believing that the Federated Trades Council has outlived its usefulness and has become nothing more nor less than a hot bed of socialism and should receive a charter from some National Socialistic Society and its charter revoked, we have, therefore, organized a new Central Body, called the Industrial Council, adopted a Constitution and By-Laws, elected permanent officers, received duly elected delegates in sympathy with us. We have placed the basis of representation at five delegates to each union, thus giving all unions an equal voice in the transaction of business, no matter what their numerical strength may be.

We therefore, for the best interest of organized labor of this city, petition you for a charter and pray that the same may be granted at an early day—Cream City Typographical Union, No. 23, Horseshoers' Union,[24] Plumbers' Union, Steamfitters Union, Steamfitters' Helpers' Union, Mason and Bricklayers' Union, Tanners' and Curriers' Union, No. 1, and Tanners' and Curriers Union, No. 2.[25]

This organization to be known as the Industrial Council of Milwaukee, organized February 28, 1894.

We urge you to give this matter your immediate attention as organized labor of this city is in a deplorable condition and is earnestly awaiting your decision.[26]

Respectfully yours, The Industrial Council,
Mike Fallon. Pres.,
Sam Godfrey, Secretary.

Address all communications to 385 Broadway.

Enclosed find a copy of the constitution with clauses marked, also a copy of the preamble and declaration of principles of the Industrial Council.

ALS, Files of the Office of the President, General Correspondence, reel 59, *AFL Records.*

1. Michael Fallon was a Milwaukee horseshoer.

2. Samuel W. Godfrey, a Milwaukee compositor, had served as recording secretary of the Milwaukee Federated Trades Council (FTC) in 1893.

3. John E. COUGHLIN was general president of the United Brotherhood of Tanners and Curriers of America (UBTCA) in the early 1890s.

4. UBTCA 1 of Milwaukee.

5. Jacob Hunger, a member of German-American Typographia (GAT) 10 of Milwaukee, was elected vice-president of the FTC in November 1893. He edited the *Milwaukee'r Arbeiter-Zeitung* in 1889 and its successor, the *Milwaukee Volkszeitung,* in 1890. He was subsequently an assistant editor of the *Wisconsin Vorwärts.*

6. Victor Luitpold BERGER edited the *Wisconsin Vorwärts* from 1893 to 1904.

7. After purchasing the *Milwaukee Volkszeitung* in 1892, Berger changed its name to the *Wisconsin Vorwärts*.

8. The United Brotherhood of TANNERS and Curriers of America.

9. GAT 10 of Milwaukee.

10. International Typographical Union 23 of Milwaukee.

11. National Association of Steam and Hot Water Fitters and Helpers of America (NASHWF) 18 of Milwaukee.

12. NASHWF 24 of Milwaukee.

13. Bricklayers' and Masons' International Union of America 7 of Milwaukee.

14. United Association of Journeymen Plumbers, Gas Fitters, Steam Fitters, and Steam Fitters' Helpers of the United States and Canada 75 of Milwaukee.

15 National Brotherhood of Electrical Workers of America 2 of Milwaukee.

16. UBTCA 3 of Milwaukee.

17. Probably George J. Eckelmann.

18. Milwaukee musicians applied unsuccessfully for an AFL charter in August 1893. In August 1894, however, the AFL chartered Musicians' Protective Union 6408 of Milwaukee.

19. The Wisconsin State Federation of Labor organized and was chartered by the AFL in 1893.

20. KOL Lake Faring Men's District Assembly (DA) 148 of Milwaukee.

21. Frank Joseph WEBER, a sailor, was president of the Milwaukee FTC in 1893 and the chief officer of the Wisconsin State Federation of Labor from 1893 to 1917.

22. John Dolan was master workman of KOL DA 148 in 1892.

23. Probably the Milwaukee branch of the Lake Seamen's Union.

24. Probably Journeymen Horseshoers' International Union 11 of Milwaukee.

25. Actually UBTCA 3.

26. See "To Louis Schroeder," Feb. 2, 1894, n. 2, above.

To Owen Miller

April 18, [1894]

Mr. Owen Miller,
604 Market St. St. Louis, Mo.
Dear Sir and Brother:—

In accordance with the suggestion contained in your favor of the 6th. inst. I shall unquestionably defer the issuance of the charter to the Colored Musicians until after the convention of the National League is held in Baltimore.[1]

I do this for more reasons than one. I have stood between a concerted effort on the part of a large number of musicians' locals throughout the country with their aiders and abettors and the National League. In consequence of the years of agitation they have obtained a large number of friends who continually urge and urge their claims for recognition and their right to receive charters.

It may seem an exaggeration but I assure you on my word of honor there are 12 charters deferred and laying in abeyance in this office and it is only on account of my stern determination to do what I can that a number of locals now connected with the League did not break away from it in consequence of the peculiar and isolated attitude that that organization takes.

A large number of working people of our country accept the attitude of the League as either inimical to the trade union movement or so entirely indifferent to it that they have often made a declaration somewhat to this effect. "If the National League of Musicians believes that it is not an organization for protective purposes, that it has nothing in common with organized labor, then organized labor in turn should so regard the National League and treat it accordingly."

I am sure if the true sentiment of the musicians of the country was to be put to the test they would ally themselves with the organized labor movement of America for mutual protection and advantage.

At the last convention of the American Federation of Labor (if it had not been for the stand I took) a rupture with the League would necessarily have occurred, and it was only by my earnest protest and the expression of my full belief that the Baltimore convention would favorably consider the affiliation, that action was deferred until after May.

You know me well enough to know that I am not indulging in either idle boasts, nor attempting any trick or coercion, but I beg of you in the interests of the musicians as well as the labor movement of our country to urge vigorously and vehemently upon the assembled delegates to give this their serious and I trust favorable consideration.[2]

Should you come East as a delegate to the convention I hope that I may have the pleasure of seeing you & showing you the applications.

With assurances of my earnest wish for your success and prosperity and that I may hear from you soon and frequently, I am,

Fraternally Yours   Saml Gompers.
President. American Federation of Labor.

TLpS, reel 7, vol. 10, pp. 480-81, SG Letterbooks, DLC.

1. The 1894 convention of the National League of Musicians (NLM) was held in Baltimore, May 1-5.

2. The 1894 NLM convention decided that the proposal to affiliate with the AFL violated a standing resolution against subordinating the NLM to another organization.

To Henry Stauffer[1]

April 19, [1894]

Rev. Henry Stauffer,
341 S. Ohio Ave. Columbus, O.
My Dear Sir:—

I am in receipt of your favor of the 17th. inst. the contents of which are carefully noted.

I beg to say in reply that to answer the five questions you propound fully and give the reasons for an answer would occupy much more time than I can at present give to the subject.

If I may be permitted to answer almost laconically, I should say to your first question, That the Churches can save the cities from wrong and wrong doers, but I have great doubts as to their doing so, not because there may be anything inherently wrong in the churches, but because as a rule the ministers are too craven to take hold of the cancerous condition and help to root out the cause of wrong and wrong doing.

To the second question I would say that the labor unions can save the cities from wrong and wrong doing, and will do it, not only for the cities but for the wrong and wrong doing of the country, towns as well as the cities. With the labor unions it is a question of their mission, it is inherent in their very existence, it is their constant struggle, and in which despite antagonism of enemies and indifference of laggards they must ultimately be successful.

3rd. The Church and the Labor Unions can be brought into closer touch with each other and united in the common struggle against wrong and wrong doers, but inasmuch as the greatest wrongs are done by those who by fair or unfair means are the possessors of nearly all the wealth of the country, I am inclined to the belief that for the reasons mentioned in my answer to your first question little will be accomplished in that direction.

4th. Your 4th. and 5th. questions could actually be condensed into one and be answered by saying that the main grievance that the working men have against the Church, is that nearly all of our Ministers seek to divert the attention of the workingmen from a redress of their present grievances to the good time to come hereafter. The ministers take no account of the intelligence of the working men and talk "down to them" instead of talking to them, catering to the vanities, frivolities and possessors of the money power of the country, and usually throw their opinions on the side of the wealth possessors as against that of the working men whenever there is a contest for a living wage, for home, for family, progress and independence. Is it any wonder under such circumstances that the Church and labor unions have drifted apart?

I beg to say however, that there are a number of ministers of the Gospel who form a noble exception to the rule, whose churches are filled because their hearts are filled with sympathy for the wrongs inflicted upon the toiling masses of our country, and whose tongues and brain give expression to the thoughts and hopes for a better day on earth "as it is in Heaven." Let us hope that as the years go on more of our friends in the ministry may become impressed with the true meaning of the "Sermon on the Mount" and look kindly and fraternally upon the efforts of the toilers to achieve justice and fair dealing and to make "man's inhumanity to man" a thing of the past.

I readily comply with your request for permission to quote anything that I have said in this letter. My only regret is as I say in the commencement of this letter, that time does not permit me to enter into the subject more fully at present.

With this I mail to your address a number of documents which may be of some advantage to you in the preparation of your address, and I kindly ask you should anything be printed in connection therewith that you will forward me a copy.

With kind regards, I am,

Yours for Justice, Right and Humanity.   Saml Gompers.
President. American Federation of Labor.

TLpS, reel 7, vol. 10, pp. 484-85, SG Letterbooks, DLC.

1. Henry Stauffer, a Congregational minister, was pastor of the Mayflower Chapel in Columbus, Ohio.

To John Commons[1]

April 26, [1894]

Prof. John R. Commons,
Prof. of Political Economy,
Indiana University, Bloomington, Ind.
Dear Sir:—

I am in receipt of your favor of the 24th. the contents of which are carefully noted.

I should like to answer your questions fully and thoroughly, but I am free to say that there are no statistics to base an accurate statement upon, hence in answering I am thrown upon my own observations and impressions as to which classes you name "the best, most persistent and useful advocates of the cause of labor" are secured from.

Of course I have in mind the proportionate number of persons constituting the various classes.

1. Members of Ethical Societies
2. Unitarians
3. Non-Believers
4. Catholics
5. Protestants
6. Jews
7. Ministers
8. Physicians
9. Lawyers

If there were any others you had enumerated, I should still have placed the latter, last.

If there is anything printed in reference to the preparation of any paper on this subject I wish you would let me have a copy of it.

Very Truly Yours   Saml Gompers.
President. American Federation of Labor.

TLpS, reel 8, vol. 11, p. 14, SG Letterbooks, DLC.

1. John Rogers COMMONS was a member of the faculty of the University of Indiana from 1892 to 1895 and a founder in 1893 of the American Institute of Christian Sociology, serving as its secretary.

An Article in the *Cleveland Citizen*

[April 28, 1894]

THE TENTH PLANK.

At the last annual meeting of the American Federation of Labor, held at Chicago last December, a political platform containing eleven planks and a recommendation that the labor organization take independent political action, was submitted to the various unions for their approval or rejection. At the same convention an official organ called the American Federationist was established for the discussion of questions of interest to the wage-earners. Now it would naturally be supposed that the official organ would see that the platform was discussed fairly pro and con. But such does not seem to be the case. It is generally admitted that plank 10 — "Collective ownership of all means of production and distribution" — is the great plank that overshadows all the others combined. Even the old parties would adopt the other planks if sufficient pressure were brought to bear on them, *but they would never adopt Plank 10.* That plank is the supreme test whether the labor organizations represented in the Federation believe that the laborer is entitled to the *full* product of his labor, and that labor, and labor only, is the creator of all wealth. It means the complete downfall of the capitalist and wage system; and it means, furthermore, that the adoption of this plank will be the dawn of New Trade Unionism, and the beginning of a grander and greater struggle for the rights of the toiler.

But look at the attitude of the Federationist toward the platform, and especially toward Plank 10. Every issue is filled with articles in opposition to that plank, written by such old political hacks as "Tackmaker" Foster of Boston, and others of his ilk, whose palms itch for the boodle they get yearly from the old political parties. It is no wonder that these men are opposed to the tenth plank; for if it is adopted, these fellows would find their occupation gone. But if this were all, we would make no complaint. The editorial tone of the paper seems to be against the New Trade Unionism. In the last issue Gompers editorially denounced Socialists,[1] and indirectly Socialism, thus implying that the organ of the American Federation of Labor would be used to defeat Plank 10 of the platform submitted to the unions. Now we object to Gompers' course as unfair. Several Socialists may have criticized Gompers unjustly, but that, in our opinion, is no excuse for his hostility to Plank 10, or favoring the opposition to that plank as editor. If the Federationist is to succeed, it must be above personal animosity, and allow a freer and broader discussion of the platform. The Foster crowd ought not to be allowed to monopolize the paper. If free discussion of the platform is encouraged in the various labor papers, and the members understand it, it is safe to say that it will be adopted by an overwhelming majority at the next convention of the American Federation of Labor.

Cleveland Citizen, Apr. 28, 1894.

1. "Unity and Progress," *American Federationist* 1 (Apr. 1894): 30-31.

To Thomas Mann

May 10, [1894]

Mr. Tom. Mann.
36 Minford Gardens, W. Kensington London, W. England.
Dear Sir and Brother:—

Your favor of the 2nd. came duly to hand, and I beg to assure you that I most heartily appreciate both the kind words contained in your letter as well as the promptness with which you comply with my request to write an article for the "Federationist." I have read it over carefully and think it very good and have taken the liberty to put the following caption on it, "Tactics, Present and Future."[1] I shall take pleasure in forwarding a half a dozen copies of the magazine containing it, and have placed your name on our mailing list so that you will receive the magazine regularly.

The American labor movement has certainly passed through a very crucial test within the past ten months, and I am more than elated by the manner in which we have withstood its fearful effects. Of course there has been a falling off in the membership of some of the organizations, but others again have increased, and I am quite sure the lessons thus taught our fellow workers will not only give them a clearer conception of their duties but will also, upon the first revival of industry, give an impetus to our movement unparalleled in the history of America.

I look forward to an increased membership for the unions in the near future similar to that resulting from the Dockers' strike of England a few years ago; and also increased interest on the part of all in the efforts of the wage workers to obtain their inalienable and unachieved rights.

In America we have something peculiar to contend against in connection with the development of an Independent Labor Party movement, and about which I will freely communicate with you in a future letter.

I certainly read with a great deal of interest the circular you enclosed, and in the main can give it my hearty approval. I note with a great deal of satisfaction that notwithstanding the fact that you are engaged in the active work of a Political Labor Party there is no attempt to underrate the importance of the trade union movement.

I wish, if you could, make it convenient to write regularly, and it would afford me pleasure to do likewise.

Again thanking you for your article and reciprocating your kind and fraternal wishes, I am,

Sincerely Yours   Saml Gompers.

President. AF. of L.

P.S. A friend J. S. King has just shown me the Leeds Evening Express of April 27 in which your name appears for nomination to a seat in the Commons. Do you expect the Liberals' endorsement? I wish you success in either event.

S. G.

N.B. Could you not persuade Comrade Hardie[2] to write a letter or article for the Federationist? I was [. . .] entered here.

S. G.

TLpS, reel 8, vol. 11, p. 37, SG Letterbooks, DLC.

1. *American Federationist* 1 (June 1894): 65-66.

2. James Keir HARDIE, a Scottish miners' leader, was editor of the *Labour Leader* (1889-1904), chairman of the Independent Labour party (1893-1900), and a Member of Parliament (1892-95, 1900-1915).

To Isidor Straus[1]

May 11. [1894]

Hon. Isidor Straus,

House of Representatives, Washington, D.C.

My Dear Sir:—

When I had the pleasure of an interview with you in Washington in reference to the subject matter of complaint made by the American Flint Glass Workers Union you suggested that I would submit the complaint in writing in order that you might have it investigated and you kindly promised to act thereon.

In compliance with the suggestion I beg leave to say that the officers of the American Flint Glass Workers Union complain that the Foreman in your glass cutting department discriminates against American workmen both in employment and in the class of labor given, that he encourages the men in violating their just obligations and duties to the Union and in many other ways uses his position and influence to hurt the organization of the Flint Glass Workers and in several instances discharged men for a slight violation of the rules while tolerating violation of the same rules by his friends or countrymen.

The officers of the American Flint Glass Workers inform me that they are engaged in a contest with an employer who seeks to cut wages and that should the firm in question succeed in enforcing the reduced scale it would be both unfair to your House as well as detrimental to the workers. In order to maintain a fair rate the members of the organizations are required to contribute towards in a measure supporting the men engaged in the controversy, and the unfair conduct of the Foreman of your establishment deprives the organization of part of the means by which the dispute for a fair scale is maintained.

There seems to be no other ground of complaint against the fairness of your dealings with the glass workers and I earnestly hope that you will take such action as will remove this unfair discrimination and encouragement of violation of duty in the cutting department.

Feeling assured that you will give this matter, early, and I hope favorable attention, I have the honor to remain,

Very Respectfully Yours   Saml Gompers.
President. American Federation of Labor

TLpS, reel 8, vol. 11, p. 41, SG Letterbooks, DLC.

1. Isidor Straus (1845-1912), a New York City department store owner and financier, was elected as a Democrat in 1894 to fill a vacancy in the U.S. House of Representatives, serving until 1895.

From Henry Stauffer

Columbus, O., May 12, 1894,

My Dear Sir—

Your favor of April 19th[1] was received in due time and should have been acknowledged before.

In reply I beg leave to say that you are partly right in your severe criticisms of the church.

But those of us who still believe in the church are glad to note a marked change for the better in many directions. I have just returned from the annual meeting of our State Association at Cincinnati,[2] and in some respects, it was a remarkable gathering. Those who took part in the discussions, and those who made formal addresses were almost all young men who are under the full influence of the new sociological ideals.

I fully believe that it will be to the advantage of the labor leaders to "labor" with the ministers in order to enlist them in their cause.

I presume multitudes of them are too hidebound to be open to conviction on the matter; but I know that many of the younger men are
anxiously seeking the right way and would be very glad to talk the
question over with men of your standing and ability.

I am persuaded that the church and the labor movement must form
a closer alliance if either is to succeed. You emphasize one fact—the
relation of a good environment to a good character. We emphasize
the value of the individual and the need of saving him, whatever may
be done or left undone, in the matter of improving the environment.
We are both looking at *facts.* We are each in danger of shutting the
eyes to what the other insists on seeing.

I hope you will not use your large influence to encourage workingmen to stay away from the churches. Would it not be better policy
to advise them to "capture" the church and use it for their purposes?

Let me remind you of the fact that the great majority of trustworthy
labor leaders in this country and England for the last fifty years have
either been all their lives members of the church or, at least, got their
training in the church.

I wish to thank you, both for your excellent letter as well as for
the literature sent me.

I enclose a clipping from yesterday's *Tribune* in which a brief notice
of my thirty minutes' address will be found. A number of ministers
express the desire that the paper be published. If this is done I shall
gladly forward you a copy of the same.

Fraternally yours,   Henry Stauffer,
Pastor, Mayflower Congregational Church.

American Federationist 1 (June 1894): 80-81.

1. Printed above.
2. The Congregational Association of Ohio held its fourth annual meeting in
Cincinnati, May 8-10, 1894.

To Edward McSweeney

May 14, [1894]

Mr. Edward. F. Mc-Sweeney,
Assistant Commission of Immigration,
Ellis Island, N.Y.
Dear Sir and Friend:—
Having the subject matter in mind which we discussed at our last

interview and desirous of co-operating with you for the purpose of running down the infamous padrone system,[1] I enclose to you herein a copy of a letter[2] I sent to Senator David B. Hill, Chairman of the United States Senate Committee on Immigration, and which you may find interesting. You have my permission to make such use of it as you may in your judgment deem most advisable to accomplish the best results.

It is needless to call your attention to the fact that the "bankers" and their "agents" are nothing more nor less than the padrones and their hirelings known under more euphonious titles. I fully believe that if the suggestions contained in the letter were carried out it would largely tend towards wiping out the traffic in human flesh which the padrones systematically conduct.

The more thought I give the subject the more fully am I persuaded that the system of government agents being on board the incoming vessels, coming over with the passengers, mingling with them, possibly taking work with them too, would be the best means of exposing and finally putting a stop to the padrone system.

I commend to your consideration the suggestion of licensing the "bankers" or putting them under bonds.

The American Federation of Labor has frequently condemned this padrone system, and I should esteem it not only a pleasure, but my duty, to render you and the Department all the aid that I can in order to see it abolished.

Wishing you every success, I am,

Very Truly Yours   Saml Gompers
President. American Federation of Labor.

TLpS, reel 8, vol. 11, p. 52, SG Letterbooks, DLC.

1. Padrones were labor bosses who served as recruiting agents for employers of unskilled Italian immigrants. The padrones occasionally facilitated passage of these workers to the United States, but most often they simply recruited immigrants coming off the boat or looking for work in the cities. Abuses of the padrone system included exorbitant charges for food, housing, clothing, transportation, and services, cheating workers out of their wages, and sometimes holding them in conditions of peonage in labor camps. Railroad and construction companies in particular made use of labor contracted through padrones during the height of Italian immigration in the 1880s and 1890s. Despite its abuses, the padrone system enabled Italian immigrants to find work and to overcome the barriers of language and unfamiliar labor practices.

2. June 23, 1893, reel 7, vol. 9, p. 198, SG Letterbooks, DLC.

From Charles Baustian[1]

Carriage and Wagon Workers' International Union of North America[2]
Chicago, May 18 1894

Dear Sir and Brother.

Yours of recent date came duly to hand and contents were noted. I may be mistaken, but it has been my belief, organization can best be put forward when workingmen are to a large degree in idleness. As soon as business becomes active, they again are satisfied, as their immediate wants are partially fullfilled. Then when they are again put into idleness they begin to think of organization, but if that organization is not started, before they again get to work, it will take some time before they think of doing something to protect themselves from further oppression.

From the little experience I have had with workingmen in the past fifteen years and most of this time I spent at work in large factories, employing several hundred men, as soon as work falls off, workmen say well boys we ought to have a Union, no one wants to make the start, for fear of losing his job. it goes by in idle talk and no action is taken, as soon as they are at work again, they say what is the good of a Union, I have got a job and getting as much as any that belong to the Union and nothing more is heard of starting a Union until a reduction in wages is made, when it results in all talk and no action. I think if some one leads the way, workmen will follow. I have taken your advice and enclosed find a letter[3] for the "Federationist," which you can fix to suit, as my experience as an author is very limited. Trusting the desired effect will be accomplished, I am.

Fraternally Yours.   Chas. A. Baustian
Sec'y—

ALS, Carriage and Wagon Workers' Union Records, reel 139, *AFL Records.*

1. Charles A. BAUSTIAN served as secretary-treasurer of the Carriage and Wagon Workers' International Union of North America from 1893 until 1907.

2. The CARRIAGE and Wagon Workers' International Union of North America.

3. Baustian's letter, which was published in the *American Federationist*, appealed to AFL organizers to form carriage and wagon workers' locals and offered to send circulars on request (1 [July 1894]: 106).

To Charles Baustian

May 24, [1894]

Mr. Chas. A. Baustian,
Sec. Carriage & Wagon Workers Intl. Union
3152 Shields Ave. Chicago, Ill.
Dear Sir and Brother:—

Your favor of the 18th. together with letter for publication in the American Federationist came duly to hand, and I earnestly hope for good results from the same.

I regret to be compelled to say that I am forced to disagree with the conclusions which you have arrived at, for not only my experience but the history of the labor movement proves the contrary.

As a matter of fact new organizations are seldom instituted among working men during dull times or periods of idleness. They may feel more keenly the absence of organization than at any other time, but they are neither in a position nor have they the courage then to organize. It is true when their interests are attacked they feel very keenly the fact that they are unorganized and wish that they were, and that is where it usually ends. Upon a revival of business it is a mistake to believe that they become satisfied. As a matter of every day experience it shows that organizations of labor are brought into existence and assume a more aggressive form as soon as employment becomes somewhat more general.

I know that there are a number of our friends who believe that the poorer workers before the better do they fight for their rights. That that is a mistake the history of the whole world teaches. The best organizations of labor are in those countries where the highest wages and the shortest number of hours and best conditions prevail and vice versa. This does not only apply to countries. It applies to states, cities or industries with equal force.

If this were not the case it should be our purpose to bring about the greatest amount of idleness and poverty among the wage-workers of our country to attain the best results.

As I say, I regret to be compelled to disagree with the conclusions you arrive at, but I think you would regard me less than a man and unworthy the position I hold if I simply acquiesced in statements made though I might be convinced they are founded upon error of judgment.

Sincerely hoping that we may be successful in bringing about a thorough organization of our fellow workers throughout the country and the world, I am,

Fraternally Yours   Samuel Gompers.

President American Federation of Labor.

N.B. I think there is great merit to the circular you have issued to the trade, and I kindly ask you to send half a dozen copies here.

S. G.

TLpSr, reel 8, vol. 11, p. 65, SG Letterbooks, DLC.

To Thomas Gruelle

June 19, [1894]

Mr. Thos. M. Gruelle,
Genl. Organizer A.F. of L.
c/o "Labor Signal" Indianapolis, Ind.
Dear Sir and Brother:—

Your favor of the 14th. to Bro. Evans came duly to hand. He will give his attention to the financial portion of it.

The other I desire to answer by saying that I am sure you do not doubt my devotion either to the Federation or the trade union movement, nor do I wish to waste time endeavoring to conciliate the disrupters of the labor movement, for I know it is worse than useless, but as an executive officer I am bound by the actions of the membership, and the Chicago convention decided to accept the invitation to the conference and selected me as one of the conferees.

Let me call your attention to the action of the K. of L. since the St. Louis conference. You should keep in mind the fact that the conference was called by the K. of L. and there were present the representatives of the Brotherhoods and Orders of Railway men, Green Bottle Blowers National Union,[1] which seceded from the K. of L., Farmer's Alliance, K. of L. and the A.F. of L., and upon the question which has divided the labor movement for years and has caused all the dissatisfaction they were outvoted by 12 to 5. The proposition submitted by me was adopted by that vote, and theirs rejected by the same vote, except that where it was pro. in one it was con. in the other.

Immediately after the adoption of the proposition the K. of L. declared in the St. Louis papers and elsewhere that they will not abide by the decision but will endeavor to "deal directly with the National and International Trade Unions."

I have known these men for years and I also know that they will not recede from their position and they are determined to undermine the trade unions if they can, and that all their declarations for unity are pretences, or the unity which could be accomplished by their annihilating or swallowing the trade unions.

After all, I am glad the conference took place for it will henceforward show clearly that they will abide by nothing which does not suit their convenience, or policy. I feel stronger than ever that the trade unions will gain in strength continually and that it will not be long before all will recognize that by and through them in our grand A.F. of L. the toilers will battle for improved conditions and secure their final emancipation.

I see you have the proper appreciation of the make up of the A.R.U.[2] It is indeed the second edition of the K. of L. except that they propose to confine themselves to the railroad men.

With the firm conviction that we are on the right road, and that success will crown our efforts and with kindest wishes to you personally and hoping to hear from you soon, I am,

Fraternally Yours Saml Gompers
President. American Federation of Labor.

N.B. I await your letter in reference to the C.L.U. affair.[3] Let me have it as soon as possible.

S. G.

TLpS, reel 8, vol. 11, pp. 113-14, SG Letterbooks, DLC.

1. The United Green GLASS Workers' Association of the United States and Canada.

2. The American RAILWAY Union.

3. Because there was some local opposition to issuing a charter to the Indianapolis Central Labor Union, SG appointed a committee consisting of P. J. McGuire and William B. Prescott to investigate. The committee gave its approval in September 1894, and the AFL issued the charter in October.

A Translation of an Excerpt from an Article in the *New Yorker Volkszeitung*

[June 21, 1894]

SLAVES OF THE PADRONI.

The congressional committee on immigration questions[1] held a closed session at the Victoria Hotel yesterday in which the padrone system was the main subject under discussion. A great number of Italian workers were interviewed, among them were Nicola Florina and Siepto Salvatore, two barbers who had only recently arrived here from Italy. Both said that they had received letters in Italy in which work had been promised to them if they came to America. They said they had indeed come here as contract workers, but had been told before their arrival how they were to act on Ellis Island and how they were to answer the questions of the officials. The Italian "banker," at whose suggestion they had emigrated, was unable to provide them with work, and now they had to live in the boardinghouse of the padrone, until he [the padrone] received a contract for delivery of workers.

In the afternoon Dr. Senner[2] provided information about the padrone system. Samuel Gompers, who appeared at the invitation of the committee, recommended several amendments to the immigration laws, which were taken into consideration by the committee.

Gompers said, among other things, that although immigration had decreased, now mostly Italians and Slavs were coming instead of desirable immigrants like the Germans and Irish. He thought it strange that now the immigrants were traveling to areas where workers were on strike and he emphasized that people were probably encouraged to go to places where strikes were in progress. Asked by Congressman Geissenheimer[3] if it were just to deny a man entrance into this country who had strong arms and was willing to work, Gompers responded that as long as 1½ million Americans were unemployed, the principle of self-preservation demanded that further competition through continued immigration be prevented. Gompers recommended that the government should appoint inspectors to travel to those countries from which emigrants were now coming, observe the emigrants there, and travel back to America with them, so that they could determine whether the contract labor law was being broken.

No information was given about the result of the hearing, but it was determined that it has been recommended to amend the law in such a way that contract workers can be held in order to act as witnesses here. At present such workers must be sent back with the same ship on which they arrived. The committee will hold a session today in Union Square. In any case, a law to fight the padrone system will be submitted to Congress.[4]

. . .

New Yorker Volkszeitung, June 21, 1894. Translated from the German by Patrick McGrath.

1. The Committee on Immigration and Naturalization of the U.S. House of Representatives.

2. Joseph Henry Senner was U.S. commissioner of the port of New York from 1893 to 1897.

3. Jacob Augustus Geissenhainer (1839-1917), a lawyer, represented New Jersey as a Democrat in Congress from 1889 to 1895.

4. Geissenhainer submitted H.R. 7897 (53d Cong., 2d sess.) on Aug. 6, 1894, to amend earlier immigration laws and amendments concerning contract labor, but Congress adopted no further legislation on contract labor until 1903.

An Editorial by Samuel Gompers in the *American Federationist*

[June 1894]

A CRIME AGAINST FREEDOM.

Not the unexpected but the to-be-deplored, has happened. The authorities at Washington have arrested the leaders of the Commonwealers,[1] and upon a charge as flimsy as it is preposterous, ridiculous and outrageous, convicted and sentenced them to twenty days each in prison.

The charge was brought that they trod on a few blades of grass, and under this pretense the whole power of government is brought to bear, to crush out the constitutional and natural rights of free speech, free assemblage and freedom of petition.

It matters little whether the Coxey movement for "good roads and non-interest bearing bonds" was reasonable or not. We are firmly convinced that so long as our law makers are either the bankers or the bankers' retained attorneys, the question of securing non-interest bearing bonds is a visionary dream, but we maintain that [it is] in the interest of the vast number of people who are unemployed, in the interest of the whole people, who require good roads. For the purpose of protecting the people from the shylocks, by the government conducting work upon the faith of the people in its honor and ability to pay its honest debts. Mr. Coxey and his "Commonweal Army" had the perfect and inalienable right to meet at Washington, and by peaceful speech and petition endeavor to influence Congress to pass his measures.

Of course, the Commonwealers could not very well hire a lobby with millions of dollars to "argue" with the members, upon the *advisability* of their voting in favor of his scheme. To be sure his bills did not affect the gambling either in "soap" or "sugar." He and his army did not come to Washington in palace cars, or appear in full evening attire. They came however, as plain citizens to plead for the poor, outraged, robbed, idle millions of America's best and truest men and friends, the men upon whom the vast fabric of our nation depends, who are at once its prop and its defenders.

The authorities and their brutal hirelings have clubbed and battered a few heads, propose to send a few more to jail, and will no doubt, with a Chesterfieldian, self-satisfied air, assume that they have "saved the country." If history teaches anything aright it wholly and conclusively demonstrates that bludgeons and prison walls have never yet prevented truth from becoming generally accepted, recognized and established. On the contrary frequently has error become enthroned simply because arbitrary power has sought to throttle it by force.

"Agitation is the mother of wisdom," and the agitation of the question of labor's rights and the functions of government, are the only means by which a solution can be reached upon the great problems confronting the people of our time. We repeat our remarks of last month upon this subject. "It is something not yet understood how perfectly safe freedom is."

American Federationist 1 (June 1894): 76.

1. The Commonweal of Christ was the official title of the marchers led by Jacob Coxey, though the press more commonly referred to them as "Coxey's Army."

To Henry Lloyd

July 2, [1894]

Mr. Henry Lloyd,
Loynbee [Toynbee] Hall, 28 Commercial St. London E.C. Eng.
Dear Friend:—

Your favor of the 16th. came duly to hand and contents noted.

It would be superfluous to say that I was exceedingly pleased to hear from you, not only that, but I was deeply interested in the matters you communicate. I was sure that your reception among the trade unionists of Great Brittain[1] would be all that could be desired, and it is indeed some gratification to learn that the foremost men in the ranks have so cordially, heartily and fraternally greeted you.

It is an ideal for which I have long struggled to establish here, that men regardless of their differences of opinion, convictions and theories, might have some respect for each other, be tolerant of each other's views, and yet be united in face of a common enemy. You will remember during the trouble at the Detroit convention I pleaded for this very toleration and unity. That it has not been achieved is lamentable, but our earnest men must still strive to accomplish it.

Of course I know that John Burns, Tom. Mann, Ben. Tillett, and Keir Hardie differ materially with Geo. Shipton,[2] Tom Burt,[3] Chas. Fenwick and Henry Broadhurst,[4] yet in fact I know that often the men of both sides do not agree entirely with each other, but the fact that they present a solid front whenever the interests of labor are at stake, is the best tribute to their honesty, earnestness and devotion to the cause of the wealth producing masses of Great Brittain. After all, it is merely a difference of opinion as to the most practical methods to be employed in securing to the laborer his just rights; and until the advent of Prof. De Leon in the Socialist movement we managed matters so that we could at least work together. This man's characteristics of intolerance to every one that does not adopt his policy, his venom and spite crop out at every opportunity that makes it impossible for any one that has any self-respect to have any dealings with him or those for whom he speaks. He has simply widened the chasm between the different wings in the labor movement. The last effort on his part is to pit the Knights of Labor against the trade unionists to intensify the differences and create bitterness among the active men in our movement.

So far as I am concerned I bear neither of them any animosity. On the contrary I hope that the time will soon be at hand when with an appreciation of each other's worth we may proceed on the even [. . .] of our way dealing the severest blows possible to the enemies of the movement.

I hope you will pardon my lengthy reference to this matter, but your letter depicting the different conditions prevailing in England almost tempted me to open the flood-gates of my tongue and expression of my regret of the conditions here. I am satisfied that the near future will bring about a better condition of affairs.

Yes, I remember very well my father speaking of his old shop mate Bill. Caiger. Some years ago I had the pleasure of writing to Mr. Ben Cooper[5] Secretary of the Cigar Makers Society. When you see them or any of our other comrades referred to in this letter or in fact all our fellow unionists don't forget to remember me kindly to them and express my utmost sympathy and fraternal and personal well wishes.

While I do not wish to interfere with your thoroughly enjoying yourself and recouping your health, I would esteem it a great favor if you could write a letter or article for publication in the magazine. Anything you care about writing will I am sure prove interesting.

If you attend the Trade Union Congress in Sept. you might convey to the delegates the earnest desire for the extension of the spirit of concord and fraternity of the trade unionists of America. I presume you will write before that event and I may have something to say again upon that subject.

Ascertain if you can what arrangements have been made for the International Labor Congress and give me some details upon it. I see no reason why the trade unionists of America should not be represented at such a Congress, of course if they consistently can, and further if they are invited.

Again expressing the hope that you will have a thoroughly enjoyable time, that you may come back to the United States with your health fully restored, robust and energetic, and that you may be in a position for many years to contribute your valuable aid in the struggles for labor's emancipation, I am,

Fraternally Yours   Saml Gompers.

President. American Federation of Labor.

N.B. Frank,[6] P.J.[7] and I were at the St. Louis conference. I mail to your address with this six copies of No. 5 of the Federationist which I hope you will find interesting. You might give a few of them [to?] our friends in the movement.

S. G.

P.S. Let me know whether the English edition of the "Review of Reviews" for July contains an interview with me. The American edition does.[8] It is rather interesting and if the English edition does not contain it, I will send a copy to you. Did you see the opening of the Tower Bridge?

S. G.

TLpS, reel 8, vol. 11, pp. 132-34, SG Letterbooks, DLC.

1. Henry Lloyd, a leader of United Brotherhood of Carpenters and Joiners 33 of Boston, was spending a holiday in England for health reasons. He addressed the Trades Union Congress of Great Britain (TUC), which met at Norwich, Sept. 3-8, 1894, on behalf of the AFL, and the TUC responded by sending two representatives, David Holmes and John Burns, to the AFL's 1894 convention in Denver.

2. George SHIPTON, a London painter, was secretary of the London Trades Council from 1872 to 1896.

3. Thomas BURT was president of the Northumberland Miners' Association (1865-1905) and a Liberal Member of Parliament (1874-1918).

4. Henry BROADHURST, a London stonemason, was a Liberal Member of Parliament (1880-92, 1894-1906).

5. Ben Cooper, a cigarmaker and secretary of the Cigar Makers' Mutual Association, was active in the London Trades Council, the TUC, and the Labour Representation Committee.

6. Frank K. Foster.

7. P. J. McGuire.

8. See "Excerpts from an Interview in the *Review of Reviews*," July 1894, below.

To the Delegates at the 1894 Convention[1] of the National Alliance of Theatrical Stage Employes[2]

July 5, [1894]

To the Officers and Delegates of the National Association
of Theatrical Stage Employes in convention assembled,
c/o Mr. Lee M. Hart,[3]
120 W. Washington St. Chicago, Ill.
Dear Sirs and Brothers:—

Inasmuch as your organization is about to hold its regular convention, my sense of duty has impelled me to communicate with you upon what I regard as an important and momentous question.

On every hand we see the capitalist class, the corporate and moneyed interests concentrating their efforts for the purpose of despoiling the people of their rights, encroaching upon our liberties and endeavoring to force the workers down in the social, economic and political scale. Allied with them are the governmental powers, national, state and municipal. Their efforts are concentrated, their actions united. Nothing is allowed to interfere with the full development of the protection and advancement of their interests.

In view of these circumstances it must impress itself upon your minds as it has upon mine, that the toiling masses, the wealth producers of our country, should unite for the common advancement of the working masses, and by our common concert of action act unitedly to protect and advance the liberties and rights of our people.

I have stated that we should unite our forces, but I do not wish it to be understood that we are to become an incoherent, chaotic mass of organized workers each entrenching upon the rights of others, or encroaching upon the reserved trade rights. On the contrary in becoming affiliated with the American Federation of Labor your organization would retain its absolute autonomy and independence in all that concerns your trade rights and trade interests and also the manner of conducting the affairs of your fellow-workers. We ask for your affiliation with the American Federation of Labor, your unity with the great band of the trade unionists of America upon the distinct understanding that your Union with the other great National and International trade unions shall in your and their trade affairs be as distinct as the billows, and in the American Federation of Labor one as the seas.

There are many things which transpire in the great struggle of the toilers for improved conditions which cannot be attended to by a single organization and which requires a common concert of action of the entire organized working men of America. In these instances the American Federation of Labor performs the great work that the individual organizations cannot accomplish.

We all agree that it is morally wrong for any workman to remain outside of the Union of his trade. We also declare that it is wrong for a local union of a trade to remain outside of the National or International Union of its trade, and if these propositions are true, and they are true, then it logically follows that it is equally morally wrong for any National or International Union to remain outside of the ranks of the great trade unions of America which are banded together under the banner of the American Federation of Labor.

In becoming affiliated with the A.F. of L. there is no loss of any right that your members as such, or your International Union surrenders. Your autonomy and independence are guaranteed and maintained. You can neither be ordered to strike, nor when on strike be ordered to return to work by any officer of the American Federation of Labor. These matters lie exclusively within your own authority, and I beg to assure you that both personally and officially we are too sincere unionists to either encourage or allow any infringement upon your trade rights.

Nor can any organization refrain from affiliation with the A.F. of L. upon the ground that the payment to it is burdensome. Each National or International Union affiliated with the A.F. of L. contributes one fourth of one cent per member each month, in other words three cents per year. In the event of a great crisis that one or more of the affiliated National Unions may be engaged in a prolonged trade dispute and requiring the financial assistance of the Federation, if we have not too many contests already on hand an assessment of two cents per member for five consecutive weeks may be levied. I desire to add that thus far in the history of the Federation only six weeks assessment have ever been levied.

There are many other matters which cannot be even referred to in a letter of this kind, and which it would afford me pleasure to reply to should inquiries be made in reference to them, but I mail to your address with this a number of documents which will give further explanation in reference to matters of interest in connection with the Affiliation of your organization with the A.F. of L. as well as many other questions of importance.

I kindly ask you to lay this matter before the delegates of your convention, and earnestly appeal to you in your own interests as well as those of the toiling masses of our country, to discuss these questions coolly, deliberately, and to take a comprehensive view of it, and finally resolve upon affiliating with the greatest organization of workers of modern times—the American Federation of Labor. Let our watch word be "Unity and Autonomy; Federation and Independence."

Fraternally Yours   Saml Gompers.

President. American Federation of Labor.

TLpS, reel 8, vol. 11, pp. 144-46, SG Letterbooks, DLC.

1. The convention was held in Chicago, July 9-12, 1894.

2. The National Alliance of THEATRICAL Stage Employes of the United States.

3. Lee M. HART was elected president of the National Alliance of Theatrical Stage Employes at its 1894 convention.

The Pullman Strike

On the morning of July 4, 1894, five companies of the 15th U.S. Infantry marched into Chicago. The Pullman strike, which was disrupting rail traffic throughout much of the nation, had reached its climax. Within days President Grover Cleveland had committed additional troops, and, in a gesture illustrating the cooperation between the railroads and the federal government, their commander, General Nelson A. Miles, established his headquarters in the Pullman Building. Because Chicago was a hub of the strike, it was also a focus of military intervention. By the time the strike had ended, the federal government had dispatched nearly 2,000 men to the city, the state of Illinois had sent in some 4,000 militia, and over 5,000 deputy marshals and sheriffs had been sworn in there.[1]

The Pullman strike grew out of a conflict between the Pullman Palace Car Co. and its employees over wages and the rents and other expenses charged to workers who lived in the "model" company town of Pullman, Ill.—over two-thirds of the workforce. Between September 1893 and May 1894, the company cut wages an average of 25 to 33 percent; in some cases they were lowered as much as 50 percent. Although the company simultaneously reduced hours because of a decline in the amount of work available during the depression, there was no commensurate reduction in the rents charged to workers who lived in Pullman or in the prices they were required to pay for food, heat, gas, and water.[2]

In the spring of 1894 the Pullman employees organized themselves into locals of the American Railway Union (ARU), and, encouraged by the ARU's success that April in its strike against the Great Northern Railroad, they took their grievances to their employers. After the company fired three members of the grievance committee, however, almost 3,000 workers walked off their jobs on May 11, and the company locked out the remaining workers. "We do not expect the company to concede our demands," strike chairman Thomas Heathcote stated on May 13. "We do not know what the outcome will be, and in fact we do not care much. We do know we are working for less wages than will maintain ourselves and families . . . and on that proposition we absolutely refuse to work any longer."[3] Despite public sympathy for the strikers, and efforts by Chicago's mayor, the city council, the Civic Federation, and others to encourage conciliation or arbitration, representatives of the company resolutely held their ground.

The ARU, whose first convention opened in Chicago on June 12, also attempted to resolve the conflict, sending a group of its own delegates on June 15, and a committee of former Pullman employees on June 16, to meet with Pullman vice-president Thomas H. Wickes. Wickes responded that the firm would not consider any proposal from the ARU and would deal with its former employees only as individuals, not as representatives of a union. Furthermore, it again rejected arbitration. "The policy of the company," the *Chicago Inter Ocean* explained, "is to maintain a dignified silence."[4] Deeply stirred by the plight of the Pullman workers and angered by the company's response to its overtures, the ARU tried unsuccessfully one last time on June 22 to resolve the dispute. Then, despite Eugene Debs's advice to proceed cautiously, and acting on instructions from their local unions, the convention's delegates voted unanimously to refuse to handle Pullman cars beginning June 26.

The General Managers' Association (GMA) of the railroads, an organization founded in 1886 and reactivated in 1892 to minimize competition and to deal with labor problems in the industry, termed the boycott "unjustifiable and unwarranted" and maintained that it was the railroads' "lawful right and duty" to resist it. Representing twenty-four railroad lines centering or terminating in Chicago, many of which were bound by contract to the Pullman Co., the GMA's members employed over 200,000 workers.[5] The Association welcomed the confrontation with the ARU, which it considered to be a growing threat, and ordered the discharge of any workers refusing to handle Pullman cars. Entire crews responded to these dismissals by walking off their jobs, however, thereby transforming the ARU's boycott into a strike affecting much of the nation's railroad system.

Having pledged to keep the trains running, the GMA assumed management of the strike for its members, established a command center in Chicago under the direction of John M. Egan, and hired strikebreakers. Simply put, the objectives of the Association were to defeat the strike and annihilate the ARU.[6] Its strategy was twofold: to create public sentiment against the strike itself and, more significantly, to involve the federal government as an ally on the grounds that the strikers were disrupting interstate commerce and the movement of the mail.[7]

The Association soon had the full cooperation of Attorney General Richard Olney in this regard. On June 28 he directed the U.S. district attorney in Chicago, Thomas E. Milchrist, to take the steps necessary to prevent obstruction of the mails, and on June 30 he appointed Edwin Walker as special federal attorney in Chicago. Ostensibly Milchrist's assistant, Walker assumed direction of affairs for the Department of Justice in Chicago. A general counsel for the GMA, Walker had been recommended to Olney for his new post by the Association and remained on its payroll during the strike. On Olney's orders, Milchrist and Walker applied on July 2 for an omnibus injunction against the leaders of the ARU. Promptly granted by federal court judges Peter S. Grosscup and William A. Woods, it provided the railroads within the court's jurisdiction with complete protection against the strike and served as a model for similar injunctions that were quickly issued elsewhere against the ARU.[8]

Up to this point there had been little violence in connection with the strike. On July 3, however, a riot broke out in the railroad yards in Blue Island, Ill. (located outside Chicago), and in response President Cleveland sent troops to Chicago, a step that both Chicago's mayor, John P. Hopkins, and Illinois' governor, John P. Altgeld, considered unnecessary. After the troops arrived, however, the level of disorder escalated considerably. Railroad property was destroyed as the ARU increasingly lost control of the volatile situation, and additional troops, both federal and state, were committed. As a result of the injunctions and the military intervention, the GMA's leaders could note with satisfaction that "so far as the railroads are concerned with this fight, they are out of it. It has now become a fight between the United States Government and the American Railway Union, and we shall leave them to fight it out." In a strongly worded telegram, Gompers protested to President Cleveland "against [the] base action [of the] judiciary and [the] improper use of [the] military."[9]

At Debs's suggestion, trade unionists in Chicago resolved on July 8 to call a city-wide general strike for July 11 if Pullman continued to refuse arbitration. They also telegraphed Gompers, insisting that he come to Chicago. Convinced of the gravity of the situation, Gompers informed the AFL Executive Council on July 9 that an "extraordinary industrial situation" required them to take action, and he called a meeting at the Briggs House for the morning of July 12.[10] He notified officers of national and international unions and the railroad brotherhoods of the Executive Council meeting and invited them to attend as well.

Meanwhile, on July 10, a federal grand jury convened by Milchrist indicted Debs and his fellow ARU officers for conspiring to interfere with interstate commerce, and the union men were promptly arrested. They were released on bail after a few hours, but not before their offices were raided and their papers and other records confiscated by federal officers. Although the GMA, now convinced that it had broken the strike, predicted that business would resume the very next day, a number of Chicago's workers, including locals of AFL affiliates, struck in sympathy with the railroad men.[11]

When Debs appeared at the Briggs House conference on the evening of July 12, he asked Gompers to deliver a proposition to the GMA on behalf of the ARU, offering to end the boycott if the Association would rehire the strikers. He also sought the conference's approval for a general strike should the GMA reject the offer. "I would make an injury to one in the cause of labor the concern of all," he declared. "My theory has always been and is now that labor ought to stand by labor, and if I were you, in your place and you in mine, I would muster all the forces of labor in a peaceable effort to secure a satisfactory adjustment of our grievances, even if we had to involve all the industrial industries of the country."[12]

Although Gompers refused to carry the union's proposal to the GMA himself, he offered to accompany Debs. The ARU leader ruled this out — "I knew I was very offensive to the general managers," he later explained, "and that no good could possibly come from any action in which I would have a part" — so the proposed meeting never took place. At the same time, the delegates to the conference decided that, under the circumstances, a general strike by unions affiliated with the AFL would be "inexpedient, unwise and contrary to the best interests of the working people."[13] From Gompers' point of view, the conference lacked the authority to take such action, and, besides, the ARU's proposal demonstrated that the Pullman strike had already been lost. The meeting pledged both moral and financial support to the ARU's leaders, but did not endorse the general strike, even though, as Gompers later acknowledged, the rank and file probably would have participated had they been asked to do so.

Following the Briggs House conference, Mayor Hopkins delivered Debs's offer to call off the boycott. Egan rebuked the mayor for permitting himself "to be a messenger boy" for the union, and the managers refused to receive the document. George Pullman then issued a statement claiming that the real question behind the strike was "the possibility of the creation and duration of a dictatorship which could make all the industries of the United States . . . hostages for the granting of the fantastic whim of such a dictator." The ARU attempted to keep up the struggle, but after Debs and other officers were rearrested and jailed July 17, charged with contempt of court for violating Grosscup's and Woods's injunction, most striking railroad workers returned to work. Debs later testified that "as soon as the employees found that we were arrested and taken from the scene of action, they became demoralized, and that ended the strike. It was not the soldiers that ended the strike; it was not the old brotherhoods that ended the strike; it was simply the United States courts that ended the strike." Within three days of the arrests, the Pullman Company had reopened its gates and the U.S. army left Chicago.[14]

With the loss of the strike, critics charged Gompers and the AFL with deserting the ARU in favor of the railroad brotherhoods. Thomas J. Morgan publicly branded Gompers a "traitor" and an "infernal rascal," who had shaken hands with the ARU with one hand and then stabbed Debs in the back with the other.[15] Others suggested that the AFL leader had ridden to Chicago on a Pullman car. Gompers denied these charges, reiterating his position that strong organization made for powerful strikes and not the reverse. Although he agreed that "the impulse of the men on strike was noble," he added that "impulses must be wisely directed." He was convinced that the AFL had served labor's long-term interests by stifling calls for a general strike, especially in the midst of an industrial depression. "We submit," Gompers answered his critics, "that when a battle is really lost, it is not the best time to stake the interests of organized labor upon that issue."[16] When the AFL convention met in Denver later in the year, Gompers again reviewed the case, noting that the actions taken by the Executive Council had been "adversely criticised."[17] He demanded and received the convention's vote of confidence. Although the convention endorsed Gompers' actions, the strike itself and the federal government's role in defeating it by means of injunctions and military intervention left a bitter legacy. The ARU was crushed, and railroad men throughout the central and western United States who had participated in the Pullman strike were blacklisted.

Notes

1. U.S. Strike Commission, *Report on the Chicago Strike of June-July, 1894. . .* , U.S. Congress, Senate, Ex. Docs., no. 7, 53d Cong., 3d sess. (Washington, D.C., 1895), p. xix.

2. U.S. Strike Commission, *Report*, pp. xxxiii-xxxiv; Almont Lindsey, *The Pullman Strike* (1942; reprint ed., Chicago, 1964), pp. 93, 98-99, 91-92; Nick Salvatore, *Eugene V. Debs: Citizen and Socialist* (Urbana, 1982), p. 127. Contemporaries estimated that rents ran 20 to 33 percent above costs for similar housing in adjacent communities (U.S. Strike Commission, *Report*, p. xxxv; Lindsey, *Pullman Strike*, p. 92).

3. Lindsey, *Pullman Strike*, pp. 123, 126. The U.S. Strike Commission estimated that 600 workers were locked out (*Report*, p. xxxviii).

4. *Chicago Inter Ocean*, June 17, 1894.

5. Ibid., June 26, 1894; U.S. Strike Commission, *Report*, p. xxviii.

6. Lindsey, *Pullman Strike*, pp. 137, 139; Salvatore, *Debs*, p. 130.

7. Lindsey, *Pullman Strike*, pp. 141-42; Salvatore, *Debs*, p. 131.

8. Lindsey, *Pullman Strike*, pp. 153-55; Philip S. Foner, *History of the Labor Movement in the United States*, vol. 2, *From the Founding of the A.F. of L. to the Emergence of American Imperialism*, 2d ed. (New York, 1975), p. 266. The document enjoined Debs and the officers and members of the ARU from "in any way or manner interfering with, hindering, obstructing, or stopping" the railroads' business. Second, it prohibited them from "compelling or inducing, or attempting to compel or induce, by threats, intimidation, persuasion, force, or violence" any railroad employees "to refuse or fail to perform any of their duties" or "to leave the service of such railroads"; nor were they allowed to attempt to prevent anyone else "from entering the service" of the railroads. Finally, Debs and the others were prohibited from "sending out any letters, messages, or communications directing, inciting, encouraging, or instructing any persons whatsoever" in connection with the strike (U.S. Strike Commission, *Report*, pp. 179-80).

9. Lindsey, *Pullman Strike*, p. 144; SG to Debs, July 5, 1894, reel 8, vol. 11, p. 147, SG Letterbooks, DLC. Debs now realized, he later testified to the U.S. Strike Commission, that the ARU confronted not only the GMA, but that the strike "had resolved itself into a conflict in which the organized forces of society and all the powers of the municipal, State, and Federal governments were arrayed against us." He called a meeting of the ARU board on July 6, which drew up a document to be presented to the Association offering to call off the strike on condition that the strikers were allowed to return to their jobs. This was the document that Debs presented to the Briggs House conference with the request that Gompers deliver it to the GMA (U.S. Strike Commission, *Report*, p. 145).

10. See, for example, SG to P. J. McGuire, July 9, 1894, reel 8, vol. 11, p. 155, SG Letterbooks, DLC.

11. Foner and Salvatore estimate that as many as 25,000 Chicago workers participated in the strike (Foner, *Founding of the AFL to the Emergence of American Imperialism*, p. 271; Salvatore, *Debs*, p. 135). Although the KOL's Grand Master Workman James Sovereign issued a general strike call on July 10, by the next day the KOL executive board announced that the call applied only to Chicago. "It does not contemplate a general strike and Mr. Sovereign has not the authority to order such strike except by the consent of a majority of the executive board. If the labor assemblies in other cities want to go on strike," the board added, "they can do so by virtue of the appeal, but the order has reference merely to Chicago" (*Rocky Mountain News* [Denver], July 12, 1894).

12. U.S. Strike Commission, *Report*, p. 155.

13. Ibid., p. 146; "A Statement Issued by the Conference of Representatives of Labor Organizations Meeting at Briggs House, Chicago," July 13, 1894, below.

14. U.S. Strike Commission, *Report*, pp. 143, 271; Ray Ginger, *The Bending Cross: A Biography of Eugene Victor Debs* (New Brunswick, N.J., 1949), p. 150. Refusing bail, Debs was released on his own recognizance on July 25, 1894. After the trial later in the fall before Judge Woods, he was sentenced to a six-month jail term and the other officers to three-month terms.

15. *Chicago Inter Ocean*, July 16, 1894; *Chicago Tribune*, July 16, 1894.

16. SG, "The Strike and Its Lessons," *American Federationist* 1 (Aug. 1894): 126.

17. AFL, *Proceedings*, 1894, pp. 11-12, 30.

An Article by Samuel Gompers in
the *North American Review*

[July 8, 1894]

On Decoration Day, May 30, 1894, Judge Grosscup,[1] of the United States Courts, in his oration commemorative of the day, took occasion to say that "the growth of labor organizations must be checked by law," yet when the sounds of his voice had scarcely died away we had in the midst of us the greatest and most extensive labor struggle that has ever taken place among the wage-workers of America, and possibly of the world.

Thousands of miles of railroads in all directions have been at a standstill, and nearly a hundred thousand workmen in voluntary idleness to secure what they regard as justice to their fellow workmen. It has been questioned whether the boycott or strike was wise or whether it was justifiable. On the first question there may be some difference of opinion. It may sincerely be doubted whether it was wise for an organization such as the American Railway Union, within a year of its formation, to attempt to inaugurate a movement which, in its inception, of necessity, assumed gigantic proportions.

The policy or wisdom of entering into so great a movement without consultation with, or against the advice of, the older railroad and *bona-fide* labor organizations of the country is open to serious question. Nor will I attempt from the usual standpoint of trade dispute to justify the strike. Sufficient for me are the facts which provoked it and to which I shall allude later; but that the railroadmen deliberately entered a contest which entailed many sacrifices and dangers in an attempt to redress grievances not of their own, but of other workmen, who, having become thoroughly enervated and impoverished, without organization or previous understanding, in sheer desperation threw down their work, is indeed to their credit.

A little more than twenty years ago George M. Pullman[2] conceived the idea of starting, in connection with his car shops, a town—one that should bear his name and hand down to posterity a monument of his enterprise and philanthropy. He built houses for his employees to live in, stores to make their purchases in, and churches to do their praying in. The workers were told their interests and Mr. Pullman's were one and the same, that what would bring him a greater prosperity would redound to their advantage. They were warned that to belong to a trade-union would be inimical to their *joint* enterprise, hence workmen who would purpose forming a union among them would be discharged, regarded as a common enemy, and driven out of town.

They were to depend entirely upon Mr. Pullman's generosity and foresight in all things.

The result was that the workers at Pullman were huddled together in the (outwardly) neat houses, for which they were required to pay higher rents than are paid for similar accommodations in Chicago. They were reduced in wages as often as the seasons would recur and opportunities either arose or were made. This was carried on until last February, when a reduction in wages was offered varying from 25 to 33⅓ and in a few instances 50 per cent.

Here are a few figures which may be taken as a fair criterion of the extent of the reduction in wages offered:

Price per piece, 1893.		Price offered, 1894.
Making trolley roofs........	$2.25	$1.40
Framework car seat.........	1.25	.79
Cutting carpets	3.00	1.50
Making mattresses double...	.25	.15
Cutting brussels carpet	2.50	1.10
Blacksmith work, platform..	4.00	2.65
Truck setting	.45	.16
Sleeping car bodies	180.00	115.50

The workmen being driven to desperation, a meeting was held. Who called it no one knows; how it came about not a vestige of evidence is at hand. It was held and a committee appointed to wait upon Mr. Pullman or a representative of the company, to show that it was absolutely impossible to live on the wages offered; that a middle ground should be sought; that if wages were to be reduced the rents should also come down. Instead of the request of the men being considered by Mr. Pullman, the committee was summarily dismissed and discharged almost instantly. Is it surprising that these men in their rude awakening, finding themselves injured and insulted and their spokesmen discharged and blacklisted, and themselves without an organization to protect or defend them, without the means of properly laying their grievances before organized labor of the country, struck work, declaring that they might as well remain idle and starve as work and slowly meet that fate?

Organized labor of Chicago becoming aware of the unusual commotion at Pullman did not hold against the workers of that town their previous refusals to organize. It was readily appreciated that these men had been wholly misled by false promises and covert threats. Relief committees were at once formed, and it is firmly declared that the average workmen of that town have fared better since they engaged in the contest and fraternized with their fellow-workmen than they have for the past two years while working.

It was during this time, when relief committees from the Pullman strikers were making their visits to organizations, that the American Railway Union was holding its first convention in Chicago,[3] and a committee called upon it for its financial and moral assistance. A committee from the convention was appointed to wait upon the company with the request that the matter in dispute might be submitted to arbitration. The committee was told that there was nothing to arbitrate and that the company refused to discuss the matter at all. Insulted, humiliated by the manner their disinterested efforts at restoring amicable relations between Mr. Pullman and his former servile employees were received, the committee made its report. The convention in a moment reflected the feelings of the committee, and though at first sullen, silent, and indignant they resolved amidst the wildest enthusiasm that unless the Pullman company either adjusted the matter in controversy with their employees or submitted it to arbitration the members of the American Railway Union would not handle Pullman cars and would ask all workmen to act likewise. No heed was given to the request, resolution, or threat (call it what you will), and the great boycott (strike) was on.

I can scarcely bring myself to the belief that the convention imagined that the movement would be as extended as it became into, nor that it would last as long as it did. Be that as it may, we certainly found ourselves in the midst of one of the greatest labor struggles.

Now comes the question repeated: Was the strike wise or justifiable? the answer to which must always depend upon the character and position of the party giving it. As to the wisdom, time only can tell. Since "nothing succeeds so well as success" in all efforts of life, I presume this element will finally set its *quietus* upon this consideration of the subject. But was it justifiable? From the standpoint of the employer, No. From the standpoint of a labor organization having an agreement with an employer whose provisions a strike would violate, No. From the standpoint of the A.R.U., having no agreement with either of the railroad companies involved, and expressing the inarticulate protest of the masses against the wrongs inflicted upon any of their brothers and their yearning for justice to all mankind, Yes; a thousand times yes.

It is something not yet fully understood how thoroughly organized labor stands as the sturdy pioneer of all the hopes of the masses for justice and humane conditions, of their aspirations for a nobler manhood resultant from an equality of opportunities. It is in consequence of these facts that organized labor feels itself frequently called upon to espouse the cause of those who have neglected their own interests, and who have even antagonized any effort to bring them within the fold of organization. Laboring men feel and know that the wealth producers would certainly avail themselves of their only means of defending and advancing their position in life were it not that they in many instances had their prejudices aroused and their ignorance of actual conditions preyed upon by the instruments of their oppression in the hands of the corporate and employing class. But the men are on strike, the police armed to the teeth are on guard to protect life and property, the militia are called out ostensibly for the same purpose, and the regular army of the United States are marshalled into the fields by order of the President to enforce injunctions, restraining "everybody" from even writing a letter, issued by the Judge who only a few days before expressed the firm conviction that the growth of labor organizations must be checked by law.

Is it not somewhat strange that the provisions of the Interstate Commerce Law, a law passed by Congress in compliance with the demand of the people of our country to protect them against the greed and outrageous discriminations of the railroads, can be distorted to such a degree as to appall its authors and promoters, and should be perverted from its true purpose, and made to do service as an instrument to oppress the parties to whom it was never intended to apply, workingmen engaged in a contest to redress grievances. One may look almost in vain for the restraint the law has put upon the avarice and injustice practised by the railroad corporations. The reform elements in our country seem to have unconsciously created their own Frankenstein, the breath of life being injected into it by plutocracy in the shape of ill-gotten gains.

There is no desire nor even a tendency on the part of organized labor to have its movement go beyond the limits of the law, but I submit that there is a standpoint from which this great problem should be considered other than a judges' injunction, a policeman's club, or the point of the bayonet. The fact of the matter is that industrial conditions have changed to a wonderful extent within the past thirty years, that wealth has been accumulated as never before, that new forces are at play in the production and transportation of wealth, and that the civil law of our States and country has simply not kept pace in becoming accommodated to the altered conditions. Do what you will, declaim as you may, industrial and commercial development cannot be confined within the limits of laws enacted to fit past decades the theories of which are sought to be applied to modern conditions.

Civilization of the past and present is based upon labor, and yet the laborer has no standing nor protection in the economy of our life. It may well be asked, if the state refuses to deal out some degree of justice and guarantee protection to labor, what interest has the laborer in the state? As a matter of fact the organizations of labor are endeavoring to secure that protection and guaranty to the workingmen which the state has failed to take cognizance of. Without organization the workmen would simply be reduced to a much worse condition than the slaves in ante-bellum days, and all attempts to strain the law, construing the exercise of natural rights to be criminal, will only react upon the heads of the legal prestidigitators.

If in monarchical England, with its old and effete traditions and crusty customs, Parliament can afford to liberalize its laws and legalize the action of workingmen engaged in the maintenance of their organizations and their effort to obtain better conditions, certainly the Republic of these United States should not only keep pace with that spirit, but advance beyond it, and not bring the entire military and civil forces to aid the strong and help crush out the weak.

Labor cannot, and will not if it could, utilize the process of securing legislation by the use of money; it relies upon the justice of its cause, the nobility of its purposes, the humanizing influences of its efforts.

Mr. Pullman, it is said, is willing to spend millions of dollars if necessary to bring his former employees "to their senses." That is to say, he is willing to spend millions of dollars to bring his workmen to the sense of their utter dependence upon him.

This is evidently his purpose. It is the purpose of many another corporation king. He and a few others may possibly win for the present, but the people of America, when once aroused to a sense of the wrong inflicted upon them, will not be slow in so shaping our laws and industrial conditions as to surprise their most supercilious critics.

We insist upon the right to organize, the right to think, to act; to protect ourselves, our homes, and our liberties, and work out our emancipation. We are confident we shall secure them, and that the world will stand surprised that they were accomplished through the means of an enlightened public opinion and by peaceful means.

North American Review 159 (Aug. 1894): 201-6.

1. Peter Stenger Grosscup (1852-1921) was U.S. district judge for the northern district of Illinois (1892-99) and later judge of the Seventh U.S. Circuit Court (1899-1911), presiding over that court from 1905 to 1911. He and Judge William A. Woods issued an injunction on July 2, 1894, enjoining Eugene Debs and other American Railway Union (ARU) officials from activities interfering with interstate commerce or the mails, and subsequently indicted them for violation of this injunction. Grosscup presided over a grand jury that convened on July 10 to consider conspiracy charges

against the ARU leaders, and his charge to that jury, virtually assuring the defendants' indictment, gained national attention.

2. George Mortimer PULLMAN was the owner of the Pullman Palace Car Co. and the founder of the company town of Pullman, Ill.

3. The ARU's convention was held June 12-23, 1894.

A Telegram Issued by the Conference of Representatives of Labor Organizations Meeting at Briggs House, Chicago

Chicago, Ill. July 12, 1894.

To the President of the United States. Washington, D.C.

The gravity of the industrial situation of the country demands extraordinary and exceptional action of a conciliatory character at the hands of all men. Recognizing this fact the Executive Council of the American Federation of Labor and the undersigned Executive Officers of National and International Trade Unions and Brotherhoods of railroad organizations of America are in conference in this city. We ask you in the name of the working people and the entire citizenship of our country to lend your influence and give us your aid so that the present industrial crisis may be brought to an end, alike to the advantage of the people of our country and the institutions under which we live. We therefore ask you to come to Chicago and meet this conference, or if the state of public business does not warrant such a course that you will deputize some one as your representative.

Executive Council American Federation of Labor.

Samuel Gompers, President
P. J. Mc-Guire, 1st. Vice-President
C. L. Drummond,[1] 2nd. Vice-President
Jas. Brettell, 3rd. Vice-President
Wm. H. Marden, 4th. Vice-President
John B. Lennon, Treasurer.
Chris. Evans, Secretary.

Geo. W. Perkins, Prest. Cigar Makers Intl. Union
Thos. I. Kidd, Sec. Machine Wood Workers Intl. Union[2]
J. W. Kenney,[3] Prest. Bro'd. Painters & Decorators of America
T. Elderkin, Sec. Seamen's Intl. Union
G. L. Horn, Sec. Bakers & Confectioners Intl. Union of A.

E. Kurzenknabe C. F. Bechtel,[4] Sec. and Assistant Secretary
Brewers Nat. Union
P. Mc-Bryde, Sec. United Mine Workers of A.
M. Carroll, Executive Int'l. Typographical Union
O. Miller, Prest. Nat'l. League of Musicians
C. Bauntian H. Dopheide,[5] Carriage & Wagon Workers Intl. Union
C. L. White,[6] Nat'l. Bro'd. Electrical Workers of A.[7]
M. M. Garland, Prest. Amalgamated Ass'n. of Iron & Steel
Workers of A.
F. Kurtzer,[8] Nat'l. Furniture Workers Union
P. H. Morrissey,[9] 1st. Vice Grand Master
Brotherhood of Railroad Trainmen
F. W. Arnold,[10] Grand Secretary & Treas. Brotherhood of
Locomotive Firemen.

TWpSr, AFL Executive Council Minutes, reel 2, *AFL Records.*

1. Charles L. DRUMMOND, a Fort Wayne, Ind., printer and journalist, was second vice-president of the AFL from 1893 to 1894.

2. The Machine WOODWORKERS' International Union of America.

3. Joseph W. MCKINNEY was general president of the Brotherhood of Painters and Decorators of America from 1892 to 1894.

4. Charles F. BECHTOLD was a secretary of the National Union of the United Brewery Workmen of the United States from 1892 until 1901.

5. Henry Dopheide was a member of the executive board of the Carriage and Wagon Workers' International Union of North America (CWWIU) and an officer of CWWIU 4 of Chicago.

6. Charles L. White was a member of National Brotherhood of Electrical Workers of America (NBEWA) 9 of Chicago. In 1895 he served on the executive board of the NBEWA.

7. The National Brotherhood of ELECTRICAL Workers of America.

8. F. Kurtzer was the organizer for International Furniture Workers' Union of America 1 of Chicago.

9. Patrick Henry MORRISSEY served as vice grand master of the Brotherhood of Railroad Brakemen (after 1890 the Brotherhood of Railroad Trainmen) from 1889 to 1895.

10. Frank W. ARNOLD served as grand secretary and treasurer of the Brotherhood of Locomotive Firemen from 1892 to 1904.

An Excerpt from an Article in
the *Rocky Mountain News*

Chicago, July 13. [1894]

OPPOSE A GENERAL STRIKE

Shortly after 10 o'clock to-day, the American federation conference began its second day's meeting at the Brigg's house. A few delegates were present to-day who were not here yesterday, among them being P. J. McGuire.[1]

The morning session immediately took up the resolutions where they were dropped the night before. The session was a hot one, and many strong speeches were made on both sides of the resolution as to whether the American Federation of Labor should order a general strike of the members in sympathy with the Pullman strikers, and at the request of the A.R.U.

Several presidents and secretaries of different labor organizations of this city came to the committee room to get instructions as to what to do. They said that all their men were out, and they had no instructions. They were refused admission, and many grew disgusted and walked away apparently sorry for the steps already taken.

A strong speech was made by M. J. Carroll of the International Typographical union, in favor of a general strike. He appealed to the feelings of the conference on the manner in which labor had been tramped upon by capital and said that the only way to force a recognition was to order a complete tie up. Messrs. McGuire and Perkins made speeches in the same line, urging most emphatically in favor of the resolutions.

Mr. Drummond took up the side of the opposition and discussed at some length the inadvisability of a general strike. He said:

"I want Debs to understand that it is unnecessary for us to order a strike. He wishes to shift the responsibility off from his shoulders and I object to it. If we should order a strike now, the financial situation of the country is in such a condition that a great many of our members would not go out, and the vacancies would be filled with non-unionists. I believe that the condition of this country is such that a general strike would not win. I do not want the reputation of having our federation lose, I am opposed to the resolution.

Mr. Garland of the iron and steel workers, said:

"We were unable to form an effective organization as long as the Pullman shops were working on the wages which they were and not until this A.R.U. strike have we been able to do anything. In our organizations we have had, and still have, great strikes both in sympathy and for grievances. I am opposed to a general strike now, because we have a certain scale of wages adopted by arbitration, and if we strike, that scale of wages will be broken, and at this time of financial depression, I believe that it would be impossible to get as good a scale of wages again as we have now, and therefore a general strike would be detrimental to our men.

"I am not in favor of complying with Debs' request. He was so very arrogant in the start, not even recognizing us, and now he wants to shift all the responsibility off on us, and blame us for losing the strike. Another thing, the Knights of Labor are in favor of a council and not of a monarchial government, as Debs favors. This country will not stand that kind of thing. I do not care how smart he is, he cannot win. I can call out the iron and steel workers, but I can see no favorable results, and therefore, I oppose the resolution."

Mr. Evans then said: "If the local organizer of the American Federation of Labor had attended to his business the A.R.U. would never have handled this strike. I am opposed to the resolutions and any action in that regard, now."

Patrick McBride, representing the coal miners, said:

"If a strike is ordered, let it be for ourselves and not for Debs. He has not managed this thing right and now he wants help, and I am not in favor of doing it. A general strike order, by this conference, in sympathy with the A.R.U., would be of no value to us, and it would break our contract, change the present arbitrated scale of wages, and be of a general disadvantage to us. While I can call out the miners, I am not in favor of it, and think it very poor policy. I am opposed to bringing any other organization into this strike. If Debs has started it, let him finish it."

The council re-assembled about 4 o'clock and the committee[2] presented for adoption an address to the public. President Gompers read it quite impressively. After arguments for and against it the address was finally adopted.

. . .

Rocky Mountain News (Denver), July 14, 1894.

1. The minutes published in the *American Federationist* indicate that, in addition to P. J. McGuire, Martin Fox of the Iron Molders' Union of North America and Andrew Furuseth of the National Seamen's Union of America arrived at the conference on the evening of July 12, 1894.

2. The committee consisted of SG, P. J. McGuire, Michael J. Carroll, Martin Fox, and Mahlon M. Garland.

A Statement Issued by the Conference of Representatives of Labor Organizations Meeting at Briggs House, Chicago

Chicago July 13, 1894.

The great industrial upheaval now agitating the country has been carefully, calmly and fully considered in a conference of the Executive

Council of the American Federation of Labor and the executive officers and representatives of the National and International Unions and Brotherhoods of railway men called to meet in the city of Chicago on the 12th. day of July 1894. In the light of all the evidence attainable, and in view of the peculiar complications now enveloping the situation we are forced to the conclusion that the best interests of the Unions affiliated with the American Federation of Labor demand that they refrain from participating in any general or local strike which may be proposed in connection with the present railroad troubles.

In making this declaration we do not wish it understood that we are in any way antagonistic to labor organizations now struggling for right or justice, but rather to the fact that the present contest has become surrounded and beset with complications so grave in their nature that we cannot consistently advise a course which would but add to the general confusion.

The public press ever alive to the interests of corporate wealth have with few exceptions so maliciously misrepresented matters that in the public mind the working classes are now arrayed in open hostility to federal authority. This is a position we do not wish to be placed in nor will we occupy without a protest.

We claim to be patriotic and law abiding as any other class of citizens, a claim substantiated by our actions in times of public need and public peril.

By misrepresentation and duplicity certain corporations assume that they stand for law and order, and that those opposing them represent lawlessness and anarchy. We protest against this assumption, as we protest against the inference that because a certain individual or a certain class enjoys a monopoly in particular lines of trade or commerce, that it necessarily follows that they are entitled to a monopoly in loyalty and good citizenship.

The trade union movement is one of reason, one of deliberation and depending entirely upon the voluntary and sovereign action of its members. It is democratic in principle and action, conservative in its demands and consistent in its efforts to secure them.

Industrial contests cannot be entered into at the behests of any individual officer of this conference, regardless of the position he may occupy in our organizations. Strikes in our affiliated organizations are entered into only as a last resort, and after all efforts for a peaceful adjustment of grievances have failed; and then only after the members have by their own votes (usually requiring a two-thirds and often a three-fourths vote) so decided.

The trade union movement has its origin in economic and social injustice, and has its history, its struggles, and its tendency well defined.

It stands as the protector of those who see the wrongs and injustice resultant of our present industrial system, and who by organization manifest their purpose of becoming larger sharers in the product of their labor, and who by their efforts contribute towards securing the unity and solidarity of labor's forces; so that in the ever present contest of the wealth producers to conquer their rights from the wealth absorbers we may by our intelligence and persistency, the earnestness of our purpose, the nobility of our cause work out through evolutionary methods the final emancipation of labor.

While we may not have the power to order a strike of the working people of our country, we are fully aware that a recommendation from this conference to them to lay down their tools of labor would largely influence the members of our affiliated organizations; and appreciating the responsibility resting upon us and the duty we owe to all, we declare it to be the sense of this conference that a general strike at this time is inexpedient, unwise and contrary to the best interests of the working people. We further recommend that all connected with the American Federation of Labor [now out on] sympathetic strike should return to work and those who contemplate going out on sympathetic strike are advised to remain at their usual vocations.

In the strike of the American Railway Union we recognize an impulsive vigorous protest against the gathering, growing forces of plutocratic power and corporation rule. In the sympathetic movement of that Order to help the Pullman employes, they have demonstrated the hollow shams of Pullman's Pharasaical paradise. Mr. Pullman in his persistent repulses of arbitration and in his heartless autocratic treatment of his employes has proven himself a public enemy.

The heart of labor everywhere throbs responsive to the manly purposes and sturdy struggle of the American Railway Union in their heroic endeavor to redress the wrongs of the Pullman employes. In this position they effectually reiterate the fundamental trade union principle that working people regardless of sex, creed, color, nationality, politics or occupation should have one and the same interests in one common cause for their own industrial and political advancement.

By this railway strike the people are once more reminded of the immense forces held at the call of corporate capital for the subjugation of Labor. For years the railroad interests have shown the lawless example of defiance to injunctions and have set aside laws to control them. They have displayed the utmost contempt for the Inter-State Commerce Law, have avoided its penalties and sneered at its impotency to prevent pooling discriminations and other impositions on the public. In this disregard of law these corporations have given the greatest impetus to Anarchy and lawlessness. Still they did not hesitate, when confronted by outraged labor, to invoke the powers of the State. The Federal Government backed by United States marshals, injunctions of Courts, proclamations of the President and sustained by the bayonets of soldiers and all the civil and military machinery of the law have rallied on the summons of the corporations.

Against this array of armed force and brutal moneyed aristocracy would it not be worse than folly to call men out on general or local strike in these days of stagnant trade and commercial depression? No, better let us organize more generally, combine more closely, unite our forces, educate and prepare ourselves to protect our interests, and that we may go to the ballot box and cast our votes as American Freemen united and determined to redeem this country from its present political and industrial misrule, to take it from the hands of plutocratic wreckers and place it in the hands of the common people.

TDp, AFL Executive Council Minutes, reel 2, *AFL Records.*

To James Linehan

July 19, [1894]

Mr. Jas. Linehan,
Sec. Trades and Labor Assembly,
418 Rand Mc-Nally Bldg. Chicago, Ill.
Dear Sir and Brother: —

In the Chicago papers of Monday morning July 16th. there appeared a statement that Mr. Thos. J. Morgan in the course of a discussion of a matter pending before the meeting of your Trades and Labor Assembly the day before stated in substance that before I left New York City I declared that I "was going to a funeral and that that funeral would in all likelihood be the American Railway Union."

In connection with this matter I desire to say that I am loath to take the public press as the authority for any statement a man in the labor movement may make, but in this instance I have had the matter verified by those who were at the meeting, and I desire to take this opportunity to assure the officers and delegates to the Trades and Labor Assembly, and through them organized labor of Chicago, that whoever published or voiced the above statement uttered what was a gratuitous and unqualified falsehood.

To prove how earnest was my sympathy with the men engaged in the railway strike I call your attention to an article which I wrote July 8th. for the "North American Review"[1] and which is republished in the current issue of the American Federationist, and also the letter I wrote to Congressman Amos J. Cummings[2] asking him to prevail upon the President not to throw the influence of his great office on the side of the corporations and against the workmen.

The men entrusted with the interests of organized labor of America have enough enemies and calumnies to contend against, and it seems to me that a man who himself has suffered as much as Mr. Morgan has from such treatment should be the last to recklessly indulge in it when it refers to others in the movement.

So far as my actions in the recent railroad strike are concerned I am perfectly satisfied to be coolly and calmly judged, and all the antagonism and bitterness that any desire to pour out on my devoted head they are perfectly at liberty to do, but I believe it is due to the Trades and Labor Assembly to know that the statement attributed to me by Mr. Morgan is not based upon truth.

Since Mr. Morgan is a delegate to the T. and L.A. and made his statement before your body I have deemed it the proper course to pursue to address this letter to you instead of to him.

Sincerely hoping that the cause of labor may be carried onward and forward to ultimate success, and with kindest wishes, I am,

Fraternally Yours   Saml Gompers.
President American Federation of Labor.

Private

N.B. Please hand enclosed letters to Mr. Hart. Read August number of American Federationist [. . . .]

TLpS, reel 8, vol. 11, pp. 173-74, SG Letterbooks, DLC.

1. Printed above.
2. July 3, 1893, reel 8, vol. 11, pp. 141-42, SG Letterbooks, DLC.

An Editorial by Samuel Gompers in the *American Federationist*

July 1894

A typical example of capitalistic anarchy comes to us from the motherland of our own "triumphant Democrat,"[1] where a crisis in the jute trade has induced the manufacturers of Dundee to consider the advisability of making an all around reduction of ten per cent. in the wages of their operatives.[2] The process of the progressive degradation of the mill workers was efficiently exposed by the president of the union at a meeting called to consider the proposal of the employers. The speaker said, "that while they had thousands of their fellow creatures on the borders of starvation many millions were worse than wasted every year in keeping soldiers and other instruments for the destruction of human life. It was a lamentable fact that in Dundee there was so little work for men. That was because the employers, wherever they could, took on women to do men's work. Proceeding further, the employers had carried out their determination to pair looms, with the result that only the strongest women were kept; the weaker no matter how skillful were shown the door. The wages paid would reveal that it was impossible for a woman to earn a week's wage unless she did two women's work. The prosperity of Dundee would ultimately result in the starvation of its people.["]

The capitalistic process was further traced at a subsequent meeting to hear the report of the delegates to confer with the employers' committee. The Rev. Henry Williamson spoke from a wagon, on which was displayed the banner of the Union, to this effect:—"Short time had been attempted, and they were now told that instead of making matters better it would to some extent make things worse; because while Dundee was idle, Calcutta was running as much as it could. The employers said that they had no alternative but in some way to reduce the cost of production, and they insisted that it was necessary to reduce wages or the trade would leave the city. In the neighborhood of Calcutta large jute mills, fitted with electric lights, were working 22 out of the 24 hours daily (by shifts), women and children being regularly employed through the night. These Calcutta mills were established by Dundee capital—money that was earned in Dundee by the hard labor of their forefathers and themselves. That money so saved up had been invested in these great mills. Further, they had in Calcutta Dundee-made machinery, Dundee managers, Dundee foremen, and Dundee overseers. Calcutta was near to the supply of jute, and her merchants had an immense market of more than two hundred millions of people in India. But now Indian jute manufacturers had crossed the seas; they had invaded and conquered Dundee's chief foreign markets. The Australian and California trade had slipped away, and Calcutta was sending goods to New York, the great emporium on the Atlantic side for the import trade of the United States, and was underselling Dundee there. The question was: Could the workers and the employers resolve to unite together, or were they to submit to see the trade leave the city and allow Dundee to become a howling wilderness?"

The same evening the member for Dundee rose in the House of Commons to ask the Indian Secretary[3] "whether it was lawful for mills owned by English capitalists, and competing with similar mills in the United Kingdom, to be worked night and day with shifts of hands." The Secretary replied "that it was not unlawful for mills to be so worked, but it was not lawful for women to be employed between 8 P.M. and 5 A.M., unless sanctioned by the government factory inspector, or for children to be employed between those hours under any circumstances whatever. He would ask the Government of India to take steps to ensure that the law is enforced."

The growth of the jute manufacturing industry in India furnishes a most impressive lesson on the existing relations of capital and labor. In 1872 there were only five mills in existence, containing 1,180 looms and 13,000 spindles. In ten years the number of mills had increased to 23, with 8,000 looms and 130,000 spindles. During the last twelve years the number of mills have not increased save but by one. The number of looms during that period, have increased by 2,200 and the number of spindles by 55,000. It will be seen that in [the] twenty-two years since 1872, the increase in looms has been about 700 per cent. while the increase in spindles has been 1,300 per cent. In 1872, about 11 spindles per loom was sufficient, but so much greater is the speed at which the looms are driven to-day that it needs the yarn from 20 spindles to keep a loom employed.

Such is the efficiency of the India mills, which up to date machinery, triple expansion engines, perfect ventilation, electric light and telephone installations, plentiful coal, skilled operatives, limitless supply of ordinary laborers whose expenses for house rent, clothing, are but nominal; the cost of whose food, rice, fish, fruit, milk and salt, is excessively low; that India to-day controls the jute market of the world. In the accomplishment of this grand stroke of capitalistic genius, more than $30,000,000 accumulated profits on the labor of Dundee operatives has been sunk and the wages of the Dundee weaver has been reduced nearly to the level of those of the Hindoo.

The systematic policy of the capitalistic class as exhibited in its persistent efforts in breaking down the ancient civilizations of India and China, the introduction of labor-saving machinery of modern methods of production in the less advanced countries of the world, is a form of deviltry far more menacing to the well being of the working class of America, than negro slavery was in Dixie. The time has arrived for the most energetic action. The call for the unity of the working class to stamp out forever this diabolical capitalistic policy, should strike like a trumpet's blast on the ear of every toiler in America, and stir him to energy like a battle cry.

For which purpose is a prohibitory tariff maintained on European goods, often the products of trade union labor, while secret treaties are made with Asiatic countries?

Why is our capitalistic class so anxious to hurry to completion an "invincible armada," in the meanwhile throwing dust in the eyes of the groundlings in the shape of catch words like "old glory," "white squadron," and by the use of every other despicable artifice of clap-trap as a substitute for true patriotism?

Why is our capitalistic class seeking a plausible pretext for the annexation of Hawaii; why is it so solicitous about the welfare of a few thousand coolies there, while one hundred and fifty thousand coal miners at home are in open rebellion against its inhuman rule?

Why is our capitalistic class so energetic in pushing missionaries into the interior of China, are there not heathens enough in the treaty ports which the capitalists of England and France have already blown open with the guns of their battle ships?

The motive is plain. The enterprise is well under way. The final result is foreshadowed in the degradation of the weavers of Dundee.

Workers will you endeavor to avert your doom before it is too late? Then organize.

American Federationist 1 (July 1894): 99-100.

1. Andrew Carnegie.
2. Women workers in the Scottish jute industry in Dundee organized the Dundee and District Mill and Factory Operatives' Union in response to a wage reduction in 1885 and elected Radical Unitarian minister Henry Williamson honorary president and spokesman for the union. Wages remained a center of contention; a brief strike in 1893 succeeded in restoring a wage cut, but in 1895 some 32,000 workers struck unsuccessfully for a wage increase.
3. Liberal party member John Leng of Dundee questioned Sir Henry Hartley Fowler (secretary of state for India, 1894-95) on June 1, 1894.

Excerpts from an Interview in the *Review of Reviews*

[July 1894]

A TALK WITH MR. GOMPERS.

In Clinton Place, New York, a few doors west of Broadway and a few minutes' walk from the offices of the *Review of Reviews*, one finds on the lintel of an old house, once a residence but now an office building, a modest sign that reads: "The American Federation of Labor, Samuel Gompers, President." The halls are rather dark and dingy, and one climbs two flights to find the rooms of the Federation. But the journey will be worth while if the caller is fortunate enough to find Mr. Gompers at his desk. He is not prone to careless absence from his place of work, but the manifold duties of his position frequently take him to distant parts of the country. The quarters of the American Federation are unadorned enough to allay any suspicion that the chief officers of this great combination of the trades unions of the country are disposed to revel in luxurious appointments. Everything is as severely plain as it can be; and the stiff common chairs invite no loiterers. Order and system are evident at a glance, and the experienced observer is quickly satisfied that the affairs of the Federation are in methodical and competent hands.

Mr. Samuel Gompers has been heard by many audiences besides those composed of workingmen and members of the constituent orders of the Federation. He is a short but massively framed man of perhaps forty-five years, with a strong and handsome face and suave manner, a business-like yet not too abrupt deportment, and a diction as discriminating and clear as one is taught to expect from a college professor. Mr. Gompers certainly exhibits great gifts of lucid expression, whether on the platform or in private conversation. He possesses a singularly well balanced temperament, the key to which seems to be a cheerful optimism tempered by natural caution and held in bounds, though not repressed, by experience and responsibility.

. . .

The editor[1] of the *Review of Reviews* made Mr. Gompers a neighborly call the other day to exchange views with him upon the coal strike[2] and upon various questions of the day that have to do with the prevailing social unrest.

His View of the Coal Strike.

"I see no immediate or early possibility," said Mr. Gompers, "of a complete agreement, in settlement of the coal dispute, that shall include all the States and mining districts that are involved. The effect of the uncontrolled competition of the Southern Illinois district with those that lie beyond it, north, south, west and east, is such that for the present a settlement all along the line seems to be out of the question. There is nothing to do but to close the strike by separate agreements in the different coal-mining territories involved, and then proceed to bring the Southern Illinois miners into a state of more perfect organization so that in future their district may not be a source of disturbance to the coal-mining interests of the entire country.

"But," Mr. Gompers continued, "although this year's coal strike is not to be terminated upon principles as sweeping in their application as one could desire, I wish to say emphatically that I regard this great strike, in spite of its numerous unfortunate incidents, as an essentially fortunate thing, not only for the cause of organized labor but also for the general economic and industrial interests of the United States. The financial panic of last year, with its attendant industrial depression, led to a general attempt on the part of capital engaged in the employment of labor to sharply curtail the consuming power of the masses of the people by diminishing their ability to purchase — that is, by a general reduction of wages. This movement against labor made its way through various great fields of employment. In the railroad world it was resisted by the strikers on the Great Northern system,[3] whose final success in arbitration has helped to check the downward tendency. But the most typical instance of the aggressive movement among the employing class against the workers was in the mining field and especially in that of bituminous coal mining. The great strike was a notice served upon capital that the whole world of organized labor had determined to take a stand, to face about, and not only to resist further aggression but to endeavor to gain back some of the ground that had been lost. With the success of this stand, — for the miners have in most of the districts concerned gained all or a considerable part of their demands, — it is evident that there is a turn in the tide. Wages in general are not to decline any further, but on the contrary are to tend upwards. And with better pay the people will require larger supplies of standard commodities and the wheels of industry will be quickened in many directions. It is not true," Mr. Gompers further continued, "that the miners have really suffered anything in the loss of wages during the weeks of enforced closing down of the mines. They will gain back all the time apparently lost by more steady employment hereafter. It is only approximately a certain volume of output that the country can consume in any case, and if through a strike the miners can secure a higher wage per ton it is clear that their total wages upon a year's output will be increased by so much."

VOUCHES FOR JOHN M'BRIDE.

Being asked to give some account of the quality and character of Mr. John McBride, the leader of the coal miners in their recent noteworthy conflict, Mr. Gompers spoke substantially as follows:

"I have no hesitation in saying that Mr. McBride is not only a strong man and an intrepid leader, but also a man who should be held free from the charge of rashness or undue excitability. He understands mining in every particular, and is as widely and minutely conversant with the mining interests of this country as any man who could be named. Personally he is urbane, courteous, and of gentlemanly, even polished, manners. He is fully deserving of the confidence of the great organization of miners over which he has been chosen to preside. Mr. McBride, in his circular accompanying the agreement,[4] expresses his opinion that one of the reasons why the effort for the full restoration of former wages was not successful was that in a few districts some of the men had forgotten or failed to abide by his urgent request not to resort to violence or violation of law. The strike itself, and the just grounds upon which it was ordered by the Miners' Convention, ought certainly by every fair-minded man to be distinguished from certain deplorable incidents that grew out of it in some mining districts where great bodies of non-English-speaking workmen have been imported by the mine operators to the detriment of those miners who were earlier on the ground.

"Mr. McBride, it should further be remembered, is not to be saddled with the responsibility for the fact that there was a strike. It was ordered instituted on the demand of the great majority of the representatives of the miners; and it then became Mr. McBride's duty to lead it as best he could. His conduct will bear the test of scrutiny."

THE SCOPE OF ARBITRATION.

Mr. Gompers was asked to express himself as to arbitration in industrial disputes, and especially as to the possibility of some form of compulsory arbitration. He replied that he was most assuredly in favor of arbitration. "As for 'compulsory arbitration,' however," he continued, "the two words seem to me antithetical. Arbitration always involves a compromise. The conditions under which it usually comes about are those which have led each of the parties in dispute somewhat to fear and somewhat to respect the other. The employing interest is usually the stronger. But when, through careful organization, the employees attain a position which commands the respectful attention of the representatives of capital, it becomes possible to confer together successfully and to secure a reference of disputes for the desired settlement by arbitration. I see no means by which legal compulsion to arbitrate could be made really beneficial to the party that is usually the weaker. It would be an instrumentality that might react dangerously against the progress of organized labor. The labor movement has too much at stake and has too slender means at its command to indulge in dubious experiments. The weapons that it now uses have been tested by long experience, and their use is understood and also their limitations."

Against the idea that an occasional outbreak or scene of disorder in connection with a strike was the essence of the labor movement, Mr. Gompers protested earnestly. "The real labor movement," said he, "goes on unnoticed by the newspapers and unwitnessed by the public. At this moment, while we discuss the question, there are probably thousands of committees of trades unions and labor organizations in conference with employers in the shops and counting rooms of the country. For every strike that occurs, scores of questions are settled by quiet conference between groups of organized workingmen and their employers. The strikes are unfortunate and to be regretted, but they are a part of the existing industrial order and serve their purpose. They should not be indulged in without great caution, but sometimes they are necessary, and their general result is beneficial upon the whole. It is always to be noticed that employers fight most stubbornly and ruthlessly in their first experience of a strike. They are much more disposed to negotiate and compromise when subsequent disputes arise."

For Free Silver, Income Tax, Short Hours.

With regard to the attitude of the American Federation of Labor upon public questions Mr. Gompers stated that the order is committed to the doctrine of the free coinage of silver at the ratio of one to sixteen regardless of the success of attempts to secure international agreement. He regarded Coxeyism and the industrial army movements rather as evidences of social unrest and incidental phenomena than as occurrences having any primary or vital significance in themselves. With Mr. Coxey's doctrine of non-interest-bearing bonds Mr. Gompers could find no theoretical fault. In fact his words were friendly rather than otherwise for the financial propositions that Mr. Coxey has advocated. As a practical matter, however, he did not consider that proposals to deal radically with the currency and the national debt are timely or advisable. In a general way, the American Federation has for some years been committed to the doctrine of an income tax. Mr. Gompers expressed himself as personally adverse to the exemption line in the pending bill,[5] and as in favor of a tax that should reach all incomes of self-supporting men, no matter how small. He would, however, employ the principle of a graduated tax, increasing the rate as incomes increased and were therefore better able to contribute to the public treasury.

The interview was ended by the following statement regarding the aims of the Federation: "The American Federation of Labor actively participates in every effort made by thinking men to secure amelioration in their condition, economically, socially and politically, and often initiates movements tending towards those purposes. But the organization, as such, is particularly committed to the shorter hours movement, or what is more popularly known as the Eight-Hour movement, the leaders all agreeing that the movement which gives the workers more leisure brings more intelligence and consequently more independence, more sterling qualities of character and truer progress. The Federation has accomplished wonders in this movement for a shorter work-day, and millions of workers now enjoy countless golden hours of rest, leisure, and opportunity as the result of the concentrated efforts of 1886 and 1890."

. . .

Review of Reviews 10 (July 1894): 27-29.

1. William Thomas Stead was a London clergyman and reformer who helped launch the Chicago Civic Federation.

2. In response to wage reductions and unequal pay and working conditions among the coal regions, the fifth annual convention of the United Mine Workers of America (UMWA), meeting in Columbus, Ohio, Apr. 10-12, 1894, called for a general strike, to commence Apr. 21 in all the coal regions represented by the union. The miners and coal operators attempted to settle the strike at a joint conference held in Cleveland, May 14-17, but the refusal of some operators to attend prevented a settlement. Threatened with the prospect that strikebreakers would be hired, and hoping to prevent further wage reductions, the union signed an accord on June 18 that accepted the traditional variation in district wage scales. Since each district had to ratify the agreement separately, the strike continued in some areas into September. In some districts the union was able to win the restoration of previous wage scales and such other concessions as union recognition or the election of check weighmen.

3. Three wage cuts over an eight-month period combined with company firings of union workers caused members of the American Railway Union (ARU) to strike James J. Hill's Great Northern Railroad on Apr. 13, 1894, demanding a restoration of wages to the level in effect on Aug. 1, 1893. The brotherhoods of firemen and locomotive engineers had already signed agreements with Hill accepting wage cuts, and resolved to abide by them; along with the railway conductors' organization, they threatened to expel any of their members involved in the strike. Despite the opposition of the brotherhoods and a federal court injunction against the strike in Minnesota and North Dakota, the strikers not only held firm but also gathered support from local farmers and small businessmen. On May 1 an arbitration panel headed by prominent St. Paul, Minn., businessman Charles Pillsbury awarded the ARU most of its wage demands, and Hill subsequently agreed to reemploy strikers without discrimination. The strike's success caused a rapid growth in ARU membership.

4. See *United Mine Workers' Journal*, June 14, 1894.

5. The Income Tax Act of Aug. 27, 1894, which was attached to the Wilson-Gorman tariff (U.S. *Statutes at Large*, 28: 509-70), instituted a 2 percent tax on all corporate and individual net incomes of $4,000 and above, exempting those whose incomes fell below this level.

To Charles Drummond

Aug. 1, [1894]

Mr. C. L. Drummond,
2nd. Vice-President A.F. of L.
358 E. Washington St. Fort Wayne, Ind.
Dear Sir and Friend: —

I am in receipt of your favor of the 30th. and although only having arrived in the city this morning from a Western trip in the interest of our movement and finding an accumulated mail and business, I hasten to reply.

You say that you have been unmercifully criticized and antagonized since your return home on account of the action taken by the Chicago conference and that an effort is being made to strike you down in the labor movement.

In connection therewith let me say that of course I am coming in for my share of abuse and criticism and so are the other participants in the conference, but I am convinced that our action was not only right and wise but decidedly in the interests of our fellow workmen and that those who now are indignant or pretend to be indignant at our action will very shortly be compelled to admit their error. Hot heads may have their sway for a while, but honesty of purpose and practical action will undoubtedly commend itself to a calmer and cooler judgment of sincere labor men.

It would indeed be unfortunate should you be made to suffer even temporarily for having performed a duty honestly and courageously in the interest of the labor movement and the working people generally, but even should ignorance or prejudice dominate now, you will have the proud satisfaction to know that these men will soon acknowledge their error and with it you will rise higher in their estimation and confidence.

One thing you should keep in mind and that is that error and wrong judgment should not be permitted to go on without a persistent and vigorous protest on your part. I commend the matter published in the Aug. issue of the American Federationist[1] to your consideration. It contains the statements of our position in this controversy, and if you think it will be advantageous I shall be pleased to send you a few copies and also a number of addresses of men in whose hands the placing of the magazines you think would do good. I think you will find not only a justification of our action in the columns of the magazine, but it will convince reasonable men that we pursued the only course open to us. Bear in mind, dear comrade, that every man who ever takes an advanced and courageous stand on what he believes to be right has always had to encounter the antagonism and prejudice of the hour.

With kindest wishes, I am,

Very Truly Yours   Saml Gompers.
President. A.F. of L.

TLpS, reel 8, vol. 11, p. 200, SG Letterbooks, DLC.

1. The August *American Federationist* printed the minutes of the Briggs House conference of July 12-13, 1894, its July 12 telegram to President Cleveland, and the statement it released on July 13. The issue also contained pieces by SG on George Pullman and the Pullman strike and a reprinting of his article from the August *North American Review* (see above, July 8, 1894).

To Gideon Tucker[1]

Aug. 2, [1894]

Hon. Gideon J. Tucker,
Constitutional Convention, Albany, N.Y.
Dear Sir and Friend: —

I have your favor of the 27th. the contents of which are carefully noted.

I shall be pleased to have an article from your pen for the Sept. issue of the American Federationist, an account of the fight now being made in the Constitutional Convention in the interest of reforming that instrument, and shall be obliged to you if you can confine it to between 800 and 1000 words and to let me have it on or before the 12th. inst.

I enclose to you herein four propositions to amend the Constitution which I think should certainly receive the attention of the convention.[2] At any rate, you may submit them and do what you can to advance them in the cause of justice and the humane principles involved.

With kindest wishes, I am,

Very Truly Yours   Saml Gompers.
President.   American Federation of Labor
[Enclosures]

IN CONVENTION

Proposition to amend Article IX of the Constitution.

Section 2: Several free industrial Colleges shall be established and maintained at the expense of this State in which minors over the age of thirteen years may enter and shall be taught a broad, liberal and practical course of study of agriculture, the manual, industrial and mechanical arts, and in the use of tools in wood and metals employed therein; and the legislature shall pass liberal laws for the purpose of carrying out the provisions of this section.

IN CONVENTION.

Proposition to amend Article IX of the Constitution.

Section 3: No minor shall be employed more than eight hours in one day; and the Legislature shall pass stringent laws for the protection of minors from injuries while so employed.

IN CONVENTION.

Proposition to amend Article IX of the Constitution.

Section 4: The Labor and employment of children under fourteen years of age is prohibited, and the Legislature shall pass stringent laws for the purpose of carrying out the provisions of this section.

IN CONVENTION.

Proposition to amend article IX of the Constitution.

Section V: The labor and employment of minors in tenement houses or houses used for dwelling purposes, is prohibited, and the Legislature shall pass stringent laws for the purpose of carrying out the provisions of this section.

TLpS and TDp, reel 8, vol. 11, pp. 208-10, SG Letterbooks, DLC.

1. Gideon J. Tucker (1826-99), a lawyer and the founder of the *New York Daily News*, served as a Democrat in the New York assembly in 1866. In 1894 he represented the New York tenth senatorial district at the state's constitutional convention, and he subsequently published an article in the *American Federationist* detailing his experiences at the convention and describing the disposition of the amendments he had proposed there (1 [Sept. 1894]: 141-42).

2. Because the Aug. 1, 1894, deadline for receiving proposed amendments had already passed, SG's suggestions were not considered by the constitutional convention.

To George Van Gülpen

Aug. 9, [1894]

Mr. G. W. Van Guelpen,
Sec. L.U. 228 C.M.I.U. of A.
368 Jessie St. San Francisco, Ca.
Dear Sir and Brother:—

Your favor of the 21st. together with enclosure came duly to hand.

In the report of the committee, which you forward, is contained the proposition that action be taken by the American Federation of Labor for the purpose of preventing the funding of the debts of the Union Pacific and Central Pacific Railroads, so that the Government of the United States may foreclose, take possession of and thus own and control these two systems of railroads.[1]

I have submitted both your letter and proposition to the Executive Council of the A.F. of L. and they direct me to make further inquiry into the matter. The proposition and the plan were favorably considered, but certain details in connection with it are necessary, and it will be necessary to make the campaign practical in order to accomplish the desired result.

It is evident that the committee of your Union has given this subject a good deal of thought resultant from their research which at this moment is not at hand here.

I would therefore ask you to write me a few details in reference to the following matters. The time of the organization of each Company; the date of the passage of the law authorizing an appropriation of money in the building of the roads; the amounts in each case appropriated and advanced; the time when the same shall become due and paid, and also the present claim for funding or refunding the debts, and any further information you may be in possession of or may learn to aid in the prosecution of the work in hand.

Assuring you of our desire to do all that we possibly can to push the entering wedge for the Government ownership and control of the railroads of the country, and with kindest wishes, and hoping to hear from you at your earliest convenience, I am,

Fraternally Yours   Saml Gompers.
President. American Federation of Labor.

TLpS, reel 8, vol. 11, p. 237, SG Letterbooks, DLC.

1. The federal government provided funding for much of the cost of building the Union Pacific and Central Pacific railroads after the Civil War. In July 1894 the Committee on Pacific Railroads of the U.S. House of Representatives reported favorably on H.R. 7798 (53d Cong., 2d sess.) to refinance the unpaid debts of the two railroads. A minority report favored foreclosing on the debts, and one member of the minority also recommended that the government assume ownership if the railroads failed to pay what they owed. Congress took no action on these or other proposals. In 1898 a syndicate of bankers led by E. H. Harriman arranged a reorganization of the Union Pacific that resulted in the payment of most of its government loans.

To Henry Demarest Lloyd

Aug. 9, [1894]

Mr. Henry D. Lloyd,
Little Compton, R.I.
Dear Sir and Friend:—

Your favor of the 30th.[1] came duly to hand, and inasmuch as the Executive Council was then about to hold a meeting in the course of a few days I preferred to submit the subject matter upon which you write to the consideration of my colleagues before replying.

It is our consensus of opinion that a conference of the nature you mention and with some of the men you suggest would certainly be working in the right direction and no doubt be productive of great good to the cause. I presume you are aware however, that some such call has already gone forth from an organization of men in Chicago.[2] I think among the number is the Civic Federation.[3]

Each of the members of the Council has some indefinite knowledge as to the holding of such a conference and gather the idea that it is to be held some time during Sept. If such a movement is on foot it would certainly be unwise to call any other conference which instead of concentrating our efforts would only diffuse them and show to the enemy the divisions which exist, while, at the same time our friends and fellow workers would become despondent.

The newspaper despatches which I saw in reference to the holding of a conference mentioned that I was to be one of those invited. When in Chicago I had a conversation with Mr. Carroll of the Eight Hour Herald and it was then that the matter of holding a conference was gone over. I assured him of my hearty co-operation, and I have already seen in the public press that a call is to be issued soon.

If it is not too inconvenient for you I wish you would make some inquiries in reference to it as to whether it has materialized or will be abandoned. After definite information upon the subject I could be more ready to act upon your suggestion.

Your telegram reached me while I was in Chicago, but I was so busily engrossed in the work in hand that I confess I could give it scarcely any thought. The times are certainly propitious for aggressive action, the public mind is in a receptive mood and we should do all we possibly can to take advantage of the situation to score a good point for labor.

Assuring you of my appreciation of your kind efforts to aid in the struggle and with kind wishes, I am,

Very Truly Yours   Saml Gompers.
President. American Federation of Labor.

TLpS, reel 8, vol. 11, p. 242, SG Letterbooks, DLC.

1. Files of the Office of the President, reel 59, *AFL Records.*
2. At the conclusion of the Pullman strike, the Chicago Civic Federation's (CCF) Industrial Department called a Congress on Industrial Conciliation and Arbitration, to be held in Chicago, Nov. 13-14, 1894. Participants included labor and business leaders, congressmen, public officials, reformers, and academics. SG, P. J. McGuire, L. S. Coffin of the Brotherhood of Railway Trainmen, and M. M. Garland of the National Amalgamated Association of Iron and Steel Workers represented labor. The participants spoke on various legal, philosophical, and practical aspects of industrial conciliation and arbitration, and the CCF published the speeches and helped secure passage of an Illinois arbitration law in 1895 based on proposals discussed at the congress. For SG's speech, see "An Address before the Congress on Industrial Conciliation and Arbitration, Chicago," Nov. 14, 1894, below.
3. The CCF was organized after a Nov. 12, 1893, mass meeting in Chicago that was called to protest widespread destitution, corruption in city government, lack of city services, and concern over a wide array of urban reform issues. The meeting created a committee on organization representing labor, business, professional, religious, educational, and civic organizations, and its work led to the incorporation of the CCF on Feb. 3, 1894. Devoted to working for reform in various areas of urban life, it developed a system of ward councils coordinated by a central council, and a series of specialized departments in the areas of relief, political and municipal reform, education, philanthropy, moral reform, and the resolution of industrial disputes.

To the Editor of the *New York World*

[August 14, 1894]

To the Editor of The World:

I am pleased to learn that the Tariff bill[1] will be passed by Congress, not because I look to any very great beneficial results, but because it will remove the question out of the arena of the present discussion, as well as convince all that they have followed a chimera.

Just about a year ago Congress was called together in extraordinary session to repeal the purchasing clause of the Sherman act upon the plea that it was necessary to save the country and to revive industry, but industry did not revive and we were simply placed so much surer in the hands of the money power both here and abroad.

The Tariff bill was then taken up with the avowed purpose of again giving an impetus to industry, and I am firmly convinced that I am not venturing my reputation as a prophet when I say that the authors and promoters of the Tariff bill, as well as those who have believed in its remedial features for our economic depression, will be sadly disappointed.

The causes of our industrial crises and stagnation lie deeper in our body politic than the repeal of silver-purchasing acts or enacting tariff bills.

Samuel Gompers
President American Federation of Labor.

New York World, Aug. 14, 1894.

1. The Wilson-Gorman tariff (U.S. *Statutes at Large,* 28: 509-70) passed Congress on Aug. 15, 1894, and became law without the signature of the president. It established a generally lower schedule of duties than had prevailed since the McKinley tariff of 1890.

To Peter Grosscup

Aug. 14, [1894]

Hon. P. J. Grosscup,
Judge of the United States Court,
Chicago, Ill.
Dear Sir:—

I have the honor to acknowledge the receipt of your favor of the 31st. inst.[1] the contents of which I have carefully noted. Possibly I should have written you earlier, but more important matters demanded my immediate consideration. I hope however, that you have suffered no inconvenience or pain of injustice done you by reason of this delay.

You say that I have misquoted you in my article in the "North American Review,["][2] in attributing to you the following words in your Decoration Day Address at Galesburg. "The Growth of Labor Organizations must be restrained by Law." Upon closer examination you will find that I did not use the word "restrained" but "checked." However, this makes little material difference, except to show that unintentionally one man may misquote another.

The words I quoted I saw in several newspaper accounts of your address, and I am exceedingly pleased that you favor me with a printed copy of it, which I have read with much interest. In perusing that address I find that you said (Page 12) "Restore to each individual, by *the enforcement of Law,* not simply his right, but if possible, a returning sense of duty to control his own personality and property. *Let us set a limit to the field of organization.*"

Of course this citation from the printed address you send me does not contain the words I attributed to you, but you say in your letter that I will not find either that you used the words or that you "expressed that sentiment." To my untutored mind there may not be that grave difference which your legal learning can discern in limiting by law the field of organization, and checking its growth by law.

I doubt that the thinking world will hold me chargeable of having done you a grave injustice, and I feel convinced after a perusal of your address that both in fact and in spirit you gave utterance to the sentiment I attribute to you, and which you either fail to remember or regret.

You say that as you stated in your charge to the Grand Jury you believe in labor organizations within such lawful and reasonable limits as will make them a service to the laboring man and not a menace to the lawful institutions of the country.

I have had the pleasure of reading your charge to the Grand Jury and have only partially been able to discover how far you believe in labor organizations. You would certainly have no objection officially or personally to workingmen organizing, and in their meetings discuss perhaps "the origin of man," benignly smiling upon each other and declaring that all existing things are right, going to their wretched homes to find some freedom in sleep from gnawing hunger. You would have them extol the virtues of monopolists and wreckers of the people's welfare. You would not have them consider seriously the fact that more than two million of their fellows are unemployed, and though willing and able cannot find the opportunity to work in order that they may sustain themselves, their wives and their children. You would not have them consider seriously the fact that Pullman who has grown so rich from the toil of his workmen that he can riot in luxury, while he heartlessly turns these very workmen out of their tenements into the streets and left to the tender mercies of corporate greed. Nor would you have them ponder upon the hundreds of other pullmans of different names.

You know or ought to know that the introduction of machinery is turning into idleness thousands faster than new industries are founded, and yet machinery certainly should not be either destroyed or hampered in its full development. The laborer is a man, he is made warm by the same sun and made cold—yes colder—by the same winter as you are. He has a heart and brain, and feels and knows the human and paternal instinct for those depending upon him keenly as do you.

What shall the workers do? Sit idly by and see the vast resources of nature and the human mind be utilized and monopolized for the benefit of the comparatively few? No. The laborers must learn to think and act, and soon too, that only by the power of organization and common concert of action can either their manhood be maintained, their rights to life (work to sustain it) be recognized and liberty and rights secured.

Since you say that you favor labor organization within certain limits, will you kindly give to thousands of your anxious fellow citizens what you believe the workers could and should do in their organizations to solve this great problem? Not what they should not do. You have told us that.

I am not one of those who regards the entire past as a failure. I recognize the progress made and the improved conditions of which nearly the entire civilized world are the benficiaries. I ask you to explain however, that if the wealth of the whole world is as you say "preeminently and beneficially the nation's wealth" how is it that thousands of able bodied, willing earnest men and women are suffering the pangs of hunger? We may boast of our wealth and civilization, but to the hungry man, woman and child our progress is a hollow mockery, our civilization a sham, and our "national wealth" a chimera.

You recognize that the industrial forces set in motion by steam and electricity have materially changed the structure of our civilization. You also admit that a system has grown up where the accumulations of the individual have passed from his control into that of representatives, combinations and trusts, and that the tendency in this direction is on the increase. How then can you consistently criticize the workingmen for recognizing that as individuals they can have no influence in deciding what the wages, hours of toil and conditions of employment shall be?

You evidently have observed the growth of corporate wealth and influence. You recognize that wealth in order to become more highly productive is concentrated into fewer hands and controlled by representatives and directors, and yet you sing the old siren song that the working man should depend entirely upon his own "individual effort."

The school of *laissez faire* of which you seem to be a pronounced advocate has produced great men in advocating the theory of each for himself and his Satanic Majesty taking the hindmost, but the most pronounced advocates of your school of thought in economics, have, when practically put to the test been compelled to admit that combination and organization of the toiling masses are essential both to prevent the deterioration and to secure an improvement in the condition of the wage-earners.

If, as you say, the success of commercial society depends upon the full play of competition, why do not you and your confreres turn your attention and direct the shafts of your attacks against the trusts and corporations, business wreckers and manipulators in the food products—the necessities of the people. Why garland your thoughts in beautiful phrases when speaking of these modern vampires, and steep your pen in gall when writing of the laborers' efforts to secure some of the advantages accruing from the concentrated thought and genius of the ages?

You charge that before a boy can learn a trade he must receive a permit from the Union and assume obligations which the Union imposes. I am sure you have read the current history of industry but superficially or you would certainly have discovered that with the introduction of modern methods of production the apprenticeship system has almost been entirely eliminated. The Professors, the learned men concerned in the welfare of our people, insist upon the maintenance of a technical knowledge of crafts and trades. They are endeavoring to substitute manual training schools in order that the youth of our country may be supplied with a knowledge of the trades and crafts of which modern methods of production have deprived them.

For the sake of your argument let me admit that what you say in connection with this matter is true. I ask you whether it is not true that before a boy can properly learn your trade, is it not necessary for him to enter a term of apprenticeship? Of course, you have a more euphonious name for it, student life I believe. Would Judges permit any one to practice law in their Courts where justice is dispensed (with) unless he could produce his working card? Pardon, I mean his diploma.

One becomes enraptured in reading the beauty of your description of modern progress. Could you have had in mind the miners of Spring Valley, or Pennsylvania, or the clothing workers of the sweat-shops of New York or Chicago, when you grandiloquently declare, "Who is not rich today when compared with his ancestors of a century ago. The steamboat and the railroad bring to his breakfast table the coffees of Java and Brazil, the fruits from Florida and California and the steaks from the plains. The loom arrays him in garments, and the factories furnish him with a dwelling that the richest contemporaries of his grandfather would have envied. With health and industry he is a prince."

Probably you have not read within the past year of babes dying of starvation at their mothers' breasts. More than likely the thousands of men lying upon the bare stones night after night in the City Hall of Chicago last winter escaped your notice. You may not have heard of the cry for bread that was sounded through this land of plenty by thousands of honest men and women. But should these and many other painful incidents have passed you by unnoticed, I am fearful that you may learn of them with keener thoughts with the coming sleets and blasts of winter.

You say that "labor cannot afford to attack capital." Let me remind you that labor has no quarrel with capital, as such. It is merely the possessors of capital, who refuse to accord to labor the recognition, the right, the justice which is the laborer's due, whom we contend with.

See what is implied by your contemptuous reference to the laborer when you ask "Will the conqueror destroy his trophy?" Whoever heard of a conqueror marching unitedly with his *trophy* as you would have them? But if by your comparison you mean that the conqueror is the corporation, the trust, the capitalist class, and ask them whether they would destroy their *trophy*, I would have you ask the widows and orphans of the thousands of men killed annually through the avarice of railroad corporations refusing to avail themselves of modern appliances in coupling and other improvements on their railroads.

Enquire from the thousands of women and children whose husbands or fathers were suffocated or crushed in the mines through the rapacious greed of stock holders clamoring for more dividends. Investigate the sweating dens of the large cities, go to the mills, factories, through the country. Visit the modern tenement houses or hovels in which thousands of workers are compelled to eke out an existence. Ask these whether the conqueror (Monopoly) cares whether his trophy (the laborers) is destroyed or preserved. Ascertain from employers whether the laborer is not regarded the same as a machine, thrown out as soon as all the work possible has been squeezed out of him.

Are you aware that all the legislation ever secured for the ventilation or safety of mines, factory and workshop is the result of the efforts of organized labor? Do you know that the trade unions were the shield for the seven-year-old children from being the conqueror's trophy until they become somewhat older? And that the reformatory laws now on the Statute Books protecting or defending the trophies of both sexes young and old from the fond care of the conquerors were wrested from congresses, legislatures and parliaments despite the Pullmans, the Jeffries,[3] the Ricks, the Tafts, the Williams,[4] the Woods,[5] or the Grosscups.

By what right, Sir, do you assume that the labor organizations do not conduct their affairs within lawful limits, or that they are a menace to the lawful institutions of the country? Is it because some thoughtless or over-zealous member, at a time of great excitement and smarting under a wrong, may violate a law or commit an improper act? Would you apply the same rule to the churches, the other moral agencies and organizations that you do to the organizations of labor? If you did, the greatest moral force in life to-day — the trade unions — would certainly stand out the clearest, brightest and purest. Because the class (for which you and a number of your colleagues on the bench seem to be the special pleaders) have a monopoly in their lines of trade, I submit that that is no good reason for their claim to have a monopoly on true patriotism or respect for the lawful institutions of the country.

But, speaking of law reminds me of the higher law of the land. The constitution prescribes that all rights not specifically granted to the general government are reserved to the states. There is another provision prohibiting the President from sending the armed forces into any state except for the purpose of maintaining "a republican form of government" and then only upon the requisition of the legislature of the state or of the governor, when the legislature is not in session. Yet, when during the recent railroad strike the President sent the troops into Illinois it was not in compliance with the request of the legislature of that state nor of the governor, but in spite of his protest. Yes, when the governor remonstrated he was practically told by the President to stop arguing the law upon the question. Pardon the simplicity of my inquiry, but does not the law require that its limits shall be observed by a President, a Judge equally, as by a labor organization?

If I remember aright you based the injunctions recently issued by you upon the provisions of the Interstate Commerce Law, a law enacted by Congress upon the demand of the farmers and shippers of our country, to protect them against the unjust exactions and outrageous discriminations imposed by the railroads. Where in that law can you find one word to justify your course applying to workingmen organized and engaged in a strike?

Read the discussions in Congress when that law was under consideration. You will not find a remote reference to the application of the law as you construe it. In fact, I am informed upon excellent authority that when the law was before the Senate in the form of a Bill, Senator Morgan[6] of Ala. proposed an amendment which if adopted would have had the effect of empowering judges to issue a mandamus of the nature you have, in the recent railroad strike, but it was not adopted! It was defeated. How then in the face of this you can issue your omnibus restraining order passes the comprehension of ordinary men.

In his last report to Congress the Post Master General recommended the passage of a law by Congress declaring that any train in which there should be but one pouch of mail matter should be considered a "mail train," thus recognizing that there was no law by which other than a regular "mail train" came under the operation of the postal laws. Hence it is not a grave stretch of the imagination to regard this latest court-made law as an invention to break the strike.

I am not versed in the law, but somewhere I read that Blackstone[7] says that a law which is not based on justice is not law; and presumably judges who distort law so that injustice is done are not the ablest or purest devotees of the "blind goddess." I do not quote this for the purpose of converting your mind to some degree of impartiality for labor but merely to show you what a sycophantic knave Blackstone was.

Year by year man's liberties are trampled under foot at the bidding of corporations and trusts, rights are invaded and law perverted. In all ages whenever a tyrant has shown himself he has always found some willing judge to clothe that tyranny in the robes of legality, and modern capitalism has proven no exception to the rule.

You may not know that the labor movement as represented by the trade unions stand for right, for justice, for liberty. You may not imagine that the issuance of an injunction depriving men of a legal as well as a natural right to protect themselves, their wives and little ones must fail of its purpose. Repression or oppression never yet succeeded in crushing the truth or redressing a wrong.

In conclusion let me assure you that labor will organize and more compactly than ever and upon practical lines, and despite relentless antagonism achieve for humanity a nobler manhood, a more beautiful womanhood and a happier childhood.

Very Respectfully Yours. Saml Gompers.
President. American Federation of Labor.

TLpS, reel 8, vol. 11, pp. 266-73, SG Letterbooks, DLC.

1. Printed in *American Federationist* 1 (Sept. 1894): 149.

2. See "An Article by Samuel Gompers in the *North American Review,*" July 8, 1894, above.

3. Probably James Graham Jenkins (1834-1921), a judge of the Seventh U.S. Circuit Court (1893-1905). Jenkins gained national attention in April 1894 when he enjoined Northern Pacific Railroad workers from striking against proposed wage reductions. Jenkins wrote: "A strike is essentially a conspiracy to extort by violence . . . , destructive to property, destructive to individual rights, injurious to the conspirators themselves and subversive of republican institutions. . . . It must ever remain the duty of the courts, in the protection of society, and in the execution of the laws of the land, to condemn, prevent, and punish all such unlawful conspiracies and combinations" (quoted in Almont Lindsey, *The Pullman Strike* [1942; reprint ed., Chicago, 1964], p. 157).

4. Henry W. Williams (1830-1899) was an associate justice of the Supreme Court of Pennsylvania for the Western District from 1887 until his death. He ruled adversely in an 1891 suit brought by Ephrata, Pa., CMIU 126 against a manufacturer for using a counterfeit label.

5. William Allen Woods (1837-1901) was a judge of the Seventh U.S. Circuit Court from 1892 until his death. He granted an injunction during the Pullman strike against interference with trains carrying the U.S. mails. He also ordered Eugene Debs's imprisonment for violation of this injunction.

6. John Tyler Morgan (1824-1907), a lawyer and Democrat, served as U.S. senator from Alabama from 1877 to 1907.

7. Sir William Blackstone.

From Henry Demarest Lloyd

Little Compton, R.I. August 14, 1894.

Dear Mr. Gompers:

I have your letter.[1] I will say to you, privately, that while I have no knowledge of the proposed convention about which you enquire, I still am confidant that if it is under the auspices of the Civic Federation, it will in no way fulfil the purposes for which a convention of the elements you could assemble would be useful. What is needed in my view is a delegate assembly of all the reform elements to give immediate direction and concentration to the acts of the people in the coming election. It should be for the whole country what the Springfield Convention[2] was for Illinois. It should be held not later than the last week of September. The time is not so short but that with the telegraph all the details can be arranged. Such a convention could make terms for the workingmen with the Peoples' Party and the Socialist Labor Party and the Single Taxers that would be equal to the fruits of ten years of agitation. If such a convention gave the word as I think it would and as I think it ought to do—*for this moment*—that all the voters of discontent should unite on the candidates of the Peoples' Party, we would revolutionise the politics of this country. The time has come for the leaders to lead. No man in history has had a greater opportunity for usefulness and glory than now begs you to embrace it. The people are scattered, distracted, leaderless, waiting for just such guidance. And the opportunity will not recur. If not taken now the reins will pass to other hands or what is more likely, no reins will be able to control the people.

It is a great crisis, meet it greatly!

Fraternally yours,   H. D. Lloyd.

TLcSr, Henry D. Lloyd Papers, WHi.

1. "To Henry Demarest Lloyd," Aug. 9, 1894, above.
2. The Illinois State Federation of Labor sponsored a convention of labor and reform organizations in Springfield, Ill., July 3-5, 1894. Lloyd proposed a compromise at the convention which overcame an impasse between socialists and populists by resolving that, pending a national convention on independent political action, the organizations represented there should support People's party candidates pledged to collective ownership of the means of production and distribution. It provided the basis for the populist-labor electoral alliance in Illinois.

To Eugene Debs

Aug. 16, [1894]

Mr. Eugene V. Debs,
Terre Haute, Ind.
Dear Sir and Friend:—

You will remember the very interesting conference had between you, Mr. P. J. Mc-Guire and myself at the Revere House Chicago Ill. on Sunday afternoon July 15th. It has left a deep impression upon my mind. I am sure that the many important topics we discussed ought and will no doubt bring forth good fruit.

You remember our mentioning the fact that at the meeting of the Executive Council of the A.F. of L. an appropriation of $500.00 had been made to be contributed towards your legal defense before the courts,[1] and that an appeal would be made for contributions towards a legal defense fund for you. In compliance therewith I enclose to you herein a check for $670.10 which in the name of the A.F. of L. and the other donors I ask you to accept with our best wishes.

In presenting this to you we desire to convey more eloquently than I can find words to express our unqualified disapproval of the attempts on the part of governmental officials and the courts in throwing the weight of their influence in favor of corporate wealth and against the most necessary, useful and liberty loving people of the country—the wage workers. We offer it to you as a protest against the exercise of class justice, and as a further protest against the violation of rights guaranteed by the Constitution and the Declaration of Independence.

It would be superfluous to say to you in this letter that the end of the struggles of the masses is not yet, that the workers must thoroughly organize upon practical lines to maintain their manhood, to prevent their liberty from being filched from them, to achieve that success for which all previous contests were but preparatory to the attainment of that justice looked forward to by all lovers of mankind.

I kindly ask you to forward two separate receipts to Secretary Chris. Evans, one for the $500.00 donated by the American Federation of Labor, and another for the balance $170.10 at your earliest convenience.

Sincerely hoping that you may be successful in confounding the enemies of labor who are trying to secure your incarceration, and with kindest wishes, I am,

> Very Truly Yours   Saml Gompers.
> President. American Federation of Labor.

TLpS, reel 8, vol. 11, p. 263, SG Letterbooks, DLC.

1. Debs and the officers of the American Railway Union were charged with contempt of court for violating the injunction issued on July 2, 1894, against interference by strikers with trains carrying the U.S. mails. The case was tried before Judge William A. Woods in the Seventh U.S. Circuit Court for the District of Chicago in November, and the defendants were found guilty; Debs was sentenced to a six-month jail term and the others to three-month terms. Their conviction was upheld by the U.S. Supreme Court in 1895.

Excerpts from Samuel Gompers' Testimony before the U.S. Strike Commission[1]

August 25, 1894

Samuel Gompers, after being first duly affirmed, testified as follows:

. . .

(Commissioner Wright). There was a conference held in this city at the Briggs House in July last relative to the strike ordered by the American Railway Union and the boycott accompanying it. If you have no objections the commission would like to know the reason for your action as a member of that conference and the general reasons which actuated or induced that action on your part.—Ans. No, I have no objections.

(Commissioner Wright). You can state whatever you wish to in your own way.—Ans. Of course I was made aware of the existence of the strike of the American Railway Union and its boycott of the Pullman cars—in various ways I was made aware of this. Some of our organizations throughout the country had been in telegraphic communication with me and desirous of ascertaining the attitude of the American Federation of Labor toward this strike and boycott.

On Sunday afternoon and evening, July 8, a conference was held in this city[2] in which a very large number of the unions affiliated with the American Federation of Labor participated. Among the number were several of the officers of national or international unions which were affiliated with the American Federation of Labor. On Monday morning I received a telegram signed by the chairman and secretary of that conference advising me of the action thereof and conveying a resolution passed by it insisting that it became my duty to be in Chicago at the earliest possible moment; that the interests of the organization, as well as of labor generally, demanded that I should heed the request contained in the resolution. I consulted with a few of the members of the executive council of the American Federation of Labor in reference to the matter, and we concluded that I should send telegrams first to the other members of the executive council of the American Federation of Labor to meet me in Chicago at the earliest possible moment, which was the morning of July 12, and, at the same time I sent telegrams to fifteen or twenty of the executive officers of national and international unions to meet in the conference with the executive council of the federation to view the situation and to decide as to the best course to pursue under the circumstances. That conference was held in the Briggs House July 12. . . .

. . .

In the interim between the conference held on the evening of July 8 and the meeting of our executive council and conference, a number of local unions in the city of Chicago had gone out on a strike in sympathy with the American Railway Union strike and boycott. From St. Louis and various places throughout Missouri, Ohio, and Colorado, I was in receipt of telegrams that they had resolved to await the word that the American Federation of Labor conference would give as to determining their action. Upon the assembling of the conference one of the local unions of Chicago appointed a delegation or committee to present the position that they were then placed in and to urge upon the conference to take such action as would either order a general strike or to recommend one.[3] The committee was heard and a number of questions were put to the committee, each tending to throw some light upon the situation. A general discussion took place as to what should or could be done and what the attitude of the trades unions represented by the American Federation of Labor should be. And since the General Government had been brought in to the side of the railroads to throw its influence upon the side of those who had the money power, we determined that it became the duty of the President of the United States to use some of his influence for an amicable adjustment of the differences existing in this great struggle.

We thought that if the present prime minister[4] of England had been delegated by the then prime minister, Mr. Gladstone,[5] to use the influence and power of the Government of Great Britain to end the great coal strike of that country, it would not be a loss of dignity for the President of the United States to do something toward relieving the unhappy situation existing in this country at that time. For that reason it was decided to send a dispatch to the President, of which the following is a copy. . . .[6]

. . .

. . . To that telegram the President did not deign to send an answer or acknowledgment.

We resolved to invite Mr. Eugene V. Debs, president of the American Railway Union, to come before our conference at a time mutually agreeable and make a statement of the situation of the strike, and also to ask him, or to have him tell us what, in his judgment, would be the most advisable course for us to pursue, or rather how we could be of any assistance to him and to the strike. It was agreed that 8 o'clock in the evening would be satisfactory to both parties. The intervening time was spent in a general discussion as to the powers of the conference, the various participants to the conference, and what could be done in order to help bring this strike to a settlement, if it could be brought to a settlement, or in how far and in what way we could aid the strike or boycott if we could aid it at all.

About 5 o'clock the conference took an adjournment, and at 8 o'clock reassembled. At that time Mr. Debs was escorted into the room and made an address, calm, dispassionate, stating, as he then saw, the situation, giving a history as to the causes which led up to the Pullman strike or the strike of the Pullman employees, and the strike of the American Railway Union in sympathy with the Pullman strikers. A number of questions were asked Mr. Debs, and answers were given to them by him. He then asked that the chairman, your humble servant, might present the document[7] to the Railroad Managers' Association[8] — the one which was subsequently published and which I believe is now in evidence here. After the discussion ensuing upon both the proposition and the condition of the strike it then got along to near 12 o'clock, and Mr. Debs asked to be excused, since it was necessary for him to get home, I believe, to meet some other men and get some rest in order to perform the duties that were assigned to him by the organization. It was the understanding that I would telephone to Mr. Debs as to the action of the conference, and that I would do so before retiring. When I say "the action of the conference," I mean that in so far as authorizing its chairman to present the document to the managers' association.

The conference continued the discussion of the statement of Mr. Debs and the proposition of the American Railway Union until about half past 1 o'clock in the morning of the 13th and then adjourned. I went to the telephone at the Briggs House and called up the Revere House, at which place Mr. Debs was stopping, and I was told by the clerk that Mr. Debs had retired and could not be disturbed, and hence I could not communicate with him as to the action of the conference and council, which was to this effect: That the president (Mr. Gompers) or any other one or more members of the conference would accompany Mr. Debs and any other number of citizens that Mr. Debs might choose, to present the document to the managers' association. The adjournment at 1.30 o'clock was had until 9.30 of the same morning.

In view of the statements made and in view of the proposition submitted by Mr. Debs, the executive council and the members participating in the conference believed it would be most unwise, as well as inexpedient, as well as detrimental to the interests of labor, to recommend a general strike in sympathy with the American Railway Union or the Pullman strikers.

It must be borne in mind that the executive council had not the power to order a strike of any one man or woman in the entire country, and any attempt to order a strike would have been a usurpation of power for which we would have been compelled to answer to our own constituents. Then again, the conference regarded the proposition made by the American Railway Union as a declaration that this strike had been lost, and that a recommendation on the part of the conference to the workingmen — to the organized labor of America — to strike was then out of the question, since the men who were engaged in the strike were asking to be permitted to return to work—of course, in a body, and that the question of the Pullman strike or the Pullman boycott was to be abandoned entirely. The conference having these facts in view prepared a statement. . . .[9]

. . .

. . . With the adoption of that report, an expression of good will and a resolution recommending to the executive council proper the appropriation of $1,000 toward a defense fund for Mr. Debs, the conference adjourned.

The executive council meeting proper was taken up and the positions reiterated simply by formal resolution, and a sum of money ($500) appropriated from the funds for the legal defense of Mr. Debs, and the authorizing of the issuance of an appeal to organized labor throughout the country to contribute toward that fund.[10]

I think I have now given you fairly and truly the business of the conference. There may be some details that I have omitted which possibly by questioning could be elicited.

(Commissioner Wright). Under what circumstances could the American Federation of Labor have a general strike?—Ans. It would be very difficult indeed except possibly by—such as was contemplated in its early days, in 1886. At a convention of the American Federation of Labor in 1884,[11] it was resolved that a movement should be inaugurated on May 1, 1886, for the establishment of the eight-hour workday in all trades and industries throughout the country.

(Commissioner Wright). That was the Baltimore convention?[12]— Ans. No; it was the Washington convention, and thereafterwards reiterated in 1885 in Chicago;[13] and at that time the organizations had previously resolved upon it, both in their local and national meetings and conventions, and at such time as the American Federation of Labor might designate. . . .

(Commissioner Wright). That would be the point, generally, on which the American Federation of Labor could act—the hours of labor?—Ans. Not necessarily, but on anything that would be a matter of discussion and matter of vote by the members of their various local organizations, and which would have to find expression at the conventions of the national or international unions of those respective trades, and then again in the conventions of the American Federation of Labor.

I should say that in 1888, at the St. Louis convention,[14] it was again decided to set a date when the unfinished portion of the establishment of the eight-hour workday should be attempted to be enforced, or, in other words, in those trades in which it was not achieved. At the subsequent convention it was decided that a general strike for the enforcement of the eight-hour workday would not be wise, and leaving it to the executive council to select any one national or international union, from among those which applied to be selected, to make the battle for the eight-hour workday. . . .[15]

(Commissioner Wright). The federation, then, has never had a general strike?—Ans. It has never had a general strike except the one which was contemplated May 1, 1886, but which unfortunately was terminated by the throwing of the bomb at the Hay Market, in the city of Chicago, and which of course killed our eight-hour movement.

(Commissioner Wright). Had the executive board of the American Federation of Labor called a strike even in its advisory capacity here in Chicago, would its members have responded to that call by coming out?—Ans. Generally, yes, sir, I believe they would.

(Commissioner Wright). Do you think it justifiable for any labor organization or association of organizations to paralyze, to any degree, the commercial industry of the country in order to settle a grievance which any part of that organization or association of organizations may have?—Ans. I believe that labor has the right—the natural as well as inherent right—to endeavor to improve its condition. The workers—the producers of the wealth of the world—have a right to a larger share of the product of their labor, and they are fast beginning to learn that that is their right, and they are going to have it. If industry or commerce is incidentally injured it is not their fault; the better course and the most reasonable course would be for the employers to grant the reasonable requests that labor usually makes, and thus avert the disaster to commerce or industry that you have mentioned.

(Commissioner Wright). Your view, then, is that the labor question crystallized, and the strike as a part of it, tend to improve the condition of the employees?—Ans. Yes, sir.

. . .

(Commissioner Wright). Is it the policy of the American Federation of Labor to welcome the creation of new organizations wherever possible?—Ans. Yes, sir.

(Commissioner Wright). So that the action of the conference had nothing to do with the policy of your order in its relation to the American Railway Union?—Ans. None whatever, sir. As a matter of fact, all these steam railway organizations were asked through their executives to be represented at our conference, although none of them were affiliated; but I might say, if I may be permitted, that one of the reasons we had in mind in asking the representatives of these organizations to meet in conference with us was this, that if we decided to recommend to organized labor that a strike should be entered into, at least those men who were clothed with responsibility as well as authority might be consulted, and that they would know what action they could or could not take.

(Commissioner Wright). You have given the labor question, in its various ramifications, a great deal of attention for a good many years. Have you arrived at any conclusion relative to methods which can be adopted, either by the State or Federal Government, looking to the avoidance of strikes and boycotts, and, if so, what are your conclusions? — Ans. So long as the present industrial and commercial system will last, so long will strikes continue. They may be diminished in number or intensity of feeling and bitterness, but, I repeat, so long as the present industrial and commercial system will last, so long will we have industrial disputes and disturbances.

I do not join this general hue and cry against strikes. I believe in diminishing the number as much as possible, and I have worked and contributed, I think, as much as any other one living man to the diminution in the number of strikes; but in the denunciation of strikes I will not join. I regard the strikes as the sign that the people are not yet willing to surrender every spark of their manhood and their honor and their independence. It is the protest of the worker against unjust conditions; and the strike has commanded the attention of the employing class, the capitalist class, and the thinkers throughout the world to the problem of labor, who would otherwise not have given the laborer a second's consideration, except as to the amount of labor that he can produce. No man would think of trying to invent some machine by which the thunderstorms could be abolished or entirely eliminated from our existence. The thunderstorm is the result of noxious gases or different gases in the atmosphere that come together and crush, and they simply purify the atmosphere, and make us feel reinvigorated and with renewed hope.

A strike is the movement of one of the forces in the industrial life and the commercial life, and gives evidence that we shall not go down further in the social and economic scale, and it is a warning that labor has more rights than it now enjoys, and a determination that it is going to secure them, if not today, some other day.

Strikes are not the failures that they are usually written down to be. Speaking of the strikes gained, the various bureaus of labor statistics, both of the General Government and the various State governments, demonstrate that a vast majority of them are gained. I am not familar with all the reports, since I am too much of a busy man to more than get that data which has been gone over by those who have gone over them before me, and I get their result, yet the reports of the bureau of labor statistics of the State of New York show that more than two-thirds of the strikes undertaken are victories for the workers, and that they involved the largest number of employees; that they are not, as a rule, against reduction of wages, but for an increase of wages or for a diminution of the hours of labor, or for improved conditions. Some four years ago I sent out a blank to our affiliated organizations, and obtained from them reports of the strikes they had had within a year, officially recognized, and the costs and results, how many involved, etc. There were more than 80 per cent of them victories, about 4 per cent compromised, and about 16 per cent which were lost.

Now, apart from the question of strikes which are won, strikes which are lost—that is, which do not succeed in obtaining the conditions which the workers started out to achieve—it is true that a strike has been lost, but there are few if any instances where some advantage has not been gained. First, the immediate advantage, the warning to the employing class generally that the workingmen will not go down further, and that any attempt to force them down will be very expensive if nothing else—very expensive, and that it would be dearer to them, even if they succeeded in enforcing a reduction, than to concede the wages or hours then paid or allowed. It can scarcely be accepted to be or to mean a diminution of production either. There are few workingmen in the entire country who do not lose from one week to three months of employment throughout the year, and I refer to those who are employed; and it is variously estimated that from one to three million wage workers in the United States who are or who have been out of employment in the last year, and, if I remember right, the Hon. Carroll D. Wright, in 1886, stated that there were then nearly a million wage workers unemployed, so that the million of unemployed workers was not the result of the commercial and financial crisis of 1893, but is now the normal condition in the United States.

I have thought this matter of strikes over very carefully, and there is another conclusion that I have come to, and that I have not seen dealt with largely or at all, and that is, whether defeated strikes do not, even in those, raise the economic condition of the people. Let me give an illustration of what I refer to. Say a railroad company whose employees are on a strike, and we will further say, against a reduction of wages. In the course of the industrial dispute the corporation gets other workers to take the place of their former employees. As a rule those from whom these new employees were recruited have been much lower in the economic scale than the position that they are about to occupy—in other words, economically they are raised—and I think that is undisputed, otherwise men would not change as a rule from equal employments to take the place of their brothers who were on a strike—engaged in a trade dispute; hence, it is true that they come from a lower strata to take the place of their striking brothers. Now, as to those who go on the strike, would they change places relatively to those who have been recruited? My experience and my inquiries demonstrate that that is not so, that a few may suffer and suffer quite a time, but that as a whole they do not go down in the social scale. I refer to employees who went on strikes; there are a few who suffered, but the whole number, as a class, have either remained where they were before the strike or are pushed higher in the social and economic scale. And thus, though the defeated strike loses the immediate object of the men who went out on the strike, yet on the whole it has benefited the whole people socially and economically. That is the result of my observation and inquiry.

I think I have already spoken of the influence on the public mind of strikes. The fact that this honorable commission was appointed to investigate the strike of the American Railway Union is an evidence of the beneficial results of the strike, although I think it was a little late in the season to have appointed the commission. The commission, if appointed during the strike, might have brought the managers' association and the officers of the American Railway Union together, and the refusal of the managers' association to meet or to speak with or discuss with the officers of the railway union the questions might have been prevented and an amicable adjustment might have been arrived at had the commission been appointed during the time of the strike; and I believe the law contemplates that the commission shall be appointed during the pendency of the trouble and with the view of endeavoring to amicably adjust the differences. It seems to me like the appointment of a coroner to hold an inquest rather than the appointment of a commission to adjudicate or endeavor to amicably adjust the differences. And that is, as I understand, the purpose of the law and the intent of the law.

. . .

(Commissioner Wright). What in your observation has been the effect of strikes, either successful or non-successful as you may choose to call them, on the membership of labor unions? Have they increased the membership as a rule?—Ans. I find that the organizations which are formed, usually in their early history they have great strikes or more strikes—I should put it this way: Unorganized workmen have an exaggerated idea of the power of the employing class and a belief of their own utter incompetency to do anything to improve their condition. On the other hand, as soon as workmen organize, for the first few weeks or months they underestimate the power of capital or capitalists and corporations and overestimate their own power; hence you will find that newer organizations usually rush in where older organizations would not dare to tread.

Strikes have various effects. On an old organization usually it has the effect of making the members more determined to remain true to it than ever. To new organizations, or rather to organizations newly formed, a failure usually has the effect of the men denouncing the organization, when, as a matter of fact, it is due to their own negligance in the failure to form unions years before, or is due to their ill preparation, their poorly organized condition. It is the difference between veterans and raw recruits.

(Commissioner Worthington). There are two or three questions that you were discussing before this last matter that I would like to ask you about. . . .

. . . Have you any unions of railroad employees, as such?—Ans. Not as steam railroad employees.

                                        . . .

. . . If they [the railroad brotherhoods] decided at their next convention to become affiliated with the American Federation of Labor they would so notify my office and receive a certificate of affiliation and be represented at our annual convention, participate in our conferences, partake of the mutual advantages which our federation gives and receives.

(Commissioner Worthington). They would have all the advantages and all the powers, as I understand you, of membership by affiliation with your federation in the way you have suggested?—Ans. Yes sir. I would say, in connection with this, that within this past week or two I have been in correspondence with the officers of the Brotherhood of Locomotive Firemen and, judging from the tenor of their letters, I should say that the day of the affiliation of that organization, and I hope of the others in the steam railway service, is not far distant.

(Commissioner Worthington). You would think that likely to be beneficial to the interest of all concerned—all employees of these different orders, would you?—Ans. Yes, sir; I think it would be to the interests of all. Our organization is conducted upon the principle that each trade is best qualified to decide for itself its trade regulations, its relations with its employers—or the employers of its members— to decide these questions for itself without the let or hindrance of the other organizations. Of course, we believe that as industry becomes developed and as labor becomes divided and subdivided, instead of having the different branches which have practically been wiped out by the development of machinery and the application of new tools, that there must necessarily be industrial divisions that will logically follow; they can not be peremptorily created; they must result from organizations existing rather than, I think, others to take their places— a matter of evolution, if you please, evolving from them — growing from them.

(Commissioner Worthington). I understood you to say that neither you as president nor the executive committee or executive council (by whichever name you call it) has authority to declare a general strike. That is correct, is it? — Ans. That is correct.

(Commissioner Worthington). And has no authority to declare a strike of any particular body of workers? — Ans. It has no such power.

(Commissioner Worthington). Has it any power to prohibit strikes?— Ans. It has not, except when any affiliated body engaged in an industrial dispute desires having the assistance, financial or moral, of the American Federation of Labor, it is within our power to give it our approval or disapproval; and while it is not an order to strike or an order not to strike, it is fair to presume that an approval carries with it considerable prestige for victory, and, on the other hand, a disapproval would mean that the organization would find it to its advantage not to enter into the strike.

(Commissioner Worthington). But that would be in the shape of moral influence, rather than a direct power on its part? — Ans. The system is governed more by moral influences than by force.

. . .

(Commissioner Worthington). I understood you to say that you thought strikes would continue as long as the present industrial and commercial system continued. Did I understand you correctly as to that? — Ans. Yes, sir.

(Commissioner Worthington). What do you mean by the present industrial system? For instance, the system of capital going into the market and purchasing labor as cheaply as it can? — Ans. I think that that rightly — and selling in the dearest market, which apparently carries with it the seal of righteousness.

(Commissioner Worthington). That is practically the condition now, is it not? Ans. Yes, sir; that is the condition. It is immaterial whether delicate women or innocent children are brought into play in competition with willing, earnest men, or whether the lives of children are thrown into the balance, so that wages shall go down and the condition of the laborer become deteriorated.

(Commissioner Worthington). While you expressed no opinion upon this point, I infer, perhaps incorrectly, from your general statements, that you do not think this is a good system?—Ans. I think it is the best we have had, but I do not think it is the best we will have.

(Commissioner Worthington). That is what I want to get at. What do you think is a better system?—Ans. That is a matter for theoreticians and speculative thought. I think that scarcely any that could be evolved out of the human mind could be much worse than that which we now have. I do not think the human family will tolerate anything worse than we have. We have grown away from things that have been worse. The question whether the Government employment of all labor—in plainer words, state socialism, is something for the future to decide, something which the future will determine, and which no man today can say. I imagine that more than likely it will be necessary for our people to go through that phase—more than likely that we will have to go through that phase whether we like it or not.

(Commissioner Worthington). The phase of state socialism?—Ans. At least a portion of it, if not entirely. I do believe, however, that the Government ownership of the railroads and of all means of transportation and communication and all other productive forces which are in those monopolies should be taken hold of by the Government. I have heard a good many objections to the Government ownership of railroads, but, as has been tersely said to you, the question was whether the Government should own the railroads or the railroads own the Government. The Government of the United States practically operates a vast number of the railroads, but simply waits until they have been bankrupted and in the hands of a receiver, and then conducts them. If the Government can conduct a bankrupt railroad why should it not be in a position to conduct a railroad which has not yet been bankrupted?

. . .

(Commissioner Worthington). Have you anything more that you desire to say?—Ans. Yes, sir; there are a few things I would like to say. I have not attempted to clearly think out in logical sequence a few thoughts that I wanted to express, but I have made a note or two, while riding along on the railroad, which I would like to speak of.

(Commissioner Worthington). You may proceed, and if we should think it was entirely outside of the scope of our investigation, we will say so. — Ans. If you think it does not come under the scope of your investigation, of course you can apply the editorial blue pencil.

In the matter of compulsory arbitration, I think that the very terms in themselves present the antithesis of each other — they are neither logical nor rational. Compulsory arbitration implies compulsory organization of the workers, for without organization of the workers compulsory arbitration is absolutely impossible. A compulsory organization would be as obnoxious as was the feudal system. The question of compulsory arbitration would be, what would be considered fair wages. In England the strike of the miners set a principle — settled a principle in the mining industry of Great Britain, and that was, that the first consideration in the cost of production was living wages; that there was a "life line" below which point wages dare not fall, no matter at what price coal was sold. Without that strike of the miners of England that principle would not have been recognized nor established. Now, in the Amalgamated Association of Iron and Steel Workers, in the trades and branches covered by that organization, they have a minimum line — in other words, a life line; there is a sliding scale, but below a certain point — that is, the life line, that they consider wages should not go, no matter at how low a price iron and steel may be sold; in other words, that the first lien on the product is a living wage; that is established fairly in the iron and steel trade; it is not so in very many other trades throughout the United States.

Where would the line of a living wage be drawn by compulsory arbitrators? A living wage is that which the working people establish for themselves; among the men in the iron and steel trade it may be $3 per day, among the miners it may by $1.25 per day. Who is going to establish for the $4 per day bricklayer the life line? If he has just come away from considering the question of a living wage for a hod carrier or a coal miner, it is more than likely, yes, it is reasonable to suppose, that the mind of the arbitrator would be influenced from having come in contact with the mine worker who received $1.25 per day, and he would consider that the strike of the bricklayer against a reduction of 50 cents per day from $4 would not be so great a hardship to the bricklayer, when, as a matter of fact, it would be striking below the living wage of the bricklayer.

In the matter of arbitration, further: Arbitration is a matter of compromise as a rule; it is not usually an award of one to the other, or of one party as against another; it is usually a compromise sought to endeavor to mollify both sides. The employing class are usually more alert — necessarily so; if they have not the brains themselves they buy them; continually on the alert, continually thinking, more watchful of events — those present and those coming; and if compulsory arbitration were in vogue it would be a question then as to who would be most alert, the workers or the employers, to make a movement, the workers for an increase, the employers for a decrease or a reduction in wages. Whoever would get there first would get their complaint considered, and the arbitrators, prompted by the spirit of compromise, I don't think the workers would get much the best of it. And another consideration: Compulsory arbitration would place the workmen in a status, a status from which we have been continually departing and to which we will not go back.

. . .

Now, in regard to the question of injunctions issued by the courts, I want to say, first, that the interstate-commerce law was the result of an agitation of farmers and shippers, and the entire reform elements, if you please, took hold of the cry and agitated the question and presented it in some tangible shape to Congress, and it was enacted by Congress. No thought was ever had at that time that that law was to be made, or was at all to apply to labor engaged in a dispute with corporations or employers—no one even hinted it.

I am informed upon very good authority that Senator Morgan, of Alabama, proposed an amendment to the law when it was before the Senate—it was a bill then—making it apply to organizations of labor; in other words, if that amendment had been adopted the injunctions issued by Judge Ricks, by Judge Taft, by Judge Williams, by Judge Woods, and by Judge Grosscup would have been based upon the law as it was understood and as it was proposed and adopted; but the amendment of Senator Morgan was defeated, plainly defeated, thus showing that the intention of Congress was that this law should not apply to the organizations of labor engaged in any trade dispute or conflict or industrial dispute with their employers, and that in granting the injunctions, so far as it applies to the interstate-commerce laws, the court is doing what the courts have too frequently done in matters when the workers have been involved, and that is, the court made law—law which does not exist, but decisions which have taken the place of law, or the absence of law, upon the subjects.

. . .

Another consideration, and that is that the trouble with us is this: More than one hundred years ago a number of the ablest and best men that the world has produced met in convention and adopted a Constitution. In the States constitutions were adopted subsequently. And at that time men knew scarcely anything of the existence of the power of steam; they knew nothing at all of electricity; they had no suspicion even in the days of Adam Smith of the steam engine and the electric motor or the telegraph, the telephone, the application of steam and electricity to industry; and yet, the laws that had been made in the period that I have mentioned are sought to be applied to modern industry and modern commerce. The fact is that there is too much rigidity—if I may so say—in the law; it is not pliable, it does not possess either elasticity enough or does not permit of the adoption of such laws as the changed industrial and commercial conditions make absolutely necessary. When labor goes to the various legislatures or goes to Congress and asks for remedial or beneficial legislation, the answer is that it is unconstitutional. The fact that it is beneficial or necessary is not denied, but it is said that it is unconstitutional.

I submit that industry and commerce can not go back to conform to old thoughts, old theories, and old crusty customs of law, but that the law, sooner, must be changed to conform to the changed industrial and commercial conditions. It was revolution that saved France, it was reform that saved England, it is a question what will save America. The trade unions stand for the reform of these conditions, and we hope by the evolutionary process to secure those changes for which we struggle and have struggled and will continue to struggle; and the very fact that our efforts are thwarted time and again instead of being met in a conciliatory spirit is what often dispels the hope of the trade unions to find a peaceable solution for this great problem.

· · ·

. . . The number of laws that we can not secure the enactment of under the plea of the legislators and Congressmen that it would be unconstitutional is marvelous, and the few laws that we do secure after years and years of agitation are declared unconstitutional; and it, as I say, simply makes men who usually look upon the bright side— makes them look almost as if it was very doubtful—become pessimistic.

· · ·

A number of men speaking of labor organizations—and Judge Grosscup, too, recently, spoke of being in favor of labor organizations within lawful limits, and which would not prove a menace to the lawful institutions of the country; and I want to say that he has written me a letter[16] in reference to that subject, and that I have answered him,[17] I hope to his conversion, if not to his satisfaction. Some of the men—and I believe our friend Judge Grosscup is among them— who have no objection to the organizations of labor provided they would discuss, probably, the origin of man or the distance of the sun or moon from the earth, but the question of their relations to their employers, the fact that there are millions of men unemployed who are willing to work, I don't think the Judge would—

Commissioner Wright. What the opinions of different persons might be is rather outside of our investigation.

Witness. I want to say this, if permitted, that an organization of labor that would resolve never to strike would be simply placing itself in the hands of the employer for him to do all the striking in the shape of reductions of wages; it would be like a regiment of soldiers that resolved immediately upon the breaking out of any war to disband.

In the industrial field, when to all appearance there is not a ripple disturbing the relationship between the workers and their employers, in other words, when there is not some gigantic strike taking place, the casual observer always regards that the labor movement is stagnant. In fact, the average man seems to think that there is a labor movement only when a great stuggle is inaugurated or in progress, and that the entire labor movement consists in nothing more nor less than strikes.

As a matter of fact, the strike is but one of the incidents, and, in truth, one of the infrequent incidents of the labor movement. Few of the people, even among observers, appreciate the fact that the labor movement is one unceasing, never-ending struggle from the beginning of one year until its end, and then a continuous repetition.

The number of strikes that have been averted by the trade unions can never be correctly recorded. The efforts to reduce wages and increase the working hours successfully checked will be but half written; the concessions gained in the matters of wages, hours of labor, conditions of employment and legislation, but grudgingly acknowledged and frequently unappreciated. As a matter of fact, the greatest victories of the labor movement are those which are achieved though unheralded and unknown to the general public. They are obtained by the unions in conference with employers or their representatives in their offices; and in many cases a condition of settlement being the fact that the victory should not be proclaimed to the world.

The trades-union movement is in the industrial field what the pioneers are to progress in their onward march. It plods along encountering whatever disasters may come and bearing the sacrifices that are to be made. Sometimes defeated, more often victorious in forging ahead without ostentation, without flaunting their successes into the faces of the world and without braggadocio; making few if any protestations of faith, but carrying on the brunt of battle for the down trodden and heavy laden, without pronunciamentos of cosmopolitanism the trades-union movement extends the hand of fraternity and establishes the bond of sympathy and unity. It overcomes national, race, color, and sex prejudices as the opportunities for the manifestation and exercise of these principles arise.

The trades-union movement exhibits the highest type of manhood and self-sacrifice in order to secure the achievement of a right or the establishment of a principle. It delves down into the deepest abysses of misery and despair and helps to bring up the young and innocent, the weak and the unfortunate, that they may be saved from the horrible consequences of our industrial disorder. It teaches to the learned and unlearned the power of organization; it brings forth the noblest qualities in the mind of man. It inculcates the duty that man owes to man, and instills a nobility of feeling and sentiment toward the oppressed everywhere, and inspires the workers with the hope and the aspiration to struggle for the dawn of a brighter and better day.

The trades-union movement is ever pressing onward and upward, and the workers are massed together in the unions of their trades. The progress made may not be as accelerated as we may wish, but it is advancing and moving forward in exactly the same ratio that the intelligence of our fellow-workers will admit, and though the day may be somewhat distant we are surely nearing it, when the humanizing influences of the trades-union movement shall be fully recognized and form the ethics of industry, society, and the state.

U.S. Strike Commission, *Report on the Chicago Strike of June-July, 1894. . .* , U.S. Congress, Senate, Ex. Docs., no. 7, 53d Cong., 3d sess. (Washington, D.C., 1895), pp. 188-205.

1. On July 26, 1894, President Grover Cleveland appointed a U.S. Strike Commission composed of Carroll D. Wright, commissioner of the U.S. Bureau of Labor, John D. Kernan, a lawyer from Utica, N.Y., and Nicholas E. Worthington, a circuit court judge from Peoria, Ill., to examine labor troubles surrounding the Pullman strike. It took testimony in Chicago from Aug. 15 through Aug. 30 and in Washington, D.C., on Sept. 26, from workers and officials of the Pullman Palace Car Co., railroad workers, representatives of the railroads' General Managers' Association, and labor leaders including SG, Eugene Debs and George Howard of the American Railway Union (ARU), P. H. Morrissey of the Brotherhood of Railroad Trainmen, and James R. Sovereign of the KOL. On Nov. 14 the commission forwarded its report to President Cleveland, recommending, among other things, that the federal government establish a permanent strike commission and that employers recognize labor organizations.

2. On July 8, 1894, representatives of Chicago's trade unions and KOL assemblies met in that city with Eugene Debs, James Sovereign, John McBride, and other national labor leaders to discuss the question of launching a general strike in support of the Pullman strike. The meeting resolved to make one more attempt to arbitrate the matter before taking that action.

3. A seven-man committee representing Chicago cigarmakers' unions appeared before the Briggs House Conference on July 12, 1894.

4. Archibald Philip Primrose (1847-1929), Lord Rosebery, a Liberal, was prime minister of Great Britain from 1894 to 1895.

5. William E. Gladstone (1809-98), leader of the Liberal party, was the prime minister of Great Britain four times (1868-74, 1880-85, 1886, and 1892-94).

6. See "A Telegram Issued by the Conference of Representatives of Labor Organizations Meeting at Briggs House, Chicago," July 12, 1894, above.

7. A copy of Debs's proposal, in which the ARU offered to call off the Pullman boycott if the company would reinstate the strikers, appeared in the *American Federationist* 1 (Aug. 1894): 133.

8. The General Managers' Association, organized in 1886 and reactivated in 1892, developed common traffic, freight, and wage policies for twenty-four railroads serving Chicago and also handled labor troubles for member railroads.

9. See "A Statement Issued by the Conference of Representatives of Labor Organizations Meeting at Briggs House, Chicago," July 13, 1894, above.

10. Printed in *American Federationist* 1 (Aug. 1894): 127.

11. The FOTLU convened in Chicago, Oct. 7-10, 1884.

12. The AFL's 1887 convention was held in Baltimore, Dec. 13-17.

13. SG has these reversed. It was the FOTLU's Washington, D.C., convention that met in 1885, from Dec. 8 to 11.

14. The AFL's 1888 convention met in St. Louis, Dec. 11-15.

15. See "The Campaign for Eight Hours," *The Early Years of the AFL*, pp. 163-64.

16. July 31, 1894, printed in *American Federationist* 1 (Sept. 1894): 149.

17. See "To Peter Grosscup," Aug. 14, 1894, above.

An Editorial by Samuel Gompers
in the *American Federationist*

[August 1894]

PULLMAN.

It is a lamentable fact that success does not always attend the right or those who struggle to achieve it. If any doubt existed as to the truth of this statement, the strike at Pullman and the strike of the American Railway Union in support of it, has dispelled that doubt. It is indeed difficult to conceive a cause in which right was more on the side of those who were defeated as in the one under consideration. We present to our readers the true story of this contest, and the cause which led up to it; and we hope to add to the contumely and contempt which every earnest, honest, liberty loving man, woman and child in the country must feel for the most consummate type of avaricious wealth absorber, tyrant and hypocrite this age, of that breed, has furnished—Pullman.

In the language of the picture drawn by Pullman, the *philanthropist* of Pullman, the town, he says: "That it is bordered with bright beds of flowers and green velvety stretches of land, that [it] is shaded with trees and dotted with parks and pretty water vistas and glimpses here and there of artistic sweeps and landscape gardening, a town where the homes even of the most modest are bright and wholesome and filled with pure air and light, a town, in a word, from which all that is ugly, discordant and demoralizing is eliminated and all that inspires to self-respect, to thrift and to cleanliness of person and of being is generally provided."

This description is unquestionably true so far as it refers to the view which the passer by sees upon the train; but back where the workers live and die, what a pitiful, horrible condition prevails. In whole blocks entire families have for years lived in one room in order that they might eke out an existence. In no community in the world, except possibly China, was there such a small proportion of families living in family privacy.

At the beginning of the contest the employees of Pullman owed $80,000 for rent without the ability to pay it. A young woman whose father worked for the Company for fifteen years died, leaving the family in destitute circumstances. He was in debt to the Company $60 for rent. The unpaid bill was sent to the orphaned girl and she was required out of her scanty wages of 30 cents per day with the assistance of her brother's wages of 70 cents per day to liquidate the unpaid rent. A man a few days before the strike received a check for his months' work which came 45 cents short of balancing his rent account and a bill was sent with the collector to his house for payment. Blacksmiths who formerly, at Pullman as well as other places, received $4.00 a day did not average $1.00.

In Pullman there was always an indefinable something telling the workers that their presence was not wanted where the flowers and fountains and velvety lawns are. The houses are not healthy and the records show an unusual number of deaths by zymotic diseases.

During the terrible suffering last winter the Company insisted that there was no destitution nor suffering in the place and with much nonchalance declared that "there could be none because it was not contemplated in the theory upon which the town was founded and controlled."

When a number of charitable ladies organized to relieve the destitution they were not permitted to carry on the work, for that would be an acknowledgment that there was need of relief.

The town of Pullman covers 350 acres estimated to be worth $10,000,000. Buildings occupied by the workers are congested as the most thickly settled residence districts of Chicago, yet Pullman pays but $15,000 on taxes. (Carnegie defrauds the government in his contracts; Pullman in taxes.)

Nor should it be imagined that the statement made by Pullman recently, that the reason he refused to arbitrate the matter in dispute with his employees was that the Company were producing cars at a loss. As a matter of fact last February, or two months before the strike commenced, the Company issued an official statement containing the following. "The day is near at hand when the $30,000,000 present capital of the Pullman Company will be covered and more than covered by the value of the 3,500 acres of land on which is built the town of Pullman." Coupled with this was the statement that the $30,000,000 capital stock had a market value of $60,000,000.

When the fact is borne in mind that Pullman has practically a monopoly in the building of his cars, is not the claim preposterous that he could not pay fair wages? Does any one imagine that if Pullman's statement of his inability to pay the wage demanded was true that he would refuse to arbitrate? No arbitrator would make an award against him if he could prove his assertions, his refusal is the best evidence of his untruthfulness. In truth out of his own statements he convicts himself.

The end is not yet. Labor will not down. It will triumph despite all the Pullmans combined; and as for Pullman, he has proven himself a public enemy. His name and memory are excoriated to-day and will be forever.

American Federationist 1 (Aug. 1894): 120-21.

To Oliver Smith

Sept. 8, [1894]

Mr. O. P. Smith,
417 S. 4th. St. St. Louis, Mo.
Dear Sir and Brother:—

Your favor of the 5th. inst. came duly to hand, and I beg to say that I was pleased to hear from you for several reasons, because it is the first time since you have written me since your departure from Logansport, and I have received a number of letters referring to you in various ways.

You may not know the awful plight you placed me in in Logansport

before and after your departure from that city. The Trades and Labor
Assembly[1] has written to me time and again. They had entrusted you
with the annual tax to be transmitted to this office and you had failed
to do so. You wrote me at that time assuring me that you had not
received the money, and also that you had not received the money
for the tickets of an affair arranged by the working girls. I defended
you to the very last until convinced of your improper action towards
your fellow workers. I remembered only the good work you did in
building up the labor movement of Logansport, and defended you
in spite of the demands of the Logansport unions.

In order to overcome some of the bitterness towards you and recognizing that you were the general organizer and the representative
of the A.F. of L. in that city we made an appropriation out of the
funds of the A.F. of L. to make good that deficiency.[2]

The next thing I heard about you was that you had shown up in
Nashville or Louisville (I am not sure which) and there came in conflict
with our general organizer[3] and had represented yourself as the general organizer for the A.F. of L. I advised our representative in that
city that it would be well for him to see you and to request you not
to take an active part in the labor movement until you had placed
yourself right with organized labor of Logansport, as well as with the
A.F. of L. In writing to him I imposed the injunction of privacy, except
that the matter should be communicated to you. I am satisfied that
if he has not seen you and spoken to you about it while you were in
the city referred to above, he has faithfully carried out my wishes in
so far as communicating the facts to no one else is concerned.

Some months ago I did receive a letter from a Union man in St.
Louis stating that you were antagonizing the trade union movement.
He made inquiries of me in reference to your antecedents. I wrote
to him without reciting the facts in the case, but advised him in the
same manner as I requested our organizer in the South. He told me
that you had joined the K. of L. and were about to use the cloak of
that organization as a cover for your attacks.

I do not think that I have a copy of that letter, but it was sent with
the simple request that its contents be made known to you only, but
that if you did not desist, its contents might be made public to organized labor. For the same reasons that I imposed secrecy in the first
instance upon my correspondent, I think you will recognize that it is
but justice to him when I say that it would be impracticable to disclose
the name of my correspondent to you.

What I stated to our organizer in the South and to my correspondent
in St. Louis I repeat to you now, and that is that before you take an

active part in the labor movement you should live down the unsavory part of the record you made in Logansport. Even to this day I remember with respect the good work you did there and was very seriously affected and hurt when made acquainted with the fact that you had sullied it all by your subsequent action.

You may rest assured that until the time that you appease the people whom you have wronged, that wrong will rise up always to confront you wherever you may be. You know the respect that I have always entertained for you and it is not entirely dead now, and that is one of the reasons why I should like you to redeem yourself and again take your position in the great struggle for labor for which your abilities fit you.

I beg to assure you that I regret exceedingly to learn that you have been so ill as you say and trust that you will soon regain your health and strength.

I have endeavored to be very frank with you in this matter and to address you rather as a friend who sees the fault of another and advises him the best course to pursue under the circumstances.

Very Truly Yours   Saml Gompers.
President. American Federation of Labor.

TLpS, reel 8, vol. 11, pp. 310-11, SG Letterbooks, DLC.

1. The Trades and Labor Assembly (TLA) of Logansport, Ind., was chartered by the AFL in 1890.
2. This was to cover the $25 AFL annual tax of the Logansport TLA that Smith had misappropriated.
3. Probably Benjamin C. Talley, a Nashville carpenter.

To Joseph Labadie[1]

New York, Sept. 13, 1894.

Personal
Mr. Joseph Labadie,
74 Buchannon St. Detroit, Mich.
Dear Friend Joe:—

Your favor of the 9th. came duly to hand and contents noted. I am pleased to learn that you will write for the American Federationist and hope you will do so at your earliest opportunity. Anything you may write, will, I feel satisfied, be read with much interest by our fellow unionists and friends.

To me the complications arising out of the decisions of the trade unions of the various localities to enter upon the political field is not an unmixed evil. It is unnecessary for me to say to you that I regret more than I can find words to express that anything should have occurred which has divided the workingmen in the various cities, such as for instance, Detroit and Chicago, but I repeat it is not an unmixed evil.

You know that at the convention of the Federation at Chicago a programme was submitted and which many believe would if adopted plunge the Federation as such, into nominating candidates etc. for public office. It is more than likely that the experience of the localities referred to while hurtful in a local sense will have its effect in the determination of the general subject for the entire labor movement. Probably I may take too optimistic a view of the situation, but I think you will agree with me that there is some grain of comfort if you view it from the standpoint I do. It may save the general movement from being dragged in the throes of a political squabble and with the same bandying of words and epithets and possibly the same ground (or groundless) for accusations of dishonesty.

The representatives to the Denver convention will have something in the nature of an experience in their localities that may deter them from taking a step they otherwise would.

I am pleased to learn that you are regaining strength and vigor and hope you will soon be all right again. As soon as I see our friends Lennon and Buchannon[2] I shall convey to them your kind wishes. Our friend Evans joins me in reciprocating your kind words.

While I shall impose no confidence in regard to this matter I prefer that the views expressed herein should remain personal since I may have occasion to say something of the same nature in an official way.

Truly Yours   Saml Gompers.

TLS, Joseph A. Labadie Papers, Department of Rare Books and Special Collections, MiU.

1. Joseph Antoine Labadie, a labor journalist, played a major role in establishing the Detroit Trades and Labor Council in 1880, becoming its corresponding secretary, and was also a founder and first president (1889-90) of the Michigan Federation of Labor. In 1893 he was appointed clerk of the Detroit Water Works, a post he held until about 1920.

2. Joseph Ray Buchanan was an organizer of the People's party and served on its national committee during the 1892, 1896, and 1900 elections.

To John O'Brien

Sept. 15, [1894]

Cap'tn. John O'Brien,
409 Stark St. Portland, Oreg.
Dear Sir and Brother:—

Your favor of the 5th. came duly to hand and contents noted. I presume by this time you will have received the letter I mailed to Mr. Poynton[1] and which was returned here. I regret this delay but I knew no other address than the one you gave me, Wardner, Idaho, and did the best I could under the circumstances. I hope that no unnecessary delay will occur in the organization and affiliation of our friends around the far Western country.

The departure of the printers you mention upon the "Oregonian" who were supplanted by the machine I find duplicated in very many other places throughout the country. In New York a move of the same kind is on foot as well as in Cincinnati and Chicago, and I presume the launching of a newspaper[2] will be the at least temporary means to find situations for the printers made "superfluous."

It is unnecessary for me to say that I earnestly hope that you will have entire success in the effort and that the paper will be a credit to the cause we have the honor of representing.

I know you will do all the work you possibly can in the interest of the movement and I feel assured Mr. Mc-Bryde as well as the other officers of the National Unions and myself appreciate that fact.

I am sorry to learn that some people are antagonizing your efforts. There is a good deal of that all over the country, more particularly in those places where they have plunged headlong into politics and neglected their unions. This local movement may possibly be a blessing in disguise as it may have quite an influence upon the Denver convention upon that same subject. You know the old proverb although it is somewhat musty that "Fools rush in etc."

I am obliged to you for the article you forward me from the "Oregonian." It matters little what adverse criticism they may have in it. I am satisfied that judgment and time will justify the course pursued, and so far as my eulogy of Mr. Debs is concerned I believe it to be true. I think him sincere and honest, but an enthusiast and mistaken. Because a man is mistaken is no reason why a fair judgment of his character cannot be formed and expressed. There are enough of labor's enemies to criticise and condemn him without my joining in the denunciation of an over zealous vidette.

Have you seen the Sept. issue of the Federationist? I commend to you my letter to Judge Grosscup which appears in that number.

The work of organization goes along slowly, yes, possibly slower than we would like to see but going on nevertheless, and I join you in the hope that we may gather the forces of labor together and soon be successful in the great struggle yet before us.

With kind wishes and hoping to hear from you soon, I am,

Fraternally Yours   Saml Gompers.
President American Federation of Labor

TLpS, reel 8, vol. 11, pp. 337-38, SG Letterbooks, DLC.

1. J. F. Poynton had written O'Brien and referred to SG in a complimentary manner. O'Brien shared the letter with SG, who then wrote Poynton on Aug. 11, 1894 (reel 8, vol. 11, pp. 249-50, SG Letterbooks, DLC), with the objective of bringing the miners of Idaho into the AFL.

2. The *Portland Sun*, operated by unemployed printers from the *Portland Oregonian*, began publication in October 1894 and continued until August 1895.

To Thomas Mann

Sept. 20, [1894]

Mr. Tom. Mann,
34 Minford Gardens, W. Kenzington, London, W. England.
Dear Sir and Friend:—

Your favor of recent date came duly to hand, but it was necessary for me to go West three times since then, and you are aware that this country is one of magnificent distances. This together with other important work in hand prevented an earlier response.

It would be a very long story to enter into the details of the railroad strike in this letter, and since I treat the matter fully in the Aug. and Sept. issues of the "American Federationist" I mail them to you with this. All that I need add is that the A.R.U. was organized less than a year when that strike and boycott was undertaken, and it was instituted not for the purpose of consolidating the existing railroad organizations, but to supplant them.

I presume you receive the "Federationist" regularly, but I take this precaution so that you may read the history of the strike, by sending the two copies as per above.

I suppose you are aware of the great success attending the efforts of one of our local organizations, the Tailors in abolishing the task and sweating system in the cities of New York, Brooklyn, Newark and

Brownsville.[1] It was short, sharp and decisive. It is being taken up now in Boston, and will no doubt reach Chicago and St. Louis, and if the fight is conducted on the same lines and with the same tenacity I believe that we will have seen the last of the sweating system in the clothing trade.

The newspapers here gave very meagre reports of the Trade Union Congress at Norwich, in fact much less was published about it than any of the previous Congresses for the past ten years.

Our friend Mr. Lloyd of Boston arrived here on the 15th. and I had the pleasure of a visit from him at this office and listened to him for nearly four hours recounting his experiences in Europe, and particularly Great Brittain. One thing pleased me more than all else, and that was to learn that the men leading the labor movement of Great Brittain though they may differ, yet retain a high regard for the personal welfare and character of their adversaries. It is one thing to differ with a man and quite another to regard him as dishonest simply because of that difference.

There is another feature which is gratifying to me, and that is that the men who are most active in the Independent Political Movement of the working men of the Old Country do not think it [necessary to destroy] the existing trade unions, but rather regard them as the basis for all progress of labor.

Mr. Lloyd informs me that he was very cordially as well as fraternally received wherever he went, but it remained for Mr. Hooker whom he met in England, to inform me by mail of the good work performed by Mr. Lloyd and the good impression he made by his public and private utterances.

I read the pamphlet you sent me and certainly think it an excellent document and which must necessarily help you in the canvass you say you will make in Yorkshire.

I am anxiously looking forward to the printed copy of the proceedings of the Norwich Congress. Mr. Lloyd states that a resolution was passed directing the Parliamentary Committee to send a representative to our Denver convention next December.[2] If that is so and it is carried out I would like to be made acquainted with it as soon as convenient so that our fellow workers of this city may be made aware of the fact.

Did Mr. Gunton[3] call to see you when in England? He is a bright man and a good worker, although in politics I have occasion to frequently differ with him.

With kindest wishes, and asking to be remembered to all our friends and hoping to hear from you as frequently as convenient, I am,

Very Sincerely Yours   Saml Gompers.

President. American Federation of Labor.

TLpS, reel 8, vol. 11, pp. 348-49, SG Letterbooks, DLC.

1. On Sept. 2, 1894, Brooklyn coat makers, including tailors, operators, and pressers, declared a general strike in the ready-made garment industry; they were joined by coat makers in New York City and Newark, N.J., the following day. The strike involved some 10,000 workers under the leadership of locals of the United Garment Workers of America, the Journeymen Tailors' Union of America, and the KOL. The main demand of the strikers was for a weekly wage instead of payment according to the "task" or "sweating" system. Through this system contractors, serving as middlemen for manufacturers, required workers to produce a specified number of coats per day, regardless of the number of hours it took to make them, in order to receive any pay. As a result, some garment workers labored up to sixteen hours a day for less than half the standard weekly wage in the industry. By Sept. 21 nearly all of the area's 500 contractors had signed agreements abandoning the sweating system for the time being.

2. John Burns and David Holmes attended the AFL convention in Denver as fraternal delegates representing the Trades Union Congress of Great Britain.

3. George GUNTON was president of the Institute of Social Economics from 1890 to 1904 and editor of the *Social Economist* (*Gunton's Magazine* after 1896) from 1891 to 1904.

To Ralph Easley[1]

Sept. 24, [1894]

Mr. Ralph M. Easley,
Sec. The Civic Federation,
Chicago, Ill.
Dear Sir:—

I have the honor to acknowledge the receipt of your favor of the 19th. instant which came duly to hand. In it you state that the Civic Federation contemplates holding a conference some time in the late Autumn for the consideration of the subjects of industrial arbitration and conciliation, and you ask my views on the advisability of holding the conference, and, if I favor it, my co-operation, and you also ask me to suggest the time, scope of programme and speakers and add the Committee's invitation for my attendance.

In reply let me say that when in Chicago in the early part of July I had a conversation with our mutual friend Mr. Michael J. Carroll who mentioned the subject to me, and I then told him what I now repeat, that in my judgment such a conference could only have beneficial results, providing the matter was properly attended to.

It seems to me however, that much valuable time has been lost in issuing the call. If the invitations are to be forwarded within the next few weeks a fair attendance could not be secured for a conference held before the latter part of Nov. and in the early part of Dec. the convention of the American Federation of Labor takes place. For that reason it would be inopportune for a large number of representatives of the trade unions to attend such a conference at the time stated. More than likely if a conference was called for the early part of Spring 1895 and arrangements made in the meantime a much better showing could be made.

Then again, while I look favorably upon the movement I cannot speak officially for the American Federation of Labor until after either the Executive Council holds its next session or after the convention. The Executive Council will meet in the early part of Oct. The convention takes place Dec. 10th. 1894 in Denver, Colo.

Before writing upon the question of the scope of programme and speakers, I respectfully submit the above to your consideration.

With kind wishes, I am,

Very Truly Yours   Saml Gompers.
President. American Federation of Labor

TLpS, reel 8, vol. 11, p. 357, SG Letterbooks, DLC.

1. Ralph Montgomery EASLEY was an organizer of the Chicago Civic Federation (serving as its secretary from 1893 until 1900) and, later, of the National Civic Federation.

To the Executive Council of the AFL

New York, Sept. 27, 1894.

To the Executive Council of the A.F. of L.
Fellow-Workmen: —

Our friend the Hon. Henry W. Blair of New Hampshire is making a canvass for United States Senator, and a number of workingmen of his State are advocating his return to the Senate.

He asks me whether it would be possible to send a man through the State to confer with some of the Union men to induce them [to] participate in the primaries so that members of the Legislature may be selected favorable to his election to the Senate. Mr. Blair says that he could do something towards the expenses of sending a man through the State, I presume meaning he will bear the expenses entirely.

It is unnecessary to call the attention of my colleagues of the Council to the fact that Senator Blair owed his second election to the United States Senate, to the officers of the Federation, and also his election to the House of Representatives two years ago, and that he has since 1883 been of incalculable benefit and service to our movement. The Council last year authorized the payment to him of quite a sum of money for services in our Eight Hour movement, and when the same was offered to him he declined to receive it asking that the same be devoted to the furtherance of our cause.

I mention these matters simply as my warrant in submitting his suggestion to your consideration.

Kindly return your vote[1] at your earliest convenience, as to whether the Senator's request shall be complied with, and oblige,

Yours Fraternally   Saml Gompers.
President. American Federation of Labor

TLpS, AFL Executive Council Vote Books, reel 8, *AFL Records.*

1. The AFL Executive Council approved SG's request to support Blair's candidacy. He was not elected to the Senate in 1894.

To Eva McDonald Valesh

Sept. 28, [1894]

Mrs. Eva Mc-Donald Valesh,
c/o "Tribune" Office, Minneapolis, Minn.
Dear Friend:—

I am in receipt of your favor of the 24th. with clipping, and I noted the contents with great pleasure and interest.

Of course congratulations are in order upon your promotion to the literary editorship on your paper,[1] but to me it is something more than the mere desire to convey a perfunctory congratulatory message, for in it I see the advancement of a friend and the appreciation of merit. I have no doubt that higher things as well as more advantageous positions are in store for you. With each step upward either you or Frank makes I seem to feel a personal interest.

You say that Frank is working hard and contemplates devoting his entire time the coming Winter to complete his law studies. If he succeeds, and I have no doubt that he will, providing he desires to attain that goal, is it not likely that the studies of both of you lying in different directions may in a measure divert the bond of sympathy now existing between you? Of course I do not mean the bond of love, and honor and duty, but that of sympathy occasioned by the similarity of studies. From what I know of you I am firmly convinced that the desire for more knowledge will lead you to research, and that you will become still more, if possible, devoted to your literary work. His study and work will lie in an entirely different direction. For my own part I should prefer to see you united rather than divided in your labors.

I know that neither you nor Frank will take exception to what I say here, and that you will believe that it is prompted by the sincerest wish for the welfare of both.

You say that the "Federationist" comes to you like a pleasant letter every month. Your Sunday page I regularly receive with pleasure as an answer, and recognizing how busy we both are I suppose we must content ourselves with these exchanges and an occasional letter, which by the way I want you to write as often as you possibly can.

In reference to your discussion of an organization for educational purposes, why not the Federal Labor Union which is what the mixed assembly was in the K. of L. and at the same time in close touch with the trade union movement. I believe there is room for widening the scope of the Federal Labor Unions which could be adopted by the Federation and be of advantage to all.

I wish we could meet some time in the near future. I would like to discuss several questions with you to our mutual advantage. One of which certainly would be the A.R.U. I am glad you and Frank will be at our Denver convention. You have both honored several of our conventions and I have come to look upon you as part of our sessions, and our chats are quite exhilarating.

I agree with you entirely in what you say about our friend Swinton's book.[2] You evidently saw my criticism in the Federationist.[3] I am glad you think so highly of the magazine. I am sure I have tried to make it worthy of our great cause.

By the way, I am strongly inclined to the belief, from what you wrote in the "Tribune" that you did not read carefully, my answer to Judge Groscup. I may be mistaken, but in order to make assurance doubly sure I want to inflict the burden upon you of reading it again, and therefore enclose a copy of it herein.

I am pleased to learn that young Frank is growing and enjoying good health, and hope that he and both of you may enjoy health and prosperity.

With kindest wishes, and hoping to hear from you soon, I am,

Sincerely Yours   Saml Gompers.

President. American Federation of Labor

TLpS, reel 8, vol. 11, pp. 379-80, SG Letterbooks, DLC.

1. The *Minneapolis Tribune.*

2. John Swinton, *Striking for Life: Labor's Side of the Labor Question* (1894; reprint ed., Westport, Conn., 1970).

3. The book received a very favorable notice in the *American Federationist* (1 [Sept. 1894]: 157).

To James Weaver

New York, Sept. 28, 1894.

Hon. James B. Weaver,
Council Bluffs, Ia.

Dear Sir and Friend: —

I learn with exceeding gratification of your nomination as a member for Congress in your district and recognizing your sturdiness in advocating reforms in the interest of labor and the masses generally, I can only join in the wish, which must necessarily be expressed by thousands, that you will be triumphantly elected.

There is no question which is so uppermost in the minds of the workers as the labor question, and I am sure your election to Congress will count a long step in obtaining reform legislation too long denied the workers—the wealth producers of our country.

Trusting that I may have the opportunity of congratulating you upon your success, I have the honor to remain,

Very Truly Yours   Saml Gompers.

President. American Federation of Labor

TLS, James B. Weaver Papers, Ia-HA.

To James Lynch[1]

Oct. 26, [1894]

Mr. Jas. E. Lynch,
Cor. Rep. L.U. 8 I.M.U.
Box 371, Albany, N.Y.

Dear Sir and Brother: —

Your favor of the 24th. came duly to hand.

You say that the daily papers have published a statement from me denouncing all the amendments to the Constitution of the State of New York, and advising working men to vote against them. You also ask me whether I have made such a statement, and if so, to give my reasons for the same.

In reply I beg to say that I have made no such statement, and any paper publishing one purporting to come from me in the direction named certainly does so without warrant. When I want to communicate with organized labor, I shall do so over my own signature.

Since I know you to be interested in the question however, I call your attention to one very dangerous amendment which practically makes every citizen in the State of New York within the ages of 18 and 45 years, a member of the militia.[2] In fact it is practically conscription and enforces military duty upon the unwilling as well as the willing. Can you conceive of any foreign power which wishes to engage in hostilities with the United States or the State of New York?

If such an event lied even in the remote future would not the people rise up and defend our country and our State? It is not that contingency which the framers of the amendment designed to meet. Mark my word for it; the future will bear out the prediction that if this amendment is adopted it will be put into operation only in the case of some dispute between some unscrupulous corporation and its outraged employes. Then the men who will refuse to perform military duty to shoot down their fellow workers, will be denounced and charged with treason to the State.

By the same mail that your letter reached me I am in receipt of one from another part of the State in which the proposed amendment to the constitution is enclosed, and I am reminded of the danger lurking in the amendment referred to. Look it up, it is Article XI, and form your own judgment upon it.

I repeat that I have not issued any statement to the press upon [. . . .] Isn't it strange that the press has kept this [. . . .]

Saml Gompers.
President

TLpS, reel 8, vol. 11, p. 429, SG Letterbooks, DLC.

1. James E. Lynch was an iron molder from Bath, N.Y.
2. The New York state constitutional convention passed the militia amendment Sept. 22, 1894.

To P. J. McGuire

Nov. 1, [1894]

Mr. P. J. Mc-Guire,
124 N. 9th. St. Phila, Pa.
Dear Sir and Brother:—

Your favor of the 31st. with vote on the Executive Council matter, and also enclosed statistical blank filled out came duly to hand, and I beg to thank you for your promptness in these matters.

You ask for my construction of Art. IX. Sec. 2 of the constitution of the A.F. of L. and also for information in reference to Art. IV. Sec. 2 and Art. VI. Sec. III.[1]

In reply permit me to say that so long as an organization affiliated with the A.F. of L. is in good standing it is entitled to representation. Good standing I should presume to mean that it is not more than three months in arrears with its per capita tax. The words "has been paid in full" admit of liberal construction and in the interest of affiliated organizations. This would lead me to the conclusion that an organization which has paid its per capita tax to Nov. 1st. would be entitled to representation in the convention.

In reference to Art. IV. Sec. II, let me say that the polling lists have been prepared in blank form before starting for the convention, allowing an opportunity for the organizations to make payments to the Secretary at the convention, and for this purpose at least "the office of the Federation" has during the period of the convention been transferred to the place where the convention is held.

In connection with this I would say that we have found that organizations have time and again paid upon a very much larger membership at the conventions than have been paid for regularly during the year, thus entitling the organizations to a larger representation, both as to delegates and voting power. Having this in mind Secretary Evans contemplates recommending to the convention an amendment to the constitution by which the voting power and representation shall be based upon the reports made to the office of the A.F. of L. on or before Nov. 30th immediately preceding the convention.[2] However, the present constitution does not deprive an organization from making its report to ["]the office of the Federation" and allowing it to representation and vote in accordance with that report.

One provision in Art. VI. Sec. III providing that the [accounts] shall close on Oct. 31st. of each year was adopted about three years ago as a matter of convenience so as to give the Secretary a better opportunity of having the financial report for the quarter and for the year printed and submitted to our affiliated organizations, and the convention. It in nowise interferes with the standing of the affiliated organizations, but simply acts as a matter of convenience and information.

I beg to assure you that I was delighted, more than I can express in words at the positive stand you have taken in your answer to the question contained in the blank. I refer of course to the suggestions asked. This is a time when it will require the exercise of our best judgment and the assertion that the trade unions shall not be made a plaything of nor diverted from their true sphere of action. The coming convention will really put the trade union movement to a very crucial test.

The fact that the convention will be held in Denver will be a great drawback. I love Denver, think it a beautiful place, and under ordinary circumstances to hold a convention in, but in these times of industrial stagnation, when so large a number of our fellow unionists are unemployed, our organizations taxed to the uttermost to maintain themselves and defend the interests of their members, they find themselves in the position that they cannot afford the financial strain involving full representation of their organizations at the convention. Many of them which may be represented, with a regard to economy will select representatives living in Denver or adjacent to it, and thus the convention may be dominated by local rather than National Union influences and environments.

You can readily understand that if the U.B. will be strained financially to be represented, what effect it will have upon younger or perhaps weaker unions.

I am using every means at my command to persuade the unions to be represented; how far I shall be successful of course the future can only tell, but these facts make it all the more necessary for you to do all that you possibly can to see that the Brotherhood is fully represented. Personality, preferences, yes everything else must sink in order to meet and grapple with the impending danger to our movement and the general interests of our fellow workers. Let our organizations be side-tracked or diverted from their purposes at the coming convention, and we shall have a recurrence of the calamity so graphically set forth by you in your sketch of the Labor Movement. (See page 38 Trant's pamphlet.)

Under date of Oct. 16th. I received a letter from Mr. Samuel Woods[3] Genl. Sec. of the Parliamentary Comm. of the British Trade Union Congress in which he says that Mr. D. Holmes,[4] Chairman, and Mr. John Burns, Vice-Chairman of the Parliamentary Committee have been chosen [as delegates?]to the Denver Convention, but although

I have written and cabled Mr. Woods as to whether these gentlemen contemplate a tour before or after the convention, I have thus far received no reply. The fact that the names of these two gentlemen have been coupled together, and the information that I received through other channels, leads me to the belief that the information you mention as having come to you is hardly authentic. However, we can talk this and other matters over when we meet and travel to Chicago.

I have written to you in connection with the trip and hope that you will be able to meet me in New York on Sunday afternoon Nov. 11th. We can go on the D.L. and W. to Buffalo and then on the Nickel Plate reaching there at nine o'clock Monday evening the 12th. inst. It is a twenty-seven hour trip and over a good road. I think I can secure tickets at a reduced rate. Will let you know in the course of a few days.

If these arrangements are agreeable to you, why not meet at the Federation office, or at Lynch's at five P.M. Sunday the 11th. Yes, the Civic Federation have notified me that they will pay the traveling expenses.

With kind wishes, and hoping to hear from you, I am,

Fraternally Yours Saml Gompers.
President. American Federation of Labor

TLpS, reel 8, vol. 11, pp. 449-51, SG Letterbooks, DLC.

1. Article IX, section 2, stated that only delegates from affiliated organizations that had paid their per capita taxes in full were entitled to be seated at the convention. Article IV, section 2, provided that delegates could cast one vote for every 100 members or "major fraction thereof" and that city and state bodies were entitled to one vote each. Article VI, section 3, described the duties of the secretary, including the responsibility to publish a financial report in the quarterly circular and to send ten copies to each affiliated body. It required that the secretary be located in the same office as the president.

2. In his report to the 1894 convention Secretary Evans suggested amending article IV, section 2, to base affiliates' representation at AFL conventions "upon the average membership during the year, from reports made to the office of the Federation not later than October 31st preceding each annual convention" (AFL, *Proceedings*, 1894, p. 19). The amendment was adopted unanimously.

3. Samuel WOODS, secretary of the Parliamentary Committee of the Trades Union Congress of Great Britain (TUC) from 1894 to 1904, was a miners' leader and a Liberal/Labour Member of Parliament.

4. David HOLMES, a weaver, was a member of the Parliamentary Committee of the TUC.

To Grover Cleveland

New York Nov. 7th [189]4.

Grover Cleveland.
President, Washington. D.C.
Without much concert of effort of organized labor the people have renounced at the polls[1] your assumption of unconstitutional and unwarrantable use of the military power to crush labor. Though the change may benefit us little the rebuke will nevertheless be appreciated and remembered.

Samuel Gompers.

ALpS, reel 8, vol. 11, p. 464, SG Letterbooks, DLC.

1. A reference to Democratic defeats in the 1894 elections.

To Robert Bandlow

Nov. 8, [1894]

Mr. Robert Bandlow,
113 Champlain St. Cleveland, O.
Dear Sir and Brother:—
The National Women's Christian Temperance Union[1] will hold its annual convention in your city Nov. 16-21,[2] and I have been invited to either attend myself as a fraternal delegate, or to send a representative. It will be impossible for me to accept the honor, and I have informed Mrs. Clara E. Hoffman[3] the Secretary that I shall send a representative.

I do so by requesting you to make a call upon Miss Frances E. Willard[4] the President, and arranging with her for some time during the convention when you can address it in the name and on behalf of the American Federation of Labor. I feel confident that you will make every effort to comply with this request.

In doing so I would suggest that you can in the name of our movement extend them fraternal greetings and commend their movement, urging upon their attention however the necessity for improved economic conditions and social surroundings for working men and women, so that they may become more temperate, rational and progressive, in all their habits, and make an earnest appeal for the support of the convention and the movement it represents, for organized labor.

You will find Miss Willard and a number of the representatives quite progressive upon the great question of labor reform.

If there is any loss of time involved in complying with this request, send in your bill and it will be honored by this office.

With kind wishes, and hoping to hear from you, I am,

Fraternally Yours   Saml Gompers.

President. American Federation of Labor

TLpS, reel 8, vol. 11, p. 476, SG Letterbooks, DLC.

1. The Woman's Christian Temperance Union (WCTU), which grew out of the Woman's Temperance Crusade of 1873-74, was founded in Cleveland in November 1874. Aiming to convince the American public that drinking was morally wrong, the organization targeted the saloon because it allegedly threatened the sanctity of the home and bred political corruption and crime. With organizations throughout the United States, the WCTU worked through educational and religious institutions, the press, and petitions for a variety of causes in addition to temperance, including prison reform, moral education, child labor, woman's suffrage, and world peace.

2. The WCTU held its convention in Cleveland, Nov. 16-22, 1894.

3. Clara C. Hoffman was recording secretary of the WCTU from 1894 to 1906.

4. Frances Elizabeth Caroline Willard was president of the national WCTU between 1879 and 1898 and founder and president (1883-98) of the World's WCTU.

An Address before the Congress on Industrial Conciliation and Arbitration, Chicago

[November 14, 1894]

. . .

The chairman[1] then introduced Mr. Samuel Gompers, President of the American Federation of Labor, who spoke as follows on "The Necessity of Mutual Organization":

Ladies and Gentlemen: —

By the theme given me by the committee[2] you will see that I am not to discuss the question of conciliation and arbitration, but that I am to discuss the question of the necessity for mutual organization, presumably of employers and employes. The gentlemen and ladies who have spoken from this platform have generally discussed the question of conciliation and arbitration, and all of them agree that organization of the workers—the organization of the employes—is an essential to successful arbitration. Then he who devotes his energy to the organization of the workers contributes the first essential to successful arbitration. I talk for organization, and if ever words of commendation have come to me or for me they have been because I have been somewhat successful as an organizer of labor.

Friends, I am not pessimistic. I do not always look upon the darkest side of life. I am not unmindful of the progress that has been made within this past half century. I do not fail to see the improvement in the condition of the worker, but this year it was the first and positive truism from which there can be no escape, that it is a crime against any man or woman who is willing and able to work when conditions deprive that man and woman of the opportunity to work. What is all our progress to the hungry man? What is life and liberty, what is the pursuit of happiness to him who has not the opportunity to earn his bread by the sweat of his brow? Let me call your attention to this fact, that last year, when heading a deputation waiting upon the Mayor of the city of New York, the Hon. Thomas F. Gilroy, and asking that some consideration be given to the workingmen, the unemployed workers of New York, that some needed public works should be carried on and started, I said to him in the course of my remarks: "Mr. Mayor, that city, that community is more inclined to peace where the workers have constant and remunerative employment," and with an assumption of dignity even strange for a Tammany sachem he says, "Do you mean that as a threat, sir?" I answered that I intended to convey no threat, but that I thought it was a truism that even the Mayor of New York should know.[3] Think of it, friends; think of the sad conditions that we witnessed in the city of Chicago last winter. We saw that which is gradually being repeated now. And don't talk, then, of the absence of sympathy! Yes, you should talk of it. It is very nearly eliminated from considerations of life today. "Business! Business! Dollars and Cents! Percentages and dividends!" Not hearts nor brains! Not men! Not women! Not innocent children!

If the working men and the working women were to blame for these conditions they would have no right to complain, but the truth is that modern society has given quite a euphonious title to the men who conduct our industries, and they are usually known as the captains of industry. If the captains of industry cannot conduct all our country so that the people, the men and women, that have brain and brawn, that have the ability to work and the willingness to work—if these captains of industry cannot conduct their industrial affairs so they can have a chance to work, then they prove their incompetency and should give it into the hands of those who can conduct it with good sense.

Speaking of strikes, I am free to say that it is a subject more largely misunderstood than any one subject that I know of. Men believe that the only existence of a labor movement is the strike, when, as a matter of fact, the strike is merely the external manifestation and the infrequent manifestation of the labor movement. The labor movement is carried on day and night. While we are here discussing the question of conciliation and arbitration, on the question of organization of workers and employers, there are committees in the offices, in the meeting rooms with employers, obtaining and receiving concessions in the shape of wages, hours and improved conditions. The strike, as I say, is but one of the eruptions of the labor movement, and one of the infrequent occurrences, considered beside the great work that the organizations of labor perform; and even these strikes, men and women who are honest desire zealously to see entirely eliminated or reduced in number. But will the denunciation of strikes prevent strikes? History has proven the very opposite to be the fact. The truth is, that when workingmen denounce strikes, when they are led by belief that strikes are completely to their injury, their attention is diverted from this means of defense, and greater advantages are taken of them by unfair, unscrupulous employers, and strikes are provoked entirely unnecessarily. An organization of labor which resolves that under no circumstances will it strike, reminds me very much of a militia regiment which resolved that upon the breaking out of war it will disband. As one who has been intimately and closely connected with the labor movement for more than thirty years — from boyhood — I say to you that I have yet to receive a copy of the constitution of any general organization or local organization of labor which has not the provision that before any strike shall be undertaken conciliation or arbitration shall be tried, and with nearly twelve thousand local trade unions in the United States, I think that this goes far to show that the organizations of labor are desirous of encouraging amicable arrangements of such schedules and conditions of labor as shall tend to peace. To urge arbitration previous to the organization of labor simply means the destruction of the interests of labor.

When Great Britain has any quarrel with Turkey, or Egypt, or Afghanistan, she simply bombards them. When there is any dispute or quarrel between Great Britain and the United States, she says, "Come, let us arbitrate." China wants to arbitrate, not Japan. And it is idle to attempt to divert the attention of the workers to arbitration before they have thorough organization.

"Compulsory arbitration?" Not if the working men of America know it. As a law-abiding citizen, as one who reveres the institutions under which we live, and wants to help in handing them down to our children unimpaired but improved, I would advise my fellow-workmen and women to rise and resist by every means within their power any attempt to force compulsory arbitration upon them. Compulsory arbitration was too well described today in an address of one of our frends to need further statement or addition from me. On that branch of the subject I fully concur with Mr. Weeks[4] and Mr. Wright.[5] I would add this however, that today labor has its risks. If compulsory arbitration were at all possible, labor would be compelled to also bear the risks of capital. Two of our friends upon the platform have explained about the relative merits of arbitration in France and England.[6] One of the gentlemen called attention to the fact that where arbitration in France was upon past questions, in England it is upon future questions, or wages to be received with hours of labor to be worked, conditions to be employed under. That is true, but there is something which your attention should be called to in connection with it. It is this: In France the question was a defense against being forced down in the social and economical scale, by reason of the laborers' comparative lack of organization, while on the part of the workmen of Great Britain it was a constant moving forward for better conditions of the workingmen.

Arbitration is not strange to English workmen. Arbitration was practiced between the workingmen of England and their employers for quite a long time, but their experience demonstrated that arbitration, so far as they were concerned, was considerably one-sided, and it is more than twenty years ago that the workingmen of Great Britain repudiated arbitration as being inimical to the interests of British workmen. And it is for that reason that with the growth of the organizations of labor there has been much more conciliation or conference, resulting in the adjustment of economic disputes. We, it appears, are going through the same phase today. Some of our representatives in Congress, and some of our friends who are fortunate enough not to be in Congress, are devising ways and means by which this question will be settled once for all. Unsettled questions are not calculated to contribute toward tranquility of mind. The question of labor is still an unsettled question, and will remain so until justice has been done the workers; and not that kind of justice when a man wearing the ermine of the Supreme Court of the United States will put his signature to a paper prepared by a corporation attorney, and then declare that he has just now issued a document that is practically a Gatling gun on paper; not that kind of justice when a general of our army, who is supposed to defend our interests, comes into a city and declares that by force of arms, if necessary, he will break a strike.

One of the matters which is seldom considered by our friends, the employers, is when they deny the right of workmen to be heard by their chosen representatives. If there is any feature of weakness more particularly weak than any other in the French system of arbitration, it is the fact that they will not permit the representatives, the chosen representatives, of the organized workingmen, or the workingmen who have a grievance, to sit in arbitration, but that the workmen of the factory, of the shop, of the store, of the building, of the mine, as the case may be, must. Why do employers usually prefer dealing with their own men; as they say, their own employes? Simply because they know that as a rule the employes of that particular firm would not as persistently represent their interests as would a chosen representative, who could lose nothing by an attempt at blacklisting on the part of the employers. I deny the right of my opponent to choose my counsel. The workingmen claim, in their economical life, in the economics of life, the same right the constitution of the United States accords to every citizen, that is, the right to be heard by counsel; and the walking delegate, abused as he is, the labor agitator, cursed as he is—they are the counsel of the working people. They are their advocates. Walking delegates have no diplomas written on parchment, but they have earned their diplomas by their devotion to the interests of their fellow-workmen.

In this labor movement there is a law of growth and development just as sure and just, as inevitable as there is in gravitation, as there is in attraction and repulsion. You will find—I wish I had a blackboard for a moment—you will find that the labor movement grows and recedes at various periods or decades. You will find, that though the labor movement recedes, it never comes back to the original starting point. The labor movement grows; and let me try to illustrate it possibly by an imaginary circle. The labor movement of fifty years ago, possibly with 50,000 workingmen organized; in 1837, with the panic, industrial stagnation, it contracted or receded until it became much less of a circle, with probably 20,000 organized workmen. With the revival of industry came a revival of organization, which could not be successful during the period of chattel slavery—but with the revival of industry the circle of organized labor grew. The law of labor growth and development was then again in operation, and then there were at least 100,000 workingmen organized. With the fall of slavery, black slavery, came free competition, free labor—wage labor, if you please—came into full operation here, and the labor movement took on wider dimensions, until there were a quarter of a million of workingmen organized. With the next depression of industry came recession—but never down to that small circle. In 1883 to 1889 there was a growth, until there were nearly three quarters of a million organized. Then, the period of depression following it immediately, there was again a recession. Then, with the revival of industry, another growth, and in the beginning of 1893 the organizations of labor extended until there were a million and a half organized workingmen and women of America; and since the period of industrial and financial stagnation of 1893, there has been a falling off in numbers, but I predict a revival of industry within a year, and with it a revival of organization, when there will be two million organized workingmen and women in America, with an impulse to obtain improvements that shall eliminate considerable of the injustice prevailing today.

You may hope to strike the organizations of labor a death blow, as was recently expected—give one good blow and the organizations of labor are crushed—but the man who attempts to crush the organizations of labor might as well attempt to dam up the Mississippi. It is more likely that he will himself be the sufferer and crushed, because of the injustice he is attempting to practice.

I intended to discuss the sliding scale, but will say only one thing in connection with the minimum wage. The minimum wage is an essential to labor. A minimum wage means a life line, a living wage; and any employer, any corporation, who or which is engaged in industry or commerce employing labor, that cannot afford to pay living wages ought to get out of business. The living wage is the first, or should be the first, consideration in the production of an article. The end of a purse—as a gentleman said here—the end of a purse, or hunger or starvation, is the end of a strike. It may be, so far as the rupture is concerned, but the influence is not dead. Though some may differ as to the merits of the strike last summer, it has had a positive result. That strike gave the employers of labor to understand that there was a limit beyond which it was not safe to drive the workingman—neither safe, let me add, nor profitable.

Some have said, "Restrict the power of the organizations of labor." I have yet to learn—even from the gentlemen who belong to them, notwithstanding they admit that organizations of employers may sometimes do an injustice—I have not yet heard anyone say that the organizations of the employers should be restricted. I do not believe in restricting the power of organization. What one man may legally do, I believe that others should have a legal right to do by agreement or concert. If that rule of law would prevail, there would be less cause for complaint, and less cause for this general irritable condition of affairs which now prevails.

The trouble is, my friends, we imagine that the industrial and commercial conditions can be confined to the limits of law passed more than a hundred years ago. The civil law must be made to conform to the changed industrial conditions. Industrial development cannot be prevented because of antiquated laws and constitutional provisions. Men are not made for constitutions. Constitutions are made for men.

There is one question and one movement to which you and all of us should bend a little of our energies. I mean the question that goes deeper down into the abyss of misery and depression than all others combined; I mean the movement to reduce the hours of labor. It increases consumption as well as production, and in answer to any objector, I would say that I would continue on that line, and urge employers as well as employes to move along and move along and move along, and reduce the hours of labor; and so long as there is one man or one woman unemployed, who cannot find the opportunity to work and is willing to work, so long are the hours of labor, of those who are employed, too long.

I have said that you cannot eliminate strikes entirely, and I repeat that you cannot eliminate strikes entirely, so long as labor's share in the production is in dispute. You can reduce the number of strikes. We do. Organization is accomplishing it. I would urge upon you to organize; employers, workingmen, encourage organization, thorough organization; and meet, as our friends have said, in council, and let us know in what we can agree and in what we disagree. Let us come together and talk over the various sides of the questions. Let us each have our men, who are honest and true, who have shown their devotion by years of work with us on both sides. Let us each plead our own cause, present the best arguments and present the facts as we can, and I am sure we will have accomplished our duty.

I regard this congress [to be] of great importance. It speaks well. It means hope for the future, when you and I, men and women who represent opposite views, can come here and talk this matter over freely, openly, and yet not lose any respect that we may have had for each other, but on the contrary make friends and friendships which must have their effect upon our general dealings in the world. Let us do in our own cities and towns, throughout the entire country, what we have said here. If you believe in the organization of labor as one of the essentials of successful arbitration, then help in the organization of labor. If you believe that the organization of employers is necessary to successful arbitration, organize employers. Let their councils and associations and unions be formed. Let us meet and discuss these great questions. This is a great question, which cannot be prayed or cursed out of existence. It is here, and like Banquo's ghost, will not down. So far as my friends, my colleagues in the labor movement, are concerned, I want to return to you and to the Civic Federation, as a body, my sincere thanks and my appreciation of their desire to do what they can in the line of right—the line of justice for the men and women who labor; and let us help in the amelioration of their condition and final emancipation.

. . .

Chicago Civic Federation, *Congress on Industrial Conciliation and Arbitration Arranged under the Auspices of the Industrial Committee of the Civic Federation, Held at Chicago, November 13 and 14, 1894* (Chicago, n.d.), pp. 88-93.

1. Jeremiah G. McCarthy, head of a painting and decorating company in Chicago, chaired the evening session on Nov. 14 at which SG spoke.

2. The Industrial Committee of the Chicago Civic Federation.

3. See "An Excerpt from an Article in the *New York World*," Aug. 23, 1893, above.

4. Joseph D. Weeks, editor of the *American Manufacturer and Iron World*, spoke to the conference on "Relations between Employers and Employes in Manufacturing Affairs."

5. Carroll D. Wright, commissioner of the U.S. Bureau of Labor, spoke on the "Distinction between Compulsory and Voluntary Arbitration" and the "Distinction between Compulsory Arbitration and Public Investigation of Labor Disputes."

6. Professor E. R. L. Gould of the Johns Hopkins University spoke on the "History of Industrial Conciliation and Arbitration in Europe and Australia," comparing conditions in England, France, and elsewhere; his talk was followed by comments from Joseph D. Weeks.

To Frank Foster

Nov. 19, [1894]

Mr. Frank K. Foster,
134 Harrison Ave. Boston, Mass.
Dear Friend: —

Your favor came duly to hand, and also the report[1] which I think very good and just to the point. I shall feel warranted however, in adding a statement in an appropriate place that the proposition of the K. of L. was rejected at the conference "of delegates specially invited by the Order to consider these matters." Let me know if you agree with this as I shall send on the same statement to friend McGuire with the same suggestion.

I am under obligations to you for your prompt compliance with my request in time.

I wish that you could be at Denver. The men who worship other gods and simply use the trade union house of worship are summoning their forces, and the trade union movement will indeed pass through its most crucial test at Denver. There it will not be so much the question of a man or an officer as it will be the root and fundamental principles of the organization. If we successfully resist it this time I have little fear for the future. If those who do not understand the trade union movement together with those who are its enemies should divert our movement from its proper channel you may rest assured that it would mean a setback for our movement, and a deterioration in the condition of our fellow-workers for more than a decade.

I propose to take a positive stand at the convention regardless of consequences to myself; at least I propose to do my duty as I see it and I can only hope that our earnest, intelligent trade unionists will view the danger as I know it to exist. Ordinarily I know there would be little to fear, but we are suffering from a fearful industrial depression, a large number of our fellow-workmen are unemployed, many of the organizations cannot afford to send delegates to so distant a city as Denver, or [if] they do send any representatives, it will be largely men who though earnest and honest yet because of their living in or near Denver, the convention will be largely controlled by local influence, and our movement will be viewed from a local standpoint.

If I thought you could come and you could obtain the [. . .] other way, I should be [glad to have] an invitation to [. . . .]

Our friend Chris.[2] tells me that he sent some organizing blanks to you, and our friend O'Sullivan[3] has a number on hand. Should you need others I will send you full sets of documents.

With kindest wishes and hoping to hear from you soon, I am,

Fraternally Yours Saml Gompers
President. American Federation of Labor

TLpS, reel 8, vol. 11, pp. 485-86, SG Letterbooks, DLC.

1. The report of the AFL's delegates to the St. Louis labor conference of June 11-12, 1894; it appears in AFL, *Proceedings*, 1894, pp. 57-59.
2. Chris Evans.
3. John F. O'Sullivan.

Excerpts from Accounts of the
1894 Convention of the AFL in Denver

[December 10, 1894]

TALK WITH THE PRESIDENT

President Samuel Gompers arrived yesterday morning with the bulk of the delegates to the federation convention and retired at once to his room in the St. James, where he remained all day attending to business and resting, for he was not feeling very well after his trip and wanted to rest himself for the work of the convention. He was seen in his rooms by a News representative and willingly submitted to the pumping process.

"I am simply tired out, and am trying to get a little rest," said the great labor leader of America, apologizing for his appearance. "I am a little run down, having been working pretty hard lately, but I shall be all right to-morrow.

"Yes, I consider this the most important meeting of the federation or of any other labor organization ever held in this country. Important for several reasons. Because of the present critical condition of the industrial world and because of the important matters to be considered."

"What will be the principal subjects discussed?"

"First, better organization of the workingman; a general movement all along the line to secure an eight-hour day; to devise plans for utilizing organized labor upon every field of action that will promise better results, both economically and politically in the interest of the wage earners. We shall also insist upon a more thorough representation in the governmental functions of the country, both in the making and the administration of the laws, not only state, but municipal."

"Will the question of indorsing a political party come up?"

Mr. Gompers shrugged his shoulders and thought a moment before replying.

"I imagine," said he finally, "that if there is any attempt to commit the American Federation of Labor to any political party, the plan will miscarry. The idea of a majority is that the organized labor of the country shall not be committed to any party, but devoted to the measures in the interests of the laboring man and the election of union men to office without regard to politics. The federation is non-partisan, and I hope it will remain so."

"Do you find the condition of labor much changed since the last convention a year ago?"

"Very little. There may be said to be a slight improvement in the conditions from a year ago, but they are so infinitesimally small that they are hardly worth considering. The term of idleness of the un-employed is a year longer, and that period has, of course, only intensified the poverty and suffering among that class. The coming winter will be very sorely felt, but I look for brighter times in the near future. We must hope on, you know."

"Will the condition of the unemployed be a subject for discussion at the convention?"

"Yes, insofar as the effort to reduce the hours of labor will benefit that class. We believe, you know, that when times are as they are now, and there are more men than labor, men who are working should not work so long and thus give an opportunity to more men to work."

"Will the silver question come up?"

"Oh, certainly it will. I shall mention the matter in my report, and I have no doubt but that strong resolutions will be adopted on the question. You know that we voted for silver at a ratio of 16 to 1 at our convention a year ago and we are all silver men."

"You are a free coinage man then?"

"Yes, sir. On that question I am a firm believer in the Denver idea — free coinage at 16 to 1."

Mr. Gompers will read his report to the convention this afternoon and it is expected to be of great interest. As to whether or not he should be a candidate for re-election as president, he declined to say, simply stating that it was a question he did not talk upon to anyone.

Rocky Mountain News (Denver), Dec. 10, 1894.

[December 10, 1894]

PRESIDENTIAL BOOMS.

The political situation among the delegates has not yet fully developed, but each new arrival at headquarters is buttonholed and asked to express himself on the possibility for president of the federation. The Gompers forces are out in full strength and are doing hard work to elect their candidate, for it is an assured fact that the president will be a candidate for re-election. A new feature in the race for the office developed in the temporary illness of President Gompers yesterday. It was acknowledged that no fight would be made against him in the event of his illness remaining through the sessions.

From indications last night the strongest opponent to President Gompers would be President Prescott[1] of the International Typographical union. Mr. Prescott, while his official residence is at the headquarters of his organization at Indianapolis, is a native of Toronto. Among some of the delegates there seemed to be an opinion that T. B. McCreath[2] of Boston was working in the interests of the typographical candidate, and would at the proper time throw his strength to Prescott.

Another possible candidate of considerable strength is Henry Weismann.[3] Mr. Weismann was nominated for the office at the last convention at Chicago, but withdrew in favor of President Gompers. It is hoped by his friends that he will consent to make a straight race this year for the reason that he is believed to be the strongest man to bind the two factions of the party. The delegates representing the glass working unions in the vicinity of the Ohio river are not as enthusiastic in President Gompers' favor as they might be, and Mr. Weismann is thought to be favored by these trades more than any other man so far mentioned.

The candidates for the office at the last convention were Gompers and John McBride. The extent of the opposition to Gompers was then shown to be stronger than was anticipated by his friends. The result of the election was: Gompers, 1,314; McBride, 1,222. The list of uncertain delegates this year is said to be unusually large, but Gompers' friends claim to see a safe majority in the distance. Ever since the last convention they have been proselytizing in a quiet way and the result of their united efforts in behalf of one candidate is believed to have been more powerful than the scattered shots of their opponents. However, they are working hard now, and in a day or two will practically know whether or not they will have a walkover for their candidate.

In the meantime Mr. Gompers is apparently doing nothing. In accordance with his expressed intention some months ago, he is allowing his friends to fight the battle and will not interfere except in case of circumstances arising which are at present unforseen.

The situation regarding the other officers has not developed sufficiently to indicate who will be candidates and what their strength may be.

There will undoubtedly be a struggle for the office of secretary now held by Chris Evans. There is some ground for the belief that if Gompers is not re-elected Evans will decline to be a candidate, it being understood that he is a strong supporter of the present president. It is possible that in the event of the election of Henry Weismann to the office of president, Delegate Elderkin[4] of Chicago will develop considerable strength for the office of secretary. Mr. Elderkin's friends also strangely hint of the possible nomination of their man for the presidency and point to the satisfactory manner in which he handled the affairs of the body on several occasions when presiding temporarily. But in this connection the Gompers men say that the work of the president is not of a parliamentary nature, but is even more than an executive matter, in the general acceptance of the word. They say that the man who has the most experience in handling the affairs of a multitude of dissimilar interests and creating the best satisfaction among these interests while rendering his decisions, is the man for the place, and they claim that Gompers has plainly shown his capability in this line.

Rocky Mountain News (Denver), Dec. 10, 1894.

1. William B. Prescott was a representative of the International Typographical Union (ITU).

2. Actually Augustine McCRAITH, a Boston printer, who was secretary (1892-95) of ITU 13 of Boston and was an ITU representative at this convention. Elected secretary of the AFL in 1894, he held that office until 1896.

3. Henry Weismann represented the Journeymen Bakers' and Confectioners' International Union of America.

4. Thomas Elderkin was a representative of the National Seamen's Union of America.

[December 10, 1894]

PRESIDENT GOMPERS' REPORT.

. . .

THE PROGRAMME.

At the last convention a programme was submitted to our affiliated organizations for discussion, to be reported upon at this convention. In connection with this matter it is but proper to say that the submission of this programme to our organizations was largely accepted by the membership as an indorsement of it by the Federation.

A number of the demands contained in that programme have been promulgated in almost every trade union throughout the world, but deftly dove-tailed and almost hidden there is one declaration which is not only controversial, but decidedly theoretical and which even if founded upon economic truth, is not demonstrable, and so remote as to place ourselves and our movement in a unenviable light before our fellow-workers, and which, if our organization is committed to it, will unquestionably prevent many sterling national trade unions from joining our ranks to do battle with us to attain first things first.

It is ridiculous to imagine that the wage-workers can be slaves in employment and yet achieve control at the polls. There never yet existed co-incident with each other autocracy in the shop and democracy in political life. In truth, we have not yet achieved the initial step to the control of public affairs by even a formal recognition of our unions. Nor does the preamble to the programme outline the condition of the labor movement of Great Britain accurately. In that country the organized wage-workers avail themselves of every legal and practical means to obtain the legislation they demand. They endeavor to defeat those who oppose, and elect those who support, legislation in the interest of labor, and whenever opportunity affords elect a *bona fide* union man to Parliament and other public offices. The Parliamentary Committee of the British Trades Union Congress is a labor committee to lobby for labor legislation. This course the organized workers of America may with advantage follow, since it is based upon experience and fraught with good results.

He would indeed be shortsighted who would fail to advocate independent voting and political action by union workmen. We should endeavor to do all that we possibly can to wean our fellow-workers from their affiliation with the dominant political parties, as one of the first steps necessary to insure wage-workers to vote in favor of wage-workers' interests, wage-workers' questions, and for union wage-workers as representatives.

During the past year the trade unions in many localities plunged into the political arena by nominating their candidates for public office, and sad as it may be to record, it is nevertheless true that in each one of these localities politically they were defeated and the trade union movement more or less divided and disrupted.

What the results would be if such a movement were inaugurated under the auspices of the American Federation of Labor, involving it and all our affiliated organizations, is too portentous for contemplation. I need only refer you to the fact that the National Labor Union, the predecessor of the American Federation of Labor, entered the so-called independent political arena in 1872 and nominated its candidate for the presidency of the United States. It is equally true that the National Labor Union never held a convention after that event. The disorganized condition of labor, with its tales of misery, deprivation and demoralization, from that year until the reorganization of the workers about 1880, must be too vivid in the minds of those who were trade unionists then and are trade unionists now to need recounting by me.

In view of our own experience, as well as the experience of our British fellow-unionists, I submit to you whether it would be wise to steer our ship of labor safe from that channel whose waters are strewn with shattered hopes and unions destroyed.

Before we can hope as a general organization to take the field by nominating candidates for office, the workers must be more thoroughly organized and better results achieved by experiments locally. A political labor movement cannot and will not succeed upon the ruins of the trade unions.

This convention is an important one, more important than any previously held. We require a comprehensive view of the field, close discrimination, wise and deliberate counsel and aggressive action, so as to enable us to overcome all obstacles in the way and achieve all the rights of labor.

. . .

AFL, *Proceedings*, 1894, p. 14

[December 14, 1894]

PLAINLY FOR SILVER

["]Resolved, That it is the deliberate judgment of the American Federation of Labor in delegate convention assembled that congress should re-enact the law of 1837,[1] which provided for the free and unlimited coinage of both silver and gold at the ratio of 16 to 1, thus restoring the American law of coinage as it was until 1873,[2] when silver was demonetized without debate and without the knowledge of the American people, and that this should be done at once, without waiting for the co-operation of any other nation in the world.

["]Resolved, further, That a copy of the above and foregoing, under the seal of the federation, be sent by the president of the federation to the president of the United States, to the speaker of the house of congress, to Secretary Carlisle, to the chairman of the finance committee of the house and to each member of the house and senate.["]

The American Federation of Labor has reaffirmed its declaration in favor of the free and unlimited coinage of silver and in terms which admit of no misconstruction. The cause of silver was the chief topic at the morning session of the convention.

President Gompers himself made a declaration which in a manner defined his position and his ally, Treasurer Lennon,[3] made the motion which in caucus it was decided should prevail. It was a sort of compromise. The Gompers delegates were playing one of their usual political schemes and allowed the matter to be passed in a nature that they expected would pacify the majority of the members who were strongly in favor of the white metal. Delegate Morgan[4] also squared himself with the crowd he was working for when he introduced the political resolutions at the Chicago convention.

The lines were closely drawn. The delegates were most interested in the charges of political trickery by Delegates Strasser[5] and Linehan[6] were in evidence again when it came to silver. Their devotion to the principles of President Gompers was simply sublime and indicated more than the usual fellow feeling. What particular influences were brought to bear upon them may be explained before the adjournment of the convention. The lines between the two factions are so clearly defined that advantage will be taken of the opponents of the present administration to use the facts for their purposes.

. . .

After the presentation of the reports on several resolutions the resolution regarding the free coinage of silver was presented.

Delegate Lloyd[7] moved that the majority report of the committee be adopted.

Delegate Kelly[8] said that he did not see why we should have either silver or gold as money metals. He thought that the proper thing to do was to have almost unlimited paper money backed by the credit of the national government.

Then some of the fine work of the experts in handling inside political affairs was started. Delegate Morgan, who grew very much excited at the session of the previous day when the matter of the Chicago political programme was introduced, inquired of Mr. Lloyd whether he could inform the convention as to the exact date of the demonetization of silver in 1873.

Mr. Lloyd said: "According to the best of my recollection it was on February 31, at a quarter before 12, midnight." This answer somewhat confused the gentleman anxious for information and also turned the applause of the delegates against him.

Then Mr. Morgan wanted to know how many panics there were in the country during the time that silver was coined as a full money metal. The speaker said he did not come to the country till 1869 but thought there had been a panic in 1857. At any rate in August, 1873, he came very near starving and spoke of the number of tramps he met on the road. He would be in favor of the resolution "at 16 to 1 or 1,600 to 1" if the government would assume control of the mines and the mineral resources of the country, but as long as private parties had anything to do with the mining of silver he would oppose the issue. He said he "would not be bothered with your miserable silver by carrying it around wearing holes in his pockets," and wanted greenbacks with the stamp of the government upon them.

Treasurer Lennon then introduced the motion which it seemed had been agreed upon as satisfactory to the president. He said that he did not agree with the tenor of the "whereases" and moved to strike out the preamble and adopt the resolution itself.

President Gompers said that if the convention was going to discuss the silver question any further it might be well to discard all other subjects and remain in session during the coming year. If the motion of Treasurer Lennon had not been made he would have felt as though it were necessary to make the same motion himself.

THE SILVER RESOLUTIONS.

Delegate Lloyd said that while he fathered the resolution before the convention it was not wholly his work. It had been gotten up by boiling down the best matter of several resolutions and submitting the result in that shape as a single resolution. He said that while the panic of 1873 might not have been caused wholly by the demonetization of silver and all the present ills of the working classes could not properly be laid to that action, he believed it to be a fact that all the panics and depressions since that time were caused by the repeal of the law making silver a money metal. He thought that one reason why the convention should adopt the resolutions as they were was because the silver issue was also a defined labor issue.

The shrinkage in values, the speaker held, which was caused by the recent action relative to silver was a trick of the capitalists. The burden fell on the shoulders of the workingmen. In Boston, he said, it was possible to get money to pay off labor only by paying 10 per cent to the banks, because the bankers had caused a shortage in money by locking up all the gold and securities. He was sick and tired of the cry of the goldbugs who wanted an international agreement on the American financial policy and wanting to go to England to get a value for money to do business with.

Mr. Lloyd said he wanted to go on record as saying that the best money we could have in the United States was a money which would be useless in any other country in the world.

Delegate Wolfson[9] confessed ignorance on the financial question but he said that in 1873, when business was thrown into a state of chaos by the repeal of the silver coinage act John Sherman came to the rescue of the country and made matters worse. The finances of the country, he said, are not in the control of the people but are manipulated by a lot of shylocks. In 1893 the money powers decided that the laboringmen had had about twelve years of prosperity and had by thrift and economy accumulated little homes. The shylocks decided to scoop them in and they did so. They gave the child a name—the Sherman bill.

Mr. Brettell[10] thought that most of the recent troubles which labor had to suffer were caused by adverse financial legislation. He favored cheap money because dear money made cheap men.

The resolutions were finally adopted by a practically unanimous vote, all the delegates apparently voting.

. . .

Rocky Mountain News (Denver), Dec. 14, 1894.

1. The act of 1837 (U.S. *Statutes at Large,* 5: 136-42) provided regulations for the U.S. Mint and for coinage, and set the value of gold to silver at a ratio of 15.988 to 1, popularly referred to as "16 to 1."

2. The Coinage Act of 1873 (U.S. *Statutes at Large,* 17: 424-36) established the gold standard for monetary value. In excluding silver, this act deflated the currency. Those favoring inflationary monetary policy labeled it the "crime of '73."

3. John B. Lennon was a representative of the Journeymen Tailors' Union of America.

4. Thomas J. Morgan represented the International Machinists' Union.

5. Adolph STRASSER was a delegate from the New Jersey State Branch of the AFL.

6. James J. Linehan was a representative of the United Brotherhood of Carpenters and Joiners of America.

7. Henry Lloyd represented the Boston Central Labor Union.

8. James T. KELLY was the delegate from the National Brotherhood of Electrical Workers of America, of which he was grand secretary-treasurer (1891-95) and grand secretary (1895-97).

9. Louis Wolfson, a laster from Lynn, Mass., was a representative of the Lasters' Protective Union of America.

10. James Brettell was a representative of the National Amalgamated Association of Iron and Steel Workers.

[December 14, 1894]

AN INTERESTING DISCUSSION
ON
A POLITICAL PROGRAMME
AT THE DENVER CONVENTION
OF THE
AMERICAN FEDERATION OF LABOR.

President Gompers: Delegates, the question of the special order is now laid before you for your consideration, it being the political programme submitted to our affiliated organizations by the Chicago convention of the American Federation of Labor:

POLITICAL PROGRAMME

Whereas, The Trade Unionists of Great Britain have by the light of experience and the logic of progress, adopted the principle of independent labor politics as an auxiliary to their economic action, and

Whereas, Such action has resulted in the most gratifying success, and

Whereas, Such independent labor politics are based upon the following programme, to wit;

1. Compulsory education.
2. Direct legislation.
3. A legal eight-hour workday.
4. Sanitary inspection of workshop, mine and home.
5. Liability of employers for injury to health, body or life.
6. The abolition of contract system in all public work.
7. The abolition of the sweating system.
8. The municipal ownership of street cars, and gas and electric plants for public distribution of light, heat and power.
9. The nationalization of telegraphs, telephones, railroads and mines.
10. The collective ownership by the people of all means of production and distribution.
11. The principle of referendum in all legislation; therefore,

Resolved, That the convention hereby indorse this political action of our British comrades, and

Resolved, That this programme and basis of a political labor movement be and is hereby submitted for the consideration of the labor organizations of America, with the request that their delegates to the next annual convention of the American Federation of Labor, be instructed on this most important subject.

. . .

Delegate Elderkin: I believe that the labor organizations affiliated with the American Federation of Labor were given instructions to bring this matter before their respective locals throughout the United States. They have all voted upon this question and sent their respective delegates here prepared to vote on this question, and if it is possible I would like to make a motion, if it be in order, that we take an informal vote on this question and thereby, perhaps, cut off all debate, or simply if the majority of the delegates here are instructed, to vote for that measure, or against that measure, you cannot change it. If it is in order for me to make that motion I would move that the political platform that was issued by the last convention of A.F. of L. for the affiliated bodies to act upon be adopted as a whole.

The motion was seconded.

. . .

Delegate Pomeroy:[1] The motion of delegate Elderkin is before the house, is it?

President Gompers: Yes sir; it is the motion to proceed to an informal vote to adopt or reject the programme as a whole.

Delegate Pomeroy: I move to amend the motion that we proceed to vote upon the political platform *seriatim.*

The motion was seconded by several delegates.

Delegate Pomeroy: I desire to tell my purpose for moving this. While there are delegates here who may favor some of these planks, there may be some who do not favor them all. We would not get an intelligent nor a correct expression of the opinions of the delegates here assembled if we voted upon this programme as a whole. The propostions are so varied, in may instances contradictory, that I believe it should be taken up *seriatim.* Again, there is another question—it is barely possible there are delegates here who do not favor either of these as a political programme. There may be delegates who are opposed to committing the American Federation to a plan of political action, and all these varied interests and varied opinions will have a chance and opportunity for expression if you take them up *seriatim.*

Delegate McArthur:[2] Now I want to see this matter decided with as little delay and discussion as possible, but I do not propose it shall be railroaded through; therefore I would move an amendment to the amendment, as follows:

"That all of these planks, with the exception of plank 10, be endorsed as an expression of the desires of the convention in whatever political action or political steps it may see fit to take."

President Gompers: The chair would say that if the question is to be taken up *seriatim,* it will be necessary also to consider the preambles as well as the resolutions. There may be a number of the delegates who would favor a number of the planks and be opposed to other planks, be in favor of all the planks and be against the preambles and the resolutions as well. In the interest of an intelligent discussion of the matter I would rule that the proposition of representative McArthur is not in order.

. . .

Delegate Bramwood:[3] I hope the motion made by Mr. Pomeroy will prevail. It is the only intelligent way to take a vote on the matter. This political platform was taken up at our convention at Louisville, was discussed and amendments made, not only plank ten but others. I believe this convention has already adopted something that comes in really in this political platform. If this matter is to be taken up in any other way except according to the motion of Mr. Pomeroy we would have to vote against it entirely, whereas we are instructed on it singly and have amendments to two or three propositions. I believe the motion of Mr. Pomeroy is the only legitimate way to proceed to discuss it and to reject or adopt this political platform and I hope the motion will prevail.

. . .

President Gompers: The question now is: "Shall the political programme be considered *seriatim.*"

The motion was put and unanimously adopted.

. . .

Delegate Strasser: I move that the preamble be stricken out, being a misrepresentation of facts.

The motion was seconded.

. . .

[Delegate Strasser:] These are entirely false and contrary to the history of the British labor movement. . . . I hold that to-day the Trades Unions of Great Britain are probably divided into half a dozen political factions. There are a whole lot of factions in the production of the national movement. It was formed of over 450 trades unions representing 144 representative trades and trades councils. They attempted to form an auxiliary, only to handle politics, but that auxiliary was never formed. How can it have been "a gratifying success" if such an auxiliary was never formed? How can they have adopted that platform if the organization never came into existence? I hold that the preamble is the boldest misrepresentation of facts ever submitted to wage earners of America and I hold in equity and justice labor organizations in America in its submission were imposed upon because it is on a false statement. It is possible that some of the factions in Great Britain have probably adopted that platform but the Trades Unions of Great Britain have never adopted it. . . .

Delegate Morgan: I might arise, Mr. Chairman, almost to a question of personal privilege as well as my right as a delegate to answer the statement to strike out. The delegate states emphatically that the preamble at the head of this political platform is one of the boldest misrepresentations ever made. That charge comes directly at me as the writer of that preamble, and in the pleasantest possible way I return the charge into the teeth of the maker, that I am as honest a man as he.

. . .

. . . There was a convention held by the British Trades Unionists in Belfast[4] and there they made this declaration for labor representation. . . . The motion was as follows: "First, that a separate fund be established for the purpose of assisting independent labor candidates in local and parliamentary elections, contributions to such fund to be optional and so forth, the selection of candidates in every case to rest with the locals in the first instance and so on." Now in the discussion that followed this matter, the question of the necessity of independent political action was the theme. Here the labor movement had progressed so far in Great Britain that a motion was made to render independent labor candidates financial assistance from the organized fund of the labor organization of Great Britain. If independent labor politics had not become an established fact in the labor movement of Great Britain would it have been possible for a member of parliament and delegates of labor convention to have made that proposition, that financial assistance should be rendered. Have you not heard John Burns in the Broadway Theatre tell you that there are twelve hundred trades and labor union men in parliament, county councils and various councils of similar organization throughout Great Britain. Have you not heard that? Is not that independent labor politics? Has he not told you that in the great municipality, London, they have completely wiped out the middleman, the contractor, and have established a system of public works done by union labor?

. . .

. . . I don't care to go further into this discussion; I simply want to say that in the statement in the preamble there is a sufficiency of truth to at least protect any man from being charged with bold misrepresentation.

Delegate Linehan: . . . That political action which was to take place at the Belfast convention, did not take place, and instead of being supported, only two organizations responded to the cards sent out, that is in the financial programme, to contribute money. And you cannot have it without money. Now, that being the case, it is a misrepresentation of facts, and while I don't believe Mr. Morgan at the time knew that it was so, it is so, and we know it, and we have a perfect right to strike it out or amend it as we please and make it right as it ought to be read.

. . .

Delegate MacArthur: . . . Now I don't concern myself as to whether the preamble here is a misrepresentation of facts or not, all I concern myself about is this, that it initiates, if adopted, a political movement in connection with trade unionism in this country. That is the situation as I conceive it. If there was a distinct understanding among the delegates here that the matter of this preamble means that political action shall be taken only as an auxiliary, as I understand that term, then I would have no objection to adopt the preamble, but it seems to me that the convention is at sea as to just exactly what that term auxiliary means and that they are prepared to accept this preamble as a statement to the effect the trades unions shall go into politics as trades unions. . . . I will tell you Mr. President and gentlemen that I have come from San Francisco to do everything in my power to conserve the union of the American Federation of Labor and to keep the virus of politics out of it. I am in favor of political action. What bothers me is how to do it. I am satisfied that we cannot do it as trade unionists and preserve the efficiency of the trades unions. It is all very well to cite our British brethren on the subject, but the illustrations are irrelevant, immaterial, "has nothing to do with the case." The British trade unionists are entirely different from the American trade unionists by virtue of the fact that they are homogeneous and we are heterogeneous and it means all the difference. The trades unions composed of Yorkshiremen, Lancashiremen, Cornwallmen, Londoners, are men belonging to distinct localities, with all the advantages, social, industrial and of every other kind, and can be got to hold together on political questions. But it is not so in America, except perhaps in one or two localities, perhaps in one or two of the New England localities, and I doubt if it exists even there. In San Francisco we have all nationalities in our unions, men who will stand together to a unit on wages and conditions generally in every craft, but if you mix politics, even a suspicion of them, the spectre of disintegration arises right there and stays there. You can not put it down afterwards. I know in San Francisco, where four years ago there was one of the strongest and most compact and efficient labor movements in the United States, to-day there is only a handful of men making a last stand against the encroachments of this very same thing. I admit hard times has had a great deal to do with it but I have positive proof of the fact that from the very moment when men began to talk about political action the membership fell off, the unionists began to disagree and they suffered all round. One moment before you stop me. I want to say this, that we are here to conserve the interests of trades unions, to do whatever is possible in that field, and when we have done that, let us undertake the political action for the reformation for the whole social problem.

· · ·

Delegate Weismann: I rise to support the motion of Brother Strasser. I am here under strict instructions of the National Bakers' Union to oppose any movement that intends to bring trades unions into political channels. I am opposed to political action in every respect outside of that political action that has always been taken by trade unionists through which we succeed in passing labor legislation in almost every State in the country. . . .

· · ·

Incidentally I would say I consider this preamble in a different light and in this discussion I do not attribute as much importance to the question whether Trades Unionists of Great Britain acted independent in politics or not. This preamble opens the way for independent political action and, passing over the list, it resolves that the convention endorse the action of our British comrades, and by the adoption of this we settle the question of independent political action and formally form an independent political party in this country, that is the question, if we endorse the list as stated in the programme and for this reason I rose to support the motion. And I claim the American Trades Union movement is not in condition to warrant so important and so radical a step as suggested by the programme. We are not in a position as our English comrades. Mr. Burns has stated here and on frequent occasions during his stay with us that in England there are 1,250,000 workingmen united under the banner of trades unionism. In England there is no such dissensions as we have between the Knights of Labor, American Federation of Labor, R.R. organizations, A.R.U. and all sorts of unions. We cannot be united on questions of political party or on questions of political authority. The only protection the American working man of this country can have is on the basic principles, the economic principles of the Trades Union movement, a movement cannot grow out of mere enthusiasm. I agree with you, the enthusiastic men who are so ready to coalesce with all political movements can enthuse but they will not be able to emancipate the labor of our country. We must come down to hard common sense, that teaches us to be successful in politics as labor men; must first become united among ourselves as trades unionists and not until that is done shall we have the least chance of securing a success. . . .

. . .

Delegate Lennon: I favor the proposition offered by Delegate Strasser to strike out the preamble for the reason that it is a matter not having been voted upon by our affiliated bodies in the submission of this question. I have talked with delegates from other organizations and am posted as regards my own. The questions voted upon were the different planks and the contents thereof and not the preamble. . . . We have in this country conditions that do not exist in Great Britain. We have the "spoils" system which is something almost unknown in Great Britain and on account of it we cannot afford to try at this time to start a political party as an adjunct with the unions. . . .

. . .

Delegate Tobin:[5] The delegates seem to dwell on the fact that the British Trades Union did not respond to the proposition and they recited the fact that only two organizations responded with the cash to carry on the campaign. I want to recite the fact that a few years ago, when the carpenters of this country had decided to appeal for an eight hour work day, an appeal was sent out for funds to assist them in that fight. Twelve thousand dollars was contributed. Is that a manifestation that the carpenters did not have the sympathy of the entire working people of this country?

President Gompers: The chair desires to interrupt the gentleman to say that money was not gotten by an appeal, but was contributed by the American Federation of Labor from its funds.

Delegate Tobin: Well, it's the same thing. The fact is cited that we have, as we have often heard, the spoils system that does not exist in other countries. Why have we the spoils system? Is it not because our secretaries and others use their positions for the purpose of advancing themselves politically? Is it not true that the leaders of this country make a practice of endorsing and recommending for positions certain labor leaders or men in the ranks of leaders for political jobs?

President Gompers: No, it is not true. I protest against sitting here and listening to such unjustifiable abuse.

Secretary Evans: So do I.

Delegate Tobin: The response is not coming from the delegates.

Delegate Tobin: I want it understood this thing is general. I don't mean to say every labor leader. (Cries among the delegates of "Mention names.")

Delegate Tobin: Because the—

Secretary Evans (interrupting): I protest as secretary against any such allusions. Mention names.

Delegate Morgan: Too much show of virtue. That must have hit pretty deep.

Delegate Tobin: The manifestation we have just witnessed is the best proof of the assertion I have just made. (Cries from the delegates of "Oh, oh!") I will cite another instance. Is it not a fact that members come before their own organizations and before the central bodies of various cities and ask for endorsement of political bodies? Is this not the case?

A delegate: You must come from a tough town.

Delegate Tobin: I came from an average kind of town.

A delegate: Name the places.

Delegate Tobin: Denver, Colorado, to begin with.

A delegate: That is not so.

Delegate Tobin: Chicago, and places like New York, Albany, Rochester, N.Y., Buffalo, N.Y., St. Louis, Mo., Cincinnati, Cleveland, O. Will I go on?

A delegate: I rise to a point of order. I claim he is not talking on the question before this meeting.

President Gompers: The point of order is well taken.

Delegate Metcalf[6] was called upon by the President to take the chair.

Delegate Tobin: Delegate Weismann has cited the fact that labor legislation has been gained in this country by trades union movement. I would like some one to answer what legislation have we that is in the interest of the wage-earners. Have we a single act upon the statute books enforced?

A delegate: Yes, sir; injunctions.

Delegate Tobin: We have heard that the labor organizations of this country are in a demoralized condition because of the introduction of politics. Now, I make the claim that that is not so. I say that the labor organization is in the condition they are to-day because they have failed to go into independent politics. And if I say independent politics—

A delegate (interrupting): I find the audience approving and disapproving of the remarks of delegates on this floor. I think it is entirely out of place and I hope the chair will call the attention of the visitors to the necessity of remaining quiet.

Chairman Metcalf: The brother is perfectly right. Those who are here visiting, have no right to manifest approval or disapproval, and if it is not discontinued the hall will have to be cleared.

Delegate Tobin: I have just one more word to say. I say we have no labor legislation in this country of interest to the working classes, and that the condition of the wage earners is because they have not taken up labor politics. What I mean by independent labor politics is not politics of labor organizations that will go to a Democrat and ask for a certain bill to be passed, and another organization go to a Republican and ask for a certain bill to be passed, and use the influence of their organizations in the interest of any one or the other of the party. What I mean is a movement by wage earners by themselves and by those in the interest of their class, and free from any endangering alliance with any other party.

Delegate Gompers: On this question I want to say just a few words. As a rule, I have found those who have been crying "stop thief" are those who try to divert the public attention from their own crooked actions. I have been in the labor movement since I have been fourteen years of age, and I defy Delegate Tobin, or I defy Delegate Morgan, who upon this floor accused us, a moment ago, of having an exhibition of virtue. I say I defy them to point to one act in my whole life, as one of the presidents and one of the leaders of the labor movement in America where I have shown a departure on a single point as to my honesty in the labor movement.

Delegate Tobin: I rise to a question of personal privilege. I want to explain myself, that if anybody—

President Gompers (interrupting): This wholesale charge against men of the Labor Movement, of presidents and secretaries of national and local unions is not true. It is not true. The virtue and honesty of the trades union leaders in this country is proverbial, except by those who are continually trying to tear down the labor movement, and trying to strike at its heart through the hearts of the trades union leaders. They have not the courage, and they have not the manhood, to denounce the trades unions which, by the way is their objective point, but they do it by this subterfuge, by attacking the men who have the courage in and out of season to defend the trades unions. That is the secret of their libel against the trades unionists. So much for that, and I hurl back, with all the vehemence that is in me the charge and the libel, the lie, that you make and utter here. Mr. Morgan once had the cowardice to say the same thing upon the floor of the trades assembly in Chicago, in my absence, but I met him face to face and made him swallow it. Yes, during the A.R.U. strike last summer when the Executive Council and the officers of the National Unions met in Chicago, and decided that it was inadvisable to extend the strike, what did Mr. Morgan do? Sustain us? Strengthen our hands? No, he denounced every man in that conference and stigmatized me as a traitor to the labor movement and the cause of labor. This of course, just like the cowardice of the man he said it in my absence, and this is the first time I met him face to face since his denunciation of me. What does he do? He sits silently in his seat and allows my actions in that strike to be unanimously, yes, unanimously endorsed.[7] Why did he not repeat here what he said of me at the time? When the committee made its report on the matter, I waited and waited, looking at him, expecting him to arise and say something to justify his unmanly and unjustifiable attack upon me, or to at least, vote against the endorsement the report gave me. But no, he sat silent. The whole year I have refused to answer the slanderous attacks upon me for I counted upon meeting these men here, and before you here defend my honor and my actions, official or otherwise, as well as the honor of the trade union leaders who are continually being maligned by such men as Morgan and Tobin who think more of doctrine and party than their trade unions or the interest of labor. These are things I want you to consider. And I want to say a word or two on the question under consideration. Since the resolutions have been adopted by the trades union congress of Great Britain, which has been only remotely referred to, there has not been a labor bill passed by the British Parliament in the interest of the workingmen of England. The preamble misrepresents the facts in so far—if it had said that it had passed the trades union congress it might be true—but when it says that it received the endorsement of the trades unionists of Great Britain, it set out to state that which is not true. The fact of it is that, as I stated in my report, the matter had been so cleverly interwoven as to almost escape attention at the Chicago convention—and I pay my compliment to the fence master who so cleverly used his foil to divert attention from the point of attack. But the truth is that it is a bold misrepresentation of facts, as has been stated. Let me say that the position that Mr. Tobin takes upon this floor is absolutely antagonistic to the position taken by John Burns. Because John Burns has stated in New York what he said practically in Denver, the official organ of the socialist party, the same party that the gentleman speaks for, but for tactical reasons does not mention—denounces trade union leaders, as it denounces John Burns as a traitor to the cause of labor and inimical to its interests. This is the spirit in which the antagonism is manifested. It is against the trade unions and against the trade union officers because they manfully defend the trade unions. The truer the union officer to his union the more does he earn the enmity of those men who call themselves Socialists, but who use socialism merely as a cloak for their disrupting tactics. The preamble is not based on truth and it should not go out as the basis of any declaration this convention desires to make. If we desire a preamble for our action we can draft one, accurate in statement and expressive of our honest belief.

. . .

[Delegate McGuire:][8] . . . what right have we to go to our members and ask them to commit themselves to a political programme, when we, before they joined, told them and guaranteed them by joining this association that there is nothing in it that will conflict with their belief or political opinions. Is that not breaking faith? I say if you want independent labor politics do as I do, go outside with other citizens and lead as I lead, as I do. I have done so since 1876, and am only too sorry there are not more trades union men and working men [who] do so. But with eight per cent. of the wage earners organized and divided on this question, to rush into an independent political party is suicidal and dangerous.

. . .

The ayes and nays having been taken, Secretary Evans announced the result of the vote as follows: Yeas 1345; nays 861.

President Gompers: The motion is adopted and the preamble is striken out.

. . .[9]

Secretary Evans then read plank 10:
"The collective ownership by the people of all means of production and distribution."

. . .

Delegate Strasser: I propose an amendment. I intend to compel the drawer of this resolution to show his colors. I am opposed to beating behind the bush. I amend section 10 to read as follows: "The collective ownership by the people of all means of production and distribution *by confiscation without compensation."*

. . .

Delegate McCraith: On behalf of the International Typographical Union, I wish to offer the following amendment or substitute: "The abolition of the monopoly system of land holding and the substitution therefor a title of occupancy and use only." The delegates of printers are instructed to offer this as a substitute.

. . .

Delegate Barnes:[10] This subject just introduced has been covered by legislation already by this convention consequently I hold it is not in order.

President Gompers: It is offered as a substitute for the plank now. It is not a question as to the rejection of the principles, but whether that substitute shall be made the plank in place of the one proposed.

Delegate Barnes: I desire to appeal from the decision of the chair.

President Gompers: The gentleman will state his appeal.

Delegate Barnes: I have never seen in legislative bodies—I have attended the sessions of a few—where such a ruling as this has been made, where subjects that have been acted upon by this convention, have not been immediately ruled out as matters already legislated upon. You will see the injustice of such a ruling being enforced as has been handed down, by the fact that if it were permitted to stand, after a motion had been acted upon, after a subject had been acted upon and according to parliamentary usage and law there should be just one other subject acted upon than the same subject, the first subject, can be reintroduced and so on to the end of time, this method might be pursued by some persons persistent in having legislation enacted or strung out at length. It is a dangerous ruling in that respect and according to my limited knowledge of affairs of this kind, without a precedent. I believe it not being germane, which is wholly unfair and foreign outside of having been previously legislated upon and I hope the good sense of members may see the point at issue and act accordingly.

The appeal was seconded.

A delegate rose to speak when President Gompers announced: The rule in this Federation is that an appeal is debatable only by the appellant and respondent.

Delegate Hohfer:[11] Where did the chair get that ruling from?

President Gompers: The gentleman will take his seat.

A delegate: Cushing's Manual—

President Gompers: The question as presented is—a proposition is before the house, a delegate offers a substitute to take the place of another proposition before the house, the claim is made that because a principle has already been decided upon by this convention that that is the reason why it cannot be offered to take the place of another proposition that has not yet been declared or decided upon. The chair has ruled that that position is untenable.

A delegate: There is an appeal pending, with no one in the chair but you, and you are interested in the appeal. You have no right—

President Gompers: The gentleman will be in order. I desire to call attention to this fact. I am perfectly satisfied to call the vice-president to the chair as a matter of courtesy, but not as a matter of right. The Speaker of the House of Representatives, or the Speaker of any Legislature, or the chairman of any legislative body, when his decision is appealed from, he occupies the chair, and there is no other rule except in a body having a rule to the contrary. I will say this: I will ask Vice-President McGuire to the chair, and I regret that I did not call him to the chair previously; it was more a matter of oversight than anything else.

. . .

. . . The chair desires to have nothing further to say on this matter, but would come to the question whether the decision of the chair will stand. The question is, "Shall the decision of the chair stand as the decision of the house?"

The matter was put and the decision of the chair sustained by a vote of 37 to 15.

. . .

Delegate McCraith: I wish to say in offering this resolution that I hold the highest regard for the men, knowing them so well as I do as good and active workers in the cause of trades unionism, I know that there are trades unionists that are socialists, I know that because the position which I have held in Boston as secretary of the union,

when on several occasions I had to call upon our socialist friends for
assistance in boycotts, strikes and so forth, but notwithstanding that,
I radically disagree with them as to the expediency, the possibility and
justice of that which is contained in plank 10. I do not believe that
plank 10, or the principles which are involved therein, would work
as it is intended to work, and even if it would I believe that it is a
menace to liberty fraught with danger. It proposes to take in the first
instance "all means of production and distribution," and I stand here
as an individual and say that that which I produce is mine against the
world regardless of governments or otherwise and I further state that
what examples we have had of socialism and what we have to-day of
government, they are not shining examples of a perfect system. We
know that by this delegation of power, by the increasing of the herds
of officialism, that the people's rights can be trampled upon and the
system, whichever system the principal party in power desires to perpetuate, can be perpetuated. We know that to-day in the Post Office,
which is held up as a shining light of socialism, we know that no one
but a Democrat or a Republican can get a position therein, and to
do so we know he has to chase some of the politicians to get there.
We know very well no Populist in the East could obtain a government
position, we know very well that any man with radical opinions is shut
out of government office. Therefore I am opposed to any legislation
which will tend to increase governmental power, especially when the
object plank 10 advocates can be obtained in another direction without
a sacrifice of personal liberty. We have been here to-day legislating
on laws and for laws which are the outcome of other laws. The proper
course for us to pursue would be for us to abolish laws which create
the evils with which we contend and battle and I stand here as representing the International Typographical Union to state we believe
that the causes of the distress of the working people are because of
monopoly in land as the primal cause and also because of the monopoly
of using that system in land and the money, we claim there would be
no necessity for these sanitary inspection laws, the eight-hour laws
and anti-convict and anti-contract labor laws. We know in the past
when we had a system of free land, and we know even the city of
Denver to-day, which we might say is on the outskirts of the country,
there is a bright prospect compared with our Eastern cities. Why?
Simply because the land around here is practically free, you see no
such poverty here as you see in the East. It is stated it is the system
under which we live. I claim we have not a competitive system, but
it is a monopoly system. I believe in the principle of competition pure
and simple, but it is not competition that we have to do with. I don't
know that I care to say any more to-day, but I wish to call attention

specially of delegates to the fact that plank 10 is decidedly a bone of contention in the labor movement and if adopted by this convention you would be running up against a very large high rock. There are many who will not vote for plank 10 under any consideration. Then why should we tie our organization to do it. I claim it would be dangerous and I therefore offered the substitute.

. . .

Delegate Penna:[12] Mr. Chairman and fellow delegates, I don't very well see how we can, at this time, amend or defeat plank 10 after having adopted planks 8 and 9. I recognize the handiwork of killing this plank with amendments and motions and substitutes. Probably had I been on your side I would have been doing the same. I am not complaining at all. I only hope the delegates here understand it. There is a great deal of opposition to this plank because of the fact that we cannot realize it; it is too far away from us, so we are told, and we are invariably called dreamers. Well, John Brown was a dreamer, and he died a dreamer, and his dreams were realized in a very short time after his death and he became a martyr, and we love to celebrate his name by song. A great philosopher of this nation, in 1851, said slavery ought to be abolished but no one would live to see it, yet in ten years afterwards chattel slavery was at an end and the war nearly over. That site of the World's Fair was made in one-tenth the time that the first mission was made that stood by the side of it. We do things faster. The accomplishments of the past are the employment with which we go on to accomplishments in the future. If the principle is right, it seems to me we are underestimating the manhood and womanhood of American citizens; we are underestimating our liberty by standing here and saying we cannot do it. . . . If it be right to own telegraphs and telephones, why not right to own coal and silver mines? If it be right to own any source of production and transportation, why not say the whole resources of the whole people shall belong to the whole people? these things of which we have been robbed. We don't want any of this legislation if you will restore these principles. Give us them, we ask nothing more. It belongs to the whole people, and the whole people ought to have it and control it. One word more. It is an injustice, it is a movement against our statutes; it was offered by my friend Strasser as a piece of sarcasm. My feelings are not hurt in the matter, but I would like to reply to that. He says "Confiscation without compensation." We don't say so, don't expect that, and whatever else has been said we are not responsible for. You have compensation to-day. You cannot deny it. A railroad corporation in Indiana took away the home of my wife's father, after years of toil; it was taken away, and he was paid the price the assessors made.

Delegate Strasser: Are you in favor of compensation to owners?

Delegate Penna: I don't care to answer that just now, it seems to be fair and I don't see why I should not be in favor of it.

. . .

Delegate Sullivan:[13] . . . Brother Penna asks why if planks 8 and 9 may be passed, plank 10 may not be passed as being in the same category. Why, for this reason, planks 8 and 9 relate to land monopoly; they do not relate to the collective ownership of all other means of production. The industries mentioned in planks 8 and 9 are inseparable from land monopoly. That is the reason why plank 10 is not to be placed in the same category, and why I should vote for plank 8 and did so and be opposed to the spirit and philosophy of plank 10. I maintain that the movement throughout Europe on the part of social reformers is not toward plank 10. There is a three-fold complexity in the movement. The first is that because a state is organized certain institutions must pass under the rule of the state, and one of these is the post office. Another, the domestic administration of the post office, cannot be carried on without the state control and management, nor can the country be defended in times of war unless the means of communication from place to place be in the hands of the government. And that is the reason the post office is in the hands of the government, and not because the people should go on and place other industries there which have no reason to be under the control of the state. The next in the three-fold complexity is simply this, that the helpless, the dependent, are wards of the state. It is the same communistic idea, but does not point to the plank 10 that all production shall pass into the hands of the state. Next our land. It has been said John Brown was a dreamer. He was; he dreamed of liberty, and so did Franklin and so did Jefferson. What did Jefferson say of government? "That government which governs the least governs the best." I shall vote for Delegate McCraith's amendment.

A delegate: In answer to my other question about the difference between 8, 9 and 10, you answer, because your vote on other questions was against land monopoly. The question I want to ask is this: Would a vote for the ownership of mines be any less a vote against land monopoly than a vote for the ownership of telegraphs and telephones?

Delegate Sullivan: I place them both in the same class.

A delegate: You place both of them in the same class?

Delegate Sullivan: Both mines, telegraphs and telephones, because they must have right of eminent domain, that is clear, and both require a franchise authorizing the owners to occupy land.

Delegate Greenhalgh:[14] "Collective ownership by the people" is a very pretty phrase indeed, but it either means ownership by the government or it means absolutely nothing. When we see that the two previous planks demand municipal ownership and national ownership respectively of some of the means of production and distribution our last doubt is set at rest and the talk which is heard on all sides about the people controlling these industries as they control the post office still further verify our conclusions. How much do the people of the United States control the post office? It is purely a machine used by the party in office to perpetuate its power. Why this post office department is so lauded is something I could never understand. In order to exist at all it has to tax all competitors out of the market. But even this tax which was specially designed to prevent competition, does not always save it. . . . Control by the government is not control by the people and never can be for the government is the natural enemy of the people. It is only in so far as we conquer the government that we progress. Once give this greatest of all monopolies the powers suggested in the tenth plank and it will be unnecessary to demand compulsory education. If you once solve the economic question such tyranny as this is useless and until you do establish equitable economic conditions any such act must be mischievous. Supposing the telegraphs, telephones, railways, etc., were placed under government control, what should we gain? Every employee of those industries would at once become an officer of the government whose interest it would be to maintain the existing state of affairs. To-day there are many good and earnest reformers in their ranks. These would be forced either to support the powers that be or give up their positions, so this kind of reform must necessarily block the way to all further progress in any direction. It is hard to realize how great this power would be until we recollect how many men are engaged in these industries. Surely the spoils system is elaborate enough to-day. Don't let us make it any worse. Did not the A.R.U. strike teach us anything? We clamored for an interstate commerce law. Yes, and we got it. Got it shot into us at Chicago and prodded into us in California with bayonets.[15] Our glorious postal system was used as another excuse for calling out the U.S. troops to drive us back to work. And yet we howl for more. Judge Woods decided that the interfering with the passage of street cars was a violation of the interstate commerce law as they carry passengers to the depot where they may start for other States. It is now in order for some one to maintain that a strike among farriers is obstructing the mails as it would prevent the U.S. horses from being shod. Give us government control of railroads, etc., and some one will issue an injunction, the latest weapon of tyrannical capitalism against the strikers in cloak factories in New York on the ground that such strikes or indeed any other may violate the U.S. railway laws, for if things are not manufactured how can they be transported and since it is the avowed object of all such strikes to prevent production, they therefore prevent transportation. Decisions far more absurd and far less logical have often been granted to prevent a strike. Perhaps government control of these industries may prevent strikes. We won't be allowed even that means of redressing our wrongs, but be driven back to work at the point of the bayonet or blown to pieces at the cannon's mouth.

Delegate Wolfson: It is expected by all that this plank and this measure under discussion is a socialistic measure. I will admit it. I will also right here give the definition of socialism by the greatest authority in the English language. Socialism is a theory of society which advocates a more precise and harmonious arrangement of the social relations of mankind than that which has hitherto prevailed. In the name of common sense and justice, what are we American workingmen made of? To-day, on the eve of the middle of the last decade in the nineteenth century, is it possible that there should be men gifted with no more intelligence than the eye of an oyster, that shall attempt to defeat or shall attempt to stop the progress or call a halt to the laws of evolution? And this is exactly what is being attempted here, and those who make this futile effort and attempt I would suggest to them that they should join membership with Mrs. Partington, who undertook to stem the incoming tide of the Atlantic with a broom. You may retard a movement, but you cannot prevent it. Remember this; you may defeat this for the working people of the world, for this year, but I can assure you by doing so none of you will have another opportunity to defeat the same again. We are told this theory is acceptable as such, but it is too remote. Let me remind you, gentlemen, in 1837 six men came together and concluded that chattel slavery in the United States is a disgrace to civilization, and in the United States of America they began an agitation which lasted until 1861. . . . I presume every one here is a mechanic, laborer or workingman of some kind. Do we own the tools we work with, outside of pincers and hammer and compass? These are not what we term the tools of production. The tools are the machinery. We claim to-day, those that are advocating these measures, that they are working on the same lines as Lovejoy,[16] Lincoln, Sumner[17] and Phillips.[18] They sought the emancipation of four million colored chattel slaves in the South. We demand the abolition of fifty-two million white slaves throughout the country, and we are going to have it, and I sincerely believe I shall live to see the day. It is not so remote, Mr. President, gentlemen and ladies, not by any manner of means. We must own the tools or else be worse off than the chattel slaves to-day. You say we are not slaves. I say we are. The only difference is, the colored slaves down South had their master. I may find a master one week, but he lets me get out of a job and I have to find another master.

Delegate Morgan: Mr. Chairman, fellow-delegates, Mr. Strasser offered an amendment to plank 10 for the purpose of, as he expressed it, of making the author of this platform show his colors. Nothing would please me more than for this convention to extend to me the opportunity to show my colors, so that you could understand them without any question or any doubt, but I am limited to five minutes unless the convention is kind enough to extend my time, and if I ask you, I promise you it will be the smallest possible amount of time in which I can condense what is to be said on this question. Let me say in answer that I have watched that platform ever since we opened this session at nine o'clock this morning, for the presence of John Burns, hoping and failing to find him there, believing he could substantiate and support me in the truth of the statement I am about to make, that relates to the British unionists. But his chair is vacant; I cannot depend upon his help, and I simply must rely upon my own and the assistance of delegates who think and act and who know me. Do I want to hide anything? For God's sake no! I want to reveal, and I have been hindered at all times rather than encouraged at showing my colors. I concede every claim made by the trades unionists of England in behalf of the movement they have employed to bring about better conditions. I concede every claim they have made, but I come to the United States and find, after all these years (and this is the 14th Annual Convention of the American Federation of Labor, and that is only in addition to the fifty years the labor unionists have put in in the United States), and what do we find? Here is a chart I have made (exhibiting a chart) that on top represents the population of the United States divided into four classes, the workers, business men, capitalists and millionaires. The bottom represents the wealth of the United States which some people say has been created by the workers. This is all the wealth of the United States, and it is divided in proportion to the classes and here is the workingman's portion of the wealth they have created. Now go ahead and hurrah for the American Federation of Labor and say this is what we are after. Here is the portion of the business men, let the business men get up and shout, they are well fixed. Look at the capitalists. Five hundred dollars for each workingman's family in the United States, under the stars and stripes, $2,000 for each business man, $130,000 for every capitalist's family, and $2,225 a day for every millionaire's family. How do you like it? You say, go back to the old country where John Burns has labored. I will tell you; put the paupers of Great Britain into a procession four deep and they will reach [a] hundred miles. Eighty thousand school children go to school in London without breakfast every morning. In Philadelphia the same old platform, the same old resolution was introduced, a resolution from the printers to make telegraphs governmental property, and another resolution to make railroads governmental property, and then you talk of another to make means of production as well as means of transportation public property, and it was beat out by two-thirds vote. The men who stood in Carnegie's works, who were foes of Pinkertons, voted solidly that those works belonged to Carnegie and not to the laborer. The position of trades unionists of the old country was made a weapon to defeat the proposition I submitted and then the very same year the unionists of Great Britain met in Belfast and here is a resolution, if you will only give me a chance to read the merits of it. I only wish I had the time to read every word set out here. I read a little. A resolution was introduced to give financial aid, financial aid to the candidates, to independent labor candidates nominated by labor men of the old country and here is where I found plank 10.* Just listen. Mr. James Macdonald,[19] evidently a Scotchman by name, added this amendment: "Candidates receiving financial assistance must pledge themselves to support the principle of collective ownership and control of all the means of production and distribution." There is plank 10 in the Trades Union Congress of Belfast a year ago and you blame it to Tommy Morgan. And here is what John Burns says. He said he had seconded—

Delegate Strasser: Let me ask a question.

Delegate Morgan: You asked me to show my colors. Mr. Burns said he had seconded an amendment of similar terms to this proposed by Mr. James Macdonald in Liverpool and that was at a prior congress. Notwithstanding the fact that the amendment—that was a year ago—was crudely drawn and in his opinion not correctly expressed, he would support it because it formed a principle that, as workingmen, they must stand or fall by it. That is the stuff for the laboring men to get at, if not now—and it is for you men, though it will take years—if not now, a few years hence. He supported it because it formed a principle which cut right to the kernel of the social problem, and the delegates shouted "Hear, hear." It charged at the House of

* Here the delegate's time was extended.

Commons and the party politicians—Hear, hear, they shouted again—
whether Liberal or Tory, whether Democrat or Republican, it is all
the same, and five or six of the bogus independent labor parties that
have come into existence. It was not a bogey, as some of the trade
unionists had represented it, for if they were to examine the doings
of the trades union congress for the 26 years it had existed, they
would find that fragment after fragment of the socialist program had
been accepted. And the delegates said "Hear, hear." They found
congress had accepted the nationalization of the land at Dundee[20] and
so on right through the whole of the socialist programme and the
delegates said "Hear, hear." If they had swelled the socialist programme bit by bit he did not see why they protested against collective
fields. The time had come when they should adopt a distinctive labor
programme. He regretted the amendment did not state what should
be done, whether they had a bright and consistent laborer on the
one side and on the other side a journalistic blackleg. He denounced
the frauds in the name of socialism going about the country doing
everything to disintegrate approved labor, and so shall I until the
independent labor party are put into existence. There was nothing
between trades unionism on the one hand and trades unionism versus
the social labor party on the other. These parties were at the present
separated but if blended together they would be invincible. And that
is the position we take to trade unions.

Here is the fact. It was agreed by a majority of 150 to 52. Bully
for the trades unionists of Great Britain in the Belfast congress. It
must have been the ozone of Ireland that stimulated them. Now we
come to the Norwich congress, and I wish I only had the chance to
read you the proceedings. It was the first thing I got hold of, after
I came from the law school, tired and weary. I sat up until three
o'clock in the morning to swallow the proceedings, so much am I
interested. And I can only just give you a column here and there and
the progress made in our direction. Here is the president[21] who has
been quoted. He must say we rely upon wise independent political
action of trades unionism for the redress of the wrongs under which
we labor, and we can point to the past year for a justification of our
faith. What do you think of that from the president in his address to
the congress? "Legislate," he says, "will become more and more our
watchword." They always used to say, organize, and here is the president saying, "legislate." I venture to think this will become more and
more our watchword in the future, until the old weapon becomes
useless by comparison. The only direction in which we can look for
the ultimate solution of our industrial problem is that of collectivism.
In the meantime all our present tokens of social reconstruction are

on the collectivist line and opposed to anarchism and individualism. And here is the last I will use to trespass on your time. Mr. J. H. Rudge, of Manchester, moved that in the opinion of this congress it is essential to the maintenance of British industries to nationalize the land monopolies and railroad lands, and that the parliamentary committee be instructed to promote legislation for the above object. He remarked, trade unionism was only a fundamental effort to carry out socialism. This was the most serious question in connection with land, and yet it had been always kept in the background. Trade unionism was not a solution of the labor problem and they ought to spend their time better than in trying to find palliatives. And another man rose and moved as an amendment that the words "And all means of production, distribution and exchange be substituted for the words 'Mines, minerals and railroads.'" He said he never could understand any argument in favor of the nationalization of land and things which did not equally apply to the nationalization of every other form of production. He said again the only true solution of the problem was to dispense with the means whereby the workers were chained, enthralled, and to introduce a system in which competition, with all its fearful results, should disappear and the genuine co-operative community take its place. The problem of the unemployed was closely bound up with the ownership of land and means of production. Plank 10 comes out in every sentence. Macdonald steps to the front and says in seconding the amendment, said it really was socialism, it represented the entire question of collectivism, socialism by having continually arisen did not hamper but accelerated the road of progress. This is the best day done by the leaders of the labor movement, fixing a higher ideal. Let us put it high above the level of the British stamp. John Burns said Englishmen justly prided themselves on having given to the world through the suffering of their fathers, social reform, political liberty and a municipal enfranchisement. What was the good of giving men political liberty, with rich men, as before the friends of the law, when social inequality, private property and monopoly caused them to be deprived of the means by which he lived. I have only a few more words and I claim your attention. He repeats the words he said in the Broadway theatre the other night. As a life-long abstainer and non smoker he declared thrift was an invention by capitalists, fellows of depraved influence, fellows of every title of property conferred. What was in trust and conferred is, I understand commercial enterprise used to promote a lack of patriotism. It was the last resource of capitalists, the Jay Goulds and Carnegies who preached thrift in order that their men might continue proud of property, their balance in the bank being in proportion to the wealth of which the workingmen were deprived. The dirty work. What had socialism done for them? Trades Unionism was the indispensible preliminary and precursor of the modern development of socialism, the work of subjugating the sharks, that was socialism and that was common sense and he stood for plank 10 and when it went to a vote what do you think? There was on adoption for the amendment 219, against 61 and plank 10 went through the British Congress! By God. It has been stated in the president's report, it has been insinuated on this floor that I skillfully, as a fence master, dovetailed this plank 10 into the programme and hid it away. Don't you men get the proceedings of the European Congress, ain't it public to you as well as I? Don't you get the *Federationist?* Friend Gompers asked me to write one of the articles and my subject was plank 10. What is plank 10? Did I hide it? No, and I say that very seriously. I wanted everybody to understand that could that when a vote was taken it should be taken intelligently and not blindly. Do you think I would try to hoodwink you leaders of the labor movement into passing something you didn't understand? That would not be progress but a work that would be discovered in a day. No, I that have been in the movement when some of you men were stuttering infants, am seeking to push this thing legitmately and not covertly. In the town I come from and the delegates know it, nobody mistakes me for anything but a socialist, nobody can listen to me without understanding I am a socialist. Do I go into politics myself other than as a socialist? Do I fight with my ballot any other than on plank 10? No, no. When we had our fight in Chicago, we Peoples' Party, we trades unionists and socialists came in on the fight. Thirty-five thousand honest voters were counted and thousands not counted were stolen and we made that fight against men that sit here, that stand high in the labor movement, that speak in the name of organized labor. The Manchester of the West fought that alone, we who stand for independent political action, who stand for socialism as embodied in the trades union platform and made our fight at the risk of our lives, because the men whose living has been in bogus politics see that their days are numbered and they fight desperately to retain their hold. But as my friend here says are we discouraged at the fact of difficulties and dangers of to-day? Will that interfere with us? No. Do you know who we have on our side? We have John Burns, unless he has gone back on us, and we have more than John Burns. Oh, you printers we will fix you, and the shoemakers and the cabinetmakers and other fellows what are being ground to death by machines, and we told you your days would come. They say to us "Oh, my friend you can't make a machine to think." No, that is true, but the machines are making you think. Do you know who we have fighting for us? Look here, see these fools, they are fighting for us; they put Debs in jail to-day. Bully for them, because these fools will make you organize an independent labor party to put judges on the bench that won't send men to jail. We have others fighting for us but the irresistible never sleeping power of progress stands behind us and urges us on. Aye, and let me say as I do, a man not belonging to the church, that I believe the Almighty God stands behind the progressive labor movement, pushing their way to spend a manhood that should be consistent with the declaration of independence, of which the American people are so proud and of which they enjoy so little.

Delegate Strasser: The gentleman who has preceded me has evaded my question. I asked the gentleman whether he favors confiscation without compensation. The gentleman at the back asked me whether I have got that from New York. I will tell you where I have got it from. I have read every socialist book issued within the last 25 years and I found in the most prominent work published by the leading Socialists in the last chapter "Confiscation without compensation." And therefore I wanted to see whether the Socialists assembled here have backbone enough to stand by their colors. They have been beating around the bush for years. They have not backbone enough to stand by their authorities and consequently I am compelled to call them cowards. Now the gentleman has asked what have the trade unionists done. I may ask another question, "What have the Socialists done for all these 30 years?" What have they done? In Germany the Socialist agitation there from 1864 up till 1875 has completely split the trades unions; and they themselves are broken into three factions, one following LaSalle and Schweitzer, the second Bebel and Liebknecht, and the third following Hirsch-Dunker, and to-day, with political agitation, the labor movement, the entire labor movement of Germany numbers not more than 225,000, and it would not number even that if a gentleman[22] who has worked in the United States, a cigar packer who went back in 1881, had not commenced to raise the flag of trades unionism. What have they done? In 1876, when the great strike was on in the city of London,[23] which cost the Stone Masons' Union of England $300,000, the Socialist press of Germany published week after week articles denouncing the trades unions of Great Britain, and saying it would be a great benefit if the masons would be whipped. What did we find? Over 600 men went to London to work on the law courts building where the stone masons were on strike. A man wrote a letter to that Socialist paper. They refused to publish it. He threatened to go to Germany and expose them. They published a garbled statement and again reiterated it would be a benefit to the Socialistic movement if strikes of trades unions could be defeated. Go to France, we find the same movement divided in two or three factions, you have the Positivists and a lot of other fellows.* I happened to be in Paris in 1888. I found a French Socialist paper and saw an article about a strike. What did they use? Precisely the same argument as used in Germany in 1876. They used the same in 1888, in other words it was the same old hash. Now we find in the United States that not many years ago the gentlemen who simply pose as such strong trades unionists published an attack in Chicago on Ira Stewart[24] and George E. McNiell and others for their advocacy of shorter hours of labor—

Delegate Morgan: I was accused through newspaper reports.

Delegate Strasser: After these gentlemen left Chicago these papers followed them. Another time, in 1883, when we had a great lockout in Chicago, these socialist friends to the number of 800 came to a mass meeting of cigar makers intending to break it up, but I was prepared for them and fired the whole 800 out. The very article the gentleman cited from Great Britain calling upon trades unionists of Great Britain calling for funds for candidates, only two unions responded. It was adopted at the Belfast Congress and does not represent the sentiment of the trades unions of England. I do not now know the names, but delegates from the largest unions spoke against it, the boilermakers and shipmakers.[25] One man said it didn't represent the sentiment of the British trades unions. Now the fact is this that that very illustration the gentleman referred to has split up the labor movement of Great Britain in four or five factions, I challenge the gentleman to deny it.

Delegate Morgan: I do deny it.

Delegate Strasser: One faction has already denounced John Burns in very severe terms. Mr. Hardie published a picture of a carriage in which Lord Roseberry was seated, and a dog was following the carriage and it was labeled John Burns. And you find in Great Britain the very same causes creating the same results as they have created in Germany. It has split up the trade union movement in so many factions. The movement in Germany cannot be compared with the movement in America, it is simply a rise in democracy and is not a labor movement in the true and strict sense of that term. The Socialists say they support Carl Marx. When he died he left papers showing the platform of the Socialists of Germany was not in harmony with the labor platform, he declared it was simply a movement to oppose the monarchical form

---

* Here the time of the speaker was extended.

of government and if successful, to change the system of monarchical form of government to a republican form of government.

A delegate asked a question in the rear of the hall.

Delegate Strasser: The same man went back to Germany and that gentleman, with a lot of others, have compelled the Socialists, after fighting trades unions for over 16 years, to change ground, that is all. There is a vast difference between socialism and socialists. The gentleman has quoted socialism. Ninety-nine Socialists out of a hundred cannot explain to you scientific socialism and I am prepared to go with anyone on the platform and I shall take their own books and beat them.

Delegate Wolfson: I accept the challenge.

Delegate Strasser: Have you the books here?

Delegate Wolfson: Aye, here (pointing to his forehead).

Delegate Strasser: In conclusion I desire to say I am in favor of going before the working people of this country with measures that can be realized within our own life. The comparison of John Brown and the slaves of the South is no comparison at all. The problem of socialism is not a national problem, it is an international problem and comprises the whole civilized world and to compare this with the abolition of slavery in the South is simply ridiculous. What I see, there is danger in this. Unite on the measures that will benefit the working people and not divide our time to discuss affairs or doctrines advanced by men in the labor movement who have been fighting the trades union movement in the United States for over 20 years. What have trades unions done? If you don't know it you ought to know it, and not continually ridicule the trades unions and belittle them. I am opposed to giving to these gentlemen the opportunity to antagonize the measures we adopt and which experience shows are for the benefit of labor.

Delegate Bramwood: I understood at the last convention these questions were submitted to the referendum and delegates were supposed to come here fully instructed as to how to vote on the questions. I find amongst men I have talked to on the questions that nearly all are instructed and have nothing else to do but to vote as instructed. I am very much interested, but I believe we are simply wasting time so far as actual good is concerned. . . .

Delegate Weismann: Mr. President, we have seen to-day a little dramatic, sometimes humorous, sometimes ridiculous exhibition on the floor of this convention, an exhibition of the pyrotechnic style of Delegate Morgan. Enthusiasm has been raised that carried a great many off their feet, but such similar meetings in the history of the American Federation of Labor, as I have had occasion to study, have never left a lasting impression upon its members. I believe the business of this meeting should be carried on by good common sense methods rather than by appeals to sentiment and prejudice. Mr. Morgan has given us a splendid arraignment of our shortcomings. I believe much what he says as absolutely correct. We know that the conditions confront us as he presents them, but the State Socialists of the country have not arrived at the reality to change these things. The State Socialists make it their business to appear not only before the working people in this country, but before the working people of all countries as the only ones that understand the question. And upon this a lot of us differ. . . .

. . .

. . . Now, as I said there are two contending factions in the German Labor movement to-day. One is growing, while the other is not growing, one representing the radical trades union spirit of Germany, and the other, the parliamentarians. In the annual meeting in Cologne[26] the question of State Socialism and trades unions was discussed and there was proposed a definition of the true position of Socialism to trades unions. When the action was subsequently taken, it was demanded that the Socialists who were wage workers should become members of their union where such trade unions exist. When that matter was submitted, it was defeated on the floor of the convention. . . .

. . .

. . . The matter I wish to call the attention of the workers of to-day to is not painting beautiful pictures of the future, but by doing something for them now. But if you will only furnish relief when it is most needed, then you will be able to bring them into your labor organization. If we are unsuccessful to rescue it out of the hands of these men who come here under disguise to cut the life out of the trades union, if we let it be surrendered into their hands, disintegration will follow. But if we can convince the workers of what labor has accomplished by organization, rather than what it failed to do, if they can realize that our cause is the cause of the wage-earners in its natural form, if we can convince them of that, the word will go broadcast all over the land, and workingmen will realize that we know exactly what we want and how we stand, and are desirous of achieving it, and how we can achieve it. I have my day dreams as well as others. I challenge any one to show me one more radical than myself. I have been in jail in San Francisco for my radicalism years ago. I have been through the radical schools, and had to come down from the lofty rungs of the ladder in order to come into feeling, into elbow touch with the workingmen I had left behind. Yet there is not an advanced sentiment that I do not still endorse and appreciate. But what is the use of us if we spring the red banner into the faces of the working people of our country without the immediate achievement of some tangible result in their interest, if we cannot count upon the great masses of our men who may not follow and who I am sure will not now follow to our heights? I have understood that of some of the cigar makers' unions, having a membership of 600 or 700 men, only 45 voted on this political platform. We know our organizations are reduced, but I feel confident I am right when I say that in the entire country, of all the unionists represented here, there were not 25,000 votes cast on this programme, and on the strength of that you will dare to provoke this dangerous dissension in the movement. . . .

. . .

Saturday, December 15. [1894]

. . .

Delegate Weismann was then given the floor and continued his remarks of the previous day. He said: I was trying to show yesterday the position taken by Mr. Morgan and his friends toward the trade unions. The argument was made that the strike had become disregarded. It is very significant of their true position. While we are not here to eulogize or endorse indiscriminate strikes, we must admit, as long as there is a difference between capital and labor, as long as workingmen have to struggle for lesser hours of labor and better wages, so long will there be a necessity for strikes. The practical development of the movement will always tend to the improvements now necessary. So it is with the boycott, and with every other weapon the trades union movement has been using to combat the employers with. If you read our socialist papers of New York, San Francisco or Philadelphia, you will find in every issue articles gloating over the defeats of organized labor in their strikes.

Delegate Barnes: I deny the accusation as to the Philadelphia *Tageblatt.* It is not true.

Delegate Weismann: Does that gentleman read the German language?

Delegate Barnes: No, but I am in connection with people who do.

Delegate Weismann: Not reading German, I don't suppose you would be a fair judge.

A delegate: I rise to a point of order. I object to such statements unless the gentleman is prepared to quote and produce.

Delegate Weismann: This is a matter of notoriety, and these so-called labor papers can't deny it.

Delegate McGuire: I read the Philadelphia *Tageblatt* and substantiate the statement.

. . .

Delegate Lloyd: I desire to move you that plank 10 be referred back to the affiliated bodies to be voted upon next year.

The motion was seconded.

Delegate McBryde:[27] . . . I have not at any period traveled away up ladders, away up so high that I was compelled to come down again in order to be in elbow touch with the rest of my fellow workingmen. I have been there all the time and I never could get away from them, they were just as ready to go ahead as I was. . . .

. . .

When I arrived in this city I had no knowledge that any feeling existed in this matter, but when the officers of the organization read their annual address I noticed there were words of warning given into the ears of the delegates in reference to our political plank and independent political action and it struck me as very plausible that it was rather a late day for to be given advice, to be locking the door after the horse was stolen, to come and advise us to be cautious of what we are doing, after the question had been submitted to our members and we are here with the votes in our pockets. I think that rather a peculiar position and then to discuss all the political platform. I find delegates who now oppose plank 10 sitting here and opposed to political action stated the "Whereases" were false, were not true, and ought to be wiped out and they were wiped out by motion, and all this was done because they did not want to go into independent political action, and then we go along and find the very same delegates that were opposed to independent action and wiping out of "Whereases" proceed to debate a platform that binds the Federation and every delegate to independent political action. That is rather a unique position we find ourselves in. Then we come down to planks 8 and 9, then we stop and get into a wrangle on plank 10. Is there any sense in all this noise? Let me ask any delegate who sits here, let me put my fingers on the minds of this country, how far are we away from plank 10 when we get telegraphs, gas and water and everything else down in planks 8 and 9? I want to say plank 10 is knocking at the door and window to get in and every one of you know it. If this question of plank 10 is opposed here simply because it is away off, what difference is plank 10 and plank 8? How much is the one further off than the other? I have not heard a word against the principle except against some individuals, say some socialists, and they are trades unionists; and the funny part of it all, I notice the very delegates that assailed socialism and claim to being pure and simple trades unionists, every one are confessed socialists. I am a trades unionist that never was anything else, and know nothing about the socialistic party or anything in connection with the disputes. We are assailed as if we were socialists, backsliders in the trades union movement. I say to you, gentlemen, it is unfair. I am prepared to vote for that resolution and I want it to be defeated. I will tell you why I am willing to vote for it. A man willing to vote for plank 10 can suffer defeat. We will exhibit no feeling in the matter; we will simply take it philosophically; we will say you have the majority, and I want us to be defeated because I see there are feelings exhibited on the other side that they cannot take defeat that way. We want to eradicate this feeling from the American Federation of Labor, and while I am instructed to vote for plank 10, in order to eradicate it and get rid of the question, I am prepared to shake hands with Brother Lloyd and refer this matter once again to the members.

Delegate Barnes: . . . Yesterday I stated that this whole subject was decided last year by an almost unanimous vote, the members here declared themselves not capable, nor did they want to take the responsibility to act at that time. They said, "Let's go back to the people, the fount of all wisdom and power, and give to them the opportunity to say what we shall do in a representative capacity," and a great number of the people have spoken on this question. Your constituents have spoken, and the majority, I believe, to-day, of the working people of the country have favored this proposition wherever it has been submitted. This may be denied, saying there has been a small percentage of the total number of votes cast to the number of organizations. That is not of any consequence whatever. The miners have some 25,000 or 30,000 persons who voted on this question at the referendum, and they voted in favor of it, with the exception of about 400 members, and instructed their delegates to vote for this. Why should not the people who made these great terms last year, and entered into this noble contract that they would abide by the decision of their members, to which it would be referred, if we are not cowards, state plainly and above board what we believe. I ask you to consider who made these propositions last year, and who, when the delegates came here instructed, used every influence in their power to try and prevent the delegates having an opportunity to express the wish of their constituents on the original subject matter or its provisions. They have introduced amendments or substitutes, and it has had the purpose, I doubt not, of confusing the minds of the members. . . .

Delegate Linehan: I desire to make a few corrections. It has been said here that the so-called political independent party of Chicago cast a vote of 34,000. I want to say in regard to that they cast a vote of 34,000 this last time 1894. Out of the total vote of 308,000 they cast 34,000. There are 308,000 registered voters in the city of Chicago, taking the city alone, of which 34,000 were cast for the Populist ticket, made up of Populists, Single Taxers, Socialists, and any other that had joined the party to get in it and many of them were non-unionists. I want to show you the conclusion you can draw in regard to it. In 1887 Butler ran for Sheriff of the county of Cook, which is virtually the city of Chicago, and out of 90,000 he received 27,000 on a labor ticket, a third of the total votes cast. If this doctrine is as powerful, if it amounts to anything, why in the name of Heaven has it not gained anything in the past five or six years, and is it not evidence that it is failing fast? Mr. Morgan ran on the labor ticket and received the largest vote of the socialists for he is considered the Jesus Christ of the Socialist party and all he received was 2,600 votes. Is not that right?

Delegate Morgan: No, the whole statement is a fabrication of false-hoods.

Delegate Linehan: It is true! . . .

. . .

Delegate Brettell: I have listened with great attention and with considerable interest to this great question now known as plank 10, which is destined, I presume, to be historical. I am certainly surprised at the turn matters have taken, there must be great apprehension in the minds of a great many of the delegates here assembled that if this plank 10 so-called is passed it will take the place of the trades union, that trades unions are to be disrupted. Now I certainly have never had that conception of the question. I do not look upon this plank 10 as taking the place of the labor union, but that it will be, as stated in the programme, an auxiliary to the trades union, a mere pendant to it. My fealty to trades unions has never yet been questioned and it has never been my idea that it would take its place. We all agree there are great evils in the land and the question is how to get rid of them. . . . I hold that when man is born into the world he brings with him certan inalienable rights which cannot legally, rightfully or justly be taken away from him. These rights are his birthrights. What are they? In that grand charter known as the Declaration of Independence we have the right to "life, liberty and the pursuit of happiness." If we have that right it brings with it the right to have a place to live and to live off the things which sustain life and which control the things that sustain life—air, water, earth. Then that man, or syndicate, controls our lives and we are their slaves, and then where are we to-day? Organize, you say; yet we have an Attorney-General who says he will break up all labor organizations.

. . .

. . . I think it is time we did something besides organize. It is all right to organize, that is the first step; but simply to organize, it is like any army organized without munition. We have the privilege to shoot and shoot at the right time. And it seems to me we should not only organize, but that we should vote, and vote men into office who are in touch with labor that will give us fair treatment. I have said all that is necessary to be said on this subject at this time.

Delegate O'Sullivan:[28] You say organize to shoot.

Delegate Brettell: That is figuratively, of course; at the ballot box I mean.

Delegate Lennon: I favor the motion of Delegate Lloyd, to re-refer plank 10 for several reasons. During the past year we have been in an industrial crisis such as never occurred in the United States since I have been grown, at any rate. Our unions all fighting upon this question, have been so diverted from its consideration in trying to keep their falling trade that they have not cast a representative vote thereon. . . . As to plank 10, as will be the case do we refer that plank alone, I am in favor of its reference because of the demonstration that has occurred in this convention. The intensity of the division as to the advisability of the adoption of plank 10 is just as intense among the individual members of our organization as it is between the individuals sitting upon the floor of this convention. And were this a local union of any trade, I ask any intelligent man upon the floor of this convention, would it be advisable for us as a local organization to adopt a policy that has shown such a strong division of sentiment, such an intense division, as to whether it is a practical means of advancing the interest of the organization? We have already adopted a number of planks that give scope for political action by our organization or by members of our organizations. I believe that the proper development of this movement for political action is first in municipal affairs. Why do I believe so? For the reason that in municipal politics partisanship can be eliminated and should be eliminated. But when this applies to State or national affairs, as would be the case if we now adopt plank 10, it becomes absolutely partisan. As to municipal affairs, as well as any other direction, I am one of those trade unionists who believe it is not wise for the trades unions officially to go into politics. I have been an independent in politics, as far as the old parties are concerned, ever since I was a voter, and I hope and trust the time will come when the organized working men of the country will see as I do, perhaps, though lots of people may not — will see as I do that we can organize, so far as our political ideas are concerned, outside of our trades unions. I find this, that in the city where we organized, or tried to organize, there were three or four or half a dozen men calling themselves philosophical anarchists; there may be some who are intensely Democratic, some prohibitionists — there are some even of that class — there may be some Republicans, but when it comes to the question of obtaining less hours of labor — when it comes to the question of getting fifty cents or a dollar more for making a garment — we must have a co-operation of the anarchists, Democrats, Republicans as well as with all the socialists or anti-socialists and the populists or any other men. But if we adopt plank 10 as the policy of the trades unions, it will be used as a means to cram it down our throat and the throat of every man working at the trade, and if he is not willing to swallow it he will be driven out of the trades union, and our efforts will be absolutely futile, and we cannot increase our compensation for our work. For that reason I desire the re-reference of the matter, because I believe it will be educational, and when the time has arrived when there is nearly a unanimous vote in our organization there will be an almost unanimous vote in the national organization.

Delegate Hysell:[29] I only desire at this time to talk to the question before the house and reserve the right in case this motion does not prevail to talk to the other. I favor a re-reference of this question and I want to give my reasons for favoring it. I happen to be well acquainted, as you all no doubt are, with the manner in which these questions are voted upon. I venture to say that when these questions went back to the miners of the United States, that there was not one-tenth of them considered the question and moreover voted upon them without consideration at all. They are read as you all know. The secretary gets up and reads them the best he can. If you are tired possibly some man moves they be adopted as a whole. It is seconded. The chair puts it without debate and it is carried and the vote comes in as unanimous. Had the way we are considering obtained among our members no such vote would have been possible upon this question. . . .

Delegate McGuire: I take the position I do to-day sensible of the responsibility I assume. At one time I was red-headed and hopeful, but to-day I am gray-headed and cautious. I have read every socialistic work which has been published in German, French and English, and up to to-day I have failed to discover if we had the disposition of the means of production and distribution how to arrange the system to hold control of it for the future on that plan. There are as many details and as many ideas as there are schools of socialism in France. Through all the various manifold divisions of labor that we have, control of the means of production is a matter away off in the future, and I don't care to deal with speculative questions in a practical organization. Some one will say he was a socialist. Yes, of the trades union kind. I remember a young man in my time, a very bright fellow, who used to write poetry, and one evening I came on him and he had this stanza at the top of the first page:

> I have soared aloft, I have soared aloft,
> And in dreamy realms I dwell.

In years after he traveled, went away from home. He had a good farm, his father's farm, but he was not content to work at it; he wanted to write poetry and become a great poet. Six years later I met him as I was going along in Connecticut. He said, "Hello, McGuire." I looked back and there he was sawing wood. I said, "Didn't you make a success of poetry?" He said:

> "I have soared aloft, I have soared aloft,
> And in dreamy realms I've dwelt.

["]But, thank God, I am back to old daddy's woodpile." And I am back to the old principles of the party pile—the trades union movement, the safest movement. What do I find? Protests from 41 locals of the Brotherhood of Carpenters against introducing this question; 7,156 members who promised to withdraw from our organization, to desolate its ranks, if we act on these questions of a speculative character. Do you mean to say by legislation that this body has the right to do anything to break up our ranks? . . . I am opposed to a re-reference of this proposition. I don't believe in agitating it in our unions for 12 months together on an abstract speculative dream; and if you re-refer it once more what do you do? You give the official stamp of this body for this question to be agitated in your unions, to the secondary consideration of other matters of pressing importance.

. . .

Now we have enough trouble and many difficulties to contend with to convert men to union principles, and why should we load ourselves with more than we can carry and offset many non-union men? Why not keep all the things we can get on with and leave out the points of disagreement until the labor movement has advanced up to the standard so much talked of by Brother Morgan? His organization, I

see, has five votes — 500 members — and a few years ago that organization had nearly 3,000 members turned over to it by the Federation
of Labor. Is that the way to increase the stand of the labor movement?
I say better go on with your work of organization. Organization
precedes education, and should go hand in hand with it, and after
our unions' doors are closed we are citizens as well as workers. Then
let us join any party, whether socialist-labor party or any other. If you
wish to go, go as citizens for this idea, but don't bring in this dissension
where there are prohibitionists, Democrats, Republicans and men of
all kinds at your work. Organize outside the unions for political party
purposes. We organize our unions, but we do not meet for the purpose
of being a cat's-paw of the socialist labor party. The men who built
us have made many self-sacrifices and hard work to bring together
the trades unions of this country, and, having brought them together,
you cannot go and say, "You have gone the wrong road; this is the
royal road and that road alone. You cannot stop and pick berries;
you must go after the heavenly manna even if you starve on the
journey.["] I have thought lots in thirty years of the movement, when
men come and say there is nothing to it. Ain't there? Look at the
brains of the people in this convention! Look at fifty-four cities where
the carpenters work eight hours and 1,521 where they work nine
hours, and all done in ten years! Look, only eighteen cities where we
have suffered reduction of wages through this panic! Mr. Morgan
cannot say that for the machinists in his organization. Stick to your
union, build it up and don't go after political will-o'-the-wisps.

Delegate Morgan: I rise to a question of personal privilege. The
delegate just seated has made assertions in regard to my organization
and myself that are not true, and I wish to correct them if I am
permitted.

President Gompers: Is it a reflection upon the delegate?

Delegate Morgan: Upon me personally and upon the organization
I represent. Isn't that in order of a reflection upon the delegate
himself?

President Gompers: Proceed.

Delegate Morgan: At the convention in Chicago I was charged by
some delegates with not building up my own organization and not
organizing. I had been working at the bench for thirty-seven years,
had never occupied an official labor position other than statistician
in the trades assembly; given up my time night and day, apart from
the shop, to the labor movement. I was a convert, a student, of this
man here (McGuire) when he was the principal organizer of the
socialist party. As I said in Philadelphia, I saw him ragged and dirty,
I was ashamed of his personal appearance —

President Gompers (interrupting): That is not a personal explanation. It is an attack upon another delegate. The gentleman will take his seat.

Delegate Morgan: I wish to say —

President Gompers: The floor is withdrawn from the gentleman for the purpose of making a personal explanation, and that is the decision of the chair.

Delegate Morgan: Will you permit me, Mr. Chairman —

President Gompers: The gentleman has requested the floor for the purpose of making a personal explanation, a question of the highest importance. The gentleman has asked the question of highest privilege, for a personal explanation. That implies that his honor has been impugned. Upon that being granted he starts in to discuss a matter entirely foreign to any reflection upon himself, on the contrary he starts out upon an attack upon another delegate in this convention. The chair has deemed it wise and right and fair to withdraw from him the privilege of the floor for the purpose of making a further explanation. Now the question is the gentleman desires to appeal from that decision. That is his right, but no other question is before the house at this moment.

Delegate Morgan: Well, then, I take an appeal from your decision. In taking my appeal from the decision of the chair I simply want to do justice to myself by completing what I intended to say, to do justice to McGuire as well as myself and to the convention so that shall not go out of the confidence of the organized body that individuals in themselves should dictate this convention. I want to say to McGuire, differing as we do, I have the greatest respect for my old friend and the statement I was about to make did not reflect against him personally, though I touched upon his personal appearance. Now I ask you to give me a chance to set myself right.

President Gompers: The chair has this merely to say in reply, that the question of personal privilege is where a delegate takes the floor away from another delegate having already secured it. If that question of the highest privilege is abused it destroys the entire right in itself. The delegate abused the right of personal privilege and for that reason, for the preservation of the right of personal privilege, as well as the preservation of the dignity of this convention the chair withdrew the privilege of the floor from the gentleman. The question is: Shall the decision of the chair stand as the decision of the house?

The question was then put and the decision of the chair was overwhelmingly sustained.

Delegate Pomeroy: In regard to the motion of Delegate Lloyd, that the matter be referred back again to the organizations, I desire to say that I am positively opposed to any such proceeding. If the delegates here could have seen, or could see the disruption that now exists in Chicago, in the State of Illinois, if they could see union men banded against union men all on account of dissensions and animosities that have grown out of this socialistic propaganda, this plank 10, no man would vote to send it back to the organizations again. It can only intensify that hate that is now leading to disruption. . . . let us advocate measures and demand of Congress and of legislative bodies, in the name of organized labor and the common people of this land, that these measures, for humane reasons, shall be adopted—and let us spread out this little plank here, let us spread out the trades union movement, catch the Democratic and Republican parties, and eventually wipe out the un-American A.P.A.,[30] who are now our most dangerous menace. I want to get a carpenter to join the trades union movement. We will say you have adopted plank 10—become a political party. This carpenter is a Grand Army[31] man, and nearly all carpenters who are old enough are Grand Army men, and he is a Republican. He says, "I am perfectly willing to join the trades unions as such, but I will not join a political party in opposition to my ideas." He is wrong, perhaps; we may all agree his political ideas are wrong, but we want him in the trades union, and you cannot get him in if he has to desert his party and adopt the policy of a new political party founded on theory, existing nowhere, in fact, and advocating against everything for which he fought during the war.* The Democrat is the same; the Populists are in many cases the same. Now, my friends, something concerning socialism. Let us advance trades unions until such time as we can display our political power, and this we all know now would only demonstrate our weakness, as has been done in this last election.

. . .

. . . The Socialists are very inconsistent. The whole framework of the propaganda is built up from interlaying laths of inconsistencies. Railing against corporations on account of its extensive power, they would further extend its power. That is inconsistency. Railing against monopoly they would build up a gigantic monopoly so powerful that no people could resist its operation, and this is the retrospection methods and inconsistencies of politics. Just the same railing against the old political parties. Have they ever done anything in the history of the socialistic labor party to prove they either have or are entitled to the confidence of the masses of the people? Carrying insidiously

* Here the time of the speaker was extended.

their politics into labor organizations, they have branded men who have refused to adopt their policies as traitors to the cause of labor. They slander them behind their backs, publish letters in their official organs concerning these men, and have even gone so far as to suggest conspiracy, and seek to expel them from the organization. Do we want men like that in control of political movements, and unless they could control it they would desert it, unless they can rule they will ruin? They have had it everywhere. It is their whole science. . . . My friends and fellow delegates, anything that tends to lessen the individual acts of man is opposed to liberty, anything that tends to destroy in man that ambition which is the guiding star of progress is opposed to liberty and progress. Imagine that beautiful condition of things wherein we are all brothers and we are all on a level and all getting our orders from the general sanitary bureau over which my friend Morgan would preside or there would be no sanitary bureau. Imagine the dead level of mediocrity to which we must descend, no hope to the few except a bloody revolution. The brains of the people would leave the land, they would fly to other lands or be thrown into jail for refusing to accept the situation the Socialist would furnish us with. You have not public opinion with you on this question and you never will have. There never will come a time in the history of this world intelligent as it is now and traveling towards an intelligence, when men of brains and sense, men of discretion, men of manhood, will permit socialism to rule in the land. Elimination alone of a chance to succeed, the desire in human nature to rise above common level will defeat it, no matter how beautiful they predict the storms or how accurately they may draw the rain above.

. . .

. . . Now this one last point. It was impossible under the submission of the programme, under the manner of its submission to get a fair test vote. If it was the case of only one candidate in the field, single tax, which is in reasonable bounds and is the proper antidote for this question, the abolition of land monopoly which will give you your money and your home and place the land at the disposal of those who are homeless and struggling, if single tax was submitted to the people, because single tax is the winning candidate before the American trade unionists to-day and place beside it plank 10 it would come back a victor by a thousand-fold vote. . . .

. . .

Delegate Mahon:[32] . . . I don't know how serious this question may be to you, gentlemen, to me it is a serious question, it is a question that I have considered, that I sat up at four o'clock this morning to consider. I went into the labor movement when I was a boy in the miners' union, and I have followed the trades unions all my life. I am still interested in the trades union movement and intend to be, I want to say. As McGuire says, I am a Socialist and I don't deny it. I have come up in the ranks of trades unionism and studied socialism according to the ideas of socialism and trades unionism, and I want to say here to-day, for the benefit of all, that I am not a Socialist after the stripe of that class of people who march in the procession of the Socialist Labor Party, not of that specific kind held out to the people of New York. I want that to be understood, with that class of Socialist I have no truck. I believed in these great questions years ago. I began to study them and often thought in discussing prison labor it was my duty to oppose the present style of boycotting labor. I thought it my duty to go further and boycott prisons. The importance of this movement is what I want to look at. I don't care to attack any of my friends. I like them on both sides. We have been fighting side by side. We have now come to a time when it appears to me that we may follow the Knights of Labor in so far that there is to be a split. We have got to a certain point in this movement and that is there is a split which I and you should look after, consider and prevent. You are at a point where the trades union is about to be split asunder and there is no denying it. I came up with instructions, but if I disregard them, I don't answer to this body, but to the people that sent me here. I don't care what the thoughts may be or what may be said in regard to my position in this convention or before this convention. I am answerable to the organization that sent me here. If I come down here and see the situation here and did not do my duty I should feel they ought to condemn me. I think it time we dropped this question. I believe in socialism, but not in that kind of socialism that wants to cram it down my fellow man's throat. It is not socialism, it is not the principles of socialism. The principles of socialism, as I understand them, are the very principles of liberty and the brotherhood of labor. . . .

. . .

Delegate Penna: . . . It is not fair to say that we have come here to break down trades unions. My friend Hysell said that last night. He did not say it deliberately. Anyone who knows him intimately never accuses him of the crime of deliberation. My friend Weismann said this morning the object of plank 10 was to disrupt trades unions. He did not believe it when he said it. It is one of those statements not made after thought and deliberation, but said on the impulse of the moment—simply made under the excitement of debate. It is not true, however, that the object of that plank is to disrupt trades unions. We are trade unionists first, last and all the time, but we believe that trades unionism should progress into open and adequate fields.* There is one class of privations we can remove by trades unionism. There is another class that can only be removed by political action, and we cannot remove anything by politics without going into politics. It is the science of government, and is not trickery and skulduggery, as most of our delegates have been in the habit of thinking. . . .

. . .

President Gompers: The written question asked by Delegate McBryde was this: "The national organizations attached to the American Federation of Labor, having complete autonomy, can the American Federation of Labor by motion, vote or otherwise impose upon its members any political platform in direct opposition to the wishes of the members." My answer is this: "The American Federation of Labor is a voluntary organization, the resolutions or platforms adopted by it at its conventions are expressive of the consensus of the opinion of the majority of the organized workers affiliated with it. The resolutions and platforms adopted cannot be *imposed* upon any affiliated organization against its wishes, but they are presumed to be observed by all organizations."

Delegate O'Sullivan: . . . My attention was called forcibly to the question of trades unionism and political action at the Detroit convention of this organization in 1890, when the Executive Council refused the charter to a political organization, practically the socialistic labor party. That matter was carried into the convention of the Federation of Labor in Detroit, and from that time on we have had more or less trouble.† We have had our legs pulled, so to speak; have been used for propaganda purposes by the socialistic labor party. Yes, they have imported men from other countries to come in here and tell us not only how to conduct our industrial but our political affairs. A man who can hardly speak the English language. From that time down to this the trades unionists who opposed the introduction of a political party into the Federation of Labor were denounced; were called boodlers, and I see among the list the names of men best known by us for their honor, their honesty and devotion to the cause of labor— Gompers, McNiell, McGuire, Foster. They were denounced as boodlers, and it is an open secret, in fact, that the slogan had gone out to stab the men in the back who had gone out to sustain the Executive Council who had refused the demand of the political party. The attack

* Here the speaker's time was extended.
† Here the time of the speaker was extended.

was a bitter one. Wherever we attempted to speak or organize a trades union, members wearing red neckties or the red badge of the socialistic party came into our meeting and did everything in their power to disrupt our meetings, particularly when we attempted to organize. . . .

. . .

Delegate McBryde: I rise to a point of order.

The delegate thereupon read the President's reply to Delegate McBryde, and added: Is the question before the house in conformity with the Constitution of the American Federation of Labor, and if not, is the present discussion in order?

President Gompers: The delegate cannot shift the entire responsibility upon the shoulders of the chair. If the delegate is opposed to the matter he should speak and vote against it. The chair declines to rule it out of order.

Delegate Lloyd: . . . I am a trades unionist. I believe in it. I will never stand up and condemn it. It will hurt our movement in Mass., the New England States. Do you know that we can scarcely approach the native Yankee yet to get him into the trades union because they say it is a foreign institution, but if we introduce the tenth plank at this time how do we expect we will reach them? We cannot do it. Not only that, but in every university there are professors, such as Ely,[33] Bailey, Bemis and others that can scarcely hold their jobs. You put the tenth plank in and advocate trades unionism and we will not have a professor in the colleges. There never was a time when we could so readily get the attention of the so-called "better classes." To-day on my way home I am billed to speak at Cornell, and I have also been invited to speak at Chicago, and who invited me? A man like W. R. Sterling, vice-president at Joliet. Still, if we get these men interested the socialists will say, "You are creeping." I am prepared to pander and creep at the feet of any man or movement if I can use him and educate him in this trades union movement for the working classes of this country. I am prepared to use his or anybody's influence, but you cannot touch these people if you put this plank in your platform. . . .

. . .

Delegate Cohen:[34] Mr. President, if the question is to refer I am opposed to it for this reason. I don't think it will do any good to the trades unions of this country to have the question referred for another year or two or three years to have discussions on a question proposed wherein it is supposed the State can carry everything. The good people seem to think the State can carry everything. They are like the bad child who has burnt fingers and runs to its mother for help, and so they run to our grandmother, the government for every single thing, they run to her notwithstanding the fact that she never gave up any thing and the only thing they ever have achieved was through trades unionism. . . .

. . .

Delegate Tobin then resumed the discussion on plank 10. He said: I don't intend to consume much time. There is one thing I want to draw your attention to. In the first place it has been stated by a number of delegates that socialists are endeavoring to enforce their peculiar ideas in trades organizations. It is not the fact. Socialism is the product of labor organization and began in labor organization in the first place. People who have been imbued with that idea have not the idea of trades unions on the old lines. I take it they are seeking for broader grounds and are looking for the right, and notwithstanding what action may be taken in regard to plank 10 justice will come in. It is not our desire to throw this down the throats of anybody. I believe this movement is going on and is bound to come to the front, and as was remarked yesterday, it is impossible to stop it, it is like endeavoring to sweep back the waves of the Atlantic Ocean with a broom. It is also claimed it will disrupt labor organizations. It will not. But it will the old labor parties, and that is where the fear exists among laboring men in this country. . . .

. . .

Secretary Evans then read plank 10 and the various substitutes and motions pending before the house.

Delegate Lloyd's substitute to refer the plank back to affiliated organizations to be discussed during the coming year was put and lost.

. . .

The question then recurred on Delegate McCraith's substitute, "The abolition of the monopoly system of land holding and the substituting therefor of a title of occupancy and use only."

The vote resulted on a roll call as follows: 1,217 ayes, 913 nays. . . .

. . .

Secretary Evans then read the resolution attached to the platform: "*Resolved,* That this convention hereby endorses this political action of our British comrades."

Delegate Pomeroy: I amend that to read as follows:

"That the convention hereby endorses the above planks as a whole," referring to the ones we have adopted.

The motion was seconded.

. . .

President Gompers: The chair desires to explain the situation, and thinks you will see the force of it. A bill before Congress is introduced. It is considered, and amended, and changed, and substituted and so forth, and at this last stage of the proceedings a member arises and moves to strike out the enacting clause or to adopt the bill as amended. If that motion is adopted, to strike out the enacting clause, or the motion to adopt the bill as amended fails, the bill is defeated. The question now is that these various planks have been adopted, and now the proposition is to endorse them as a whole. If that is defeated that strikes at them all and defeats them all as a programme. The chair thinks the explanation will show you there is not at least on the part of the chair any other desire than that the matter may be fully understood. The chair cannot question the motives of any delegate, nor has he a right to asperse them, but the motion is to adopt them as a whole, and to vote that down is to defeat them.

. . .

Delegate Pomeroy's resolution was then put to the vote.

Secretary Evans announced the result of the vote as follows: Ayes, 735; nays, 1,173.

. . .

The question then recurred upon the original resolution which was lost.

. . .

A delegate: I move we close all debate on this political platform and go on with other business.

Delegate McCraith: Would it not be better to have definite postponement, so it would be brought up again? I move that as an amendment that the whole matter be definitely postponed.

The motion was seconded.

A delegate: We have adopted these planks *seriatim;* we have refused to accept it as a whole. Where do we stand? Why not adopt this resolution, or, if necessary, I will move to re-consider plank 10.

Delegate McCraith: I insist on my motion that the whole matter be definitely postponed. The motion was seconded and adopted.

. . .

AFL, *A Verbatim Report of the Discussion on the Political Programme, at the Denver Convention of the American Federation of Labor, December 14, 15, 1894. (Reported by an Expert Stenographer.)* (New York, 1895), pp. 1, 3-13, 25-48, 50-52, 56-57, 59, 61-64.

1. William C. Pomeroy represented AFL Phoenix FLU 6257 of Chicago.

2. Walter MACARTHUR, business manager (1891-94) and editor (1895-1900, 1901-13) of the *Coast Seamen's Journal,* represented the San Francisco Labor Council.

3. John W. BRAMWOOD, a printer, was president of International Typographical Union (ITU) 49 of Denver from 1895 to 1896, and was one of the ITU's representatives at this convention.

4. The Trades Union Congress of Great Britain (TUC) met in Belfast, Ireland, Sept. 4-9, 1893.

5. John F. TOBIN, a Rochester, N.Y., shoe worker, was the delegate of the Boot and Shoe Workers' International Union.

6. Richard Henry METCALF was chairman of the Executive Board of the Iron Molder's Union of North America (IMUNA) from 1890 to 1895 and was a representative of the IMUNA at this convention.

7. In his report to the convention SG discussed the "considerable adverse criticism" directed at himself and the AFL Executive Council because of their decision not to order a general strike in support of the Pullman boycott. "We have the right to and do insist that this convention shall in emphatic terms either approve or disapprove the course taken by us," he told the convention. "I shall certainly accept your verdict as either a vote of confidence or a want of confidence" (AFL, *Proceedings,* 1894, p. 11). The convention unanimously approved a resolution endorsing their action.

8. P. J. McGuire was a representative of the United Brotherhood of Carpenters and Joiners of America.

9. The delegates then discussed and voted on the first nine planks of the political program. Planks 1, 4, 5, 6, 7, and 9 were adopted without amendment. Planks 2 and 11 were combined to read, "Direct legislation through the initiative and referendum," and were adopted as plank 2. Plank 3 was amended to read, "A legal work day of not more than eight hours" and plank 8 was amended to read, "Municipal ownership of street cars, water works, gas and electric plants"; both were then adopted.

10. John Mahlon Barnes was a representative of the CMIU.

11. Philip A. Hofher, a member of St. Louis CMIU 44, represented the St. Louis Central Trades and Labor Union.

12. Philip H. Penna was a representative of the United Mine Workers of America (UMWA).

13. James W. Sullivan represented the New York State Branch of the AFL.

14. Charles Greenhalgh of Denver represented AFL Core Makers' Union 6355.

15. Workers on the Southern and Central Pacific railways in California stopped handling Pullman cars on June 27, 1894, in response to the American Railway Union boycott. Within a few days rail traffic in California was tied up by work stoppages and raids on company property. Two regiments of state militia entered the struggle in Sacramento, and a series of clashes followed. One striker was shot, and the sabotage of a train escorted by the military led to the death of an engineer and four soldiers. The strike collapsed on July 16, after which 130 strikers were arrested on various charges. Most of those arrested were eventually released. One, S. F. Worden, was sentenced to be hanged for murder as a result of the sabotage incident, but his sentence was commuted to life imprisonment after a mass petition campaign by California unions. The railroads maintained a blacklist of union members until 1896.

16. A reference either to Owen Lovejoy (1811-64), an Illinois Congregational minister and abolitionist who served as a Republican in the Illinois legislature in 1854 and as a U.S. congressman from 1857 until his death, or to his brother Elijah, who was killed in 1837 by a mob in Alton, Ill., because of his abolitionist sentiments.

17. Charles Sumner (1811-74), a Massachusetts abolitionist leader, was elected to

the U.S. Senate in 1851 as a Democratic and Free Soil candidate; in subsequent elections he ran as a Republican, serving until his death.

18. Wendell Phillips.

19. James Ramsay MacDonald (1866-1937) was a member of the Executive Committee of the Fabian Society (1894-1900) and of the Independent Labour party. He later served as a Labour party Member of Parliament (1906-18, 1922-35) and as prime minister of Great Britain (1924, 1929-35).

20. The Trades Union Congress of Great Britain met in Dundee, Sept. 2-7, 1889.

21. Frank Delves, president of the Norwich and District Trades and Labour Council and a member of the Amalgamated Society of Engineers, presided over the 1894 meeting of the TUC.

22. Johann Adolph von ELM.

23. Members of the stonemasons' union went on strike against contractors building new law courts in London in July 1877, demanding increased wages and a reduction in hours; the strike spread, eventually involving builders throughout the country. The importation of German strikebreakers by building contractors helped to defeat the eight-month strike, which concluded in March 1878.

24. Ira STEWARD was a leader of the eight-hour movement.

25. The United Society of Boilermakers and Iron Shipbuilders, founded in 1832, was the strongest union in the British engineering, metal, and shipbuilding trades in the 1890s. Among wooden shipbuilders, the Associated Society of Shipwrights, founded in 1882, had the largest membership.

26. During the annual conference of the Sozialistische Arbeiterpartei Deutschlands (Socialist Labor Party of Germany [SAPD]) in Cologne in November 1893, delegates debated whether unions should be subordinated to the SAPD as auxiliaries to the socialist political movement or operate independently and emphasize economic improvements. Carl Legien, leader of the Generalkommission der Gewerkschaften Deutschlands (General Commission of German Trade Unions), advocated the independent economic position in opposition to the views of August Bebel and other party leaders.

27. Patrick McBryde was a representative of the UMWA.

28. John F. O'Sullivan represented AFL Federal Labor Union (FLU) 5915 of Boston.

29. Nial R. HYSELL, an Ohio miner, was a representative of the UMWA.

30. The American Protective Association (APA), a secret, anti-Catholic society, was founded in Clinton, Iowa, in 1887. It received much of its early support from disaffected KOL members opposed to the power of Catholics in the Order and in politics and from railroad workers feeling the competition of Irish laborers. Its main strength lay in the urban areas of the Midwest, but during the depression that began in 1893 it made headway in cities of the East and the West and grew to a membership of about one million. APA members boycotted Catholic-owned businesses and discriminated against Catholics in hiring. Its program included support for the free public school system, immigration restriction, and a prolonged period of naturalization. After 1894 internal factionalism weakened the organization, and it had disintegrated by the end of the decade.

31. The Grand Army of the Republic, a Civil War veterans' mutual benefit association, was founded in 1863. By the mid-1880s it had become a powerful lobbying group particularly concerned with veterans' pensions, and was allied with the Republican party.

32. William D. MAHON was president of the Amalgamated Association of Street Railway Employes of America (after 1903 the Amalgamated Association of Street

and Electric Railway Employes of America) from 1893 to 1946, and represented that union at the convention.

33. Richard Theodore ELY was director of the University of Wisconsin's School of Economics, Political Science, and History.

34. Henry L. Cohen, the recording and corresponding secretary for Denver Journeymen Tailors' Union of America (JTUA) 3, was a JTUA delegate at this convention.

[December 18, 1894]

GOMPERS NOT IN IT.

The battle at the morning session was between the Gompers forces and the opposition, composed largely of the socialistic element of the convention. After the smoke of conflict had cleared away there remained little of the proud array of Gompers men. The socialists had won and Gompers was beaten. About the only Gompers men elected were P. J. McGuire, first vice president, and John B. Lennon, treasurer. The others, with the president, were left in the cold. As a foretaste of the defeat which followed, the headquarters of the federation were moved to a city against which President Gompers was unalterably opposed and the city of his choice was left. It was a sweep, the results of which organized labor affiliated with the federation will await with some wonder. The element against which Gompers has waged fierce war almost since the inception of the organization will now be in control, and, though President Gompers offers his mightiest efforts in behalf of the incoming administration, the policy will not be as in the past.

After the routine business of opening the session was dispensed with the matter of a new location for the headquarters was taken up.

The name of Louisville was withdrawn, leaving the fight between Washington, Indianapolis and Brooklyn—the latter being out of the race, however. The result of the vote was: Indianapolis, 1,290, Washington, 929, and Brooklyn, 8.[1] The names of the delegates voting for Washington displayed almost the strength of the vote for President Gompers. The delegates representing the largest number of individual votes were against him. An effort was made to prevent the removal of the headquarters for a period of three or five years, but the convention declined to take action that future conventions could change at will.

THE ELECTION IN ORDER.

On motion of Delegate Allen,[2] seconded by Delegate McCallin,[3] the convention then took up the matter of election of officers. President Gompers called President Prescott of the International Typographical union to the chair.

Delegate Eickhoff,[4] amid some applause, placed in nomination the name of President Gompers.

Delegate Penna who last year made the same nomination, placed before the convention the name of John McBride. This brought cheers from the majority and sealed the doom of the administration. The nomination was seconded by Delegate Cohen of the Journeymen Tailors' union.

Delegate Tracey[5] placed in nomination the name of E. L. Daly,[6] who withdrew in favor of President Gompers. A. McCraith of Boston was also nominated, but withdrew in favor of Gompers. Several members were absent when the roll was called and desired to vote after the ballot was closed. The chair decided otherwise and time was lost in taking an ineffectual appeal to the convention.

The ballot resulted as follows:

For Gompers. . . 937.

For McBride. . . 1,162.[7]

The ballot disclosed several changes since last year's election. For instance, P. J. McGuire, who last year voted for McBride and who also when nominated for the office of president at Chicago withdrew in favor of McBride, was yesterday among the friends of President Gompers. Others were Valentine,[8] Brettell and Fox.[9]

After the result of the ballot had been announced President Gompers moved that the election of McBride be made unanimous. This was agreed to and so recorded.[10] There were no remarks or demonstrations beyond applause when the election of a successor to Gompers was known, the delegates waiting for more game before gloating over their victories or bewailing the losses.

GOMPERS' CONGRATULATIONS.

President Gompers, in addressing the convention on the election of John McBride to the office of president, said he desired to express to the convention his feeling of relief. He had held the office so long that it had told upon him physically and made him, a comparatively young man, a comparatively old one. President Gompers continued: "I believed that I stood for a principle and have fought the fight for that principle, and in fighting I did not believe I should lie down; I preferred to be mowed down. Since the inception of the American Federation of Labor at Pittsburg in 1881 I have given my undivided time and attention to trades unionism and I have no regrets to express for any of my actions during that time. I will further state that with the close of this convention my official connection as an officer will cease, but that will not close my devotion to the cause of organized labor. If defeat had come at the Chicago convention I would have gone out of the office of president broken hearted. I feel that now I have left it, although by an adverse vote, with a record as clear as the noonday sun.

"Mr. John McBride has been elected in the place I have held, and as an evidence of how I feel about his election I have sent him the following telegram:

John McBride,
Columbus, Ohio.

Congratulations on election to presidency of Federation of Labor. None will be more loyal than I to aid you to make your administration successful.

Samuel Gompers.

"And I propose to do it, and the man or men who attempt to drag down John McBride as the president of the American Federation of Labor, or strike the heart of the federation through him, will find me a more bitter fighter for him than I have been or could have been for myself.

"Never in my whole life have I felt freer, and I can come back to the next convention and advocate more strenuously what I believe to be right. I hope to have the pleasure of meeting a number of the present delegates at that convention. I do not believe there has been any bitterness between myself and those who have opposed me, except as our ideas would clash, and I hope we will unite to advance the cause for which we are all associated."

For the office of first vice president there was no contest worth mentioning. Mrs. T. J. Morgan[11] and P. J. McGuire were in the field and the result was: McGuire, 1,865; Mrs. Morgan, 226. Mrs. Morgan moved that the election of McGuire be made unanimous.

. . .

GOMPERS VINDICATED.

One of the inside facts connected with the election for president of the federation last year was given out last night by a man high in the councils of the federation. He stated that last year the election of Samuel Gompers was caused by the socialists, who were disgusted with some of the charges[12] alleged to have been brought in executive session by P. J. McGuire. It was stated that charges reflecting against the honesty of President Gompers had been brought in executive session and were found to be entirely groundless. In order to thoroughly acquit President Gompers of the charges and also to demonstrate that such actions were in opposition to fair play, several of the prominent socialists voted for Mr. Gompers and turned the result. This is borne out by the fact that T. J. Morgan and others were on the side of Mr. Gompers. It was to this event that President Gompers referred yesterday when he said that had he been defeated last year he would have retired broken-hearted. The result was a complete vindication of Mr. Gompers and he was satisfied.

This fact also had some influence yesterday when Gompers and McGuire were on the same ticket for election as fraternal delegates to the trades congress[13] of Great Britain. Several delegates thought it would hardly be the proper thing to have Mr. McGuire serve with Mr. Gompers, whose election was certain, and they accordingly voted for other candidates or voted for only one candidate. The final result, however, resulted in McGuire's election.

Rocky Mountain News (Denver), Dec. 18, 1894.

1. The tally as printed in the convention proceedings was: Indianapolis, 1,290; Washington, D.C., 937; Detroit, 8. Brooklyn is not mentioned (AFL, *Proceedings*, 1894, p. 41).

2. Joseph B. Allen was a member of Brotherhood of Painters and Decorators of America (BPDA) 32 of Philadelphia and a delegate from the BPDA.

3. Andrew McCallin, a plasterer, represented the Denver Trades and Labor Assembly.

4. Henry J. Eikhoff represented the Metal Polishers', Buffers', and Platers' International Union of North America.

5. Thomas F. TRACY, a Boston cigarmaker, was fourth vice-president of the CMIU from 1896 to 1906.

6. Edward L. Daley was a representative of the Lasters' Protective Union of America.

7. The tally printed in the convention proceedings was: Gompers, 976; McBride, 1,170 (AFL, *Proceedings*, 1894, pp. 41-42).

8. Joseph F. VALENTINE was vice-president of the Iron Molders' Union of North America (IMUNA) from 1890 to 1903 and was one of its delegates at this convention.

9. Martin Fox represented the IMUNA.

10. The convention proceedings report that this motion was not adopted (AFL, *Proceedings*, 1894, p. 42).

11. Elizabeth C. Morgan represented AFL Ladies' Federal Labor Union 2703.

12. See "Gompers Is Elected," Dec. 17, 1893, in "Excerpts from News Accounts of the 1893 Convention of the AFL in Chicago," above.

13. The 1895 meeting of the Trades Union Congress of Great Britain convened in Cardiff, Wales, Sept. 2-7.

An Article in the *Labor Leader*

[December 22, 1894]

GOMPER'S DEFEAT

The news of the defeat of Samuel Gompers for president of the A.F. of L., while not unexpected, was received with keen regret by a host of the trade unionists of the country who have learned to appreciate the sturdy and whole-souled qualities of the man who has been so long at the head of the trade union movement of America.

There were various reasons which conspired to bring about the defeat of Mr. Gompers, the two most potent being the feeling that he had held the office for a sufficiently long period, and that a new man would be less handicapped in the performance of the duties of president; and, secondly, the even stronger feeling that it was advisable for some other section of the country than New York City to be represented in the president's chair.

Personal antagonisms played a comparatively minor part in the election, although Mr. Gompers, in common with most men of positive convictions, is honored by the hostility of a few malcontents, who are always ready to assist in throwing somebody down.

Still less may his defeat be regarded as in any sense a Socialistic victory, for his successor, John McBride, is even less acceptable to the leaders of the S.L.P. than Samuel Gompers, and has been, even within a few months, more bitterly attacked in their official organ.

The western delegates, or many of them, have long sought to gain control of the administration of the Federation, and have steadily gained in strength as the trade union movement has developed west of the Alleghenies.

The comparison naturally suggests itself between the enforced retirement of Mr. Powderly last year in the K. of L. and that of Gompers this year, but there are many and radical points of difference. Powderly, in common with Gompers, had been identified with the organization of which he was the head for a long period, almost from the commencement of its existence, but there the resemblance ends.

When Mr. Powderly was defeated, the once great order of which he was the chief had gone far on the downward path as the direct result of the intolerant policy to which he had too often lent a tacit acquiescence. He left an order rent with factional strife, fast dwindling into an insignificance which it has still further achieved.

On the contrary, President Gompers has had the satisfaction and honor of having his policy ratified, even by the convention which defeated him, and leaves the Federation stronger than at any time in its existence, powerful both in numbers and unity of purpose.

No taint of suspicion rests upon any official act during his long term of office, and even his bitterest foes are forced to admit that he never used his high office for personal profit or private gain.

The Federation of Labor has been very much a part of the life of Samuel Gompers. He has been zealous in its interest, untiring in defence of its rights and unswerving in his devotion to its principles.

President Gompers has been charged with being an ultra conservative, but those who know him best know that this charge is not well founded. Wisely conservative he has been, and the great responsibility of his office has demanded and obtained at his hands a judicial faculty which the Federation will be fortunate indeed if his successors are able to emulate.

Sam Gompers is neither a rhetorician or tactician. There are more brilliant orators on the labor platform, but none whose grasp of the economics and ethics of the labor movement is sounder. There are labor leaders who are more skillful in winning adherents to their support, but none who are more careless of personal triumph when a principle is at stake.

As Mr. Gompers said in his closing address to the delegates, he has little to regret as to his official acts. He has given all there was in him to the trade union movement, he has been an honest and upright leader, he will always remain a true and loyal worker in the trade union cause.

No one recognizes better than he how much greater the labor movement is than any one man, and none realize better than his personal friends how much greater the labor movement would be if each individual member was inspired by the same high ideal which has animated the man who for thirteen years has been the standard bearer of the American Federation of Labor.

Labor Leader (Boston), Dec. 22, 1894.

To John McBride

December 24th. [1894]

Mr. John Mc-Bride,
President United Mine Workers of America.
53 Clinton Bldg. Columbus, O.
Dear Sir and Brother:—

Pursuant to a resolution of the recent convention of the American Federation of Labor, held at Denver, Colo., I wired that which I now communicate in a more formal manner, informing you of your election as President of the American Federation of Labor, for the term commencing January 1st. 1895.

Upon that date, in accordance with the constitution of the A.F. of L., my term as President of the American Federation of Labor, expires, and it would afford me pleasure to be enabled on that date to turn over to you all the books, papers, and other property belonging to the American Federation of Labor. There are also very many things and duties connected with the office of the Presidency, which are not generally known, and if you could make it convenient to call here a day or two before January 1st, I should deem it not only my duty but a pleasure to acquaint you therewith, and place you in possession thereof.

As per the accompanying notice you will observe that by resolution of the Executive Council, a meeting of the Executive Council-elect has been called to take place at the office of the A.F. of L. 14 Clinton Place, New York City, N.Y. at ten o'clock in the morning of January 1st, 1895, and there to meet the retiring President and Secretary for the purpose of arranging the transfer of all business and property belonging to the A.F. of L.

I should say that an amendment to the constitution was adopted directing the President and Secretary-elect to hire suitable offices at Indianapolis, Ind. where the head quarters of the American Federation of Labor will be until ordered otherwise.

May I kindly suggest that you would place yourself in communication with Mr. August Mc-Craith, the Secretary elect, No. 12 Pearl Street, Boston, Mass. and (informally) endeavor to secure offices at Indianapolis, Ind.

Sincerely hoping that you will be in attendance at the meeting of the incoming Executive Council January 1st. 1895, and trusting that your health may be improved over that of the last report which reached me, I am,

Fraternally Yours   Saml Gompers.

President. American Federation of Labor.

N.B. Permit me to repeat in substance what I stated in my telegram, that I shall endeavor to aid all that I possibly can to make your administration successful.

S. G.

TLpS, reel 8, vol. 12, pp. 14-15, SG Letterbooks, DLC.

To Edward McSweeney

December 27th. [1894]

Hon. Edward F. Mc-Sweeney,
Assistant Commissioner of Immigration,
Ellis Island, N.Y.

Dear Sir and Friend:—

I presume you read in the papers of my return on the 24th. instant, but I was so fatigued with the journey and the work incident to the convention, that it was absolutely impossible for me to give any attention to my correspondence before this morning, and among the many expressions of good will I find your esteemed favor of the 21st. instant.

It should be needless to say that I appreciate sincerely the many pleasant references you make to me and my services to the labor movement, but I beg to assure you that with all my experience I can look back and truly say I have nothing to regret. Let those who bear the responsibilities for whatever is to come have the satisfaction that may come from my defeat. It is more than pleasant to find, however, that there are a large number who recognize some merit in me notwithstanding my failure of reelection.

Yes, you are right, my own interests have been my last consideration, and financially I am in about as good a position as I was when working at the bench, except that after Jan. 1st, I shall not have that. As a consequence I shall be in need of a position for the maintenance of myself and those depending upon me. Of course if such a position is of a character congenial to my convictions and whatever abilities I may be possessed of, I should much prefer it, than to those which most any man of fair ability could fill, and it goes without saying that I am under deep obligations to you for your offer to aid me in this.

My term of office ends with the first of the year and I am engrossed with the work of issuing the Jan. number of the American Federationist, and finishing up the work and correspondence. If it were not for these matters I should certainly call upon you at once. However, if you can make it convenient to drop in here during the course of the week I shall be under additional obligations to you for the many kindnesses you have done me.

Reciprocating your kind wishes, and trusting that Christmas may have been pleasant, and your New Year happy and prosperous, I am

Very Truly Yours   Saml Gompers.

President

TLpS, reel 8, vol. 12, p. 17, SG Letterbooks, DLC.

An Editorial by Samuel Gompers in the *American Federationist*

New York, Dec. 31st, 1894.

A PARTING WORD.

The Denver convention elected Mr. John McBride, of the United Mine Workers of America, President of the A.F. of L. As a consequence my term of office expires this day, and having been so long officially associated with the trade unionists of America it does seem to me not entirely inappropriate to bid all a direct and official good bye.

I do not ask the readers of this magazine nor my fellow unionists to imagine for a moment that in leaving the office of President of the A.F. of L. that I sever my connection with the labor movement, for as a matter of fact, even if I so desired, I doubt that I should be enabled to carry it out. I am now nigh upon forty-five years of age, and have been in the labor movement for more than thirty years. Of this, actively more than twenty-six, hence the labor movement and the labor cause have grown to be part of my existence, part of my very nature. To speak for it, to write for it, to work for it has been my highest hope, my inmost aspiration. Beyond it I have seen nothing, and success outside of it has seemed to me to be impossible.

At all times advocating the cause of the wage-workers who were struggling for ameliorative measures and emancipation, and at times speaking in defense of those who perhaps had neither the courage nor the opportunity to speak for themselves, and perhaps even again pleading for some who, in their demoralized condition, have been forced to repudiate the authority to speak in their name, hence it is not presuming too much when I repeat that the labor movement and the labor cause is part of my very being, and from which it is difficult, if not impossible, to depart.

Of course I have made enemies. I expected to when I first entered actively in the struggle, and any man who imagines for a moment that he could be in active participation in this combat for the right without incurring the enmity and ill-will of some, had better not enter the arena, for if any such thought is entertained it were better both for the beginner as well as the movement that his attentions be directed to another and less controversial channel.

To always act for the right without fear or favor or as to personal consequences is to run counter to schemes of all kinds. Having set the maxim and watchword the truth and the right for my guidance, it is but natural that I should have come in conflict with the weak-kneed, the trickster as well as those who have well formed but different opinions.

I have always held that every trade unionist should have one of two elements in his make-up, and which seemed to me were necessary essentials to success. The first was a thorough knowledge of the trade union movement, its history, its struggles, its tendencies, and for what it stands, or in the absence of this knowledge that it required absolute faith in the ability of the trade unions to accomplish the amelioration in the condition, and the final emancipation of labor. Talk as one will, but if either one of these two characteristics is not the dominating influence of a trade union leader or member success is an impossibility.

It is therefore not unnatural that men who lack the knowledge of the trade union movement, and who have no faith in it, but who look upon it as a secondary consideration in the struggles of labor, merely to be used for personal or ulterior purposes should have felt dissatisfied with me, recognizing that I was always ready and anxious to prevent the use or abuse of our movement by those who appeared either under the mask of friendship, or as its open and avowed enemies.

For office in the movement I care and cared nothing. To me the movement was greater than any man or set of men, and believing as I did and do, that the trade union movement is the natural class organization of the wage-workers in which they must seek present improvement as well as future disenthrallment, I have dared to fearlessly express my convictions regardless of who it hurt or benefited.

No one can truthfully say that I have ever entered into any caucus for any purpose whatsoever. I never entered into any deals, or bargains or combinations, either to elect myself or any other man to office, or to even advance legislation or propositions which I favored or to defeat men or measures to which I was opposed. I stood for a cause, and was willing at all times to bear the full brunt of antagonism and opposition that could be manifested against it or myself.

I have not been re-elected, and can fairly say that I have no regrets to express. I feel the consciousness of having performed my duty to the very best of my ability and with a single purpose, to benefit my fellow wage-workers. There is nothing that I have done in the cause that I would seek to undo, or words that I have expressed that I would unsay, except to do and say them with greater force and emphasis.

I beg to assure my successor as well as all unionists that I shall, so far as in me lies and opportunities present themselves, help to place our organization and our movement upon a higher plane of advantage and success, in the sincere hope that the day of labor's emancipation may be so much nearer at hand.

Appealing to all wage-workers to unite, to federate and mutually pledge to each other fraternity and solidarity, in which I cheerfully join, I have the honor to remain for all time,

Yours in the cause of labor,   Samuel Gompers.

American Federationist 1 (Jan. 1895): 256-57.

To the *People*

#308 E 125 St. New York. Dec. 31st 1894.

The People
#184 Williams St City
Comrade:—

Although no longer President of the A.F. of Labor I am deeply anxious to remain in direct touch with the labor movement of the Country, and I know of no way better than the close scrutiny of the labor and reform press. Had I accumulated money during my long Connection with the movement I would not ask you what I am now compelled to and that is that you will kindly place my name on your mailing list.

Appreciating your many kindnesses to me, and trusting that you will see your way Clear to comply with my request for which I thank you in anticipation, I am,

Yours, for the cause

Saml Gompers.

ACS, Socialist Labor Party Papers, WHi.

GLOSSARY

ALEXANDER, D. L., of Reedsville, Pa., helped organize the Axe and Edge Tool Makers' National Union of America and was its general secretary from 1890 to 1891.

ALTGELD, John Peter (1847-1902), was born in Germany and immigrated with his family to Ohio in 1848. After service in the Union army he worked as a teacher in Missouri, practiced law, and in 1874 was elected state's attorney for Andrew Co., Mo. In 1875 he moved to Chicago where he became active in Democratic politics, running unsuccessfully for Congress in 1884. He served as judge of the Superior Court of Cook County between 1886 and 1891, retiring as chief justice. Altgeld was elected governor of Illinois in 1892, and in 1893 pardoned the three surviving Haymarket defendants. He also opposed President Grover Cleveland's use of federal troops in the Pullman strike in 1894, although he later authorized the use of state troops. Altgeld was not reelected in 1896 and ran unsuccessfully as an independent candidate for mayor of Chicago in 1899.

ARCHIBALD, James Patrick (1860-1913), an Irish-born paperhanger and member of the Irish National Land League, was an officer in the New York City Central Labor Union and its successor, the Central Federated Union, from 1882 to 1904, with the exception of one year. He was prominent in the KOL in the late 1880s, representing District Assembly 49 and paperhangers' National Trade Assembly (NTA) 210 in the General Assembly and organizing for the Knights in England, Scotland, and Ireland. He served as district master workman of NTA 210 from 1888 to 1890. In 1895 he helped found the National Paperhangers' Protective and Beneficial Association, serving for seven years as its president. This union was unable to compete with the AFL's affiliate in the trade, the Brotherhood of Painters, Decorators, and Paperhangers of America, and merged with it in 1902. Archibald then served the Brotherhood as general organizer, local and district officer, and AFL delegate. In politics Archibald moved from leadership in the Henry George New York City mayoralty campaign in 1886 to support of Grover Cleveland and a leading place in the New York state Democratic party. He served as warden of the Ludlow Street Jail in 1895, was active after the turn of the century in the New York City Civic Federation, was president of the Democratic Association of Workingmen of Greater New York, and for several years was the city's deputy commissioner of licenses. Archibald served as a lobbyist and officer of the Workingmen's Federation of the State of New York and the New York State Federation of Labor.

ARNOLD, Frank W. (1851-1917), born in Columbus, Ohio, began working as a brakeman for the Pennsylvania Railroad at the age of sixteen and later became a fireman, joining Brotherhood of Locomotive Firemen (BLF) lodge 9 of Columbus, Ohio. In 1879 he was admitted to the Ohio bar. He served as grand master of the BLF from 1879 to 1885, and as grand secretary and treasurer from 1892 to 1904. After leaving union service he became a businessman and later an examiner for the Interstate Commerce Commission.

ARTHUR, Peter M. (1831-1903), a Scottish immigrant, was grand chief engineer of the Brotherhood of Locomotive Engineers (BLE) from 1874 until his death. He was a charter member of BLE Division 46 in Albany, N.Y., was its chief engineer in 1868, and represented it in BLE conventions from 1866 to 1874. Arthur served as second grand assistant engineer of the BLE from 1869 to 1874. As grand chief engineer he maintained the BLE's independence from the AFL and other labor organizations.

AVELING, Eleanor Marx (1855-98), daughter of Karl Marx, was born in London and became a literary reviewer, writer, editor, and translator, much of her work involving socialist literature and themes. She became a member of the Social Democratic Federation in 1883, and in 1884 helped found the Socialist League, remaining a member until 1888. Aveling was active in the gas workers' and dock workers' strikes in 1889 and in that year organized the first women's branch of the National Union of Gas Workers and General Labourers of Great Britain and Ireland; she served on the national union's executive board from 1890 to 1895.

BANDLOW, Robert (1852-1911), manager of the *Cleveland Citizen* from 1891 to 1910, was the son of German immigrants who came to America in 1854. Trained as a printer, he helped organize the Cleveland Gutenberg Society, which became German-American Typographia 6 shortly after its founding in 1873. Bandlow held various posts in the Cleveland Central Labor Union (CLU): secretary from the late 1880s to 1893, president in 1893-94, and treasurer from 1898 to 1902. He served as treasurer of the CLU's successor, the United Trades and Labor Council of Cuyahoga County, from 1902 to 1910. Bandlow became a socialist in the mid-1890s, served on the national committee of the Socialist Party of America from 1908 to 1909, and ran regularly, though unsuccessfully, for city and state office on the socialist ticket.

BARNES, John Mahlon (1866-1934), a cigarmaker born in Lancaster, Pa., was a member of the KOL in the 1880s. He joined the CMIU in 1887 and served as secretary of CMIU 100 of Philadelphia (1891-93, 1897-1900) and of CMIU 165 of Philadelphia (1903-4). In 1902 he was elected first vice-president of the Pennsylvania State Federation of Labor. He joined the SLP in 1891 and served as corresponding secretary of the Philadelphia Central Committee and as an organizer for the Philadelphia American Branch of the SLP in the 1890s. He helped form the Socialist Party of America (SPA) in 1901 and served as the secretary of its Philadelphia branch and as the Pennsylvania representative on its National committee in the early years of the decade. He was elected executive secretary of the SPA in 1905, a position he held until 1911. In 1912 and again in 1924 he was the party's campaign manager.

BARONDESS, Joseph (1867-1928), a Russian-born cloakmaker, spent several years in England as an active trade unionist before immigrating to the United States in 1888. He worked as a knee-pants maker in New York City, joined the SLP, and became a union organizer associated particularly with the United Hebrew Trades. He was a leader in the New York City cloakmakers' strike of 1890, in the course of which he helped organize Operators' and Cloakmakers' Union 1. In 1891 he received a prison sentence for accepting a $100 check from the firm of Popkin and Marks as part of the settlement of a strike against that company, although he contended that the money was not intended for his personal use. Released on bail, he organized the short-lived International Cloakmakers' Union of America, and he continued his organizing work after Governor Roswell Flower pardoned him in June 1892. He became a Zionist in 1903 and was a founding member of the American Jewish Congress; he later served as one of its delegates to the Paris Peace Conference of 1919. Barondess was a member of the New York City Board of Education from 1910 to 1918 and in his later years worked as an insurance broker.

BAUSTIAN, Charles A. (b. 1864?), was born in Iowa. He served as secretary of Carriage and Wagon Workers' International Union of North America (CWWIU) 3 of Chicago in 1892 and 1893. He was elected to the Executive Board of the CWWIU in 1892 and became secretary-treasurer in 1893, serving until 1907.

BECHTOLD, Charles F., was secretary of St. Louis local 6 of the National Union of the United Brewery Workmen of the United States (NUUBW) from 1888 to 1892. In 1892 he was elected secretary of the NUUBW, holding the position jointly with Ernst Kurzenknabe until 1899 and with Julius Zorn from 1899 to 1901.

BERGER, Victor Luitpold (1860-1929), was born in Nieder-Rehbach, Austria, and attended the universities of Vienna and Budapest before immigrating to the United States in 1878. He lived in Bridgeport, Conn., for two years, working as a boiler mender, metal polisher, and salesman, and then moved to Milwaukee where he taught German in the public school system. In 1892 he resigned and bought the *Milwaukee Volkszeitung.* He changed its name to *Wisconsin Vorwärts* in 1893 and edited it until 1904. In 1897 he helped form the Social Democracy of America and in 1898, the Social Democratic party, which became the Socialist Party of America (SPA) in 1901. He served on the SPA's executive board from 1901 until 1923. He edited the weekly *Social Democratic Herald* from 1901 to 1913, and the daily *Milwaukee Leader* from 1911 until his death. In 1910 he was elected alderman-at-large for Milwaukee and later that year was elected as the first SPA congressman, serving from 1911 to 1913. Sentenced to twenty years imprisonment in February 1919 because of his vocal criticism of American involvement in World War I, he nevertheless ran successfully for Congress later that year, though Congress refused to seat him. The U.S. Supreme Court overturned Berger's conviction in 1921, and he was elected to Congress again the following year, serving from 1923 until his defeat in 1929.

BISHOP, Michael J. (1856-1903?), was general worthy foreman of the KOL from 1893 to 1896. A baker and cook born in Brooklyn, N.Y., he joined KOL bakers' Local Assembly (LA) 2872 in 1882 and was active in District Assembly (DA) 49. After moving to Massachusetts in 1885, he was briefly associated with shoe and harness makers' LA 2766 in Haverhill. By the spring of 1886 he was a member of bakers' LA 5296 in Boston. During the next decade and a half he was a book canvasser and life insurance salesman, pursued a business venture in the West Indies, and worked as an advertising agent and a cook. He was elected district statistician of DA 30 in 1887 and subsequently served as KOL state organizer and worthy foreman in 1891, and as secretary-treasurer for DA 30 of Massachusetts (1893) and for the KOL Massachusetts state assembly (1893-94). He edited the *Weekly Index,* apparently a KOL paper, from 1892 to 1894.

BLOCK, George G. (1848-1925), secretary of the Journeymen Bakers' National Union (JBNU) from 1886 to 1888, was born in Bohemia and immigrated to New York City in 1870. Moving to Philadelphia in the 1870s, he worked as a pocketbook maker and a journalist, joined the Social Democratic Workingmen's Party of North America, and, during 1877, was organizer for the Philadelphia American section of the Workingmen's Party of the United States. Block returned to New York City in the early 1880s where he joined the staff of the *New Yorker Volkszeitung*. He helped found the New York City Central Labor Union and was secretary of the Executive Committee of the Henry George campaign. In 1885 he established the *Deutsch-Amerikanische Bäcker-Zeitung* through which he helped generate interest in organizing the JBNU in 1886. He served as editor of the journal until 1889. Around 1889 he went into the liquor business.

BLOETE, Charles George (1839-1908), a Prussian-born cigarmaker, came to New York City in 1866, joining CMIU 90. He became a member of the United Cigarmakers of New York soon after its organization in 1873 and was subsequently a prominent member of CMIU 144, serving successively as German recording secretary, auditor, and treasurer for the union between 1877 and 1881. He represented his local in the Amalgamated Trades and Labor Union of New York and Vicinity, where he served as financial secretary during 1882, and in the New York City Central Labor Union during 1886 and 1887. In 1887 he was appointed special agent of the New York Bureau of Labor Statistics and held that office until 1904.

BOHM, Ernest (1860-1936), secretary of the Central Labor Federation of New York City from 1889 to 1899 and of the Central Federated Union of New York City from 1899 to 1921, was born and educated in New York. He was a compositor, clerk, and manager of a cloak operators' union early in his career, becoming secretary of the Excelsior Club of the KOL in 1881 and corresponding secretary of the New York City Central Labor Union in 1882. During the 1880s and 1890s he was active in the organization of the brewery workers. He supported Henry George in his campaign for the mayoralty of New York City in 1886, participated in the formation of the United Labor party, and served as secretary of the Progressive Labor party in 1887. Bohm was a member of the SLP and, from 1896 to 1898, secretary of the General Executive Board of the Socialist Trade and Labor Alliance. During World War I he worked with the American Peace League, but then allied with SG in the prowar effort. After the war he served as secretary of the New York City Farmer-Labor party (1919-21). From 1921 he was a leader of the Bookkeepers', Stenog-

raphers', and Accountants' Union—AFL Federal Labor Union
12646—holding several positions including the presidency.

BRAMWOOD, John W. (1857?-1932), was born in England and immigrated to Fall River, Mass., at the age of four. He was apprenticed
in the printing trade and at age sixteen moved to Longmount, Colo.
He served as president of International Typographical Union (ITU)
49 in Denver from 1895 to 1896. In 1896 he was elected secretary-
treasurer of the ITU, moving to Indianapolis. He held the position
until 1908 when he resigned to buy an interest in Cohea Affiliated
Publications, an Indianapolis concern, which became Cohea-Bram-
wood Press. In 1911 he assumed control of the company and changed
the name to Bramwood Press.

BRETTELL, James (b. 1844), was born in England and immigrated
to the United States in 1868. He settled in Mingo Junction, Ohio,
and joined National Amalgamated Association of Iron and Steel Workers 22 of the second district, serving as that union's corresponding
representative in 1888. He served as third vice-president of the AFL
from 1893 to 1894. Brettell later became an insurance and real estate
agent.

BROADHURST, Henry (1840-1911), a leader of the London stone-
masons, was secretary of the parliamentary committee of the Trades
Union Congress of Great Britain (1875-90) and a Liberal Member of
Parliament (1880-92, 1894-1906).

BUCHANAN, Joseph Ray (1851-1924), was born in Missouri and
moved to Denver in 1878, where he became an editor and an organizer of the International Typographical Union. In 1882 he helped
organize KOL Local Assembly 2327 and began publishing the *Labor
Enquirer.* The following year Buchanan helped form the Rocky Mountain Division of the International Workingmen's Association. Between
1884 and 1886 he organized western railroad workers and led several
successful railroad strikes. Buchanan was a member of the KOL General Executive Board from 1884 to 1885 and of the KOL auxiliary
board in 1886. He served as district master workman of KOL District
Assembly 89 from 1885 until he moved to Chicago in January 1887.
In that year the KOL expelled him as a result of his disagreement
with the decision to force CMIU members to leave the Knights.
Buchanan moved to New Jersey in 1888 and twice ran unsuccessfully
for Congress. In 1892 he helped organize the People's party, serving
on its national committee during the 1892, 1896, and 1900 elections.
He was labor editor of the *New York Evening Journal* (1904-15) and a

member of the conciliation council of the U.S. Department of Labor (1918-21).

BURGMAN, Charles F., a tailor and a socialist, was a delegate to the 1881 FOTLU convention from the Representative Assembly of Trades and Labor Unions of the Pacific Coast and second vice-president of the FOTLU Legislative Committee during 1881-82. At the 1881 convention he successfully advocated the passage of a resolution prohibiting further Chinese immigration. In 1882 Burgman worked with Burnette G. Haskell in founding the Pacific Coast Division of the International Workingmen's Association, and between 1883 and 1885 he served as business manager of Haskell's paper, *Truth*. Burgman operated a tailoring establishment in San Francisco into the late 1890s.

BURNS, John Elliott (1858-1943), a British machinist and a leader of the 1889 London dockers' strike, joined the Amalgamated Society of Engineers in 1879. He was a member of the Social Democratic Federation from 1884 to 1889, the year he was elected to the London County Council. In 1892 he was elected to Parliament as an Independent Labour candidate, and he was reelected until 1918 (beginning in 1895 as a Liberal/Labour candidate). He was one of the fraternal delegates from the Trades Union Congress of Great Britain to the 1894 AFL convention in Denver, and in 1895 SG helped him set up a speaking tour of American cities to promote the principles of trade unionism. In 1906 Burns became a cabinet member in the ruling Liberal government; he resigned his post in 1914, however, in protest against Britain's entry into World War I.

BURT, Thomas (1837-1922), was born in England and began work in the mines at the age of ten. He first became active in trade union work in 1863, and served the Northumberland Miners' Association as president (1865-1905), agent (1905-13), and subsequently as an advisor. From 1874 to 1918 he was a Liberal Member of Parliament, serving as secretary to the Board of Trade from 1892 to 1895. He was a member of several parliamentary committees and commissions concerned with labor conditions, including the Royal Commission on Labour (1891-94). He was president of the International League for Peace from 1882 to 1914.

CAHAN, Abraham (1860-1951), a major interpreter of the Yiddish-American experience as an editor of the Yiddish press and as a writer, was born in Lithuania and attended the Vilna Teachers' Institute from 1877 to 1881. His involvement with the anti-czarist underground movement after 1880 eventually forced him to flee the country and he immigrated to New York in 1882. There he worked in the cigar and tin industries before becoming an evening school English instructor in 1885. He was associated with the anarchist movement in the 1880s, and beginning in 1884 helped organize unions of Jewish workers in the garment trades. By 1886 he had joined the SLP and during that year founded, and for several months published, a Yiddish socialist periodical, *Di Neie Tseit* (*Die Neue Zeit*). He also took an active part in the Henry George mayoralty campaign in 1886. In 1890 he and Morris Hillquit founded the Yiddish weekly *Arbeiter Tseit* (*Arbeiter Zeit*) as the official organ of the United Hebrew Trades as well as the official Yiddish organ of the SLP. In 1891 Cahan was temporarily president of Operators' and Cloakmakers' Union 1 during the absence of its regular president, Joseph Barondess, who was serving a jail sentence. Cahan edited the *Arbeiter Tseitung* (*Arbeiter Zeitung*) from 1891 to 1894, and *Di Tsukunft* (*Die Zukunft*), the monthly of the SLP's Jewish sections, from 1894 to 1897. In 1897 he and other leaders of the Jewish sections left the party, forming local 1 of the Social Democracy of America and launching the socialist *Jewish Daily Forward*. Cahan served as its first editor in 1897 and over the following five years wrote for several papers, including Lincoln Steffens's *Commercial Advertiser*. He served as editor of *Jewish Daily Forward* again for six months in 1902 and then returned to hold the position from 1903 until his death.

CARNEY, William A. (1860?-1906?), born in England, immigrated to the United States around 1884 and settled in Pittsburgh where he worked in the iron mills as a rougher. He was a member of Monongahela Valley Lodge 53 of the National Amalgamated Association of Iron and Steel Workers of the United States (NAAISW), serving as its corresponding representative in the late 1880s, and vice-president of NAAISW District 1 from 1890 to 1895. From 1891 to 1893 he was second vice-president of the AFL, and he served as an AFL organizer through the mid-1890s. Between 1895 and 1898 Carney organized workers for the NAAISW in Pennsylvania and West Virginia and assisted in strikes.

CAVANAUGH, George (b. 1841), a New York City carpenter, immigrated to the United States from Canada in 1856. He was secretary of the American District of the Amalgamated Society of Carpenters and Joiners in 1890 and 1891.

COHEN, Fanny (Femmetje) Gompers (b. 1836), SG's aunt, married Jacob Cohen, a union cigarmaker. They immigrated to the United States and had three sons and five daughters.

COMMONS, John Rogers (1862-1945), a leading economist and reformer, was born in Ohio and raised in Indiana. From 1883 to 1887 he worked as a printer in Cleveland, becoming a member of International Typographical Union 53. He completed an undergraduate degree (1888) and masters (1890) at Oberlin College and did advanced work at Johns Hopkins (1888-90) before teaching at several universities during the 1890s. In 1893 he helped found the short-lived American Institute of Christian Sociology, serving as its secretary. He worked for the U.S. Industrial Commission in 1900 and was statistician for the National Civic Federation (1902-4) before joining the faculty of the University of Wisconsin (1904-32).

The writings and activities of Commons and his students were widely influential in the field of industrial relations and contributed substantially to developing a framework for governmental regulation of the economy. Commons was closely identified with the Progressive movement in Wisconsin, particularly as an advisor to the administration of Governor Robert M. LaFollette (1901-6). He was a founder of the American Association for Labor Legislation in 1906 and a member of the National Civic Federation's public utilities commission from 1906 to 1907. He drafted in 1907 Wisconsin's public utility act and, in 1911, the law creating the Wisconsin Industrial Commission. He served on both that commission and the Milwaukee Bureau of Economy and Efficiency between 1911 and 1913. He also contributed to the shaping of state regulatory legislation in such areas as unemployment and health insurance, civil service, minimum wages for women, and child labor. From 1913 to 1915 he was a member of the U.S. Commission on Industrial Relations, and in 1917 he was elected president of the American Economics Association. In the post–World War I period he served as a member of the Wisconsin minimum wage board (1919), associate director of the National Bureau of Economic Research (1920-28), chairman of the Unemployment Insurance Board of the Chicago Clothing Trades (1923-25), and president of the National Consumers' League (1923-35). He was the author of many publications and produced, with associates, the ten-volume *Documentary History of American Industrial Society* (1910-11) and the four-volume *History of Labour in the United States* (1918-35).

COUGHLIN, John E. (1853?-99), was born in Massachusetts. He was a currier in Chicago during the 1880s and was president of the National Tanners' and Curriers' Union in 1881. Living in Milwaukee during the 1890s, he served as general president of the United Brotherhood of Tanners and Curriers of America and as president of the Milwaukee Federated Trades Council.

CUMMINGS, Amos Jay (1841-1902), a native of Conkling, N.Y., and longtime member of International Typographical Union 6 of New York City, served in the Union army during the Civil War and afterward held editorial positions on the *New York Tribune, New York Sun,* and several other New York City newspapers. He was elected as a Tammany Democrat to the U.S. Congress in 1886, serving with two brief interruptions from 1887 until 1902.

DALEY, Edward L. (1855-1904), was born in Danvers, Mass., and apprenticed in the shoemaker's trade at age thirteen. A member of KOL Local Assembly 715, Daley organized the Lynn, Mass., Lasters' Protective Union in 1878 and was its first secretary. He was the general secretary of the New England Lasters' Protective Union (subsequently the Lasters' Protective Union of America) from 1885 to 1895. In 1891 he was elected to a single term in Congress as a Democrat.

DALY, James J., served as general president of the Mosaic and Encaustic Tile Layers and Trade National Union in the early 1890s. After that union ceased to exist he was involved in the Mosaic and Encaustic Tile Layers of New York and Vicinity. In the early 1900s he served as president of Ceramic, Mosaic, and Encaustic Tile Layers' and Helpers' International Union (CMETL) 30 of New York City, and later he was a member of CMETL 52 of New York City. In 1918 he was elected general president of the CMETL, serving until the union amalgamated with the Bricklayers', Masons', and Plasterers' International Union of America later that year.

DEBS, Eugene Victor (1855-1926), born in Terre Haute, Ind., entered railroad work as an engine-house laborer and became a locomotive fireman. He was elected first secretary of Vigo Lodge 16— the Terre Haute local of the Brotherhood of Locomotive Firemen (BLF)—in 1875 and became grand secretary and treasurer of the BLF and editor-in-chief of its journal, the *Firemen's Magazine* (after 1886 the *Locomotive Firemen's Magazine*), in 1880. Debs resigned as an officer of the Brotherhood in September 1892 to begin building a single union for all workers employed in the industry; he resigned the editorship in 1894. He founded the American Railway Union (ARU) in 1893 and served as its president, leading it in a victorious strike against the Great Northern Railroad in 1894. The same year he was arrested and imprisoned for defying a federal court order in connection with the refusal of ARU members to handle Pullman cars while Pullman Co. workers were on strike. The Pullman strike effectively destroyed the ARU.

After six months in prison Debs turned his energies to political activity, first supporting the populist campaign of 1896, and then publicly embracing socialism at the beginning of 1897. He organized the Social Democratic Party of the United States (SDPUS) in 1897, and in 1900 he polled 100,000 votes as the presidential candidate of the SDPUS and a wing of the SLP led by Morris Hillquit. In 1901 Debs participated in the creation of the Socialist Party of America (SPA). He ran for president as the party's candidate in 1904, 1908, 1912, and 1920, making his best showing in 1912 with 6 percent of the vote. Debs joined with William D. Haywood and other radicals in 1905 to form the Industrial Workers of the World, a revolutionary syndicalist industrial union that he hoped would function as the economic arm of the SPA; he resigned three years later because of tactical differences.

During World War I, Debs became the most famous individual prosecuted under the Espionage Act, receiving a ten-year sentence because of a 1918 speech in which he questioned the sincerity of capitalist appeals to patriotism. SG supported the campaign for clemency that culminated in a presidential pardon in 1921. After his release, Debs attempted to rebuild the SPA, which had been devastated by government repression inspired by the party's pacifist position during World War I.

DELABAR, August, a German immigrant, was secretary of San Francisco Journeymen Bakers' National Union (JBNU) 24 from 1886 to 1887 and in 1888 was elected secretary of the JBNU (after 1890 the Journeymen Bakers' and Confectioners' International Union), serving until 1892. In 1890 he ran for mayor of New York City on the SLP ticket.

DELAHAYE, Victor (1838-97), was a French mechanic and socialist. After serving in the navy for five years, he moved to Paris in 1863 where he worked as supervisor of bridges and roads until 1870. As president of the syndicat des mécaniciens (union of mechanics) in Paris he took part in the Paris Commune in 1871. Living in London from 1871 to 1879, he was active in the circle of political refugees and socialists around Marx and Engels. After his return to Paris, Delahaye established himself as a small manufacturer of telegraphs, but he also became active in a local mechanics' union which he represented at the founding convention of the Fédération nationale des syndicats (National Trade Union Federation) in 1886. He was a socialist city councilman from 1883 to 1888 and was appointed to the Conseil supérieur du travail (Supreme Council on Labor) in 1883. Delahaye was frequently sent abroad as a delegate for his union; he visited the United States in 1876.

DELEON, Daniel (1852-1914), was the leading figure in the SLP from 1891 until his death. Born in Curaçao, he was educated in

Germany in the late 1860s and studied medicine in Amsterdam until 1872 without completing his course of study. Between 1872 and 1874 he immigrated to the United States, working as a school teacher in Westchester, N.Y., until he entered the Columbia College School of Law in 1876. He earned his law degree in 1878 and practiced in Brownsville, Tex., until 1882 and in New York City from 1882 until at least 1884. From 1883 to 1889 he was a lecturer at the Columbia College School of Political Science and active in reform and radical movements. He supported the mugwump campaign of 1884 against the Republican presidential candidacy of James G. Blaine, worked in the mayoralty campaign of single-tax reformer Henry George in 1886—remaining a single-tax adherent until 1888—was a member of KOL Local Assembly 1563 from 1888, and participated in the utopian socialist Nationalist movement from 1889 to 1890, when he joined the SLP. He ran for governor of New York on the SLP ticket in 1891.

DeLeon never held a major national office in the SLP, but in 1891 he became editor of the SLP's official organ, *People,* a position he held until shortly before his death, and this journal formed the foundation of his leadership in the SLP. In 1891 his local assembly elected him as its delegate to KOL District Assembly (DA) 49, and from this base he played a prominent role in the KOL general assemblies between 1893 and 1895. In coalition with People's party adherents in DA 49, whose slate he supported in the 1893 state elections, he helped engineer the replacement in 1893 of KOL general master workman Terence Powderly by James R. Sovereign. The alliance with Sovereign dissolved in 1895, however, in a dispute involving Sovereign's refusal to allow the SLP to nominate the editor of the KOL's journal. The 1895 General Assembly rejected the credentials of DA 49's delegates, and DeLeon launched an alternative labor federation, the Socialist Trade and Labor Alliance (STLA), in December of that year. The *People* served as the STLA's official organ, and DeLeon was a member of its general executive board, functioning as its leader. In conformity with the principles of the "new trade unionism," the STLA accepted the affiliation of SLP branches as well as trade unions; after 1898, however, it functioned as a weak adjunct of the party, centered increasingly in New York City, until it merged with the Industrial Workers of the World (IWW) in 1905. DeLeon helped frame the constitution of the IWW at its 1905 founding convention in Chicago and was active until he was denied a seat at the 1908 convention, culminating a struggle with the organization's syndicalist faction. While DeLeon's supporters withdrew and set up a second IWW in Detroit, he discouraged the establishment of the new organization and was never active in it.

DILLON, William J., secretary of the American Flint Glass Workers' Union (AFGWU) from 1886 to 1893, was born in Newark, N.J., and became a glass worker in Brooklyn. He served as president of Brooklyn AFGWU local 1 before assuming national office and moving to Pittsburgh. Dillon resigned his position in 1893 to become a glass manufacturer in Hyde Park, Pa.

DOLD, Charles (b. 1860), immigrated to the United States from Germany in 1873 and settled in Aurora, Ill., in the mid-1880s, working as a cigarmaker and joining CMIU 41. He served on the executive committee of the Illinois State Federation of Labor in 1888 and as financial secretary of CMIU 41 in 1891. Moving to Chicago about 1892, he was financial secretary of CMIU 14 from 1893 to 1895 and was active in the mid-1890s in the Chicago Labor Congress, a short-lived rival to the Trade and Labor Assembly of Chicago. The state federation elected him president in 1898.

Dold helped organize Chicago piano makers into AFL Piano Makers' and Piano Varnish Finishers' Union 7143 in 1898, and was general organizer of the Piano and Organ Workers' International Union of America from its founding in 1899 until 1904, when it was renamed the Piano, Organ, and Musical Instrument Workers' International Union of America (POMIU). He was president of the POMIU and editor of its journal from 1904 to 1911, when the journal was suspended, and was serving as president of the POMIU as late as 1920. In 1917 Dold was secretary of the Public Ownership League of America, and in 1918 he served as chairman of the Chicago Labor party. He was the unsuccessful Farmer-Labor party candidate for Illinois lieutenant-governor in 1920. During the 1920s and 1930s he owned a piano store in Chicago.

DRUMMOND, Charles L. (1864-1900), a printer and a journalist born in Huntington, Ind., moved to Fort Wayne in 1885 where he worked for the *Fort Wayne Gazette* and later for the *Fort Wayne Sentinel.* A member of International Typographical Union 78, he served as its financial secretary from 1888 to 1891, and as its president in 1895. He was a delegate to the Fort Wayne Trades and Labor Council from its founding in 1889 until 1896 and served as president in 1893. The 1893 AFL convention elected him second vice-president; he served for one term. A Democrat, Drummond played an active role in local politics. Between 1891 and 1896 he was connected with the free silver paper *Monday Morning Times*. He was elected to represent Allen Co. in the Indiana legislature in 1900 but died before taking office.

DULLEA, John D. (1861-1919), born in New Jersey, was a member of Boot and Shoe Workers' International Union (BSWIU) 71 of Boston and the BSWIU's assistant general secretary in early 1894. Later that year he became general secretary of the BSWIU, leading the organization into a merger in 1895 that created the Boot and Shoe Workers' Union (BSWU). By 1900 he was living in Lynn, Mass., where he was briefly a member of BSWU 300 and then was associated with BSWU 205. He became the business agent of BSWU Joint Council 4 in Lynn about 1907 and still held that position as late as 1916.

DUNCAN, James (1857-1928), a granite cutter born in Scotland, immigrated to the United States in 1880. He joined the Granite Cutters' National Union (GCNU) in 1881 and in the early 1880s served as an officer of GCNU locals in New York, Philadelphia, Richmond, and Baltimore, where he settled in 1884. He subsequently served as Maryland state organizer for the GCNU, general organizer for the AFL, and president of the Baltimore Federation of Labor (1890-92, 1897). Duncan was an officer of the GCNU (after 1905 the Granite Cutters' International Association of America) from 1895 to 1923 (secretary, 1895-1905; international secretary-treasurer, 1905-12; and international president, 1912-23). He edited the *Granite Cutters' Journal* from 1895 to 1928. He served the AFL as second vice-president (1894-1900) and first vice-president (1900-1928) and was acting president of the Federation during President John McBride's illness in 1895. He represented the AFL at the 1898 British Trades Union Congress in Bristol and the International Secretariat in Budapest in 1911. President Wilson appointed him envoy extraordinary to Russia in 1917 and a member of the American labor mission to the peace conference in Paris in 1919.

DYER, Josiah Bennett (1843-1900), granite cutters' leader, was born in England and came to the United States in 1871. He was an early member of the KOL in Boston and helped organize a branch of the Granite Cutters' International Union in Graniteville, Mass., in 1877. The following year he was elected secretary of the Granite Cutters' International (later National) Union, serving in that office until 1895.

EASLEY, Ralph Montgomery (1856-1939), was born in Browning, Pa. He founded a daily newspaper in Hutchinson, Kans., and then moved to Chicago to work as a reporter and columnist for the *Chicago Inter Ocean*. He helped organize the Chicago Civic Federation (CCF) in 1893, leaving the *Inter Ocean* to serve as the CCF's secretary. He resigned from that position in 1900 and moved to New York to organize the National Civic Federation (NCF); SG became its first vice-president. As chairman of the Executive Council of the NCF,

Easley organized a series of conferences and programs bringing together prominent leaders of business and labor organizations in cooperative reform efforts and in the settlement of labor disputes. In his later years he increasingly devoted himself to opposing radical labor organizations and social movements.

EDMONSTON, Gabriel (1839-1918), a founder and the first president of the Brotherhood of Carpenters and Joiners of America (1881-82), was born in Washington, D.C., and served in the Confederate army. He helped organize Washington carpenters in 1881 and was carpenter of the House of Representatives in the 1880s. A member of the FOTLU Legislative Committee from 1882 to 1886, he was elected its secretary in 1884. He introduced a series of resolutions at the FOTLU 1884 convention calling for the inauguration of the eight-hour movement. From 1886 to 1888 Edmonston served as treasurer of the AFL.

EIKHOFF, Henry J. (1861-1925), a stove polisher, was born in Michigan and was active in the Detroit Trade and Labor Council before helping organize the Metal Polishers', Buffers', and Platers' International Union of North America in 1891. He served as the first vice-president and, during the latter part of 1894, as president of the national union. After 1897 he was a Michigan state factory inspector and played a major role in the passage by the Michigan legislature of the first blower law requiring removal of dust in polishing rooms. He later opened a private factory inspection bureau.

ELDERKIN, Thomas J. (b. 1853), a London-born sailor, came to the United States in 1869, working in Scranton, Pa., and Buffalo, N.Y., before settling in Chicago. In 1878 he helped organize the Lake Seamen's Benevolent Association (variously the Lake Seamen's Union), serving several terms as its president in the 1890s. In 1892 he was a founder of the National Seamen's Union of America (after 1895 the International Seamen's Union of America) and was elected its first general secretary, serving until he resigned the office in 1899. The 1894 AFL convention elected him fourth vice-president; he served for one term. In the late 1890s Elderkin was serving as a vessel dispatcher in Chicago, and he was living there as late as 1917.

ELLIOTT, John T. (1836-1902), a founder of the Brotherhood of Painters and Decorators of America (BPDA), was born in Baltimore. Following the Civil War he moved to Philadelphia and joined the International Workingmen's Association (IWA). The IWA General Council in New York City elected him U.S. general secretary for 1871-72, and this brought him actively into socialist and reform politics and relief efforts in the city during the depression of the 1870s. He was involved in organizing the Grand Lodge of Painters of America in 1871, the first national painters' union, which lasted until 1876.

Returning to Baltimore in 1879, Elliott organized KOL Local Assembly 1466 and served as secretary of District Assembly 41. He resigned from the Knights in 1882, and in 1887 helped organize the BPDA and was elected general secretary-treasurer. Elliott presided over the BPDA during years of factionalism, in which the painters divided into two groups, Elliott's based in Baltimore, and another in Lafayette, Ind. Poor health forced him to retire in 1900.

ELM, Johann Adolph von (1857-1916), born in Hamburg, a cigarmaker and an active socialist and trade unionist, immigrated to the United States in 1878 in the face of the Bismarckian anti-socialist laws and during his four years in New York became friends with SG. Returning to Germany in 1882, he became secretary of the Verband der Zigarrensortierer (Cigar Packers' Union) and was instrumental in arranging its merger with the Deutscher Tabakarbeiter-Verband (German Cigarmakers' Union). When the official ban on socialist and labor activities eased in 1890, Elm took part in the founding of the Generalkommission der Gewerkschaften Deutschlands (General Commission of German Trade Unions) and from 1894 to 1907 served as a member of the Reichstag representing the Sozialdemokratische Partei Deutschlands (Social Democratic Party of Germany). Elm was also prominent in organizing and managing several cooperative ventures and an insurance plan linked with the German trade unions. When SG visited Europe in 1895, Elm served as his liaison with the German labor movement.

ELY, Richard Theodore (1854-1943), an economist at the Johns Hopkins University and from 1892 director of the University of Wisconsin's School of Economics, Political Science, and History, was a leader in the "new school" of reform-oriented economics and one of the founders of the American Economics Association. Ely was an advocate of trade unionism and believed in positive government intervention in the economy.

EMRICH, Henry (b. 1846?), a cabinetmaker born in Prussia, immigrated to New York in 1866 and joined the Cabinet Makers' Union two years later. Emrich was active in the political organization of the New York City Central Labor Union in the 1880s. He served as secretary of the International Furniture Workers' Union of America between 1882 and 1891 and was its delegate to the FOTLU and AFL conventions between 1885 and 1889. He was elected sixth vice-president of the FOTLU in 1885 and treasurer of the AFL in 1888 and 1889.

EVANS, Christopher (1841-1924), an Ohio miners' leader and AFL secretary from 1889 to 1894, was born in England and immigrated to the United States in 1869. He helped found the Ohio Miners' Amalgamated Association, serving as its president in 1889, and the National Federation of Miners and Mine Laborers (NFMML). As secretary of the NFMML from 1885 to 1888, he participated in joint conferences between miners and operators to establish annual scales of prices and wages in the Midwest coal region. After 1895 he became an organizer for the United Mine Workers of America (UMWA) and the AFL, and in 1901 he was appointed UMWA statistician.

FEHRENBATCH, John (1844-1930), was born in Rochester, N.Y., where he apprenticed as a blacksmith. In the early 1860s he apprenticed as a machinist in Peterboro, Ont., and then worked in Ohio and Indiana, joining International Machinists and Blacksmiths of North America (IMBNA) 5 of Evansville, Ind., in 1864, and IMBNA 4 of Indianapolis later that year. He was vice-president of the latter before serving on a U.S. military railroad during the Civil War. After returning to Indianapolis in 1865, his union elected him special corresponding secretary to work in the eight-hour movement, and he was elected secretary of the Grand Eight-Hour League of Indiana. In 1868 he was a delegate to the National Labor Union convention in New York City. He moved to Rochester, N.Y., in 1870 to rebuild IMBNA 7, and in 1871 was elected president of the IMBNA; he was reelected in 1872. He was elected president of the Industrial Congress of the United States in 1873, and to a single term as a Republican in the Ohio legislature in 1875.

FIELDEN, Samuel (b. 1847), born in Lancashire, was a cotton mill worker in England. After coming to the United States in 1868, he worked as an itinerant laborer, hauling stone and working the canals, railroads, and levees of the Midwest and South. He settled in Chicago in 1871, was involved in labor organization among teamsters, and by the early 1880s was a prominent labor agitator. He joined the anarchist International Working People's Association in 1884. Fielden was convicted of murder in connection with the Haymarket incident. His sentence was commuted to life imprisonment by Governor Richard J. Oglesby, and he was pardoned by Governor John P. Altgeld in 1893.

FORAN, Martin Ambrose (1844-1921), Democratic congressman from Ohio (1883-89), was a Cleveland cooper, an organizer in 1870 of the Coopers' International Union, and its president for three years.

During the early 1870s he was active in the movement to form a federation of national trade unions. He became a lawyer in 1874 and served as prosecuting attorney of Cleveland between 1875 and 1877. As a congressman, he supported labor legislation, and in 1884 he introduced a bill to prevent the importation of contract labor.

FOSTER, Frank Keyes (1855-1909), was born in Massachusetts and worked as a printer in Connecticut before settling in Boston in 1880. He was active in the International Typographical Union and represented the Boston Central Trades and Labor Union at the 1883 FOTLU convention, where he was elected secretary of the Legislative Committee. A member of KOL Local Assembly 2006, he was elected secretary of District Assembly 30 and a member of the Knights' General Executive Board in 1883. In 1884 he began editing the KOL organ in Massachusetts, the *Laborer* (Haverhill). Foster ran unsuccessfully for lieutenant-governor of Massachusetts in 1886 on the Democratic ticket. In 1887 he helped found the Massachusetts State Federation of Labor and served as treasurer (1887), secretary (1889-95), and chairman of the legislative committee (1892-93, 1900-1907). He founded the *Labor Leader* (Boston) in 1887 and was its editor until 1897.

FOX, Martin (1848-1907), president of the Iron Molders' Union of North America (IMUNA) from 1890 to 1903, was born in Cincinnati, and there joined IMUNA 3 in 1864. For most of his career he belonged to IMUNA 20 of Covington, Ky. He began serving as a trustee of the IMUNA in 1878 and was a clerk in the IMUNA president's office from 1880 to 1886. In 1886 he was elected secretary of the union, holding that position until he became president. Fox represented the AFL at the Trades Union Congress of Great Britain in 1897. Following his retirement from the IMUNA presidency, he was a paid consultant to the organization until 1907. Fox was also active in the National Civic Federation from its founding in 1900, serving on its administrative council and in its division of conciliation and mediation.

FUHRMAN, Alfred (b. 1863), was active in the organization of seamen and brewers on the West Coast. Born in Germany, he immigrated to the United States in 1881. He organized local 16 of the National Union of the United Brewery Workmen of the United States (NUUBW) in San Francisco and served as its general secretary in 1889-90. He was also associated with the Coast Seamen's Union as a member and organizer. Fuhrman was secretary (1889-90) and president (1890-91) of the Representative Council of the Federated Trades and Labor Organizations of the Pacific Coast. In 1890 the NUUBW suspended his local and the AFL suspended the Representative Council in a dispute that saw Fuhrman organize the rival United Brewery Workmen's Union of the Pacific Coast, of which he became general secretary. The San Francisco brewers rejoined the national organization in 1892. In 1891 Fuhrman helped organize and served as the first president (1891-93) of the Council of Federated Trades of the Pacific Coast. He became a lawyer and left the labor movement in 1893.

GAGE, Lyman Judson (1836-1927), a Chicago banker, played an active role in the movement to pardon the Haymarket defendants. A member of the board of directors of the World's Columbian Exposition, he served as its president from 1890 to 1891. He was president of the American Bankers' Association and the first president (1894-95) of the Chicago Civic Federation, and served as secretary of the U.S. Treasury from 1897 to 1902 under McKinley and Roosevelt.

GARLAND, Mahlon Morris (1856-1920), president of the National Amalgamated Association of Iron and Steel Workers (NAAISW) from 1892 to 1898 and fourth vice-president of the AFL from 1895 to 1898, was born in Pittsburgh, Pa. An iron puddler and heater, he joined the NAAISW in the late 1870s. He was fired in 1878 for union activities and found work in several midwestern cities before returning to Pittsburgh in 1880. There he joined NAAISW South Side Lodge 11 and in the mid-1880s served two terms on the city's select council. From 1890 to 1892 he was assistant president of the NAAISW, before assuming its presidency. He resigned from office in 1898 and accepted an appointment as U.S. collector of customs for Pittsburgh, retaining that post until 1915. Garland was a Republican congressman from 1915 until his death.

GEORGE, Henry (1839-97), a Philadelphia-born journalist, labor reformer, and anti-monopolist, began his newspaper career in 1860 as a printer and then worked as an editor for several San Francisco papers. George published *Progress and Poverty*, his most influential work, in 1879 and *The Irish Land Question* in 1881, and subsequently served in the British Isles as correspondent for the *Irish World*. In 1886 he ran second as the liberal and labor candidate in a three-way contest for mayor of New York City against Theodore Roosevelt and the victorious Abram S. Hewitt. His supporters gave serious consideration to a presidential race in 1888, but their hopes were dashed by his disappointing showing in the 1887 campaign for secretary of state of New York. In the campaign's aftermath supporters launched the single-tax movement, based on George's tax reform theories. George meanwhile continued his writing, edited the *Standard* from

1887 to 1890, undertook several speaking tours, and traveled extensively. In 1897, against medical advice, he again ran for mayor of New York City; he died four days before the election.

GOLDMAN, Emma (1869-1940), was born in Kovno, Russia, and immigrated to the United States in 1885. She settled in Rochester, N.Y., where she worked in a clothing factory and was married briefly. She first became interested in anarchism after the execution of the Haymarket defendants in 1887. She moved to New York City in 1889 where she met anarchist leader Johann Most and her long-time collaborator, Alexander Berkman, and became active in the anarchist movement and in union organizing in the clothing industry. After addressing a mass meeting of unemployed workers in 1893, she was arrested and sentenced to a year in prison for inciting to riot. In 1895 she traveled abroad and studied nursing and midwifery in Austria. She returned to the United States in 1896 and for the next few years lectured throughout the country. In 1906 she founded an anarchist journal, *Mother Earth,* which she published until 1918 when it was suppressed by the government. She was jailed for fifteen days in 1916 for lecturing on birth control and for two years in 1917 for opposing conscription. Goldman's sole claim to American citizenship rested on her earlier marriage, and when the government successfully challenged her former husband's citizenship in 1909, she lost hers at the same time. In December 1919 the government deported her to the Soviet Union. After she broke with the Bolsheviks in 1921, she lived in various European cities before settling in Canada in 1926. She continued to lecture and write prolifically until her death.

GOLDWATER, Samuel (1850-98), was born in Poland and immigrated to New York City in 1859, apprenticing as a cigarmaker and joining CMIU 15. He was active in the labor movement and the SLP in Chicago in the 1870s and 1880s, helping form the Chicago Trade and Labor Council (later the Trade and Labor Assembly of Chicago), serving as president of CMIU 11, and running for local offices of the SLP ticket. Moving to Detroit in 1886, he was twice elected president of the Detroit Trade and Labor Council and helped organize the Michigan Federation of Labor. He also served as a CMIU vice-president in 1895 and as a delegate to two AFL conventions. Goldwater was elected city alderman as an independent Democrat in 1894 and 1896, and twice ran unsuccessfully for mayor, dying in the midst of his second campaign.

GOMPERS, Abraham Julian (1876-1903), was the son of SG and Sophia Gompers; he worked in New York City in the clothing industry as a cutter. In 1901, after he contracted tuberculosis, his parents sent him to convalesce at the Denver home of Max Morris, secretary and treasurer of the Retail Clerks' International Protective Association. Abraham worked briefly for the association before his death.

GOMPERS, Alexander (1857-1926), SG's brother, was born in London and immigrated with the family to the United States in 1863. He was a cigarmaker and an early member of CMIU 144. He married Rachel Bickstein, who was born in London, and they had six children.

GOMPERS, Alexander Julian (1878-1947), was the son of SG and Sophia Gompers. He was a cigarmaker and cigar manufacturer in New York City and in Washington, D.C. From 1914 to 1947 he served as an official of the New York State Department of Labor. He and his wife, Ella Appelbaum Gompers, had three children: Esther, Sophia, and May.

GOMPERS, Henry (b. 1853), SG's brother, was born in London and immigrated with the family to America in 1863. A cigarmaker and member of the CMIU, he married Sarah Wennick, a Dutch immigrant, and they had two sons.

GOMPERS, Henry Julian (1874-1938), was the son of SG and Sophia Gompers. In 1887 he was the AFL's first office boy, and he later became a granite cutter. About 1914 he moved from New York City to Washington, D.C., where he ran Gompers' Monumental Works. He and his wife, Bessie Phillips Gompers, had four children: Sophia, Samuel, Alexander, and Louis.

GOMPERS, Jacob (1863-1906), SG's brother, was born in London and immigrated with the family to America in 1863. A diamond polisher and first president of the Diamond Workers' Union of America, he married Sophia Spero, and they had three sons and two daughters.

GOMPERS, Louis (1859-1920), SG's brother, was born in London and immigrated with the family to the United States in 1863. He became a Brooklyn cigar manufacturer and president of the Retail Tobacco Dealers' Association. He married Sophia Bickstein, and they had seven children.

GOMPERS, Samuel Julian (1868-1946), was the son of SG and Sophia Gompers. Born in New York City, he left school at the age of fourteen to work in a New York City print shop. He moved to Washington, D.C., about 1887 and worked as a printer in the Government Printing Office, a compositor in the U.S. Department of Commerce and Labor, and a clerk in the U.S. Census Office. He was a member of the Association of Union Printers and the Columbia Typographical Union

(International Typographical Union 101). In 1913 he became chief of the Division of Publications and Supplies of the U.S. Department of Labor, and in 1918 he became chief clerk of the Department of Labor, a position he held until 1941. Gompers and his wife, Sophia Dampf Gompers, had one child, Florence.

GOMPERS, Simon (1849-96), SG's uncle and close childhood companion, was born in London and was a union shoemaker. Immigrating to the United States in 1868, he married Elizabeth Tate; they had six sons and two daughters.

GOMPERS, Simon (1865-1953), SG's brother, was born in New York and worked there as a sheet metal worker. He married Leah Lopez, and they had five children. The family moved to Norwalk, Conn., in 1924.

GOMPERS, Sophia Dampf (1870?-1959), was born in New York City and moved to Washington, D.C., after her marriage to SG's son, Samuel Julian Gompers, in 1892.

GOMPERS, Sophia Julian (1850-1920), SG's first wife, was born in London and immigrated to the United States about 1858. She was living with her father and stepmother in Brooklyn and working as a tobacco stripper in a cigar factory when she married SG in 1867. Between 1868 and 1885 she and SG had at least nine children, six of whom lived past infancy: Samuel, Rose, Henry, Abraham, Alexander, and Sadie.

GREENAWALT, Elmer Ellsworth (1862-1920), was born in Lancaster, Pa., where he became a cigarmaker and a member of CMIU 257. In 1893 he was elected president of the short-lived Pennsylvania Federation of Labor. After the organization reformed in 1902, Greenawalt served as its president from 1903 to 1912. He edited the *Labor Leader* in Lancaster for twenty-three years. He was an unsuccessful Democratic candidate for Congress in 1912 and then served as commissioner of conciliation. He was appointed commissioner for immigration for the port of Philadelphia in 1914, a position he held until his death.

GRUELLE, Thomas M. (b. 1855), was editor and publisher of the *Labor Signal* (Indianapolis) from 1887 until the paper's demise in 1894. He was born in Kentucky, and lived in Minnesota and Illinois before moving to Indianapolis about 1882. Working as a printer in that city he joined KOL Alpha Assembly 1712 and International Typographical Union 1. He was active in the Indiana Federation of Trade and Labor Unions as its lecturer and organizer in 1890 and its president from 1891 to 1893. He also served as president of the Indianapolis

Central Labor Union (1889-92) and as a general organizer for the AFL (1891-94). Gruelle continued as a printer until about 1910, and in the subsequent decade worked as a journalist, salesman, and cabinet maker.

GUNTON, George (1846-1919), was born in England and immigrated to the United States in 1874. He settled in Fall River, Mass., where he worked as a weaver and served in 1875 as secretary of the Weavers' Protective Association. Blacklisted that year after an unsuccessful strike, he moved to Boston where he worked with George McNeill and Ira Steward in the eight-hour movement and the organization of the International Labor Union (ILU) in 1878. A member of the ILU's provisional central committee, he returned to Fall River in 1878 where he helped organize textile workers for the ILU and managed the *Labor Standard* from 1878 to 1882, initially as the ILU's official organ. He ran unsuccessfully for the Massachusetts legislature in 1880 on the Greenback ticket. In 1885 he moved to New York City and in 1887 his *Wealth and Progress* was published, a widely known work based on Ira Steward's unfinished manuscripts. Gunton served as president of the Institute of Social Economics from 1890 to 1904, and as editor of the *Social Economist* (*Gunton's Magazine* after 1896) from 1891 to 1904, when it ceased publication.

HARDIE, James Keir (1856-1915), a Lanarkshire, Scotland, miner, was secretary of the Ayrshire Miners' Union (1886-90) and a founder in 1888 of the Scottish Labour party. He founded the *Miner* in 1887 and edited it until 1889 when he launched the *Labour Leader,* editing the latter as a monthly until 1894 and as a weekly thereafter until 1904. In 1892 he was elected to Parliament as an independent candidate, serving until his defeat in 1895. In 1893 he helped organize the Independent Labour party (ILP); he was the ILP's chairman from 1893 to 1900. Hardie helped form the Labour Representation Committee in 1900, serving on it until it evolved into the Labour party in 1906. He was a Member of Parliament from 1900 to 1915 and chairman of the Labour party (1906-7, 1913-15).

HARDING, John C. (b. 1859), a Chicago printer, emigrated from England in 1882. He was active in International Typographical Union 16 as president (1892-93) and secretary (1906-9) and was a delegate to the Trade and Labor Assembly of Chicago. From 1890 to 1892 he was president of the Illinois State Federation of Labor.

HARRIS, Daniel (1846-1915), a Civil War veteran and cigarmaker, was born in England and immigrated to the United States in the early 1860s. During the 1877-78 cigarmakers' strike the Central Organization of the Cigarmakers of New York appointed Harris to its Committee on Organization for Pennsylvania. In the late 1880s Harris was president of CMIU 144. He served as president of the New York State Workingmen's Assembly from 1892 to 1897 and of the New York Federation of Labor in 1899 and from 1906 until his death.

HART, Lee M. (1862-1916), was born in Maryland and worked as a theatrical stage employee in Chicago in the early 1890s. He was elected treasurer of the newly formed National Alliance of Theatrical Stage Employes in 1893 and president in 1894, serving a one-year term. In 1895 and 1896 he served as president of the Illinois Brotherhood of Theatrical Stage Employes. Elected secretary-treasurer of the national union in 1898, he held this position until he retired in 1914.

HAYES, John William (1854-1942), was born in Philadelphia. By the 1870s he lived in New Jersey where he was initiated into the KOL while employed as a brakeman with the Pennsylvania Railroad in 1874. Soon after joining the Order he was commissioned as an organizer and, after the loss of his right arm in an 1878 railroad accident, became a telegrapher. Losing his position in 1883 because of union activities, he entered the grocery business. He was a member of the KOL General Executive Board from 1884 to 1916, serving as general secretary-treasurer from 1888 until 1902 and as the Knights' last general master workman from 1902 until the Order closed its central office in 1916. Hayes took an active part in the People's party in the early 1890s. He was manager of the Atlantic Gas Construction Co. in Philadelphia and, later, president of the North Chesapeake Beach Land and Improvement Co.

HILL, David Bennett (1843-1910), a Democrat, served as governor of New York from 1885 until 1892 and as a U.S. senator from 1892 until 1897.

HOLMES, David (1843-1906), was president of the Amalgamated Weavers' Association (1884-1906) and a member of the Parliamentary Committee of the Trades Union Congress of Great Britain (1892-1900, 1902-3).

HORN, George L. (b. 1863?), was born in Germany and immigrated to the United States in 1877. He settled in Indianapolis where, in the early 1890s, he was a member of Journeymen Bakers' and Confectioners' International Union (JBCIU) 18. He was elected secretary of the JBCIU in 1892 and moved to Detroit in 1893 before settling in Brooklyn in 1894. He resigned as secretary in 1895 and was working as a factory inspector in Brooklyn as late as 1903.

HYSELL, Nial R. (b. 1854), was born in Ohio where he worked as a coal miner. In 1884 he was elected vice-president of the Ohio Miners' Amalgamated Association, a position he held for three years. He was also a member of the Executive Board of the National Federation of Miners and Mine Laborers (1886-87). He served in the Ohio General Assembly as a Democrat (1888-92; Speaker of the house, 1890-91). Hysell undertook the study of law in 1890 and was admitted to the bar in 1893. He served a term as a state senator from 1896 to 1897 and was later a hotel proprietor and broker in Columbus.

IVES, Harry M. (b. 1856), born in Iowa, graduated from Iowa State Agricultural College and moved to Topeka, Kans., in 1881 where he worked as a printer. He was elected president of International Typographical Union 121 in 1889 and a director in 1890. In 1892 and 1893 he served as president of the short-lived Kansas State Federation of Labor and in 1893 worked as an organizer for the AFL. In 1905 Ives started a commercial printing establishment, H. M. Ives and Sons, where he worked until retirement in 1924.

JOHNSON, William Lee Andrew (1863-1934?), was born in Leavenworth, Kans., and worked in coal mines and on a farm before apprenticing as a boilermaker in Kansas City, Mo. He was active in the KOL in the 1880s and joined the National Brotherhood of Boiler Makers of the United States of America (NBBM) in 1891, becoming its vice-president in 1892. After the NBBM merged with the International Brotherhood of Boiler Makers and Iron Ship Builders' Protective and Benevolent Union of the United States and Canada to form the International Brotherhood of Boiler Makers and Iron Ship Builders of America in 1893, he was elected grand president of the new organization. He held the position until 1897 when he was appointed state labor commissioner of Kansas. He was elected secretary of the Kansas State Society of Labor and Industry when it was founded in 1898, and held that office until 1911. Subsequently he served as an arbitrator for the Southwest Inter-State Coal Operators' Association and the United Mine Workers of America.

JONAS, Alexander (1834-1912), was born in Berlin and immigrated to the United States in 1869, becoming a journalist. He joined the Social Democratic Workingmen's Party of North America in the early 1870s and in 1877 was elected to edit the official organ of the SLP, the *Arbeiter Stimme*. In 1878 he founded the *New Yorker Volkszeitung*, with which he was associated as an editor (1878-89) and as a member of the editorial board (1878-1912). He was the SLP's candidate for mayor of New York in 1878, 1888, and 1892, for state senator in 1891, and for state assemblyman in 1894.

JONES, Jerome (1855-1940), was born in Nashville, Tenn., where he worked as a reporter, printer, and editor for several newspapers, including the *Nashville Herald,* the *Nashville Sun,* and the *Journal of Labor.* He joined the International Typographical Union (ITU) in 1876 and later served as president of the Nashville Federation of Trades and, from the early 1890s, as an AFL organizer. In 1898 he established the *Journal of Labor* in Atlanta, serving as its editor until 1940. He was active in ITU 48 in Atlanta and helped organize the Georgia Federation of Labor (GFL) in 1899. The *Journal of Labor* became the official organ of the GFL, and Jones served two terms (1904-5, 1911-12) as the Federation's president. He was a founder of the Southern Labor Congress in 1912 and its president until its demise in 1919. He also served a term as president of the Atlanta Federation of Trades.

KEAN, Edward J. (b. 1851), a New York City printer, was born in Maryland. He served as president of the Amalgamated Trades and Labor Union of New York and Vicinity and as editor of International Typographical Union 6's organ, the *Boycotter.* Kean was chief clerk of the New York Bureau of Labor Statistics between 1885 and 1891.

KELLY, James T. (1862-1930), was born in Overton, Pa. He was one of the founders of AFL St. Louis Wiremen's and Linemen's Union 5221 in January 1891, serving as that organization's vice-president until he helped form the National Brotherhood of Electrical Workers of America (NBEWA) in November of the same year. He was grand secretary-treasurer (1891-95) and grand secretary (1895-97) of the NBEWA. In 1892 he established the *Electrical Worker,* acting as editor until 1897. After 1897 Kelly remained active in NBEWA 1 of St. Louis, serving as press secretary for many years.

KENNEY, Mary. See Mary Kenney O'SULLIVAN.

KEUFER, Auguste (1851-1924), was general secretary of the Fédération française des travailleurs du livre, the French typographical union, from 1885 to 1920. He was a leading positivist and in 1895 was one of the prime movers in the founding of the Confédération générale du travail, serving as its first treasurer. SG met with him on several occasions both in the United States and abroad.

KIDD, Thomas Inglis (1860-1941), a woodworker, immigrated to the United States from Scotland in 1884, residing in Nebraska before moving to Denver at the end of the decade. He helped organize woodworkers in Nebraska, Colorado, and Minnesota and was elected general secretary-treasurer of the newly formed Machine Woodworkers' International Union (MWWIU) in 1890. He held this position for the next five years and continued as general secretary of the MWWIU's successor, the Amalgamated Wood Workers' International Union from 1895 to 1905. In these positions he edited the union's journal, the *Machine Woodworker* (retitled the *International Woodworker* in 1895). Kidd moved to Chicago in 1892 and played a prominent role in the Populist-labor alliance in Illinois. He was the AFL's sixth vice-president from 1898 to 1900 and its fifth vice-president from 1900 to 1905. In 1907 he became a New York sales representative for the Milwaukee-based Brunswick-Balke-Collender Co. and in 1913 became branch manager in Milwaukee.

KILGALLAN, John C. (1862-97), a national secretary (1892-95) and secretary-treasurer (1895-97) of the National Amalgamated Association of Iron and Steel Workers (NAAISW), was born in Ireland and moved to England as a child. In 1880 he came to the United States where he worked as an iron puddler in several Pittsburgh mills and joined NAAISW Ever Faithful Lodge 51. He was assistant secretary of the NAAISW from 1890 to 1892.

KING, Edward (1846-1922), a type founder, immigrated from Scotland about 1870 and organized in his trade. He was one of a small group of New York City positivists. During the 1880s he served as a delegate to the New York City Central Labor Union and proved an ardent supporter of both trade unionism and independent political action on the part of the workers. In the late 1880s King became active with SG in the Social Reform Club which included trade unionists, employers, and members of the middle class who were interested in improving working conditions and the relationship between the classes. He was involved in the New York settlement movement from its beginning, living and working at the University Settlement House for many years, where he taught classes in Greek and Roman history. He was also a member of the Advisory Council of the People's Institute of the Ethical Culture Society, which organized clubs to discuss social problems.

KIRCHNER, John S. (1857-1912), a cigarmaker, was born in Maryland and became active in the labor movement in 1877 when he joined a Baltimore local assembly of the KOL. After moving to Philadelphia he was recording secretary of KOL Local Assembly 53 for several years. He helped organize CMIU 100 and filled various offices (financial secretary, president, and corresponding secretary) in the new union during the 1880s. He was financial secretary of the Philadelphia Central Labor Union in 1886 but resigned that position because of his duties as CMIU organizer for Pennsylvania as well as CMIU fourth vice-president (1885-87). In 1886 the FOTLU Legislative Committee appointed him secretary of the FOTLU upon the death of William H. Foster.

KLIVER, William H. (1846-1914), an Ohio-born carpenter and Civil War veteran, came to Chicago in 1884 and became a member of KOL Local Assembly 1307 and Brotherhood of Carpenters and Joiners local 28. He was president of the Trade and Labor Assembly of Chicago in 1887 and first vice-president of the Illinois State Federation of Labor in 1888. In 1888 he also became fifth vice-president of the United Brotherhood of Carpenters and Joiners and two years later was elected general president, serving until 1892. Kliver moved to Gary, Ind., in 1904 and was elected as a Republican to a two-year term in the Indiana legislature in 1908. He was building commissioner of Gary from 1909 until 1914.

KOENEN, Bernard (variously Bernhard), was born in Germany in 1850 and immigrated to the United States in 1881. He settled in Brooklyn, working as a cabinetmaker and joining International Furniture Workers' Union of America (IFWU) 7 of New York City. He served as corresponding secretary of the IFWU (1891-92), recording secretary (1893-95), and editor (1891-95) of the union's journal, the *Furniture Workers' Journal* (retitled the *Wood Workers' Journal* in June 1891). Koenen was an SLP nominee for Brooklyn alderman at large in 1893. He later owned a hardware store in Brooklyn.

KURZENKNABE, Ernst (1860?-1927), was national secretary of the National Union of the United Brewery Workmen of the United States (NUUBW) from 1888 to 1899 and held this position jointly with Charles Bechtold after 1892. A former secretary of NUUBW 1 of New York City, Kurzenknabe moved to St. Louis during his tenure as national secretary. Between 1900 and 1920 he worked variously as a saloonkeeper, cashier, and bookkeeper before becoming a reporter for *Amerika*, a German-language paper, about 1921.

LABADIE, Joseph Antoine (1850-1933), born in Paw Paw, Mich., was apprenticed to a printer in South Bend, Ind., in 1866. After settling in Detroit in 1872, he joined International Typographical Union 18 and in 1878 became a KOL organizer. He was also active in politics, running unsuccessfully for mayor on the Workingmen's party ticket in 1879 and playing an active role in the SLP. In the early 1880s Labadie worked as a labor journalist for several papers and was one of the publishers of the *Labor Review* and the *Times,* a trade union paper. He played a major role in establishing the Detroit Trades and Labor Council in 1880, becoming its corresponding secretary, and was also a founder and first president (1889-90) of the

Michigan Federation of Labor. Labadie became a philosophical anarchist in 1883 and was a close associate of Benjamin Tucker, a leading anarchist thinker; he frequently wrote for Tucker's journal, *Liberty,* until its demise in 1908. In 1893 Labadie was appointed clerk of the Detroit Water Works, a post he held until about 1920.

Lappard, John (b. 1853), was born in Ireland and immigrated to the United States in 1870. He worked as a currier in Chicago and was general secretary and treasurer of the United Brotherhood of Tanners and Curriers of America in 1894. He later became a letter carrier.

Law, William J., was president of the Amalgamated Association of Street Railway Employes of America (AASREA) from 1892 to 1893. A streetcar conductor, he was a traveling delegate in 1892 for AFL Detroit Street Car Employes' Association 5391, and its delegate to the AASREA's founding convention that year. A secession movement in the AASREA's Detroit local 3 consumed most of Law's attention during his year as president, and he was defeated for reelection in 1893. He later became a doorkeeper for a Detroit hotel.

Legien, Carl (1861-1920), was born in Marienburg, Prussia, and raised at an orphanage in nearby Thorn. He apprenticed to a woodcarver at the age of fourteen. After three years of compulsory military service and two years as a traveling journeyman, Legien settled in Hamburg and joined the local union of woodcarvers in 1886. He was elected president of the Vereinigung der Drechsler Deutschlands (Union of German Woodcarvers) at its founding in 1887. In 1890 he stepped down from this office to become secretary of the newly founded Generalkommission der Gewerkschaften Deutschlands (General Commission of German Trade Unions). He led this organization (renamed Allgemeiner Deutscher Gewerkschaftsbund [General German Federation of Trade Unions] after 1919) until his death. He also edited its official organ, the *Correspondenzblatt,* from 1891 to 1900. Under his leadership the German trade union movement grew from a regionalized group of craft unions to the most powerful centralized industrial union movement in Europe. A member of the Sozialdemokratische Partei Deutschlands (Social Democratic Party of Germany), Legien served as a socialist deputy in the Reichstag from 1893 to 1898 and from 1903 until his death. As a social democrat, Legien was instrumental in integrating the concerns of the German union movement into the political program of the Social Democratic party. He also became an important figure in the international trade union movement when he helped inaugurate the annual meetings of the International Secretariat of Trade Union Centers (after 1913, the

International Federation of Trade Unions) in 1900. He was secretary of this organization from 1903 to 1919.

LENNON, John Brown (1850-1923), president and subsequently general secretary of the Journeymen Tailors' National Union of the United States (JTNU; later renamed Journeymen Tailors' Union of America), was born in Wisconsin and raised in Hannibal, Mo. He moved to Denver in 1869 where he helped organize a tailors' union and the Denver Trades Assembly and held offices in both. In 1883, Lennon's local affiliated with the newly formed JTNU; Lennon subsequently served as president of the national union (1884-85), General Executive Board member (1885-87), and general secretary and editor of the *Tailor* (1887-1910). He was treasurer of the AFL from 1890 to 1917, a member of the U.S. Commission on Industrial Relations (1913-15), and of the Board of Mediators of the U.S. Department of Labor (1917).

LEVY, Sarah Gompers (b. 1842), SG's aunt, married Marcus Levy in 1863; they immigrated to New York City in 1865.

LLOYD, Henry (b. 1855), was the general president of the United Brotherhood of Carpenters and Joiners of America (UBCJA) from 1896 to 1898. He was born in Albany, N.Y., and moved to Toronto in 1864, joining the Millwrights' Union of Toronto in 1876 and local 27 of the UBCJA in 1884. During the 1880s he was active in the Toronto Trades and Labour Council. In 1888 the UBCJA elected him first vice-president, and he held this position until 1890. He moved to Boston in that year and joined UBCJA 33, functioning as its president for two terms. He took an active role in the Boston Central Labor Union, serving as its president in 1896. In 1895 he ran unsuccessfully for the Boston School Board on the Workingmen's Political League of Boston ticket. The 1898 AFL convention elected him a delegate to the Trades Union Congress of Great Britain. About 1900 he began to sell insurance and moved to the Boston suburb of Somerville; as late as 1915 he continued to work as an insurance agent in Boston.

LLOYD, Henry Demarest (1847-1903), was born in New York City where he became a lawyer in 1869. His opposition to monopoly power and special privilege drew him to the American Free-Trade League, and he served as league secretary as well as editor of its journal— the *Free Trader*—from 1869 to 1872. Moving to Chicago in 1872, he became financial editor and then chief editorial writer of the *Chicago Tribune*. His economic self-sufficiency, based largely on a financially advantageous marriage, enabled him to leave the *Tribune* in 1885 and devote himself independently to reform causes. Lloyd achieved prominence through his long campaign to reform the Chicago Board of Trade and through his exposé, published in the *Atlantic Monthly* in 1881, detailing the monopolistic practices of Standard Oil. Among his major works he later published an acclaimed book-length treatment of Standard Oil, *Wealth against Commonwealth* (1894). He was also associated closely with labor causes. He sought commuted sentences for those convicted in connection with Chicago's 1886 Haymarket incident, became a central figure in the effort to build a labor-populist alliance in the early 1890s, and wrote extensively in sympathy with labor. Lloyd ran unsuccessfully for Congress as a National People's party candidate in 1894.

LOEBENBERG, Abraham B. (1842?-1911), was a founder and early leader of the Retail Clerks' National Protective Association of America (RCNPA; renamed Retail Clerks' International Protective Association [RCIPA] in 1899). Born in Germany, he immigrated to the United States in 1857. After a brief time in West Virginia, he settled in Indianapolis and became a store clerk. In 1882 he helped organize a clerks' early closing society, which affiliated with the KOL as Commercial Assembly 8032. In 1889 the assembly reorganized as the Salesmen's Union of Indianapolis and was chartered by the AFL as local 3695. Loebenberg represented that union at the 1890 AFL convention where he helped form the RCNPA; the Indianapolis union became local 1 of the new national. Loebenberg was elected national organizer for the Retail Clerks at its founding, a post he held until it was eliminated in 1894. He frequently represented the organization at AFL conventions until 1908. In 1899 he moved to Decatur, Ill., where he belonged to RCIPA 493.

LOSKY, Woyt, a Denver waiter, was general secretary of the Hotel and Restaurant Employees' National Alliance (HRENA) from 1893 until 1896, and he was a member of HRENA 14.

MACARTHUR, Walter (1862-1944), was business manager (1891-94) and then editor (1895-1900, 1901-13) of the *Coast Seamen's Journal*, published by the Coast Seamen's Union (later the Sailors' Union of the Pacific Coast) and the National (later International) Seamen's Union. He was born in Glasgow, Scotland, where he received one year of university education before serving in the British merchant marine (1876-86). As a member of the U.S. merchant marine (1886-91), he came to San Diego in 1887 and joined the Coast Seamen's Union in 1889. He was elected president of the San Francisco Federated Trades Council in 1892, secretary of the Council of Federated Trades of the Pacific Coast in 1893, and chaired the committee that organized the AFL's California state labor federation in 1901. MacArthur wrote numerous books and pamphlets on seamen's laws and maritime affairs, and from 1913 to 1932 was U.S. shipping commissioner for the port of San Francisco. He was also active in the National Civic Federation.

McBRIDE, John (1854-1917), the only person to defeat SG for the presidency of the AFL, presided over the formation of the United Mine Workers of America (UMWA) and was its second president. The son of an Ohio miner, he was elected president of the Ohio Miners' Protective Union in 1877 and master workman of KOL District Assembly 38 in 1880, and served as president of the Ohio Miners' Amalgamated Association from 1882 to 1889. In 1885 he was a founder and first president of the National Federation of Miners and Mine Laborers and in 1886 presided over the founding convention of the AFL, declining the Federation's nomination for president. He served as president of the National Progressive Union of Miners and Mine Laborers in 1889 and was a leader in merging that union with KOL National Trade Assembly 135 in 1890 to form the UMWA. He became president of the UMWA in 1892 and served until 1895.

McBride served as a Democrat in the Ohio legislature from 1884 to 1888, was commissioner of the Ohio Bureau of Labor Statistics from 1890 to 1891, and later became active in the populist movement. He was elected president of the AFL over SG in 1894, and narrowly lost to SG the next year. McBride purchased the *Columbus Record* in 1896, and subsequently pursued various occupations including editor, saloonkeeper, and federal labor conciliator.

McBRYDE, Patrick (1848-1902?), secretary-treasurer of the United Mine Workers of America (UMWA) from 1891 to 1896, was born in Ireland and raised in Scotland, where he became active in local miners' organizations. He came to the United States in the late 1870s, working for several years before returning to the Scottish mines. About 1884 he immigrated to the United States, settling in the Pittsburgh area where he joined KOL Local Assembly 151. McBryde represented KOL National Trade Assembly 135 at the founding convention of the National Progressive Union of Miners and Mine Laborers and served as its secretary-treasurer (1888-90). In 1890 he was elected to the National Executive Board of the newly founded UMWA. After retiring from the miners' union in 1896, he served as commissioner for mine operators in Ohio.

McCRAITH, Augustine (1864?-1909), was born in Canada. He moved to Massachusetts, where he joined International Typographical Union (ITU) 61 of Cambridge at the age of nineteen. After living for a short time in Boston, he moved to New York in the mid-1880s before returning to Boston in 1887. There he served as president (1891-92) and secretary (1892-95) of ITU 13. Between 1894 and 1896 he was secretary of the AFL. Later he moved to New York City, where he was an active member of ITU 6.

McGILL, James (b. 1862), general president-secretary of the Horse Collar Makers' National Union from 1889 to 1893, was born in Ireland and moved to the United States in 1867. Settling in Louisville, Ky., he worked as a horse collar maker and became active in the local labor movement. He served the Trades and Labor Assembly of Louisville and Vicinity as recording secretary (1890, 1894) and sergeant-at-arms (1892-93), and in 1894 helped organize the Louisville Central Labor Union, serving as recording secretary (1895) and president (1897-99). In 1896 he helped organize AFL Federal Labor Union 6873 in Louisville. McGill worked as a storekeeper and gauger for the U.S. surveyor of customs in Louisville from 1895 to 1898 and as the assistant wharfmaster for the city in 1899. From 1901 to 1904 he edited the *Journal of Labor* and in the latter year was president of the Kentucky State Federation of Labor. From 1906 until at least 1921 he worked as a collar maker.

McGLYNN, Edward (1837-1900), a New York–born Catholic priest, was appointed pastor of St. Stephen's parish in 1866. He was a member of the American Land League and came into conflict with Archbishop Michael Corrigan for his outspoken support of Henry George in the 1886 New York mayoral campaign. As a result, early in 1887 he was transferred from St. Stephen's and later that year was excommunicated. During the next five years McGlynn regularly lectured about the single tax at meetings of the Anti-Poverty Society, of which he was the first president. In 1892 the papal representative in the United States reinstated McGlynn, and in 1894 he was named pastor of St. Mary's church in Newburgh, N.Y.

McGREGOR, Hugh (1840-1911), was an English-born jeweler. He served as a volunteer with Garibaldi's army and immigrated to the United States in 1865. During the 1870s he was a member of the International Workingmen's Association and a founder and active organizer of the Social Democratic Workingmen's Party of North America. He served as secretary of its New York branch in 1875 and its Philadelphia branch in 1876, returning to New York in the spring of that year to edit the new English-language organ of the party, the *Socialist*. A participant in the Economic and Sociological Club, he apparently left the socialist movement and became active in a small circle of New York City positivists. During the late 1880s he served as SG's secretary, directing the AFL office during the president's absence. He helped organize seamen on the Atlantic coast and between 1890 and 1892 served as secretary of the short-lived International Amalgamated Sailors' and Firemen's Union. He later worked briefly in the AFL's Washington office.

McGUIRE, Peter James (1852-1906), chief executive officer of the United Brotherhood of Carpenters and Joiners of America (UBCJA), was born in New York City. He joined a local carpenters union there in 1872 and became a member of the International Workingmen's Association. He was involved in relief efforts in New York City during the depression of the 1870s and played a major role in organizing the Tompkins Square demonstration of January 1874. In 1874 he helped organize the Social Democratic Workingmen's Party of North America and was elected to its Executive Board; that same year he joined the KOL. During the late 1870s McGuire traveled widely, organizing and campaigning first on behalf of the Workingmen's Party of the United States and then for the SLP. After living for a time in New Haven, Conn., he moved to St. Louis in 1878 and the following year was instrumental in the establishment of the Missouri Bureau of Labor Statistics, to which he was appointed deputy commissioner. He resigned in 1880 to campaign for the SLP and for the Greenback-Labor party. In 1881 he was elected secretary of the St. Louis Trades Assembly and, as a member of the provisional committee to organize a carpenters' national union, began editing the *Carpenter.* Through that journal he generated interest in organizing the Brotherhood of Carpenters and Joiners (later the UBCJA); he was elected secretary of the union at its founding convention later that year and held the position until 1901. McGuire moved to New York City in 1882, was a founder of the New York City Central Labor Union and became a member of Spread the Light KOL Local Assembly 1562. He subsequently moved to Philadelphia. He served as secretary of the AFL from 1886 to 1889, second vice-president from 1889 to 1890, and first vice-president from 1890 to 1900.

McKINNEY, Joseph W. (1856-1917?), was born in Chicago where he joined a local painters' union in 1873. Active in KOL Local Assembly 1940, he joined Brotherhood of Painters and Decorators of America (BPDA) 147 in 1891. He served as general president of the BPDA from 1892 to 1894 and was elected general secretary-treasurer in 1894 but, in a dispute with the incumbent, was unable to take office. He then led in the formation of a rival faction of the painters' union, which established its headquarters in Lafayette, Ind.; he was the general secretary-treasurer of this so-called western faction until resigning in 1897.

MCNEILL, George Edwin (1837-1906), a Boston printer born in Massachusetts, was secretary of the Grand Eight-Hour League and president of the Boston Eight-Hour League. He helped lobby for the establishment of the Massachusetts Bureau of Statistics of Labor and served as its deputy director from 1869 to 1873. McNeill was an officer of the Sovereigns of Industry, president of the International Labor Union in 1878, and secretary-treasurer of KOL District Assembly 30 from 1884 to 1886. He was editor or associate editor of several papers including the *Labor Standard* in Boston, Fall River, Mass., and Paterson, N.J., and in 1887 published *The Labor Movement: The Problem of To-Day*. He helped organize the Massachusetts Mutual Accident Association in 1883 and was elected its secretary and manager in 1892. In 1897 he served as the AFL's fraternal delegate to the Trades Union Congress of Great Britain.

MCSWEENEY, Edward F. (1864-1928), general president of the Lasters' Protective Union of America (LPUA) from 1890 to 1893, was born in Massachusetts. He was editor of the *Laster* from 1888 to 1893 and for about the same period was secretary of the Marlboro, Mass., branch of the LPUA. In 1893 he moved to New York to serve as assistant commissioner of immigration at Ellis Island, holding the post until 1902. After returning to Massachusetts, he edited the *Boston Traveler* (1905-10), served on the Massachusetts Industrial Accident Board (1912-14), and was chairman of the directors of the port of Boston (1914-17).

MCVEY, George H. (b. 1846), was president of the United Piano Makers' Union in 1887 and financial secretary of the New York City Central Labor Union in 1886 and 1887. He was active in Henry George's New York mayoralty campaign and was elected secretary of the New York State Workingmen's Assembly in 1887. From 1892 to 1894 he served as treasurer of the New York City Central Labor Federation. McVey continued to work as a pianomaker and lived in Brooklyn until the early twentieth century.

MADDEN, Stephen (b. 1855?), was a leader of the National Amalgamated Association of Iron and Steel Workers (NAAISW) from 1887 to 1899. He was born in Wales and immigrated to the United States in 1864, settling in Pittsburgh where he worked as a puddler. For most of his years in the NAAISW's leadership he was assistant secretary (1887-90, 1893-94, 1896, 1899), with intervening periods as secretary (1890-92) and secretary-treasurer (1897-98). From 1904 to 1927 he served as chief clerk of the bureau of electricity of Pittsburgh.

MAHON, William D. (1861-1949), was born in Athens, Ohio, and worked as a coal miner in the Hocking Valley district. He moved to Columbus, Ohio, in the late 1880s where he worked as a mule car driver and helped to organize street railway workers in the early 1890s. In 1893 he was elected president of the Amalgamated Association of Street Railway Employes of America (AASREA) and shortly thereafter moved to Detroit. He served as president of the AASREA (after 1903 the Amalgamated Association of Street and Electric Railway Employes of America) until retiring in 1946. Mahon was presiding judge of the Michigan State Court of Arbitration (1898-1900), a member of the Executive Committee of the National Civic Federation, and a member of the AFL's Executive Council (1917-23, 1935-49).

MANN, Thomas (1856-1941), a British machinist, was a member of the Amalgamated Society of Engineers (ASE) and, until 1889, of the Social Democratic Federation. A leader of the London dock strike of 1889, he became president of the Dock, Wharf, Riverside, and General Labourers' Union at its founding in mid-September of that year, serving until 1892. In 1891 he was one of seven trade unionists on the Royal Commission on Labour, which was formed to discuss the question of industrial relations. Mann was secretary of the Independent Labour party from 1894 to 1896. In 1916 he joined the British Socialist party and in 1920 helped found the British Communist party, remaining a member until his death. From 1919 to 1921 he was secretary of the Amalgamated Engineering Union, successor to the ASE. Mann stood unsuccessfully for Parliament four times.

MANUEL, Joseph C. (b. 1864), served as the first secretary of the Amalgamated Association of Street Railway Employes of America (AASREA) from 1892 to 1893. Born in Canada, he moved to the United States in 1885, becoming a brass caster in Detroit. In 1891 and 1892 he was secretary of AFL Detroit Street Car Employes' Association 5391 and represented that organization at the founding convention of the AASREA in 1892. In the mid-1890s he became a railroad clerk, an occupation he held until his retirement in the 1930s.

MARDEN, William Henry (1843-1903), a leader of the Massachusetts shoemakers, was born in that state and served in the Union army. He was secretary of the Knights of St. Crispin Lodge in Stoneham, Mass., and became a member of KOL Local Assembly 2340. Marden was general treasurer of the New England Lasters' Protective Union in the late 1880s and continued in that office after the organization changed its name to the Lasters' Protective Union of America (LPUA) in 1890. He remained general treasurer of the LPUA until it merged with other shoe workers' unions in 1895 to form the Boot and Shoe Workers' Union. In 1893 he was elected fourth vice-president of the AFL, serving one term. He was a member of the Massachusetts House of Representatives from 1895 to 1899.

MARTIN, William (1845-1923), emigrated from Scotland in 1868 and was secretary of the National Amalgamated Association of Iron and Steel Workers from 1878 to 1890. As secretary of the Columbus, Ohio, Lodge of the Iron and Steel Roll Hands' Union, he helped found the Amalgamated in 1876; he later moved to Pittsburgh. Martin served as second vice-president of the AFL from 1886 to 1888 and as first vice-president from 1889 to 1890. In 1891 he accepted a position as head of the Bureau of Labor of Carnegie Brothers and Co. (subsequently the Carnegie Steel Co.). After leaving Carnegie in 1893, he became a varnish manufacturer and later held a variety of positions including insurance agent and night foreman.

MEE, John (d. 1907), worked as a laborer in Philadelphia in the late 1870s before organizing local unions of hotel and restaurant workers in Philadelphia, Boston, Louisville, Ky., New York, and other places, and in 1892 was elected national organizer for the Hotel and Restaurant Employees' National Alliance at its first national convention. He was elected president at the union's 1893 annual meeting. In 1894 the convention abolished the office of president. Mee was elected third vice-president in 1900 and continued to be an active organizer for the union.

MENCHE, Adam (b. 1849?), was born in Vermont and moved as a boy to Syracuse, N.Y., where he worked with his father in the salt works. He later became an apprentice cigarmaker and in 1865 joined the CMIU. Moving to Denver by 1890, he served as an AFL organizer throughout the first half of the decade and was the Denver Trades and Labor Assembly's delegate to the AFL's 1890 convention. About 1896 he moved to Chicago and was president of CMIU 14, secretary-treasurer of the Chicago Union Label League, and, from 1901 to 1903, president of the Illinois State Federation of Labor.

METCALF, Richard Henry (1855-1928), was born in Uxbridge, Ont. At the age of sixteen he became an apprentice iron molder in Toronto, and in 1876 joined Iron Molders' Union of North America (IMUNA) 28 of that city. As corresponding representative of local 28, he attended the 1886 IMUNA convention and was elected a member of the union's Executive Board. He became chairman of the Executive

Board in 1890. In the early 1890s Metcalf moved to Cleveland where he became active in IMUNA 218. He retired from the Executive Board in 1895 upon his election to the newly created office of financier, a position he held until his death.

MEYERS, John C. (d. 1896?), of St. Paul, Minn., served as president of the Journeymen Barbers' International Union of America (JBIUA) from 1890 to 1894. He moved to St. Louis with the transfer of the JBIUA's headquarters there in 1893. Defeated for reelection in 1894, he attempted to form a rival organization based in Chicago. As a result, the JBIUA expelled him in 1895.

MILLER, Henry (1858-96), was born in Gillespie Co., Tex. From the age of seventeen he worked as a lineman in the Southwest, and in January 1891 he became president of AFL Wiremen's and Linemen's Union 5221 of St. Louis. He helped organize the National Brotherhood of Electrical Workers in November 1891 and served as that organization's first grand president from 1891 to 1893. In 1893 he was elected grand organizer. He was killed in a job-related accident while working in Washington, D.C.

MILLER, Owen (1850-1919), a musicians' leader, was born in New Jersey. He enlisted in the U.S. army at the age of twenty-one and transferred to St. Louis in 1873, serving for the next ten years in the arsenal band. He became president of the Musicians' Mutual Benefit Association (MMBA) of St. Louis in 1885, serving for thirty years. In 1886, when the MMBA joined the KOL as Local Assembly 5938, he was its master workman. The MMBA also apparently became local 8 of the National League of Musicians (NLM), which organized in 1886. NLM 8 affiliated with the AFL as MMBA 5579 in 1891, even though the NLM refused to join the Federation. Miller served as president of the NLM in 1891-92 and 1894-95, and in 1896 led a contingent out of the League to form a rival union, the American Federation of Musicians (AFM). He also helped organize the St. Louis Central Trades and Labor Union in 1887, serving seven times as president, and in 1888 he was elected to the Missouri senate on the Union Labor ticket. He served from 1889 to 1893.

Miller served as president of the AFM between 1896 and 1900 and as its secretary from 1900 to 1918. He was editor of the *International Musician* from 1901 to 1919. Besides his activities with the musicians, he was a delegate to the Missouri State Federation of Labor, a Democratic member of the St. Louis Charter Revision Board in 1914, and a member of the St. Louis draft board during World War I.

MITCHELL, Samuel (1867?-1932), who married SG's daughter Rose in 1891, worked in New York City as a letter carrier and postal clerk, eventually becoming a clerk foreman. While a letter carrier, Mitchell belonged to branch 36 of the National Association of Letter Carriers.

MORGAN, Elizabeth Chambers (b. 1850), a labor organizer and reformer, was a founder of AFL Ladies' Federal Labor Union (FLU) 2703. Born in Birmingham, England, and a mill worker from the age of eleven, she married Thomas J. Morgan in 1868, and they immigrated to Chicago in 1869. She and her husband became socialists during the depression of 1873. She was a charter member of the Sovereigns of Industry and in 1881 joined KOL Local Assembly 1789, later becoming its master workman. In 1886 she was elected delegate to the Trade and Labor Assembly (TLA) of Chicago and two years later helped organize Ladies' FLU 2703 and the Illinois Women's Alliance, a coalition of women's organizations working for woman suffrage and government protection of women and children from industrial exploitation. The report she wrote on sweatshop labor for the Chicago TLA served as a basis for the successful campaign for passage of the Illinois Factory and Workshop Inspection Act of 1893, and she subsequently testified before Congress on the sweating system. She later worked as a bookkeeper in her husband's law office.

MORGAN, Thomas John (1847-1912), a Chicago machinist and brass finisher, was born in Birmingham, England, where he married Elizabeth Chambers. They immigrated to the United States in 1869, and he worked for the Illinois Central Railroad, joining the International Machinists and Blacksmiths of North America in 1871, and serving as president of his local in 1874. Beginning in 1876, he was active in the Social Democratic Workingmen's Party of North America and its successor, the Workingmen's Party of the United States. He was an organizer and officer of the Chicago American Section of the SLP and ran unsuccessfully as its candidate for alderman in 1879 and 1881. He helped found the Council of Trades and Labor Unions of Chicago in 1877, joined Local Assembly 522 of the KOL in 1879, helped organize the Chicago Central Labor Union in 1884, and founded the Machine Workers' Union of Chicago in 1886. In 1891 Morgan helped organize the International Machinists' Union, serving as its general secretary in 1894 and 1895. He was a founder of the United Labor party in Chicago in 1886, and he ran unsuccessfully for mayor of the city on the SLP ticket in 1891. Morgan left the Illinois Central in 1893 to study law, and in 1895 was admitted to the bar. In 1894 he took a leading role in forging a labor–People's party alliance. He helped launch the Social Democratic party in 1900, serving as secretary of its national campaign committee and running unsuccessfully as its nominee for state's attorney of Cook Co. He became a leader in the Socialist Party of America, running unsuccessfully for a variety of offices including U.S. senator in 1909. From 1909 until his death he was editor and publisher of the *Provoker.*

MORRISSEY, Patrick Henry (1862-1916), began working for the railroads as a call boy and was a founding member of Brotherhood of Railroad Brakemen lodge 62 of Bloomington, Ill., in 1885. He served as an officer in his lodge and as vice-grand master (1889-95) and grand master (1895-1909) of the brotherhood (after 1890 the Brotherhood of Railroad Trainmen). After retiring from office, he was president of the Railway Employes' and Investors' Association and assistant to the vice-president in charge of operation for the the Chicago, Burlington, and Quincy Railroad Co.

MURCH, Thomas Henry (1838-86), born in Penobscot Co., Me., spent some time at sea before learning the stonecutters' trade. He was secretary of the Granite Cutters' International Union from 1877 to 1878 and edited the *Granite Cutters' Journal* in 1877. He was elected to the U.S. congress as a Greenback-Labor candidate and served from 1879 to 1883. Losing his bid for a third term, he worked as a businessman until his death.

NEEBE, Oscar W. (b. 1850), a tinsmith born in New York City, became involved in the labor movement in Chicago after moving there in 1875. He was a member of the anarchist International Working People's Association and was operating a yeast business in 1886. He was convicted of murder in connection with the Haymarket incident and was sentenced to fifteen years in prison; he was pardoned by Governor John P. Altgeld in 1893.

NORTON, George L. (b. 1852), secretary of St. Louis Marine Firemen's Protective Union 5464, was born in Tennessee. The AFL Executive Council appointed Norton as an AFL general organizer in May 1892 and SG sent him on a month-long mission to organize black workers along the Ohio and Mississippi rivers. Norton later operated a saloon and boardinghouse in St. Louis.

O'BRIEN, John (1840?-1931), a printer, was born in Ireland and immigrated to the United States in 1843, settling in Connecticut. He served in the Union army during the Civil War and, following his discharge, moved to San Francisco. Resettling in Portland, Ore., in 1887, he joined the staff of the *Portland Oregonian* and became president (1889-90, 1891-92) and vice-president (1890-91) of the Multnomah Typographical Union (International Typographical Union [ITU] 58). He was also a member of the ITU national executive committee (1888, 1893-94). From the late 1880s through 1891 he served as president of the Portland Federated Trades Assembly, and he was an AFL general organizer during the 1890s. In 1894 he helped found the *Portland Sun* to provide work for unemployed union printers. He continued to work as a printer in Portland until his retirement in 1907.

O'CONNELL, James (1858-1936), born in Minersville, Pa., learned his trade as a machinists' apprentice and later worked as a railroad machinist. Active in the KOL, O'Connell acted as a Knights' lobbyist in Harrisburg, Pa., in 1889 and 1891. He joined National Association of Machinists (after 1891 International Association of Machinists [IAM]) lodge 113 of Oil City, Pa., around 1890, became a member of the IAM general executive board in 1891, and served as grand master machinist of the IAM from 1893 to 1911. He moved to Chicago in 1896. O'Connell was third vice-president of the AFL from 1895 to 1913, second vice-president from 1914 to 1918, and president of the AFL Metal Trades Department from 1911 to 1934; he represented the AFL at the Trades Union Congress of Great Britain in 1899. He also served on the U.S. Commission on Industrial Relations from 1913 to 1915, and on the Council of National Defense committee on labor in 1917.

O'DEA, Thomas (1846-1926), an Irish immigrant and Civil War veteran, served as secretary of the Bricklayers' and Masons' International Union of America (BMIU; 1884-87 and 1888-1900) and was the first editor of the *Bricklayer and Mason* (1898). After retirement from the BMIU, O'Dea worked in Cohoes, N.Y., as a contractor.

O'SULLIVAN, John F. (1857-1902), a Boston journalist and labor organizer, was born in Charlestown, Mass. He wrote on labor for the *Boston Labor Leader* and *Boston Herald* before joining the *Boston Globe* in 1890 as a reporter and labor editor. In the late 1880s he became active in organizing sailors, serving as treasurer of the Boston sailors' union. He was president of the International Amalgamated Sailors' and Firemen's Union from 1889 to 1891, and of the Atlantic Coast Seamen's Union from its founding in 1891 until his death. He was active in the Boston Central Labor Union and served two terms as its president in the early 1890s. He also was active in the Massachusetts Federation of Labor as a member of the legislative committee. In 1894 he married Mary Kenney. O'Sullivan was secretary of Newspaper Writers' Union 1 of Boston from 1896 until his death and served the International Typographical Union as an organizer, fifth vice-president (1897-1902), and fourth vice-president (1902).

O'SULLIVAN, Mary Kenney (1864-1943), the first AFL national organizer for women, was born in Hannibal, Mo. She apprenticed to a dressmaker but eventually became forewoman in a printing and binding company. In the late 1880s she moved to Chicago where she worked in local binderies and became active in AFL Ladies' Federal Labor Union (FLU) 2703, working with Elizabeth Morgan. She served as the FLU's delegate to the Trade and Labor Assembly of Chicago and became a leader in organizing women binders into an organization of their own—the Chicago Bindery Workers' Union.

In 1892 Kenney served for five months as an AFL organizer for woman workers, concentrating her efforts in New York and Massachusetts. Returning to Chicago, she continued to organize women workers and successfully lobbied for a state factory law regulating the employment of women and children. After its passage, she became a deputy to Chief Inspector Florence Kelley.

In 1894 Kenney married John F. O'Sullivan, labor editor of the *Boston Globe*. They lived in Boston, and over the years she wrote articles for the *Globe* on women, trade unions, and labor issues. She continued to organize women workers with the support of the Women's Educational and Industrial Union and also helped found and served as executive secretary of the Union for Industrial Progress, a group studying factory conditions.

At the 1903 AFL convention she was one of the founders of the National Women's Trade Union League (NWTUL), serving as its first secretary (1903) and later as its vice-president (1907-9); she resigned from the NWTUL in 1912. In 1914 she became a factory inspector for the Massachusetts Department of Labor and Industries, holding that post until her retirement in January 1934.

PENNA, Philip H. (1857-1939), was born in England and immigrated to the United States in 1881, working in coal mines in Brazil, Ind. He was president of the Federated Association of Miners and Mine Laborers of Indiana in 1888 when that organization became District 11 of the National Progressive Union of Miners and Mine Laborers, and he continued as president of the district until 1890. He helped form the United Mine Workers of America in 1890, serving as its vice-president (1891-95) and president (1895-97). In the following decade he became secretary of the Indiana Coal Operators' Association, holding that post until his retirement in the 1920s.

PERKINS, George William (1856-1934), longtime president of the CMIU, began his career in the union by joining Albany, N.Y., local 68 in 1880. He was first vice-president of the CMIU from 1885 to 1891, acting as president for six months in 1888-89. In 1891 he was elected president, an office that he held for the next thirty-five years. Perkins worked closely with SG in the CMIU and the AFL. In 1918 he was appointed to the AFL's Commission on Reconstruction and represented the American labor movement at the International Federation of Trade Unions conference. He became the president of the AFL Union Label Trades Department in 1926, serving until his death.

PINNER, Reuben E. (1846-1916), a New York–born cigarmaker, served as financial secretary of local 144 in 1878 and 1879 and as a trustee of the CMIU during 1880.

POMEROY, William Curtis, born in Kentucky, worked as a waiter on riverboats between New Orleans and St. Louis before moving to Chicago in the mid-1880s. There he helped organize the catering trades into KOL Local Assembly 7475 in 1886 and was a founder of the Waiters' League of Chicago, which affiliated with the AFL in 1890. Pomeroy became active in the Trade and Labor Assembly (TLA) of Chicago as its financial secretary in 1886 and was the dominant figure in the TLA and the Illinois State Federation of Labor in the early 1890s. He was an AFL organizer from 1893 to 1894 and in 1896. In 1891 he helped found the Waiters' and Bartenders' National Union (after 1892 the Hotel and Restaurant Employees' National Alliance and after 1898 the Hotel and Restaurant Employees' International Alliance and Bartenders' International League of America). Pomeroy held official positions with the Alliance as editor of its journals, the *Purveyor* (1893-94), the *American Caterer* (1896-98), and the *National Purveyor* (1897-99), and as its vice-president (1896-99). He was also active in politics, fielding a Labor party ticket in the 1892 Chicago city elections and establishing his own People's party for the 1894 elections; he worked closely with Mark Hanna in William McKinley's presidential campaign of 1896.

Throughout the 1890s Pomeroy faced repeated charges of corruption. In 1896 the AFL convention rejected his credentials as a delegate after a challenge from the Illinois State Federation of Labor, and in 1897 the AFL received complaints from locals of the Alliance that culminated in formal charges before the AFL Executive Council in 1898. The following year, Pomeroy formed a rump organization; in 1900, however, the Alliance expelled him.

POWDERLY, Terence Vincent (1849-1924), general master workman of the KOL, was born in Carbondale, Pa. Apprenticed as a machinist, he moved to Scranton, Pa., and joined the International Machinists and Blacksmiths of North America in 1871, becoming president of his local and an organizer in Pennsylvania. After being dismissed and blacklisted for his labor activities, Powderly joined the

KOL in Philadelphia in 1876 and shortly afterward founded a local assembly of machinists and was elected its master workman. In 1877 he helped organize District Assembly 5 (number changed to 16 in 1878) and was elected corresponding secretary. He was elected mayor of Scranton on the Greenback-Labor ticket in 1878 and served three consecutive two-year terms. At the same time he played an important role in calling the first General Assembly of the KOL in 1878, where he was chosen grand worthy foreman, the KOL's second highest office. The September 1879 General Assembly elected him grand master workman, and he continued to hold the Order's leading position (title changed to general master workman in 1883) until 1893. Active in the secret Irish nationalist society, *Clan na Gael,* Powderly was elected to the Central Council of the American Land League in 1880 and was its vice-president in 1881. He became an ardent advocate of land reform and temperance and, as master workman, favored the organization of workers into mixed locals rather than craft unions, recommended that they avoid strikes, encouraged producers' cooperatives, and espoused political reform.

In 1894 Powderly was admitted to the Pennsylvania bar, and in 1897 President William McKinley, for whom he had campaigned, appointed him commissioner general of immigration. President Theodore Roosevelt removed him from his position in 1902 but in 1906 appointed him special representative of the Department of Commerce and Labor to study European immigration problems. Powderly was chief of the Division of Information in the Bureau of Immigration and Naturalization from 1907 until his death.

POWERS, Richard (1844?-1929), an Irish-born sailor, came to New York City in 1861 and, after Civil War service, settled in Chicago and worked as a sailor on the Great Lakes. He helped organize a lumber vessel unloaders' union in 1877 and a sailors' union (known both as the Lake Seamen's Benevolent Association of Chicago and the Lake Seamen's Union) in 1878, serving as president of the latter organization from its founding into the 1890s. He was a member of the Legislative Committee of the FOTLU from 1881 to 1885, and that body sent him to Washington, D.C., to lobby for seamen's measures. He was also active in the KOL, representing District Assembly 136 at the 1886 General Assembly, and in the *Clan na Gael,* a secret Irish nationalist society. From the late 1880s Powers worked variously as inspector of drains, clerk, vessel dispatcher, saloonkeeper, deputy collector of internal revenue, and real estate salesman.

PRESCOTT, William Blair (1863-1916), was born in Ontario, Canada, and in 1883 joined International Typographical Union (ITU)

91 of Toronto. He served as president of the ITU from 1891 to 1898 and then worked as a proofreader for newspapers in Indianapolis and Baltimore.

PRINCE, Samuel (1852-1914), a cigar packer and member of CMIU 251 of New York City, emigrated from England in 1864. He was prominent in both the city and state labor movements and was an AFL organizer in 1900 and 1901. Prince represented the sixteenth district in the state assembly as a Democrat from 1900 to 1904. He held the post of deputy commissioner of licenses from 1910 to 1914.

PULLMAN, George Mortimer (1831-97), an inventor and railroad car manufacturer, was born in New York where he worked as a cabinet maker and building contractor. He moved to Chicago in 1855 where he began remodeling railroad day coaches into sleeping cars for the Chicago and Alton Railroad. After working as a storekeeper in the Colorado mine fields, where he had investments, from 1859 to 1863, he returned to Chicago and developed such innovations as folding berths for railroad sleeping cars, the combined sleeping and restaurant car, the day car, and the vestibule car. In 1867 he organized the Pullman Palace Car Co. and within a few years was operating plants in several states; he was the founder of the "model" company town of Pullman, Ill. Pullman also owned the Eagleton Wire Works and served as president of the Metropolitan Elevated Railroad in New York City.

RAE, John B. (b. 1835?), a Scottish-born miner, immigrated to the United States in 1875 and settled in Pennsylvania. In 1888 he was elected worthy foreman of KOL National Trade Assembly 135, subsequently serving as its master workman and leading it into a merger with the National Progressive Union of Miners and Mine Laborers in 1890 to form the United Mine Workers of America (UMWA). Rae served as president of the UMWA from 1890 to 1892. He later became a physician and moved to Bowling Green, Ohio.

REICHERS, Charles F. (1850?-1929), a New York City garment worker and one of the founders in 1891 of the United Garment Workers of America (UGWA), served as that organization's general secretary (1891-95) and president (1895-96). Reichers was born in New York and was an active member of UGWA 5 of Brooklyn throughout the 1890s. He left the union in 1896 to start a children's clothing business but returned to the UGWA as an organizer when his venture failed shortly thereafter. With a group of UGWA members he launched a cooperative clothing company in 1898, heading the company until 1921 when he retired to California.

RIST, Frank Leonard (1858-1918), a printer born in Cincinnati, apprenticed with the *Cincinnati Volksfreund* and later worked for the *Cincinnati Enquirer.* He became a member of German-American Typographia 2 in 1878 and joined the KOL, subsequently becoming a leader of International Typographical Union 3 and the Cincinnati Central Labor Council (CLC). In 1892 he founded the *Chronicle,* official organ of the CLC, serving as editor and manager until his death. He was also a long-time organizer for the AFL.

SANIAL, Lucien Delabarre (1836-1927), a French-born journalist, came to the United States in 1863 as a war correspondent for *Le Temps.* A prominent leader of the SLP, he drafted the party's platform in 1889, edited its organs the *Workmen's Advocate* (1889-91) and the *People* (1891), and ran for mayor of New York on the SLP ticket in 1894. Around 1902 Sanial left the SLP; he later joined the Socialist Party of America, remaining an active member until breaking with the party in 1917 over its opposition to World War I. Sanial spoke at the founding convention of the American Alliance for Labor and Democracy in 1917.

SCHWAB, Michael (b. 1853), a bookbinder born in Kitzingen, Germany, and a member of the Sozialdemokratische Arbeiterpartei, immigrated to the United States in 1879 where he became a member of the SLP. In the early 1880s he was a reporter in Chicago for the *Chicagoer Arbeiter-Zeitung* and organized the socialist clubs that participated in the founding of an American branch of the anarchist International Working People's Association in 1883. He was convicted of murder in connection with the Haymarket incident. His sentence was commuted to life imprisonment by Governor Richard J. Oglesby, and he was pardoned by Governor John P. Altgeld in 1893.

SHEVITCH, Sergius E. (variously Sergei E. Schewitsch; 1848-1911), was born in Russia and came to the United States in 1877. Because of his facility in three languages, he was an important figure in the SLP in New York City during the 1880s. He was a member of the *New Yorker Volkszeitung* editorial board after 1878 and edited the paper in 1890. He also edited the *Leader* in 1887. In 1887 he ran for mayor of New York City on the Progressive Labor party ticket. Shevitch left the United States in 1890 and after an interlude in the Baltic provinces took up residence in Munich.

SHIPTON, George (1839-1911), was secretary of the London Amalgamated House Painters (later London Amalgamated House Painters and Decorators) from 1866 to 1889. He served as secretary of the London Trades Council (1872-96) and was secretary of the Parliamentary Committee of the Trades Union Congress of Great Britain (1875-82, 1883-84, 1885-90).

SKEFFINGTON, Henry J. (1858-1927), a shoemaker born in California, joined Philadelphia KOL Local Assembly (LA) 64 in 1878. He became master workman of LA 64, organized female carpet weavers in Philadelphia into the KOL's first assembly of women, and helped found the Executive Council of Shoe and Leather Workers, linking together various KOL shoe workers' trade districts. In 1887 he helped organize KOL shoe workers' National Trade Assembly 216, serving as its master workman and striving to establish its jurisdiction over shoeworkers within the Order. He led the secession of shoemakers from the KOL in 1889 and the amalgamation of these seceding local assemblies to form the Boot and Shoe Workers' International Union (BSWIU). He served as the BSWIU's secretary-treasurer in 1889, and as both general secretary and general treasurer from 1890 to 1894. He was also U.S. deputy immigration officer (1885-89) and chief immigration inspector (1894-97) for Boston and immigration commissioner for New England (1913-21). In the early 1920s he was a contract labor inspector in Providence, R.I., and a conciliation commissioner for the U.S. Department of Labor.

SORGE, Friedrich Adolph (1828-1906), a leading American socialist, was born in Saxony. He participated in the Revolution of 1848 and the Baden uprising in 1849, and after a brief period of imprisonment in 1849, he settled in Geneva. Swiss authorities forced him to leave the country in 1851 and he immigrated to New York City in 1852, living there for about two years before moving to Hoboken, N.J.

In 1857 Sorge helped found the Communist Club in New York, which corresponded with Karl Marx. He embraced the idea that trade unions had to play a central role in the emancipation of the workers and rejected the emphasis placed by followers of Ferdinand Lassalle on the primacy of political action. In 1868 he became the leader of the Social Party of New York and the designated U.S. spokesman for the General Council of the Marx-led International Workingmen's Association (IWA). He became secretary of Section 1 of the IWA in the United States in 1869 and first corresponding secretary of the IWA's Central Committee for North America at its establishment in 1870. He also served as the delegate of his section to the National Labor Union between 1869 and 1871. When the 1872 Hague Congress of the IWA moved the organization's General Council from London to New York City, Marx supported Sorge's appointment as IWA general secretary, a position Sorge held until resigning in 1874.

In 1876 Sorge participated in the founding of the Workingmen's

Party of the United States, but he withdrew in 1877 after the political faction gained control. He helped form the International Labor Union (ILU) in 1878. In 1883, after the ILU had dwindled to a single branch in Hoboken, he reorganized that body as the International Labor Union of Hoboken; it dissolved in 1887. For the remaining years of his life, Sorge supported himself as a music teacher and wrote articles for labor publications including, on SG's request, a serialized history of the U.S. labor movement that appeared in *Die Neue Zeit* (Stuttgart) between 1891 and 1895.

SOVEREIGN, James R. (b. 1854), was born in Grant Co., Wis., and grew up on a farm in Illinois. After working in the Midwest as a cattle driver and a bridge and tunnel construction worker, he became a marble carver in 1874. He joined the KOL in 1881 and in the 1880s was active in the Knights as a labor journalist and lecturer. He was appointed commissioner of labor statistics for Iowa in 1890 and reappointed in 1892. A representative of the Iowa state assembly to the KOL General Assembly in the early 1890s, he was elected general master workman in 1893 and served until 1897. He took an active part in the populist movement, serving on the national executive committee of the People's party in 1896 and helping run the party's Chicago branch headquarters during the 1896 presidential campaign. In 1898 Sovereign was living in Wallace, Idaho.

STEWARD, Ira (1831-83), leader of the movement for the eight-hour workday, was born in Connecticut and apprenticed as a machinist, becoming a leading figure in the International Machinists and Blacksmiths of North America. During the mid-1860s in Boston he helped organize several associations devoted to the establishment of the eight-hour workday, and he successfully promoted the passage of a Massachusetts ten-hour law for women and children in 1874. During the 1870s he developed close ties with New York City trade unionists in the International Workingmen's Association, and he helped found and served as an organizer for the International Labor Union. Steward formulated the theoretical basis for the eight-hour movement in the United States. He believed that freeing workers from long hours of labor would stimulate their desire for a better life and facilitate their education and organization, leading eventually to the abolition of the wage system. His ideas were disseminated in pamphlets and through the writings of his disciples, most notably George McNeill and George Gunton.

STRASSER, Adolph (1843-1939), was born in Hungary and immigrated to the United States about 1872. He became a cigarmaker, helped organize New York City cigar workers excluded from membership in the CMIU, and played a leading role in the United Cigarmakers. Strasser was a member of the International Workingmen's Association and, in 1874, helped organize the Social Democratic Workingmen's Party of North America, serving as its executive secretary. He was also a founder of the Economic and Sociological Club. In 1876 he was a delegate to the unity congress that organized the Workingmen's Party of the United States, and he aligned with the trade unionist faction of the party. During 1876 and 1877 he worked to establish a central organization of New York City trade unions, and his efforts culminated in the founding of the Amalgamated Trades and Labor Union of New York and Vicinity in the summer of 1877. Strasser was elected vice-president of the CMIU in 1876 and president in 1877 and successfully promoted the reorganization of the union in the late 1870s and early 1880s. After retiring as president in 1891, he continued to work for the CMIU as an organizer, auditor, and troubleshooter. In addition he served as an AFL lecturer, member of the Federation's legislative committee, and AFL arbitrator of jurisdictional disputes. He ended his labor career in 1914, becoming a real estate agent in Buffalo, and in 1919 he moved to Florida.

SULLIVAN, James William (1848-1938), a printer from Carlisle, Pa., moved to New York City in 1882 after serving his apprenticeship in Philadelphia. He worked for the *New York Times* and the *New York World* and joined International Typographical Union (ITU) 6, becoming a leading figure in the ITU. He was a strong supporter of land reform and edited the *Standard* with Henry George from 1887 to 1889. A close associate of SG, he participated in the Social Reform Club and the People's Institute of the Ethical Culture Society. He served with SG in the National Civic Federation, accompanied him to Europe in 1909, helped to edit the *American Federationist,* and served with SG on the Advisory Commission of the Council of National Defense during World War I. His European travels encouraged him to support the movement for direct legislation through the initiative and the recall. He opposed labor movement involvement in socialist political activities, publishing *Socialism as an Incubus on the American Labor Movement* (New York, 1909) and a report critical of English socialism (in Commission on Foreign Inquiry, National Civic Federation, *The Labor Situation in Great Britain and France* [New York, 1919]).

SWINTON, John (1830-1901), a Scottish-born journalist, emigrated in 1843 and apprenticed as a printer in Montreal. He was on the editorial board of the *New York Times* throughout the 1860s, and the *New York Sun* from 1875 to 1883 and again from 1892 to 1897. He published the influential New York City labor reform newspaper *John*

Swinton's Paper between October 1883 and August 1887. Active in New York City politics, he ran for mayor in 1874 on the Industrial Political party ticket and worked in the mayoralty campaign of Henry George in 1886.

TAKANO, Fusataro (1868-1904), was born in Nagasaki and attended lower school in Tokyo before moving to Yokohama where he worked in his uncle's store and attended commercial school. In 1886 he came to San Francisco and in 1890 he helped organize the Shokkō Giyū-kai (Fraternal Society of Workers) to study American trade union methods with an eye to labor problems attending Japan's industrialization. He returned to Japan in 1896 and became editor of the English-language *Japan Advertiser.* In 1897 he helped reconstitute the Shokkō Giyū-kai in Japan and in the same year was appointed to head the new Rōdō Kumiai Kisei-kai (Society for the Promotion of Trade Unions) as its secretary. He founded Kyōeisha, a consumers' cooperative, in 1899. In 1900, discouraged by the Japanese government's opposition to trade unions, he traveled to North China as a correspondent for the *Japan Advertiser.* He died there four years later.

TALBOT, Thomas Wilson (1849-92), was born in South Carolina and went to work in a shoe factory when he was ten. In 1865 he became an apprentice in a Florence, S.C., railroad machine shop, and worked as a machinist and engineer before opening his own machine shop in Sumter, S.C., in 1874. Joining the KOL, he served as a master workman and state organizer. In 1887 he moved to Atlanta and in the following year helped organize the Order of United Machinists and Mechanical Engineers of America. In May 1889 Talbot was elected grand master machinist of the National Association of Machinists, as the Order was renamed, and he was reelected the following year. He resigned in July 1890.

THORNE, William James (1857-1946), a British laborer and gas stoker, was a founder and general secretary from 1889 to 1934 of the National Union of Gas Workers and General Labourers of Great Britain and Ireland (after 1924, the National Union of General and Municipal Workers). He joined the Social Democratic Federation in 1884, served on the West Ham town council (1891-1910) and as alderman (1910-46), and was a member of the Parliamentary Committee of the Trades Union Congress (TUC) of Great Britain (1894-1933) and chairman of the TUC (1896-97, 1911-12). In 1898 Thorne attended the AFL convention in Kansas City, Mo., as a TUC fraternal delegate. From 1906 to 1945 he was a Labour Member of Parliament.

TILLETT, Benjamin (1860-1943), a British seaman and dock worker, helped organize the Tea Operatives' and General Labourers' Association in 1887 and was a leader of the London dock strike of 1889. In its aftermath he was a founder of the Dock, Wharf, Riverside, and General Labourers' Union of Great Britain and Ireland and its general secretary until 1922. In 1910 he helped organize the National Transport Workers' Federation. He was a member of the Parliamentary Committee of the Trades Union Congress of Great Britain (1892-95) and a founder of the Independent Labour party in 1893, serving on its executive council during its first year. In 1900 he helped establish the Labour Representation Committee, direct predecessor to the Labour party. Tillett stood unsuccessfully for Parliament four times before serving as a Labour Member from 1917 to 1924 and 1929 to 1931.

TOBIN, John F. (1855-1919), was born in Guelph, Ont., where he attended school and apprenticed in the shoe trade at the age of fourteen. He worked in various Canadian cities before moving to the United States in 1881, where he worked chiefly in Buffalo and Rochester, N.Y. He first joined the Knights of St. Crispin when he was sixteen and joined the KOL in 1884 and the Boot and Shoe Workers' International Union (BSWIU) in 1890. Blacklisted because of his union activities, he ran his own cobblers' shop in Rochester for a time, and later moved to Quincy, Mass. When the BSWIU and the Lasters' Protective Union amalgamated to form the Boot and Shoe Workers' Union in 1895, Tobin was elected general president, holding the office until his death.

TRACY, Thomas F. (1861-1916), was born in Massachusetts and worked as a cigarmaker in Boston. President of CMIU 97 in 1894, he also served as a member of the Massachusetts State Federation of Labor's Legislative Committee. He was fourth vice-president of the CMIU from 1896 to 1906 and then second vice-president until his death. In 1910 Tracy moved to Washington D.C., to serve as secretary-treasurer of the AFL's Union Label Trades Department, a position he also held until his death.

VALENTINE, Joseph F. (1857-1930), was born in Baltimore where he apprenticed as an iron molder. After moving to San Francisco, he joined Iron Molders' Union of North America (IMUNA) 164 and served as the local's president from 1880 to 1890. Achieving prominence as a leader of a difficult strike in 1890, he was elected first vice-president of the IMUNA that year, serving until 1903. He moved to Cincinnati in 1891 to assume his duties. In 1903 he became president of the IMUNA (known after 1907 as the International Molders' Union of North America) and continued in office until he retired in

1924. He was a vice-president of the AFL from 1905 to 1924 and first vice-president of the AFL's Metal Trades Department from 1908 to 1924. In 1927 he returned to San Francisco.

VALESH, Eva McDonald (1866-1956), a printer, journalist, and labor organizer, was born in Maine and moved to Minneapolis in 1877. She worked for the *Spectator,* had become a member of the International Typographical Union and the KOL by the 1880s, and headed the labor department of the *St. Paul Globe,* writing a series on working women for that paper in 1887 and 1888. She became the manager of the industrial department of the *Minneapolis Tribune* and in 1891 was a state lecturer and treasurer for the Minnesota Farmers' Alliance and a lecturer for the National Farmers' Alliance. In 1891 she married Frank Valesh, a state deputy commissioner of labor. About 1898, she moved to New York City where she worked for the *New York Journal* and served as an AFL organizer. From 1900 to 1909 she was managing editor of the *American Federationist,* and she served in the women's section of the National Civic Federation in 1909. She subsequently edited the *American Club Woman* magazine and for about twenty-seven years was a proofreader for the *New York Times* prior to her retirement in 1952.

VAN ETTEN, Ida M. (1867?-94), was born in Van Ettenville, N.Y., and moved to New York City in 1887. In 1888 she helped organize the New York Working Women's Society, was elected secretary, and for several years was a leading figure in organizing women workers in New York. She frequently lectured and published articles on the industrial status of women, and she lobbied before the New York legislature for the abolition of the sweating system and for passage of the Fassett bill providing for female factory inspectors. In 1889 she helped organize women feather workers and women cloakmakers in New York City and at the 1891 AFL convention served as secretary of a women's committee that recommended commissioning a woman organizer. She went to Europe in 1893 to gather material for a series of articles and died the following year in Paris.

VAN PATTEN, Simon Philip (b. 1852?), a draftsman and architect, was born in Washington, D.C., but was living in Chicago as Philip Van Patten as early as 1873. In 1876 he became national secretary of the Workingmen's Party of the United States. He continued in that office after the organization became the SLP in 1877, serving until 1883 and moving with its headquarters to Cincinnati, Detroit, and finally New York City. By the early 1880s Van Patten was also active in the KOL. In 1883 he left the SLP, moving to Hot Springs, Ark., where he operated his own architectural firm under the name Simon

P. Van Patten. In the early 1890s Van Patten served on the state committee of the People's party in Arkansas. He continued to reside in Hot Springs through World War I.

VOGT, Hugo, a notary public and later a lawyer, was a leader of the SLP in New York City. He served as acting secretary of the SLP in 1883, supported Henry George's mayoralty campaign, and was active in the United Labor party. In the 1880s and 1890s he ran for the New York assembly several times. Together with Daniel DeLeon and Lucien Sanial, Vogt led the SLP in the 1890s, serving as secretary of its New York American Section, editing the *Vorwärts,* and serving as manager of the *Daily People.* He was active in KOL District Assembly 49 and also was a founder in 1895 of the Socialist Trade and Labor Alliance. Vogt left the SLP about 1902 after a dispute with Daniel DeLeon.

VOLDERS, Jean (1855-1896), a Belgian socialist leader, was a founder of the Parti Ouvrier Belge (POB; Belgian Workers' Party) in 1885. He was a former bank employee and a writer for *Le National Belge* before founding and editing *Le Peuple,* organ of the POB. He organized the Brussels congress of the Second International in 1891.

WATCHORN, Robert (1858-1944), an English-born miner, immigrated to the United States in 1880, settling in Ohio. He worked as a miner in Pennsylvania and New York, became a member of the KOL, and in 1888 was elected president of the Pittsburgh division of KOL National Trades Assembly 135. He was elected secretary-treasurer of the newly formed United Mine Workers of America in 1890, but resigned in 1891 to become chief clerk to Pennsylvania Governor Robert Pattison. He helped secure passage of the 1893 amendments to the Pennsylvania factory inspection law and was appointed that year as the first chief factory inspector of the state. In 1895 he accepted a position as an inspector with the U.S. Bureau of Immigration. He became commissioner of immigration at Ellis Island in 1905, retaining that office until 1909. In 1910 Watchorn moved to California where he became treasurer and a director of the Union Oil Co. Moving to Oklahoma in 1913, he purchased substantial holdings in several oil companies, forming his own company in the 1930s, and engaged in extensive philanthropic activities.

WEBER, Frank Joseph (1849-1943), was born in Milwaukee and became a sailor on the Great Lakes at an early age, joining a seamen's union in 1868 and subsequently becoming a member of the KOL. He helped organize the Milwaukee Federated Trades Council (FTC) in 1887 and the following year organized local unions of cargo handlers and carpenters. He was the FTC's chief officer as president in 1893 and as general secretary from 1902 to 1934. In 1893 he was instrumental in the formation of the Wisconsin State Federation of Labor, serving until 1917 as its chief officer (president, 1893; state organizer, 1894-1917). He also worked as an AFL organizer for several years beginning in the mid-1890s. Weber was active in the People's party and served as a socialist assemblyman in the Wisconsin legislature for six terms betweeen 1907 and 1925.

WEIHE, William (1845-1908), president of the National Amalgamated Association of Iron and Steel Workers from 1884 to 1892, was born in Pennsylvania. He served as a local officer of the Sons of Vulcan before becoming a member of the executive committee of the Amalgamated in 1876. He served as a Democrat during the 1883-84 term of the Pennsylvania state legislature; he later became a Republican. Weihe was employed as a deputy immigration inspector for New York from 1896 until his death.

WEISMANN, Henry (1863-1935), was born in Bavaria and immigrated to the United States, settling in San Francisco at the age of eighteen. He became a member of Burnette Haskell's anarchist International Workingmen's Association (known as the Red International) and worked with Haskell in publishing the *Truth* from 1882 to 1884. Weismann joined KOL Progressive Assembly 2999 in 1884 and helped found the Representative Council of the Federated Trades and Labor Organizations of the Pacific Coast. While serving as president of the Anti-Coolie League, Weismann was imprisoned for several months on charges of possessing explosives. Following his release he organized San Francisco locals for the Journeymen Bakers' National Union and helped organize coast seamen and brewers as well. He moved to New York City in 1890 and the following year became editor of the official organs of the Journeymen Bakers' and Confectioners' International Union (JBCIU), the *Bakers' Journal* and the *Deutsch-Amerikanische Bäcker-Zeitung;* the union merged the two publications in 1895. The JBCIU combined the offices of editor and international secretary in 1895 and selected Weismann to fill the joint position. Weismann remained the chief executive officer until resigning in 1897 and leaving the labor movement. He became active in Republican politics in Kings Co. (Brooklyn) and Suffolk Co., and from 1901 to 1903 served as first deputy county clerk of Kings Co. In 1903 he graduated from the Brooklyn Law School and acted as a lawyer for the Boss Bakers' Association. From 1915 to 1918 he was president of the New York State and Brooklyn branches of the German-American Alliance. After 1918 he continued to practice law as the senior member of the firm of Weismann and Holland. He also served as justice of the peace and as town clerk in Smithtown, N.Y.

WHITE, Henry (1866-1927), general secretary of the United Garment Workers of America (UGWA) from 1895 to 1904, was born in Baltimore and lived in Rochester, N.Y., before moving to New York City about 1886. In 1891 he helped form the UGWA, and he was a leader in the New York clothing cutters' union that became UGWA 4. During the early 1890s White was active in the New York City labor movement as secretary (1891-92) of the short-lived New York (City) Federation of Labor; in 1893 he was secretary of his local union, a member of the executive board of UGWA locals 4, 5, and 28 (clothing cutters' unions), a member of the General Executive Board of the UGWA, and the UGWA's general auditor. He became the editor of the UGWA's official organ, the *Garment Worker,* in 1893, retaining that position until 1903 and continuing as the editor of the journal's successor, the *Weekly Bulletin of the Clothing Trades,* until 1904. In 1904 he resigned as general secretary in a dispute over his intervention to end a general strike against the open shop. He subsequently continued his career as an editor and writer on economic and labor issues, particularly for the garment trade publication the *Clothing Designer and Manufacturer* and its successor, the *Clothing Trade Journal.*

WISDOM, Thomas J. (b. 1861), was born in England and immigrated to the United States in 1885. He settled in Pittsburgh where he joined Iron Molders' Union of North America (IMUNA) 46. He served as second vice-president of the IMUNA from 1890 to 1895.

WOODS, Samuel (1846-1915), a British miners' leader, was president of the Lancashire and Cheshire Miners' Federation (1881-1915) and vice-president of the Miners' Federation of Great Britain (1889-1909). He served as secretary of the Parliamentary Committee of the Trades Union Congress of Great Britain from 1894 to 1904, and as a Liberal/Labour Member of Parliament (1892-95, 1897-1900).

WRIGHT, Carroll Davidson (1840-1909), born in New Hampshire, studied law in Vermont and moved to Boston in 1871 after service in the Civil War. He was elected to the Massachusetts Senate as a Republican in 1871 and served as chief of the Massachusetts Bureau of Statistics of Labor from 1873 to 1888 and as commissioner of the U.S. Bureau of Labor (after 1888, the Department of Labor) from 1885 to 1905. During the last four years of his life he was president of Clark College.

ORGANIZATIONS

The International Union of the ARCHITECTURAL Iron Workers' Industry of North America organized in 1891.

The AXE and Edge Tool Makers' National Union of America organized about 1890 when it affiliated with the AFL. It disbanded by 1893.

The Journeymen Bakers' National Union of the United States was organized in 1886, participated in the formation of the AFL that year, and was chartered by the AFL in 1887. In 1890 it adopted the name Journeymen BAKERS' and Confectioners' International Union of America and, in 1903, it became the Bakery and Confectionery Workers' International Union of America.

The Journeymen Barbers' National Union, founded in 1887 by unions formerly affiliated with the KOL, affiliated with the AFL in 1888 as the Journeymen BARBERS' International Union of America.

The International Brotherhood of BLACKSMITHS organized in 1889 and affiliated with the AFL in 1897. In 1903 it absorbed the AFL's federal labor unions of blacksmiths' helpers and changed its name to the International Brotherhood of Blacksmiths and Helpers. In 1919 it amalgamated with the Brotherhood of Drop Forgers, Die Sinkers, and Trimming Die Makers to become the International Brotherhood of Blacksmiths, Drop Forgers, and Helpers.

Bookbinders seceded from the International Typographical Union (ITU) in 1892 and joined with independent bookbinders' unions to form the International Brotherhood of BOOKBINDERS (IBB). In 1894 the ITU recognized the IBB's jurisdiction, and the Bookbinders affiliated with the AFL in 1898.

The BOOT and Shoe Workers' International Union of America (BSWIU) was organized in 1889 by seceding locals of shoemakers' National Trade Assembly (NTA) 216 of the KOL; it affiliated that year with the AFL. In 1895 the BSWIU merged with another AFL affiliate, the Lasters' Protective Union of America, and with the remnant of NTA 216 to form the Boot and Shoe Workers' Union.

The National Union of Brewers of the United States organized in 1886 and affiliated with the AFL as the Brewers' National Union in March 1887. Later that year it changed its name to the National Union of the United BREWERY Workmen of the United States, and it became the International Union of the United Brewery Workmen of America in 1903. After a prolonged series of jurisdictional disputes the AFL revoked the union's charter in 1907; it reinstated the Brewers in 1908. In 1917 the union became the International Union of United Brewery and Soft Drink Workers of America, and in 1918, the International Union of United Brewery, Flour, Cereal, and Soft Drink Workers of America.

The BRICKLAYERS' and Masons' International Union of America was organized in 1865 and changed its name to the Bricklayers', Masons', and Plasterers' International Union of America in 1910. It did not affiliate with the AFL until 1916.

Delegates from AFL federal labor unions organized the International BROOM Makers' Union in 1893, and it affiliated with the AFL the same year. In 1905 it became the International Broom and Whisk Makers' Union.

The Brotherhood of Carpenters and Joiners of America was organized in 1881 and was chartered by the AFL in 1887. In 1888 the Brotherhood and the United Order of American Carpenters and Joiners merged, forming the United Brotherhood of CARPENTERS and Joiners of America.

The CARRIAGE and Wagon Workers' International Union of North America organized in 1891 and was chartered by the AFL that year. In 1912 the union changed its name to the International Union of Carriage, Wagon, and Automobile Workers of North America. The AFL suspended the union's charter in 1918 in a dispute involving its claim to jurisdiction over automobile workers.

The Cigar Makers' National Union of America was organized in 1864 and changed its name to the CIGAR Makers' International Union of America in 1867. It participated in the formation of the FOTLU in 1881. The following year, seceding New York City locals formed the Cigarmakers' Progressive Union of America; the Progressives rejoined the International in 1886. The AFL chartered the CMIU in March 1887.

The Retail CLERKS' National Protective Association of America was organized in December 1890 as an AFL affiliate. It changed its name to the Retail Clerks' International Protective Association in 1899.

The Coopers' International Union organized in 1870 and in 1881 participated in the formation of the FOTLU. After a period of dormancy in the 1880s, it reorganized as the COOPERS' International Union of North America in 1890 and the following year affiliated with the AFL.

The National Brotherhood of ELECTRICAL Workers of America was organized in 1891 and affiliated with the AFL in the same year.

In 1899 it became the International Brotherhood of Electrical Workers.

The American FLINT Glass Workers' Union of North America was organized in 1878 by locals formerly affiliated with the KOL. It affiliated with the AFL in 1887.

The Gewerkschafts Union der Möbel-Arbeiter von Nord Amerika (Furniture Workers' Union of North America) was organized in 1873, and in 1882 it changed its name to the International FURNITURE Workers' Union of America. It affiliated with the AFL in 1887 and in 1896 merged with the Machine Wood Workers' International Union of America to form the Amalgamated Wood Workers' International Union of America.

The Tailors' National Protective Union joined with members of KOL Garment Cutters' National Trade Assembly 231 in 1891 to form the United GARMENT Workers of America. The new union affiliated with the AFL the same year.

The Independent Druggist Ware Glass Blowers' League (founded in 1867) divided in 1884 into the eastern or Green Bottle Blowers' League, and the western or Green Glass Workers' League, and the two organizations affiliated with the KOL in 1886 as District Assemblies 149 and 143, respectively. They merged as National Trade Assembly 143 in 1889. In 1891 the organization withdrew from the KOL and formed the United Green GLASS Workers' Association of the United States and Canada. It changed its name to the Glass Bottle Blowers' Association of the United States and Canada in 1895, and affiliated with the AFL in 1899.

The Granite Cutters' International Union of the United States and the British Provinces of America was formed in 1877. In 1880 it changed its name to the GRANITE Cutters' National Union of the United States of America, and in the following year participated in the formation of the FOTLU. It joined the AFL in 1888, but left the federation in 1890, rejoining in 1895. In 1905 it adopted the name Granite Cutters' International Association of America.

The HOTEL and Restaurant Employees' National Alliance. See the WAITERS' and Bartenders' National Union.

The National Amalgamated Association of IRON and Steel Workers of the United States was organized in 1876 and in 1887 was chartered by the AFL. In 1897 it changed its name to the National Amalgamated Association of Iron, Steel, and Tin Workers and in 1908 dropped "National" from its name.

The Pen and Pocket KNIFE Grinders' and Finishers' National Union of America was founded in 1891 and affiliated with the AFL the same year. It reorganized under a new charter in 1905 as the Pocket Knife Blade Grinders' and Finishers' National Union. In 1917 the union dissolved, some of its members joining the Metal Polishers', Buffers', Platers', and Helpers' International Union.

The Spring KNIFE Makers' National Protective Union of America affiliated with the AFL in 1892 and withdrew in 1895.

The New England Lasters' Protective Union was organized in 1878 and affiliated with the AFL in 1887. It changed its name to the LASTERS' Protective Union of America in 1890, and in 1895 merged with KOL National Trade Assembly 216 and the Boot and Shoe Workers' International Union to form the Boot and Shoe Workers' Union.

The locomotive engineers organized the Brotherhood of the Footboard in 1863. In 1864 the organization became the Brotherhood of LOCOMOTIVE Engineers.

The Brotherhood of LOCOMOTIVE Firemen organized in 1873, and in 1878 merged under its name with the International Firemen's Union. In 1906 it adopted the name Brotherhood of Locomotive Firemen and Enginemen.

The International MACHINISTS' Union of America (IMUA) was established in 1891 and chartered that year by the AFL. The AFL's 1895 convention revoked the IMUA's charter, as the International Association of Machinists had affiliated with the Federation earlier in the year.

The Order of United Machinists and Mechanical Engineers of America organized in 1888 and the following year changed its name to the National Association of MACHINISTS. It changed its name to the International Association of Machinists in 1891 and in 1895 affiliated with the AFL.

The National Progressive Union of Miners and Mine Laborers and KOL National Trade Assembly (NTA) 135 united in 1890 to form the United MINE Workers of America (UMWA), which affiliated with both the AFL and the KOL. The merger recognized the Progressives and NTA 135 as equal partners in the UMWA. NTA 135 retained its name, structure, and practice of secrecy, and officers' titles such as president and master workman were often used interchangeably. Gradually the UMWA outgrew these residual divisions, and in 1894 the Knights' General Assembly excluded NTA 135 on the grounds that it was dominated and controlled by the UMWA.

The National League of MUSICIANS of America (NLM) was founded in 1886 and dissolved in 1902. It was superceded by the AFL's American Federation of Musicians, founded in 1896 by dissidents who disagreed with the NLM's belief that musicians were professionals rather than workers.

NATIONAL Trade Assembly (NTA) 135, the KOL miners' assembly, was organized in May 1886, eight months after the founding of the National Federation of Miners and Mine Laborers. The two organizations competed for jurisdiction. In December 1888 a minority of NTA 135 seceded and joined the Miners Federation, which was reorganized as the National Progressive Union of Miners and Mine Laborers. NTA 135 and the Progressives united in 1890 as the United Mine Workers of America (UMWA), affiliated with both the AFL and NTA 135 of the KOL. In 1894 the Knights' General Assembly excluded NTA 135 on the grounds that it was dominated and controlled by the UMWA.

The Representative Council of the Federated Trades and Labor Organizations of the PACIFIC Coast was organized in 1886. It originated at a Pacific Coast anti-Chinese convention called by the San Francisco District Assembly of the KOL. As originally conceived, it was to be a federation of all western unions with an authority over them similar to that of a national trade union over its locals. It failed to achieve significant influence outside San Francisco, and by the end of the decade was generally referred to as the San Francisco Federated Trades Council (FTC). In 1891 the Council of Federated Trades of the Pacific Coast was founded in another attempt to establish a West Coast labor federation; it held its last convention in 1894. The FTC was superceded in 1892 by the San Francisco Trades and Labor Council, which changed its name to the San Francisco Labor Council in 1893.

The Brotherhood of PAINTERS and Decorators of America (BPDA) was organized in 1887, affiliating with the AFL the same year. In 1891 the union withdrew from the Federation, but it reaffiliated the following year. In 1894 the BPDA split between western and eastern factions headquartered, respectively, in Lafayette, Ind., and Baltimore. The factions merged in 1900, forming the Brotherhood of Painters, Decorators, and Paperhangers of America.

The PAVING Cutters' Union of the United States and Canada was organized in Baltimore in 1887. The national union declined in the

1890s, prompting its remaining locals to affiliate directly with the AFL. In 1901 several of these locals organized the Paving Cutters' Union of the United States of America (renamed the International Paving Cutters' Union of the United States of America and Canada in 1904) in affiliation with the AFL.

The Brotherhood of Railroad Brakemen of the Western Hemisphere organized in 1883. In 1886 it changed its name to the Brotherhood of Railroad Brakemen and in 1890 to the Brotherhood of RAILROAD Trainmen.

The Conductors' Union, organized in 1868, changed its name to the Conductors' Brotherhood at its first annual convention in 1869. In 1878 the union became the Order of RAILWAY Conductors of America.

Eugene Debs played a leading role in creating the American RAILWAY Union (ARU) in early 1893; the organization was then formally launched at a meeting in Chicago in June of that year. Its purpose was to replace the existing railroad brotherhoods, abolish craft distinctions in organizing railway workers, and bring into one union all railway workers regardless of skill; membership dues were one dollar a year. At its first convention in June 1894, delegates narrowly voted to limit membership to white workers, while encouraging the organization of blacks into separate unions. Following its victory in the Great Northern Railroad strike in the spring of 1894, the ARU's membership swelled to 150,000. Some of its members came over from the existing brotherhoods, but most came from among the 75 percent of the railway workers who were unorganized. The ARU's defeat in the Pullman strike in the summer of 1894 brought on its decline, and it disbanded in June 1897.

Seamen and firemen established the International Amalgamated SAILORS' and Firemen's Union, an AFL affiliate, in 1889. It dissolved in 1891 with the seamen founding the Atlantic Coast Seamen's Union (ACSU) and the firemen, the Watertenders', Pilers', and Firemen's Benevolent Association. The next year the ACSU joined with other seamen's organizations to form the National Seamen's Union of America.

The National SEAMEN'S Union of America organized in 1892 as a federation of several regional sailors' unions including the Sailors' Union of the Pacific, the Lake Seamen's Union, the Gulf Coast Seamen's and Firemen's Union, and the Atlantic Coast Seamen's Union.

The following year it affiliated with the AFL and in 1895 changed its name to the International Seamen's Union of America.

The Amalgamated Association of STREET Railway Employes of America was established in 1892 and affiliated with the AFL in 1893. It absorbed the Brotherhood of Surface Car Employes in 1894. In 1903 it changed its name to the Amalgamated Association of Street and Electric Railway Employes of America.

The SWITCHMEN'S Mutual Aid Association of the United States of America organized in 1886 and disbanded in 1894. It was succeeded by the Switchmen's Union of North America, founded later in 1894.

The Journeymen Tailors' National Union of the United States, composed of custom tailors, was organized in 1883 and was chartered by the AFL in 1887. It changed its name in 1889 to the Journeymen TAILORS' Union of America and in 1913 to the Tailors' Industrial Union. The following year it merged with the Amalgamated Clothing Workers of America (ACWA) but in 1915 seceded from the ACWA and reassumed the name Journeymen Tailors' Union of America.

In 1881 the National Tanners' and Curriers' Union participated in the formation of the FOTLU. It was not until 1891, however, that a successor organization, the United Brotherhood of TANNERS and Curriers of America, affiliated with the AFL. This organization survived at least through 1895.

The National Alliance of THEATRICAL Stage Employes of the United States was organized in 1893 and affiliated with the AFL in 1894. It became the National Alliance of Theatrical Stage Employes of the United States and Canada in 1899, the International Alliance of Theatrical Stage Employes of the United States and Canada in 1902, and the International Alliance of Theatrical Stage Employes and Moving Picture Machine Operators of the United States and Canada in 1915.

The Mosaic and Encaustic TILE Layers and Trade National Union was organized and received a charter from the AFL in 1890, but became inactive after 1893. Another tile layers' union, the Mosaic and Encaustic Tile Layers' International Union, was formed in 1897.

The TIN, Sheet Iron, and Cornice Workers' International Association organized in 1888 and affiliated with the AFL the following year.

The TRADES Union Congress of Great Britain, the central organization of that country's trade union movement, was founded in 1868.

The National Typographical Union was organized in 1852 by a group of locals that had held national conventions in 1850 and 1851 under the name Journeymen Printers of the United States. In 1869 it adopted the name International TYPOGRAPHICAL Union (ITU). Although ITU members participated in the formation of the FOTLU in 1881 and in the organizing of the AFL in 1886, the union did not affiliate with the Federation until 1888.

The WAITERS' and Bartenders' National Union organized and affiliated with the AFL in 1891. The following year it changed its name to the Hotel and Restaurant Employees' National Alliance and in 1898 to the Hotel and Restaurant Employees' International Alliance and Bartenders' International League of America.

The Machine WOODWORKERS' International Union of America organized in 1890 and affiliated with the AFL the same year. It merged with the International Furniture Workers' Union of America in 1895 to form the Amalgamated Wood Workers' International Union of America, which merged with the United Brotherhood of Carpenters and Joiners of America in 1912.

INDEX

Names of persons or organizations for whom there are glossary entries are followed by an asterisk.

Italics indicate the location of detailed information. While this index is not cumulative, it does include references to substantive annotations in volumes one and two that are relevant to this volume but are not repeated here; these appear first in the index entry. The reference to Ernest J. Arundel's annotation in volume one, for example, appears in this index as *1:414n*.